THE POLITICAL ECONOMY OF HUNGER

T0323656

WIDER

Studies in Development Economics embody the output of the research programmes of the World Institute for Development Economics Research (WIDER), which was established by the United Nations University as its first research and training centre in 1984 and started work in Helsinki in 1985. The principal purpose of the Institute is to help identify and meet the need for policy-oriented socio-economic research on pressing global and development problems, as well as common domestic problems and their interrelationships.

The Political Economy of Hunger

Edited by

JEAN DRÈZE AND AMARTYA SEN

Volume 1

Entitlement and Well-Being

CLARENDON PRESS · OXFORD

OXFORD

UNIVERSITY PRESS

Great Clarendon Street, Oxford, OX2 6DP,
United Kingdom

Oxford University Press is a department of the University of Oxford.
It furthers the University's objective of excellence in research, scholarship,
and education by publishing worldwide. Oxford is a registered trade mark of
Oxford University Press in the UK and in certain other countries

Published in the United States of America by Oxford University Press
198 Madison Avenue, New York, NY 10016, United States of America

British Library Cataloguing in Publication Data
Data available

Library of Congress Cataloging in Publication Data
Data available

ISBN 978-0-19-828635-6 (Hbk.)
ISBN 978-0-19-886017-4 (Pbk.)

In fond memory of
Sukhamoy Chakravarty

FOREWORD

The first fruits of WIDER's programme in the theme area of 'Hunger and Poverty—The Poorest Billion' initiated in 1985 were presented in August 1986 at a research conference in Helsinki on 'Food Strategies'. The research was co-ordinated by WIDER's Research Adviser on this theme, Amartya Sen, now Lamont University Professor at Harvard University. The focus of the research project was on identifying 'what feasible opportunities exist' for changing a situation where inordinately large numbers of people go hungry.

A common background to many of the papers presented at the conference was provided by an approach that sees famine and hunger as arising not primarily from a lack of availability of food but from failure of entitlement to food. Another key focus of the conference was on the public intervention issue, namely, how does a country with a low per capita income reach high levels of physical quality of life in terms of literacy rates, life expectancy, and infant mortality. Besides the country studies, other issues addressed in the research include strategies of famine prevention, international interdependence, gender inequalities, the role of food production, and the functions of an active press.

The conference papers have been brought together in three volumes, edited by Jean Drèze and Amartya Sen, of which this is the first. In addition to editing these three volumes, Jean Drèze and Amartya Sen have themselves written a separate monograph entitled *Hunger and Public Action* (Oxford University Press, 1989), which closely relates to the themes and concerns of this book.

Lal Jayawardena
Director, WIDER
August 1989

PREFACE

This collection of twenty-six papers, presented in three volumes, represents the result of work undertaken at and for the World Institute for Development Economics Research (WIDER) in Helsinki. This programme of joint research was initiated in the summer of 1985. The first versions of most of the papers were presented at a WIDER conference on 'food strategies' held in Helsinki in July 1986. The papers as well as the research programme as a whole were subjected to close scrutiny at that conference. Those discussions strongly influenced the work that followed—both extensive revisions of the papers presented and the undertaking of new studies, which are also included in these volumes.

The objective of this programme has been the exploration of a wide range of issues related to hunger in the modern world. The papers are concerned with diagnosis and causal analysis as well as policy research. The focus is particularly on Africa and Asia, but there are also two papers on hunger and deprivation in Latin America and a few contributions on more general theoretical issues. The full list of papers in the three volumes can be found at the beginning of each volume. Our 'Introduction' to the three volumes, discussing the papers and their interrelations, is included in full in volume 1, but the parts relevant for the subsequent volumes are also included in the respective volumes, i.e. volumes 2 and 3.

The tasks of revising the papers and carrying out the follow-up studies proved to be quite challenging, and the entire project has taken much longer than we had hoped. We are extremely grateful to the authors for their willingness to undertake substantial—and in some cases several rounds of —revisions, and for putting up with long lists of suggestions and requests. The revisions have been enormously helped by the contributions of the discussants who participated in the 'food strategies' conference in July 1986, including Surjit Bhalla, Susan George, Keith Griffin, S. Guhan, Iftekhar Hussain, Nurul Islam, Nanak Kakwani, Robert Kates, Qaiser Khan, Henock Kifle, Stephen Marglin, Siddiq Osmani, Martin Ravallion, Sunil Sengupta, Mahendra Shah, Nick Stern, Paul Streeten, Megan Vaughan, and Samuel Wangwe. Carl Eicher's comments and suggestions contributed greatly to the improvement of a number of papers. Very helpful comments and suggestions were also received after the conference from Sudhir Anand, Susan George, Judith Heyer, Nurul Islam, Robert Kates, B. G. Kumar, and François-Régis Mahieu.

For their participation in the conference, and their help in planning these studies, we are also grateful to Frédérique Apffel-Marglin, Juha Ahtola, Tuovi Allén, Lars-Erik Birgegaard, Pekka Harttila, Cynthia Hewitt de Alcantara, Eric Hobsbawm, Charles Kindleberger, Michael Lipton, Kaarle Nordenstreng, Kimmo Pulkinnen, Shlomo Reutlinger, Tibor Scitovsky, Darrell Sequiern, Heli Sirve, Marjatta Tolvanen, Matti Tuomala, Tony Vaux, and Hannu Vesa.

For editorial and logistic assistance, we are greatly in debt to Asad Ahmad, Robin Burgess, Nigel Chalk, Jacky Jennings, Shantanu Mitra, Sanjay Reddy, Sangeeta Sethi, Pekka Sulamaa and Anna-Marie Svedrofsky. We would like to thank Judith Barstow for doing the subject index.

Finally, we are grateful to WIDER for its generous support. We owe special thanks to Lal Jayawardena, the Director, for being immensely helpful at every stage of this project.

J.D.
A.S.
November 1989

CONTENTS

LIST OF PAPERS

Volume 1: Entitlement and Well-Being

Volume 2: Famine Prevention

Volume 3: Endemic Hunger

LIST OF CONTRIBUTORS

SUDHIR ANAND is University Lecturer in Quantitative Economic Analysis at the University of Oxford, and Fellow and Tutor at St Catherine's College.

KAUSHIK BASU is Professor of Economics at the Delhi School of Economics, and currently Visiting Professor of Economics at Princeton University.

PARTHA DASGUPTA is Professor of Economics at the University of Cambridge, and Professor of Economics and Philosophy at Stanford University.

MEGHNAD DESAI is Professor of Economics at the London School of Economics.

JEAN DRÈZE, formerly Lecturer in Development Economics at the London School of Economics, is now a freelance development economist.

CHRISTOPHER HARRIS is University Lecturer in Public Economics at the University of Oxford, and a Faculty Fellow of Nuffield College.

BARBARA HARRISS is University Lecturer in Agricultural Economics at Queen Elizabeth House, University of Oxford, and Fellow of Wolfson College.

JUDITH HEYER is Lecturer in Economics at the University of Oxford, and Fellow and Tutor at Somerville College.

FRANCIS IDACHABA is Vice-Chancellor of the University of Agriculture, Makurdi, on leave of absence from the Department of Agricultural Economics, University of Ibadan.

S. M. RAVI KANBUR is Editor of the World Bank Economic Review and Senior Adviser on the Social Dimension of Adjustment at the World Bank, on leave from Professorship in Economics at the University of Warwick.

B. G. KUMAR is Associate Fellow at the Centre for Development Studies, Trivandrum, Kerala, India.

S. R. OSMANI is Research Fellow at the World Institute for Development Economics Research, Helsinki, Finland.

KIRIT S. PARIKH is Director of the Indira Gandhi Institute of Development Research, Bombay, and from 1980 to 1986 was Program Leader of the Food and Agriculture Program of the International Institute for Applied Systems Analysis, Austria.

JEAN-PHILIPPE PLATTEAU is Professor of Economics at the Facultés Universitaires, Namur, Belgium.

N. RAM is Associate Editor of *The Hindu*, a leading national daily newspaper in India, based in Madras.

MARTIN RAVALLION is Senior Economist in the Agricultural Policies Division of the World Bank, Washington DC, on leave from the Australian National University, Canberra, Australia.

DEBRAJ RAY is Professor, Planning Unit, Indian Statistical Institute, New Delhi.

CARL RISKIN is Professor of Economics at Queens College, City University of New York, and Senior Research Scholar at the East Asian Institute, Columbia University.

IGNACY SACHS is Professor at the Écoles des Hautes Études en Sciences Sociales, and Director of its Research Center on Contemporary Brazil in Paris.

AMARTYA SEN is Lamont University Professor at Harvard University.

REHMAN SOBHAN was formerly the Director of the Bangladesh Institute of Development Studies, Dhaka, with which he is still associated.

PETER SVEDBERG is a Senior Research Fellow at the Institute for International Economic Studies, Stockholm.

SAMUEL WANGWE is Profesor of Economics at the University of Dar es Salaam.

ANN WHITEHEAD is Lecturer in Social Anthropology at the University of Sussex, England.

LIST OF TABLES

1
Introduction
Jean Drèze and Amartya Sen

The facts are stark enough. Despite the widespread opulence and the unprecedentedly high real income per head in the world, millions of people die prematurely and abruptly from intermittent famines, and a great many million more die every year from endemic undernourishment and deprivation across the globe. Further, hundreds of millions lead lives of persistent insecurity and want.

While all this is quite obvious, many things are unclear about the characteristics, causation, and possible remedies of hunger in the modern world. A great deal of probing investigation—analytical as well as empirical—is needed as background to public policy and action for eradicating famines and eliminating endemic undernutrition. In this collection of twenty-six papers in three volumes, serious attempts have been made to address many of these momentous issues.

1.1. Organization and structure

These studies were initiated in 1985 when the World Institute for Development Economics Research (WIDER) was established in Helsinki. First versions of most of the papers were presented at a conference on 'food strategies' held at WIDER in July 1986. In that meeting there were extensive discussions of the analyses presented in the various papers, and some of the debates continued well beyond the conference. The papers have been revised in the light of these exchanges, and further discussions among the authors and the editors. A few new studies were also undertaken during 1986–8 to fill some identified gaps. This book of three volumes represents the fruits of these efforts. It is meant to be a wide-ranging investigation of the causal antecedents, characteristic features, and policy demands of hunger in the modern world. The focus is primarily on sub-Saharan Africa and South Asia, but the experiences of several other countries—from China to Brazil—have also been examined.

Though three of our own essays are included in these volumes, our role has been primarily organizational and editorial. We have, however, also written a monograph of our own, *Hunger and Public Action*,[1] which deals with related

---

[1] Also published by Oxford University Press in the series of WIDER Studies in Development Economics: Drèze and Sen (1989a).

issues, and there is a clear connection between the two works. The planning and the design of these three volumes of essays, *The Political Economy of Hunger*, have been closely related to the approach explored and developed in *Hunger and Public Action*, and in turn, in that book, we have drawn on the results of the studies presented in these three volumes.

We should, however, emphasize the obvious. We, as editors, must not be identified with all the views that have been expressed in these essays. These three volumes of essays, which are mainly revised conference papers, present investigations and conclusions that deserve, in our view, serious consideration. But although we have been involved at every stage of these studies, and have also presented our critical comments on the various versions, it was not our aim to soldier on with requests for revision until we all agreed. The analyses and the views are those of the respective authors.

1.2. *Political economy*

The essays in the first volume deal with 'general matters'—including the nature and diversity of the problem of world hunger. They set the background for the analysis of government policy and public action. The second volume includes studies of famines and of anti-famine strategies, and altogether there is an attempt here to identify what is needed for the eradication of famines. The third volume takes up endemic deprivation and undernourishment, discusses successes and failures of different lines of action, and investigates the lessons for public policy aimed at eliminating persistent hunger. The different volumes, thus, deal with distinct but interrelated aspects of what we have called 'the political economy of hunger'.

The meaning of the expression 'political economy' is not altogether unambiguous. To some it simply means economics. It is indeed the old name of the discipline, common in the nineteenth century, and now rather archaic. To others, political economy is economics seen in a perspective that is a great deal broader than is common in the mainstream of the modern tradition. In this view, the influences of political and social institutions and ideas are taken to be particularly important for economic analysis and must not be pushed to the background with some stylized assumptions of heroic simplicity. Political economy thus interpreted cannot but appear to be rather 'interdisciplinary' as the disciplines are now standardly viewed.

Even though the two interpretations are quite distinct, there is a clear connection between them in the sense that the dominant tradition of economics is much narrower now than it was in the classical political economy of Adam Smith, Robert Malthus, David Ricardo, Karl Marx, John Stuart Mill, and others.[2] Thus the old and archaic term for economics as such is also a reminder

---

[2] On this issue, see Sen (1984, 1989a).

of the breadth of the earlier tradition of the subject. Many of the analyses of the kind that are now seen as interdisciplinary would have appeared to Smith or Mill or Marx as belonging solidly to the discipline of political economy as a subject.

It does not, of course, really matter whether political, social, and cultural influences on economic matters are counted inside or outside the discipline of economics, but it can be tremendously important not to lose sight of these influences in analysing many profoundly important economic problems. This is particularly the case with the problem of hunger. The title of the book, *The Political Economy of Hunger*, is meant to be an explicit reminder of the need to adopt a broad perspective to understand better the causation of hunger and the remedial actions that are needed.

1.3. *Entitlements and political economy*

As was mentioned earlier, the essays included in the first volume of this book deal with rather general matters that serve as background to policy analysis. The topics covered include the characteristics and causal antecedents of famines and endemic deprivation, the interconnections between economic and political factors, the role of social relations and the family, the special problems of women's deprivation, the connection between food consumption and other aspects of living standards, and the medical aspects of undernourishment and its consequences. Several contributions also address the political background of public policy, in particular the connection between the government and the public, including the role of newspapers and the media, and the part played by political commitment and by adversarial politics and pressures.[3]

Chapter 2, 'Food, Economics and Entitlements' by Amartya Sen, is concerned with some very elementary issues. It points to the need for focusing on the 'acquirement' of food by the respective households and individuals, and the fact that the overall production or availability of food may be a bad predictor of what the vulnerable groups in the population can actually acquire. The 'entitlement approach', already presented elsewhere (see Sen 1977, 1981), concentrates instead on the forces that determine the bundles of commodities over which a family or an individual can establish command. A person can be reduced to starvation if some economic change makes it no longer possible for him or her to acquire any commodity bundle with enough food. This can happen either because of a fall in endowment (e.g. alienation of land, or loss of labour power due to ill health), or because of an unfavourable shift in the conditions of exchange (e.g. loss of employment, fall in wages, rise in food prices, drop in the price of goods or services sold by the person, reduction of social security provisions).

---

[3] On these questions see also Drèze and Sen (1989a).

The chapter then proceeds to use the entitlement perspective to analyse a number of specific policy issues: famine anticipation and warning; famine relief (particularly the use of employment and payment of cash wages to regenerate lost entitlements); the use of food imports; the role of public distribution (of food and other necessities including health care); and the need for diversification in the production structure (particularly in the context of encountering African famines and hunger). Many of these issues are further investigated in other contributions in these volumes.

1.4. *Food commands of countries and regions*

Ravi Kanbur in Chapter 3 examines the regional pattern of food commands in the world. By extending entitlement analysis from the level of individuals and households to nation states and regions, the global position of food production and needs is supplemented by the analysis of each nation's and region's ability to command food. Kanbur also examines the problems of data availability underlying the corresponding estimations.

Not only does this 'intermediate' level of disaggregation provide a different perspective on the trends of food balances in the world, it also directs attention to crucial variables that influence a country's ability to command enough food, e.g. international prices of non-food exports, the possibility of substitution between commodities in production and consumption.

The analysis of hunger has to be, ultimately, thoroughly disaggregative, and the food entitlements of regions and countries cannot by themselves tell us whether many people will go hungry and who they will be. But between the extreme aggregation of global food analysis (popular in some economic as well as journalistic traditions) and the totally disaggregated picture of the entitlements of families and individuals, there is an important intermediate focal point of regional and country-specific food entitlements. Kanbur's investigation concerns that intermediate stage, and he points to the connection between that stage and the ultimate concern with the deprivation of families and persons. In this context, Kanbur also argues for the possibility of making good use of nutrition-based poverty measures supplemented by sensitivity analysis of different cut-off levels of nutritional norms.

1.5. *Politics and the state*

In Chapter 4 Rehman Sobhan extends entitlement analysis in a different —more political—direction. Although he is generally concerned with the diverse political factors—national and international—that govern the entitlements of households, he concentrates specifically on the determination of the entitlements against the state that particular households may have.

Indeed, the state is, to a great extent, a direct instrument for providing entitlements through such mechanisms as public distribution of food and health care, the generation of public employment, the provision of relief in distress situations, the offer of subsidies on particular productive inputs and consumption goods. Sobhan provides a broad-ranging analysis of the political forces that determine the public provision of these entitlements, thereby supplementing the usual concentration in the literature on entitlement analysis in the market economy.[4] He also presents an analysis of the politics of food aid—drawing partly on the experience of Bangladesh.

Sobhan's paper brings out *inter alia* the need for many governments to propitiate influential interest groups and the important effects that this can have on entitlements.[5] The analysis can be extended in other directions as well. The provisions made by the state respond not only to pressures of vested interests, but also to general political pressures. There is some evidence that organized political opposition can be quite effective in influencing state policy even in rather authoritarian states. For example, hard-to-suppress opposition groups may have made quite a substantial contribution to the populist (and, to some extent, welfare-oriented) policies in South Korea and in post-Allende Chile.[6] In general, the positive role of 'adversarial' politics deserves clearer recognition than it tends to get in the literature on world hunger. The tradition of thinking about public action only in terms of policy choice by the government (e.g. in the literature on 'optimal' policy decisions) needs to be supplemented by bringing in the action of the public itself. Public action is action not only *for* the public but also—in an important sense—*by* the public.[7]

1.6. *International policies of the rich countries*

While Sobhan's political analysis draws attention *inter alia* to one aspect of international relations (connected with aid, leverage, and 'food politics'), Kirit Parikh in Chapter 5 examines the influence of the protectionist economic policies of the rich countries on hunger in the Third World. This is done with the help of an 'applied general equilibrium' model, based on explicitly stated—if somewhat exacting—assumptions.[8]

One of the results of his model is that the poor are forced into the role of being 'the adjustors', in the sense that fluctuations of supply—whether in the developed or developing countries—have to be absorbed by the poor (through

---

[4] In this sense the issues taken up by Sobhan can be seen as complementary to those—related to the functioning of markets—investigated by Ravallion (1987*a*).

[5] On the need to consider the influence of vested interest groups in the context of the analysis of the Indian economy, see also Jha (1980) and Bardhan (1984).

[6] On this see Drèze and Sen (1989*a*: ch. 10, 12).

[7] These and related issues have been discussed in Drèze and Sen (1989*a*, 1989*b*).

[8] The models used have been more extensively presented and discussed in Parikh and Rabar (1981).

adjustments of their consumption). The intuition behind the result may be explainable by noting the likelihood that the richer people will be able to keep up their consumption of as vital a commodity as food even when things are generally short, so that the losers would have to be those who are overwhelmed in the competition of the market.[9]

Another result concerns the interesting—and rather comforting— conclusion that the protection of agricultural producers in the rich countries on the whole reduces hunger in the poorer countries. Parikh also shows how the protection of the labour market in the richer countries through immigration control has—of all the international policies considered—the largest adverse effect on world hunger. That conclusion is not counter-intuitive, but the political possibility of a real change in this respect is bound to be extremely slim in the near future.

1.7. The role of the press and the media

The role of the news media—the press in particular—in the prevention of famines and hunger is examined by the distinguished journalist and editor N. Ram in Chapter 6. Ram's analysis importantly expands our understanding of one of the most neglected aspects of the prevention of hunger—an aspect that has only recently begun to receive attention. By providing information on likely famine threats and pressuring the government to act without delay, an active newspaper system can lead to early and effective intervention by the government. One of the roles of the press is to make it 'too expensive' in political terms for the government to be callous and lethargic, and this can be decisive since famines are extremely easy to prevent by early intervention. Indeed, it appears that no country with a free press *and* scope for oppositional politics has ever experienced a major famine.

The contrast is especially striking in comparing the experience of China and India. The particular fact that China, despite its much greater achievements in reducing endemic deprivation, experienced a gigantic famine during 1958–61 (a famine in which, it is now estimated, 23 to 30 million people died) had a good deal to do with the lack of press freedom and the absence of political opposition.[10] The disastrous policies that had paved the way to the famine were not changed for three years as the famine raged on, and this was made possible by the near-total suppression of news about the famine and the total absence of

---

[9] Determined public action can, in some circumstances, succeed in shifting a substantial part of the burden of downward adjustment from the poor to the relatively prosperous classes (see Jean Drèze's chapter 'Famine Prevention in India' in vol. 2). But this may call for far-reaching measures of protection of the entitlements of the vulnerable groups, and such measures do not belong to Parikh's model. See also ch. 9 in this volume, on the observed priority that consumers evidently give to maintaining food expenditure.

[10] On this see Sen (1983), Ashton *et al.* (1984), Peng (1987). See also Carl Riskin's chapter ('Feeding China') in vol. 3 of this book.

media criticism of what was then happening in China. It is also arguable that the persistence of famines in sub-Saharan Africa has much to do with the absence of media freedom and the suppression of oppositional politics in many countries in that subcontinent. In fact, the differences between the experiences of various African countries—some with more open press and politics than others—also bring out the important role that the media and oppositional politics can play in preventing famines.[11]

However, it appears that even an active press, as in India, can be less than effective in moving governments to act decisively against endemic undernutrition and deprivation—as opposed to dramatically visible famines. The quiet persistence of 'regular hunger' kills millions in a slow and non-dramatic way, and this phenomenon has not been much affected, it appears, by media critiques. There is need for an analysis here of what explains the difference.

While Ram begins his investigation by referring to international coverage of famines and distress, the focus of his paper is on the role of the national media. Ram distinguishes between the 'credible-informational' role of the press (including the fact that an active and efficient press can be an excellent early warning system against famines) and its 'adversarial' or 'destabilizing' role (in putting pressure on the government to act rapidly to combat famines and persistent undernutrition). Both can be extremely important in famine prevention and *potentially* also in combating endemic undernutrition.

Ram's empirical illustrations come mostly from the history of the Indian press. He shows that the Indian press—by informing the public and by pressuring the government—has indeed been able to play quite a positive part in the prevention of some types of hunger (e.g. open starvation and famines). On the other hand, it has been less successful in dealing with the type of deprivation that requires deeper economic, social, and medical analysis (e.g. endemic deprivation). Ram identifies the problems arising from 'a tendency to dramatize and sensationalize the coverage of poverty and hunger on a mass scale while missing out deeper structural features and processes' (p.188). Imprecision, oversimplification, and dilettantism also take their tolls.

If the explanation, as Ram argues, of the ineffectiveness of the Indian press in combating endemic undernutrition (as opposed to famines) lies in the more complicated nature of the phenomenon, the remedy sought would have to go beyond guarding the freedom of the press (important though it is) into ways of improving the quality of news analysis and journalism. Ram's essay suggests some crucial directions in which effective improvements can be made (including greater interaction between academic research and journalism). These particular pointers as well as Ram's general analysis deserve serious attention, given the potential importance of the role of the news media in combating world hunger.

[11] On this and related matters, see Drèze and Sen (1989a: chs. 5, 8, 11, 13), and also Jean Drèze's chapter 'Famine Prevention in India' in vol. 2 of this collection.

1.8. *Nutrition, adjustment, and adaptation*

The complexity of the phenomenon of undernourishment is not only a difficulty for good journalistic coverage of endemic deprivation, it can also create problems for the professional literature on hunger and nutrition. Indeed, there have been several protracted—and heated—debates among nutritionists on the criteria for undernourishment. The traditional 'intake norms' approach involves the specification of certain nutritional norms of 'required intakes', and a diagnosis of 'undernourishment' if the actual intakes of people fall below these norms. This approach has been subjected to a good deal of criticism in recent years.[12] The need for some types of nutrients (e.g. the 'protein requirements' of adults) has been shown to be exaggerated in the usual specification of nutritional standards. Even for 'calorie requirements', grave doubts have been raised about the scientific basis and practical usefulness of comparison with prespecified intake norms.

Some reasons for doubting the wisdom of mechanical use of the 'intake norm' approach are clear enough. First, there is much evidence of *inter-individual* variations in metabolic rates and other factors influencing calorie needs. Any statistical analysis of intake observations must take note not only of such variations, but also of the possibility that some of the people with low nutritional needs may in fact *choose* low-intake diets.

Second, there is often a good deal of *intertemporal* variations in intakes, with low calorie consumption in some periods being balanced by higher consumption in others. Thus, the observation of low intake in a given period is no proof of undernourishment.

Third, there is considerable evidence that nutritional differences bring about adjustments of some kinds, e.g. children being shorter and lightly built. What is not clear is how these adjustments impair well-being and working ability (if at all). This has been a field of much debate—with positions taken varying from uncritical acceptance of the contribution of anthropometric factors to good living (e.g. the common presumption that 'taller is better') to attaching no importance at all to those factors (e.g. the general acceptance of the commonness of being 'small but healthy').

Fourth, some nutritionists have argued that the body can in fact 'adapt' to low intakes by cutting down the nutritional needs without any effect on body size and other physical features and without any impairment of bodily functionings. If the thesis of costless adaptation is biologically sound and widespread in its application, the 'intake-norm' approach would be thoroughly undermined. The adaptationist thesis would also suggest a redirection of policy priorities towards concentrating only on severely deficient intakes —beyond the scope for adaptation—with no need for worrying about those

---

[12] See in particular Sukhatme (1977, 1982*a*, 1982*b*).

with smaller shortfalls who are automatically protected by adaptation. The 'adaptationists' have tended to argue that the magnitudes of nutritional deprivation are much exaggerated in standard estimates.

It should be obvious from this quick summary that the more serious points of medical argumentation are likely to be the last two, and in particular adaptation as a phenomenon would be immensely important if it were widely applicable and quantitatively significant. In Chapter 7, Partha Dasgupta and Debraj Ray argue, on the basis of reviewing the relevant medical literature, that the biological evidence does not favour the thesis of costless adaptation. Both interpersonal differences in nutritional requirements and intertemporal variations in intakes are accepted as real possibilites (though it is also pointed out that because of the 'waste' involved in storage, a fluctuating intake pattern tends to raise the average requirement). But the possibility of costless adaptation is strongly disputed on empirical grounds.

Dasgupta and Ray then go on to investigate the implications of undernourishment for labour markets, including the effects of inadequate nutrition on low work capacity, unemployment, and continuing poverty. They discuss how a 'poverty trap' can operate, with undernourished people finding it hard to get employment because they are weak, and remaining weak because they are unemployed.[13] The role of anti-hunger policy, thus, extends well beyond that of preventing escapable mortality or morbidity into achieving a major economic transformation.

Siddiq Osmani in Chapter 8 provides a wide-ranging assessment of the nutritional literature on food intakes and health, and it complements Dasgupta and Ray's analysis of biological evidence. On the specific subject of adaptation, Osmani's conclusions are sceptical, though less critical and decisively dismissive than those of Dasgupta and Ray ('the hypothesis of intraindividual adaptation in requirement is not yet substantiated by scientific evidence, although the possibility cannot be ruled out').

Osmani also investigates the detrimental effects of adjustment to lower nutritional intakes, and finds some 'association' between low intake and impairment (though here too his conclusions are more conditional and qualified than those of Dasgupta and Ray). He also goes into a number of other—related—issues, e.g. the importance of health planning and hygiene in food policy (particularly since food requirements *and* the ability to absorb food depend on a person's health), and the relevance of the nutritional debates for the measurement of poverty (especially for poverty defined as the failure of basic nutritional capabilities).[14] Osmani argues that some of the debates on nutritional economics do not quite have the policy relevance that has been

---

[13] On this see also Dasgupta and Ray (1986, 1987).

[14] A number of papers on these and related themes were presented at a Conference on 'Nutrition and Poverty' at the World Institute for Development Economics Research in July 1987, and these papers will be published in a volume edited by Siddiq Osmani: Osmani (forthcoming).

claimed, but he separates out those parts of the debate that are really central to policy choice.

Those who have argued for taking note of the possibility of adaptation and other forms of costless adjustment have often emphasized the case for concentrating on really serious nutritional deprivation as opposed to relatively minor shortfalls that may come out in the wash. It is indeed possible to argue that an exaggeration of the number of the undernourished may distract attention from the urgent need to concentrate on remedying the conditions of those who are tremendously deprived. That point remains relevant even if costless adaptation or adjustment is absent (or possible but uncommon). The actual harm that nutritional shortfall does can rise at an increasing rate, *whether or not* there is costless adaptation. That is a different issue and should be seen as such.

1.9. *Food and living standard*

The analyses presented by Dasgupta and Ray, and by Osmani, push us in the direction of paying greater attention to the problem of nutritional deprivation, and its manifold medical, economic, and social effects.[15] One of the recurrent themes in the studies included in these three volumes concerns the *interconnections* between the problem of hunger and the broader economic and social concerns.

These connections can work in different directions. The need to link hunger to the failure of economic entitlements indicates one connection—economic penury has to be seen as a major predictor of hunger. For much the same reason, the observation of hunger can also be seen as an indicator of a family's general poverty. Indeed, since there are good reasons to believe that the family would typically give priority to food in its consumption allocation, the expenditure on food may be a better guide to the family's overall economic solvency and opulence than more variable indicators, such as total income or even total expenditure.

In an innovative model, Sudhir Anand and Christopher Harris have analysed in Chapter 9 the way food expenditure can be used as an indicator of the general living standard of a family. If a family's income fluctuates over time, the observation of its income at any point of time may be a very misleading basis for judging its ordinary level of opulence. For reasons that have been discussed by Milton Friedman, among others, there may be more stability in the family's total consumption expenditure, which may be based on long-term average income (the so-called 'permanent income'). But a family may not give equal priority to preserving all types of expenditure, and given the importance of food, it is not unreasonable to expect that it would attach the highest priority to preserving the expenditure on food.

---

[15] See also the papers presented at the Conference on 'Nutrition and Poverty': Osmani (forthcoming).

Equipped with this insight, Anand and Harris present both an analytical model to investigate these connections and also an empirical study of Sri Lankan data. It is shown that if the economic opulence of the family is judged not by the observation of its short-run income, but by the size of food expenditure per capita, the behaviour of consumers becomes much easier to explain (including the observed chronic 'dissaving' of the poorest sections of the people classified in terms of per capita income or per capita total expenditure).

Of the four possible indicators of living standard that Anand and Harris consider (namely income per capita, total expenditure per capita, food expenditure per capita, and the share of food in total expenditure), food expenditure per head seems to give the best guidance to the family's economic opulence. The finding has implications for economic policy—including subsidies and taxation—and it can be seen as an important aid in using short-run data for informed analysis of the economic condition of the people. Observing a family's food expenditure tends to tell more about its general economic conditions than we can find out by observing its short-run income, or total expenditure.[16] Anand and Harris comment on some of the far-reaching implications of the relations analysed.[17] The perspective of food is important not only for the analysis of nutrition, but also for an understanding of general economic conditions and for interpersonal comparisons of the economic state of different families. This broader consideration extends the scope and use of the political economy of hunger.

1.10. *Women's deprivation and intrafamily distribution*

In the analysis of hunger, the divisions of classes and occupation groups are obviously important, and their roles have been recognized for a long time. The fact that gender can also be a crucial variable had not received due acknowledgement until fairly recently. There can be systematic differences between the command over resources and commodities that men and women respectively enjoy. The differences can show up in the levels of undernourishment, morbidity, and mortality respectively experienced by women and men.

There are, in fact, very asymmetrical survival patterns of men and women in different parts of the world. There is fairly strong evidence that if women and men receive similar nutritional and medical attention, women tend to live significantly longer than men. Women seem to be more resistant to disease and more able to deal with hardship, and the survival advantages are particularly

[16] Anand and Harris also consider the proportionate share of food in total expenditure as a basis of classification and find that it is a less useful indicator of living standard than total food expenditure per head. A family would try to preserve its total command over food, but need not particularly worry about maintaining the same ratio of food expenditure to other expenditure.

[17] The authors have explored the implications more extensively in a monograph; see Anand and Harris (forthcoming).

significant for advanced age and also at the other end, especially in the neo-natal period (and even *in utero*).[18] It is, therefore, not surprising that, in Europe and North America, women have a much higher life expectancy at birth than men, and that—because of the greater survival rates of women—the female–male ratio in the total population is around 1.05 or so on the average.[19]

However, the female–male ratio is significantly lower than unity in many parts of the world. The ratio is around 0.93 or 0.94 in South Asia, West Asia, and China.[20] It is also lower than unity—though not by much—in Latin America, and quite a bit less in North Africa. Given the natural, i.e. biological, advantages of women *vis-à-vis* men (when they receive the same nutritional and medical attention), this shortfall of women would tend to indicate a really sharp difference in social treatment (i.e. in the division of necessities of life such as food and medical attention). The shortfalls amount to millions of 'missing women' in Asia and North Africa compared with what would be expected on the basis of the European or North American female–male ratio, and even on the basis of the ratio for sub-Saharan Africa.[21] If India had the female–male ratio that obtains in sub-Saharan Africa (around 1.02), then—given the number of Indian males—there would have been 37 million more women in India in the mid-1980s. The number of 'missing women' in China, similarly calculated, is 44 million.[22] There is need for an explanation as to why women's survival pattern has been so adverse in these countries.[23]

The motivation behind Barbara Harriss's investigation in Chapter 10 can be understood in this context. How much evidence is there of intrafamily inequality in hunger in South Asia, in particular India and Bangladesh? She examines a variety of empirical information, including anthropometric comparisons of women and men, but concentrates on the actual nutrient intakes of different members of a family in relation to the respective nutritional 'norms'. She also investigates the intrafamily distribution according to age, especially the shares of the very old and the very young. As background to these empirical studies, Harriss examines the methodological problems that make such comparisons so difficult. She also throws light on the material and cultural factors

[18] See Waldron (1983).

[19] This despite the fact that the 'sex ratio' at birth goes the other way, namely, 105 or 106 male children are born per 100 female children, more or less everywhere in the world.

[20] While Pakistan seems to have the lowest female–male ratio (around 0.90) among all the sizeable countries in the world, there are states in India which have still lower female–male ratios. Uttar Pradesh and Haryana have ratios around 0.88, while in the Indian state of Kerala the ratio is higher than 1.03 (and thus quite close to the female–male ratio in Europe and North America).

[21] See Sen (1988a).

[22] See Drèze and Sen (1989a: ch. 4).

[23] See also Harriss and Watson (1987). There are also 'subtler' patterns of anti-female differences related to such factors as birth order. For example, Monica Das Gupta (1987) has found, with data from Punjab, that while the bias against the first daughter seems to be little, the discrimination becomes quite sharp as later birth-order girls are considered.

that may influence the intrafamily distribution of food, and their relevance for public action.

Barbara Harriss finds rather mixed evidence of intrafamily discrimination in the intakes of nutrients. The inequalities have some regional pattern.[24] There are strong interconnections between differences related to age and gender. Inequalities also differ with socio-economic class. Harriss's conclusions, based on what is probably the most extensive empirical investigation of the available data on food intakes related to gender and age, cover a wide range of questions. In general, however, they indicate that it would be a mistake to diagnose a general pattern of anti-female bias in the intrafamily distribution of nutrients in India, though there are some specific differences connected with age, class, and region.

Given the absence of a general diagnosis of intrafamily inequality of nutrient intake, the question may be asked why there is such a strong pattern of excess female mortality in India for most age groups until the age of the late thirties.[25] In answering this question, two issues have to be borne in mind. First, morbidity and mortality are affected not only by food intake, but also by health care and parental attention. There is some direct evidence of anti-female discrimination in these respects in much of Such Asia, both for women vis-à-vis men, and for girls vis-à-vis boys.[26] As Barbara Harriss notes, intrafamily inequalities in health care, medicine, and general attention can yield, on their own, excess female mortality rates.

Second, one can go further and question whether we really learn enough about gender discrimination in nutrition by concentrating on nutrient intakes. Ultimately, nutritional well-being is concerned with the ability to achieve certain 'functionings', and depends on a variety of factors (including personal characteristics, activity levels, epidemiological environment, access to health care, etc.) of which nutrient intake is only one.[27] Gender bias in this context would take the form of different levels of accepted debilitation for the respective sexes (e.g., tolerating more health dysfunctioning in the case of girls compared with boys). Whether this is occurring or not cannot be deduced simply by comparing actual intakes with a set of intake 'norms' that cannot

[24] Regional contrasts within India of anti-female discrimination have been discussed by Boserup (1970), Bardhan (1974, 1987), Miller (1981, 1989), among others.

[25] The overall life expectancy at birth of women has, it appears, caught up at last with that of men in India (though it remains lower in Pakistan and Bangladesh). But this aggregate index is much influenced by the higher age-specific mortality rates of Indian men beyond the age of 40 (this is in line with the situation in most countries). Below that age, for many of the age-groups, women still have a higher age-specific mortality rate in India. Oddly, there is some evidence that in China, where women's life expectancy had become larger than men's, there has been a movement in the opposite direction since the economic and social changes of 1979. Female life expectancy in China has again fallen below that of the male in the early 1980s (on this see Banister 1987: Table 4.12).

[26] See e.g. Chen et al. (1981), Kynch and Sen (1983), Sen (1984), Das Gupta (1987).

[27] On this see Sen (1984, 1985), and Drèze and Sen (1989a: chs. 1–4). See also chs. 7 and 8 below.)

allow for possible variations in the other influences relevant to nutritional well-being. We would need other data that take direct account of the *effects* of differences in intakes, such as clinical signs of undernourishment and morbidity rates.[28]

This observation is not meant as a criticism of Harriss's paper, since her investigation concentrates quite explicitly on nutrient intake patterns rather than on the broader question of gender discrimination in nutritional well-being. But we do need to note that the latter question cannot be adequately addressed without going into the functioning space at some stage of the exercise. The important questions that motivate Barbara Harriss's study can be properly answered only by broadening the informational base.

1.11. *Food production and African women*

In contrast with South Asia, West Asia, North Africa, and China, where women are vastly outnumbered by men, in sub-Saharan Africa there are many more women than men. In terms of survival rates, sub-Saharan African women do better than men (even though the absolute levels of life expectancy of both males and females are often quite low in Africa). Also, sub-Saharan African women have a much bigger role in the production process and in work outside the household than women in the bulk of Asia and North Africa. There has been some discussion as to whether these two facts are related, and whether the larger economic role and the correspondingly greater independence of women in sub-Saharan Africa help to give them a better deal in the intrafamily divisions of commodities and privileges.[29] While that particular hypothesis would demand more examination and scrutiny, the general picture of African women's work and economic role has been far from clear. The need for a better understanding of that picture has become particularly important in the context of assessing the relation of African food problems with the nature of work that African women perform. The links involved include not only the question of gender discrimination (discussed in the preceding section), but also the general relevance of women's work for food strategies and in particular for food production.

Ann Whitehead in Chapter 11 examines this issue with empirical information and conceptual analysis. Whitehead argues that many of the common beliefs about African women's role in food production (e.g. that African agriculture can be neatly divided into a 'female/subsistence' sector and a 'male/commercial' sector) are myths. A substantial part of her paper is devoted to debunking some common myths, and disputing generalizations that have been taken for granted.

[28] On this see Chen *et al.* (1981) and Kynch and Sen (1983).

[29] On this see Boserup (1970), Kandiyoti (1988), Sen (1988*a*, 1989*b*), Drèze and Sen (1989*a*: ch. 4).

A second objective of Whitehead's paper is to assess the effect of development of projects on women in sub-Saharan Africa, and this is supplemented by her analysis of the roles that women can play in expanding African agricultural output. Among other issues, she discusses the assumption of an 'unproblematic unity of interests of household members' on which development strategies have frequently relied. The modelling underlying the development projects has tended to ignore the 'dual' role of African women in production, i.e. women's independent farming as well as women's recruitment as household labour (including 'peasant wives' family labour'). It is the latter that has received priority in the development projects, thereby making it harder for African women to preserve and expand their role as independent producers.

While there are many variations in that general theme (and Whitehead goes into several related issues in her extensive investigation), the nature of the main policy mistake is, in her view, clear enough. The neglect of women's role as independent producers worsens the relative position of women (as Whitehead puts it, 'development planners, perhaps unwittingly, are making it very hard for women' (p.460)), and it may also be counterproductive for raising agricultural output generally. There is scope for expansion based on a greater use of women's role as independent producers. Whitehead ends her paper with a discussion of policies for the future in line with her diagnostic analysis. Problems of production incentives and ways of removing constraints are assessed in that light.

1.12. *Famines and famine prevention*

The ten chapters in the first volume cover general grounds on the economic, political, and social background to hunger and deprivation. They are not meant, of course, as exhaustive studies of all the relevant issues. They are purposeful investigations of some specific problems that have to be addressed for a better understanding of hunger and related deprivations in the modern world. The two volumes that follow are more directly concerned with public policy and action.

The six chapters in volume 2 deal primarily with starvation and famines (problems of endemic undernutrition are taken up in volume 3). Sub-Saharan Africa receives much of the attention, since it is there that famines have persistently continued to occur. But there is discussion also of famines and famine prevention in South Asia.

1.13. *The Indian experience*

Jean Drèze's chapter 'Famine Prevention in India', scrutinizes India's achievement in preventing droughts, floods, and other natural disasters from developing into famines as they used to in the past. A major step was taken in that direction in the 1880s when the 'Famine Codes' were formulated. These codes included instructions for recreating lost incomes through wages to be paid in public works programmes, supplemented by some unconditional relief for those who could not be employed. Food trade was left almost entirely to private traders throughout the pre-independence period.

The Famine Codes, though clear-headed in analysis, were only a partial success in practice. Sometimes the relief offered was too little and too late, and in one notorious occasion—the Bengal Famine of 1943—the Famine Codes were not even invoked (the famine was simply 'not declared'). In post-independence India the relief system has become more systematic and extensive, but no less importantly, the governments—pressured by the news media and opposition parties—do not any longer have the option of ignoring famine threats. The last major famine in India occurred in 1943, preceding independence in 1947.

Drèze presents a discussion of the rationale of the Famine Codes (and other insights of the Famine Commission Reports), and he also investigates the changes that have been brought about since independence. Aside from a major political transformation, the latter include a considerable increase in the real resources devoted to famine relief, a broadening of the range of support measures, direct state involvement in food trade without eliminating private traders, and the maintenance of a substantial volume of food in public stock. Food management in India seems to have produced a large measure of food price stability, but India's success in famine prevention is still thoroughly dependent on the recreation of lost entitlements through wage-based employment, supplemented by unconditional relief.[30]

Jean Drèze provides two specific case-studies, namely the food crisis of 1966–7 in Bihar and the non-famine of 1970–3 in Maharashtra despite a disastrous drought. Finally, he examines the lessons that can be derived from the Indian experience for famine prevention elsewhere.[31]

1.14. African successes in famine prevention

India's success in the eradication of famines is fairly widely acknowledged, even though the reasons for this success are often misunderstood.[32] In

---

[30] There are few empirical studies of the role played in practice by unconditional relief measures. The interregional contrasts within India in this respect are important. For further discussion and some empirical material relating to the 1987 drought in Gujarat, see Drèze (1988).

[31] Drèze also points to the limitations of the Indian anti-hunger policy, which eliminates famines but tolerates massive endemic undernutrition. See also Drèze (1988).

[32] It is often presumed that famines have been eliminated in independent India through a revolutionary increase in food production. There certainly has been some rise in food production per capita since independence (and the 'green revolution' has been effective in the production of wheat in particular), but the increase in food production per head has not been very large. Indeed, the average per capita food availability in India today is not substantially greater than in the late

contrast, the experiences of successful famine prevention in sub-Saharan Africa are often unacknowledged and ignored. The harrowing tales of unprevented famines in that subcontinent seem to dominate the international perception of what has been happening in Africa.

In his second chapter in volume 2 ('Famine Prevention in Africa: Some Experiences and Lessons'), Jean Drèze concentrates specifically on recent success stories in sub-Saharan Africa, and examines the lessons that can be drawn from them. The case-studies include experiences of averted famines in Botswana, Cape Verde, Kenya, and Zimbabwe. At a very general level, these experiences confirm that public policy for recreating lost entitlements provides a major clue to success in famine prevention. Neither rapid economic growth (as in Botswana), nor rapid growth of agriculture (as in Kenya), nor even rapid growth in food production (as in post-independence Zimbabwe), are by themselves an adequate safeguard against famines. The distinguishing achievements of these countries (as well as of Cape Verde) really lie in their having provided direct public support to their populations in times of crisis.

Aside from this general observation, there are many other lessons to learn from the experiences examined by Drèze. The lessons are partly concerned with the strategy of entitlement protection, and partly with the politics of early action.[33] Regarding the former, Drèze discusses a range of policy issues including the role of food supply management in famine prevention, the question of early warning, the case for greater use of cash support and employment provision, the interconnections between private trade and public distribution, and the long-run importance of economic diversification. As far as early action is concerned, the case-studies presented in the chapter confirm that, in Africa no less than in India, the response of governments has been more a question of political incentives to intervene against a famine than one of relying on formal 'early warning techniques' to anticipate a crisis. There is some diversity in the precise nature of political incentives that have prompted the governments of these African countries to counter resolutely the threat of famine. But one of the features that does emerge again in this context is the importance of public accountability in making it hard for a government to allow a famine to develop.

19th century (a decline over the first half of this century having been balanced by an increase after independence). The causes of success of Indian famine prevention policy have to be sought elsewhere—in the process of entitlement protection through various measures of income generation and price stability, and the compulsion generated by adversarial politics that ensures early public intervention. On this last see ch. 6 below.

[33] See also Drèze and Sen (1989a: chs. 5–8).

1.15. Famines in Ethiopia

The success stories from Botswana, Cape Verde, etc. have to be contrasted with failures in famine prevention elsewhere. The case of Ethiopia is often cited in this context. In the third chapter of volume 2 ('Ethiopian Famines 1973-1985: A Case-Study'), B. G. Kumar examines the famines in Ethiopia during 1973-5 and 1982-5. The former set of famines began during Haile Selassie's rule and, in fact, he was deposed during those famines. But the government that followed has not been able to eliminate famines from Ethiopia.

Kumar explains the occurrence of famines and the composition of destitutes by examining the collapse of entitlements to food of different occupation groups. He also argues, however, that there were substantial declines in food availability in each of the famines, and these declines were among the factors that had a major influence on the entitlements of different groups.[34] Kumar also investigates the demographic and social impacts of the Ethiopian famines.

On matters of policy, Kumar's analysis underlines the usefulness of employment creation and the use of cash wages. He also emphasizes the importance of an early response. In this respect Kumar attaches some importance to bettering formal 'early warning' systems, but argues that the main delays in responding have been caused by political factors rather than by technical inadequacies. These lessons have clear affinity with those emerging on the 'other' side, from case-studies of success in India and in sub-Saharan Africa.

1.16. Early warning systems

There is general agreement on the need to act quickly to defeat threatening famines. 'Early warning systems' are aimed at making it possible to act without

---

[34] As far as the 1973 famine is concerned, earlier discussed in Sen (1981), Kumar disputes Sen's view that the famine was not caused by any significant decline in food availability. Sen's diagnosis referred to food availability in Ethiopia as a whole, whereas Kumar's point is about a decline in food availability specifically in the famine province of Wollo (this was, in fact, noted and discussed by Sen, pp. 88–96). Since there was no ban on food movement between the different provinces during the famine of 1973, the question as to whether Wollo's low food supply should be treated as an endogenous variable governed by local food production in Wollo (as Kumar suggests), *or* as being governed by the low purchasing power of the Wollo population connected with the local agricultural decline (as Sen suggests), turns on the physical possibility of transporting food across the boundaries of Wollo with the rest of Ethiopia. In this context, the undisputed existence of a major highway linking Dessie (the capital of Wollo) to Addis Ababa and Asmera (the highway was in fact used for moving some food *out of* Wollo to elsewhere, on which see Sen 1981: 94), *is* crucial to the point at issue. Further, the fact that food prices in Dessie did not rise and remained roughly similar to those in Addis Ababa and Asmera (Sen 1981: 95–6), despite the famine conditions in and around Dessie, would seem to support the view that the food available in the rest of Ethiopia could not be pulled into Wollo because of the lack of purchasing power of the Wollo population (not because of a transport bottleneck).

delay by making policy makers aware of famine threats. Unfortunately, there is also some agreement that the existing formal systems of early warning are seriously defective.

From here we can go in one of two different directions. One is to abandon the search for an adequate 'early warning' model, and to concentrate on getting the necessary warnings in other ways, e.g. through an active news media reporting early cases of hardship and worsening hunger.[35] The other way is to try to improve the models that have been so far devised. Meghnad Desai takes the second route in his chapter ('Modelling an Early Warning System For Famines'), and suggests ways in which the exercise of early warning can be much improved. He also goes into the use of such systems in determining the timing of policies.

One of the reasons why formal analysis of early warning is difficult is the fact that a famine can develop from a variety of causes. The initiating factor can be a natural phenomenon (e.g. a drought), or an economic one (e.g. widespread loss of employment and income), or a socio-political event (e.g. a civil war). Desai discusses how these processes can respectively—in different ways—affect the economic system and lead to the collapse of entitlements of vulnerable groups.

Desai's analysis throws much light on the requirements of a good early warning system.[36] There may be some scope for doubt as to whether these requirements can be typically fully met given the complexities of the relations involved and the need for speed in data gathering and analysis. That question remains somewhat open at this stage. But even if a fully adequate system of early warning were not to emerge rapidly, the connections that Desai explores can be of a great deal of use in devising anti-famine policies. An analytical system of early warning, of the kind that Desai has explored, relies on unpacking the different components involved in the collapse of entitlements, and those components have to be clearly understood for the formulation of effective policies of entitlement protection and famine prevention. Thus, the scope of Desai's chapter is considerably broader than the title suggests.

1.17. *Anti-hunger policy and market responses*

In the fifth chapter in volume 2 ('Market Responses to Anti-hunger Policies: Effects on Wages, Prices, and Employment'), Martin Ravallion takes up the complex issue of how market responses affect the effectiveness of various public measures to combat hunger of particular groups. This investigation draws on general-equilibrium analysis of the kind that Ravallion has already

---

[35] On this see chs. 2 and 6 below and the chapters by Drèze in vol. 2. See also Drèze and Sen (1989a).

[36] See also Desai (1988), and the chapter by d'Souza (1988) in the same volume.

used very successfully in his previous studies of famines (particularly in his book *Markets and Famines*, Ravallion 1987a).

Ravallion considers the major types of measures that have been used in this field, including pure transfer payments, wages for relief work, public grain storage, food price policies, foreign trade, and public information and famine forecasting. In each case, he investigates the ways in which the markets may respond, and their implications for public policy. For example, the overall transfer benefits (inclusive of 'multiplier effects') of public employment programmes will be larger when the wage elasticity of demand for labour is small, and this provides one argument for providing such employment at times when it competes with other employment, rather than just in lean seasons. Of course, these particular considerations have to be integrated with other elements of a full assessment of alternatives, including in this case the 'stabilization benefits' that may be associated with income generation in lean seasons (when incomes are scarce) particularly if opportunities for borrowing are restricted.

Ravallion puts particular emphasis on the less obvious elements of anti-hunger policy. In contrast with the much-discussed cases of relief work and pure transfers, he also investigates the considerable benefits for the poor and the hungry that may result from price stabilization policies, improvement of rural credit, etc. The relative effectiveness of these different lines of action has to be assessed in the light of their respective market responses. Altogether Ravallion has provided an important exploration of alternative anti-hunger policies, the effects they may have (operating *inter alia* through the market), and how their effectiveness may be respectively assessed. The lessons have relevance in combating endemic hunger as well as in devising policies of famine prevention.

1.18. *Policy variables and structural constraints*

One of the issues facing public policy analysis to combat famines and hunger in sub-Saharan African concerns the assignment of responsibility for its present predicament. Policy mistakes in the past have often been identified as the major offenders in bringing Africa to its present plight. For example, African governments typically have much control—direct and indirect—over prices of agricultural goods in general and food prices in particular, and it has been frequently argued that it is the tendency to keep these prices artificially low that has been a major cause of low food production in Africa.[37]

In so far as the problems of sub-Saharan Africa are seen as arising primarily or largely from policy mistakes, there may be some reason to hope that a

---

[37] This position has been forcefully presented in several contributions by the World Bank and its policy analysts; see e.g. World Bank (1986), Ray (1988).

solution of these problems may be readily available in the form of reversing these policy-mistakes. For example, 'getting prices right' has appealed to many as an obvious and sure-fire way of liberating Africa from its present predicament.

While there is clearly some truth in the diagnosis of policy errors, and while price incentives can indeed be important, it is not easy to see a ready salvation for Africa through a simple 'policy reversal'. For one thing, each of these policies has many aspects. For example, high food prices may give more production incentives, but they also make it harder for the poor to acquire food, and a substantial proportion of the African poor have to rely on the market—rather than on home production—for getting the food they eat. For another, the remedy of African poverty calls for a rapid increase in production and incomes in general, and the demands of this have to be distinguished from the policy imperatives of maximizing food production as such. Even though there have undoubtedly been policy mistakes that have contributed to Africa's present problems, straightforward remedies, such as raising food prices, may not be as promising and unproblematic as they have been made to look.[38]

What is at issue is not merely the effectiveness of changes in prices and of other policy variables that the governments can easily control, but also the need to address the harder and less easily influenceable features of the economy and the society. Platteau's chapter ('The Food Crisis in Africa: A Comparative Structural Analysis') discusses many of the structural features that have had a profound bearing on famines and hunger in Africa, particularly through influencing food production. The domain of Platteau's investigation is wide, and he identifies the important influences exercised by land tenure and other institutions, technological constraints, political limitations, and even cultural obstacles. His analysis of Africa's predicament draws on a long-ranging study of history, and he argues strongly in favour of taking fuller note of structural parameters and constraints in understanding African hunger and in seeking effective and lasting remedies.

Platteau's institutional analysis importantly supplements the concentration on easily influenceable policy variables in many other studies. The recurrence of famines in Africa has many aspects and it relates to different antecedent circumstances. The demands of rapidity and durability in remedying the situation include the need for attention being paid to policy issues of widely different kinds.

The chapters in volume 2, taken together, provide a fairly comprehensive investigation of the underlying issues and the different considerations that have to be taken into account in eradicating famines from Africa. While there is scope for much optimism, especially in view of the successes already achieved

---

[38] We have gone into these issues in Drèze and Sen (1989a), particularly in chs. 2, 9, and 13. There is an extensive literature on this; see e.g. Lipton (1987), Streeten (1987), Pinstrup-Andersen (1989).

in some parts of sub-Saharan Africa and elsewhere, the need for deep-rooted, constructive changes cannot be overemphasized.[39] The call for rapidity should not be confused with a search for the 'quick fix'.

1.19. *Endemic undernourishment and deprivation*

While the focus of volume 2 is primarily on eliminating famines, the third volume deals with the challenge of combating persistent want and hunger. Two cases of notable success—China and Sri Lanka—are discussed in some detail. In both these cases a major reduction of deprivation and expansion of life expectancy and related indicators have been achieved despite very low gross national product per capita.

In another book (Drèze and Sen 1989*a*), we have compared and contrasted two different—though not unrelated—general strategies for eliminating endemic undernourishment and deprivation. The approach of 'growth-mediated security' involves rapid economic expansion, including that of GNP per head, and the use of this achievement to eradicate regular hunger and privation. In this general strategy, the fruits of growth are widely shared partly through a participatory growth process (involving, in particular, a rapid and sustained expansion of remunerative and worthwhile employment), but also through the use of the resources generated by economic growth to expand public support of health, nutrition, education, and economic security for the more deprived and vulnerable. In contrast, the approach of 'support-led security' involves going in for public support measures without waiting for the country to become rich through economic growth. Examples of support-led security include, in addition to China and Sri Lanka, such countries as Costa Rica, Cuba, Chile, Jamaica, and the State of Kerala in India.

There is a real contrast between these two strategies, but it is important to recognize that the extensive use of public support measures plays a crucial role in both. While public support is the primary and immediate instrument of action in the strategy of support-led security, it is also an important ingredient of the success of growth-mediated security. Indeed, in the absence of public involvement to guarantee that the fruits of growth are widely shared, rapid economic growth can have a disappointingly poor impact on living conditions.[40] The distinctiveness of the strategy of support-led security is not the *use* of public support to improve living conditions, but the *temporal priority* that is attached to this instrument of action even when the country in question is still quite poor.

It may be asked how poor countries can afford to have extensive public

---

[39] The positive opportunities that can be effectively used have also been discussed in Drèze and Sen (1989*a*: chs. 5–8).

[40] On the role of public support measures in the recent experiences of growth-mediated security, see Drèze and Sen (1989*a*: ch. 10).

support systems. Part of the answer lies in the labour intensive nature of many of these measures of public delivery—particularly in health care and education—making them cheaper in poorer economies. But some of the explanation also relates to the scope for reorienting the focus of delivery away from providing an enormous lot—expensive and advanced services—to a few (the relatively affluent) to securing minimal basic services for all (including the worst off).[41] Indeed, the fractions of their relatively low GNP per head devoted to public programmes of health care and education in China, Sri Lanka, Kerala, Cuba, and other adopters of the general strategy of support-led security have not been remarkably higher than in countries that have treated education and medicine as the entitlement of the rich and the privileged.

1.20. China's record

Carl Riskin's chapter ('Feeding China: The Experience since 1949') is an illuminating account of China's experience in combating hunger since the revolution.[42] While a problem of undernourishment in many rural areas continues to exist, China has been in general remarkably successful in reducing the reach and magnitude of undernourishment across the country. Food production has generally grown faster than population over these years, but between the 1950s and the reforms of 1979, not by very much.[43] China's success in reducing deprivation is particularly connected with public policies involving relatively egalitarian distribution and widespread public support of health and nutrition. Riskin also discusses in some detail the mechanisms of food distribution in China—between the provinces, between the urban and rural areas, and between different families and persons.

One terrible blot in China's otherwise impressive record is the occurrence of a large famine during 1959–61, in the wake of the failure of the so-called Great Leap Forward. Riskin discusses the factors that contributed to this calamity, including the limited information that the central government had about food production and consumption in the provinces. In the comparison between China and India, on which we commented earlier in this Introduction, it would appear that India has done much worse than China in the reduction of

---

[41] There are many other factors involved in this complex question. On this and related matters (including the considerations involved in the choice between the two general strategies), see Drèze and Sen (1989a: chs. 10–12).

[42] See also Riskin (1987).

[43] Oddly, in the post-reform period, between 1979 and the mid-1980s, while agricultural and food production per head have rapidly increased, the mortality rate has also gone up and there has been a considerable reduction in life expectancy (on this see Banister 1987). These changes are not yet fully studied, but among the factors implicated are general financial stringency and some withdrawal of wide-coverage rural health services, and the introduction of compulsory birth control measures, leading to a neglect (if not worse) of female children. These matters have been discussed in Sen (1988b) and Drèze and Sen (1989a: ch. 11).

endemic undernourishment, but has been more successful in eradicating famines.

The fact that China could have such a famine despite its excellent general record in the reduction of endemic deprivation and normal mortality under-lines the need to see the battle against hunger as one with many facets. It also indicates that the eradication of hunger benefits not only from having a dedicated and determined government committed to that objective, but also from having a system that permits participatory and adversarial involvement of the general public.[44] Given the recent developments in China, the relevance of these considerations may extend well beyond the limited field of anti-hunger policy.

1.21. *Public support in Sri Lanka*

Sri Lanka's achievements in raising life expectancy and the quality of life have been the subject of much attention among economists (even though these achievements are in some danger of being overshadowed by the violence and strife into which Sri Lanka has recently been plunged). A life expectancy of 70 years for a country with the low GNP per head that Sri Lanka has is no mean feat. Indeed, its life expectancy is still marginally *higher* than that of South Korea despite the latter's remarkable economic expansion leading to a GNP per capita many times that of Sri Lanka.

Sri Lanka's use of public support measures goes back a long way. Expansion of primary education took place early in the century. A rapid expansion of health services occurred in the mid-1940s. Sri Lanka moved to a system of free or subsidized distribution of rice in 1942. Between 1940 and 1960, its crude death rate fell from above 20 per thousand to around 8 per thousand.

Sri Lanka's radical and innovative public support measures have played a substantial part in its achievements.[45] In their chapter ('Public Policy and Basic Needs Provision: Intervention and Achievement in Sri Lanka'), Sudhir Anand and Ravi Kanbur have provided a probing and far-reaching account of that connection. By using time-series data pertaining to the relevant variables, they have indicated how and when direct public intervention has contributed to reducing deprivation and to enhancing the quality of life in Sri Lanka. These

---

[44] On this see also Drèze and Sen (1989*a*). Also ch. 6 below and the chapters by Drèze in vol. 2.

[45] Some observers (e.g. Bhalla and Glewwe 1986, Bhalla 1988) have argued that Sri Lanka's high level of life expectancy and other achievements may not have been related to its public support measures and in support of this view they have pointed to its unexceptional expansion of life expectancy and other indicators in the period *since 1960* (compared with other countries). Aside from some methodological problems in the analysis (on which see Isenman 1987, Pyatt 1987, Ravallion 1987*b*, among others), this line of argument overlooks the fact that the expansion of public support measures in Sri Lanka substantially predates 1960, and that in the period of rapid expansion of public support (particularly from the mid-1940s) Sri Lanka's death rate did fall quite fast. On this and related matters, see Drèze and Sen (1989*a*: ch. 12).

lessons have considerable bearing on future policy as well, since public support measures have been under severe scrutiny in Sri Lanka—as elsewhere—on the grounds of their being expensive, and there has been some withdrawal (also analysed by Anand and Kanbur) from an interventionist strategy in recent years.

Anand and Kanbur's econometric analysis suggests that the expansion of health services has been rather more effective than food subsidies in bringing about mortality decline in Sri Lanka. The policy issues to be faced in Sri Lanka—and elsewhere—not only concern the recognition of the role of public support measures in general, but also call for a discriminating assessment of the choices to be faced *within* a general strategy of public intervention. Anand and Kanbur have provided an authoritative account of the diagnostic and policy issues concerning one of the most interesting experiences of combating hunger and deprivation in a poor country.

1.22. *Brazil and unaimed opulence*

While Sri Lanka provides an example of what can be achieved even with a low real income per head and moderate economic growth, Brazil provides an illustration of how little can happen in removing poverty and deprivation even with remarkably rapid growth of GNP per head. In his chapter 'Growth and Poverty: Some Lessons from Brazil', Ignacy Sachs provides a lucid account of this contrary experience.

Brazil's economic growth has not only been fast, it has also been sustained and technologically rich (with widespread use of modern technology). Brazil has also emerged as one of the largest exporters of industrial products in the world, and the incomes generated in production for domestic and foreign markets have raised the level of average income in the country to levels that are very much higher than obtained a few decades ago. And yet there is a good deal of endemic undernutrition in Brazil and there is persistent poverty affecting a substantial section of the population. Sachs discusses how and why rapid economic growth has failed to improve the lives of so many million Brazilians, and why their entitlements have been so little influenced· by the newly generated incomes. Identifying inequality as the major villain in all this, Sachs has also briefly explored the scope for 'growth with redistribution' in Brazil.

As we discussed earlier in this Introduction (and more fully in Drèze and Sen 1989a), growth of GNP *can be* a major contributor to removing undernourishment and deprivation, and the strategy of 'growth-mediated security' specifically focuses on this connection. But that recognition should not be confused with the claim that growth of GNP per head must invariably and automatically bring about removal of deprivation across the board. What is at issue is not merely the quality of growth—in particular its participatory nature—but also the willingness of the government to use the fruits of growth to provide public support with comprehensive coverage—guaranteeing basic health services, education, and other basic amenities to all sections of the population, including the most vulnerable and deprived groups. In both these respects the experience of growth-mediated security in, say, South Korea contrasts sharply with the 'unaimed opulence' of Brazil.[46]

1.23.   *Latin American poverty and undernourishment*

While Sachs concentrates on Brazil, Ravi Kanbur's chapter 'Malnutrition and Poverty in Latin America' has a much wider coverage. Kanbur identifies the extent of undernourishment in Latin America, which is obviously much less severe than in South Asia or sub-Saharan Africa, but which is far from negligible in magnitude.[47]

Kanbur goes on to discuss the extent to which economic growth on its own can be expected to eliminate undernourishment in the Latin American countries. Here Kanbur's broader analysis supplements the more concentrated study of Brazil by Sachs. Kanbur shows that the 'crossover time' (i.e. the number of years required for the average poor person to cross the poverty line if his or her income grows at the average rate of growth of per capita GNP of the past twenty years) tends to be remarkably high. This takes Kanbur to the question of the *aiming* of economic expansion and the *targeting* of the increase of incomes and consumptions. He outlines some necessary characteristics of a well-targeted policy for alleviating poverty and undernourishment.

Crucial to Kanbur's analysis is his identification of the contrasts between socio-economic groups in terms of vulnerability to deprivation. Throughout Latin America, the incidence of poverty is much higher in the rural areas than in the urban (though the urban slum dwellers form one of the more deprived groups). Within the rural areas, the landless workers and those with tiny holdings are most prone to suffer. Kanbur finds the size of the family to be an important parameter as well, indicating the relevance of population policy. His analysis of targeting in removing undernourishment draws on the results of these diagnostic analyses. The important issue is to replace 'unaimed opulence' by using growth as a mediator of security.

1.24.   *The extent of undernourishment in sub-Saharan Africa*

Peter Svedberg's chapter 'Undernutrition in Sub-Saharan Africa: A Critical Assessment of the Evidence' is concerned with the diagnostic question as to

---

[46] The contrast between 'growth-mediated security' and 'unaimed opulence' is discussed in Drèze and Sen (1989a: ch. 10).

[47] While the proportion of people in poverty in Latin America is comparable to that in East Asia in terms of income deprivation, Latin America's record is much worse than that of East Asia in terms of living conditions, including the expectation of life.

how much undernourishment exists in sub-Saharan Africa. Svedberg deals with both methodological and substantive issues. He argues that the methodologies used to measure the extent of undernourishment in sub-Saharan Africa have frequently been faulty and have involved the use of unreliable data. He also indicates that the extent of undernourishment has been very often exaggerated.

Svedberg makes extensive use—*inter alia*—of anthropometric evidence to establish his substantive conclusions. There are interpretational problems here too, but Svedberg's critical assessment of the unreliability of the usual high estimates is certainly quite robust. It is important not to read his conclusions as grounds for smugness, since even his own estimates indicate a substantial problem of deprivation and undernourishment in sub-Saharan Africa.

Svedberg's chapter can be seen as an argument for not exaggerating what is in any case quite a momentous problem. It can be added that, by exaggerating the extent of the problem, well-meaning scholars have sometimes inadvertently encouraged a sense of hopelessness and fatalism about hunger in sub-Saharan Africa. This can be changed by a more realistic assessment of the extent of the challenge, followed by a determination to deal with it effectively. Svedberg's essay serves this dialectic purpose in addition to the methodological and diagnostic functions on which he himself concentrates.

1.25. *Institutions and policies for sub-Saharan Africa*

In removing the true—unexaggerated—prevalence of endemic undernourishment in sub-Saharan Africa, the expansion of its agriculture will undoubtedly play an important part. This is not merely because food comes primarily from agriculture, but also because the entitlements of the majority of Africans depend—directly or indirectly—on the functioning of the agricultural sector, and this situation can change only relatively slowly. Despite the importance of distinguishing between the problems of food entitlement and those of food production as such, the crucial contributory role of food production in particular and agricultural production in general can scarcely be denied.

In his chapter 'Policy Options for African Agriculture', Francis Idachaba has provided a broad-ranging analysis of ailments of sub-Saharan agriculture and the policy options that exist. Rather than concentrating on some simple 'remedies', Idachaba surveys the whole gamut of specific issues—social institutions, technological research, rural infrastructure, agricultural prices. It is in this wide setting that he assesses what the governments can do and what policies seem most promising.[48] Idachaba also considers the role of external

---

[48] There is a discussion in Drèze and Sen (1989a: ch. 9) of these issues, including the importance of diversification and the balance of food production *vis-à-vis* the production of cash crops and industrial goods.

assistance and the parts—negative as well as positive—played by international institutions such as the World Bank.

1.26. *Kenyan agriculture and food deprivation*

While Idachaba takes on the whole of sub-Saharan Africa as his field of investigation, Judith Heyer looks specifically at smallholder agriculture in Kenya ('Poverty and Food Deprivation in Kenya's Smallholder Agricultural Areas'). The incidence of poverty among people engaged in smallholder agriculture in Kenya is, of course, very high, and Heyer considers the ways in which this situation can be changed.

Although Heyer examines various internal reforms within smallholder agriculture, she comes to the conclusion that, in bringing about a major change, an important part will have to be played by developments *outside* the sector—in non-agricultural activities and in large-scale farming. Heyer identifies intersectoral interconnections that are important, but which are frequently overlooked in viewing smallholder agriculture on its own. Her argument for a broader economic analysis with an eye to social consequences can be seen as a corrective to some of the prevailing preconceptions in this field.

1.27. *The industrial connection*

Samuel Wangwe's chapter ('The Contribution of Industry to Solving the Food Problem in Africa') has close links with Judith Heyer's broad-based approach. Wangwe looks specifically at the contribution of industry to combating hunger (in this his concentration is rather narrower than that of Heyer), but he does not confine his analysis to any particular country (his focus is, in that respect, broader than that of Heyer).

Given the importance of employment in securing entitlements, Wangwe devotes a good deal of attention to the need for generating opportunities of employment—in off-farm activities and in industry in addition to farm employment. Another industrial connection that receives much attention in Wangwe's paper is the part played by the production, acquisition, and use of agricultural equipment. He also goes on to discuss the role of industry in agricultural processing.

The contributions of Heyer and Wangwe supplement the analysis presented by Idachaba, and help to underline the important fact that the solution of the so-called 'food problem' in sub-Saharan Africa will require a good deal more than a concentration on the internal problems of the food-producing sector. The persistence of endemic undernourishment in sub-Saharan Africa calls for a wide range of remedial actions involving institutional changes and economic reforms both within the food sector and outside it.[49]

[49] See also Mellor *et al.* (1987), Lipton (1987), Eicher (1988), Pinstrup-Andersen (1989). See also Drèze and Sen (1989a).

1.28. *Hunger in Bangladesh*

Sub-Saharan Africa is not only plagued by endemic deprivation, it also suffers from the persistence of recurrent famines. In this respect the situation in South Asia is rather less desperate in that famines have rarely occurred in recent years in any of the South Asian economies. The one exception is Bangladesh which experienced a major famine in 1974.[50] But despite this relative absence of famines, the extent of regular undernourishment seems to be, if anything, *larger*—even in proportion to its population—in South Asia than in sub-Saharan Africa.[51]

Among the major countries in South Asia, Bangladesh is not only the poorest, it also has the largest proportion of hungry and undernourished people according to most estimates. In his chapter 'The Food Problems of Bangladesh', Siddiq Osmani has provided a helpful and authoritative account of the problems of undernourishment and famines in Bangladesh. Despite the international perception of the enormous and seemingly incurable nature of Bangladesh's problems (it has frequently been referred to as 'a basket case'), Bangladesh's achievements are far from negligible. It has achieved a growth rate of per capita income of about 2 per cent per year over the fourteen years or so since the famine of 1974,[52] and it has successfully avoided famines despite natural calamities of rather larger dimension than in 1974 (including the widespread and severe flooding of 1988). Osmani discusses the changes that have taken place and the major tasks that remain.

Osmani comes to the conclusion that, despite actually avoiding famines since 1974, Bangladesh's vulnerability to them remains. There is a lack of system in famine prevention and too much reliance on muddling through.[53] As far as endemic hunger is concerned, Osmani also argues that current food policies have the effect of accentuating rather than relieving this problem. The relatively successful overall economic growth has not been adequate in eliminating regular undernourishment.[54]

It is interesting that despite a much faster overall growth of aggregate real income compared with the growth of food production and consumption

[50] On this see Alamgir (1980) and Sen (1981: ch. 9).

[51] This is so even according to standard estimates (see Kanbur's chapter 'Malnutrition and Poverty in Latin America' for some comparative figures). Svedberg's criticisms have the effect of indicating that the actual extent of undernourishment is less in sub-Saharan Africa than these estimates suggest.

[52] On this see also Osmani (1989).

[53] It is also possible to argue that the more restricted nature of adversarial politics in Bangladesh compared with India is a factor that keeps the former country more vulnerable to famines arising from the lack of alertness and speed in anti-famine public policy.

[54] There has, however, been a considerable reduction in mortality, morbidity, and clinically diagnosed undernourishment in Bangladesh, connected with better delivery of health services.

(nutritional intake per head has not materially increased over the last two decades), food prices have not risen relative to other prices (in fact, the contrary has happened[55]). This is one result of the fact that Bangladesh's continuing problems have much to do with the persistence—even accentuation—of inequality, and the distribution of ownership and power that lead to unequal results. Osmani discusses the lines of reform that would be needed to meet the major challenge of continuing hunger in Bangladesh.

1.29.   *Public support and South Asia*

While Osmani's chapter concentrates on Bangladesh, the chapter by Kaushik Basu ('The Elimination of Endemic Hunger in South Asia: Some Policy Options') considers the problems of South Asia as a whole. The inadequacy of relying only on overall economic growth resurfaces here again in this context. Basu outlines the need for—and the actual possibility of—effective policies of 'direct action' to remove poverty and regular deprivation.

Basu illustrates his arguments with empirical illustrations from the experiences of Sri Lanka, India, and Bangladesh. He also provides a probing scrutiny of various 'poverty alleviation programmes' in use in South Asia, including 'food-for-work' schemes. While many of these programmes have failed in diverse ways, Basu outlines the promising nature of some of these policies if they are effectively planned and implemented.

The 'direct action' programmes take the form of economic action, but their success depends greatly on their political background—in particular the ability to remove the political constraints that often make them ineffective or degenerate. In addition to providing economic analysis of poverty removal, Basu's paper goes into the political requirements of entitlement protection and promotion. Both Osmani and Basu go explicitly into the political factors on which the effectiveness and success of economic policies significantly depend.[56] Here again political economy, in the broader sense outlined earlier, becomes the crucial analytical apparatus.

1.30.   *A concluding remark*

This collection of twenty-six papers has ranged over many different aspects of the battle against famines and endemic deprivation. While the responsibility for the views and analyses presented in them is ultimately that of the respective authors, it should be clear even from this Introduction that there are many interlinkages in the arguments and approaches contained in these papers. The challenge of hunger in the modern world calls for close scrutiny of many different issues in the political economy of hunger. These papers constitute elements of such a scrutiny.

---

[55] On this see Osmani (1989).

[56] On this see also Drèze and Sen (1989a: esp. ch. 13).

References

ALAMGIR, M. (1980), *Famine in South Asia* (Cambridge, Mass.: Oelgeschlager, Gunn & Hain).

ANAND, S., and HARRIS, C. (forthcoming), *Food and Nutrition in Sri Lanka* (Oxford: Oxford University Press).

ASHTON, B., HILL, K., PIAZZA, A., and ZEITZ, R. (1984), 'Famine in China, 1958–61', *Population and Development Review*, 10.

BANISTER, J. (1987), *China's Changing Population* (Stanford, Calif.: Stanford University Press).

BARDHAN, P. K. (1974), 'On Life and Death Questions', *Economic and Political Weekly*, 9 (Special No.).

——(1984), *The Political Economy of Development in India* (Oxford: Basil Blackwell).

——(1987), 'On the Economic Geography of Sex Disparity in Child Survival in India: A Note', paper presented at the BAMANEH/American SSRC Workshop on Differential Female Mortality and Health Care in South Asia, Dhaka.

BHALLA, S. (1988), 'Is Sri Lanka an Exception? A Comparative Study of Living Standards', in Srinivasan, T. N., and Bardhan, P. K. (eds.), *Rural Poverty in South Asia*, vol. ii (New York: Columbia University Press).

——and GLEWWE, P. (1986), 'Growth and Equity in Developing Countries: A Reinterpretation of the Sri Lankan Experience', *World Bank Economic Review*, 1.

BOSERUP, E. (1970), *Women's Role in Economic Development* (London: Allen & Unwin).

CHEN, L. C., HUQ, E., and D'SOUZA, S. (1981), 'Sex-Bias in the Family Allocation of Food and Health Care in Rural Bangladesh', *Population and Development Review*, 7.

DAS GUPTA, M. (1987), 'Selective Discrimination Against Female Children in Rural Punjab', *Population and Development Review*, 13.

DASGUPTA, P., and RAY, D. (1986); 'Inequality as a Determinant of Malnutrition and Unemployment: Theory', *Economic Journal*, 96.

—— ——(1987), 'Inequality as a Determinant of Malnutrition and Unemployment: Policy', *Economic Journal*, 97.

DESAI, M. (1988), 'The Economics of Famine', in Harrison (1988).

DRÈZE, J. P. (1988), 'Social Insecurity in India', paper presented at a Workshop on Social Security in Developing Countries held at the London School of Economics, July.

——and SEN, A. K. (1989a), *Hunger and Public Action* (Oxford: Oxford University Press).

—— ——(1989b), 'Public Action for Social Security', Discussion Paper No. 20, Development Economics Research Programme, London School of Economics; to be published in Ahmad, S. E., Drèze, J. P., Hills, J., and Sen, A. K. (eds.) (forthcoming), *Social Security in Developing Countries* (Oxford: Oxford University Press).

D'SOUZA, F. (1988), 'Famine: Social Security and an Analysis of Vulnerability', in Harrison (1988).

EICHER, C. (1988), 'Food Security Battles in Sub-Saharan Africa', paper presented at the VIIth World Congress for Rural Sociology, Bologna, 25 June–2 July.

HARRISON, G. A. (ed.) (1988), *Famines* (Oxford: Oxford University Press).

HARRISS, B., and WATSON, E. (1987), 'The Sex Ratio in South Asia', in Momsen, J. H., and Townsend, J. (eds.), *The Geography of Gender in the Third World* (London: Butler and Tanner).

ISENMAN, P. (1987), 'A Comment on "Growth and Equity in Developing Countries: A Reinterpretation of the Sri Lankan Experience" by Bhalla and Glewwe', *World Bank Economic Review*, 1.

JHA, P. S. (1980), *India: The Political Economy of Stagflation* (Bombay: Oxford University Press).

KANDIYOTI, D. (1988), 'Bargaining with Patriarchy', *Gender and Society*, 1.

KYNCH, J., and SEN, A. K. (1983), 'Indian Women: Well-Being and Survival', *Cambridge Journal of Economics*, 7.

LIPTON, M. (1987), 'Limits of Price Policy for Agriculture: Which Way for the World Bank?', *Development Policy Review*, 5.

MELLOR, J. W., DELGADO, C. L., and BLACKIE, C. L. (eds.) (1987), *Accelerating Food Production in Sub-Saharan Africa* (Baltimore, Md.: Johns Hopkins).

MILLER, B. (1981), *The Endangered Sex: Neglect of Female Children in Rural North India* (Ithaca, NY: Cornell University Press).

——(1989), 'Changing Patterns of Juvenile Sex Ratios in Rural India, 1961 to 1971', *Economic and Political Weekly*, 24.

OSMANI, S. (1989), 'Food Deprivation and Undernutrition in Rural Bangladesh', paper presented at the 9th World Crongress of the International Economic Association, Athens, Aug.

——(ed.) (forthcoming), *Nutrition and Poverty* (Oxford: Oxford University Press).

PARIKH, K., and RABAR, F. (eds.) (1981), *Food for All in a Sustainable World* (Laxenburg: IIASA).

PENG, X. (1987), 'Demographic Consequences of the Great Leap Forward in China's Provinces', *Population and Development Review*, 13.

PINSTRUP-ANDERSEN, P. (1989), 'Assuring a Household Food Security and Nutrition Bias in African Government Policies', paper presented at the 9th World Congress of the International Economic Association, Athens, Aug.

PYATT, G. (1987), 'A Comment on "Growth and Equity in Developing Countries: A Reinterpretation of the Sri Lankan Experience" by Bhalla and Glewwe', *World Bank Economic Review*, 1.

RAVALLION, M. (1987a), *Markets and Famines* (Oxford: Oxford University Press).

——(1987b), 'Growth and Equity in Sri Lanka: A Comment', mimeo (Washington, DC: World Bank).

RAY, A. (1988), 'A Response to Lipton's (June 1987) Review of "World Development Report 1986"', *Development Policy Review*, 6.

RISKIN, C. (1987), *China's Political Economy: The Quest for Development since 1949* (Oxford: Oxford University Press).

SEN, A. K. (1977), 'Starvation and Exchange Entitlements: A General Approach and its Application to the Great Bengal Famine', *Cambridge Journal of Economics*, 1.

——(1981), *Poverty and Famines* (Oxford: Oxford University Press).

——(1983), 'Development: Which Way Now?', *Economic Journal*, 93.

——(1984), *Resources, Values and Development* (Oxford: Basil Blackwell).

——(1985), *Commodities and Capabilities* (Amsterdam: North-Holland).

——(1988a), 'Africa and India: What Do We Have to Learn from Each Other?', in Arrow, K. J. (ed.), *The Balance between Industry and Agriculture in Economic Development*, i: *Basic Issues* (London: Macmillan).

——(1988*b*), 'Food and Freedom', Sir John Crawford Memorial Lecture, to be published in *World Development*.

——(1989*a*), 'Economic Methodology: Heterogeneity and Relevance', *Social Research*, 56.

——(1989*b*), 'Women's Survival as a Development Problem', talk given at the American Academy of Arts and Sciences, published in the *Bulletin* of the Academy.

STREETEN, P. (1987), *What Price Food?* (London: Macmillan).

SUKHATME, P. V. (1977), *Malnutrition and Poverty* (New Delhi: Indian Agricultural Research Institute).

——(ed.) (1982*a*), *Newer Concepts in Nutrition and Their Implications for Policy* (Pune: Maharashtra Association for the Cultivation of Science).

——(1982*b*), 'Measurement of Undernutrition', *Economic and Political Weekly*, 17.

WALDRON, I. (1983), 'The Role of Genetic and Biological Factors in Sex Differences in Mortality', in Lopez, A. D., and Ruzicka, L. T. (eds.), *Sex Differentials in Mortality: Trends, Determinants and Consequences* (Canberra: Australian National University).

World Bank (1986), *World Development Report 1986* (Washington, DC: World Bank).

2

Food, Economics, and Entitlements

Amartya Sen

2.1. *Economics and the acquirement problem*

What ·may be called 'instant economics' has always appealed to the quick-witted layman impatient with the slow-moving economist. This is particularly so in the field of hunger and food policy. Of course, the need for speed is genuinely important in matters of food, and the impatience is, thus, easy to understand. But instant economics is also highly deceptive, and especially dangerous in this field. Millions of lives depend on the adequacy of the policy response to the terrible problems of hunger and starvation in the modern world. Past mistakes of policy have been responsible for the death of many millions of people and the suffering of hundreds of millions, and this is not a subject in which short cuts in economic reasoning can be taken to be fairly costless.

One common feature of a good deal of instant economics related to food and hunger is impatience with investigating the precise mechanisms for acquiring food that people have to use. People establish command over food in many different ways. For example, while a peasant owning his land and the product of his labour simply owns the food produced, a wage labourer paid in cash has to convert that wage into a bundle of goods, including food, through exchange. The peasant does, as it were, an exchange with 'nature', putting in labour, etc., and getting back the product, namely food. The wage labourer does repeated · exchanges with others in the society—first, his labour power for a wage and then, the wage for a collection of commodities including food. We cannot begin to understand the precise influences that make it possible or not possible to acquire enough food, without examining the conditions of these exchanges and the forces that govern them. The same applies to other methods of acquiring food, e.g. through share-cropping and getting a part of the produce, through running a business and making a profit, through selling services and earning an income, and so on. I shall call the problem of establishing command over commodities, in this case food, the 'acquirement problem'. It is easy to

This is a shortened version of the fourth Elmhirst Lecture given at the triennial meeting of the International Association of Agricultural Economists, in Malaga (Spain), on 26 Aug. 1985. The paper was prepared at the World Institute of Development Economic Research in Helsinki. The author is grateful for discussions with Lal Jayawardena, Glenn Johnson, and Nanak Kakwani. An earlier version (the fourth Elmhirst Lecture) was published in the *Proceedings* of the conference (Maunder and Renborg 1986) and also in *Lloyds Bank Review*, 160 (Apr. 1986).

establish that the acquirement problem is really central to questions of hunger and starvation in the modern world.

The acquirement problem is often neglected not only by non-economists, but also by many economists, including some great ones. For example, Malthus in his famous *Essay on the Principle of Population as it Affects the Further Improvement of Society* (1798) leaves the acquirement problem largely unaddressed, though in his less-known pamphlet *An Investigation of the Cause of the Present High Price of Provisions* (1800), which deals with more short-run questions, Malthus is in fact deeply concerned precisely with the nitty-gritty of this problem.[1] The result of this neglect in the former work is not without practical consequence, since the popularity of the Malthusian approach to population and food, and of the particular metric of food output per head extensively used in the *Essay on Population*, has tended to give that metric undue prominence in policy discussions across the world.

Malthusian pessimism, based on the expectation of falling food output per head, has not been vindicated by history. Oddly enough, what can be called 'Malthusian optimism', i.e. *not* being worried about the food problem so long as food output grows as fast as—or faster than—population, has often contributed substantially to delaying policy response to growing hunger (against a background of stationary or rising food output per head). This is a serious enough problem in the case of intensification of regular but non-extreme hunger (without starvation deaths but causing greater proneness to morbidity and mortality), and it can be quite disastrous in the context of a famine that develops without a decline in food output per head, with the misguided focus leading to a hopelessly delayed response of public policy. While Malthus's own writings are by no means unique in focusing attention on the extremely misleading variable of food output per head, 'Malthusian optimism', in general, has been indirectly involved in millions of deaths which have resulted from inaction and misdirection of public policy.[2] While fully acknowledging the great contribution that Malthus has made in highlighting the importance of population policy, this negative feature of his work, related to his own bit of instant economics, must also be recognized.

The neglect of the acquirement issue has far-reaching consequences. For many years rational discussion of the food problems of the modern world was distracted by undue concentration on the comparative trends of population growth and the expansion of food output, with shrill warnings of danger coming from very respectable quarters.[3] The fear of population outrunning

---

[1] On the importance of the latter document, which has received much less attention than the former, see Sen (1981a).

[2] This issue is discussed in Sen (1982).

[3] The Club of Rome, despite its extremely distinguished leadership, had been responsible for some of the more lurid research reports of doom and decline. However, a later study sponsored by the Club, undertaken by H. Linnemann (1981), shows the picture to be both less gloomy and more easily influenced by policy. See also Parikh and Rabar (1981), especially on the role of policy.

food output on a global scale has certainly not been realized, and world food output per head has steadily risen.[4] This has, however, gone hand in hand with intensification of hunger in some parts of the world. In many—though not all—of the affected countries, food output per head has in fact fallen, and the anxiety about these countries has often been anchored to the statistics of food output per head, with Malthusian worries translated from the global to the regional or country level. But a causal analysis of the persistence and intensification of hunger and of the development of famines does, in fact, call for something more than attention being paid simply to the statistics of food output per head.

I shall have more to say on the policy questions presently, but before that I would like to discuss a bit further the nature and implications of the acquirement problem. I shall also discuss some arguments that relate to studying food and hunger in terms of what in my book, *Poverty and Famines*,[5] was called the 'entitlement approach'.[6] That approach has been extensively discussed, examined, criticized, applied, as well as extended, and I have learned a lot from these contributions.[7] But the approach has also been occasionally misinterpreted, and given the importance of the subject of food policy and hunger, I shall permit myself the self-indulgence of commenting—*inter alia*—on a few of the points that have been made in response to my earlier analysis.

2.2. Famines and entitlements

The entitlement approach provides a particular focus for the analysis of famines. It does not specify one particular causation of famine—only the general one that a famine reflects widespread failure of entitlements on the part of substantial sections of the population. Such failure can arise from many different causes.

The entitlement of a person stands for the set of different alternative commodity bundles that the person can acquire through the use of the various legal channels of acquirement open to someone in his position. In a private ownership market economy, the entitlement set of a person is determined by his original bundle of ownership (what is called his 'endowment') and the various alternative bundles he can acquire starting respectively from each initial endowment, through the use of trade and production (what is called his

---

[4]   See e.g. FAO (1985).

[5]   See Sen (1977, 1981a, 1981c); see also Ravallion (1987).

[6]   Note that the use of the expression 'entitlement' here is descriptive rather than prescriptive. A person's entitlements as given by the legal system, personal circumstances, etc. need not command any moral endorsement. This applies both to the opulent entitlements of the rich and to the meagre entitlements of the poor.

[7]   Particularly from Seaman and Holt (1980), Arrow (1982), Bliss (1982), Griffin (1981), Hayter (1981), Joshi (1981), Lipton (1981), Desai (1984), Solow (1984), Kahn (1985), Kumar (1985), Ravallion (1985, 1987), Snowdon (1985), among others.

'exchange entitlement mapping'). This is not the occasion to go into the formal characterisations of endowments, exchange entitlement mappings, entitlement sets, etc., which were discussed in *Poverty and Famines*.

A person has to starve if his entitlement set does not include any commodity bundle with enough food. A person is reduced to starvation if some change either in his endowment (e.g. alienation of land, or loss of labour power due to ill health), or in his exchange entitlement mapping (e.g. fall in wages, rise in food prices, loss of employment, drop in the price of the goods he produces and sells), makes it no longer possible for him to acquire any commodity bundle with enough food. I have argued that famines can be usefully analysed in terms of failures of entitlement relations.

The advantages of the entitlement approach over more traditional analysis in terms of food availability per head were illustrated with case-studies of a number of famines, e.g. the Bengal famine of 1943, the Ethiopian famines of 1973 and 1974, the Bangladesh famine of 1974, and the Sahel famines in the early seventies.[8] In some of these famines food availability per head had gone down (e.g. in the Sahel famines); in others there was no significant decline —even a little increase (e.g. in the Bengal famine of 1943, the Ethiopian famine of 1973, the Bangladesh famine of 1974). That famines can occur even without any decline in food output or availability per head makes that metric particularly deceptive. Since food availability is indeed the most commonly studied variable, this is a source of some policy confusion. It also makes 'Malthusian optimism' a serious route to disastrous inaction. But the point of entitlement analysis is not only to dispute the focus on food availability, but more positively also to provide a general approach for understanding and investigating famines through focusing on variations in endowments and exchange entitlement mappings.

Famine can be caused by various different types of influences, and the common predicament of mass starvation does not imply any one common fundamental cause. Droughts, floods, general inflationary pressure, sharp recessionary loss of employment, and so on can all in their own way deprive large sections of the population of entitlement to adequate food. A decline in food output or availability can, of course, be one of the major influences on the development of a famine, but even when that is the case (indeed even when food availability decline is the primary proximate antecedent), a serious study of the causal mechanism leading to the famine and the precise form it takes will require us to go into the behaviour of the determinants of the entitlements of the different sections of the population.

In *Poverty and Famines* two broad types of famines were distinguished from each other, namely *boom famines* and *slump famines*. A famine can, of course, occur in a situation of general decline in economic activity (as happened, for

---

[8] See Sen (1981a: chs. 6–10).

example, in the Wollo province of Ethiopia in 1973, due to a severe drought). But it can also occur in overall boom conditions (as happened, for example, in the Bengal famine of 1943, with a massive expansion of economic activity related to war efforts). If economic expansion is particularly favourable to a large section of the population (in the case of the Bengal famine, primarily the urban population including that of Calcutta), but does not draw into the process another large section (in the Bengal famine, much of the rural labouring classes), then that uneven expansion can actually make the latter group lose out in the battle for commanding food. In the food battle the devil takes the hindmost, and even a boom condition can lead to some groups losing their command over food because of the worsening of their relative position *vis-à-vis* the groups favoured by the boom.

2.3. *The entitlement approach and economic traditions*

It is important to emphasize that the entitlement approach is consistent with many different detailed theories of the actual causation of a famine. While the approach identifies certain crucial variables, different theories of the determination of the values of these variables may all be consistent with the general entitlement approach. For example, the entitlement approach does not specify any particular theory of price determination, but relative prices are quite crucial to the entitlements of various occupation groups. The entitlement approach by itself does not provide—nor is it intended to provide—a detailed explanation of any famine, and such an explanation would require supplementation by more specific theories of movements of prices, wages, employment, etc., causing particular shifts in the entitlements of different occupation groups.[9]

What the entitlement approach does is to take up the acquirement problem seriously. Rather than arbitrarily making some implicit assumption about distribution (such as equal division of the available food, or some fixed pattern of inequality in that division), it analyses acquirement in terms of entitlements, which in a private ownership economy is largely a matter of ownership and exchange (including of course production, i.e. exchange with nature). I would claim that this is not in any way a departure from the old traditions of economics. It is, rather, a reassertion of the continuing concern of economics with the mechanism of acquiring commodities. If I had the courage and confidence that Gary Becker shows in his distinguished work in calling his own approach '*the* economic approach',[10] I would have called the entitlement approach by the same bold name. While the price of timidity is to shy away from such assertive naming, I would nevertheless claim that economic tradi-

---

[9] See Sen (1981a: chs. 6–10). See also Svedberg (1984), Ravallion (1985), and Khan (1985).

[10] See Becker (1976, 1981).

tions stretching back centuries do, in fact, direct our attention to entitlements in analysing problems of wealth, poverty, deprivation, and hunger.

This is clear enough in Marx's case,[11] but the point is often made that Adam Smith was a great believer in the simple theory of food availability decline in explaining all famines, and that he would have thus had little patience for discussion of entitlements and their determinants. Indeed, it is true that in his often-quoted 'Digression Concerning the Corn Trade and Corn Laws' in Book IV of the *Wealth of Nations*, Adam Smith did remark that 'a dearth never has arisen from any combination among the inland dealers in corn, nor from any other cause but a real scarcity, occasioned sometimes, perhaps, and in some particular places, by the waste of war, but in by far the greatest number of cases, by the fault of the seasons'.[12] However, in understanding the point that Adam Smith is making here, it is important to recognize that he is primarily denying that traders could cause famine through collusion, and he is disputing the view that famines often follow from artificial shortages created by traders, and asserting the importance of what he calls 'a real scarcity'. I shall have the occasion to take up this aspect of Smith's observation presently when I discuss the issue of anti-famine policy.

We have to look elsewhere in the *Wealth of Nations* to see how acutely concerned Adam Smith was with the acquirement problem in analysing what he called 'want, famine, and mortality'. I quote Smith from the chapter called 'Of the Wages of Labour' from Book I of the *Wealth of Nations*:

But it would be otherwise in a country where the funds destined for the maintenance of labour were sensibly decaying. Every year the demand for servants and labourers would, in all the different classes of employments, be less than it had been the year before. Many who had been bred in the superior classes, not being able to find employment in their own business, would be glad to seek it in the lowest. The lowest class being not only overstocked with its own workmen, but with the over-flowings of all the other classes, the competition for employment would be so great in it, as to reduce the wages of labour to the most miserable and scanty subsistence of the labourer. Many would not be able to find employment even upon these hard terms, but would either starve, or be driven to seek a subsistence either by begging, or by the perpetration perhaps of the greatest enormities. Want, famine, and mortality would immediately prevail in that class, and from thence extend themselves to all the superior classes.[13]

Here Adam Smith is focusing on the market-based entitlement of labourers, and its dependence on employment and real wages, and explaining famine from that perspective. This should, of course, come as no surprise. In denying that artificial scarcity engineered by collusive traders can cause famine, Adam Smith was in no way closing the door to the economic analysis of various

---

[11] See e.g. the discussion on wages and capital in Marx (1887), Parts VI and VII.

[12] See Smith (1776).

[13] Smith (1776: Book I, ch. VIII, 26, pp. 90–1).

different real influences on the ability of different groups to command food in the market, in particular the values of wages and employment.

Perhaps it is useful to consider another argument presented by another great classical economist, namely David Ricardo, attacking the view that a famine cannot occur in a situation of what he calls 'superabundance'. This was in a speech that Ricardo wrote for delivery in Parliament in 1822, using the third person for himself as if the speech is reported in *Hansard*, though in the event Ricardo did not actually get to deliver the speech. The reference is to the famine conditions then prevailing in Ireland, and Ricardo examines the point made by another member of Parliament that this could not be the case since there was superabundance of food in Ireland at that time.

But says the honble. gentn. the people are dying for want of food in Ireland, and the farmers are said to be suffering from superabundance. In these two propositions the honble. gentn. thinks there is a manifest contradiction, but he Mr. R. could not agree with him in thinking so. Where was the contradiction in supposing that in a country where wages were regulated mainly by the price of potatoes the people should be suffering the greatest distress if the potato crop failed and their wages were inadequate to purchase the dearer commodity corn? From whence was the money to come to enable them to purchase the grain however abundant it might [be] if its price far exceeds that of potatoes. He Mr. Ricardo should not think it absurd or contradictory to maintain that in such a country as England where the food of the people was corn, there might be an abundance of that grain and such low prices as not to afford a remuneration to the grower, and yet that the people might be in distress and not able for want of employment to buy it, but in Ireland the case was much stronger and in that country there should be no doubt there might be a glut of corn, and a starving people.[14]

There is indeed nothing surprising in the fact that economists should be concerned with the acquirement problem, and dispute the instant economics that overlooks that aspect of the food problem based on confusing supply with command, as the 'honourable gentleman' quoted by David Ricardo clearly did. It is a confusion that has recurred again and again in actual discussions of the food problem, and the need to move away from instant economics to serious analysis of the acquirement problem and the entitlement to food is no less today than it was in Ricardo's time.[15]

It is not my purpose to assert that the entitlement approach is flawless as an economic approach to the problem of hunger and starvation. Several 'limitations' of the entitlement approach were, in fact, noted in *Poverty and Famines*, including ambiguities in the specification of entitlement, the neglect of non-legal transfers (e.g. looting) in the disposition of food, the importance of tastes and values in causing hunger despite adequate entitlement, and the relevance of disease and epidemic in famine mortality which extends far beyond the groups whose entitlement failures may have initiated the famine.

[14] See Ricardo's papers in Sraffa (1971: 234–5).
[15] See Taylor (1975) for an illuminating critique.

To this one should also add that in order to capture an important part of the acquirement problem, to wit, distribution of food within a family, the entitlement approach would have to be extended. In particular, notions of perceived 'legitimacy' of intrafamily distributional patterns have to be brought into the analysis, and its causal determinants analysed.[16]

Further, if the focus of attention is shifted from famines as such to less acute but possibly persistent hunger, then the role of choice from the entitlement set becomes particularly important, especially in determining future entitlement. For example, a peasant may choose to go somewhat hungry now to make a productive investment for the future, enhancing the entitlement of the following years and reducing the danger of starvation then. For entitlement analysis in a multi-period setting the initial formulation of the problem would require serious modification and extension.[17]

These changes and amendments can be systematically made without losing the basic rationale of introducting entitlement analysis to understand the problem of hunger and starvation in the modern world. The crucial motivation is to see the centrality of the acquirement problem and to resist the short cuts of instant economics, no matter how respectable its source.

2.4. *Policy issues*

(a) *Famine anticipation and action*

Focusing on entitlements and acquirement rather than simply on food output and availability has some rather far-reaching implications for food policy. I have tried to discuss some of these implications elsewhere, but I would like to pick a few issues here for brief comment. In particular, the problems of famine anticipation and relief are among the most serious ones facing the turbulent and traumatic world in which we live, and I shall comment on them briefly from the perspective that I have been outlining.

So far as famine anticipation is concerned, the metric of food output and availability is obviously defective as a basis, for reasons that follow from the preceding discussion. In fact, the anticipation of famines and their detection at an early stage have often in the past been hampered by undue concentration on this index, and specifically by what we have been calling 'Malthusian optimism'. Early warnings, as they are sometimes called, may not come at all from

[16] The consequences of particular perceptions of 'legitimacy' of intrafamily distributions do have something similar to those of legal relationships. Using that perspective, 'extended exchange entitlement' relations, covering both interfamily and intrafamily distributions, have been explored in an integrated structure in Sen (1985). The interrelations may be of real importance in understanding sex bias, e.g. the effect that outside earnings of women have on the divisions within the family. On this see also Boserup's (1970) pioneering study, and Sen (1984: essays 15, 16, 19, and 20).

[17] See Sen (1981a: n. 11). For some important and original ideas in this direction, see Svedberg (1986).

the output statistics, and it is necessary to monitor other variables as well, which also influence the entitlements of different vulnerable groups. Employment, wages, prices, etc. all have very direct bearing on the entitlements of various groups.

It is also important to recognize that famines can follow from many different types of causal processes. For example, while in a boom famine food prices will sharply rise, in a slump famine they may not. If the economic change that leads to mass starvation operates through depressing incomes and purchasing powers of large groups of people, food prices may stay low—or rise only relatively little, during the process of pauperization of these groups. Even when the slump famine is directly related to a crop failure due to, say, a drought, there may possibly be only a relatively modest rise in food prices, if the supply failure is matched by a corresponding decline in purchasing power due to the same drought. Indeed, it is easy to see that in a fully peasant economy in which food is eaten precisely by those who grow it, a crop failure will subtract from demand what it deducts from supply. The impoverished peasants would of course be later thrown into the rest of the economy —begging, looking for jobs, etc.—but they will arrive there without purchasing ability, and thus need not cause any rise in food prices even later. Actual economies are not, of course, that pure, but the impact on prices is very contingent on the relative weights of the different types of system and organization that make up the affected economy.[18]

Neither food output, nor prices, nor any other variable like that can be taken to be an invariable clue to famine anticipation, and once again there is no substitute for doing a serious economic analysis of the entitlements of all the vulnerable groups. All these variables have possible significance, and it is a question of seeing them as contingently important in terms of what they could do to the ability of different groups to acquire food. The search for some invariable indicator on the basis of which even the economically blind could see an oncoming famine sufficiently early is quite hopeless.

One of the major influences on the actual prevention of famine is the speed and force with which early hunger is reported and taken up in political debates. The nature and freedom of the news media, and the power and standing of opposition parties, are of considerable importance in effective prevention of famines.[19] But if the aim is to anticipate a famine even before early reports of hunger, that object cannot be satisfied by some mechanical formula on an 'early warning system'. The various information on prices, wages, outputs,

---

[18] In the Ethiopian famine in Wollo in 1973, food price rises seem to have been relatively moderate. Indeed, in Dessie, the capital of Wollo, the mid-famine food prices seem to have been comparable with prices outside the famine-affected province. There was more of a price rise in the rural areas, but again apparently not a catastrophic rise, and prices seemed to come down relatively quickly. On the importance of prices as a monitoring device for famine anticipation, see Seaman and Holt (1980) and Cutler (1984). See also Snowdon (1985).

[19] On this see Sen (1983).

etc. has to be examined with an economic understanding of the determinants of the entitlements of the different occupation groups and of the rich variety of different ways in which the entitlements of one group or another can be undermined.

The different processes involved not only vary a good deal from each other, they may also be far from straightforward. For example, in various famines some occupation groups have been driven to the wall by a fall in the relative price of the food items they sell, e.g. meat sold by pastoral nomads in Harerghe in the Ethiopian famine of 1974, fish sold by fishermen in the Bengal famine of 1943. These groups may survive by selling these food items and buying cheaper calories through the purchase of grains and other less expensive food. A decline in the relative price of meat or fish will, of course, make it easier for the richer parts of the community to eat better, but it can spell disaster for the pastoralist and the fisherman. To make sense of them as signals of turmoil, the observed variables have to be examined in terms of their specific roles in the determination of entitlements of vulnerable groups.

(b) Relief, food, and cash

Turning now from the anticipation to the relief of famines, the traditional form of relief has, of course, been that of providing free food in relief camps and distribution centres. There can be no doubt that relief in this form has saved lives in large scale in various famines around the world. But to understand precisely what free food distribution does, it may be useful to distinguish between two different aspects of the act of providing, which are both involved in the food relief operation. One is to give the destitute the ability to command food, and the other is to give him this ability in the actual form of food itself. Though they are integrated together in this form of relief, they need not in general be thus combined. For example, cash relief may provide the ability to command food without directly giving the food.

A person's ability to command food has two distinct elements, namely, his 'pull' and the supplier's 'response'. In the price mechanism the two elements are integrally related to each other. But in terms of the logistics of providing the person with food, the two elements may, in some contexts, be usefully distinguishable. If a person has to starve because he has lost his employment and has no means of buying food, then that is a failure originating on the 'pull' side. If, on the other hand, his ability to command food collapses because of absence of supply, or as a result of the cornering of the market by some manipulative traders, then this is a failure arising on the 'response' side.

One way of understanding what Adam Smith was really asserting (an issue that was briefly touched on earlier) is to see his primary claim as being one about the nature of 'response failure' in particular, saying nothing at all about 'pull failure'. His claim was that a response failure will only arise from what he called 'a real scarcity', most likely due to natural causes, and not from manipulative actions of traders. He may or may not have been right in this claim, but it is important to note that in this there is no denial of the possibility of 'pull failure'. Indeed, as is shown by his own analysis of 'want, famine, and mortality' arising from unemployment and falling wages (I quoted a passage from this earlier), Smith did also outline the possibility of famine originating on the 'pull' side. There is nothing particularly puzzling or internally inconsistent in Smith's various pronouncements on famine, if we distinguish between his treatment of pull and that of response. It is not the case, as is often asserted, that Adam Smith believed that hunger could not arise without a crop failure. Also he was not opposed to public support for the deprived, and in particular he was not opposed to providing relief through the Poor Laws (though he did criticize the harshness of some of the requirements that were imposed on the beneficiaries under these laws).

Smith's point that response failure would not arise from collusive action of traders has a direct bearing on the appropriate form of famine relief. If his point is correct, then relief could just as easily be provided by giving the deprived additional income and leaving it to the traders to respond to the new pull through moving food to the cash recipients. It is arguable that Smith did underestimate the extent to which traders can and do, in fact, manipulate markets, but at the same time the merits of cash relief do need serious examination in the context of assessing policy options.

Cash relief may not, of course, be quick enough in getting food to the starving in a situation of severe famine. Directly moving food to the starving may be the only immediate option in some situations of acute famine. There is also the merit of direct food distribution that it tends to have, it appears, a very immediate impact on nutrition, even in non-famine, normal situations, and it seems to do better in this respect than relief through income supplementation. These are points in favour of direct relief through food distribution. There is the further point that cash relief is arguably more prone to corruption, and that the visibility of direct food distribution does provide a better check. And the point about the possibility of manipulative actions of traders cannot, also, by any means be simply dismissed. These are serious points in favour of direct food distribution. But cash relief does have many merits as well.

First, the government's inefficiency in transporting food could be a considerable barrier to famine relief, as indeed some recent experiences have shown. In addition to problems of bureaucracy and red tape, there is the further problem that the transport resources (i.e. vehicles, etc.) in the possession of the private sector may sometimes be hard to mobilize, whereas they would be drawn into use if the actual trading and moving is left to the profit-seeking private sector itself. There is here a genuine pragmatic issue of the speed of response, and it cannot be brushed aside by a simple political judgement one way or the other.

Second, as was observed in the Wollo famine in 1973 and the Bangladesh famine of 1984, and most spectacularly in the Irish famines of the 1840s, food often does move *out of* the famine-stricken regions to elsewhere. This tends to happen especially in some cases of slump famine, in which the famine area is short of effective demand. Since such 'food countermovement' tends to reflect the balance of pulls of different regions, it may be preventable by distributing cash quickly enough in the famine-affected region.

Third, by providing demand for trade and transport, cash relief may help to regenerate the infrastructure of the famine-stricken economy. This has some merit in contrast with *ad hoc* use of transitory public intervention, which is not meant to continue, and the lasting benefits from expansion of normal trade and transport may be considerable for the local economy.

Fourth, it is arguable that cash relief is more usable for development investment needed for productive improvement, and this cannot be sensibly organized in relief centres. Even 'food for work' programmes, which can help in this direction, may sometimes be too unwieldy, given the need for flexibility for such investment activities.

Fifth, living in relief camps is deeply disruptive for normal family life as well as for pursuing normal economic activities. Providing cash relief precisely where the people involved normally reside and work, without having to move them to relief camps, may have very considerable economic and social advantages. Judging from the experience of an innovative 'cash for food' project sponsored by UNICEF in Ethiopia, these advantages are indeed quite real.[20]

This is not the occasion to try to form an overall judgement of the 'net' advantage of one scheme over another. Such judgements would have to be, in any case, extremely contingent on the exact circumstances of the case. But the general distinction between the 'pull' aspect and the 'response' aspect of entitlement failures is of immediate relevance to the question of the strategy of famine relief. Adam Smith's long shadow has fallen over many famines in the British Empire over the last two hundred years, with Smith being cited in favour of inaction and letting things be. If the analysis presented here is accepted, then inaction reflected quite the wrong reading of the implications of Smith's economic analysis. If his analysis is correct—and the honours here are probably rather divided—the real Smithian issue in a situation of famine is not 'intervention versus non-intervention', but 'cash relief versus direct food relief'. The force of the arguments on Smith's side cannot be readily dismissed, and the experience of mismanagement of famine relief in many countries has done nothing to reduce the aptness of his question.

(c) Food supply and food prices

In comparing the merits of cash relief with food distribution, it was not assumed that there would be more import of food with the latter than with the former. That question—of food imports from abroad—is a quite distinct one from the form that relief might take. It is, however, arguable that in a famine

---

[20] See Kumar (1985). See also Bjoerck (1984) and Padmini (1985).

situation direct food distribution is more thoroughly dependent on food import from abroad than a cash relief scheme need be. This is to some extent correct, though direct food distribution may also be based on domestically acquired food. But if we compare food distribution combined with food imports, on the one hand, and simple cash relief without such imports, on the other, then an arbitrary difference is brought into the contrast which does not belong there. In fact, the issue of food import is a separate one, which should be considered on its own.

This relates to an issue that has often been misunderstood in trying to work out the implications of the entitlement approach to hunger and famines, and in particular the implications of recognizing the possibility that famines can occur without any decline in food availability per head. It has sometimes been argued that if a famine is not caused by a decline in food availability, then there cannot be a case for food imports in dealing with the famine.[21] This is, of course, a *non sequitur*, and a particularly dangerous piece of nonsense. Consider a case in which some people have been reduced to starvation not because of a decline in total supply of food, but because they have fallen behind in the competitive demand for food in a boom famine (as happened, for example, to rural labourers in the Bengal famine of 1943). The fact is that the prices are too high for these victim groups to acquire enough food. Adding to the food supply will typically reduce prices and help these deprived groups to acquire food. The fact that the original rise in prices did not result from a fall in availability but from an increase in total demand does not make any difference to the argument.

Similarly, in a slump famine in which some group of people has suffered a decline in their incomes due to, say, unemployment, it may be possible to help that group by reducing the price of food through more imports. Furthermore, in each case import of food can be used to break a famine through public relief measures. This can be done either directly in the form of food distribution, or indirectly through giving cash relief to the famine victims combined with releasing more food in the market to balance the additional demand that would be created. There are, of course, other arguments to be considered in judging pros and cons of food imports, including the important problem of incentives for domestic food producers. But to try to reject the case for food imports in a famine situation on the simple ground that the famine has occurred without a decline in food availability (if that is the case) is to make a straightforward mistake in reasoning.

A more interesting question arises if in a famine situation we are, for some reason, simply not in a position to get more food from abroad. Would a system

---

[21] For a forceful presentation of this odd belief, see Bowbrick's paper (with a truly flattering title), 'How Professor Sen's Theory Can Cause Famines', presented at the Agricultural Economics Society Conference, 1985, at the Annual Conference of the Development Studies Association. (A revised version was later published in *Food Policy*; see Bowbrick (1986, 1987) and Sen (1986, 1987).)

of cash relief then be inflationary, and thus counter-productive? The answer is it would typically be inflationary, but not necessarily counter-productive. Giving the famine victims more purchasing power would add to the total demand for food. But if we want a more equal distribution of food, with some food moving from others to the famine victims, then the only way the market can achieve this (when the total supply is fixed and the money incomes of others cannot be cut) is through this inflationary process. The additional food to be consumed by the famine victims has to come from others, and this may require that prices should go up to induce others to consume less, so that the famine victims—with their new cash incomes—can buy more. Thus, while having a system of cash reliefs is not an argument against food imports in a famine situation, that system can have some desirable consequences *even when* food imports are, for some reason, not possible. If our focus is on enhancing the entitlements of famine victims, the creation of some inflationary pressure —within limits—to redistribute food to the famine victims from the rest of the society may well be a sensible policy to pursue.

(d)   Entitlements and public distribution

So far in this essay my concentration on policy matters has been largely on what may be called short-run issues, including the anticipation and relief of famines. But it should be clear from the preceding analysis, with its focus on acquirement and entitlements, that long-run policies have to be geared to enhancing, securing, and guaranteeing entitlements, rather than to some simple formula like expanding food output.

I have discussed elsewhere the positive achievements of public food distribution policies in Sri Lanka and China, and also in Kerala in India, along with policies of public health and elementary education.[22]

The role of Sri Lanka's extensive 'social welfare programmes' in achieving high living standards has been the subject of some controversy recently. It is, of course, impossible to deny that judged in terms of such indicators of living standard as life expectancy, Sri Lanka's overall achievement is high (its life expectancy of 69 years is higher than that of any other developing country —even with many times the GNP per head of Sri Lanka). But by looking not at the *levels* of living but at their rate of *expansion* over a selected period, to wit 1960–78, it has been argued by Surjit Bhalla and others that Sri Lanka has performed only 'in an average manner'. Armed with these findings (based on international comparisons of expansion of longevity, etc. over 1960–78), the positive role of Sri Lanka's wide-based welfare programmes has been firmly disputed (asking, on the contrary, the general question: 'when does a commitment to equity become excessive?').[23]

The basis of this disputation, however, is extremely weak. 1960–78 is a

[22]   See Sen (1981*b*, 1983).
[23]   See Bhalla (1988).

period in which Sri Lanka's social welfare programmes themselves did not
grow much, and indeed the percentage of GNP expended on such programmes
came down sharply from 11.8 in 1960–1 to 8.7 by 1977.[24] If the expansion of
sowing is moderate, and so is the expansion of reaping, that can scarcely be
seen as a sign of the ineffectiveness of sowing!

The really fast expansion of Sri Lanka's social welfare programmes came
much earlier, going back at least to the forties. Food distribution policies (e.g.
free or subsidized rice for all, free school meals) were introduced in the early
1940s, and health intervention was also radically expanded (including taking
on the dreaded malaria). Correspondingly, the death rate fell from 21.6 per
thousand in 1945 to 12.6 in 1950, and to 8.6 by 1960 (all this happened *before*
the oddly chosen period 1960–78 used in Bhalla's much-publicized 'international comparisons' of expansions). There is nothing in the picture of
.'expansion' that would contradict the fact of Sri Lanka's exceptional performance, if one does look at the right period, i.e. one in which its social welfare
programmes were, in fact, radically expanded, which happened well before
1960.[25]

The diverse policy instruments of public intervention used in Sri Lanka
relate closely to 'food policy' in the wider sense, affecting nutrition, longevity,
etc., going well beyond the production of food. Similar relations can be found
in the experience of effective public distribution programmes in other regions,
e.g. China and Kerala. It is right that the 'food problem' should be seen in these
wider terms, involving not only the production of food, but also the entitlements to food and to other nutrition-related variables such as health services.

(e) Production and diversification

The problem of production composition is achieving economic expansion is
also, *inter alia*, an important one in long-run food policy. This complex
problem is often confounded with that of simply expanding food output as
such, treating it as largely a matter of increasing food supply. This is
particularly so in the discussions of the so-called African food problem. It is, of
course, true that food output per head in sub-Saharan Africa has been falling in
recent years, and this is certainly one of the major factors in the intensification
of hunger in Africa. But food production is not merely a source of food supply
in Africa, but also the main source of means of livelihood for large sections of
the African population. It is for this reason that food output decline tends to go
hand in hand with a collapse of entitlements of the masses in Africa.

The point can be easily seen by comparing and contrasting the experience of
sub-Saharan Africa in terms of food output per head with that of some

---

[24] These figures are given by Bhalla himself in a different context. He does not give the figure
for 1978, but in his table the percentage had further dropped to 7.7 by 1980. Other sources confirm
these overall declining trends during the 1960s and 1970s taken together.

[25] My reply to Bhalla's note (Sen 1988), spelling out the methodological issues as well as
empirical ones, is included in the same volume, with a further rejoinder by Bhalla.

countries elsewhere. Take Ethiopia and the Sahel countries, which have all suffered so much from famines. Between 1969–71 and 1980–2, food output per head fell by 5 per cent in Chad and Burkina Faso, 7 per cent in Senegal, 12 per cent in Niger, 17 per cent in Mali, 18 per cent in Ethiopia, and 27 per cent in Mauritania.[26] These are indeed substantial declines. But in the same period, and according to the same source of statistics, food output per head fell by 5 per cent in Venezuela, 15 per cent in Egypt, 24 per cent in Algeria, 27 per cent in Portugal, 29 per cent in Hong Kong, 30 per cent in Jordan, and 38 per cent in Trinidad and Tobago. The contrast between starvation in sub-Saharan Africa and nothing of the sort in these other countries is not, of course, in the least difficult to explain. Unlike the situation in these other countries, in sub-Saharan Africa a decline in food output is associated with a disastrous decline in entitlements, because the incomes of so many there come from growing food, because they are generally poor, and because the decline of food output there has not been outweighed or even balanced by increases in non-food (e.g. industrial) output. It is essential to distinguish between (1) food production as a source of income and entitlement, and (2) food production as a source of supply of the vital commodity food. If the expansion of food production should receive full priority in Africa, the case for it lies primarily in the role of food production in generating entitlements rather than only supply.

There are, of course, other reasons as well for giving priority to food production, in particular the greater security that the growers of food might then have since they would not be dependent on market exchange for acquiring food. This argument has been emphasized by many in recent years, and it is indeed an important consideration, the relevance of which is brought out by the role of market shifts in contributing to some of the famines that have been studied. But this type of uncertainty has to be balanced against uncertainties arising from other sources, in particular those related to climatic reasons. In the very long run the uncertainty of depending on unreliable weather conditions in parts of sub-Saharan Africa may well be eliminated by irrigation and afforestation. However, for many years to come this is a serious uncertainty, which must be taken into account along with other factors in the choice of investment policy in sub-Saharan Africa. An argument that is often encountered in public discussion in various forms can be crudely put like this: 'Food output in parts of sub-Saharan Africa has suffered a lot because the climate there is so unreliable for food production; therefore let's put all our resources into food production in these countries.' This is, of course, a caricature, but even in somewhat more sophisticated forms, this line of argument as a piece of economic reasoning is deeply defective. One does not put all one's eggs in the same highly unreliable basket. The need is surely for diversification of the production pattern in a situation of such uncertainty.

[26] *World Development Review 1984* (Oxford University Press, 1984), Table 6.

2.5. *Concluding remarks*

I have tried to comment on a number of difficult policy problems. The entitlement approach on its own does not resolve any of these issues. But by focusing on the acquirement problem, and on the major variables influencing acquirement, the entitlement approach provides a general perspective that can be fruitfully used to analyse the phenomenon of hunger as well as the requirements of food policy. I have tried to illustrate some of the uses of the entitlement approach, and have also discussed what policy insights follow or do not follow from it. The policy issues discussed have included problems of anticipation and relief of famines, forms of relief to be provided (including food distribution versus cash relief), the role of food supply and food prices in famine relief, and long-run strategies for eliminating vulnerability to famines and starvation (with particular reference to Africa).

I have also claimed that the entitlement approach is, with a few exceptions, in line with very old traditions in economics, which have been, in their own way, much preoccupied with the acquirement issue. The challenges of the terrible economic problems of the contemporary world relate closely to those traditional concerns, and call for sustained economic analysis of the determination and use of entitlements of diverse occupation groups.

References

ARROW, K. J. (1982), 'Why People Go Hungry', *New York Review of Books*, 29.

BECKER, G. S. (1976), *The Economic Approach to Human Behaviour* (Chicago, Ill.: Chicago University Press).

——(1981), *A Treatise on the Family* (Cambridge, Mass.: Harvard University Press).

BHALLA, S. (1988), 'Is Sri Lanka an Exception? A Comparative Study of Living Standards', in Srinivasan, T. N., and Bardhan, P. K. (eds.), *Rural Poverty in South Asia*, vol. ii (New York: Columbia University Press).

BJOERCK, W. A. (1984), 'An Overview of Local Purchase of Food Commodities (LPFC)' (UNICEF).

BLISS, C. (1982), 'The Facts about Famine', *South*, Mar.

BOSERUP, E. (1970), *Women's Role in Economic Development* (London: Allen & Unwin).

BOWBRICK, P. (1986), 'The Causes of Famine: A Refutation of Professor Sen's Theory', *Food Policy*, 11.

——(1987), 'Rejoinder: An Untenable Hypothesis on the Causes of Famine', *Food Policy*, 12.

CAMPBELL, R. H., and SKINNER, A. S. (eds.) (1976), *Adam Smith: An Inquiry into the Nature and Causes of the Wealth of Nations* (Oxford: Oxford University Press).

CUTLER, P. (1984), 'Famine Forecasting: Prices and Peasant Behaviour in Northern Ethiopia', *Disasters*, 8.

DESAI, M. (1984), 'A General Theory of Poverty', *Indian Economic Review*.

FAO (1985), *The State of Food and Agriculture 1984* (Rome: FAO).

GRIFFIN, K. (1981), 'Poverty Trap', *Guardian*, 7 Oct.

HAYTER, T. (1981), 'Famine For Free', *New Society*, 15 Oct.

JOSHI, V. (1981), 'Enough To Eat', *London Review of Books*, 19 Nov.

KHAN, Q. M. (1985), 'A Model of Endowment Constrained Demand for Food in an Agricultural Economy with Empirical Applications to Bangladesh', *World Development*, 13.

KUMAR, B. G. (1985), 'The Ethiopian Famine and Relief Measures: An Analysis and Evaluation', mimeo (UNICEF).

LINNEMANN, H. (1981), *MOIRA: A Model of International Relations in Agriculture* (Amsterdam: North-Holland).

LIPTON, M. (1981), 'The Analysis of Want', *The Times Literary Supplement*.

MARX, K. (1887), *Capital*, vol. i (London: Sonnenschein).

MAUNDER, A., and RENBORG, V. (eds.) (1986), *Agriculture in a Turbulent World*, proceedings of the 19th International Conference of Agricultural Economists, Malaga, Spain, 26 Aug.–4 Sept. 1985 (Aldershot: Gower).

MYINT, H. (1985), 'Growth Policies and Income Distribution', Discussion Paper, World Bank, Mar.

PADMINI, R. (1985), 'The Local Purchase of Food Commodities: "Cash for Food" Project', mimeo (Addis Ababa: UNICEF).

PARIKH, K., and RABAR, F. (eds.) (1981), *Food for All in a Sustainable World* (Laxenburg: IIASA).

RAVALLION, M. (1985), 'The Performance of Rice Markets in Bangladesh during the 1974 Famine', *Economic Journal*, 95.

SEAMAN, J. A., and HOLT, J. F. J. (1980), 'Markets and Famines in the Third World', *Disasters*, 4.

SEN, A. K. (1977), 'Starvation and Exchange Entitlements: A General Approach and its Application to the Great Bengal Famine', *Cambridge Journal of Economics*, 1.

——(1981a), *Poverty and Famines* (Oxford: Oxford University Press).

——(1981b), 'Public Action and the Quality of Life in Developing Countries', *Oxford Bulletin of Economics and Statistics*, 43.

——(1981c), 'Ingredients of Famine Analysis: Availability and Entitlements', *Quarterly Journal of Economics*, 95.

——(1982), 'The Food Problem: Theory and Policy', *Third World Quarterly*, 4.

——(1983), 'Development: Which Way Now?', *Economic Journal*, 93.

——(1984), *Resources, Values and Development* (Oxford: Basil Blackwell).

——(1985), 'Women, Technology and Sexual Divisions', *Trade and Development (UNCTAD)*, 6.

——(1986), 'The Causes of Famine: A Reply', *Food Policy*, 11.

——(1987), 'Reply: Famines and Mr. Bowbrick', *Food Policy*, 12.

——(1988), 'Sri Lanka's Achievements: How and When', in Srinivasan, T. N., and Bardhan, P. K. (eds.), *Rural Poverty in South Asia* (New York: Columbia University Press).

SMITH, A. (1776), *An Inquiry into the Nature and Causes of the Wealth of Nations*, repr. in Campbell and Skinner (1976).

SNOWDON, B. (1985), 'The Political Economy of the Ethiopian Famine', *National Westminster Bank Quarterly Review*, Nov.

SOLOW, R. M. (1984), 'Relative Deprivation?', *Partisan Review*, 51.

SRAFFA, P. (ed.) (1971), *The Works and Correspondence of David Ricardo*, vol. v (Cambridge: Cambridge University Press).

SVEDBERG, P. (1984), 'Food Insecurity in Developing Countries: Causes, Trends and Policy Options', mimeo (UNCTAD).

——(1986), 'The Economics of Food Insecurity in Developing Countries', mimeo (Stockholm: Institute for International Economic Studies).

TAYLOR, L. (1975), 'The Misconstrued Crisis: Lester Brown and World Food', *World Development*, 3.

3

Global Food Balances and Individual Hunger: Three Themes in an Entitlements-Based Approach

S. M. Ravi Kanbur

3.1. *Introduction*

While there is considerable disagreement about the actual number of hungry people in the world today, there is almost universal agreement that the current situation is unacceptable. Too many individuals are subject to periodic reductions in their food intake—which leaves many dead—and even among those not subject to such transitory reductions, there is too low a level of average food intake. What is the role of global food balances in determining this pattern of individual hunger? The object of this paper is to introduce and elaborate upon three themes which emphasize the regional element in the link between global food balances and individual hunger in an entitlements-based approach. The first of these themes is an extension of Sen's (1981) entitlements approach to hunger to the case of nation states in a global setting. The second theme is based around the nature of the world food market as an interlinked system of markets in internationally traded and non-traded food crops. The third and final theme emphasizes the essential and inherent conflict between net sellers and net buyers of food, in an international and national system of market-based entitlements.

Sen (1981) has introduced us to the role of 'entitlements' in determining the link between endowment and hunger. Alternative rules of social organization and exchange allow alternative linkages between endowment and command over food. In a market economy this link is simply the food-purchasing power of the market value of the endowment at current prices. As Sen (1981) shows, individual hunger can increase at a given level of total food availability, if market-based entitlements change because of relative price changes. Viewing nation states as individual actors in a global setting, a similar entitlement-based approach can be applied to an analysis of global food balances and regional hunger. Hunger can occur in a country not only because of a decline in total world food availability, but also because of a drop in the value of goods the country has to sell in exchange for food. Although important to the hungry, food is only one part of the world economy, and the capacity of a nation to feed

I am grateful to participants to the WIDER Conference on Food Strategies for helpful comments. In particular, I would like to thank Jean Drèze, Nanak Kakwani, Robert Kates, and Amartya Sen.

its hungry depends as much on developments in the non-food part of the world economy as on global food balances.

Returning to food, let us consider the impact of global food balances on hunger. In principle of course there need be no direct connection. If the world food market was segmented, with very little in the way of flows between the different submarkets, then the total supply of food in the world could remain the same with individual submarkets moving up and down. If the decline in supply occurred in markets where hunger was not a problem at all, then world hunger would not be affected significantly. At the other extreme, if the world market in food was essentially unified, then changes in the world supply or demand would feed through to price in every region of the world and affect hunger, unless counteracting measures were taken. In fact, the actual picture is somewhere in between these two extremes. Some food crops, like wheat, are traded goods in the world market and, despite various types of government intervention, changes in supply and demand do feed through to 'the world price'. Other food crops, like many root crops in Africa, are essentially non-traded so that supply and demand have to be looked at market by market. The situation is further complicated by the fact that the traded and non-traded crops are often substitutes in production and/or consumption, so that changes in the price of one do feed through to changes in the price of the other. The link between global food balances and individual hunger is thus mediated by internationally traded and non-traded food crops, and any analysis of the problem should take these into account.

It is a fact of economic life that a change in the price of a commodity affects net buyers and net sellers in diametrically opposite ways. Thus an increase in the price of food, *ceteris paribus*, benefits net sellers of food at the expense of net buyers. A decrease in the price of food benefits net buyers at the expense of net sellers. But the hungry of the world consist of both net sellers and net buyers of food. Added to this is the complication that many of the net buyers of food rely on net sellers of food for employment. The relationship between the price of food and hunger is thus not as simple as it may seem. It is not clear that a secular decline in the world price of food will necessarily benefit all of the hungry in the world—or even most of them. What is certain is that in a system of market-based entitlements it will disadvantage some of them, unless compensating measures are taken.

The plan of this chapter is as follows. Section 3.2 begins the analysis with a review of current estimates and projections both of global food balances and of global hunger. Sections 3.3, 3.4, and 3.5 take up each of the three themes of this chapter—nation states in a global setting, traded versus non-traded food crops, and conflicts between net buyers and net sellers—in turn. Section 3.6 concludes with a summary of the main policy implications, and a discussion of the pressing needs for further research.

3.2. Global food balances and global hunger

As a prelude to an analysis of the links between food balances at the global level and hunger, we will review the current evidence on food balances and on the extent of hunger in the world. Both areas of investigation are bedevilled by data problems and by conceptual problems. On the food balances side, there is the question of an appropriate framework for projection and the quality of the database. On hunger, there is the question of the appropriate definition of minimal food requirements. We will deal with each of these in turn.

(a) Global food balances

There are two major sources of data on food supplies at the world level: the Food and Agriculture Organization of the United Nations (FAO), and the United States Department of Agriculture (USDA). As documented by Paulino and Tseng (1980), there are significant differences in the coverage and collection of these data, and significant differences in the actual estimates of area under production, total output, and trade for different crops. The country coverage of the two sources is different (USDA reports on fewer countries than FAO), as is the reference time period. It should be clear how the latter can give rise to major differences in estimates of output, particularly during periods in which production fluctuates dramatically or when a sharp shift occurs in trend. Paulino and Tseng (1980) carry out a comparison of production and trade data from the two sources for the years 1965, 1970, and 1975 and conclude that 'as

Table 3.1 Wheat: production and trade, 1984 (selected countries)

Countries	Production (1,000 metric tons)		Net exports (+) or net imports (−) (1,000 metric tons)	
	USDA	FAO	USDA	FAO
United States	66,009	70,638	(+) 38,018	(+) 43,515
Canada	26,914	21,199	(+) 20,500	(+) 21,623
France	24,785	32,884	(+) 12,980	(+) 15,272
Australia	22,000	18,580	(+) 12,000	(+) 10,631
Argentina	12,000	13,000	(+) 9,500	(+) 7,406
Soviet Union	78,000	76,000	(−) 20,000	(−) 25,348
China	81,390	87,682	(−) 10,000	(−) 10,955
Egypt	1,996	1,815	(−) 6,800	(−) 7,034
Japan	695	741	(−) 5,300	(−) 5,643
Brazil	2,100	1,830	(−) 4,400	(−) 4,868

Notes: 'Production' refers to wheat only, while 'Trade' refers to wheat and flour (in grain equivalent).

FAO data refer to the calendar year. USDA trade data refer to the 12 months following 1 July 1983. USDA production data refer to the season 1983/4.

the major sources of international agricultural statistics, FAO and USDA should undertake more joint efforts to reconcile their data'.

Paulino and Tseng's analysis is for production and trade a decade ago. To see if their suggestion was indeed taken up and reflected in the data, let us consider Tables 3.1 and 3.2, which present production and trade figures, for wheat and rice, for the latest year available. From Table 3.1 it can be seen that discrepancies in production figures are large for the largest producers. In comparison with USDA figures, FAO figures overstate production by 7 per cent for the US and for China, 8 per cent for Argentina, and an extraordinary 32 per cent for France. Similarly, FAO figures understate production by 12 per cent for Brazil and 21 per cent for Canada. In fact, the only country for which the discrepancy is under 5 per cent is the Soviet Union. On the trade side, FAO figures overstate US exports by 14 per cent and French exports by 17 per cent, while Soviet imports are overstated by over 26 per cent.

The picture for rice is similar, but the discrepancies are lower. The production discrepancy for China, by far the world's largest producer, is 7 per cent, and the large discrepancies are for the smaller producers—FAO figures understate Iraq's production by 52 per cent. On the trade side, FAO figures overstate exports of the biggest exporter (Thailand) by 24 per cent, and understate the exports of the second biggest exporter (US) by 5 per cent. The imports of Indonesia are understated by an enormous 64 per cent, while the imports of Nigeria are understated by 35 per cent. In fact, the discrepancies are

Table 3.2 Rice: production and trade, 1984 (selected countries)

Countries	Production (1,000 metric tons)		Net exports (+) or net imports (−) (1,000 metric tons)	
	USDA	FAO	USDA	FAO
Thailand	18,000	19,200	(+) 3,700	(+) 4,619
United States	4,523	6,216	(+) 2,230	(+) 2,113
Pakistan	5,210	5,009	(+) 1,299	(+) 1,265
Burma	14,800	14,500	(+) 750	(+) 721
China	168,870	181,028	(+) 475	(+) 1,107
Indonesia	34,503	37,500	(−) 1,175	(−) 414
Nigeria	1,280	1,100	(−) 701	(−) 450
Iran	1,400	1,230	(−) 680	(−) 710
Saudi Arabia	3	0	(−) 500	(−) 490
Iraq	200	95	(−) 473	(−) 487

Notes: USDA trade figures include milled, semi-milled, broken, and rough rice in terms of milled equivalent. FAO's Commodity Notes indicate that trade figures are also in converted milled equivalent units. Production data is for rough rice.

FAO and USDA trade data refer to calendar years. For production, FAO data refer to calendar years 'in which the entire harvest or the bulk of it took place', while USDA data refer to crop year beginning 1 Aug. 1983.

such as to alter even the rankings of the countries by volume of imports: Indonesia, Nigeria, Iran, Saudi Arabia, and Iraq according to USDA; Iran, Saudi Arabia, Iraq, Nigeria, and Indonesia according to FAO.

The overall conclusion must be that major discrepancies remain between FAO and USDA data. It should be clear that without further detailed work we cannot pronounce on which of the two data sets is 'better'—the answer will probably be country specific. Such an agnostic conclusion is also reached by Paulino and Tseng. Bearing in mind these data problems, let us now consider different estimates and projections of food supplies per capita. A number of these estimates and projections are available, but we focus on three studies: (1) FAO's 'Agriculture: Toward 2000', (2) 'The Global 2000 Report to the President', see Barney (1982), and (3) the International Food Policy Research Institute (IFPRI) projections reported in Mellor and Johnston (1984). The most pessimistic of these is the report by Barney (1982), which sees demand outstripping supply over the years to the end of the century, and food prices rising dramatically. However, Johnson (1983) takes this report to task for making claims unsubstantiated by historical trends. Thus, for example, the study projects an increase in food prices at the rate of 2.25 per cent per annum, when in actuality the trend price of food has remained constant or even declined slightly.

The projections reported by Mellor and Johnston (1984), which are based on a series of studies by the International Food Policy Research Institute, rely on extrapolations of trends between 1961 and 1977. For the world as a whole during this period, staple food production stayed comfortably above population growth rate, so that per capita world food availability increased. However, there were substantial regional differences, with sub-Saharan Africa showing a dramatic gap of 15 per cent between production growth and population growth. On the other hand, developed countries as a whole expanded their production more than two and a half times as fast as population growth rates (see Mellor and Johnston 1984). It is not surprising, then, that the developed countries became net exporters of food staples and the developing countries became net importers of food staples, a state of affairs which is projected to intensify in the last two decades of this century.

The FAO's 'Agriculture: Toward 2000' paints a similar picture, of gradually increasing per capita food supplies at the global level, with growing imports by developing countries and growing exports by developed countries. While expressing satisfaction with the overall trend in supplies, both the FAO and Mellor and Johnston (1984) express concern about growing imports by developing countries. It is not clear why this should cause concern, since the overall trend in supplies must mean lower prices in an integrated world market, unless the worry is that developing countries will not have enough foreign exchange either to sustain this trend level of imports or to insulate food consumption against periodic fluctuations. This latter issue will be taken up in section 3.3.

(b) *Global hunger*

How many hungry people are there in the world? The answers to this question are many and varied. On the one hand we have the scepticism of Poleman (1983), that the question is unanswerable: 'Let me make clear at the outset that there is no way to specify with certainty the extent of world hunger.' On the other hand, we have the well-known estimates of Reutlinger and Selowsky (1976): 'Based on average calorie consumption data in the mid-1960's, it is estimated that 56 per cent of the population in developing countries (some 840 million people) had calorie-deficient diets in excess of 250 calories a day. Another 19 per cent (some 290 million people) had deficits of less than 250 calories a day.' A recent World Bank (1985) estimate, based on the Reutlinger–Selowsky methodology, brings the figures up to date:

In 1980, probably somewhere between 340 million and 730 million people in the developing countries (excluding China) did not have incomes which allowed them to obtain sufficient calories from their diet. The estimate of 340 million is based on a calorie requirement standard that would prevent serious health risks and stunted growth in children. If the standard is enough calories for an active working life, however, the estimate of those with chronically deficient diets rises to 730 million.

The Reutlinger–Selowsky methodology for estimating the numbers of the hungry involves several stages, each of which can be criticized. The first stage

Table 3.3 Share and size of population with energy-deficient diets, 1980

Region[a]	Population with energy-deficient diets			
	Below 90% of FAO/WHO requirement		Below 80% of FAO/WHO requirement	
	Share in population (%)	Population (m.)	Share in population (%)	Population (m.)
All developing countries (87)[b]	34	730	16	340
Sub-Saharan Africa (37)[b]	44	150	25	90
East Asia and Pacific (8)[b]	14	40	7	20
South Asia (7)[b]	50	470	21	200
Latin America and Caribbean (24)[b]	13	50	6	20
Middle East and North Africa (11)[b]	10	20	4	10

[a]The 87 countries had 92% of the population in developing countries in 1980, excluding China.
[b]Numbers in parentheses are the number of countries in the sample.

Source: World Bank (1985: Table 1.1).

is the establishment of energy requirement standards. This they do by taking the FAO/WHO standards (see FAO 1973), which are based on intake required for normal energy expenditure and for normal growth, and which are country specific to take account of demographic differences. The second stage is the estimation of a relationship between energy in the daily diet and income. The third stage is the estimation of income distribution in the year in question. The fourth and final stage is to read off, from the income distribution, the numbers with income below that level which, given the energy–income relationship, could not provide the minimum specified requirement of calories. Let us take each one of these stages in turn.

Poleman (1983) has criticized the minimum requirement standards used by Reutlinger and Selowsky (1976) as being too high, based as they were on FAO/WHO standards. The World Bank (1985) study meets this criticism by setting the standard at either 90 per cent of the FAO/WHO requirement, or at 80 per cent of this requirement. Table 3.3 reproduces their results at a regional level of disaggregation. As can be seen, overall the figures are lower than in Reutlinger and Selowsky (1976), and this is partly due to the lower standards used. What is interesting, however, is that the ranking of regions remains largely unchanged, in terms of percentage of population suffering from hunger, when the different requirement levels are considered. Sub-Saharan Africa and South Asia change rankings, suggesting that extreme hunger is more of a problem in the former, but otherwise the relative positions remain unchanged. In terms of policy guidance as to which of the regions should be favoured relative to the others, the use of different cut-offs makes only a small difference. A similar picture is seen when changes between 1970 and 1980 are considered. Table 3.4 shows that the rankings as between the five regions remain largely unchanged, except that sub-Saharan Africa and South Asia change places as before. With the lower requirement, developments in sub-Saharan Africa look worse.

Srinivasan (1981, 1983) has become a persistent critic of another aspect of the Reutlinger–Selowsky method, namely, the fact that the FAO/WHO requirements are *average* norms:

Even if the energy requirements of a randomly chosen man from a population of reference men is a fixed number, since the published norms are the *average* norms of the individuals in the population, it is obvious that half of the population of healthy reference men will have intakes (which equal their requirements, since they are healthy) below the average. (Srinivasan 1983; emphasis in original)

Such a criticism applies equally well to studies by Dandekar and Rath (1971), FAO (1977), Altimir (1982), and others. Given the lack of information on requirements by individuals, the use of average norms is something we may have to live with. Kakwani (1986) provides some estimates of how far wrong we can go in using such average norms. But there is a further point, of adjustment of individuals to low intake, which leads Srinivasan to argue against the notion

Table 3.4 Changes between 1970 and 1980 in the share and size of the population
with energy-deficient diets

Region	Below 90% of FAO/WHO requirement		Below 80% of FAO/WHO requirement	
	Change in share of population	% change in number of people	Change in share of population	% change in number of people
All developing countries (87)[a]	−0.06	+10	−0.02	+14
Sub-Saharan Africa (37)[a]	+0.01	+30	+0.04	+49
East Asia and Pacific (8)[a]	−0.27	−57	−0.14	−57
South Asia (7)[a]	+0.03	+38	+0.02	+47
Latin America and Caribbean (24)[a]	−0.07	−15	−0.04	−21
Middle East and North Africa (11)[a]	−0.25	−62	−0.14	−68

[a]Numbers in parentheses are the number of countries in the sample.
Source: World Bank (1985: Table 1.2).

of a nutritional 'requirement' for individuals. The key question here is the time frame, and the severity of the adjustment. It is perhaps true that a slow and prolonged change in economic and dietary conditions will lead the body to adapt. But if such adaptation takes place relatively slowly—say over a period of decades—we still have to take into account the discomfort of prolonged hunger at a low level, or the short sharp shock of a famine. The body clearly cannot adapt fast enough to avoid death by starvation. Surely in such a case the notion of a minimum requirement makes sense—however low that standard is set. Difficulties in drawing a line based on nutritional standards should not engender a nihilistic attitude. A line has to be drawn, and sensitivity analysis should be carried out in testing how crucial the actual cut-off is for policy recommendations.

Of course, it goes without saying that discussion of poverty requires a cut-off—whether based on nutritional or other criteria. Indeed Sen (1981) codifies this requirement in his 'focus axiom'. Having rejected energy requirement as a basis for analysis of hunger and poverty, Srinivasan (1983) turns to what he terms a 'pragmatic approach', as illustrated for India:

It would appear that in rural areas a *sustained* decline in the share of food in total expenditure and the share of starchy staples in calorie intake starts from a per capita monthly expenditure of 43 rupees (Rs.). In urban areas, the corresponding figure is Rs. 34. Interestingly, the rural cutoff point of Rs. 43 per capita per month happens to equal the official poverty expenditure of Rs. 15 per capita per month at 1960–61 prices—a poverty line that has gained authority through its use in several studies of rural poverty in India (Ahluwalia, 1978; Srinivasan and Bardhan, 1974). This pragmatic approach leads to classifying around 42 percent of rural households and a little over 9 percent of urban households as having inadequate food intakes to *some degree*. To avoid any misunderstanding, it should be emphasized that one *should not infer* that these proportions represent households whose members are malnourished in a clinical or biomedical sense. Inadequacy of food intake in this approach is as perceived by the household and reflected in its consumption pattern. In any case, almost by definition, inadequacy of food intake is associated with poverty. (emphasis in the original)

It is not clear what guidelines emerge from the above argument. Should the cut-off be chosen on the basis of the food consumption pattern, or on the basis of a poverty line that has gained authority (this latter line may itself have been defined with reference to some nutritional norms)? What happens if the authoritative line and the consumption pattern line conflict? The example illustrates the fact that the same cut-off can be justified on different grounds. There is an identification problem here—there clearly exists a fixed average energy requirement along FAO/WHO lines which would give the same number of people below the cut-off as Srinivasan's pragmatic line. Thus, while accepting his strictures against a precise, 'pseudo-scientific', definition of hunger, it seems that the best defence is still to carry out sensitivity analysis using a range of cut-offs—some of which could be based on the FAO/WHO guidelines. Atkinson (1985) and Foster and Shorrocks (1985) have already made a start on the theory of rankings using a range of poverty lines.

The second stage of the Reutlinger–Selowsky methodology, the determination of a calorie consumption–income relationship, can be equally criticized for imposing an average relationship on the population in identifying those who fall below the cut-off. Given enough detailed information we can directly calculate the calorie intake of each household, and will not need the relationship to income. But in the absence of such information, at least for some countries, it is difficult to see an alternative to the Reutlinger–Selowsky method. The best we can do is to get an idea of the bias that can arise. The third stage of the calculation involves equally heroic assumptions regarding income distribution. In World Bank (1985), income distribution data were used directly for thirty-five countries. For these, the Reutlinger–Selowsky method is to apply the Kakwani–Podder (1976) technique of fitting a Lorenz Curve to available survey data. For the remaining countries, the percentages of population below the minimum requirement were *extrapolated* by first regressing this variable on per capita energy in diet and per capita energy requirement for the thirty-five countries, and then using this regression to arrive at the percentage of population below the requirement for other countries. There are clearly problems with such extrapolation and it may well be that these problems dominate the conceptual critique of average norms for calorie intake.

While the estimates of Reutlinger and Selowsky (1976) and the World Bank (1985) can be criticized on a number of grounds, it is not clear how, given the information we have, they can be substantially bettered. Closer attention to econometric detail and procedure would help, as would an indication of the biases the method might entail under different statistical specifications. However, if we are in the game of linking global food balances and global hunger then perforce we have to project food balances and hunger at the global level. The criticisms levelled against current methods should indicate caution rather than nihilism.

3.3. *Nation states in a global setting: an extension of the entitlements approach*

Sen (1981) has introduced us to the simple yet powerful idea that hunger is caused not necessarily by there not being enough food to eat; it may also be caused by the fact that the existing social and economic conditions and institutions may not give an *entitlement* to an adequate amount of food:

The entitlement approach to starvation and famines concentrates on the ability of people to command food through the legal means available in the society, including the use of production possibilities, trade opportunities, entitlements *vis-à-vis* the state, and other methods of acquiring food. A person starves either because he does not have the ability to command enough food, or because he does not use this ability to avoid starvation. The entitlement approach concentrates on the former, ignoring the latter possibility. Furthermore, it concentrates on those means of commanding food that are legitimized by the legal system in operation in that society. While it is an approach of some generality, it makes no attempt to include all possible influences that can in principle cause starvation, for example illegal transfers (*e.g.* looting), and choice failures (*e.g.* owing to inflexible food habits).

While in a subsistence economy entitlement to food is given by what one grows and by what one perhaps has customary rights over, and in a market economy it is given by what one can acquire through trade and exchange of one's endowments, in a mixed economy food entitlements depend both on market-based exchange and on entitlements society has created through various means of social security. In most developing countries, the government can and does influence both market-based entitlements and direct entitlements to food. It is not surprising, therefore, that a major determinant of individuals' access to food in a national setting is their government's access to food in an international setting.

The entitlements approach to the relationship between a government and individuals in the country can be extended to nation states in a global setting. If we characterize each nation as having a certain 'food requirement', we can consider how each government can set about meeting this requirement from the international market. What are a nation state's food entitlements? There are two main forms of entitlements under the current institutional setting. Firstly, the country can purchase food on international markets. Global food balances are clearly relevant here. If growth in world supply lags behind world demand, there will be a general increase in the price of food and, *ceteris paribus*, a decline in the country's food entitlement. However, the value of what a country sells in order to purchase food is also important. Secondly, the country may have access to food on concessional terms—the various food aid provisions relate to this.

Given the value of its 'endowment' on world markets—essentially the foreign exchange that it can earn by selling other, non-food, goods to the world—the country's access to food is determined by the international price of food and by the extent of food aid available. A decline in its endowment value, an increase in the world price of food, or a decrease in food aid will increase the degree of food deprivation in the country if internal policy is unchanged. This tells us why forecasts of a static or declining trend in the world food price do not offer grounds for complacency. Many developing countries are facing severe declines in the value of the goods they can sell abroad, compounded by the tightness of borrowing conditions on world markets. Food aid is tied up to surplus disposal in developed countries, and there are pressures (budgetary or otherwise) to reduce farm surpluses in these countries. Such a reduction would at the same time reduce appropriations available for food aid shipments, and reduce market supplies—thereby leading to an increase in world price. On the demand side, the growing prosperity of middle-income developing countries increases effective demand—which increases the temptation among developed countries to sell their stocks at market prices rather than supply at concessionary prices, and also generally tigthens the market for food at the international level. This increases the burden on the poorest of the poor.

The gap between a country's entitlements and its requirements will eventually be translated into hunger for at least some of its citizens. However, this calculation can be turned on its head and we can estimate what the entitlements will have to be to meet the requirements. This is the basic approach followed, although with some differences, by USDA (1982, 1983), IFPRI (1983), and FAO (1983a) in forecasting food aid requirements of developing countries.

The USDA analysis is short term in nature and provides estimates of food aid requirements for the coming season by forecasting import requirements and the ability to import. Import requirements are derived as the difference between food production and the aggregate food consumption which would (1) meet recent per capita calorie intake or (2) meet the FAO/WHO nutritional standards for the population as a whole. Not surprisingly, the latter method gives a higher figure for consumption requirement. Given the import requirement, the next step is to ascertain how much the country could import to meet the gap. This is a difficult calculation not only because the foreign exchange earnings of a country have to be forecast, but also because the proportion of this allocated to food imports is a policy choice variable. USDA assume that to be a fixed ratio, based on the recent experience. In 1983/4, for a total of 67 countries, the higher estimate of cereal import requirements was 48.5 million tons of which the food aid requirement was estimated to be 33 million tons.

IFPRI (1983), while recognizing the importance of foreign exchange availability in meeting food import requirements, simply assumed a figure of 2 per cent (and 5 per cent) as the fraction of export earnings that would be allocated to cereal imports. On this basis, their forecast of food aid requirements in 1990 for 57 countries came to 35.4 million tons if the objective was to meet the FAO/WHO standard. The differences between the IFPRI and USDA findings lie not only in different country coverage and the different time periods considered, but also in the method of calculating foreign exchange available for cereal imports. FAO (1983a) further criticized both of these studies for not disaggregating between different categories of food aid: project aid, non-project aid, and emergency aid. However, it did not provide an alternative methodology for assessing project aid requirements (but see WFP 1979).

In the FAO (1983a) study, the non-project aid requirement was estimated essentially along the USDA/IFPRI lines. But an 'effective demand' approach was taken in deriving consumption requirements—translating projections of private consumption expenditure into demand for food using elasticities estimated from household expenditure surveys. (While this may seem to be different from using the FAO/WHO minimum standard, in some cases 'account was taken of known targets of national development plans in developing countries', which may of course reflect the minimum standard.) A similar market orientation is seen in their calculation of commercial cereal imports —this was done by estimating elasticities of commercial cereal import demand with respect to export earnings for 1970 to 1981. On this basis the cereals food aid requirement in 1985, for 111 countries, was estimated to be 14.2 million tons. The major reason for the large difference between the FAO estimates on the one hand and the USDA and IFPRI estimates on the other is of course that FAO uses 'effective demand' as the basis of consumption requirement while USDA and IFPRI have used 'minimum nutritional standard' requirement. When IFPRI used the effective demand method, their forecast of food aid requirement came to 16.6 million tons in 1990.

To these studies we should add the projections in World Bank (1985). For seven countries (Bangladesh, Burkina Faso, Ethiopia, Mali, Nepal, Tanzania, and Uganda) for which even equal distribution of per capita energy intake would be insufficient to satisfy 90 per cent of FAO/WHO requirements, this study forecast cereal imports on the basis of meeting the FAO/WHO requirements in full. These imports were compared to projected export earnings in 1990, and the ratios ranged from 0.19 for Burkina Faso to 0.86 for Ethiopia and 1.27 for Bangladesh. In other words, Bangladesh cannot, in the foreseeable future, meet its food requirements on the basis of market forces. Even if one revises the standard downwards dramatically, allowing for inequality of food consumption will tend to restore these high figures. Added to this is the fact that food production has been assumed to grow in these countries at the optimistic rate of 3 per cent per annum.

However, projections for 31 other countries reveal a less pessimistic future.

For these countries required food imports are projected to be less than 10 per cent of export earnings. The crucial factors explaining this difference are (1) lower population growth and (2) better prospects for export earnings. These comparisons highlight the strong regional/national element in the link between global food balances and hunger. The current precarious balance at the global level does *not* mean an even-handed distribution of hunger across the developing world. Some countries can afford to pay for their food, others cannot. For these countries, market-based entitlements can only lead to greater hunger. If the trend value of their 'endowments'—the goods they sell—is not to be improved, then their only other entitlement to food is on a non-market, concessionary basis. This must be one of the strongest arguments for maintaining and expanding current levels of food aid commitments by the rich countries.

Alongside the trend movements of market and non-market entitlements, we also see, from time to time, sharp fluctuations in global economic conditions and hence in these entitlements. What is important to realize is that a sharp drop in food entitlements can occur not necessarily because of developments in the food market, but by developments in the non-food markets as well. Sharp declines in the value of non-food exports can equally well cause starvation in a country—this is the central message of the entitlements approach. FAO (1983a) calculated emergency food aid requirements by stipulating a shortfall of cereal production below trend which would be classed as an emergency and hence be eligible for emergency food aid. The critical shortfall specified varied from 10 per cent for middle-income countries and 5 per cent for low-income countries. These were then applied to the twelve-year period 1970 to 1981 and an annual average of emergency requirements in this period was calculated.

Table 3.5 Emergency and non-emergency food aid requirements in 1985

Region	Emergency aid (m. tons)	Non-emergency aid (m. tons)	Emergency/ non-emergency (%)
All food aid recipient countries	3.00	14.2	21.1
North Africa/Near East	1.10	4.3	26.6
Sub-Saharan Africa	0.50	3.1	16.1
Asia/Pacific	1.00	4.3	23.3
Latin America/Caribbean	0.35	0.3	116.7
Others	0.05	—	—
Low-income food-deficit countries	1.40	12.0	11.7
Other food aid recipient countries	1.60	2.2	72.7

Source: FAO (1983a: Table 1 and Table 3).

Table 3.5 reproduces the FAO results. The 3 million tons of cereals required on average every year are to be added to the 14.2 million tons for trend food aid. As can be seen, there is once again considerable regional variation in both the absolute level of emergency aid requirements, and its relation to non-emergency aid requirements.

The most striking feature of the FAO (1983a) calculation of emergency aid, at least from the point of view of the entitlements approach, is its narrow focus on variations in food supplies. This is particularly surprising given that the trend calculations of food aid do go beyond this and take into account the capacity of the country to purchase food. A similar concentration on the food import bill is to be found in WFC/FAO (1983), which argues for special balance of payments support to finance temporary increases in the *food* import bill. But exactly the same situation can arise with fluctuations in prices of export commodites and hence export earnings. Given current capital market constraints, temporary shortfalls in export earnings are bound to be reflected in reduced food imports by the poorest developing countries. Simple as it is, this insight of the entitlements approach sheds new light on international commodity price stabilization schemes. These have been criticized by Newbery and Stiglitz (1981)—but see Kanbur (1984, 1986b)—as being inefficient ways of improving consumer and producer welfare. The food security view would be one line of argument against their conclusions. More generally, equal attention must be paid to *export* prospects in the battery of indicators that FAO (1983b) suggests as signals of acute and large-scale food shortages, and as part of its global early warning system.

3.4. *Traded and non-traded food crops*

In a world without government intervention, the pattern of transport costs and comparative advantage would determine which commodities were traded across national boundaries and which were not. The significance of this distinction between traded and non-traded goods lies in the implications of global food balances for regional hunger. If the market for a particular food crop were integrated on a world-wide level, so that it was a traded good for all countries, then it would have a single world price which responded to the global food balance. To the extent that the world market was segmented at the regional and national levels, the extreme of which is that the food crop was a non-traded good for each country, then there would be an array of prices responding to the regional or national food balance, with the global picture having little or no effect.

Government intervention alters this neat distinction between 'naturally' traded and non-traded goods. Whether such intervention is optimal or not can be analysed using standard welfare economics. For a small open economy which takes world prices as given and which has competitive markets in those goods which are not 'naturally' traded, we know that free trade will achieve a

Pareto-efficient outcome in a world of certainty. However, it is well known that in a second-best world, where some markets do not satisfy the competitive requirements, intervention in the form of trade taxes which reduce trade may well be optimal. Intervention may also be optimal if the government cares about distribution but does not have the lump sum instruments to alter the distribution in a non-distortionary manner. The same arguments hold in a world of uncertainty where individuals do not have access to insurance markets. In such situations governments can, and do, insulate domestic food markets from global changes for commodities which are 'traded'. They do this by interventions which divorce domestic supplies from international supply conditions—by discouraging exports in a period of global shortage and high prices, to maintain domestic supplies and low domestic prices, or by discouraging cheap imports in a period of global excess supply and low prices, to protect the incomes of farmers. The presence of a government also means that effectively there is no such thing as a non-traded good—imports or exports of the good can always be subsidized and encouraged. The cost of turning a non-traded good into a traded good, and vice versa, is borne by the exchequer, and it is the budgetary costs of food intervention that have been causing concern during the last decade (see, for example, Scobie 1983). In a world where national governments pursue active policies designed to protect national food intake, global conditions affect not necessarily the consumption of the poor, but the budget of governments—which then have to make adjustments in other parts of the economy to compensate (e.g. cutting down on public investments).

Table 3.6 presents figures for net exports (including processed trade) as a percentage of domestic production for selected commodities and countries. The figures are 1979–81 averages taken from the FAO's food balance sheets. Six cereal crops and four root crops are chosen, and five countries each from Asia, Latin America, and Africa have been selected. An asterisk indicates that total domestic supply was less than 500 metric tons, i.e. that the commodity is basically irrelevant to the country under consideration. As can be seen, the fewest asterisks appear among the cereal crops while most appear among root crops. However, what is also interesting is how many zeros appear in the root crop columns—a zero indicates significant domestic production but no exports or imports. Out of the 60 possible cells in the root crop categories, there are 14 asterisks, and of the remaining 46 cells no fewer than 22 have zeros. Out of the 90 cells in the cereals categories, 7 are asterisks, and of the remaining 83 only 7 have zeros.

Overall, out of the 129 significant cells, 29 (i.e. around 20 per cent) are non-traded in the sense that they have significant domestic production but no exports or imports. If we extend the category to include not only zeros but absolute values of less than 1, then the percentage of non-traded significant cells rises to 70 per cent among root crops, 19 per cent among cereals, and 37 per cent overall.

Table 3.6 Net exports as a percentage of production: 1979–1981 average for selected commodities and countries

Crop/country	Wheat	Paddy rice	Barley	Maize	Millet	Sorghum	Cassava	Sweet potatoes	Potatoes	Yams	Non-traded calories as % of total
Bangladesh	-142.6	-1.6	-16.7	0.0	*	-∞	-∞	0.0	-0.2	*	2.0
China	-18.3	0.8	-1.9	-2.8	0.2	-0.1	31.0	0.0	0.9	*	50.2
India	-1.4	1.1	0.7	-0.1	0.0	0.0	0.0	0.0	0.2	*	16.9
Indonesia	-∞	-7.1	-∞	-0.8	*	*	14.4	0.0	-0.5	*	9.6
Pakistan	-9.8	34.1	30.2	-0.3	0.0	5.1	-∞	0.0	5.1	*	4.5
Argentina	53.4	54.2	36.7	66.3	45.7	62.0	0.0	0.0	-2.6	*	1.0
Brazil	-162.6	-6.0	-386.2	-6.9	-∞	2.3	0.1	0.0	-0.8	2.8	8.3
Chile	-108.2	-21.6	28.2	-67.1	*	-∞	*	0.0	-0.2	*	3.4
Colombia	-874.0	2.0	-52.5	-12.8	*	-13.3	0.0	*	0.2	4.4	9.1
Mexico	-36.9	-18.6	-20.1	-21.2	*	-42.7	0.0	-2.0	-0.3	*	0.8
Egypt	-280.8	5.8	-10.4	-28.8	0.0	*	*	4.3	8.0	*	1.1
Kenya	-18.4	-33.3	1.3	-4.9	0.0	0.0	0.0	0.0	0.0	*	14.6
Nigeria	-4,945.8	-76.5	-∞	-10.8	-0.9	-0.1	0.0	0.0	0.0	0.0	49.0
Senegal	-∞	-547.7	-∞	-31.7	0.3	-∞	13.6	0.0	-220.0	*	25.9
Tanzania	-64.8	-41.5	-250.0	-17.0	10.3	7.7	0.7	0.0	2.1	0.0	30.5

Notes: * = information not reported because domestic supply does not exceed 500 metric tons.
-∞ = finite net imports with zero production.

Source: FAO (1984), calculated from individual country tables.

Table 3.6 is a first attempt at providing a breakdown of food crops by country according to the traded/non-traded category. It shows that, if we take the broader definition of 'non-traded', then around two-fifths of the commodity–country cells in Table 3.6 represent non-traded goods. Of course, there are problems with this representation. The cells are not weighted in any sense. It would, for example, be interesting to compute what fraction of a nation's total calorie intake was accounted for by non-traded goods. The last column in Table 3.6 does just this. It calculates the total calories provided by the cells with a net exports to production ratio of less than 1 per cent and takes this as a ratio of total calorie supply. It can be seen that there is considerable variation across countries. The Latin American countries all have dependence on non-traded food of less than 10 per cent, while the four sub-Saharan African countries (Nigeria, Tanzania, Kenya, and Senegal) have a large dependence on non-traded food and this is mainly due to their dependence on root crops. In Asia the picture for any country is influenced greatly by rice. China depends for a large fraction of its calories on rice which is non-traded. Using our criterion, India and Bangladesh are just on the boundary of having rice classified as a non-traded commodity. If rice was included in this category for these commodities, they would show substantial non-traded food dependence for calories.

There is of course the problem that, in using the extended definition of 'non-traded', we have neglected the fact that a very small level of exports or imports could still be consistent with domestic prices being determined internationally and hence by global balances in that food crop. This leads us to the observation that the natural test for non-tradedness is the relative independence of domestic price from international price. Policy interventions notwithstanding, the collection and analysis of such data would enhance our appreciation of the extent to which calorie intake—particularly of the poor —was vulnerable to global balances even after allowing for non-traded foods.

Despite these caveats, Table 3.6 does represent a start in formulating the implications of the traded/non-traded distinction for the links between global food balances and regional hunger. Wheat is seen as being largely a traded food crop for the fifteen countries considered (representing the bulk of the developing world's population). Root crops are predominantly non-traded, while cereals like millet show a mixed picture. In the absence of policy intervention, changes in the global balances of wheat would feed through fairly quickly into domestic price changes for all of these countries. Put another way, if there was to be policy intervention to insulate the domestic price of wheat, the budgetary consequences for developing country governments of a change in the global balance would be significant. However, changes in the global balance of root crop production and consumption would not feed through directly to the regional or national level. A substantial part of the calorie supply in sub-Saharan countries is thus insulated from direct effects of global food supply conditions.

However, this is not to say that indirect linkages between traded and non-traded food crops do not exist. If the food crops are substitutes in consumption (which they are at the national level) and/or substitutes in production, then global changes in traded good conditions can feed through to the non-traded sector. Such interlinkages are explored by Braverman and Hammer (1984) in their 'multi-market' approach to agricultural pricing (see Braverman and Kanbur 1985 for an analysis of the implications of such linkages for shadow pricing of agricultural projects). Let us take the case of Senegal, shown in Table 3.6 and also considered by Braverman and Hammer (1984). As is seen from the table, Senegal is an importer of rice, but millet is largely domestically produced and consumed. In fact, from the Senegal table in FAO (1984) it is clear that out of the total calorie supply in Senegal of 2,346 calories per capita per day, 624 calories came from rice and 605 from millet. An increase in the world price of rice, if not counteracted by policy, will feed through to the domestic price of rice in Senegal. However, rice and millet are substitutes in consumption. Thus there will be significant shift of demand into millet consumption and the price of millet will rise. This will encourage extra production of millet till a new equilibrium is established with a higher price of millet than ruled previously. Thus the increase in world price of rice (brought about by changes in *global* balances in this food crop) has fed through to the price of a commodity which is not traded on world markets, but which is nevertheless as important as rice in the calorie supply of Senegal. Under specific conditions, in particular countries, there could be further chain effects of commodities that were, for example, substitutes in production for millet. Any analysis of the implications of global food balances for regional, national, and individual hunger that does not take into account the disaggregation between traded and non-traded goods could, therefore, turn out to be seriously misleading.

3.5. *Food prices and conflicts: net sellers versus net buyers*

What would be the consequences of lower food prices as the result of a change in global food balances? We will look at this question first of all from the point of view of poverty, and then from the point of view of hunger. It is sometimes argued that lower food prices would be good for the poor, and the argument does make some sense. But it should be obvious that this line of argument focuses solely on net buyers of food and ignores net sellers. It is a characteristic feature of market-based entitlements that they give net sellers and net buyers of a commodity diametrically opposed interests. Any decrease in the price of a commodity benefits net buyers of the commodity. But it must, *ceteris paribus*, hurt net sellers. At the national level, it should be clear from Tables 3.1 and 3.2 that Argentina and Brazil would have very different views about the price of wheat, and that Thailand and Nigeria would have opposed interests with regard to the price of rice. The relationship of global balances to the conflicting interests of selling and buying nations translates itself into the relationship of national balances to the conflicting interests of net sellers and net buyers of food within a country. The argument that high food prices at the national level might actually *help* the poor has some support in the African context where net food sellers are typically smallholders in the rural sector, while net food buyers are mainly urban sector dwellers.

One way of formulating and quantifying this conflict is to consider explicitly the effect on a poverty index of a change in the price of a particular food commodity. This is done in Besley and Kanbur (1986), using the Foster, Greer, and Thorbecke (1984) measure of poverty defined on the equivalent income of net sellers and net purchasers. If $f(y)$ is the frequency density of 'income' y and the poverty line is z, then the FGT measure is:

$$P_\alpha = \int_{y'}^{z} \left(\frac{z - y}{z} \right)^\alpha f(y) dy$$

where y' is the lowest value of y and α is a parameter which defines members of this class of measures. The measure is essentially a summation of normalized poverty gaps $(z - y)/z$, each raised to the power α. When $\alpha = 0$ the measure becomes the headcount ratio; when $\alpha = 1$ it is simply the normalized poverty gap; and when α is greater than one the measure is 'transfer sensitive' to the appropriate order (see Foster, Greer, and Thorbecke 1984). From our point of view the usefulness of this measure lies in the fact that it is decomposable across population subgroups. Thus if the population can be divided into two mutually exclusive and exhaustive subgroups of net sellers and net producers of food then we can write

$$P_\alpha = \lambda_1 P_{1,\alpha} + \lambda_2 P_{2,\alpha}$$

where λ_i is the proportion of population in group i ($\lambda_1 + \lambda_2 = 1$) and $P_{i,\alpha}$ is the P_α measure for group i alone. While there are other poverty measures in the literature (the most famous of which is the Sen (1976) measure), the usefulness of the FGT measure lies in its flexibility and its decomposability, which allows us to aggregate subgroup poverty effects up to the national level.

It is shown in Besley and Kanbur (1986) that the effect of a small change in the price of food, q, is given by:

$$\frac{dP_\alpha}{dq} = \lambda_1 \frac{\alpha}{z} \int_0^z \left(\frac{z - y}{z} \right)^{\alpha - 1} x f_1 dy$$

$$+ \lambda_1 \frac{\alpha}{z} \int_0^z \left(\frac{z - y}{z} \right)^{\alpha - 1} [-n] f_2 dy$$

where f_i is the frequency density of income in group i, x represents net consumption of different consumers, and n the net supply of different producers. The two components of the expression reflect the conflicting forces in play. If α = 1, then:

$$\frac{dP_1}{dq} = \frac{1}{z} \left[\lambda_1 H_1 \bar{x}^P - \lambda_2 H_2 \bar{n}^P \right]$$

where H_i is the incidence of poverty in group i and $\bar{x}^P$ and $\bar{n}^P$ are mean net consumption of the poor and mean net supply of the poor. *Ceteris paribus*, the greater the incidence of poverty among net producers the more likely it is that poverty will increase when food is made cheaper.

The expressions derived above and in Kanbur (1985, 1986a) provide a way of quantifying the essential conflict between food producers and food consumers in a market-based system of entitlements. The disaggregation can be as detailed as the data allow, and other effects can be modelled as well. It provides a method whereby income distribution data disaggregated by producer and consumer type can be used to follow through the impact of global balances on individual poverty, via the interventions of policy at the national level.

Binswanger and Quizon (1984) have built and simulated a general equilibrium model of the effects increasing food supplies in the Indian context. The results are summarized in World Bank (1985):

An increase of wheat imports equal to 10 percent of the existing supply led to price declines in domestic foods: wheat went down 15 percent; rice 6 percent; and coarse grains 5 percent. There was also a 5 percent drop in wheat production and a slight increase in rice and coarse grains production. As a result, for the lowest quartile in the urban population, real income and cereal consumption rose about 5 percent. For the lowest quartile of the rural population, the net effect on the real income and cereal consumption was also positive, though much less so. Significantly, the lower food prices more than compensated the poorest rural group for the drop in employment and wages. The second quartile in the rural population neither gained nor lost.

Although the Binswanger–Quizon (1984) exercise does not start from a change in global wheat balances, it should be clear that their analysis would be equally applicable in this case. In fact, one scenario which might allow an increase in wheat imports with a given government budget constraint is precisely a fall in world wheat prices as the results of a change in global balances. In any event, their argument illustrates the difference between the Asian context and the African one, because of the presence in the former of the large landless class in the rural area. These benefit directly from lower wheat prices, but suffer indirectly as the result of reduction of employment and wages in the wheat production sector. In an African context, with predominantly smallholder agriculture and a small landless rural class, the conclusions would be different. The Latin American case, with higher degrees of urbanization and substantial landless labour, would approximate the Asian case better.

We have so far concentrated on the effects of food prices on poverty. How is the analysis altered if our interest is in food deprivation rather than general poverty? In this case there seems to be a basic soundness to the view that lower food prices are good. Net buyers of food benefit in terms of their overall welfare and, if food is not a Giffen good, their consumption of food will increase. Even with net sellers, although a fall in the price of food reduces their overall welfare since they can now buy less in exchange than they previously could, so long as food is a single commodity and is not a Giffen good they too will increase their consumption of food. If the focus is on food intake then clearly an improvement in global food balances which lowers the price of food is a good thing.

However, there are several ways in which this conventional wisdom may need to be modified. In the first instance many of the net buyers of food may depend on net sellers for employment. At the theoretical level, Drèze and Stern (1987) have argued that in a wide class of models the impact of a change in the price of a commodity on social welfare can be represented as the difference between the 'distributional characteristic' of the commodity, which captures how society views the effects on different individuals, and the 'index of ficti- tious discouragement', which essentially captures the general equilibrium feedback effects. In fact, in our earlier discussion we derived the distributional characteristic of food for the particular, poverty-orientated, social welfare function we were using. As already seen, Binswanger and Quizon (1984) show that general equilibrium feedbacks are unlikely to overturn the first round effects. While the simulation analysis of Binswanger and Quizon, and the theoretical argument of Drèze and Stern, relate to welfare in general, it is clear that similar conclusions would follow for food deprivation in particular.

Intertemporal considerations may force further modifications to the con- ventional wisdom on low food prices and hunger. Recall that our objective is to trace through the implications of a change in global food balances which lowers the price of food to a country which has no market power and takes this price as given. But if there are year-to-year fluctuations in the output of individual peasants in this country a low price of food in a normal year will lower income and hence the ability to save enough to withstand a possible downturn in production next year. Even from the point of view of food deprivation, therefore, there appears to be a conflict between encouraging food consump- tion among poor net buyers through lower prices and increasing the income of net sellers sufficiently to allow them to build a cushion against food deprivation in drought years. The line of argument here is the same as the case where the commodity sold by net sellers is not the sole source of nutrition for them. Then a fall in the price of the food commodity they sell will reduce their income, which will feed through to lower consumption of other foods and hence lower nutritional intake on this account. Improved global food balances for particu- lar commodities need not, therefore, improve the nutritional intake of all individuals.

There is another argument which we need to take into account. This is that high food prices are good because they encourage more food production and hence lower food prices in the future. It is clear that the argument relies on a general equilibrium feedback at the global level—it cannot apply to a price taking small open economy. Even at the global level, the argument must rely on high prices today enabling various production, technology, and credit constraints to be overcome. But why will these constraints not reappear once the current expansion leads to lower prices in the future? We seem to have the making of a cycle here, and even if it is accurate as a description of global food balances, it seems unlikely that we can base the normative case in favour of high food prices on these arguments (which in any case depend on high food prices leading to low food prices!).

To conclude, then, an 'improvement' in global food balances may well be a mixed blessing. At the national level, food exporters would lose out, and to the extent that the poor live in such regions and countries, their position is made more vulnerable. If the price effects of global changes are allowed to feed through to the economy, then again it is not clear that a food price decline is necessarily a good thing for all. Some are bound to lose, and at the very least policy makers should be aware of this fact and be able to quantify the extent of loss. The next step might be to target expenditures towards losers so as to compensate them for these losses. In fact, the price of food is one instrument for targeting the poor. While within the consuming group it is a good instrument because of Engel's Law (see Besley and Kanbur 1986), like all prices it has the property that it has opposite effects on producers and consumers. It follows that its efficacy will depend on the characteristics of these groups, and that its use as a targeting instrument should be conditioned by this information.

3.6. *Conclusions and further research*

The suggestions for further research follow directly from the main conclusions of this chapter:

1. Major data discrepancies still exist between USDA and FAO publications. In the absence of a programme of reconciliation, which would in itself be a major task, one area of further research is appropriate sensitivity analysis on the effects of using the two data sources for global projections. However, the data problems do give support to those who would suggest a redirection of interest away from aggregate food supply accounting towards more micro-economic variables such as the local price and the local wage in terms of food.

2. The much maligned nutrition-based measures of poverty still have their uses. In particular, it is not clear what better alternatives exist, and in so far as all criteria are eventually translated into income and expenditure requirements so that the extent of food poverty can be read off from the income distribution, there exists an identification problem—different methods can give the same cut-off in income or expenditure space. In such a situation the appropriate

procedure is to do sensitivity analysis using different cut-offs—it is a little premature to jettison the nutrition-based analyses altogether.

3. The entitlements approach to food deprivation draws our attention to how much food an individual has entitlement to, from market or non-market sources. In the specification of market-based food entitlements, one should look not only at the price of food being purchased, but at the price of commodities the individual has to sell. The entitlements approach can be fruitfully extended to the context of nation states in a global setting. An immediate, and obvious, implication is the importance of non-market-based entitlements to food in preventing transitory food deprivation, and the availability of food aid is crucial for at least some countries even over the secular time horizon. A less obvious implication of the entitlements approach is that in constructing early warning systems of approaching food problems, it is important to focus on the prices of non-food exports of a country. A sharp decline in the value of these can bring on food deprivation without any essential change in global *food* balances. The elaboration and implementation of this argument is an important area for further research.

4. At least for some countries, a significant portion of nutrition supply is accounted for by non-traded food crops, i.e. crops whose domestic prices are not affected directly by global food balances. However, there can be significant *indirect* effects if (as is usually the case) various traded and non-traded food crops are substitutes in production and/or in consumption. Then the prices of basic staples, like root crops in Africa, can be influenced by global changes in the price of traded food crops. Further research could usefully focus on the quantification of these links.

5. A fall in the price of food is a mixed blessing. In a system of market-based entitlements, when the price of a commodity falls, net buyers gain and net sellers lose. The overall outcome in terms of aggregate poverty depends on how poverty is distributed between net food sellers and net food buyers. This is an empirical question, and demands further research. While recently suggested decomposable measures of poverty can help by providing a convenient framework of analysis, there is no substitute for a detailed investigation of the distribution of income disaggregated by producers and consumers of different types of food. Only then will we be able to forge a direct and quantifiable link between global food balances and hunger.

References

AHLUWALIA, M. S. (1978), 'Rural Poverty and Agricultural Performance in India', *Journal of Development Studies*, 14/3.

ALTIMIR, O. (1982), 'The Extent of Poverty in Latin America', World Bank Staff Working Paper No. 522 (Washington, DC: World Bank).

ATKINSON, A. B. (1985), 'On the Measurement of Poverty', mimeo.

BARNEY, G. O. (1982), *The Global 2000 Report to the President* (New York: Penguin Books).

BESLEY, T., and KANBUR, S. M. R. (1986), 'Food Subsidies and Poverty Alleviation', mimeo.

BINSWANGER, H., and QUIZON, J. (1984), 'Distributional Consequences of Alternative Food Policies in India', Report No. 20 (Agricultural Research Unit, Agriculture and Rural Development Department, World Bank).

BRAVERMAN, A., and HAMMER, J. S. (1984), 'Multi-market Analysis of Agricultural Pricing Policies in Senegal', in Singh, I., Squire, L., and Strauss, J. (eds.), *Agricultural Household Models: Extensions, Applications and Policy* (World Bank/ Johns Hopkins).

——and KANBUR, S. M. R. (1985), 'Agricultural Price Reform, Devaluation and the Shadow Cost of Labour in the Presence of Urban Bias', unpublished (Washington, DC: World Bank).

DANDEKAR, V. M., and RATH, N. (1971), *Poverty in India* (Bombay: Sameeksha Trusts).

DREZE, J., and STERN, N. H. (1987), 'The Theory of Cost Benefit Analysis', in Auerbach, A., and Feldstein, M. (eds.), *Handbook of Public Economics* (Amsterdam: North-Holland).

FAO (1973), *Energy and Protein Requirements*, Report of a Joint FAO/WHO *ad hoc* Expert Committee (Rome: FAO).

——(1977), *Fourth World Food Survey* (Rome: FAO).

——(1981), *Agriculture: Toward 2000* (Rome: FAO).

——(1983a), 'Assessing Food Aid Requirements: A Revised Approach', Economic and Social Development Paper No. 39.

——(1983b), 'Approaches to World Food Security', Economic and Social Development Paper No. 39.

——(1984), *Food Balance Sheets: 1979–81 Average* (Rome: FAO).

——(1985a), *Production Yearbook, 1984* (Rome: FAO).

——(1985b), *Trade Yearbook, 1984* (Rome: FAO).

FOSTER, J., GREER, J., and THORBECKE, E. (1984), 'A Class of Decomposable Poverty Measures', *Econometrica*, 52.

——and SHORROCKS, A. F. (1985), 'Poverty Orderings', mimeo (University of Essex).

IFPRI (1983), *Closing the Cereals Gap with Trade and Food Aid*, by B. Huddleston (Washington, DC: IFPRI).

JOHNSON, D. G. (1983), 'The World Food Situation: Recent and Prospective Developments', in Johnson and Schuh (1983).

——and SCHUH, G. E. (eds.) (1983), *The Role of Markets in the World Food Economy* (Boulder, Colo.: Westview Press).

KAKWANI, N. C. (1986), 'On Measuring Undernutrition', Working Paper No. 8 (Helsinki: WIDER).

——and PODDER, N. (1976), 'Efficient Estimation of the Lorenz Curve and Associated Inequality Measures from Grouped Observations', *Econometrica*, 44.

KANBUR, S. M. R. (1984), 'How to Analyze Commodity Price Stabilization?', *Oxford Economic Papers*, 36.

——(1985), 'Budgetary Rules for Poverty Alleviation', Discussion Paper No. 257 (University of Essex).

——(1986a), 'Poverty: Measurement, Alleviation and the Impact of Macroeconomic Adjustment', Departmental Memorandum, Fiscal Affairs Department, International Monetary Fund.

——(1986b), 'The Economic Analysis of International Commodity Price Stabilization', paper prepared for the Food and Agriculture Organization of the United Nations.

MELLOR, J. M., and JOHNSTON, B. F. (1984), 'The World Food Equation: Interrelations Among Development, Employment, and Food Consumption', *Journal of Economic Literature*, 22, June.

NEWBERY, D. M. G., and STIGLITZ, J. E. (1981), *The Theory of Commodity Price Stabilization: A Study in the Economics of Risk* (Oxford: Oxford University Press).

PAULINO, L. A., and TSENG, S. S. (1980), 'A Comparative Study of FAO and USDA Data on Production, Area and Trade of Major Food Staples', Research Report No. 19 (IFPRI).

POLEMAN, T. T. (1983), 'World Hunger: Extent, Causes, and Cures', in Johnson and Schuh (1983).

REUTLINGER, S. (1985), 'Food Security and Poverty in LDCs', *Finance and Development*.

——and SELOWSKY, M. (1976), *Malnutrition and Poverty: Magnitude and Policy Options*, World Bank Staff Occasional Papers, No. 23.

SCOBIE, G. M. (1983), 'Food Subsidies in Egypt: Their Impact on Foreign Exchange and Trade', Research Report No. 40 (IFPRI).

SEN, A. K. (1976), 'Poverty: An Ordinal Approach to Measurement', *Econometrica*, 44.

——(1981), *Poverty and Famines: An Essay on Entitlement and Deprivation* (Oxford: Oxford University Press).

SRINIVASAN, T. N. (1981), 'Malnutrition: Some Measurement and Policy Issues', *Journal of Development Economics*, 8.

——(1983), 'Hunger: Defining it, Estimating its Global Incidence, and Alleviating it', in Johnson and Schuh (1983).

——and BARDHAN, P. K. (1974), *Poverty and Income Distribution in India* (Calcutta: Statistical Publishing Society).

USDA (1982, 1983), *World Food Aid Needs and Availabilities* (Washington, DC: USDA, Economic Research Service).

——(1985), *Agricultural Statistics 1984*.

WFC/FAO (1983), 'World Food Security: The Need for Balance of Payments Support to Meet Exceptional Variations in Food Import Bills', document prepared in Dec. 1979 for submission to the IMF, repr. in FAO (1983b).

WFP (1979), 'Food Aid Requirements and Food Aid Targets in the Eighties', (UN/FAO Committee on Food Aid Policies and Programmes).

World Bank (1985), 'Ensuring Food Security in the Developing World: Issues and Options' (Washington, DC: Agriculture and Rural Development Department, World Bank).

4

The Politics of Hunger and Entitlement

Rehman Sobhan

4.1. *Introduction*

It is widely recognized today that hunger originates in 'entitlement failures'. Access to food is not only a function of food supply, but is influenced by a variety of factors that affect the capacity of particular households and social groups to establish entitlement over food.[1] Access to food—and other commodities—in a market economy depends both on 'direct entitlements' based on production (e.g. the access of peasants to the food that they produce) and on 'trade entitlements' derived from the capacity of households to exchange what they have to sell (e.g. labour power or farm products) for goods and services in the market. The factors influencing these entitlements and the related features of the market have been extensively studied in recent years.

However, entitlements are influenced not only by production and market transactions, but also by the political power of households. Indeed, the state itself is a source of much entitlement creation, e.g. through aid, loans, subsidies, and, more generally, the public distribution of commodities and incomes. The ability of a household or a social group to benefit from these entitlements depends on the political power of the household in question and also of the group of households to which it belongs. Even the opportunity of using transaction possibilities in the market (and the vulnerabilities that are generated by exclusive reliance on that one political economic institution) must be seen in the broader setting of legal and political institutions. Markets function within a legal system of rights, contracts, and guarantees enforced by the power of the state. The nature and reach of state power are—directly or indirectly—crucial to every aspect of entitlement analysis.

In turn, the capacity of the state to influence entitlements, and the direction that this influence takes, must be seen as depending on external as well as internal political influences. The state's external alignments, the political preferences of donor countries, and the global political climate can all have quite a profound impact on the exercise of state power in a developing country. No country can be treated in isolation from the rest of the world, and it would

I would like to acknowledge gratefully the powerful and extensive comments made by Susan George on my paper. I have greatly benefited from her suggestions, and if I have not done full justice to her comments, it is because that exercise would tempt me to develop the paper into a book. I also acknowledge my debt to the comments made by Amartya Sen and others who took part in the discussion following my paper.

[1] On this see Sen (1981).

be particularly hopeless to try to understand the process of entitlement determination in a developing country without taking note of the external influences that operate on it.

4.2. *The framework*

Such a perspective on the determinants of poverty and hunger is hardly original. It is more a question of providing adequate emphasis on this aspect of the problem. This chapter sets itself the limited task of highlighting crucial aspects of the causal relationship between politics and entitlements. This is done by schematically presenting the determinants of entitlements of particular households within a society and then focusing on the political forces that can operate on them at the national and global levels. A schematic presentation of this kind enables us to differentiate the contributions of political forces embodied in legal systems, market regimes, social institutions, and specific policy interventions of the state—all influencing the determination of entitlements of different groups.

Presented schematically, the following determinants of household entitlements may be identified: (1) direct entitlements (dependent on production conditions and capacities); (2) trade-related entitlements (reflecting terms of trade); and (3) contributions of the state to household entitlements (through the provision of employment, commodities, and incomes to particular households).

This schematic presentation provides the analytical framework for the study of the influence of politics on household entitlements. Such an exercise may be a prelude to country studies, which can more fully explore the causal connections. This chapter itself is more elementary and conceptual, drawing on a limited range of evidence to illustrate the argument. This evidence draws quite a bit on the experience of Bangladesh with which this writer is more familiar, even though information regarding other countries has been drawn upon to the extent that this has been readily available and clearly relevant.

It should be obvious that a detailing of the political influences operating on all three aspects of the determination of entitlements would be a major research endeavour.[2] In this chapter attention has been focused particularly on the political influences on the state's *direct* contribution to entitlements, i.e. on the last of the three determinants identified above. This is done to keep the chapter within manageable proportions, rather than on the basis of any belief that this is the only aspect that deserves systematic probing. There are a great many

---

[2] It should be remembered that each aspect has its historical antecedents which also need investigation. For example, the entitlements of share-croppers or peasants in Bangladesh would reflect *inter alia* the influence of land legislation over several generations, and these in turn can be interpreted and explained only by examining the contemporary political factors that operated on those respective legislations.

other issues that would need exploration and scrutiny.[3] For example, the political economy of international markets is itself an area of profound consequence, deserving serious investigation.[4] The focus of this chapter is largely guided by feasibility, and should thus be seen as one part of a wider class of studies on the politics of entitlements.

4.3. The state as a direct source of entitlements

The state directly contributes to entitlement bundles of households in a variety of ways. Drawing by way of illustration from the experience of Bangladesh, the state operates a Public Food Distribution System (PFDS). Under this system the state commits itself to delivering food at fixed prices to a variety of social/institutional categories of the population. This includes urban residents of the principal cities of the country, all public employees both civil and military, all employees of large-scale enterprises, all public school teachers, and certain defined categories of the rural poor.[5] Since the food is sold to these groups, the income transfer can be measured by the extent to which the state fails to cover the costs of its distribution programme from such sales of food. Since a part of this food usually comes in as a grant in aid from foreign donors, we have to distinguish between the actual subsidy as reflected as a charge on the exchequer and the notional subsidy derived from attributing a value to donated food.

Outside of the PFDS the state may distribute food to the rural poor in exchange for work. It may also directly distribute food as relief. This may be done on a regular basis as with the Vulnerable Group Feeding Programme (VGFP) which channels food donated under specific programmes to some destitute women and children. It may be done on a larger scale in times of emergency. Thus during the Bangladesh famine of 1974, 5,860 gruel kitchens were opened to feed famine victims on a bare subsistence diet.[6] Similar examples of relief camps to feed famine victims have been in evidence in the Ethiopian and Sahel famines of the 1970s and more recently in Kampuchea after 1979.

In Bangladesh the state has emerged as a major source of employment under a variety of rural public works programmes.[7] These may involve the direct distribution of food in exchange for work, or the payment of cash wages. Some

[3] On this see George (1976).

[4] There are also a variety of influences relevant to the operation of the markets and related production structures. For example, the entitlements of jute growers in Bangladesh are influenced by political decisions of importing countries (e.g. whether to allow free imports, whether to replace jute by other products), state decisions in developing countries (e.g. affecting acreage, production conditions, and processing of jute), and international compacts (e.g. the decisions of the Third World jute exporters to regulate supply and price of raw jute and jute goods).

[5] Abdullah and Murshid (1986).   [6] Khondker (1984).

[7] FAO (1983).

may be financed from sale of food aid, as was the case with the US PL-480 food aid programme to East Pakistan (now Bangladesh) in the 1960s. Others may simply be financial grants to the government, where cash foreign exchange is made available on a reimbursible basis for expenditure on particular public works programmes.

These contributions by the state to the entitlement bundle of each household involve major allocative policy decisions and thus reflect the interplay of political forces within the polity. To the extent that a significant part of the food distributed directly by the state originates from abroad in the form of imports and aid, the politics of global food distribution also emerge as an important determinant of entitlements in Bangladesh and other countries.

It is argued in this section that the mechanisms for distributing food, the identification of beneficiaries, the pricing policy adopted, and the means of financing government programmes emerge out of a complex interplay of political forces. This political dimension to the problem tends to be underplayed in discussions relating to public food policy and its impact on entitlements.

4.4. *The Public Food Distribution System*

The notion that the state should participate at all in the distribution of food reflects a political decision of some importance. In societies dominated by private landowners and traders, the public distribution of food was itself a challenge to the social power of these entrenched groups. The willingness of the state to intervene in the market thus reflected an emerging sensitivity to the interests of food consumers. The decision to intervene, as for instance in the repeal of the Corn Laws in Britain in the nineteenth century, represented the ascendancy of the emergent capitalist class who saw cheap corn as a mechanism to keep down real wages. The repeal of the laws was thus a result of a change in the balance of power in England from the landowning gentry to the new bourgeoisie.

The search for cheap food has over the years and across countries established an *entente* between the various classes of the urban population where both capitalist and worker, for their diverse reasons, have come together. In more recent times, however, a new recruit to this urban-based *entente* has been the rural landless or land-poor classes. The fact that 50 per cent of the rural population of Bangladesh are without cultivable land, while another 25 per cent have land insufficient to ensure subsistence, means that a sizeable proportion of the rural population of Bangladesh are net buyers of foodgrains. The constituency for cheap food is thus nation-wide in many developing countries. The emergence of the state in the arena of food distribution is a direct acknowledgement of the power of this constituency.

Since most if not all national governments are located in urban metropolitan centres, the feeding of the cities is seen as an essential part of the survival of the regime and indeed of its viability. Urban bias is thus built into the perspectives of virtually every government whatever be the character of their respective socio-economic systems. In very few societies, socialist or capitalist, does the allocative regime of a state reflect the democratic urge of the rural majority.

The decision by the state to intervene in the food market has, however, not always been commensurate with its organizational capacity to do so. The state needs a mechanism to identify intended beneficiaries, procure grain from home or abroad, stock it, and deliver it when and where needed. Surprisingly, very few developing countries have fully developed this capacity. The PFDS in South Asia is something of an exception. The distributional shambles which characterized famine relief in Kampuchea, the Sahel countries, and Ethiopia reflected the lack of any public machinery to distribute large quantities of grain.[8] This may well have reflected the fact that serious food shortages in these countries were a contemporary phenomenon, and that traditionally market-based channels of distribution sufficed to deliver food to consumers. In contrast, the development of an elaborate and moderately efficient PFDS in South Asia is a measure of its historical experience with famines and the need to feed a growing urban population at stable prices.

In the countries of South Asia this PFDS has ensured that, if adequate supplies were available to the PFDS, it had the capacity to counter the threat of serious entitlement failures. This is not to say that the PFDS was able or indeed tailored to eradicating hunger for all citizens. What it could do was to deliver food to a large number of people at fixed prices, provided that resources and food were available to feed its distributional mechanisms.

The one significant failure of the PFDS in South Asia occurred in Bangladesh in 1974. It has been argued elsewhere that this was a failure of supply into the PFDS arising out of a political decision by the US government to suspend food aid to Bangladesh.[9]

4.5.   The politics of public food distribution

The structure of the PFDS reflects the political compulsions of the government of the day. Most governments, being city-centric, recognize that their primary obligation is to feed the employees of the public sector and their dependants. The real incomes of public officials remain under constant pressure due to the inflexibility of public compensation. As they do not have the advantage of the indexing of wages practised in some Latin American countries, public officials in South Asia (along with other fixed-income groups) easily become victims of

---

[8] Shawcross (1984).

[9] Sobhan (1979, 1984). On public intervention during the 1974 famine in Bangladesh, see also Siddiq Osmani, 'The Food Problems of Bangladesh', in the third volume of this book.

inflation. The complex structure of public compensation, and the enormous budgetary constraints in increasing this compensation, have meant that upward adjustment of wages becomes an attenuated process. This exposes public servants to considerable erosion in real incomes during the interim period. This affects both morale and integrity. Extra-legal compensation becomes for many public servants a part of their survival strategy. In these circumstances, the tendency to mitigate the effects of inflation on public compensation through guaranteeing a fixed quota of basic wage goods at stable prices is standard practice in many developing countries.

It is rare that these gestures to stabilize prices and thereby contain declines in real wages are adequate to their task. Bangladesh, for example, has witnessed protracted agitation from all categories of public servants to increase their nominal wages to keep up with price rises.

The compulsion to restore and maintain a shattered administration, and to ensure the survival of the regime, appeared also to have been an essential element of the PFDS in Kampuchea after the overthrow of the Khmer Rouge regime by the Vietnamese military intervention. In his study of disaster relief in Kampuchea, Shawcross argues that a significant part of the relief aid channelled into Kampuchea went to feed the army and civil servants rather than those in more dire need.[10] The evidence in support of this remains less than definitive. However, what fragmentary evidence has been put together on the period of Khmer Rouge rule suggests that the traditional production and distribution system for food was destroyed and replaced with a variant of a command economy which disrupted all links between production and consumption.[11] The market as a mechanism of distribution ceased to exist. What was produced, and where, was determined as a politico-administrative decision. Who consumed how much was a political decision. Reports of large-scale deaths, part of which may have been attributed to an insufficiency of food rather than of work, indicated that effort was not necessarily related to reward. The breakdown of Khmer Rouge authority after the Vietnamese entry into Kampuchea created not just a politico-administrative vacuum but a structural hiatus where both production and distribution mechanisms had to be recreated. The new regime thus obviously needed time and resources to set in place an institutional mechanism which could establish political authority and economic recovery. If such an interpretation of post-Khmer Rouge Kampuchea is accepted, it is hardly surprising that the new regime placed regime building as its principal priority and sought food aid as the means to buy time to accomplish this task.

Regime survival is the first priority of any government, which usually gets precedence over that of satisfying the basic needs of all its citizens. The post-Khmer Rouge regime would not be the first regime so to order its priorities. The enforced procurement of foodgrains during the phase of War

[10] Shawcross (1984).   [11] Kiernan and Boua (1982).

Communism was seen by the Bolshevik leadership as indispensable to the survival of the revolution.[12] The British government viewed the containment of the Japanese armed forces in 1943, after the fall of Burma, as essential to the survival of British rule in India, and its food policy was in tune with this perspective. History could produce many more examples of the use of food as an integral part of the process of political survival.

Most Third World regimes calculate that the primary threat to their regime will come from a restive urban population. Of these, public servants, organized industrial workers, students, and the armed forces are likely to be the most organized and hence politically the most dangerous. These groups are usually singled out for benefits from the public distribution system. The weightage of benefits between contending groups naturally depends on the balance of power and threat perception of the regime in question. It is not surprising that where PFDS are in use the armed services remain the most privileged beneficiaries of the system so that their real compensation is, relatively speaking, subject to the least erosion. Public officials come second in the priority list. Here again in particular countries some categories may be more privileged than others.

Beyond these two well-defined categories, the identity of the targeted beneficiaries of a PFDS becomes a useful barometer of the political balance of power. In Bangladesh the PFDS, aside from public employees, covers employees of large industrial establishments. This usually means enterprises with trade unions who are capable of organizing strikes and participating in political movements against the regime. The next category has been the student population. This group has in Bangladesh (and indeed in many developing countries) been the vanguard of most political movements, and has contributed to the downfall of not a few regimes.

More recently, the primary school teachers of Bangladesh have demonstrated an impressive capacity for organized action. Since they maintain a nation-wide presence in the rural areas, a restive community of teachers located in the villages of Bangladesh is seen as a potent political threat to the stability of the realm. By way of concession, the teachers have been included in the PFDS.

The outer limits of these political constituencies of the PFDS extend to the populations of the main metropolitan centres. It is recognized that apart from organized groups the very congruity of an urban population constitutes its own political hazard. Opposition leaders can appeal to a larger constituency than just students and industrial workers. The unorganized informal sector, employees of private establishments, rickshaw pullers, and other social categories add up to a sizeable segment of the urban population. It is this amorphous mass which, if mobilized, can bring down most regimes, and needs to be propitiated. Here again the PFDS has been seen as the most convenient instrument for this purpose.

[12] Carr (1966).

The loosely defined nature of such populations obviously exposes the more indiscriminate PFDS to much abuse. Supplies are appropriated by various intermediaries, usually with the participation or connivance of public officials and people of political influence. The very prospect of becoming a dealer under the PFDS is a by-product of patronage which recognizes the prospect of extra-legal income. Many legitimate claimants on the PFDS are excluded.[13] The floating and unsettled population of most fast-growing Third World metropolitan centres precludes a clear identification of their inhabitants. Thus phantom ration card holders coexist with large numbers of the rural poor failing to get access to the PFDS. This means that the objectives of the PFDS often remain unrealized. The assured beneficiaries of the PFDS thus remain the targeted social groups covered by the statutory rationing system.[14]

4.6. Hunger and revolution

Direct pressures from the rural poor to seek redress of their deprived condition have had a limited impact in most developing countries. There is no evidence that famines tend to precipitate an uprising of the rural poor to overthrow the regime, let alone the social order which contributes to their condition. Hunger marches of the rural poor have rarely surfaced as a national phenomenon even in such politically conscious areas as Bengal in 1943, or Bangladesh in 1974. Cases of such marches or looting of food stores by famine victims have been episodic, local phenomena, largely reflecting the labours of some localized political activists. There have been no records in contemporary history of social revolution being triggered off by mass hunger, though it has been argued that at the time of the Russian Revolution the gradual breakdown in the authority of the Provisional Government under Kerensky between March and October 1917 owed something to the withholding of grain supplies from country to town, and the social tensions caused by the resultant failure of entitlements in the towns.[15] The successful peasant revolutions in China and Vietnam may have been sustained by the deprivation and anger of the peasantry. But the circumstances proximate to their victory, as was the case with the Russian Revolution, had more complex causes, not least of which was the impact of World War.[16]

However, while sudden failures of entitlement may not precipitate uprisings, the loss of credibility in a regime which permits this to happen has longer-term political implications. The military coup which toppled the long-established Ethiopian monarchy in 1974 originated in the loss of author-

---

[13] Abdullah and Murshid (1986); Chowdhury (1986).

[14] In this paper the term 'statutory rationing system' will be used to refer to the permanent and quasi-legal entitlements of specific groups (such as public servants and the army) to public distribution.

[15] Gill (1979).   [16] Carr (1966), Skocpol (1979).

ity from the famine the year before.[17] And the coup makers in Bangladesh in 1975 took courage from the erosion in popularity experienced by the regime in Bangladesh as a consequence of the 1974 famine.[18] The rural poor generally tend to remain dispersed, unorganized, and hence voiceless in most Third World countries. However, in societies where some form of social revolution has taken place, as in some of the socialist countries, the compulsion to be responsive to the basic needs of the entire population is more apparent. Most such regimes have committed themselves to providing a minimum calorific intake to the entire community through a system of guaranteed work and/or income and food at stable prices. In many socialist countries, the price of basic staples for the whole population has been kept stable virtually since the revolution. This applies, for instance, to China, where it is estimated that food subsidies cost the country the equivalent of $US16.6 billion a year, which is 42 per cent of the national revenue budget.[19]

The policy of guaranteeing food to the rural population is in these circumstances integral to the social origins and ideology of the regime, and the institutional apparatus and allocative decisions reflect this. This is not to say that such regimes have not discriminated against their rural populations (*vis-à-vis* the urgan-industrial sector) in the allocation of resources, and have not used the rural areas as a source of accumulation for the national economy.[20] However, this has been sustained by guaranteeing basic needs and ensuring that within each community such sacrifices are more equitably shared than is the case in non-socialist societies. Failures of entitlement have thus been community rather than household-specific failures.

4.7. *Democracy and entitlements*

In contrast to the few countries which have experienced a social revolution and a change in the balance of power within the society, most Third World regimes remain urban biased.[21] Few of these regimes have any representative status. Many of them have assumed power through military coups d'état. Some may have overthrown feudal and comprador regimes. But many have come to power through the overthrow of elected governments. Most such military regimes have remained committed to the building of capitalism under state patronage, and to creating a more congenial base for the operation of multinational corporations (MNCs) in their national economies. Civilian regimes made up of military regimes which have shed their uniform, or with a strong military backing, remain generally unrepresentative. Such regimes tend either to avoid elections or to predetermine the outcome of such elections.

---

[17] Shawcross (1984).   [18] Lifschultz (1979).

[19] See the special issue of *Far Eastern Economic Review* (Mar. 1986), on China, especially the section on 'Agriculture'.   [20] Lewin (1968).   [21] Lipton (1977).

Now it may be argued that regimes which have to go to the countryside to seek votes are likely to be more responsive to meeting the consumption needs of their constituents. This argument has been advanced as the reason why India has faced no famines since 1947.[22] It would account for such programmes as the Maharashtra Employment Guarantee Scheme. Sri Lanka has guaranteed a minimum food intake under the PFDS to its entire population. After a regime change in 1977, this programme has been modified to a system of food stamps directed to those in more dire need.[23] However, even this modification ensured coverage to a majority of the population. Thus all political parties in Sri Lanka have remained sensitive to the concerns of the voters.

A counterpart of the significance that is often attached to the representative character of an elected government is the notion that those regimes which do not seek votes need not care about their constituents' basic needs. These views, however, would seem to represent an oversimplification. Indeed, in societies with regular elections it may well be that the rural élite emerges as the 'vote bank' which needs to be propitiated. We thus have the prospect of alliances between the urban élites and the surplus farmers who monopolize public resources to the exclusion of the rural poor and indeed use public resources to reinforce their control over the poor.

In contrast, non-representative regimes without the need to propitiate rural hierarchies may be more sensitive to the needs of the poor. This was indeed proffered as the underlying political premise of the Filipino agrarian reform carried through by Marcos after declaring Martial Law in 1972.[24] It was argued that an elected parliament controlled by landlords could never enact a meaningful land reform and that it was only when electoral considerations were eliminated that a reform bill catering to the interests of the tenant farmer could be enacted. This argument has surfaced time and again as the rationale for military coups. It has, however, remained unproven that the agrarian reforms have either realized a significant redistribution in landownership or eroded the power of the erstwhile landowning class, whether in the Philippines under Marcos, or in Pakistan after 1960 (when the Martial Law regime initiated a land reform).[25]

Apart from the limited capacity of unrepresentative regimes to carry through agrarian transformation, not all such regimes have been insensitive to the need to keep a rural population content. This compulsion may derive from the need to discredit all representative institutions as urban-centred and thus oblivious of the needs of the rural areas. This has been a much favoured

---

[22] Sen (1981). See also Jean Drèze, 'Famine Prevention in India', in the second volume of this book.

[23] World Bank (1986a). On Sri Lanka's experience of public intervention and social achievements before and after 1977, see Sudhir Anand and Ravi Kanbur, 'Public Policy and Basic Needs Provision: Intervention and Achievement in Sri Lanka', in the third volume of this book.

[24] Wurfel (1983).   [25] Bokhari (1986).

argument by military regimes in Pakistan and Bangladesh, which invoke the concerns of a hypothetical peasantry in contrast to an order dominated by urban-centred lawyer-politicians.[26] Rhetoric about decentralization, local government, and rural development tends to be much in vogue in such regimes.[27] Again, there is no clear evidence that allocations to agriculture increase under such regimes, or that the rural poor prosper, or that genuine political devolution ensues. Instead we may find the same rural élite which sustained the old order now active in the service of the new order and becoming the creatures and instruments of the patronage disbursed by the central government.

4.8.   The PFDS in rural areas

Whether due to ideology or opportunism, most contemporary political leaderships have recognized the need to raise the entitlements of the rural poor. To this end the PFDS where it exists has been extended to the rural areas. In some cases (as in Sri Lanka, India, and Bangladesh), a sizeable off-take from the PFDS now gets through to the rural areas and within these to some of the rural poor. In Bangladesh, for example, there are three heads under which the rural poor have regular access to the PFDS. These are (1) the system of Modified Rationing, which delivers a bimonthly quota to those listed in the village revenue records as the two lowest income categories, (2) the Vulnerable Group Feeding Scheme, which delivers food to poor women and children, and (3) the Food for Work programme, which provides food to the landless and land-poor who are without prospect of sufficient work, particularly in the slack season.

What is significant about these programmes is that they remain a function of the availability of food aid. To the extent that food aid is sufficient to meet the needs of statutory ration beneficiaries, and then to extend itself to the rural areas, the PFDS in Bangladesh can lay claim to a national constituency. But when resources become scarce and aid is not readily available, it is less clear how a prioritization under the PFDS would take place. In 1974, it was the rural component of the PFDS which became the first casualty of the deceleration in food imports and the reduction in public distribution.[28]

In recent times, when foodgrain supplies in the market have been sufficient, it has been possible to raise PFDS prices in Bangladesh in closer proximity to market prices. This has meant that the statutory rationing system has lost some of its importance in feeding even the urban population categories.[29] Thus the PFDS has been able to focus on the special urban target groups, and to expand the distribution under the Food for Work Programme, and the Vulnerable Group Feeding Programme. The significance of using food as a source of employment will be discussed subsequently. Here it is argued that the

[26] Khan (1967).   [27] Haider (1986).   [28] Sobhan (1979).
[29] Chowdhury (1986).

distributive orientation of the PFDS is to be seen as a function of both political priority and supplies. Where supplies are sufficient, it can cater to a variety of constituencies both urban and rural. Where supplies are constrained, it will respond to its most immediate political compulsions. The scope for distributing the shortfall in food supplies more equitably will depend again on the ability of the regime to contain potential dissent from those who have to surrender some claim to PFDS supplies. It is here that regimes with a strong popular base, and a political machinery to communicate with the public and persuade it of the importance of such reallocations, would have greater flexibility to cope with such emergencies. The regime in Bangladesh in 1974 did bring about a modest cut in the statutory ration.[30] But in mid-1974 its once massive popular appeal had been sufficiently eroded to make it hesitant to effect a significant redistribution of resources under the PFDS from the statutory ration areas to the famine areas.[31] As a result, the main constraint on feeding these areas became the pace with which food could be imported and distributed through the PFDS.

4.9. Distributive implications of the PFDS

Entitlements against the state must by their very nature be seen as a privilege. Outside of the socialist states there are few PFDS which actually guarantee entitlements to all those in need. Exceptions to this have been the Sri Lankan system of a guaranteed rice quota and the Maharashtra Employment Guarantee Scheme. Presumably if all governments, even unrepresentative ones, could afford it, they would guarantee sufficient entitlements to their populace to meet basic needs. Most governments in developed countries have assumed this responsibility since the Second World War.[32] Since the escalation in oil revenues after 1974 most oil-exporting countries, especially the capital surplus countries, have also assumed such a responsibility.[33]

For most other developing countries, resource constraints compel the regime in power to make political choices. Few regimes can afford to distribute free food to all their populace. An alternative is to require all the beneficiaries to pay for all or most of the cost of the PFDS. This is rarely feasible since the PFDS is designed to increase the entitlements of certain social groups who are either deprived or feel that their position in the polity merits higher entitlements than those on offer to them in the market-place. The distributive element in the PFDS thus means that a source other than the beneficiary must finance the system. This has important political implications. The PFDS thus has to be highly selective in its categorization of beneficiaries and/or discriminate through the terms of access to public distribution.

---

[30] Khondker (1984).   [31] Sobhan (1979).   [32] Sen (1981).

[33] FAO (1984).

Once such distributive choices have to be made, the trade-off between politics and need becomes much more sensitive to the character of the regime. Ideally under conditions of resource scarcity food should be delivered to those most in need. Unfortunately, needs being absolute, to introduce the concept of relativity into the policy concerns of a regime poses formidable political problems. Thus in the case of Bangladesh there is no doubt that a rural landless labourer is worse off than a clerk or janitor in a government office in Dhaka. The janitor would certainly have an income which puts him well below the poverty line.[34] But he in turn would have an income above that of the landless labourer. It could therefore be argued that the PFDS should deliver food only to the rural labourer at subsidized prices and either exclude the janitor from the system, or make him pay the opportunity cost for the food. Since such a gesture would in effect reduce the real income of a person already below the poverty line it is most likely that such a move would generate political resentment.

The steady rise in statutory ration prices in Bangladesh has in practice reduced the real incomes of all public employees except perhaps the members of the armed forces who have a separate statutory price regime. This as we have observed has meant periodic unrest and political action by all categories of public employees.

It has been observed elsewhere that attempts to raise food prices in societies where large sections of the population have for a long period benefited from stable prices, as in Egypt or Tunisia, have met with a severe political response in the streets. In both cases the government had to reverse its decision to increase food prices. In Egypt, stabilization of food prices has extended to a wide range of commodities which cover consumption of the rural and urban areas.[35] This has required massive and rising subsidies, with a high opportunity cost in terms of deficit financing and exchange rate depreciation. Rising import costs and foreign exchange constraints have a cost in terms of falling industrial output. There is thus a trade-off between subsidies, industrial employment, and general price stability. All this would appear to be a cogent case for reducing subsidies. Attempts to do so by raising prices unfortunately led to riots because both the rural and urban poor were affected. To reduce subsidies by restricting the beneficiaries to only the poor, or very poor, would, however, pose the same problem as in Bangladesh, that the less poor feel deprived and victims of declining real incomes.

In both Bangladesh and Egypt it may be argued that only the rich should be excluded from the PFDS subsidized benefits. Such was the objective of replacing the guaranteed rice ration in Sri Lanka with food stamps. But the Sri Lankan experience has shown that once a line is to be drawn it tends to be drawn so close to the top that few people are excluded. Such would be the case in Bangladesh or Egypt where virtually everyone, from university teachers to

---

[34] Sobhan (1979).   [35] World Bank (1986c).

army lieutenants, would make a persuasive case for being retained within the target group.

The problem of establishing relative degrees of deprivation becomes more difficult in societies where state policies consciously foster social and economic inequalities. Where such policies as in Bangladesh or Egypt have led to the emergence of an affluent élite, seen as creatures of state-sponsored policies and patronage, it becomes more difficult to persuade bank clerks in nationalized commercial banks, or stenographers in government offices, to accept redistributive measures in favour of those poorer than themselves.[36] It would appear that where the rich tend to be largely outside the tax net and indeed are massive beneficiaries of public subsidies and credits, any interference with the structure of benefits offered through the PFDS, or through input subsidies, becomes highly difficult. The capacity to go through with reduction in such benefits thus tends to be dictated less by the merits of the argument than by the mobilizational strength of the affected parties and their voice in the corridors of power.

4.10. *Financing the PFDS*

The distribution of the benefits of the PFDS is closely related to its mode of financing. If it becomes difficult to get the beneficiaries to pay then some other source of funding has to be found. This may come from within the society. The cost may be directly borne by taxes imposed on the rest of the community. To the extent that taxpayers consist mainly of the rich making payment through direct taxes, or of the general populace making payment through indirect taxes, a redistribution of income takes place. Politically, however, it becomes much more difficult to mobilize taxpayers to correlate the transfer of income from taxes imposed on them to benefits received by the beneficiaries of the PFDS, particularly where the beneficiaries may themselves be payers of indirect taxes. In spite of tax collection, meeting food subsidies usually also requires some deficit financing, or the reduction of other expenditures. The burden of deficit finance, to the extent that this generates inflationary pressure, may be borne by all segments of the population. However, as with taxes, it becomes difficult to establish who exactly pays for this. While people may be politically mobilized against high prices, the victims of price increases are less likely to include in their demands the goal of eliminating food subsidies, particularly where this is itself seen as a relief against inflation.

When other expenditures are forgone, their opportunity cost becomes a crucial issue. Arguments against food and input subsidies in Bangladesh are often advanced on grounds that a more efficient and equitable use could be made of such funds.[37] This again may or may not be true. However, opportunity cost arguments cannot limit themselves to trade-offs between food

[36] Sobhan (1985*b*).   [37] World Bank (1985).

subsidies and other alternative benefits to the poor. There are many less needful and efficient uses of public resources than a programme of food subsidies. It may be argued that defence expenditure, or a large diplomatic establishment, are low-priority expenditures for many developing countries. If one ran through a public development budget prioritizing all public expenditures it would be difficult to place food subsidies very low down on such a list.

A further option to help the financing of PFDS is to reduce procurement costs. To the extent that depressed food prices act as a disincentive to production, both the direct entitlements of food producers and the exchange entitlements of those who work in the agricultural sector may go down.[38]

Aside from this problem, the prospects of actually enforcing low procurement prices are often limited. In most developing countries, since the government is only a limited buyer, it is the market which is more likely to influence the price of grain.[39] Where in fact official procurement prices are well below the market price, as was the case in Bangladesh in 1973–5, the PFDS nets very little of the marketed surplus since food tends to be diverted to the open market where selling prices are much higher than under the PFDS. Unless food procurement can be made compulsory and enforceable it is a futile policy.

The only regimes which have run successful procurement policies at below the opportunity cost of grain have been socialist regimes. Apart from the greater control exercised by such regimes, the fact that production and distribution are monopolized by collectivist institutions was an essential element in the viability of the programme. But even socialist systems have accepted that an excessive transfer of resources out of agriculture through compulsory grain deliveries cannot be indefinitely sustained. Peasants will be persuaded to increase and surrender their grain surplus if the society reciprocates the contribution of the farm sector by channelling budgetary resources into the rural sector. In most developing countries, however, the urban bias of the pricing and distribution system is reinforced by the neglect of the rural sector in the allocation of public expenditure.

It is thus hardly surprising that successful procurement programmes have really been price support programmes benefiting the surplus farmers. The disincentive effect on production where it does arise, as is reported to be the case in Africa today, originates in large-scale grain imports, usually through aid, which keep the relative price of food low.[40] But this is an altogether different argument since it assumes that market prices are kept low through supply side pressures exercised by imports rather than food prices being kept low because of subsidies. Bangladesh invested massively in food subsidies, particularly in the early 1970s when food imports were also heavy, but neither subsidies nor imports could do much to keep foodgrain prices low.[41]

[38] World Bank (1986a).   [39] Streeten (1987).   [40] World Bank (1986b).
[41] Osmani and Qasem (1985).

Our discussion of the PFDS suggests that the policies and distributive regime which underwrite it reflect the political compulsions of the regime. The price at which food is bought and sold by the PFDS reflects the respective power of the surplus farmers versus the coalition of urban consumers and (where they exist) the food-deficit households in rural areas. The food-deficit households can, however, be realigned with the surplus farmers through the influence of the hierarchical rural power structure and the prospect of more employment opportunities within a more dynamic agricultural sector stimulated by high procurement prices.

Where the contradiction between these two constituencies cannot be reconciled we tend to find that the financial cost has to be carried by the budget and paid for through reallocative decisions within the budget as well as through inflationary deficit finance. The victims of this process, being dispersed and unorganized, also tend to be voiceless.

4.11. *The state as an employer*

Apart from direct entitlement guarantees through the PFDS, the state promotes entitlements through various employment generation programmes. The state in many developing countries is a major source of employment in the administration and in other quasi-governmental agencies. Its compensation payments to its employees account for a sizeable generation of entitlements. Fluctuations in the size of the state budget thus become a major variable in the determinants of entitlements.

In such circumstances the size of the public sector becomes an important political variable. It reflects a shift in allocative power from the hands of property owners operating through the market to the state whose allocative decisions are politically determined. These allocative decisions over who will get work in what sectors and regions will be far more responsive to the specific political compulsions of particular decision makers. Such compulsions may frequently coincide with the allocative preferences of property owners as a class. However this may not always be so and may lead to serious political conflicts within the ruling élite.

All compensation provided by the state is designed to pay for specific services. In practice most governments carry in varying proportions a load of redundant employees whose elimination would in no way affect the workings of the administration, except to contribute to the social problem of unemployment. The state has thus already arrogated to itself, without formally acknowledging this, the task of creating employment to provide entitlements to large numbers of people who would otherwise subsist with reduced incomes. This is a form of work sharing or welfare payment which is dictated by the political compulsions of the state. These compulsions derive from a general obligation to alleviate deprivation lest the conditions of extreme distress accentuate social tensions which threaten the stability of the regime and/or its electoral prospects.

It follows that the state may extend its commitment to protect entitlements to explicit programmes designed for employment generation. The most visible of these are the varieties of public works programmes which seek to create jobs, usually of a labour intensive nature. Such programmes have been carried through by governments from ancient times, when the state assumed the obligation to provide work either in times of temporary entitlement failure, or on a regular basis to those with a permanent deficiency of entitlements. In more contemporary times this obligation has grown in size along with the growing numbers of the poor.

The capacity to sustain large public works programmes is constrained by the resources available to the state. The Keynesian model of using public works as a counter-cyclical policy instrument financed from budget deficits designed to stimulate the use of idle capacity is obviously not open to most developing countries. Here deficiency of employment is itself a characteristic of under-development, and the state has to create new resources in order to provide new employment.

The massive resources required to sustain employment programmes may be provided from local resource mobilization, whether through voluntary mobilization or through taxes or savings committed in cash or kind. This implies important allocative political decisions about who pays for such programmes.

Some states, socialist states, seek to avoid this choice by making the prospective beneficiaries of these Rural Public Works Projects (RPWP) invest their own labour to create these assets. Labour is usually mobilized within specific institutional mechanisms such as the commune which plans for the use of labour time and treats it as a specific resource in its investment planning.[42] Such projects may be part of a national project where costs are shared between the centre and local authority, or they may be purely local projects. In most cases, however, the project confers specific benefits on the community. To the extent that all households have an equitable stake in the productive assets of the community, they will face an enhancement in their direct entitlements from such collective investments. Most households are thus likely to be more willing to donate labour, or to offer it on sub-market terms for such output enhancing public works.

However, the more conventional employment generation programmes in most developing countries, while having investment objectives common to those in socialist countries, have to be financed from budgetary sources. Since the direct entitlement benefits of such investments in rural infrastructure largely accrue to those who own land, while those who work on these projects are usually the landless, there is no collective perception of benefits from such

---

[42] Strong (1964).

investments. Thus those who work on these projects need to be compensated for their labour in cash or kind. In rare cases this may come from the savings or taxes of the rich and/or potential beneficiaries of such public works, and thus pose no political problems. In most cases, however, RPWP have to be paid for out of the national exchequer as part of the nation-wide employment generation programme. At a national level, to sustain such programmes requires domestic resource commitments. When those with resources are unwilling to surrender these for projects which may be of no immediate benefit to them, the state has to look for some external donors seeking to help the rural poor of the Third World to underwrite such projects. This makes rural employment generation into a painless affair much favoured by both DC governments and donors.

The very fact that such rural public works projects have to be financed from the national budget and beyond that from foreign donors gives them a high opportunity cost. The size of these programmes thus tends to be dictated by the availability of external resources rather than by local needs and resource mobilization. Indeed the availability of external resources may become a positive disincentive to mobilize local resources. The source of local funding, the rural landowners, whose direct entitlements may rise substantially through the creation of productive assets under RPWP, may, under certain circumstances, be willing to pay for the investment. But if aid will finance it for them, if not today then tomorrow, they would be inclined to invest their surplus elsewhere, or to consume it.

Given the fact that the limited resources of the state have to satisfy multiple claimants on the budget, the benefits it can confer, whether from general employment creation or through such programmes as the RPWP, are limited. The state and its local representatives thus see such investments in direct employment creation as a vital source of patronage to be used to enhance the political authority of those who dispense it. RPWP by its nature thus becomes an instrument of local patronage. The state looks to a class of local power-brokers to act for the regime as political agents in their local sphere of influence in exchange for the patronage resources invested in them through the RPWP.

While such a political perspective tends to inform most RPWP, this argument was made particularly explicit in Pakistan in the 1960s. At that time Field Marshal Ayub Khan was seeking a rural support base to the Martial Law regime ushered in by him in 1958, particularly in the more restive province of East Pakistan (now Bangladesh). He sought to build his political base through creating a class of local beneficiaries of state patronage drawn largely from the rural affluent classes. The chosen instrument for this was the Basic Democracies (BD) system made up of the elected local council members.[43] It was under the 1962 constitution designated as the electoral college for election to the Presidency and to the national and provincial parliament.

[43] Sobhan (1968).

To secure the political allegiance of this BD electorate it was necessary to invest state resources to expand patronage in their hands. The RPWP of East Pakistan was the most significant instrument for channelling state resources to the BDs. The project was a large-scale job-creating rural public works programme financed from the counterpart funds created from the sale of US PL-480 foodgrains through the PFDS. To place resources in the range of $200 million into the hands of hitherto resource-starved local institutions gave those who controlled such resources extraordinary political power in the local community. They were thus quite willing to vote for Ayub Khan to become civilian President in 1960 and to re-elect him in 1964.

The identification of the fortunes of the BDs and the RPWP with the political viability of the Ayub regime proved hazardous. When the Ayub regime abdicated power in 1969 in the face of a mass mobilization the BD system and the RPWP in its original conception faded away with the *ancien régime*.[44]

In more contemporary times, as in Bangladesh, the RPWP has been reincarnated in a variety of forms, the principal of these being the Food for Work programme funded largely by the World Food Programme and USAID. Such programmes continue to be channelled into the rural areas through the rural élite. This class, in spite of the severance of the formal constitutional link with the state as an electoral college, still remains a powerful political instrument of the state. Most local authority chairmen see the public expeditures of the state as their principal political capital. Even though a number of opposition party leaders are elected to local bodies, the massive patronage within the control of the state compels a local leader, for reasons of political survival, to declare his allegiance to the government so as to stake some claim on aid resources, particularly those which are distributed through the RPWP. Thus even though RPWP in Bangladesh provides some long-term benefit to its immediate beneficiaries,[45] and generates considerable employment,[46] it retains its role as a political resource available to the regime of the day to secure the political allegiance of the local élite.

The scope of a regime to use its control over the allocation of employment (whether under RPWP or throughout the general administration) as a political resource depends on the specific circumstances of each country. Where public resources are a major source of new employment and provide monetized resources, the potency of this strategy will be high. However, if the resources are limited and the constituency large then the political benefits may be short lived. The Pakistan experience showed that charges of corruption and misuse of RPWP funds were used by opponents of the incumbent local officials to defeat them in the next round of local elections.[47] Where the direct beneficiaries of the project are outnumbered by the many who cannot be reached,

[44] Sobhan (1969).   [45] Hossain and Qasem (1985).   [46] Sobhan (1986).
[47] Sobhan (1968).

the idea of conferring entitlements on some while excluding many more may buy relief but at high long-term political cost. One of the virtues of a socialist system is that it attempts to embrace within its allocative regime the entire community. This may mean that the incidence of benefits remains less dramatic, but at least the deprivation and mutual benefits are more equitably shared.

4.12. *Disaster response*

Apart from general and specific employment-generation programmes, the state enhances entitlements through a variety of relief and charity programmes. These may be institutionalized, as in the case of the Vulnerable Group Feeding Programme in Bangladesh and other such programmes which provide a school meal or feed lactating mothers, infants, orphans, widows, or destitutes. Other programmes may be more *ad hoc* in nature, in response to temporary distress. Such responses are common to all societies. Such welfare programmes seek to confer entitlements on those who cannot work and/or remain permanently undernourished due to failure of entitlements. The incidence of such programmes is by its nature more limited than that of various employment-creating programmes. Such programmes are not without political motive. In Bangladesh, all beneficiaries of the VGFP are mobilized to swell the crowds at political meetings addressed by the incumbent President and his Ministers. It is not clear whether this is translated into votes at the polls. But there is some evidence that the threat of exclusion from the programme is used by local political agents to deliver their votes to the official candidate.

Of far greater significance is the use of state resources to protect entitlements where social or national disasters threaten to lead to entitlement failures. Natural disasters which totally destroy crops and earning opportunities, or political disasters such as war or political persecution which drive away populations from their normal environment, vest a special responsibility on the state. In such circumstances, the state has to provide immediate succour to victims who face death from starvation, disease, and exposure in the absence of such assistance.

The Bangladesh Liberation War uprooted 10 million people from their homes and compelled them to take shelter in India in refugee camps around the border. The famines in Bengal, Bangladesh, Sahel, Ethiopia also saw large numbers of starving people moving out of their homes in search of food. When the state set up relief camps many moved there, or were attracted to these camps directly from their homes. The capacity of the state to sustain such assistance is again limited by the resources available to it and the political costs of mobilizing such resources.

The assumption of responsibility by the state to prevent temporary entitlement failures assumes that the PFDS can command real resources from those who control these and can redirect them to those in need. The state may use its own food resources, or it may acquire food on the market to distribute to the resourceless, or it may make cash income transfers to them so that the market mechanism can be used to redistribute food in favour of the affected population. In conditions of price stability, as in the Ethiopian famine of 1973, where there was evidence of entitlement failures due to decline in the earnings of famine victims, cash transfers to famine victims may bring more grain to the market.[48] However, in Bangladesh in 1974, when entitlement failures originated in price increases, injections of money into the hands of the famine victims could have aggravated these price increases. In such cases there may be a case for bypassing the market and directly delivering food to the victims through direct relief, or Food for Work programmes. This was the strategy followed by way of famine relief in Bengal and Bangladesh in 1943, 1974, and 1984. The size of such a programme depends on the resources directly available to the PFDS.

The capacity of the PFDS to command resources is itself politically determined by the nature of the state. The prevailing social order determines who controls the surplus. If the required resources are institutionally vested in the hands of private producers and traders then the political system again determines on what terms these resources may be appropriated by the state. A state which is politically sensitive to the concerns of surplus farmers will seek to reallocate its budgetary expenditures to pay the hoarders the market price to unlock hoarded foodstuffs. However this may require, for reasons indicated earlier, more resources than are available to the state due to the high social opportunity cost of such reallocations. The state may thus aim, as was attempted in Bangladesh in 1974 with rather modest results, to use administrative fiat to unlock these hoards where the market mechanism has failed to do so.[49]

The use of administrative fiat to reallocate resources is a political decision which demands a clear political choice on the part of the regime between gainers and losers from this decision. A regime which sees the deprived classes as its primary constituency, and indeed could politically organize them, is more likely to be able to locate and seize hoarded food stocks. In most local communities it is generally known who holds such stocks, not least to the foodless. Such was the case in the USSR after the Bolshevik Revolution, when poor peasants could be organized into Committees of Poor Peasants to track down such hoards.[50] However, in a system hitherto dependent on market incentives to bring surpluses to the market, a regime which intervenes in the market-place in a politically motivated direction may pay a heavy price for this assault on the surplus farmer. The ongoing political confrontation between the Bolshevik regime and the surplus farmer or kulak throughout the 1920s had its origins in the forced seizure of grain during the period of War Communism.[51]

It follows that extra market assaults on grain surpluses are more meaningful where such surpluses are already socialized and thus within the control of the

[48] Sen (1981).   [49] Khondker (1984).   [50] Carr (1966).   [51] Dobb (1952).

state. However, the Chinese famine of the early 1960s suggests that where there are absolute shortages, the state as manifested in local authorities and as a national authority may come into conflict. At that time the whole of China was placed under a draconian system of rationing while grain was being transferred from surplus to deficit provinces.[52] Such redistribution had its physical and political limits so that localized entitlement failures or famine resulted, even under socialism.[53]

While socialist states may be better positioned to respond to the threat of entitlement failures, from antiquity there has always been an element of redistribution of grain from those with surpluses to those in dire need.[54] This may be part of the 'moral economy', where the community feels that it is responsible for meeting extreme distress through material transfers to the needy.[55] Sharing food and/or work where the deprived are not in excessive numbers was thus not just a pre-socialist but a pre-capitalist response to temporary entitlement failures.[56] However the survival of the moral economy depends on the degree of market orientation of the economy and the extent of the entitlement failure. Bengal in pre-British days and in 1943 or 1974 were two different societies where the moral economy had long been eroded by the exposure to market and demographic forces.[57]

Given the limits of moral initiatives and the political constraints on realizing a sufficiently large-scale reallocation of resources within the domestic economy, food imports remain, at the margin, the best available response to a temporary entitlement failure. However imports may remain constrained by foreign exchange shortages. Entitlement failures apply as much to nations as to households. The crisis in 1974 faced by Bangladesh arose not just from a natural disaster but also from the fact that its terms of trade had sharply deteriorated.[58] Not only had grain import prices risen but so had the price of energy and all other commodities. At the same time exports had been seriously affected by a low jute crop while the grain import bill had risen due both to the fall off in aid and the rise in prices. The macro entitlement failure was measured in terms of the bankruptcy of its external reserves. Priorities were such that more foreign exchange could not be released to import more food without risk to other areas of the economy on whom such cuts in imports might have been imposed. As it transpired all sections of the development budget were cut and exchange scarcity was faced by all ministries and all other sectors of the economy. Whether the decision makers had freedom of choice to close down sectors of the economy to release resources for grain imports is an arguable point. At that time they felt they could not. The decision was political and derived from the self-imposed institutional constraints of the system.

---

[52] Suyin (1980).   [53] Sen (1982).   [54] Khondker (1984).

[55] Thompson (1971).   [56] Khondker (1984).

[57] Bardhan and Rudra (1986) have recently challenged this view in the West Bengal context.

[58] Sobhan (1984).

Apart from the possible inflexibilities of the macroeconomy, the PFDS carries its own politically determined rigidities. It has been argued that in Bangladesh in 1974 more grain could have been released for delivery to the famine-affected areas by cutting the grain ration to the urban statutory card holders and other politically defined priority groups.[59] Grain stocks under the PFDS were subject to centralized decisions on food policy. Here again presumably the regime felt politically too insecure to cut rations to groups benefiting from statutory rationing, or to divert grain from the less to the more seriously affected areas. High prices were at that stage a national phenomenon. Households even in ration areas were having to buy some grain on the market. The implicit decision to make ration beneficiaries more dependent on the market by cutting their ration was deemed too politically hazardous for a regime already under severe political attack for the sharp escalation in prices. Thus food aid then and since has in Bangladesh, and indeed in many Third World countries, become politically the least expensive means of protecting the entitlements of the poor in times of crisis.

4.13. *Aid and entitlements*

In situations where it is financially and/or politically expensive for the state to mobilize domestic foodgrain surpluses for use within the PFDS, aid becomes the principal option to respond not just to temporary entitlement failures, but to more pervasive entitlement insufficiency. Aid dependence is in this context a response not only to entitlement failure, but to political failure which is built into the institutional parameters of the state. This failure is measured by the incapacity of the system to redistribute grain from surplus to deficit households.

This dependence on aid generates a second dimension of political problems. So far we had defined politics as an endogenous variable within the system. Now we have to take account of the external political relations of the regime and beyond that of the internal and global political perspectives of the aid donors. It may of course be argued that even external political options are endogenous to the character of the state. Politically weak, unrepresentative regimes whose very assumption to and survival in power depends on patronage from outside may really be said to have fewer policy choices. There is no shortage of Third World regimes or indeed First and Second World regimes which could be so categorized. It would be useful to trace the scope for external political choice to the nature of a particular state, but we will eschew this temptation and simply take this external dependence as given and review some of the implications for access to food.

In many Third World countries, aid dependence is high and food dependence even more so.[60] For the purpose of this chapter we will focus on food aid

---

[59] Alamgir (1980).   [60] FAO (1985).

and its political implications. To the extent that only a few countries can in effect supply food aid, this aid dependence is even more focused. Of the five principal food aid donors, Canada, Australia, and the EEC have shown no discernible tendency to use aid as an instrument of external policy. However, in all three cases, the capacity to offer food aid is very much influenced by domestic political factors affecting the food production policies of the countries in question.[61] Indeed there are significant political conflicts between the principal food donors which constrain their respective food policies. It would again be a useful exercise to study the domestic political constraints of the principal food-exporting countries and the conflicts between the exporters to trace out how far this influences the volume, price, and direction of food exports and overall availability of food aid.

The fourth major food aid donor, the World Food Programme (WFP), may itself be more apolitical in its disposition. But the WFP does not grow food. It mobilizes it from the principal donors. Thus its own supply capabilities depend on the political compulsions of its donors who will have to take the initial political decision as to the part of their food aid they wish to retain within their own aid regime and that which they are willing to disburse through multilateral channels. Again those who tend to commit aid through multilateral institutions, whether food or otherwise, keep a watching brief on the allocative decision of these institutions and the conditions under which they dispense the aid.

Amongst the principal donors and exporters of food, aid as a derivative of domestic farm policy is an explosive political issue. However, of these donors it is the United States which has carried the issue of food aid into its external political concerns. As the principal exporter of food and principal food aid donor, the United States has always seen food as an instrument of foreign policy. It has thus used or sought to use food exports as a political sanction in its global political relations. As a case in point its decision to cut off contracted food exports to the USSR following the Soviet military involvement in Afghanistan was a purely political decision. Earlier decisions to extend guaranteed sugar export quotas at extra-market prices to various of its Central American allies were invoked as a political weapon to influence their relations first with Cuba after the Castro revolution and more recently with the Sandinista regime in Nicaragua.

Obviously the capacity of the United States to enforce the writ of food supply sanctions depends on the vulnerability of the countries in question. The USSR remained quite unaffected by President Carter's grain embargo. Any number of countries including NATO allies of the US in the EEC and Argentina were willing to come forward and fill the import gap of the USSR. Embargo on food and then all trade with Iran after the seizure of hostages by the Khomeni

---

[61] Petit (1985). On the relationship between food policies in rich countries and hunger in poor countries, see also ch. 5 below.

regime was matched in Iran by a combination of import austerity and import diversification pursued by the Khomeni government.[62] The embargo imposed by President Reagan on economic relations with Libya was being undermined by other European and Third World countries ready to fill Libya's trade gap.

4.14. *US food politics in Bangladesh*

Where, however, the United States food aid is, at the margin, a major source of food supply, as it was in Bangladesh in 1974, its political leverage is both significant and potentially lethal. The United States had been the principal supplier of food and indeed economic aid to Pakistan through the 1950s and 1960s. This gave it an ascendent political position in Pakistan over two decades which was institutionalized in a bilateral mutual security pact and in regional military alliances such as SEATO and CENTO. This political leverage was reflected in the visible presence of US economic advisers who through the Harvard Advisory Group exercised significant influence on policy making in Pakistan.

The emergence of Bangladesh as a sovereign nation state in 1971 was a conspicuous set-back for US policy in Pakistan.[63] The Nixon–Kissinger administration, however, sought to recoup its fortunes in Bangladesh by feeding the narcotic dependence of Bangladesh on food aid which has traditionally characterized US–Bangladesh relations. India emerged as an alternative source of food supply in the first half of 1972 when US–Bangladesh relations were still tenuous and the US was putting in limited quantities of aid through multilateral agencies. The government of India, which could even at that time hardly afford to do so, made a sizeable political investment in the stability of the newly incumbent regime by moving in foodgrains to Bangladesh on an emergency basis between December 1971 and December 1972.[64] These grain supplies were critical to keep the PFDS viable and to avoid massive entitlement failures during 1972.

The role of India as an aid donor was, however, a one-off affair since India's food reserves at that stage were still rather precarious. Bangladesh's other ally in the liberation war, the USSR, was hardly a food aid donor and was itself a major food importer. At one stage in 1974 the USSR in response to an emergency appeal from the Bangladesh government diverted 200,000 tons of commercial imports from the US to Bangladesh.[65] But this eventually had to be paid for by Bangladesh and was thus not aid but a short-term loan.

Bangladesh's dependence on the United States as a principal source of food aid was thus a fatal contradiction in its external policy. While it sought a

---

[62] Sobhan (1980). [63] Lifschultz (1979). [64] Sobhan (1984).
[65] Faaland, Islam, and Parkinson (1981).

genuinely non-aligned foreign policy, it did nothing by way of either internal
institutional change or diversification of its dependence on food aid to achieve
some resilience in its relations with the United States.

I have discussed elsewhere how the United States had already put Bangladesh under pressure by delaying fresh commitments of food aid at the end of
1973.[66] Indeed, since August 1973 the US government had made no fresh aid
commitment of any sort to Bangladesh. Its decision to suspend PL-480
shipments to Bangladesh against pre-committed food aid on grounds of
Bangladesh's miniscule exports of jute goods to Cuba should thus be seen not
just as an attempt to constrain the regime's external relations, but as a direct
assault on the viability of the regime. The political motivation underlying this
embargo may be derived from the fact that at that time Kissinger sought a
special dispensation for Sadat's Egypt to continue exporting cotton to Cuba
while receiving US PL-480 commodity aid. Whether this assault on the
stability of the Bangladesh regime, through creating a crisis in the local food
market, was itself the prelude to the dislodgement in August 1975 of the
post-liberation regime in Bangladesh remains open to fuller enquiry,[67] though
there is some circumstantial evidence to suggest that such might have been the
premise to US economic policy towards Bangladesh in 1973–5.[68]

The immediate outcome of this withholding of food aid by the US government at a time when deliveries to the PFDS in Bangladesh were severely
constrained by foreign exchange shortages and grain prices were already rising
out of schedule triggered off the rapid escalation in grain prices in 1974.[69] To
the extent that high grain prices were the immediate cause of entitlement
failures during the 1974 famine, the roots of the famine may be traced to US
foreign policy decisions and not just floods.[70] However, as we have observed,
this total dependency on US food aid was itself derived from the prevailing
political compulsions of the Bangladesh state which was institutionally inhibited from redistributing available grain hoards and indeed grain within the
direct control of the PFDS.

4.15. *The politics of disaster relief in Kampuchea*

The Bangladesh experience with the politics of food aid is one of the more
conspicuous examples of the influence of donor politics on food entitlement.
However the food crises both in Kampuchea after 1979 and, more recently, in
Ethiopia are also powerful illustrations of the complex political motives which
underlie ostensibly humanitarian concerns.

It has been discussed at length elsewhere how emergency aid to Kampuchea
was influenced by the diverse political concerns of the principal actors.[71] The

---

[66] Sobhan (1979, 1984).   [67] Lifschultz (1979).   [68] Sobhan (1979).
[69] Ibid.   [70] Rothschild (1977) and McHenry and Bird (1977).
[71] Shawcross (1984).

Vietnamese-backed Heng Samrin regime needed food aid to feed the Kampu-cheans facing famine due to the ravages of the Pol Pot regime and the subsequent economic dislocation arising out of the Vietnamese military inter-vention to overthrow this regime. It has been argued by Shawcross that the extent of the food shortage in Kampuchea was greatly exaggerated by the Heng Samrin regime so as externally to mobilize enough food aid at its disposal to feed the machinery of government and the war machine, in order to consolidate its position within the country. To enter into a debate on the empirical basis of this argument is not possible without more detailed knowledge of the actual production and distribution system in Kampuchea. The sources citing this argument themselves have no conclusive evidence to support this hypothesis beyond the fact that massive entitlement failures, measured by famine deaths, did not take place on any appreciable scale in Kampuchea at that time, in spite of food aid falling well short of proclaimed requirements. Supportive evidence remains anecdotal and largely speculative.

The international agencies entrusted with mobilizing and delivering food to Kampuchea were under perpetual pressure from the principal donors, led by the United States, to ensure that food aid was directed to those facing famine and not used to consolidate the Heng Samrin regime. To this end there was an ongoing conflict between the principal donor agencies seeking to provide disaster relief to Kampuchea and the Heng Samrin government over the extent to which the donor representatives should actually participate in the aid delivery process. While the Heng Samrin regime did make some concessions in permitting entry to representatives of various international agencies, it con-stantly asserted its sovereign right to distribute food through its own distribu-tive system and according to its own notions of domestic allocative priority. It has been argued that the refusal of the Heng Samrin regime to give a bigger say to the international agencies was the principal factor in limiting the volume of food aid going directly into Kampuchea.

If this be so then the political compulsions of the donors were as relevant as the political compulsions of the Heng Samrin regime in determining food entitlements. Obviously in less politically embattled situations, as for instance in Bangladesh in 1974 or 1979 or 1984, aid donors do not insist on their right to monitor food aid distribution. It thus became apparent that some of the principal contributors to disaster relief, such as the United States, had their own political stake in the aid programme.

The United States and its local allies, China and Thailand, appear to have been motivated by the political goal of keeping alive a military resistance to the Vietnamese presence in Kampuchea.[72] Apart from the military support to the Khmer Rouge and other less effective resistance forces extended by the United States and China, there was the need to feed the resistance. In his study of disaster relief Shawcross provides persuasive evidence to suggest that a

[72] Ibid.

sizeable part of this relief, intended to feed Kampuchean refugees within camps in Thailand or located on the Thai–Kampuchean borders, was used to provision the military resistance to the Heng Samrin regime. Thus food aid became a significant political variable in the political and military viability of the resistance to the Heng Samrin regime. The international agencies such as the UNHCR and the International Red Cross seemed powerless to ensure that disaster relief intended for refugees did not serve a military purpose.

The political orientation of the donors may be measured by the fact that between October 1979 and December 1981, out of \$US634 million of disaster relief designated for Kampuchea only 53 per cent went directly into Kampuchea.[73] In contrast 47 per cent was distributed directly by the international donor agencies to Kampuchean refugees and insurgents and to the Thai administration. It was reckoned that in per capita terms this meant that on average \$659 went to each refugee seeking aid outside Kampuchea as compared to \$48 per capita disbursed inside. How much of this in turn went to sustain armed combatants on either side remains uncertain.

4.16. Disaster relief in Ethiopia

The recent Ethiopian famine appears to have generated similar political conflicts. The present regime in Ethiopia has for the last several years been fighting separatist insurgencies in some of its provinces. In this conflict, as in most such conflicts, access to food is seen as an important military variable. Thus famine relief in combat areas becomes both a political and logistical problem. The fact that the Ethiopian regime proclaims itself to be socialist, and has strong political ties with the Soviet bloc, has aroused the concern of the more politically orientated food aid donors, such as the United States, that disaster relief will not only reinforce the authority of the Ethiopian regime but also help it to starve out the resistance forces in Tigre and Eritrea.[74] The debate over the resettlement of famine victims goes on. The United States is reluctant to countenance any long-term measures to stimulate local production and indeed to give any aid which could stimulate longer-term development because it finds the Ethiopian regime politically unpalatable. It is thus only willing to offer emergency aid for current consumption and wants greater say over the distribution of aid. As in Kampuchea this generates tensions between the donors and the regime. Ironically the Soviet Union and some of its East European allies have become the main source of logistical support for the distribution of disaster relief in Ethiopia.[75] The regime, therefore, appears to be drawing upon the support of both the superpowers.

[73] Ibid.   [74] Ibid.
[75] Reports of UN officials in Ethiopia.

4.17. Food aid and policy leverage

It must further be recognized that apart from the use of aid as a short-term political weapon donors, both bilateral and multilateral, have been inclined to use aid in the service of ideology. This is designed to persuade regimes to change their domestic policies in a direction which is more favourable to the promotion of private enterprise and market forces. In Bangladesh recent US PL-480 agreements have explicitly written-in clauses which, *inter alia*, specify that in order to be eligible for aid the GOB should:[76]

- encourage the active participation of private grain dealers in foodgrain procurement,
- phase out major elements of the public food distribution system by the time foodgrain self-sufficiency is achieved,
- develop a private spinning industry,
- carry out wholesaling and retailing of soyabean/cotton seed oil through the private sector.

This form of conditionality is rationalized on grounds of efficiency. While this proposition appears arguable, the ideological element is evident. The objective results of this policy again appear to be designed to tilt the political balance in favour of a class of private traders and businessmen who emerge as the immediate beneficiaries of aid used in the service of ideology. The Bangladesh experience is again not unique. There is a tendency to promote similar policies in Africa where the entire policy promoted by the World Bank of injecting massive aid appears to have a politically derived policy package attached to it.[77]

4.18. The political economy of food aid

The cases of Bangladesh, Kampuchea, and Ethiopia could be elaborated upon to trace out the ramifications of donor politics and indeed the varying political perspectives of the different international agencies concerned with disaster relief. Many more cases of US food aid politics could be discussed to discern a pattern of political behaviour.

For the purposes of this chapter, however, the evidence cited suggests that vulnerability to food politics is up to a point self-imposed. Its incidence is a measure of the economic weakness and political failure to seek systemic changes within the Third World countries. This exposes such countries not just to the vicissitudes of the global market, but also to the greater uncertainties of internal political conflicts in donor countries relating to farm policy.

This internal weakness puts an exaggerated premium on the need for the

---

[76] Sobhan and Bhattacharya (1988).   [77] World Bank (1986*b*).

more vulnerable Third World aid recipients to keep their political relations with their principal donors in good repair, particularly if they cannot realize a more diversified pattern of aid dependence. Thus Bangladesh in 1974 fell a victim to the US aid embargo while Egypt continued to receive PL-480 food and retained its option to export cotton to Cuba.[78] Such options may not, however, be equitably distributed since the strategic value of Egypt to the US Middle East policy in 1974 was significantly greater than Bangladesh's. Thus the luxury of self-assertion in the global and domestic arena against the inclinations of a major donor may demand domestic political mobilization to compensate for strategic insignificance.

Fortunately for the world, and for the politically weak and strategically insignificant countries, not all food exporters are also superpowers who see their aid and commerce as an instrument of foreign policy. The United States has chosen to exploit the dependence of many economically and politically weak countries to effect modifications in their external alignments, in domestic economic policy choices, and in the internal political balance of power. The capacity to withstand such external pressures remains a function of the internal political regime in particular Third World countries. However the willingness to exploit its advantageous economic position is also a measure of both ideology and political choice within the arena of domestic politics in the United States. This too merits study in its own right.

4.19. *Conclusions for policy and research*

The argument presented in this chapter leads us to the conclusion that attempts to raise the entitlement levels of all households would require significant action of a political character. This is not to suggest that other variables, such as the forces of nature or hard work and skills of the household, would not affect its entitlements. But our analysis focuses on the underlying political forces which influence these efforts to raise entitlements. By way of illustration we may trace the nature of such policy interventions in the Bangladesh context.

Raising entitlements to land would involve the enactment of some form of land reform which imposes a ceiling on land ownership and redistributes all surplus land holdings to those households whose entitlements are insufficient to ensure subsistence. To the extent that this redistribution would still leave a number of households without land, some form of minimum wage legislation or improved crop sharing terms would be needed.

To improve the productivity of those with land and to provide fuller and more diverse employment opportunities for those without sufficient land or any land at all would require major allocative decisions to provide public resources to develop the rural infrastructure, rural industry, and labour

---

[78] Sobhan (1979).

intensive activities. This intervention may have to be at the expense of the prevailing concentrations of investment in the urban sector and in capital intensive industry.

Capital may need to be provided through public financial institutions on sub-market terms to rural producers along with complementary inputs to raise yields. This would again require allocative decisions in the credit market diverting capital away from traders and industrialists towards smallholders and rural industry.

The market regime would need to be transformed through state or co-operative institutions of small producers which ensure stable prices of inputs and remunerative prices for output. To the extent that a sufficiency of wage goods and stable prices need to be guaranteed to those with insufficient land, or indeed in exchange for surrendering the produce of their land, a regime of budgetary subsidies would be needed to the point where an acceptable social equilibrium between the conflicting interests of producers and consumers is established in the market-place. Such interventions in the market would need to be extended to develop commodity stabilization programmes to insulate producers against fluctuations in the domestic and global market.

Such programmes of subsidy and stabilization will have significant budgetary implications. Even when subsidy policies are designed to benefit the needy in a cost-effective way, the political compulsions of a regime may still leave sizeable claims on the exchequer. This would again have allocative and hence political implications where presumably subsidies would have to be paid for at the expense of the defence or some other sector budget.

For Bangladesh, or indeed any other developing country, the policy interventions indicated above have obvious political implications. Redefining the title to land and to the terms of its cultivation would meet resistance from landowners. Interventions in the market-place would generate contradictions with commodity traders, middlemen, and usurers. Decisive budgetary and credit reallocations to deploy public resources in the service of the poor would antagonize the traditional monopolists of such resources, big business, bureaucrats, military, and rich farmers. Where MNCs exercise significant control over productive assets, natural resources, and trade, such an intervention would generate contradictions at an international level with the countries from which the MNCs originate. In such conflicts the entrenched dominant class would be able to exploit conflicts among the poor. Conflicts between small landowners who hire in some labour and landless farm labourers, conflicts between those in search of cheap food and small farmers with some surplus, exploitation of primordial loyalties based on ethnic, caste, kinship, or patron–client ties, could and indeed do militate against developing a coherent and organized constituency of the poor against the dominant classes.

In such circumstances it is for political activists, policy makers, and analysts to assess the specific historic conditions under which a coalition of forces will emerge whereby a policy regime favourable to the poor can be realized in any society. It would be a truism to state that a society dominated by the working classes would realize such a policy regime. Though even here it merits analysis as to whether and under what circumstances such a regime's allocative biases are actually more successful in meeting the basic needs of the poor compared to more traditional social orders at similar levels of development and resource endowments. However, assuming that such a reconfiguration of political power in society can serve the poor, is it to be presumed that this can only be realized through fundamental systemic changes brought about in the wake of a social revolution? If such be the assumption then the logical course for poverty studies is not merely to diagnose the basis of poverty but to analyse the concrete circumstances where social revolution becomes both necessary and possible. Some of the significant studies in this area analyse the circumstances in which social revolutions take place.[79] These however do not adequately indicate whether specific policy interventions demand revolution, nor does the conceptualization of social transformation developed in these studies encompass the contemporary circumstances of many countries of the Third World.

In the absence of a major social upheaval it must be recognized that society does not stand still. In different societies, policies favourable to the poor or some of the poor are being enacted and resources are being allocated to improve their entitlements. Much of this recognition of the interests of the poor is being realized at the instigation of foreign aid donors and through aid financing, thereby making it relatively costless to the affluent classes.[80] Indeed where such investments as in RPWP improve the rural infrastructure it is strongly supported by rich farmers who save on investment and appreciate that social unrest amidst the poor is alleviated by such aid-financed programmes.

However, even outside of the aid regime resources do flow to the poor. To effect this redeployment of resources social and political coalitions are forming and reforming. In some urban centres working-class unity and organization may raise the entitlements of some segments of the working class. Landless labourers may organize for political action to seize land or to improve terms of access to land. Such pressures, if manifested on a more pervasive scale, may lead to some minimum wage or tenurial reform legislation. Though here again the efficacy of implementation may be determined by the correlation of forces at the local level. Such coalitions may even cut across class lines. An alliance of some groups of the urban middle classes with the net buyers of food in the rural areas could reinforce the constituency for food subsidies. These may in turn coalesce with surplus farmers demanding price support to press jointly for budgetary appropriations to the detriment of expenditures on defence. It would thus appear that for each policy intervention policy makers would have to determine the adjustments in the political balance of power needed to push this through.

The perspective underlying this chapter is presumably part of the intuitive

---

[79] Moore (1966), Skocpol (1979).   [80] Sobhan (1986).

apparatus of working politicians and political activists. It informs local political struggles and national and global policy debates. The tendency for multilateral donor agencies, or indeed academic analysts, to underplay the political premise of policy making does not just reduce the viability of their contributions, but erodes their credibility as policy advisers.[81] Analyses of hunger and poverty could therefore benefit greatly from an interaction between analysts and activists to understand better the political costs of policy change and the limits of the political system to realize substantive changes in the conditions of the poor.

This chapter should thus be seen as a preliminary exercise to define the causal nexus between politics, hunger, and entitlement. It should lead on to empirical studies of the political dynamics of policy making and the preconditions for systemic change. These studies may move on to compare different political systems as to their efficacy in alleviating hunger and poverty. Such exercises will place in some empirical perspective the role of politics as a variable in understanding why hunger and poverty prevail today in the world.

[81] World Bank (1986a).

References

ABDULLAH, A., and MURSHID, K. A. S. (1986), 'The Distribution of Benefits from the Public Food Distribution System', mimeo (Dhaka: Bangladesh Institute of Development Studies).

ALAMGIR, M. (1980), *Famine in South Asia* (Cambridge, Mass.: Oelgeschlager, Gunn and Hain).

BARDHAN, P., and RUDRA, A. (1986), 'Labour Mobility and the Boundaries of the Village Moral Economy', *Journal of Peasant Studies*, 13.

BOKHARI, A. S. (1986), 'Evaluation of Agrarian Reform Measures in Pakistan', mimeo (Dhaka: CIRDAP).

CARR, E. H. (1966), *The Bolshevik Revolution 1917–23*, vol. ii (London: Pelican Books).

CHOWDHURY, N. (1986), 'Public Foodgrain Distribution in Bangladesh in the Post-liberation Period: A Historical Profile', mimeo (Dhaka: Bangladesh Institute of Development Studies).

DOBB, M. H. (1952), *Soviet Economic Development* (London: Routledge).

FAALAND, J., ISLAM, N., and PARKINSON, J. B. (1981), *Aid and Influence: The Case of Bangladesh* (London: Macmillan).

FAO (1983), *Review and Analysis of Programmes for the Rural Poor in Bangladesh* (Rome: FAO).

——(1984), *Agricultural Price Policies in the Near East: Lessons and Experience*, paper prepared for the 17th FAO Regional Conference for the Near East, Aden, Mar.

——(1985), *Food Aid and Food Security* (Rome: FAO).

GEORGE, S. (1976), *How the Other Half Dies* (Harmondsworth: Penguin).

GILL, G. J. (1979), *Peasants and Government in the Russian Revolution* (London: Macmillan).

HAIDER, Y. (1986), *Development the Upazilla Way* (Dhaka: Prokashan).

HOSSAIN, M., and QASEM, A. (1985), 'The Effect on Agricultural Production and Household Income', in BIDS-IFPRI, *Development Impact of the Food for Work Programme in Bangladesh* (Dhaka: Bangladesh Institute of Development Studies, and Washington, DC: IFPRI).

KHAN, A. (1967), *Friends Not Masters* (Karachi: Oxford University Press).

KHONDKER, H. H. (1984), 'Government Response to Famine: A Case Study of the 1974 Famine in Bangladesh' (Ph.D. dissertation, University of Pittsburgh).

KIERNAN, B., and BOUA, C. (1982), *Peasants and Politics in Kampuchea, 1942–81* (London: Zed Press).

LEWIN, M. (1968), *Russian Peasants and Soviet Power* (Evanston: Northwestern University Press).

LIFSCHULTZ, L. (1979), *Bangladesh: The Unfinished Revolution* (London: Zed).

LIPTON, M. (1977), *Why Poor People Stay Poor: Urban Bias in World Development* (London: Temple Smith).

McHENRY, D., and BIRD, K. (1977), 'Food Bungle in Bangladesh', *Foreign Policy*, 27.

MOORE, B. (1966), *Social Origins of Democracy and Dictatorship* (London: Beacon Press).

OSMANI, S. R., and QASEM, A. (1985), 'Pricing and Subsidy Policies in Bangladesh Agriculture', mimeo (Dhaka: Bangladesh Institute of Development Studies).

PETIT, M. (1985), 'Determinants of Agricultural Policies in the United States and the European Community', Research Report No. 51 (Washington, DC: IFPRI).

ROTHSCHILD, E. (1977), 'Food Politics', *Foreign Affairs*, 54.

SEN, A. K. (1981), *Poverty and Famines* (Oxford: Oxford University Press).

——(1982), 'How is India Doing', *New York Review of Books*, 29.

SHAWCROSS, W. (1984), *The Quality of Mercy* (New York: Simon & Schuster).

SKOCPOL, T. (1979), *States and Social Revolutions* (Cambridge: Cambridge University Press).

SOBHAN, R. (1968), *Basic Democracies, Works Programme and Rural Development in East Pakistan* (Pakistan: Oxford University Press).

——(1969), 'East Pakistan's Revolt against Ayub', *Round Table* (London).

——(1979), 'Politics of Food and Famine in Bangladesh', *Economic and Political Weekly*, 14.

——(1980), 'The Political Economy of Petro-dollar Recycling: The Significance of Ayatollah Khomeini', *Asian Affairs* (Dhaka).

——(1984), *The Crisis of External Dependence* (London: Zed).

——(1985a), 'South–South Cooperation: The Asian Experience', paper presented at a Conference on South–South Cooperation, Harare.

——(1985b), 'Planning for the Poor: The Role of the State in Bangladesh', presidential address to the 7th Biennial Conference of the Bangladesh Economic Association, Dhaka.

——(1986), 'Rural Employment Strategies and Policies in Bangladesh', paper presented at the ILO Seminar on Rural Employment Promotion Strategies, Beijing, Apr.

——and BHATTACHARYA, D. (1988), 'Aid Conditionality in Bangladesh: The Case of U.S. PL 480 Food Aid', *Journal of Contemporary Asia* (Manila).

STREETEN, P. (1987), *What Price Food?* (London: Macmillan).

STRONG, A. L. (1964), *The Rise of the Chinese People's Communes* (Beijing: New World Press).

SUYIN, H. (1980), *My House has Two Doors* (London: Jonathan Cape).

THOMPSON, E. P. (1971), 'The Moral Economy of the English Crowd in the 18th Century', *Past and Present*, 50.

World Bank (1985), *Bangladesh Economic and Social Development Prospects*, 4 vols. (Washington, DC: World Bank).

——(1986a), *World Development Report 1986* (Washington, DC: World Bank).

——(1986b), *Financing Adjustment with Growth in Sub-Saharan Africa 1986–90* (Washington, DC: World Bank).

——(1986c), *Poverty and Hunger: Issues and Options for Food Security in Developing Countries* (Washington, DC: World Bank).

WURFEL, D. (1983), 'The Development of Post-War Philippine Land Reform: Political and Sociological Explanation', *View from the Paddy*, ii (Manila: IPC).

5

Chronic Hunger in the World: Impact of International Policies

Kirit S. Parikh

5.1. *The background and the issues*

(a) *In spite of progress chronic undernutrition still persists*

Significant progress has been made in meeting people's needs for food in the world. Only a few centuries ago, hunger was a threat to most people everywhere and a daily reality for the majority of them. Nowadays a large part of the world's population enjoy secure and adequate food supplies. Progress in providing food security for a major part of a much larger world population is one of the outstanding achievements of our times and further progress continues to be made.

With progress in providing food security, other indicators suggest improvement in the human condition. Life expectancy at birth in developing countries has increased from less than 40 years to around 55 years over the last three decades. A number of developing countries have joined the ranks of developed countries in this period. The per capita production of foodgrains in the developing countries (except for some parts of Africa) has increased over these years in spite of unprecedentedly high growth rates of population in these countries.

This progress notwithstanding and despite the fact that globally, and even regionally, adequate food is produced, several hundred million people are suffering from chronic undernutrition, i.e. from hunger. Moreover, their number still appears to be increasing, although their share in the population of developing countries, and of the world, continues to decline.

The problems of defining what constitutes an adequate calorie intake and of measuring what people actually eat lead to differing estimates of the number of persons suffering from hunger in the world. The difficulties of defining calorie intake norms, arising due to homeostasis, human adaptation, and interpersonal and intertemporal (for an individual) variability of calorie intakes have been emphasized by many (see Sukhatme 1977, and Sukhatme and

This paper reports on the work of many people in the Food and Agriculture Program of IIASA. Among my colleagues on this IIASA project I want particularly to thank Günther Fischer, Klaus Frohberg, Michiel Keyzer, Ferenc Rabar, T. N. Srinivasan, and Wouter Tims for their contributions to all aspects of the program. The paper has also benefited from the comments of the participants at the seminar at WIDER, particularly those by the discussants, Surjit Bhalla and Nanak Kakwani. Written comments by Amartya Sen and an anonymous referee have been valuable in revising the paper. Needless to say, I alone am responsible for whatever shortcomings remain.

Margen 1978). Following this, Srinivasan (1981) has emphasized the problems of estimating the extent of undernutrition from nutritional intake of household consumption surveys when medical examination is not simultaneously carried out to find clinical signs of undernutrition.

Keeping these difficulties of definitions, measurements, and estimations in mind, to get an idea of the extent of chronic undernutrition in the world, one may look at two recent estimates given in Table 5.1 of undernutrition in the world by the World Bank (1986) and the FAO (1985). It is seen that with a critical calorie intake norm of 1.2 BMR (basal metabolic rate) below which a person may be considered as undernourished, both the estimates give comparable results. However, for a critical limit of 1.35 BMR the World Bank estimates are much larger than the FAO estimates with a critical limit of 1.40 BMR (whereas one would expect that with a higher calorie intake norm the number of persons below it should be larger). This is in spite of the fact that both sets of estimates are based on the same data and differ mainly in the details (and not the spirit) of the estimation procedure.

Thus estimates of number of persons in chronic undernutrition have a large uncertainty. None the less there is a general agreement that chronic undernutrition exists in the world and that the problem is sizeable.

(b) *Chronic undernutrition is affected by policies of own and other governments*

The problem of chronic undernutrition is the problem of poverty. The chronically hungry are, by and large, people from households with too little income to be able to buy all the food they need. Their incomes are small because they own insufficient productive resources of capital, land, and skills. Households use the resources of capital, land, and skills which they own for production activities or exchange them in factor markets. This generates their income. This income is received as income entitlements in the form of cash, as payments in kind, as commodities produced for own consumption or for sale. These income entitlements are then exchanged on the goods and services

Table 5.1 Estimates of undernutrition

Estimate by	Critical limit (BMR)	Population with calorie deficiency (below critical limit) (millions)	
		1970	1980
World Bank	1.2	300	340
	1.35	600	730
FAO	1.2	335	325
	1.4	495	470
FAP model[a] Reference run			510

[a] Based on a simplified FAO approach.

market to obtain a final consumption bundle of goods and services, including food items.

This description of economic processes schematically shown in Fig. 5.1 suggests a number of ways in which a household's final consumption bundle may not contain adequate quantities of food for meeting the biological needs of the members of the household.

The final consumption bundle attained by the household is directly affected

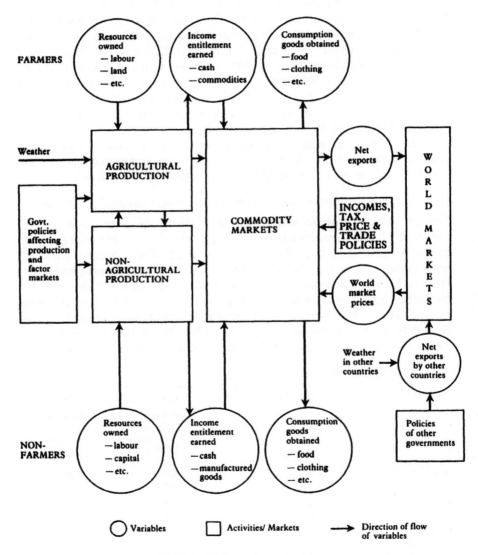

Fig. 5.1. Hunger: the processes

by the policies of the national government. These policies affect domestic relative prices and hence real incomes of the households. They also affect factor markets as well as goods and service markets. Growth and development policies influence the direction and pace of development of the economy and, particularly in a developing country, that of agriculture which can change significantly the income earning opportunities of the poor. And, of course, incomes and redistributive policies affect directly the incomes of the poor household.

However, policies of national governments depend also on the policies of other governments. Policies of other governments get reflected in the world market prices. World market prices are in turn transmitted to domestic markets to varying degrees depending on the policies of the national government. Even when a government insulates domestic prices from the world market prices, the poor cannot escape the influence of the world markets. If, for example, domestic prices are maintained through the use of variable levies when world market prices have changed, the tariff income of the government will change. This may be significant for many developing countries and may result in changes in other taxes, or in investment levels, leading to altered employment opportunities for the poor.

World market prices for agricultural products are affected not only by the trade policies of other countries but also by weather in other countries. The richer countries tend to protect domestic consumers against the influences of weather disturbances through trade. Thus the influence of weather is exported on the world market and the burden of adjustment is passed on to the poor countries. Within these countries, in turn, the poorest may have to adjust the most. The influence through the world markets can be substantial as the markets for agricultural products are dominated by a few countries, and only a relatively small part of the world's agricultural output is traded internationally, amounting to about 15 per cent. The fraction of production traded varies from commodity to commodity. For example, whereas some 15 per cent of global wheat production is traded, the share for rice remains below 5 per cent in most years. Still, international prices do influence domestic prices in producing and consuming countries.

The countries with influence on the world market are a small number of large exporters who sell to high income importers (Table 5.2). The exporters fall into two groups. The 'New World' countries (Canada, US, Argentina, Brazil, Australia, New Zealand, South Africa, and Zimbabwe) and the 'Old World', Europe.

The countries which harbour the hungry play only a modest role in international food trade, because they lack the financial means to import large amounts of food. Also the physical infrastructure to participate in international trade is lacking in some of these countries. Consequently, these countries' policies have little impact on world markets and world prices, while being affected by these prices. Developing countries have in the main become more

Table 5.2 Shares in global net exports of major exporters in selected commodity markets in 1980 (%)

	Wheat	Rice	Coarse grains	Bovine and ovine meat	Dairy products	Other animal products	Protein feeds
Argentina	6	4	6	21		4	9
Australia	18		5	20	7		
Brazil				11		2	19
Canada	22		4	31		20	
EC	7				65		
Japan		12					
New Zealand					23		
Thailand		28	2				
USA	45	31	79	7			65

Source: FAP data bank based on FAO Supply Utilization Account.

dependent on the international market as importers of food. Moreover, as exporters of agricultural products their role has declined.

The richer countries have substantial influence on the world prices of agricultural products, not only because they are able to export domestic production fluctuations on the world market where they get amplified, but also because the rich countries protect their agriculture more, as Fig. 5.2 shows.

This protection, apart from affecting the world market prices, also alters the trading opportunities of the poorer countries. What is the net impact of such policies on hunger in the world?

Finally, the most important protective policy pursued by the rich countries is protection of their labour markets. This eliminates a major option for the poor—emigration to a more productive environment—that the European poor had in the last century.

(c) The questions posed and the approach

The observations made above indicate that policies of other countries can have consequences for the extent of hunger in a country. However, one would like to know how important these effects are. Do they make a small difference or a large one?

Some aspects of this question are explored in this chapter. In particular we pose the following questions:

1. To what extent does protection by the rich countries of consumers against price fluctuations that may, in the absence of such protection, result from production disturbances affect hunger in poor countries? Is the impact comparable to the impact of production disturbances in the poor countries themselves?
2. What is the impact of protection (to be general, distortions) provided to

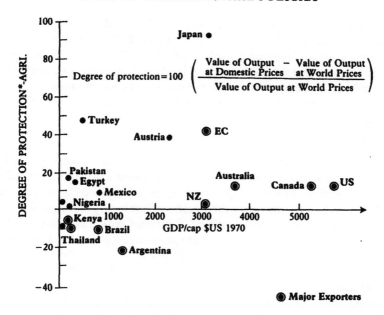

Fig. 5.2. Per capita GDP and agricultural protection

agricultural producers in the rich countries on hunger in the poor countries? And specifically, what is the impact on hunger of the distortions introduced in agricultural trade by the OECD countries?

3. What is the extent of loss in global output due to protection of labour markets in the world? What does it imply for the extent of hunger in the world?

These questions are explored with the help of the basic linked system (BLS) of national models developed by the Food and Agriculture Program (FAP) of the International Institute for Applied Systems Analysis (IIASA). The basic objectives and approach of FAP are described by Parikh and Rabar (1981). The BLS is a general equilibrium model of the global economy with emphasis on food and agriculture, with mainly national models as its constituents which are, in turn, also general equilibrium models.

In section 5.2, the modelling system is briefly described. In sections 5.3 to 5.5 results of scenarios are described which address the questions raised above. Finally some concluding comments are made in section 5.6.

5.2. A brief description of the BLS

A detailed description of the system, mathematical specifications, empirical elaborations, and its properties are given in Fisher, Frohberg, Keyzer, and Parikh (1988), and only a brief description is given here.

The system of linked national agricultural policy models was developed by the FAP of IIASA with the help of a network of collaborating institutions. It constitutes a system which lends itself to study the effect of alternative policy measures on the domestic food situation in given countries. These measures may be taken by their own governments, by the governments of other countries, or by international organizations which operate under specified international agreements.

(a) The BLS of national models

The system of linked national models is called the basic linked system (the BLS). The national models in the system cover more than 80 per cent of the world's food attributes like land, population, demand, production, trade, and so on. The remaining countries of the world are covered by fourteen simplified models comprising groups of countries. Countries which are likely to have similar relations with the world market are grouped together, like poor calorie importers of Africa, poor calorie self-sufficient African countries, Middle Eastern oil exporters, etc. Currently in the basic linked system there are three types of models:

1. models with common structure: Argentina, Australia, Austria, Brazil, Canada, EC, Egypt, Indonesia, Japan, Kenya, Mexico, New Zealand, Nigeria, Pakistan, Thailand, Turkey;
2. models with country-specific structure: CMEA, China, India, United States;
3. regional group models: African oil exporters, African medium-income exporters, African medium-income importers, African low-income exporters, African low-income importers, Latin American high-income exporters, Latin American high-income importers, Latin American medium-income countries, South-East Asian high–medium exporters, South-East Asian high–medium importers, Asian low-income countries, South-West Asian oil exporters, South-West Asian medium–low income countries, Rest of the World.

The common structure models are models developed at IIASA. Though they have a common structure they are individually estimated. The parameters are separately estimated for each country from country-specific data. Then there are some detailed models which are built outside IIASA/FAP which have not necessarily followed the common structure. These models have also relied on country-specific data and they embody much more country-specific policy structures. The third set of models consists of the country groups.

Though national models may have greater commodity detail, the international exchange among the national models takes place at the level of the following ten commodities: wheat, rice, coarse grains, bovine and ovine meats, dairy products, other animal products, protein feeds, other food, non-food agriculture, non-agriculture. The BLS is a dynamically recursive simulation model solved in yearly time steps.

(b) The nature of the BLS

The basic purpose has been to permit realistic policy analysis with the model and thus to find out what each national government might need to do for the cause of food security for all. It is far from easy to come to grips with the intricacies of national policies and to model those. This meant that we had to involve well-informed national modellers. In order to account for specific policy instruments and the responses of the various actors in each national system, actors should be distinguished, including the government, and their behaviour should be integrated through the classical accounting identities of quantities and financial flows. Thus each of the national models as well as the international system linking them has a general equilibrium framework. The major features of the approach are that it is a quantitative approach, that the parameters are empirically estimated, that it includes behavioural responses, that it is a general equilibrium framework which is comprehensive in the sense that it includes the whole economy, and the whole world without any unaccounted supply sources or demand sinks. This feature implies that there are no free lunches in this system. Moreover, it distinguishes nations and within nations various economic agents.

In the system national governments are important actors with a wide range of permitted policies. Taxes and transfers, tariffs, quotas, rationing, partial or total, are all permitted. Though one talks about determination of prices, it is not necessary in this system, or in the approach followed, that governments only select price as their adjusting instrument. Governments may decide to fix prices and let other things adjust. The models determine relative prices. Also there is no demand for money or foreign exchange, and the models are independent of exchange rates. The solution of the system does not only give a global agricultural balance sheet of commodity flows, but also traces how these come to be what they are, and under the influence of which policies. Not only does it provide international trade flows, but it also identifies the domestic supply and demand forces that determine exports and imports. Thus the system constitutes a tool to assess the impact on each country's domestic food situation brought about by a country's own government's policies as well as by policies of other governments.

Again one should emphasize what the basic linked system is, and what it is not. It is a powerful analytical engine to explore and to understand the impact of alternative policies. It is not, and one cannot emphasize this enough, a forecasting tool. If forecasting had been the main objective, a different model would have been built with more emphasis on statistical fits and less on economic structure.

(c) A typical national policy model of the FAP

The building blocks of the FAP model system are the national policy models. Each national model has to reflect the specific problems and characteristics of

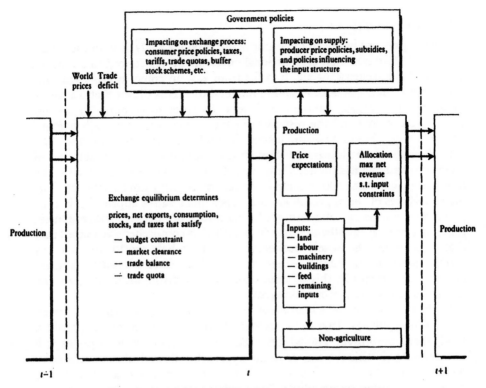

Fig. 5.3. Information flow in a typical national model

that particular nation. Although the national models do not differ in their structure, they are country specific in their contents, particularly in their descriptions of government policies. The model system of the FAP permits linking of such diverse models but requires that all national models meet a few conditions. They have to have a common sector classification at the international trade level (nine agricultural and one non-agricultural sectors, and some fairly reasonable additional technical requirements. For example, net exports have to be continuous functions of relative world prices and independent of their absolute level. Even though the national models differ from each other, the broad structure is common to most models. In some food supply and demand are distinguished by various income groups. The information flow in a typical model is shown in Fig. 5.3.

Past prices and government policies affect production decisions. The domestic production in each of the sectors of the economy accrues to each of the sectoral groups. The income this amounts to is determined by the price that these products command. For example, if farmers have grown two million tons of wheat and one million tons of rice, they would have an income of twice the price of a million tons of wheat plus the price of a million tons of rice, minus the cost of producing wheat and rice. These initial entitlements of the different products for the various groups may be redistributed by government policies.

Given these entitlements and world prices, groups trade among themselves under the influence of government policies, which include national market policies (price, buffer stock, trade), public finance policies (balance of payments, public demand, direct tax), and international market and finance policies (agreements on price, buffer stock, trade, financing).

The large variety of policy instruments available to governments in the model, as in reality, cannot be arbitrarily selected. For example, domestic production, domestic prices, stock changes, and trade levels are related. A domestic price target and a trade target cannot both be realized unless necessary stock changes are feasible. This problem is handled in the models by specifying target levels of various policy instruments along with upper and lower bounds on them, and prescribing a hierarchy of adjustments among these instruments. For instance one may let the stock level adjust first till it hits a bound, then let the trade level adjust till it also hits a bound, when the price must adjust. One may note that different specifications of this hierarchy imply different policies (Keyzer 1981). Once government policy is specified the resulting exchange equilibrium determines the domestic prices, net exports, tax rates, and the consumption patterns of different income groups whose demand behaviour is characterized by a linear expenditure system. In the process of exchange all the markets are cleared within the (national) balance of trade constraint and the income and resource constraints faced by the various actors. In the scenarios reported in the system, except for the US model, governments set price targets as functions of world prices, domestic self-sufficiency levels, and past prices. These functions transmit changes in world prices to domestic prices and were estimated from time-series data. No trade bounds were specified. Thus price targets are always realized. However, it may be noted that during each iteration of the international linkage described below, domestic price targets change as world prices vary. For the US model (Abkin 1985) instead of price transmission functions, a different scheme was used to reflect US practice.

(d) The international linkage

A first round of net exports of all the countries is calculated for an assumed set of world prices, and international market clearance is checked for each commodity. World prices are then revised using a non-differentiable optimizing algorithm and transmitted to the national models. Next, these generate new domestic equilibria and adjusted net exports for all countries. This process is repeated until the world markets are cleared in all commodities. The procedure is shown schematically in Fig. 5.4. At each stage of the iteration the domestic markets are in equilibrium. It may be noted that any international agency—such as a buffer stock agency—can be represented as a country, and

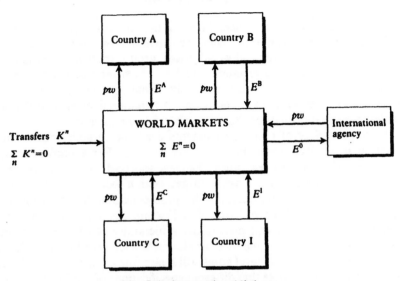

Fig. 5.4. International linkage

the effectiveness of its policies can be evaluated within a framework in which country policies react to the policies of the agency.

This process yields international prices as influenced by government policies. The outcome of this process is examined by governments who may change their policies for the next period. As agents in the model do not formulate expectations about government policies, issues of time consistency and the like do not arise in our models.

Since these steps are taken on a year-by-year basis a recursive dynamic simulation results. Simulations over fifteen-year periods are used to project the consequences of various policies, not only for individual countries but also for the entire system. The methodological approach and algorithms are described in Keyzer (1981).

(e) Difficulties of implementation, limitation, validation, and tuning

A major difficulty of general equilibrium models is that data are seldom available to estimate empirically the parameters of all the equations, and at the same time the model closure is not complete without all the equations.

Clearly, to the extent possible, parameters should be estimated empirically from time-series data (not benchmarked from a single year's synthetic SAM). In developing the BLS, we have as far as possible done so. Still some parameters had to be specified in an *ad hoc* way or based on 'engineering' information. Would it have been better to leave these equations out and settle for a partial analysis? The answer to this depends on the importance of what is left out.

If the parameters of a particular equation seriously affect the results of the problem being analysed, then one cannot leave that equation out of the system. Partial analysis which assumes away the impact of such an equation should also be suspect. One may have to admit that nothing meaningful can be said about the problem until better information is available.

Another difficulty raised against general equilibrium models is that they are too complex. The interdependences involved are so many that the results are not immediately transparent, and often one feels that almost any result can be obtained from such a system. Could one believe such results? While transparency is important for effectively communicating results, analytically it is not relevant. With experience and better understanding even complex systems become transparent. If the complexity exists in the economic system one has to understand it fully before a satisfactory simple caricature is made. Yet the issues raised above call for a thorough validation of the model.

In validating and tuning the models emphasis was placed on the fact that the primary purpose of developing the BLS is to obtain a medium-term policy analysis model and not a short-term forecasting one. Therefore it was considered unnecessary to incorporate short-term variations due to weather for any speculative behaviour resulting from such variations. However, in estimating the parameters weather effects were often accounted for. For policy analysis we want the BLS to track the central tendencies correctly.

The model system was 'validated' in three phases. In the first phase individual national models which were mostly estimated using data for the period 1960–76 were tested in a stand-alone mode (i.e. unlinked to other models) with given world prices over the period 1970 to 1980. For each of some seventy endogenous state variables generated by the model, values were regressed against the observed values. Ideally, the slopes of these regressions should be 1.0 and their intercept zero. The frequency distribution of the slopes estimated from regressions on which zero intercept condition was imposed was used to judge the model. These distributions for the different national models were considered satisfactory.

In the second phase the country models were run up to the year 2000, again in a stand-alone mode with given world prices.

In the last phase of the validation process a series of 'linked runs' with full interaction between the individual national models within the global exchange system were carried out.

The objective in phases 2 and 3 was to test whether the models behave reasonably. Since this is a very subjective notion, specifications and parameters were changed in individual models only in case of extreme results. The outcome of this process was to generate certain base runs.

(f) Exogenous and endogenous variables in the BLS

A number of important variables remain exogenous, though for a large and complex model system such as this the exogenous variables form only a small part of the total. The more important of these are discussed in summary form below:

- *Population* and its growth is taken from the latest UN and ILO sources (median projections), but for some individual countries, e.g. India, these have been adjusted by the latest national information and projections. Similarly, the participation rate in the total labour force is defined exogenously, but the allocation of the labour force between agriculture and the rest of the economy is endogenized.
- *Land* available for cultivation is exogenous and the data are taken predominantly from FAO sources and from specific national estimates. This also includes the development of land over time.
- *Rates of total investment* as a share of the GDP are estimated from the historical period and after a period of adjustment in the early 1980s they are kept constant. Some exceptions exist to this, e.g. India, where the investment rate changes exogenously over time.
- A number of important exogenous assumptions are made for the '*Rest of the World*', i.e. the group of residual countries which are modelled only in groups for inclusion in the system. These include growth rates for both agricultural and non-agricultural production based on past performance. The outputs, however, do respond to changes in world prices.

(g)   The reference scenario, welfare indicators, and comparisons for policy evaluation

As is usual in such analysis, results of simulated policy scenarios of the model will be compared with those of a reference scenario. Since the reference scenario provides only a basis of comparison, it need not be described in detail. Suffice it to say that it assumes continuation of present policy regimes, and generates growth from 1980 to 2000 comparable to that realized over the 1970s.

The simulations are carried out over 1980 to 2000 and policy changes are introduced over 1982–5 depending on the scenario.

Comparisons in general are expressed as a percentage change of the particular variable from its value in the reference scenario. Moreover, three-year averages of the values of the variables are taken for comparison. The indicators used to compare scenarios are as follows:

(i)   *Gross domestic product*   Gross domestic product (GDP), with all its well-known limitations, is the most commonly used and widely known indicator of economic development. However, before comparing the GDPs of two scenarios one should note that such a comparison suffers from all the well-known index number problems. The outcome of the comparison can be affected by the prices used.

In aggregating GDPs of different countries, base year (1970) world market prices are also used. Aggregation using 1970 domestic prices and exchange rates, in the reference run situation where countries have different protection levels on the same commodity, could lead to substantially different weights being given to similar production activities in different countries.

The following GDP indicators are calculated:

1. GDP at constant domestic prices using the divisia price index with 1970 as the base year;
2. per capita GDP in $US based on 1970 domestic prices and exchange rate;
3. GDP at 1970 world prices in $US.

(ii) *Equivalent income*   Equivalent income corresponding to a consumption bundle is defined as the income required under a reference set of prices to obtain the same utility as is provided by the given consumption bundle.

The equivalent income corresponding to alternate consumption bundles may be compared. The one with higher equivalent income provides a higher level of utility and thus indicates improvement in consumer welfare.

If the consumer demand systems have an underlying utility function, equivalent income can be calculated.

It may be noted that this notion is similar to Hicksian equivalent variation measure.

(iii) *'Real income': consumption cost comparisons*   Not all the national models of the BLS have demand systems with explicitly defined utility functions behind them. It is therefore not possible to calculate the equivalent income measure for all the national models. Because of this difficulty, a 'real income' comparison is also made between the costs of the consumption bundles purchased in the two situations or scenarios. If at the prices prevailing in a policy scenario, say a trade liberalization scenario, the cost of the actual consumption basket is greater than the cost of the consumption basket of the reference run, one can say that consumers are better off in the policy scenario. This is because they could have purchased the reference run consumption basket had they wanted to.

A similar comparison is also made at the reference run prices. The two comparisons should be consistent, otherwise an inconsistency in the demand system is indicated. Let P_t, P_r and C_t, C_r be prices and consumption in the policy scenario and reference scenario respectively. The possibilities are summarized in Table 5.3.

The real income comparisons are made for the consumers of the country as a whole as in most of the models consumers are not separated into different

Table 5.3 Real income: consumption cost comparison

	$P_t C_t > P_t C_r$	$P_t C_t < P_t C_r$
$P_r C_t > P_r C_r$	C_t better than C_r	Indeterminate
$P_r C_t < P_r C_r$	Inconsistent	C_r better than C_t

income groups. Thus it is possible that even when the aggregate real income in a country goes up, the poor in it may become worse off.

(iv) *Calorie and protein intakes per capita* While average calorie and protein intakes are important determinants of the nutritional status of the population, by themselves (i.e. without information on nutritional norm and income distribution) they do not give a precise indication of hunger, though changes in them across scenarios do suggest the direction of change in it.

(v) *Population suffering from hunger* In order to evaluate the impact on hunger in different countries and in the world it would be useful to generate an indicator. Excepting for the model of India, the models do not endogenize income distribution. Moreover, comparable estimates of persons in hunger are not available for most countries for more than a year or two.

Thus, we lack adequate independent observations to postulate and estimate a relationship between the number of hungry persons based on the variables generated in the model. None the less to evaluate the impact of policies on social welfare an indicator on hunger is needed.

Country-wise estimates of the number of hungry persons have been given by FAO's (1977) *Fourth World Food Survey*. Their estimates have been obtained by stipulating that calorie consumption distribution in a country is skewed and can be represented by a beta distribution. The parameters of these distributions are estimated for each country based on certain assumptions, country-specific data, and some cross-country comparisons. The same procedure, in principle, can be embodied in the model to generate estimated number of hungry persons. Since the estimated parameters of the beta distributions are not reported in the FAO study and since the procedure uses judgement in some cases, it is difficult to use it in a simulation model.

Instead, what is done is to fit a cross-country regression to FAO estimates to recover the FAO methodology in a reduced form which can be easily used in simulation. Using the data for the years 1969–71 for fifty-eight countries for which FAO provides estimates of percentage of population in hunger, the following regression was estimated.

$$\text{HUNGRY} = \begin{cases} 100 & \text{for CALAR} \leq 52.1 \\ 0.01338(138.6 - \text{CALAR})^2 & \text{for CALAR} \leq 138.6 \quad R^2 = 0.87 \\ 0 & \text{for CALAR} > 138.6 \end{cases}$$

where

HUNGRY: percentage of the population with calorie intake levels of less than 1.2 times the basal metabolic rate;

CALAR: calorie availability as a percentage of requirement estimated by FAO food balance sheet information for availability and FAO/WHO nutritional standards' minimum average requirements.

The functional form chosen implies that the percentage of population in hunger becomes zero when CALAR reaches 138.6. It may be noted that this value was estimated. The high value of R^2 should be no surprise as the left-hand side variable used in the regression was generated in the first place by the FAO based on the right-hand side variable and income distribution.

5.3. *Impact on hunger of consumer protection against price fluctuations in the rich countries*

To explore the impact on world hunger of the rich countries' protection of their consumers against domestic price fluctuations, two scenarios are generated. In these scenarios weather shocks lead to crop failures, in one scenario in the developed countries and in the other in the developing countries.

If there is a drought in a poor country more people will suffer from hunger than in a year of normal weather. If, however, there is a food production failure in a rich country, that will also probably result in similar increases in the number of hungry persons in the same poor country. Changed circumstances in the world agricultural system caused by food shortages require all economic agents to adapt their behaviour accordingly. Consumers in rich countries where food constitutes a relatively small share of total expenditures have a wide range of choices to minimize the loss in their perceived utility. Poverty, on the other hand, leaves no choice but hunger (apart from violence and political upheaval) as the only way of adjustment. Two BLS scenarios have been formulated to demonstrate the effects of bad harvests in rich developed countries on one hand as well as production failures of a similar magnitude in developing countries on the other hand. A 5 per cent reduction in crop yields has been applied in developed countries of the northern hemisphere, i.e. Austria, Canada, Japan, Turkey, United States, EC, CMEA, and the group 'Rest of the World' (mainly consisting of European countries). In the second variant of the 'weather shock' scenario the same 5 per cent reduction of crop output has been implemented in the OECD countries of the southern hemisphere (Australia and New Zealand) and all developing countries except China. The model of China (see Neunteufel 1985) used in the BLS may be looked at as a generator of consistent scenarios but does not contain all the feedback mechanisms desirable for this scenario.

It has to be noted that the shock scenarios have been implemented by curtailing current crop output in specific years by 5 per cent. Therefore, in the first year of the three-year shock period production will be lower by exactly that amount compared to the reference scenario R0. In the subsequent years, however, higher prices on the world market generally also lead to higher supply, thereby partly counteracting the output reduction due to the shock.

In both the scenarios, termed WS-NORTH (weather shock in the North) and WS-SOUTH (weather shock in the South), the shocks are applied over two periods of three consecutive years each, namely 1983–5 and 1993–5.

The weather shocks result in lower crop production and higher world market prices as shown in Table 5.4. Note that the last three agricultural commodities in Table 5.4 (protein feed, other food, and non-food agriculture) also include considerable amounts of animal by-products like offals, fish meal, animal fats, and wool, which explains why the supply reduction for these aggregate commodities is far below 5 per cent, since our scenario implementation only affects the respective crop sectors.

The changes in world market prices are different in the two scenarios as can be expected from the unequal shares of each country group in global production.

Aggregate agricultural prices rise steeply during the shock years. They fall after the shock years below the reference run value because of the larger investments made in agriculture during the high price years of the weather shock. A production shortfall in the North is mostly transmitted to the world market and not absorbed domestically, whereas a production shortfall in the developing countries is largely absorbed domestically. Thus agricultural prices rise (and fall) much more in the WS-NORTH scenario than in the WS-SOUTH.

The reduced availability of food and consequent higher prices can be expected to reduce calorie intake and increase the number of hungry people. Table 5.5 shows that the calorie loss in developing countries is similar in both the weather shock scenarios.

Table 5.4 Percentage change in production and world market prices in the 'weather shock' scenarios relative to reference run, averaged over 1983–1985

Commodity	Weather shock in the north				Weather shock in the south			
	Price	Production			Price	Production		
		Total	North	South		Total	North	South
Wheat	35	−3.1	−4.3	−0.1	10	−1.2	−0.4	−4.7
Rice, milled	13	−0.4	−4.9	−0.0	38	−2.1	0.8	−3.6
Coarse grains	50	−2.7	−4.3	2.5	15	−1.0	−0.1	−4.6
Bovine and ovine meat	8	−0.3	0.0	−0.7	5	−0.2	0.1	−0.6
Dairy products	11	−0.5	−0.3	−1.5	5	−0.3	0.1	−1.0
Other meat and fish	5	−0.7	−1.0	−1.1	2	−0.4	−0.5	−0.7
Protein feed	25	−0.6	−1.0	0.7	6	0.0	2.0	−4.3
Other food	11	−0.6	−1.6	0.7	13	−1.0	1.3	−2.8
Non-food products	6	−0.3	0.0	−0.6	4	−0.4	−0.1	−0.7
Total agriculture	15	−1.3	−1.8	0.1	11	−0.7	0.3	−2.7
Net calorie prod.		−2.2	−5.0	1.4		−1.4	0.9	−4.2

Note: −0.0 means the value was not exactly zero.

Table 5.5 Percentage change in average daily calorie consumption in the 'weather shock' scenarios relative to reference run (1983–1985)

Country group	WS-NORTH (%)	WS-SOUTH (%)
Developing (excl. China)	−1.5	−1.5
Middle-income	−1.5	−1.2
Low–middle-income	−0.9	−1.1
Low-income	−1.9	−2.0
Developed market economies (excluding USA)	−0.2	−0.2
CMEA	−0.1	−0.0

Note: −0.0 means the value was not exactly zero.

The number in hunger (see Table 5.6) is larger in a number of developing countries in the case of WS-NORTH than in WS-SOUTH. One reason is that the size of the shock is larger in WS-NORTH. Moreover, as mentioned earlier, prices also rise more in WS-NORTH. In particular wheat and coarse grain prices increase much more when the shock is in the North and many developing countries rely on imports of these grains.

The impact of these weather shocks on different expenditure classes is even more tellingly demonstrated in the model of India. The policy model for India (Narayana, Parikh, and Srinivasan 1987, 1990) used in the BLS distinguishes five rural and five urban income classes permitting a thorough analysis of income and nutritional impacts within and across sectors of the Indian economy. For each of the ten classes an equivalent income indicator is calculated which expresses per capita income needed for a particular class to obtain a consumption bundle at a reference set of prices which would provide the same utility as provided by the current consumption bundle. Per capita income in a given population class depends on equilibrium prices, ownership of commodity endowments, tax levels, and also on procurement and distribution of foodgrains by the government. In the Indian model the amount of grains distributed to poor urban consumers at subsidized prices reacts to absolute levels as well as to changes in domestic grain production. Whenever foodgrain supply per capita improves, distribution per capita is reduced and vice versa. Similarly, procurement of cereals at prices below the market prices rises with higher government grain distribution levels and falls as production goes down. These model features imply for our 'weather shock' scenario that foodgrain distribution by the government will increase and procurement will fall with respect to the reference run in the case of a domestic crop failure (WS-SOUTH) but will hardly change when developed countries experience the supply shocks. Consequently, poor consumers are exposed to price increases resulting from crop failures in developed countries, whereas some compensation is given to them when domestic crop production fails. In both

Table 5.6 Number of people in hunger: scenarios WS-NORTH and WS-SOUTH relative to reference scenario in 1983–1985

Country	Reference run	WS-NORTH change in scenario		WS-SOUTH change in scenario	
	m.	m.	%	m.	%
Argentina	0.6	0.0	5.5	0.0	6.4
Brazil	10.7	0.6	5.6	0.6	5.2
Egypt	0.6	0.1	11.4	0.0	3.3
India	211.7	21.8	10.3	4.8	10.3
Indonesia	13.5	0.0	−0.1	1.5	11.3
Kenya	5.7	0.5	9.1	0.3	5.4
Mexico	3.5	0.3	10.0	0.4	10.3
Nigeria	19.2	0.6	3.3	1.2	6.4
Pakistan	9.1	0.5	5.2	0.5	5.8
Thailand	7.3	0.2	2.4	0.6	7.8
Turkey	1.0	0.0	3.4	0.0	2.1
Regional groups	207.4	15.7	7.6	15.0	7.2
Developing	490.0	40.4	8.2	42.1	8.6
Middle-income	43.0	6.0	14.1	4.5	10.5
Low–middle	101.0	6.6	6.5	8.8	8.7
Low-income	346.0	27.8	8.0	28.9	8.4

cases balance of payments constraints cause price changes to be transmitted to them. Table 5.7 shows how equivalent income and food consumption (measured in terms of average daily calorie intake) of different income groups are affected in comparison to the levels observed in the reference scenario.

Table 5.7 shows that the poor in both rural and urban areas suffer more when the crops fail in the North than when they fail in India. When crops fail in the South, the Indian government knows in advance, as India is part of the South, that the harvest is poor and it steps up its subsidized public food distribution programme, insulating somewhat the poor consumers against higher price of food. When crops fail in the US, the Indian government may not take such measures until after the world prices increase. Even then, balance of payments constraints hamper imports and thus the price increases get reflected in prices in India.

The simulation results support quite impressively the previous statement that the nutritional consequences of a crop failure, wherever it occurs, will always be borne by poor consumers in developing countries. A crop failure by definition leads to an increase in the relative price of food. However, the increases in relative magnitudes of relative prices and hunger due to crop failures in different parts of the world are important for evaluating alternative policies. The model scenarios provide this information for different countries and that is the worth of the model. The effect in the different scenarios may not

Table 5.7 Change in equivalent income and average daily calorie consumption of rural and urban income classes in India: 'weather shock' scenarios relative to reference run in years 1983–1985

	Population share:	Equivalent income			Calories per day		
	Reference run (%)	Reference run (Rs[a]/person)	Change in scenario WS-North (%)	WS-South (%)	Reference run (Kcal/cap/per day)	Change in scenario WS-North (%)	WS-South (%)
Rural classes							
Lowest	28	132.1	−2.4	−1.7	1,007[b]	−6.8	−3.3
Low to middle	64	249.2	−2.4	−2.0	1,699	−5.4	−3.3
All classes	100	485.1	0.3	−1.5	2,182	−2.8	−2.7
Urban classes							
Lowest	26	346.1	−2.2	−1.5	1,790	−4.0	−2.8
Low to middle	60	492.6	−1.7	−1.4	2,072	−2.8	−2.4
All classes	100	773.7	−1.2	−1.3	2,424	−1.9	−2.0

[a] 1970 prices, $US1 = 7.5 Rs.

[b] The very low calorie intake for the poorest groups may not include all the calories consumed by them. The household consumption surveys in India, on which the demand system is based, ascribes consumption to those who pay for it. Thus payments in kind, such as food eaten by an employee in the employer's house, may be ascribed to the employer rather than the employee.

be the same for a particular country or a particular income class within a country, yet on an aggregate scale the statement seems to hold. Just as it matters little to the dead whether the origin of his demise was in the West or in the East, the poor are hurt by high world market prices regardless of what has brought those about. The protection against domestic food price fluctuations that the rich countries provide to their consumers accentuates increases in the world market prices that result from crop failure in any part of the world. The higher world prices of food increase the number of hungry people in the world.

5.4. *Protection of agricultural producers in the OECD countries: impact on hunger in the developing countries*

As pointed out earlier the rich countries protect their agricultural producers more than the poor countries do. Positive protections reflect themselves in increased supplies of agricultural commodities to the world market which are produced at relatively high cost and require subsidies for final buyers. This reduces the scope and attractiveness of export sales for low-cost producers, particularly if their resources are inadequate to provide export subsidies also. In this sense, the market climate has deteriorated progressively over the years for wheat, coarse grains, dairy products, sugar, and meat. In addition, these distortions have caused others in their wake: high domestic sugar prices and low maize prices in the US give a competitive edge to the production of high-fructose corn syrup. Its by-product, maize-gluten, is exported to the EC where it is a cheap grain substitute for feeding animals and adds indirectly to cereal surpluses to be exported with subsidies by the EC.

Similarly, dairy surpluses are provided as aid to India, depressing local milk prices to producers and slowing the growth of domestic milk production. At the same time India exports animal feeds to the EC where these fetch a high price due to expensive cereals in the EC with which they compete. Although India could produce four times the amount of milk received from the EC if it used presently exported animal feeds domestically, this is unlikely to happen as the present pattern of trade and production is benefiting India's balance of payments.

There are numerous examples of this kind, showing how countries are either hurt as competing exporters of agricultural products, or reap a benefit for their consumers through cheap imports, or gain from the distortions through exports of substitutes for protected products. Long-term effects in terms of changes in production and consumption patterns may be equally diverse, and depend for their continuity on the requirement that prevailing protectionist policies are not changed. In turn this implies that a lowering of protective barriers will have both positive and negative effects on other countries and that the results are far from easy to predict.

Removal of agricultural protection by OECD countries would alter world market prices of agricultural commodities. In general one would expect food prices to increase. The impact on a developing country would depend on the extent to which these increases in the world market prices are transmitted to domestic markets, the changes in relative domestic prices, changes in factor allocations between sectors, and the resulting changes in its GDP and growth. Even when income increases (decreases) the poor may be worse (better) off if food prices move adversely (favourably).

To explore these impacts a scenario in which the OECD countries remove their agricultural trade protection is simulated. We have presumed that:

- protective barriers affecting agricultural trade are entirely abolished, not just reduced somewhat, for all agricultural commodities at the same time, without exceptions;
- only distortions relating to trade are removed and input subsidies, production quotas, etc. are not removed except in the US (where policies relating to land set aside, loan rates, etc. are liberalized) and Canada (where milk production quota is removed);
- for the non-agriculture sector protective barriers are maintained.

Thus in this scenario trade liberalization is partial. Trade distortions among all agricultural commodities are fully removed, but that between the agricultural sector and the non-agricultural sector is only partially removed. Since, at least for the developed market economies, protection rates for the non-agriculture sector as a whole are very small, trade liberalization as defined here should capture much of the impact of liberalization.

Liberalization is carried out over a five-year period beginning from 1982 so that 1986 is the first year of full liberalization. With trade liberalization by the OECD countries[1] the world market prices of agricultural products relative to non-agriculture would be higher by 9 per cent by the year 2000 compared to the reference run (see Table 5.8). This modest average increase, however, is misleading because its modest level is strongly influenced by the very small increase in the price of the commodity group with a high weight and facing relatively low protection in the OECD countries, namely 'other food', dominated by fruits, vegetables, and tropical products.

In fact, for the commodities of primary importance to the producers in OECD countries, such as cereals, protein feed, and animal products, the world market price increases compared to the reference scenario are of the order of 10 to 20 per cent and, for dairy products, more than 30 per cent.

How do these price changes affect the developing countries? As developing countries do not change their protection policies in the OECD free trade scenario, the higher world market prices influence their domestic markets as

[1] The countries that liberalize in this scenario are: Australia, Austria, Canada, EC, Japan, New Zealand, and USA, for which explicit models exist in the BLS. Turkey is excluded from liberalization in this scenario as one of the less developed OECD countries. The other OECD countries included in a country group model also liberalize.

Table 5.8 Changes in world market prices and global net exports in 2000 in the OECD free trade scenario (% of reference scenario value in 2000)

	Relative prices	Global net exports[a]
Wheat	18	−2
Rice	21	37
Coarse grains	11	−5
Bovine and ovine products	17	35
Dairy products	31	13
Other animal products	−0	17
Protein feed	13	5
Other food	5	10
Non-food agriculture	−2	5
Total agriculture[b]	9	—
Non-agriculture	0	17

[a] Changes in quantities; Global net exports are defined as sum of net exports of countries who are net exporters; for total agriculture change in aggregate export index weighted by 1970 world prices is reported.
[b] Price weighted by production.
[c] −0 means value was not exactly zero.

determined by the price transmission mechanisms and the production structure. Hence, there is a great variation in the resulting domestic price increase, from a few percentage points in most cases to around 10 per cent in some cases, such as for Argentina and Kenya. The resulting changes in sectoral GDPs and factor use are summarized in Table 5.9 for the year 2000.

As expected agricultural price relative to that of non-agriculture increases in most developing countries modelled explicitly in the system. More labour and capital are used in agriculture and agricultural GDP at 1970 prices goes up. Since total capital stock is larger in most countries, GDP at 1970 prices also increases in many countries but not all.

OECD trade liberalization increases global GDP in the year 2000, calculated at 1970 world prices, by 0.22 per cent (see Table 5.10). Though 0.22 per cent is a small amount it is not negligible. In absolute terms the 0.22 per cent increase amounts to nearly $US25 billion 1970. Valued at 1980 $US this would amount to $US50 billion whereas official development assistance given by OECD countries in 1980 was around $US27 billion. The gain for the OECD countries in GDP valued at 1970 world prices is 0.57 per cent in 2000 which is nearly $US30 billion 1970. At these prices the loss of developing countries is only 0.02 per cent of GDP in 2000.

The small effect on the global GDP at constant prices can also be an outcome of the fact that agriculture in the OECD countries is a small part of the economy. The efficiency gains to be realized by removing agricultural trade distortions may be expected to be small. Another indicator of global welfare that is generated in the scenarios is per capita calorie intake. The calorie intake

Table 5.9 Changes in sectoral GDPs and factor use: OECD free trade over reference scenario for the year 2000 (%)

	P_A/P_{NA} Relative prices of agriculture	GDP70$_{ag}$ Agricultural value added[a]	GDP70$_{NA}$ Non-agricultural value added[a]	L_{ag} Agricultural labour input	Agricultural capital stock	Total acreage	Total capital
Developed countries							
Positively protected							
Japan	−35	−5	0.4	−5	−22	−6.0	−0.6
EC	−9	−7	0.4	−12	−5	−2.2	−0.1
USA	−2	2	0.1	—	—	2.5	—
Negatively protected							
New Zealand	16	14	−0.0	3	30	—	4.5
Canada	16	17	−0.5	20	21	2.4	0.1
Australia	14	3	0.1	4	14	4.3	0.9
Austria	8	1	—	2	2	−0.0	0.3
Developing countries							
Argentina	12	14	−1.4	15	20	1.4	1.5
Kenya	11	5	0.6	—	12	—	3.8
Brazil	8	1	−0.3	1	10	4.4	0.1
Thailand	8	3	−0.3	—	7	—	1.0
Egypt	5	2	−1.6	2	6	3.2	0.1
Turkey	1	6	−1.2	3	7	1.3	0.5
Pakistan	1	3	−1.2	2	3	0.6	0.5
Indonesia	2	0	−0.0	0	2	−0.0	0.5
India	3	0	0.1	0	—	0.0	0.5
Nigeria	0	7	0.1	5	8	4.6	2.2
Mexico	−1	4	−2.4	6	3	−0.0	−1.0

[a]At 1970 prices.

Table 5.10 · Percentage change in GDPs due to OECD trade liberalization compared to reference scenario ($US10⁹ 1970)

	World		OECD		CMEA		Developing countries	
	Reference scenario	% change	Reference scenario	% change	Reference scenario	% change	Reference scenario	% change
1990	7,558	0.17	4,034	0.30	1,218	−0.09	1,492	0.12
2000	10,841	0.22	5,433	0.57	1,777	−0.40	2,503	−0.02

ªGDP calculated using 1970 *world* prices.

Table 5.11 Per capita calorie intake and hunger under OECD trade liberalization in developing countries

	1990		2000	
	Reference scenario	% change	Reference scenario	% change
Calorie intake Kcal/person/day	2,510	−0.13	2,640	−0.3
Persons hungry (10^6)	470	3.30	400	3.6

calculations do not suffer from the index number problem to the same extent as the GDP measure does.

The average per capita calorie intake in the developing countries decreases under agricultural trade liberalization by OECD countries and consequently the incidence of hunger increases (see Table 5.11). Though at the global level the impacts of trade liberalization by OECD countries are small, at the level of individual countries they could be significant. The country-wise impact for the developing countries is shown in Table 5.12.

It may be noted that the large percentage changes in the number of hungry persons for some of the countries (e.g. Argentina and Nigeria in 2000) result from low levels of hunger in the reference scenario.

These results, further details of which are given in Parikh, Fischer, Frohberg, and Gulbrandsen (1988), show that even when a country gains in

Table 5.12 Impact on developing countries of agricultural trade liberalization by OECD countries

Country	% change over the reference scenario					
	GDP at 1970 world prices		Equivalent income		Persons hungry	
	1990	2000	1990	2000	1990	2000
Argentina	1.1	1.0	0.7	2.1	18.4	6.7
Brazil	−0.3	−0.3	−0.9	−0.9	10.1	12.3
Mexico	−0.8	−2.0	−0.9	−1.9	12.4	8.8
Egypt	0.3	−0.9	−0.3	−1.2	0.0	0.0
Kenya[a]	0.3	1.7	1.0	2.5	−8.1	−8.8
Nigeria	1.5	1.9	0.0	1.5	4.0	−47.4
India	0.2	0.1	−0.5	−0.2	3.1	5.6
Indonesia	−0.9	−0.4	−2.6	−1.5	1.0	0.0
Pakistan	2.3	1.2	1.3	1.0	18.8	8.1
Thailand[a]	0.7	0.7	1.3	1.2	−1.3	1.0
Turkey	0.2	−0.3	0.1	−0.1	4.6	1.7

[a] Refers to consumption cost comparison instead of equivalent income.

consumer welfare on the average (as reflected in equivalent income) it may have a larger number of hungry people, as is seen for Argentina, Pakistan, and Thailand. Also even when a country increases its GDP consumers may be worse off and hunger may increase.

Thus what is seen is that removal of current protection on agricultural commodities by the OECD countries would increase the number of hungry in the world by 3 to 4 per cent. Though this may seem a marginal increase, for people on the margin of existence, marginal impacts can be deadly. The impact on hunger for some of the individual developing countries is not so marginal. Thus one has to conclude that the policies of OECD countries to protect their agriculture are in general beneficial to the hungry in the world.

It must be emphasized, however, that in our model some of the commodities of interest to developing country exporters such as sugar and beverages are part of a large aggregate called other food. The impact of such protective policies on particular developing countries that export these commodities, including the impact on hunger in these countries, can be significantly adverse.

Another qualification that needs to be emphasized is that liberalization by OECD countries of trade in agricultural commodities in this scenario does not include liberalization of textiles and other manufactured products. Removal of protection from such products can be of a much greater and different consequence for the developing countries.

5.5. *Protection of labour markets: loss in global output and implication for hunger*

How did the countries which are now able to provide more than adequate food to all of their inhabitants escape from the predicament of hunger? In fact large parts of their populations were vulnerable to food shortages two centuries ago, or even more recently. Part of the story can be told in terms of the internal factors that were at work: technological progress, rising marginal productivity of labour, larger markets for new products, and finally such a demand for labour that social welfare systems could be established which provide food security for all.

But one should not neglect the external factors at work which helped to maintain the economic expansion and eased a number of frictions away. International trade in a liberal environment was important, as was the supply of cheap raw materials from newly acquired colonies. Nor should it be forgotten that labour surpluses could find their way into new lands abroad; entire continents, only sparsely populated, were there to be settled by Europeans who abandoned their agricultural livelihood but could not be absorbed in the industrialization process at home, and therefore crossed the oceans in search of more secure income opportunities. It is not an accident that the countries which were settled by them have become the largest agricultural exporters, particularly of staple crops. Nor is it an accident that these migrants have gradually closed the doors behind themselves.

By now, natural resources including land have been completely carved up into nation states and massive migration is no longer an option: today there is no longer a new world to go to. Natural resources are distributed quite unevenly as compared to the distribution of people. This applies to fertile land and to minerals. Is it reasonable to expect, under these circumstances, that poor countries could follow the example of the rich? In a world divided by fences, some to keep people out from where resources are abundant, others to keep them in where the endowment is poor, their chances to escape from poverty are severely limited, even when the international framework for trade and capital flows is a fairly liberal one. The modelling system presented here can be used to illustrate why, even in a world with free mobility of all goods, services, and capital, poverty could persist as long as labour markets are protected.

If for socio-political reasons the fences are kept, then one should realize that these work in the same way as any other import quota in international trade and that compensation of the losers is a relevant economic issue. If one accepts the neo-classical model as free trade advocates do, one should also recognize the fact that all arguments from welfare theory which advocate free trade in commodities and open capital markets will hold *a fortiori* for labour services. Opposition to migration then amounts to opposition to free trade.

Though our modelling system does not have some of the features needed to explore satisfactorily scenarios of international migration, with some assumptions, admittedly heroic ones, it was possible to generate some scenarios. It was assumed that

1. migrants acquire the skills and life-style of the country to which they have immigrated as soon as they have arrived there;
2. the costs of migration are negligible;
3. large-scale migration would be tolerated and would not disrupt the economies of the countries of origin and destinations and the migrants do not repatriate any of their earnings;
4. migration was driven by the differences in per capita incomes between country and the global average.

In a scenario in which nearly 300 million persons were relocated over a fifteen-year period, the sum of the GDP at 1970 world prices of the countries of the world at the end of this period increased by more than 20 per cent, which amounts to more than $US1,000 billion at 1970 prices. This admittedly very crude estimate indicates how large the extent of the global economic loss is.

The level of hunger in the developing countries from which migration takes place gets reduced by nearly 50 per cent by the year 2000. In the scenario no repatriation by migrants of their earnings was assumed. A modest level of repatriation would amount to large flows to developing countries which could make a dramatic reduction in the level of hunger in the world.

What one can conclude is that the policy of developed countries that has the most impact on hunger in the world is protection of their labour markets.

5.6. *Concluding comments*

These scenarios have not only demonstrated that policies of developed countries to protect their agricultural producers and consumers affect hunger in the LDCs, but have also given ideas of the size of these effects.

Protection of domestic consumers against food price fluctuations by the rich countries results in a global food system in which the poor always adjust to fluctuations in supply be they in the developed countries or in the developing ones. Whenever there is a supply shortfall, whether in the North or in the South, hunger in the poor countries increases. When there is a fall in domestic food production, the rich countries import more food, increase the world market prices, and the food-exporting developing countries export more food and food-importing countries import less food. In either case domestic food availability declines and the number of persons in hunger increases.

Protection of agricultural producers in the rich countries on the whole reduces hunger in the world. Though the reduction in number of hungry in the world is only around 3 to 4 per cent, some countries benefit much more, and hunger in some countries increases as well.

Removal of these protective policies will increase hunger in the world, though in some countries hunger will be reduced by it. Protection of agricultural producers increases food supply on the world market and lowers world market prices. Lower food prices benefit the poor and hunger is reduced.

Protection of domestic labour markets by the developed countries is the protective policy that affects the poor countries most. Removal of such protection can lead to a dramatic reduction of hunger (nearly 50 per cent in the developing countries out of which migration was permitted in the scenario). Protection of labour markets is the most important form of protection in the world as far as hunger is concerned. Removal of such protection is politically extremely difficult. What other policies can help reduce hunger in the world? A number of other international and national policies were explored with the BLS to assess their impact on hunger. These results are described in detail in a forthcoming monograph, Fischer, Frohberg, Keyzer, Parikh, and Tims (1990). Here it is possible to give only a brief summary of these results.

(a)   *No solution through markets*

The various scenarios dealing with alternative international measures to change the working of the world food system clearly reveal the problem. Any attempt to operate through national and world food markets fails for the simple reason that, lacking purchasing power, the hungry are only marginal participants in the market. Attempts to reach them through the markets leads to adjustments elsewhere and in the new equilibrium the poor usually remain as badly off as before.

In short the market mechanism creates a world food system which is resilient for the rich, but intractable for the starving. Chronic hunger is a stubbornly persistent feature of a market-orientated food system.

(b) Increases in global food supply do not help

Policy interventions specifically designed to improve global food supplies do not increase adequately the food consumed by the poor. The system adjusts to provide food at reasonable cost to those who have the money to buy it, but does not increase adequately the food consumed by the hungry. This finding applies to a number of popular notions about ways to improve the food intake of the poor, as demonstrated by a set of scenarios which increase agricultural supplies in the world market. These include increased production in the developed countries, letting farmers in those countries take care of the hungry; scenarios which assume reduced waste and overconsumption, or missing a meal; reducing meat consumption to save on feedgrains and to increase cereal availability for people instead.

Why are measures to increase global supplies not effective? Model simulations show that:

- additional food supplies on the world market are absorbed through adjustments of the behaviour of producers, consumers, and governments who are endowed with purchasing power; the hungry do not improve their incomes and consequently do not eat more food;
- consumption reductions in the rich countries lead to adjustments of prices, trade, and production which together nullify any additional food supplies to the poor.

(c) Policies that increase domestic food supplies in developing countries also help little

The results of additional incentives to farmers in developing countries are disappointing or even negative. Simulations show that:

- production in the developing countries indeed is raised, but partly for additional exports, whereas consumers are worse off due to higher prices;
- agricultural trade liberalization in both industrial and developing market economy countries increases relative prices of agriculture and changes sector proportion significantly in some countries but these 'right prices' have a very small impact on aggregate GDP and only negligible effects on the poor; whereas
- agricultural trade liberalization by the developing countries alone has somewhat larger (though still marginal) beneficial effects.

This is not surprising, as poverty and hunger relate to limited resource endowments and these are not really changed by price policies alone. Price policies may in fact increase the value of the resources not in the hands of the poor relative to the resources—mainly labour—which they do have.

(d)   Non-market measures by the developing countries can work but are
limited by resource availability

Subsidized food rations, rural works programmes or other schemes to benefit unemployed labour can give the poor more income and better access to food markets.

It is obvious that the problem is the constraint on resources. Both finance and managerial ability are scarce resources, and their diversion to programmes to alleviate poverty retards overall economic growth. Explorations with some national models of developing countries show that the trade-off between growth and redistribution is significant. Redistribution that can significantly reduce hunger would result in a drastic fall in growth, and is unlikely to be politically acceptable in the developing countries.

(e)   Non-market measures with external assistance: a solution that works

The next question is whether interventions to meet the food needs of the poor can be financed from external resources and how much additional aid is required. The emphasis is on aid, not on commercial capital flows, as the latter follow opportunities for economic and financial returns which the poorest countries hardly appear to offer. Thus the question is: how much aid should be given to finance non-market interventions in the food and labour markets for the benefit of the hungry?

The analysis provides the following results

- additional aid, equivalent to 0.5 per cent of the GDP of the rich countries, given in inverse proportion to per capita incomes but not specifically tied to spending on behalf of the poorest groups, reduces the number of the hungry by 32 per cent in the year 2000;
- if additional aid is fully added to investment, initially there is only a small reduction in hunger, but by the year 2000 it reaches the same level of 32 per cent fewer hungry people. This reduction in hunger persists even if aid is discontinued after fifteen years;
- when additional aid is given, as in the first case, without being tied to specific spending, hunger is immediately reduced but is very sensitive to discontinuation of aid;
- if additional aid can be fully used for meeting the food needs of the poor, with additional aid at half the levels in the other scenarios, eradication of hunger is possible before 2000 without reducing economic growth.

In summary: a combination of targeted aid and targeted food programmes can eradicate hunger at small financial cost and without reducing overall economic progress in the developing countries.

References

ABKIN, M. (1985), 'The Intermediate United States Food and Agriculture Model of the IIASA/FAP Basic Linked System: Summary Documentation and User's Guide', WP-85-30 (Laxenburg: IIASA).

FISHER, G., FROHBERG, K., KEYZER, M., and PARIKH, K. S. (1988), *Linked National Models: A Tool for International Food Policy Analysis*, FAP of IIASA (The Netherlands: Kluwer Academic).

—— —— —— ——and TIMS, W. (1990), *Hunger: Beyond the Reach of the Invisible Hand*, forthcoming book, FAP of IIASA.

FAO (1977), *Fourth World Food Survey* (Rome: FAO).

——(1985), *Fifth World Food Survey* (Rome: FAO).

KEYZER, M. (1981), 'The International Linkage of Open Exchange Economies' (doctoral dissertation, Free University, Amsterdam).

NARAYANA, N. S. S., PARIKH, K. S., and SRINIVASAN, T. N. (1987), 'Indian Agricultural Policy: An Applied General Equilibrium Model', *Journal of Policy Modeling*, 9/4.

—— —— ——(1990), *Agriculture, Growth and Redistribution of Income: Policy Analysis with a General Equilibrium Model* (New Delhi: Allied; Amsterdam: North-Holland).

NEUNTEUFEL, M. (1984), 'A Simple Model of Chinese Agriculture', WP-85-18 (Laxenburg: IIASA).

PARIKH, K. S., FISHER, G., FROHBERG, K., and GULBRANDSEN, O. (1988), *Towards Free Trade in Agriculture*, FAP of IIASA (The Netherlands: Martinus Nijhoff Publishers).

——and RABAR, F. (1981), 'Food Problems and Policies: Present and Future, Local and Global', in *Food for All in a Sustainable World: The IIASA Food and Agriculture Program*, SR-81-2 (Laxenburg: IIASA).

——and TIMS, W. (1986), 'From Hunger Amidst Abundance to Abundance without Hunger: An Overview of the Policy Findings of the Food and Agriculture Program', Executive Report 13 (Laxenburg: IIASA).

SRINIVASAN, T. N. (1981), 'Malnutrition: Some Measurement and Policy Issues', *Journal of Development Economics*, 8.

SUKHATME, P. V. (1977), *Malnutrition and Poverty*, Ninth Lal Bahadur Shastri Memorial Lecture, (New Delhi: Indian Agricultural Research Institute).

——and MARGEN, S. (1978), 'Models of Protein Deficiency', *American Journal of Clinical Nutrition*, 31; 1237–56.

World Bank (1986), *Poverty and Hunger: Issues and Options for Food Security in Developing Countries* (Washington, DC: World Bank).

6

An Independent Press and Anti-hunger Strategies: The Indian Experience

N. Ram

6.1. *The problem from a media standpoint and some wider issues*

The idea that information, and specifically the news media, can play a substantive and even a crucial role in shaping public policy for combating hunger is an appealing one in intellectual and socio-political terms. This discussion focuses on the role that a relatively independent press plays with respect to the phenomenon of hunger and distress resulting from a crisis (drought, other kinds of situations leading to 'food riots' or related mass-scale disturbances in society, and, where the situation is allowed to get out of hand, famine) and also regular, chronic hunger and subhuman poverty. In doing this, it calls attention to the need for a wider framework for the analysis of such media-related issues and suggests some reference points for such a framework.

The discovery that timely and relevant information on such vital matters makes a substantive difference to the way public opinion is shaped and official policy is made to respond is somewhat flattering to the self-image of professional journalism. In a sense, it begs a much larger question. It depends, obviously, on the kind of independent, or relatively independent, role that newspapers are allowed to play in society; and this in turn depends, equally obviously, on the political system and practice that prevail in the country in question.[1]

Journalism in the Third World—presumably the arena of mass hunger and

I am grateful to several people for contributing research assistance, notes, raw material, ideas, and encouragement for this essay: in particular, to Elizabeth Alexander, V. K. Ramachandran, and colleagues at the *Hindu* for either active research assistance or specific references; to the editorial departments of the *Statesman* and the *Times of India* for print-outs from old microfilms; to Lal Jayawardena for talking me into this venture; to Amartya Sen for providing ideas for the framework and for suggesting, 'have fun with it'; and to Steve Marglin for his critical evaluation as discussant when these ideas were presented in somewhat longer form at the WIDER conference on Food Strategies.

[1] Some media and communication specialists such as Hamelink (1983) have called attention to what they consider 'a constantly occurring distortion' in various discussions of the new world information order—the identification of information and mass media with news and press, the strong emphasis on the press, the news, and journalists 'as if they are the key actors in international communication'. In their view, this approach leaves the crucial questions concerning control over economic, technological, and marketing structures in international communication untouched. While legitimately attempting to correct the balance, such analyses probably undervalue the actual role independent newspapers and journalists play in a developing country, especially in the political arena. In any case, the role being analysed in this essay is not in the field of international communication; it is essentially in the arena of national politics and internal policy making.

battles over access to food that we are most concerned with—forms very much of a mixed bag. Third World journalism comes in such a pluralism of shapes and colours, historical experiences, socio-cultural, educational, infrastructural, and professional backgrounds as well as ideological and political persuasions that it becomes virtually impossible to distinguish its recent history, its practice, and its future as a meaningful category of experience in the manner this can be done for journalism as a professional field in America or Europe.[2]

At a rather obvious level, the character of the press, and therefore its role, bear the stamp of diverse, uneven environments. Third World journalists live as part of societies and cultures that, on the world map, present distinctive patterns. The histories they go back to, or take inspiration from, do not follow a uniform pattern, for among other things the civilizations they are part of extend from mankind's most ancient to the relatively recent, and their modern historical development involves significant divergences. They live in societies with quite different orders of per capita income, quality of life indices, human resource development, and institutional and infrastructural endowments. They live under systems which differ sharply in their basic structural features —in a handful of instances socialist, in the overwhelming majority of cases capitalist, in exceptional cases perhaps in some state of transition from one to the other, and only in a minority of situations (despite the encouraging progress registered recently in Latin America and also, to an extent, in Asia following the Philippine developments) providing their people with a measure of real democracy in the sense of a minimum 'bundle' of socio-economic, political, cultural, and intellectual rights being available to different sections of the people. Given these diversities, what can we say about the roles they play, and have played, in the past?

Generalizations can and must be attempted on the role of news media in overall developmental activity in the developing countries as a whole, necessarily in the context of the political, economic, and technological structures that increasingly shape this sensitive role in a situation of markedly unequal or unbalanced media resource development. But it is clear that such an exercise would need to wait for research on a wider and more systematic basis, if we are to go beyond impressions and, at best, tentative, fragmented analysis. In this essay, we advisedly restrict our discussion of the role of information and the press more or less to the Indian case. This experience seems to have both the breadth and depth of field to make possible a substantive consideration of the qualitative issues relating to anti-hunger strategies in a wider context. We begin with a brief reference to the contrasting experience of Africa where, in the main, the kind of role played by India's independent and pluralistic press in

---

[2] The experience of participating in the first media conference of the non-aligned (NAMEDIA) in the capacity of co-chairman of the conference's 'commission on imbalances—retrospect and prospect' brought this point about the extreme variability of Third World press situations home to this journalist.

relation to mass hunger and distress has seemed, if not absent, very weakly developed.

The case of the African famine, 1984–1985

The most important recent experience that provides a set of reference points for our broader discussion is that of the Ethiopian and African famine of 1984–5—specifically, the way it became an international media event and the results of that transformation. The effects of television coverage, in late-1984, of a full-blown crisis and what it actually meant for tens of thousands of Ethiopians are now fairly well known.

Activists of voluntary relief agencies, such as the Save the Children Fund and Oxfam, and a small number of sensitive reporters (and analysts of such organizations as the London-based Relief and Development Institute and, at a more substantive level, the World Bank group), were quite aware of the deepening of the crisis in Ethiopia and in the Sahel countries well before the African famine became the international media event of 1984–5. *South* magazine, based and published in London and run with an intelligently sustained sensitivity to Third World quality of life, development, and socio-political problems, had indeed featured on its cover 'Hunger: Who's to Blame?' (March 1984) and declared, in a factual analysis, Africa to be 'a continent at risk'. But since at this stage the impact of the specialist information network, and the media coverage, was not noticeable, such reporting, analyses, and warnings appear, upon media and scholarly resurrection today, marginal additions to what cynics might consider a we-told-you-so brand of development literature.

In his study of the challenge of hunger in Ethiopia, Hancock (1985), former East Africa correspondent of *The Economist*, sees the transmuting role of the October 1984 television coverage thus:

Reports of what was happening in Ethiopia made television news several times during the first nine months of 1984, but public reaction was small and editors gave the story little play. On 23 October, however, a seven-minute film by Visnews cameraman Mohamed Amin, with commentary by reporter Michael Buerk, was shown throughout the day on BBC news bulletins, and was subsequently picked up and networked around the world. This film, shot on location in the towns of Makalle and Korem in northern Ethiopia, portrayed a horrific human disaster on a scale that readily summoned up images of Hiroshima and Nagasaki, a disaster of hunger and suffering so great that it seemed to call into question the entire international system of aid, cooperation and control by which mankind governs its affairs in the late twentieth century . . . To this supplication . . . the international community has now responded by constructing a tremendous juggernaut of emergency aid and setting it rolling in the direction of Ethiopia.[3]

As Hancock relates it,[4] one of the harrowing elements of the prime time story told by the Amin visuals lay in the fact that at Makalle 150 starving people

[3] Hancock (1985: 7–8).   [4] Hancock (1985: 8–9).

were grouped 'for no special reason' in 'a patch of ground, like a sheep-pen, surrounded by a low stone wall about four feet high' while 'outside the wall there were about 10,000 other people, just as starved, just as near to death, who were not going to get fed that day, or the next day, or maybe were not going to get fed at all because there was almost no food in Makalle at that time'. Amin was particularly disturbed by the attitude of the people beyond the wall who 'just stood there and watched what was happening without any kind of greed and resentment. I think it was this calmness, this passivity, that got to me because I knew that if I had been in their position . . . I would have done anything, rioted, killed, to get the food I needed.' In Korem, the situation was a good deal worse:

about 60,000 starving people . . . camped in an open field outside the town. There was almost no food, and no real shelter, and the nights up there are cold, with temperatures falling to around zero . . . There was this tremendous mass of people, groaning and weeping, scattered across the ground in the dawn mist. I don't really know how to describe it but the thing that came to my mind at the time was that it was as if a hundred jumbo jets had crashed and spilled out the bodies of their passengers amongst the wreckage, the dead and the living mixed together as you couldn't tell one from the other. It still shatters me when I think back on what I saw. During the night, while I had slept, people had been slowly and steadily dying of exposure, and they were in this field—a mother cradling a dead child, a brother holding tight to the body of his dead sister, a husband and wife, dressed in rags, dead together on the ground. I went and filmed in the mortuary . . .

Such sensitive, professionally high-calibre reporting of the catastrophe in Ethiopia, and the feelings of solidarity brought into it, do help us to empathize with the powerful impact that hundreds of thousands of television viewers in Western countries felt when they watched the Amin and subsequent visuals or were exposed to more detailed press coverage. Information available from the BBC shows that the Buerk–Amin footage from northern Ethiopia was shown by 425 of the world's broadcasting organizations 'with a potential audience of 470 million people'.[5] We know that this television coverage made such a difference to public opinion in Western countries as to call for a very important official and voluntary life-saving response.

An important point to note is that journalism did not initiate either the insights or the campaign that brought about such positive results in terms of relief as well as understanding of the issues involved. In the words of Gill (1986), a participant journalist:

When Ethiopia's famine hit the headlines, it did so because of the relationship between private relief agencies and the television companies . . . In news coverage in October (1985) and beyond, the relief agencies provided most of the reference points—up-to-date information, places to visit, interviews in the field and at home, and a means of

<hr>

⁵ Gill (1986: 91).

response for concerned viewers. Our own *TV Eye* film 'Bitter Harvest' . . . had its origins in Oxfam's decision to purchase large quantities of grain for Ethiopia.[6]

The experience of organizing Live Aid, Sports Aid, and various other world-wide or nation-wide humanitarian projects, which have probably made a significant difference to the number of deaths in the African famine, is instructive; the whole experience provides valuable guidance for both analysis and practice.

In her often insightful essay on photography, Sontag (1978) takes on this question of impact and some determinant or shaping factors. For example: 'A photograph that brings news of some unsuspected zone of misery cannot make a dent in public opinion unless there is an appropriate context of feeling and attitude . . . Photographs cannot create a moral position, but they can reinforce one—and can help build a nascent one.'[7] She makes the point that there must be, ideologically speaking, 'space' for the impact to be made and also 'the existence of a relevant political consciousness' so that a moral impact is possible.[8]

An objection can be raised to Sontag's approach to the question of photo-graphic or media impact, which appears to undervalue the initiative or trigger that the photo/media coverage can provide by way of influencing public opinion, or the public mood, in a particular direction. Nevertheless, the analysis helps us steer clear of exaggerated notions of the impact of media coverage, by itself, on the development of mass-scale phenomena or cata-strophes such as famine or threatened famine. Alert, sensitive media coverage, if it is to be effective, must form part of an ideological and political context of attitude, feeling, and critical democratic values and practice. The role of the media within such a context in developing countries is clearly an under-researched area, certainly in the case of Africa. But we do know, from the empirical observation of those reasonably familiar with the situation in several African countries hit or threatened by famine, that neither the officially controlled mass media nor newspapers, which are usually controlled and manipulated by the state or otherwise severely restricted,[9] seem to perform the

---

[6] Gill (1986: 93).   [7] Sontag (1978: 17).   [8] Sontag (1979: 18–19).

[9] The case of Nigeria seemed to constitute a vigorous exception until the 1983 coup affected independent journalism. There are various sporadic discussions of the failure of the African press to perform a role considered vital to democratic practice. According to a report done for the Independent Commission on International Humanitarian Issues (1985), the Ethiopian govern-ment instituted in the wake of the 1972–4 famine 'the most complete early warning system of its kind in Africa', but its recurrent annual warnings lacked credibility with the aid donors. On the other hand: 'It is suggested that the reason there has not been a major famine in India since 1943 is not just because of the improved food production, but also because it has a free press functioning in a democratic framework. If an area within the country starts to slip towards crisis, victims can make their voice heard. Newspapers kick up a fuss, thus stirring the concern of the central authorities. Hence timely action. In Africa, regrettably, there is rarely the same link between countryside and urban politicians. In general, there is a lack of representative structures which allow rural voices to be heard. During the present famine, many of those in other continents who have seen starving people on television have been closer than many in Africa to what is happening'

role that the Indian press has played in relation to famine, drought, or other types of 'food crisis' over an extended historical period.

Towards analysis   The markedly dissimilar situations might be worth exploring more systematically. In some readings, the existence and flourishing of an independent, critical, watchdog press is usually regarded as a sensitive indicator of the level of civil society attained. Realization of this, in a context of being able to influence public policies in relation to issues such as mass hunger and poverty, gives the 'credible-informational' function a new, substantive content. Under certain circumstances, this makes for an 'adversarial', perhaps even a 'destabilizing',[10] role in the sense that the press tilts effectively against what begins, as a result of the communication impact or influence, to be popularly and politically perceived as unjust or otherwise unacceptable government policy. It is only in the latter sense that an independent press, by exposing facts on the ground relentlessly and by providing some kind of

---

(p. 43). As for the responsibility of the Ethiopian government, it 'had certainly been sounding the alarm internationally for over a year before a television team suddenly brought the crisis alive and galvanised international aid in October 1984. But the government had not come clean with its own people about the famine' (p. 43). In a commentary, 'Holding Back the Facts of Famine', *South* magazine (Dec. 1984) noted that while the government of Col. Mengistu Haile Mariam had 'not adopted a callous attitude to the famine', it had nevertheless 'up to a few months ago' been reluctant to 'reveal the true extent of the crisis'. For example, the head of state in a six-hour speech marking the tenth anniversary of the Ethiopian revolution in Sept. 1984 did not make a single reference to the catastrophe which was even then claiming the lives of tens of thousands of his people. Gill (1986), who is very critical of the attitude of Western governments towards the Ethiopian famine of 1984–5, refers to the phenomenon of official attention in mid-1984 being 'simply directed away from the likelihood of severe famine to the political priority in hand, the establishment of the new party and the anniversary celebrations' (p. 10). He refers to the fact that the government-run *Ethiopian Herald* did not focus on the famine raging in Ethiopia (pp. 4–15) and that while a new television transmitter costing some half a million pounds was opened in Makelle, the capital of Tigre (which along with Korem provided some of the most searing images of mass starvation on Western television screens in the autumn of 1984), the tasks on the political, economic, and social front designated officially for the expanded media 'did not include coverage of the famine' (p. 11).

[10] Some reservations have been expressed to this journalist about the use of the term 'destabilizing' in this context, and indeed Amartya Sen, in a written comment, suggested that 'the purpose of press activism may be to reform the government rather than to destabilise it even when it is acting in an "adversarial" role. In fact I like your term "adversarial" much better, as being less open to misinterpretation.' The point is persuasive; nevertheless, while characterizing the second function as 'adversarial' in the main, the question is kept open about the precise impact by the use of the term 'destabilizing' in a carefully qualified context. This usage carries none of the loaded, emotional connotations it has in the contemporary political vocabulary of, say, South Asia. Its essential content is not caught by the evocative phrase so familiar to the history of American journalism, 'muckraking'. But the term certainly covers the socio-political situation where what is legitimate and quite the professional-ethical thing to do for the press might naturally appear 'motivated destabilization' to an intolerant government. The accusation by the Rajiv Gandhi administration and the ruling Congress (I) party that the media disclosures relating to the Fairfax and defence deal controversies were part of a motivated plot to 'destabilize' the Indian government, the Indian Republic, and national security provide interesting confirmation of the typical tendencies of governments in trouble, or under pressure, to target the independent press. In Apr. 1987, when this note was written, it was a still developing story in India.

hunger-related discourse with policy implications, can prevent a government from pursuing disastrous policies and thus, in concert with other democratic institutions, can 'guarantee . . . the avoidance of acute starvation and famine'.[11] Thus in a deeper sense, the 'adversarial' or 'destabilizing' role makes for the relative stabilization of crisis-averting policies if the democratic rules of the game work reasonably. So far as a government is concerned, the second role might help to 'reform' its practice or, perhaps, to 'destabilize' it—this depends very much on the nature of the government, its attitude to democratic opposition and criticism, and the character of the policies it pursues.

In fact, it might be useful to make an analytical distinction between the 'credible-informational' and 'destabilizing' functions of an independent press in a developing country context, without attempting in any way to contrapose the functions. The first appears to be a prerequisite for the second; but without the latter, which on account of the content might imply some kind of 'adversarial' role in relation to government under typical circumstances, the former is not likely to thrive and develop, especially if it insists on living off historical memories, or on formalisms that might be sustained even in a substantively non-independent context for the press (as in Sri Lanka today). On the other hand, frequently heard complaints about the 'negative' role of the press from those in authority in countries such as India (where the system makes what must be recognized, by developing country standards, as an impressive allowance for an independent watchdog press) usually mean that the surface-level 'credible-informational' function and the more substantive 'adversarial' or 'destabilizing' political-developmental function in respect of unjust or wrong-headed or inadequate official policies relating to the vital affairs of society are being performed rather effectively.

Historically, of course, the 'credible-informational' function has something to do with a rule of law tradition which a particular colonialism, for all its barbarities and savage effects, was able to transplant to a particular country (in contrast to another colonialism in another country), but this function is also capable, it must be assumed, of being 'learned' or acquired consciously in a post-colonial context. Yet the more substantive and more progressive 'adversarial' role that a press may be able to play with respect to mass entitlements and their defence and expansion (and, at least at the conscious level, this might have nothing to do with the fight to overthrow one system and to replace it by another) needs much stronger nourishment in terms of ideological and political experience, context, institutions, and perceptions—such as those associated with a 'nationalist' or liberation movement, a struggle to consolidate and expand the content of independence, a major campaign for the people's socio-economic and political rights, a movement to overthrow authoritarianism in a post-colonial context, and so on. But lest this should sound too

[11] Sen (1985a: 77).

romantic a notion of journalism, we hasten to add that there appears to be a certain autonomy to the development of the profession in the sense of availability of indigenous media and intellectual resources, a stabilized practice with its own critical professional values and yardsticks, technological capabilities, advertising support to secure a measure of independence from the government, sophistication in production values, and so on. These might be present in one developing country and not in another, and this factor could make a vital difference to the role of the press.

The Indian press in relation to famine

At a conscious institutional and theoretical level, the idea that the independent press, and perhaps even professionally conscientious sections of the officially controlled electronic media, the journalism of 'sight and sound', can play a substantive role in anti-hunger strategies has come into its own in India only recently. There has been, of course, a kind of understanding of what this role means, and this is derived from long empirical experience. The Indian press—whose institutional memory goes back well over a century in the sense that major newspapers have files and archives going back to the 1860s and 1870s and also in the sense that there are to be encountered here and there inveterate long-term readers and newspaper veterans who can recall from their personal experience the way the press covered India's last famine, the Bengal famine of 1943—has a long-standing and fairly solid record in relation to situations where large-scale starvation and famine threatened. Over time, it has tended to bring out the facts in the field with elements of vivid descriptive and human interest detail; and to expose the failure of government authorities to recognize the problem, its causes and early symptoms, and to respond quickly and adequately in terms of crisis prevention, management, and relief.

By sensitizing and influencing public and political opinion in this way and also through editorial campaigns—especially in the strongholds of its influence or circulation, for example Calcutta and eastern India for the *Statesman*—the Indian press has tended to force public policy over time to face the challenge of crises which threaten to develop into famines. Developing in some sort of pre-historical or early form in the 1870s and gathering force and substance towards the end of the last century, this role became quite prominent during the first two decades of the twentieth century, as our case-study of the part played by an independent nationalist newspaper of record during the widespread 1918 'food riots' and related disturbances in the Madras Province makes clear.

But although the empirical practice and the institutional memory go back quite a long way, the substantive importance of the role played by newspapers in making it virtually impossible for governments and the political system to pursue obscurantist or otherwise damaging policies which might cause or usher in famine (or a mass-level food crisis) has hardly figured in media discussions in India.

It required the economist Amartya Sen to spotlight this role—so reassuring and so flattering to the self-image of Indian journalism—and even assign it central importance in an analysis of food crises and threatened famine. In his well-publicized 1982 Coromandel Lecture in New Delhi, Sen brought to national intellectual attention this somewhat surprising finding on the importance of the Indian press in the arena of mass access to food. At that time it might have appeared somewhat impressionistic, raised in a context of contrasting the situations of India and China, and substantiated chiefly in relation to the Bengal famine of 1943 and the role of the *Statesman*.[12] The strength of—as well as the apparent problem with—the formulation was that it seemed based on a clear-cut or unambiguous dichotomy between the Chinese and Indian situations, to which objection has indeed been raised. But the logic of the argument, and the fact that the Indian press found its way into a major economic theory of poverty and famine and into international discussions of it,[13] was persuasive.

The idea that independent newspapers in contrast to a controlled or manipulated press—along with genuine opposition parties—can, in a pluralistic political system, prevent a government from failing to intervene promptly in a crisis to avert famine is one that Indian journalists have warmed to, especially in a context where they have frequently heard homilies and lectures from those in authority to the effect that their practice was not 'positive', 'relevant', or 'development-orientated'.[14] The influence of the finding (and of a theoretical perspective which has influenced international policy thinking on access to food issues) on the self-awareness and practice of Indian journalism is difficult to measure, even as the impact made by the press on public opinion, official policy, and, in general, anti-hunger strategies is not at all easy to measure. But that the argument has had an influence on the profession and its internal perceptions and stances need not be doubted.

Indeed Sen's qualified tribute to the role of the Indian press seems to have struck such sympathetic or responsive chords in the better-informed sections of Indian journalism that there have been attempts to return the compliment in a rather obvious way. One is impressed by the variety and contexts of recent reports and articles (some by journalists, others by academics and pseudo-

---

[12] The contrast with China was presented in Sen (1982); and the observation on the positive role of the *Statesman* had appeared in Sen (1981: 195).

[13] See e.g. Independent Commission on International Humanitarian Issues (1985), esp. p. 43.

[14] This criticism was recorded on numerous occasions in the 1970s and 1980s by Prime Minister Indira Gandhi. After the highly damaging impact of Emergency policies on democratic institutions in India had become clear, and after the results of the very negative experience of censorship during 1975–6 which dissolved some 'liberal' illusions had been undone, the Indian press (in an institutional sense) increasingly saw the central government in an adversarial role, with Prime Minister Indira Gandhi consciously introducing strains and an element of stridency into press–government relations. With Prime Minister Rajiv Gandhi, the experience was mixed, although a tendency to blow hot and cold was recorded (in press columns) in his case also.

academics) in Indian newspapers which make reference to, or imply, the idea of 'entitlements' or their collapse, sometimes in ways that would surprise the author. Popularization of an analytical and theoretical concept can be expected, after all, to proceed in this way—especially if we take into account the inherent tendencies of journalism which appears (from the analytical literature that derives from countries where it is practised seriously as a profession) as a state of incessant oscillation or interchange between the banal and the brilliant with some worthwhile attempts to find a middle ground.[15]

6.2. An Indian case-study

The Indian press is widely regarded as the most pluralistic, the least inhibited, and the most assertive or independent in all the Third World.[16] In terms of the number of newspapers published in a country, it ranks fourth in the world. The journalistic and production values of its most advanced contingents are rated among the better anywhere, even if the severe space constraint, reflecting major problems of government policy-dictated access to reasonably priced physical inputs—above all, newsprint—militates against editorial development and the comprehensiveness or relative completeness of coverage that might, otherwise, be possible. The fading out of the newspaper of record tradition in Indian journalism, and the increasingly visible incompleteness of news reporting and editorial featuring, are weaknesses that reflect the situation on the ground. One aspect of the pluralism is the considerable unevenness in professional and production quality among Indian newspapers and periodicals. And despite the relative sophistication and development of independent professional journalism and the substantial circulations and influence built up by major newspapers, including, more recently, several Indian language newspapers,[17] coverage of the population is not impressive even after making

---

[15] This is not meant to be as light-hearted a generalization as it might sound. Serious practitioners of journalism in various parts of the world recognize the problem in an intellectual sense and see several inherent weaknesses in the profession. Futile attempts in India and elsewhere to evolve or impose 'codes of conduct' on journalism reflect the dilemma. Given journalism's inherent tendency towards flashiness and making an impact, the pursuit of 'brilliance' cannot legitimately be blocked; the banal must, of course, be combated; but the 'middle ground' is probably the best bet for the profession in so far as it aspires to better intellectual (as distinct from entertainment world) standards.

[16] See e.g. the cover feature on 'The Indian Press' in the Far Eastern Economic Review, 18 July 1985. The review begins by noting: 'Among the world's largest and oldest, though not necessarily the best, the Indian press remains unmatched in the Third World . . . Indian publications are the most free of all their counterparts (in the developing world) . . .' This feature also takes note of the tensions between the press and government, various objective constraints such as 'the low diffusion rate in the rural areas', and the internal weaknesses of Indian journalism including, allegedly, 'the conformist ethos of the daily press'.

[17] Notable examples of rapid growth, over the last decade, of Indian language journalism would be two or three Malayalam daily newspapers, notably Malayala Manorama; some Bengali newspapers, notably Ananda Bazar Patrika; some Hindi newspapers; and perhaps most spectacularly Eenadu, a recently started Telugu newspaper.

allowance for the low literacy level. On the basis of officially collected circulation figures it has been estimated that the current dailies-to-people ratio in India is around 1:40, which compares unfavourably with the relevant statistics for a number of other developing countries, for example Malaysia and Sri Lanka. There are other constraints and handicaps, including the fact that remuneration and rewards in journalism— reflecting newspaper economics but also conservative management policies—are such that they do not make it easy for newspapers to compete for the best available educated or trained skills and talent, especially intellectual resources, in an increasingly diversified and sophisticated national recruitment pool.[18]

Overall, it appears that since the long-established tradition of free-wheeling pluralism and the independence of the Indian press which so impresses outsiders can be taken for granted (and this is in notable contrast to the regressive monotony and the narrowly construed propagandistic tone of state-owned and state-regimented television and radio, which are equally taken for granted) in the Indian democratic and political context, complaints against adversarial fiscal and import control policies of the government,[19] and self-criticism and implied criticism of others (usually competitors), seem to dominate the internal debate on the state of the Indian press.[20] Taken outside the very specific context in which the grievances and the self-criticism are expressed, the response would appear exaggerated, even misleading. In other words, the constraints, handicaps, and self-limiting factors (which can be attributed to slow-changing newspaper management as well as editorial development policies) should not make us lose sight of the fact that, in qualitative and historical terms, the practice of independent journalism in India is very nearly unique in the developing world.

[18] There is no systematic information available on recruitment policies and practices in newspapers relating either to journalists or to the non-journalistic workforce. A general editorial complaint pertains to the quality of the fresh input into journalism even if, in an objective evaluation, it might not be possible to substantiate a 'decline in standards' thesis. Many journalists would appear to be 'overqualified' in formal educational terms; and the induction of an increasing number of science and technology graduates into the profession points in a healthy direction in that it indicates an internal perception that journalism requires more rigorously trained skills (in the streaming out process in Indian higher education, students in science, technology, and professional fields are, as a group, rated higher than their counterparts in the 'arts', the humanities, and the social sciences). With respect to technical production departments such as photocomposition, offset printing, facsimile, and so on, the Indian newspaper industry has the advantage of being able to draw upon a fairly large pool of highly qualified skills, especially electronics engineers and technicians. However, the technological practices vary considerably even among the big newspapers and the overall situation with respect to the adoption of modern newspaper technology in India is extremely uneven.

[19] These are presented in numerous memoranda and representations by the Indian Newspaper Society (INS) to the central government over the past five years.

[20] At the media conference of the non-aligned (NAMEDIA) in 1983, several participants from outside South Asia appeared frequently taken by surprise by the sharp divergences in the views expressed by Indian participants on various media issues that came up in the discussions in the commissions into which the conference divided.

An attempt to evaluate and analyse the role of the independent Indian press in anti-hunger strategies must take into careful, balanced account the considerable historical and current strengths of this press, and also the constraints on its influence and 'powers', *vis-à-vis* public opinion and the making of official policy. But if, in balance, it is used analytically as a model against which to compare or evaluate other press traditions or experiences in the Third World, the role needs to be broken down in terms of the quality of response to essentially different types of situations of hunger on a mass scale.

One entry point into such an exercise would be offered by the kind of 'dichotomy' highlighted by the Sen (1982) analysis of the essential experiences of India and China. On the one hand,

India's record in eliminating endemic, non-acute hunger is quite bad and contrasts very unfavourably with the record of some other countries such as Sri Lanka and China . . . the astonishing tolerance of persistent hunger in India is greatly helped by our inclination to take a low-key approach to these deadly conflicts. It is indeed amazing that in a country with as much politicisation as India has, the subject of persistent hunger of a third of the rural population can be such a tame issue . . . non-acute, regular starvation . . . does not attract much attention in newspapers. These standard events in India seem to be not newsworthy . . .

On the other hand,

there is . . . one respect in which India has really turned a page on the food front. This refers not to the much publicised self-sufficiency of India in food, since the so-called self-sufficiency co-exists with—indeed survives on—keeping a large class of people in a position of having little entitlement to food in the market. The real achievement relates to the elimination of sudden large-scale starvation and famines. Given the . . . political system in India, including the ability of newspapers and opposition parties to pester the central and state governments, it is essential to avoid famines for any government keen on staying in power, and famines . . . are very easy to prevent if the government acts intelligently and in time.

India, the analysis goes on,

has not had a famine since independence, and given the nature of Indian politics and society, it is not likely that India can have a famine even in years of a great food problem . . . newspapers play an important part in this, in making the facts known and forcing the challenge to be faced. So does the pressure of opposition parties. In the absence of these pressures and free newspapers, famines can develop even in countries that normally perform much better than India.

Some elements in the analysis of the Chinese experience of 1959–61, and of the factors behind the development of the famine, have been questioned and indeed K. N. Raj has challenged the analysis on the ground that while 'I have no disagreement with Prof. Sen on the role that democratic institutions can play in checking tyranny and injustice in all forms . . . the precise relation of that set of issues to this specific question of political responsibility for the famine that took place in China is not so obvious as he seems to assume'.[21]

The academic controversy on this issue has been useful in that, among other things, it has posed rather sharply the problem of measuring the influence of the press and other democratic institutions on government policy and on the mass-scale socio-economic realities it is supposed to respond to. For the Indian press in a situation of weak coverage, historically and currently, of the population (as expressed by readership rates) but presumed strong influence on public policy, the problem of measurement of influence is particularly difficult. We shall not attempt to resolve this problem in terms of cause-and-effect relationships, but shall confine the present exercise to looking at the type of response and the quality of coverage by the independent press of issues relating to hunger, or problems of access to food, which affect very large numbers of people.

The historical experience: origins and continuities

The historical origins of an independent, critical, 'watchdog' role for the Indian press in relation to a sudden outbreak of hunger on a mass scale or to other kinds of 'food crisis' in society have not been precisely researched, even if the press has been tapped extensively in some fields of historical research as 'source'. Here the 'little traditions' in different parts of the country would be of obvious interest in so far as they might provide insights into a preparatory or 'pre-historical' phase. But in a generalized, institutional sense—involving in the main continuities, but also a few discontinuities—this role would appear to have taken shape in the late nineteenth century during a period of acceleration of the freedom movement in India.

While nascent nationalist newspapers saw themselves as performing this role consciously in relation to the rights and entitlements of the Indian people and in the face of what was perceived in the initial stages as benevolently inadequate, and increasingly as wrong-headed, callous, and unjust, official policies, it must not be assumed that the Anglo-Indian newspapers which generally aligned themselves with the Raj and its policies against the freedom struggle (and against the press associated with it) did not play such a role. Indeed for a later period, the way in which the *Statesman*, a British-owned newspaper, 'distinguished itself in its extensive reporting of the [1943 Bengal] famine and its crusading editorials'[22] throws light on a complex role for the Indian press with its 'credible-informational' and 'adversarial' or 'destabilizing' traditions. The high quality, and authoritativeness,[23] of the role is

[21] K. N. Raj, letter to the editor, published in the *Hindu* of 7 Feb. 1983, under the heading 'China and Food Issues'.   [22] Sen (1981: Appendix D, p. 195).

[23] P. C. Mahalanobis, it is known, played a role in informing and influencing the line of the *Statesman* and in providing the newspaper with statistical information relating to famine deaths. This input from an academic who was engaged in empirical research on the famine doubtless provided authority and stature to the editorial assessment. I am grateful to a veteran in the profession, Nikhil Chakravartty, editor of *Mainstream*, for this information.

reflected in the editorials of 14 and 16 October 1943 titled 'Seen from a Distance' and 'The Death-Toll' respectively. It does suggest a certain autonomy for the role of journalism as a professional activity in the pre-independence period, which cannot simply be explained in terms of a political distinction between a nationalist press and a with-the-Raj or loyalist press. This factor is clearly a historical and institutional advantage for the development of independent Indian journalism.

There is a paucity of information on the precise role of newspapers in covering the terrible famines of the late nineteenth century and our sampling of the columns of *The Hindu* (founded in 1878) during the 1897–8 famine in different parts of the country, including the south, appears to suggest a formative, inchoate role for the independent press at this stage. Nevertheless, the spread and intensity of the 1897–8 famine—in which it reported that an estimated 150,000 people perished in the Central Provinces alone—was the topic of considerable editorial comment in the nationalist newspaper.

Reflecting the early stirrings of 'economic nationalism', some of the editorials relate the famine (in extremely general terms) to the wider consequences of British rule: '. . . but for the extreme costliness of British rule and the drain of millions of Indian money every year as the price of the good government that the country enjoys, India would be far more prosperous than she is, and there would be no such thing as famine' (*The Hindu*, 15 March 1897, 'Indian Famine and the British Exchequer'). Unlike famines which periodically occurred in the past, those of 'modern times'—which were spread over a wide area and affected millions of people—are attributed in large measure to the 'faults and errors of British rule'.

Within this broad framework, the editorials make a critical assessment of official attitudes, the 'niggardly outpourings' of British charity towards the Famine Fund, and the various difficulties relating to, and the tardy progress of, famine relief operations (points made in two editorials of 25 February and 1 March 1897, titled 'Governor and the Famine' and 'The Distribution of Famine Relief' respectively). The editorials express scepticism about the various Commissions appointed only in times of great distress:

When famine on a large scale is found to exist, the Government makes efforts to afford relief to suffering people, partly out of its own resources and partly by begging from other people. The moment the distress passes away the Government is quiet and happy again, and does not concern itself with the condition of the ryot until another similar calamity happens. Of course a Commission is now and then appointed; but the recommendations, so far as they interfere with the convenience of officials, are never carried out. ('The Starving Ryot', *The Hindu*, 24 March 1897)

Again to go by a limited sampling, the reporting is not vivid or detailed or sufficiently factual; the 'newspaper of record' function that was so strongly expressed by the same newspaper during another type of 'food crisis' a couple of decades later had not evolved during these famines. But the reports are indicative of a serious, factual approach to independent journalism. The reports in the nationalist newspaper on the 1897–8 famine refer to the proximate causes of the phenomenon, the slow pace of official response to the widespread distress, and various specific problems involved in famine relief works. Illustrative of this type of coverage is the report from South Arcot ('Notes from South Arcot') published in the newspaper on 15 July 1898:

The general outlook in the district is sufficiently gloomy, though the authorities are very slow and still unwilling to recognise the gravity of the situation and move betimes to the rescue of the suffering from the jaws of starvation and death. The price of rice, the simple article of food, has already risen to famine rates, when we see that five measures per rupee have succeeded in keeping many of those in the low strata of society beyond the reach of an adequate quantity of food-supply, nay in not a few instances of any food-supply at all. The supply of other foodgrains is not plentiful in the market. The famishing population is daily on the increase, and swarms of beggars have begun to infest our society.

This type of journalism has an old-fashioned ring to it, in relation to the confident, factually aggressive approach and style of 1918 dealt with subsequently, but it raises the relevant issues and points in a healthy direction. Research into newspaper coverage, in various parts of the country, of the famines of the late nineteenth century should throw more light on this point.

Responding to the 'food riots' and related disturbances in southern India, 1918:
a new type of role

A new, far more substantive role is indicated for the independent nationalist press in response to another type of 'food crisis'—not famine or even threatened famine in this case, but the very extensive militant actions, protests, and 'disturbances' that broke out in Madras Province in 1918. The crisis, in fact, was expressed in the 'spate of looting and grain riots' which 'like the influenza, left hardly a town or district of the province untouched'.[24]

In his excellent little study of 'Looting, Grain Riots and Government Policy in South India 1918', Arnold (1979) brings out these features of the situation. The crisis, described as one of the two 'epidemics' of the time, surfaced in 1918 and its signs continued sporadically until the end of 1919. The bulk of the looting and related disturbances—numbering about 120 instances, in Arnold's count—occurred between the middle of May and the end of September 1918. The 'peak of unrest' was the first fortnight of September when 'serious looting [was] reported from fifteen of the twenty-five districts and three days of attacks on grain bazaars and warehouses in Madras city, the provincial capital'.

Arnold's analysis underlines the fact that although the partial failure in 1918 of the south-west monsoon was 'clearly of considerable economic and psycho-

[24] Arnold (1979: 111).

logical significance in the spreading of the looting epidemic', this factor does not adequately explain the origin and character of the crisis.

The failure of rains in this or any other part of India did not automatically provoke widespread rioting. The causes lay in a conjunction of factors, economic and social as well as climatic. Looting and rioting were expressions of the bewilderment, panic and anger felt by the poorer classes of the province when faced with abrupt price rises or the sudden disappearance of foodgrains from the bazaars while large quantities of grain were known to be stacked in warehouses or barges and in railway yards ready for export elsewhere . . . the poor of southern Indian reacted much as their counterparts in France, England and Scotland had done . . .

Arnold's study sheds light on the social composition of the looters and those involved in related disturbances, and this in turn provides insights into the basic features of the development of the crisis and also into the character of public policy and the role of an independent press in relation to the challenge. In sum, translating for the purpose of the argument into a conceptual framework that Arnold does not use, there was a widespread and alarming deterioration, if not collapse, of *entitlements* among various sections of the working people, calling for an emergency response from government and public policy. The role of the press in this situation—in making inputs into, although not perhaps shaping, colonial policy—was important. Factual reporting of the incidents of looting surfaced freely, especially in September 1918, in the columns of the nationalist press, notably *The Hindu, New India, Desabhaktan, Andhrapatrika, Swadesamitran,* and the *West Coast Spectator*; even the Anglo-Indian press, especially the *Madras Mail*, came up with accounts and, occasionally, criticism of the official handling of the crisis.

Before we come to our detailed study of the coverage of this crisis by *The Hindu*, let us make the general point that without such extensive reporting of the looting, the grain riots, and the related disturbances in far-flung parts of southern India, the influence of the event on public opinion and the element of pressure on official policy would have been significantly weaker. It is likely that the absence of a diverse and pluralist nationalist press, speaking in a range of narrative and critical editorial voices, would have tended to keep knowledge of the scope, the spread, the causes, and the gravity of the disturbances away from province-wide and nation-wide public awareness; officialdom, which was criticized by the press for attempting to underestimate or cover up the gravity of the situation and was itself engaged in an internal debate which is recorded in detail,[25] would have found it much easier to keep sensitive information on the

[25] This documentation is available in the Tamil Nadu Archives, Madras. For example, GO No. 593, dated 23 Sept. 1918, Miscellaneous Series, Revenue (Special), Confidential, includes correspondence from the Madras City Policy Commissioner's office to the Chief Secretary vacationing in Ooty, and also notes from the office of the Director of Civil Supplies, Madras, and other British bureaucrats. The documentation reveals a considerable variance in the approaches to this crisis.

crisis secret or fragmented in an attempt to manipulate public opinion and shape public policy in a direction which it deemed desirable.

This positive role of the press in relation to burning socio-economic issues in the Madras Province contrasts sharply with the role allowed to the nationalist newspapers around the same time by Sir Michael O'Dwyer in the Punjab. In an editorial published on 29 March 1920 titled 'The Agony of the Punjab', *The Hindu* raised this point bluntly on behalf of the nationalist press:

The 'Punjab manner' has become to the rest of India—bureaucratic India of course —an envious aspiration. If the people in their ignorance did not know what was good for them, heroic remedies must be adopted. The bane of their life is education . . . the kind of education which breeds what Kipling in his graphic way calls the 'beggar-taught' which teaches them ideas above their proper stations . . . when a man is bent on getting things done, getting them done quickly and getting them done regardless of consequences, it may easily be imagined how fierce must be his hatred of the formalities of procedure, how impatient he must be of criticism and how in the end he could have arrived at a hatred of what he must have considered hampering influences, amounting to a positive obsession. That, stripped of excessive verbiage, is his conception of the theory of Government . . . Sir Michael . . . interned hundreds of local men with little or no cause. He gagged the vernacular press, prevented the Nationalist papers edited outside the Punjab from circulating in the province, as for instance *New India*, the *Amrita Bazar Patrika*, the *Independent*; he prohibited the circulation of even pre-censored vernacular papers and brought a stage of things, whereby it became practically impossible for the people of the province to have free interchange of independent views, or a free ventilation of their grievances in the public press; and, having prevented free speech and free writing, he allowed himself to think, and gave outsiders to understand that the people of the Punjab were the happiest under his rule.

In contrast, in the Madras Province around this time, the nationalist newspapers, aside from publishing detailed factual reports of what happened at a particular place on a particular day, were able to sound warnings and draw lessons. For example, *New India* of 10 September 1918 noted in a dispatch (cited by Arnold):

Most of the poor obtain their supplies in the evening and have their only hot meal at night. The disturbances stopped all sales, and many families had to starve on Sunday night. Riots were therefore inevitable on Monday, if some plan were not arranged to supply the daily requirements.

At times, a note somewhat sympathetic to the looters was sounded. The *Madras Times* of 9 September 1918 noted, for example, on the Madras incidents (cited by Arnold):

One feature of the looting which deserves attention is that for the most part there was no attempt to steal goods from the shops looted. The looters seem to have contented themselves with destroying and spoiling goods, their motive presumably to cause loss to the shopkeepers, to deprive them . . . [of] the equivalent of what they regarded as their ill-gotten gains.

Using a number of methods to force the government to recognize, investigate, and do something about the crisis was not the only role the independent press played during this period. Arnold (1979) detects a surprising tendency in the press responses and relates this to the attitude of a section of district-level officialdom. Before 'the climactic riots of September 1918' triggered government repression, many district officials showed 'an unmistakeable sympathy' for popular complaints against traders' profiteering and, 'if they intervened at all, it was invariably on the side of the public' to ask traders to sell at more reasonable prices. Arnold observes that the newspapers, in their editorials, dispatches from correspondents, and letters from readers, repeatedly came out against high prices, artificial shortages, and gross profiteering; 'hardly a word was to be heard or read in the merchants' defence', and until the September 'riots' made the salaried middle classes 'more wary', looting was held to be 'the inevitable and not unreasonable response of the desperately poor'. Arnold's unambiguous finding is that 'the press and officialdom helped to focus discontent against the "avarice" and the "indecent profiteering" of the merchants'.

The role played by an independent press under such circumstances, especially in a society with a very poor literacy rate, must not, of course, be exaggerated to make out that this was a determining element.

Arnold's analysis appears to underestimate the influence of the nationalist or freedom movement in providing a focus to the spontaneous grievances. Indeed in Arnold's story of popular responses to the 1918 crisis, the ending is less than inspiring. The government of Madras charged that 'nationalist agitation' had contributed to the extent of the disturbances and the violent character of the looting in its latest stages; cracked down in an increasingly repressive way on the protesters; declined to admit the consequences of its own policies; ridiculed, and refused to adopt, 'heroic remedies', choosing instead the line of least interference in the grain trade; and hardened its law and order posture. Nevertheless, the role indicated for the press is a highly positive one. And this includes the function of contributing to the 'destabilization' of the situation by making a posture of official complacency or stupidity relatively difficult to maintain—unless, of course, top officialdom adopted 'the Punjab manner' of Sir Michael.

How precisely did *The Hindu*, a nationalist newspaper which had taken on the clear function of a newspaper of extensive record, cover the crisis and the popular and official responses? Our detailed account is intended not just to highlight the role of the independent press in a socio-economic crisis but also to probe how a newspaper of record covers the events. The purpose is to provide insights into the role and method of actively independent professional journalism which is given scope and which comes alive in response to extraordinary circumstances.

This section is based on a reading of microfilms of issues of *The Hindu* from 3 September to 25 September 1918, the three-week period during which mass action against a sudden rise in the prices of rice and other foodgrains, edible oil, chilli, tamarind, cloth, and other essential commodities—the 'food riots' of 1918—was at its peak. Information on the agitation and opinions on the events are available in daily reporting, in editorials, and in letters to the editor of the newspaper. Our account and assessment are based on material from the first two sources, reportage and editorials.

Reportage   By 1918, *The Hindu* was the region's pre-eminent newspaper and it served for the Madras province and the region as a newspaper of record. This role is brought out sharply in the content of the reports that appeared on the food agitation.

As high prices and unrest spread, reports on different aspects of the events—high prices, unrest, looting, attempted looting, looting averted, and measures to deal with the situation—came in from all parts of the region. An idea of the regional spread of reporting can be had from a summary listing of the places regarding which reports (of varying length, from a paragraph to two columns, and detail) were filed from 3 September to 25 September 1918: Madras; Chingleput, Conjeevaram, and Saidapet (Chingleput District); Arakkonam (North Arcot); Villupuram and Cuddalore (South Arcot); Salem; Coimbatore and Erode (Coimbatore District); Trichinopoly, Samayapuram, and Karur (Tiruchi District); Tanjore, Mayavaram, Kuttalam, Koranad, Shiyali, Negapatam, Mannargudi, Adirampatnam, and Kumbaconam (Thanjavur District); Madura; Kamuthi and Paramakudi (Ramnad District); Tinnevelly, Tuticorin, and Viranallur (Tirunelveli District); Ellore, Venkatagiri, Sullurpet, Nellore, Guntur, and Tirupati (all in the Telugu-speaking districts); as well as Coonoor, Bangalore, Mysore, Robertsonpet (the Kolar Gold Fields), Malabar District, and Cochin. Many of the reports included the names of surrounding villages from which agitators came to towns and weekly markets.

Considerable space was given—in what was then an eight-page newspaper —to these reports. Reports were regular and sequential, in that successive dispatches from a single centre attempted to follow up previous reports. Many of the reports are characterized by considerable detail: they state the scenes of action (the towns, quarters and streets of towns, the names of surrounding villages and hamlets), describe the sequences of events, often bringing the incidents alive through graphic reporting, and always explicitly state the (perceived) *cause* of looting—the sudden and calamitously steep rise in the prices of foodgrains and other necessaries of life. The reports bring out the fact that the price rise of the period was more than 'normal' inflation; prices rose sharply over the course of one, two, or a few days.

The targets of the looters were generally the shops and establishments of merchants, traders, and retailers and, in the districts, the weekly markets or shandies. (In Kamuthi, in Ramnad District, as *The Hindu*'s correspondent noted, the stress of the events of the market-place was compounded by the simmering conflict between the merchant-dominated Nadar community of the town and the Maravars of the surrounding villages, who on the day of looting shot dead two policemen and injured the rest, ransacked the market, and finally turned on residential buildings.) The reports also serve, incidentally, to underscore Arnold's (1979) point that the target of the agitators was not the government or government officials and we cite an example, from Madurai, further down, of the crowd turning to local officials for succour against those whom they had identified as profiteers.

These are some extracts from the body of reportage of our three-week reference period; they are meant to convey some of the vividness of 1918 food riot reporting by a nationalist newspaper of record.

(i) 'Attempted Looting in Madura' (FOOC)

Madura, September 3: Consequent on the heavy rise in the price of foodgrain and other commodities in the town, rumours had been widely circulated within the last two or three days, that looting of shops was under contemplation and was to be resorted to by the people. This had caused great panic and yesterday about 12 noon, the rumour had gathered considerable momentum. Looting was in the air and the shopkeepers one by one began to close their business . . . suddenly the news spread like wild fire that a paddy go-down in the Pattaraikara street had been looted; and people in town were running in groups to the place. I hastened to the scene and found a large concourse of people collected together in that broad street to a length of nearly two furlongs . . . Just about 1 o'clock some dozen persons, all robust and well built, went into a paddy go-down and enquired the price at which the paddy was sold. The answer came . . . that it sold at six measures a rupee. The previous day the rate was seven measures a rupee and the enquirers demanded the special reasons for inflating the prices so suddenly and at so short an interval. Hot words began to be exchanged between the sellers and purchasers; and the result was a huge commotion. A very large number of people had collected themselves in the *pettai* [locality] and these men were pushed outside and the gates were closed and locked against them. Great uproar was raised, the mob mad with fury then threw stones, big and small, on the gates and made an attempt to break into the go-down and commit looting inside . . . Mr. G. F. Paddison, I.C.S., the Collector . . . was driving in his motorcar from his residence . . . a number of people . . . laid themselves flat on the ground with a view to preventing the car from passing straightaway . . . The crowds . . . represented to him that the merchants in Madura were by a combination inflating the prices every day and it had now become impossible for the poor people to buy things and get on in life. Profiteering was going on to an enormous extent; and if something was not done to control the prices, they said, looting would become the order of the day. They prayed that the good and sympathetic Collector who recently intervened on behalf of the Mill strikers and gave redress to their grievances, might likewise alleviate their grievance by promulgating an order fixing the rate at which the merchants should sell to them cloths, foodstuffs and other necessaries of life.

(ii) 'Looting and Unrest at Madras: Madras under Military Guard'

September 2, 1918: For the last four days loud complaints have been heard that prices of cloth, rice and chillies have risen very high and there was a persistent rumour that very soon the rice mandies in Wall Tax Road and the cloths bazaar in Devaraja Mudali Street would be looted. It would appear that even hand bills were circulated that such looting would occur. Vague rumours were also afloat that some of the mill hands in Choolai and some of the men to be sent to Basra would take part in the loot . . . rice and other [items] were thrown out into the street to be picked out by the mob . . . [at Pursewalkam] . . . another set of looters attacked the rice bazaar and cloth bazaar . . . but an alarm being raised a large crowd gathered and the Police also arrived on the spot . . . at Kotwal bazaar three shops selling rice, chillies, etc. were looted. Cocoanuts from a cocoanut shop were thrown in different directions and most of them destroyed. Vegetables, plantains, leaves etc. were trodden underfoot, shopkeepers were panic stricken and fled for their lives leaving the shops to their fate . . . the party that was driven back from the level crossing near the Salt Cotaurs rushed to Periamet along the Sydenham Road and arming themselves with bamboos kept on the road side in bundles for sale, attacked two or three marwari shops but no damage worth mentioning was done. Disappointed at this, they went into the Moore Market. The gates of the main building were closed. Birds were set free from their cages. A number of birds were killed and others were picked up by the mob. They then ran to the eastern building (Evening Bazaar) where several shopkeepers suffered heavy loss. Glasses, spectacles, toys, China wares, photos, etc. were destroyed. Shopkeepers in a body offered great resistance, and hand to hand fighting ensued. The police arrived on the spot and arrests were made.

(iii) 'At Tinnevelly'

Tinnevelly, September 19—A Correspondent writes:

The infection of food riots has spread to Tinnevelly. At Viravanallur it is reported on Tuesday night a mob surrounded the bundles of paddy dealers who had just then purchased a stock and on their refusal to sell paddy, looted six bandy loads of paddy. The rioters were mostly peaceful and plodding Sowrashtra weavers who were reduced to the utmost destitution owing to high price of yarn and dyes . . . Some merchants of Tuticorin have received anonymous warnings to reduce their price lest they should share the fate of Madras profiteers. The police have conferred with the merchants and advised them against the danger of charging inflated prices.

Some of the reports attempted an occupational description of the people in the crowd. When they were from among the rural working people, they were often described in terms of caste: 'people belonging to the Mala and Madiga class' (report from Ellore, *The Hindu*, 4 September 1918); 'Pallars of the hamlets of Kannanur and Narsingamangalam' (report from Samayapuram, Tiruchi District, *The Hindu*, 9 September 1918); 'a mob of about 5000 people, mostly pariahs' (report from Shiyali, present-day Sirkazhi, *The Hindu*, 20 September 1918). There were weavers, in Koranad (Thanjavur District) and Viravanallur (Tirunelveli District), and, in urban centres, industrial workers.

In Madras, textile workers were among the crowd; from Tanjore a report on the situation in Negapatam, described as a 'storm-centre of violent disturbances', warned that 'amongst the permanent population there are a considerable quantity of explosive material in the easily excitable and furiously ungovernable temperament of the workmen in the Railway shops and in the Harbour and business firms on the beach' (Report from Tanjore, *The Hindu*, 14 September 1918).

The opinion reflected in the reporting varied, of course, with the reporter. The 'mob' was a frequently used term for groups of agitators; and while the Madura correspondent could refer to the 'some dozen persons' at the paddy godown as 'robust and well-built' and a Madras correspondent described the crowd as 'on the whole a good-natured one', there were also reporters whose social predilections were explicit in their description of 'rowdies' or 'urchins'.

An important feature of our material is that as spontaneous protest spread to different regions, the response of the independent nationalist newspaper to the agitation *began to take on the character of a campaign*. This is most clearly reflected in editorial policy, but also shows itself in the way reportage was handled in the columns of the paper.

From 9 September, news of the agitation was published under a column titled 'Looting and Unrest'; on 17 September, the column title was quietly changed to 'High Prices and Unrest'. There is another interesting example of a neat intervention from the news desk: on 19 September, at the end of the 'High Prices and Unrest' column, after the reportage from the districts a small item was inserted, separated by a line but with no separate headline, of another food riot situation where the concerned Governor *had* intervened and the police played a somewhat non-traditional role: 'The rice riots in Japan are reported to have been noted for the presence of women among the mob in Kyoto. The Governor secured a supply of cheap foreign rice for sale and the police sympathise with the mob' (*The Hindu*, 19 September 1918). (This is followed by a report of places where 'disturbances and looting' took place.)

The editorials   There were five editorials, no less, on the subject of the food crisis and the people's agitation over the three-week period and they are characterized by an increasingly trenchant position *vis-à-vis* the government.

It is a characteristic of the editorials that they did not condemn the people's actions; the looting was seen as a response to the unbearable price situation:

The rise in prices of one article leads to a sympathetic rise in the rest. Chillies have gone up abnormally in prices. For what we paid 4 as. odd three months ago, today we are called upon to pay Rs. 1.10; black grams similarly has risen by about 50 percent, salt has gone up, we hear, by six annas a measure, a rise of 100 percent; rice also shows a marked tendency to rise; ghee and oils are characterised by the same feature . . . There is a belief which is, we think, justified in many cases, in many places in the mofussil especially, that profiteering remains unchecked on an immense scale. This, if it is a fact, must be put down with firmness; if it is not possible to do so by persuasion, compulsion must be unhesitatingly resorted to. The responsibility for eliminating profiteering and reducing the suffering of the people to a minimum rests on the Government . . . (editorial, 'The Food Problem', *The Hindu*, 5 September 1918)

Another editorial observed:

The Government have never had the high prices problem in hand. They are probably now considering the matter seriously. That prohibitive prices were prevailing Government have long been aware and only the other day a *communique* was issued on the sale of salt. But man does not live by salt alone, and we cannot conceive why Government have not dealt with the other necessaries of life in the same way. Their attentions have been directed to the matter over and over again, and these representations have resulted in a dissertation on the economic laws of supply and demand and a cut-and-dry programme for the publications of price lists through the cumbrous official machinery. Fine words butter no parsnips nor do statistical tables, which the proletariat never see nor care to see, stave off starvation, and the result is looting; not only in Madras but in other parts of the Presidency . . . (editorial, 'Looting in Madras', 10 September 1918)

Referring to the 'doings of a certain body in the City' charged with the supervision of mercantile activity:

Strange should be the constitution of the mind which, in spite of such unmistakeable signs of acute distress and depressing poverty, seeks to argue that no action is needed on the part of Government, that prices, though high, are not famine prices and that compulsory regulation of the trade in cloth and grain would alarm the merchants and create a panic. Such kind consideration for merchants may enable the merchants to clear huge profits part of which may be invested in war funds, but it is an altogether perverse and heartless view to take and speedy steps should be taken to see that the interests of the public do not suffer by such reactionary counsels being allowed to be made. (editorial, 'The Food Situation', 11 September 1918)

And another editorial pointed out:

Whatever may be the defects of Lord Pentland's Government, the charges at least cannot be laid at its doors that it ever acts with undue precipitation . . . The *Laissez faire* theory is so comfortable a one to hold that we need not be surprised at the assiduity with which our local Government pursues the great act of doing nothing. An endless supply of red tape, however, offers but indigestible fare for a population on the verge of starvation . . . (editorial, 'The Food Crisis', 19 September 1918)

The government was continuously faulted in the editorials and, as the campaign built up, in progressively stronger terms for mishandling the situation. It was faulted for not keeping prices in check and effectively controlling the market; for not ensuring supplies and clearing the bottlenecks in transportation; for not keeping the public informed about the measures it was taking to deal with the situation; and for a certain Olympian indifference, vividly captured by the fact that its major representatives continued their Hot Weather sojourn at the summer capital of Ootacamund while the crisis was at its peak. The editorial of 10 September 1918 stated clearly that the answer to the situation was to solve the food crisis, not to turn the police and army on the people. The editorials also stressed that the agitation sprang spontaneously from crisis conditions, and was not organized by the Home Rulers.

The other policy recommendations by the newspaper are worth noting. The first appeared in the editorial of 3 September, when the paper called for *state control* of the market in essential commodities during a period when a 'legitimate level' of prices was 'exceeded abnormally'. The second was a suggestion that a system of *food zoning* be introduced during a period of crisis. While acknowledging that this was a suggestion that the Madras government had made earlier, *The Hindu* picked up a statement by the Collector of Guntur during this period to call attention to the point:

Mr. Davies pointed out virtually that Guntur had to starve in the midst of plenty, because the Director of Civil Supplies would not allow him to restrict exports . . . The curious thing . . . is that though the Director refused to restrict exports, he consented to allow imports from the north. In fairness to the Madras Government, they appear to have recommended the prohibition of export of products whenever it was deemed that the exporting area would thereby suffer acute distress. The Government of India . . . overruled the Local Government's decision to prohibit exports, on the extraordinary ground that the whole of India constituted a single economic unit! (editorial, 'The Government and Prices', 12 September 1918)

This was also the period when a major preoccupation of the government was the war effort, and its representatives were busy raising the Second War Loan which was advertised on the newspaper's front page every day of our three-week period. The editorials intertwined references to war with discussions of the crisis in the Presidency. The editorial of 10 September mentions the war effort only to observe that the activity of raising the War Loan was matched by inactivity on the food front, putting the observation down to what 'the people say':

Meanwhile the people say that when the Government want money for the war loan or soldiers for the King, the Governor finds it convenient to tour to Calicut and to preside at meetings at which the wealthy subscribe liberally, while, when the poor are suffering and unable to make two ends meet, the Governor and his Councillors are enjoying the climate of Ootacamund and are oblivious to their suffering. (editorial, 'Looting in Madras', 10 September 1918)

The last Indian famine: Bengal, 1943, and the role of the press   India's last famine was the Great Bengal Famine of 1943 in which an estimated three million people died, with a particularly heavy toll among agricultural labourers, fishermen, transport workers, and non-agricultural labourers in rural areas. Sen (1981) finds the role of the *Statesman* very significant. It highlighted 'the conspicuous failure of the Government to anticipate the famine and to recognise its emergence' and its 'powerful campaign with news reports, photographs and editorial comments on the calamity' won praise later from the

Famine Inquiry Commission and also contributed an important insight into the role of an independent professional press in relation to famine and poverty.[26]

The two editorials from the *Statesman* (of 14 and 16 October 1943) referred to by Sen (1981) demonstrate the high competence, the critical initiative, and the active nature of the role. The colonial authorities were virtually indicted by this British-owned newspaper (edited by Ian Stevens) for grave misjudgement of the crisis and for covering up the facts. In the editorial of 14 October, titled 'Seen from a Distance', the Secretary of State for India was pulled up thus:

Mr. Amery's speeches would be more acceptable in this country were they less habitually smug. His Parliamentary utterance last Tuesday on what he euphemistically called the Indian food 'situation' seems, from the long cabled text, intended to suggest to the British public that, so far as the Government of India and the India Office were concerned, all that could have been done was . . . Nasty words such as famine, starvation, corpse or cholera were carefully avoided. The Central Government's unexplained and amazing omission to establish a Food Department for a full year after Japan's declaration of war gained no mention.

As for citizens' feelings, they had been roused by the remarkably insensitive content and tone of Amery's speech and mounting evidence of a much higher famine toll than the authorities had accepted earlier. Referring to Amery's boast that it was largely due to the central government's exertions that 'a situation of widespread distress' has been confined to Bengal, Cochin, Travancore, and parts of the Deccan, the *Statesman* commented: 'As an example of the politician's art of smoothly evasive meiosis this takes memorably high place. Bengal alone contains a population larger than Britain's . . . Yet the distant Mr. Amery can imply that her distress does not by itself justify such adjectives as serious or widespread.'

The second editorial, 'The Death-Roll' (16 October 1943), is an outstanding example of informed, precise journalism. It looks closely at the government's figures on the weekly death-roll in the light of different aspects of the evidence. The newspaper deplored 'the continuous appearance of effort on the part of persons somewhere within India's Governmental machine, perhaps out here, perhaps in Whitehall, to play down, suppress, distort, or muffle the truth about Bengal' (even if a somewhat loyalist note was sounded through the remark that such an attitude was 'dragging the fair name of the British Raj needlessly low' and a somewhat sweeping assertion was recorded to the effect that during the famines near the end of the nineteenth century, 'the heyday of British imperial responsibility', no effort was spared 'to probe and proclaim the truth about any maladministration, so that it might be promptly dealt with and the blot on the honour of the Indian Empire removed').

The *Statesman*'s factual reporting, exposés, and editorial campaign had much value in the situation; they reflected both the active function of

---

[26] See Sen (1981: 52–85 and also 195–216).

independent journalism and the professional credibility and influence of a serious newspaper. But what can we say about the role of nationalist publications during this period? To call attention to another approach and perspective, we cite an editorial from the Birla-owned *Eastern Economist* belonging to the *Hindustan Times* group (the editorial, titled 'The Bengal Famine: India and Her People on Trial', was published in the issue of 5 November 1943). The perspective adopted in this editorial is not loyalist in any way; it is the perspective of contraposing the inherent tendencies and the interests of British colonial rule to the interests of the Indian nation. Apart from indicting the British government for 'such a woeful lack of imagination and efficiency that they have allowed a situation to develop which has gone out of control', it asserted that it was 'not the scarcity of food during the last few months alone' that had brought about the tragedy. The causes were clearly 'more deep-seated'.

The editorial analysis moved without inhibition into the field of economics: today it reads like a somewhat old-fashioned admixture of instant economics and perceptive political economy-orientated concerns. There is an element of exaggeration or overblown rhetoric and a lack of precision and nuance which were later to become one of the inherent features of Indian journalism in covering droughts and other types of 'food crisis'. 'Bengal's famine', the editorial assertion ran, 'is only a portent. Famine stalks all through the land and is not confined to Bengal, though it is seen at its worst in that province. In Travancore, Cochin and Malabar the situation is, if anything, worse than in Bengal, as the Dewan of Travancore has pointed out. In the Ceded Districts in Madras, in Orissa and in parts of Bombay conditions are as near famine as one can think of.'

Aside from the burden of contributing financially to the war, policy-related weaknesses in handling India as one integrated economic unit, transport bottlenecks, and the poor distribution system were blamed as factors that had contributed to the terrible crisis. The prescription concentrated on the short-term and long-term responsibility of the state in controlling famine and preventing its appearance in the same region or in other areas. 'Preventing the recurrence of famine', noted the editorial in the *Eastern Economist*, 'requires a complete reversal of our financial and economic policies. The country should not be asked to undertake any further responsibility for feeding the armed forces quartered in India. A big production drive should be organised . . . India should be administered as one economic unit, and no amount of provincial autonomy should be allowed to make inroads into the economic integrity of India.'

The editorial emphasized that while there was an imperative for emergency famine relief and famine combat measures, 'the after-famine problem is even more important'. It called for basic measures to tackle such massive problems as 'the pauperisation of millions of people', for a determination to go beyond the miserable inadequacy of the 'gruel kitchen' approach, for plans to make the economy more productive in both agriculture and industry and provide for the 're-employment of all labour that is seeking employment'.

The role of the nationalist press, and of conscientious independent investigation, in relation to the great crisis of 1943 is brought out vividly in a collection compiled by Santhanam (1943). It includes cartoons by Shankar and a moving collection of photographs assembled with the co-operation of the publications *People's War*, Bombay, the *Amrita Bazar Patrika*, and the *Hindustan Standard*, and organizations such as the Cyclone Relief Committee, Contai, the All-India Women's Association, Calcutta, and the Friends' Ambulance Unit, Calcutta. (Some of these searing images of human suffering and desperation have resurfaced in the attempts by Satyajit Ray and also Mrinal Sen to recreate through the cinematic medium the experience and essence of the Great Bengal Famine of 1943.)

Necessarily characterized by unevenness, elements of propaganda in defence of people's rights against the policies of the Raj, and an inclination towards instant economics, the Santhanam collection offers valuable documentary insight into the strong and aggressive role various sections of the independent press played during India's last real famine.

Current role and tendencies: vis-à-vis *two kinds of hunger*   The phenomenon of hunger and poverty on a mass scale and in specific places finds a great deal of coverage in Indian newspapers and magazines today. Reports, semi-investigative feature articles, occasional interventions by economists and other specialists, editorial observations, and letters from readers dealing with the subject in one form or another would, for the Indian press as a whole, run into tens of columns per day. This coverage, as is to be expected, gets significantly expanded during a period of widespread drought covering several states and affecting millions of people and their basic conditions of life and work. It goes without saying that given the pluralism of the press on the one hand and of society and politics on the other in a country as vast as India, coverage of the phenomenon of hunger and poverty is quite uneven. For the sake of manageable analysis, it may be assumed that about twenty influential newspapers and magazines—among daily newspapers, say the *Indian Express*, the *Times of India*, *The Hindu*, the *Statesman*, the *Telegraph*, plus several Indian language newspapers such as *Malayala Manorama* and *Mathrubhumi* of Kerala, *Eenadu* of Andhra Pradesh, *Ananda Bazar Patrika* of West Bengal, *Gujarat Samachar* of Gujarat, and a couple of newspapers active in the Hindi-speaking belt, and among the magazines *India Today, Frontline, Sunday, Illustrated Weekly*, plus a couple of mass-circulated periodicals published in Indian languages—would constitute a useful sample of current coverage of hunger and poverty. Such a sample is likely to miss out much in the experience of Indian journalism, which is characterized by a tremendous diversity in standards and resources available to publications, but since the sample would be very influential in terms of circulation and the impact on the decision-making process it would be strong in serving our purpose. We do not attempt a systematic content analysis, but offer instead a preliminary description and a somewhat impressionistic assessment of the current role and tendencies of the independent Indian press in relation to the phenomenon of hunger and poverty.

How valid is the 'dichotomy' in the role observed by Amartya Sen in his analysis of famine and poverty and brought to the fore in his 1982 Coromandel Lecture in New Delhi? The current contribution made by the press in reporting extensively on the drought is in line with the historically well-observed role and the important place it is given in Sen's analysis. On the other hand, the criticism that Indian newspapers have not been sensitive or responsive to 'regular', chronic hunger and subhuman poverty has been heard frequently from inside the journalistic profession. At one level, the criticism is obviously valid, although—for what it is worth—the Indian press is inclined increasingly to wrestle with the enormous challenge of discovering and doing something about the phenomenon of poverty and hunger in a country that has, for all its advantages, a greater mass of it than probably any other. From a sensitive or progressive social science standpoint, however, this coverage does appear 'low-key' or 'tame', aside from proving frequently incompetent.

The reasons for this would need to be looked for at several levels of the newspaper field: policy orientation and bias, entrenched professional routine and habits, the ideological and political predilections of journalists and the influential and trendy currents of the national and international literature they are exposed to, a variety of mundane practical constraints, the quality of resources available to the press, and so on. But as a generalization applicable to most of the field, it would be probably accurate to say that the basic problem is not that the rules of the game tie the press's hands in some unwritten way in relation to this sensitive subject. It is that the intellectual and methodological resources and competence required to investigate the complex, mixed-up socio-economic realities of India in anything other than superficial terms, to handle data and sources meticulously and critically, to make sense in a popular medium of a body of sophisticated but sharply varying analyses, findings, and prescriptions available to it, in principle, from the academic field, and to do all this interestingly, would demonstrably be beyond the press's current level of capability or competence. In the concluding section of this essay, we propose a line of achievable advance based on the strengths and capabilities available to the Indian press from the quite developed resource pool of certain branches of Indian social science—notably economics which has paid much empirical, and a certain amount of theoretical, attention to hunger and poverty across the land. In relation to the wealth of poverty studies in India, the coverage in what is supposed to be an increasingly sophisticated medium is underdeveloped.

Coverage of drought, 'food crisis' and anticipated famine There is no doubt that the phenomenon of hunger and distress resulting from the recent spells of drought affecting several states and millions of people, especially agricultural labourers and other sections of the rural poor, has been given major attention in both the national and local press in various parts of the country. Reporters have turned up a considerable amount of descriptive detail from the field, sympathetic accounts of rural distress and even desperation reflected in the migration of thousands of families and in distress cattle sales, human interest stories focusing on individuals, and exposés of official incompetence, insensitivity, and cover-up tendencies. The itinerary of Prime Minister Rajiv Gandhi's visit in 1985–6 to areas of extreme poverty, hunger, and distress was as often as not influenced by press coverage which could at times be 'hyped-up journalism'. But the field reports have generally been valuable: they have tended, in state after state, to challenge official claims relating to drought relief efforts, the efficacy and destination of funds spent on creating employment and elementary purchasing power in a situation of near-collapse of the economy of the afflicted households, and in general the drought policies of the state and centre. So much so that a general political theme encountered in the campaign conducted by opposition parties and independent critics in various states against official drought management policies was that newspapers showed up the realities on the ground in the face of official untruths and suppression of facts. This applied to the situation in Congress (I)-ruled states such as Maharashtra, Gujarat, Rajasthan, and Orissa as much as it did to the exceptionally severe and recurrent drought in Janata-ruled Karnataka, and the situations in Telugu Desam-ruled Andhra Pradesh and AIADMK-ruled Tamil Nadu.

A cover story in the Sunday magazine section of the national daily the *Indian Express* (of 1 June 1986), reviewing the situation of the 1985–6 drought in four states—Maharashtra, Gujarat, Rajasthan, and Karnataka—and official responses to the crisis, noted that Karnataka witnessed 'the distress sale of tens of thousands of cattle last winter. The cattle population affected by the drought has been estimated as 107.39 lakhs while the human population exposed to it has been about 210.32 lakhs . . . the State's economy is in a shambles.' The article noted, in this connection, that 'it was only in the last two months of 1985 that the State Government took note of the serious shortage of fodder, and *that too after* newspapers carried detailed reports on cattle sales' (emphasis added). The newspapers referred to were local Kannada newspapers, such as *Samyuktha Karnataka*, and national dailies like *The Hindu* and the *Indian Express*.[27]

What is the kind of socio-economic and human interest detail that Indian newspapers bring to the attention of their readers in such circumstances? A sampling of reports from national dailies and magazines published in English is revealing:

[27] Some of the coverage, especially in the Kannada newspaper *Samyuktha Karnataka*, which is associated with the Congress (I) party, reflected oppositional politics. This bears out Sen's (1982) impression that the pressure from the independent press combined with campaigns by opposition parties would make it virtually impossible for any government keen on staying in power to shut its eye to a major crisis and to avoid pursuing famine-averting policies.

The story is the same every year—only the dates and the statistics are different. The vocabulary, too, remains unchanged . . . the same tired phrases are conjured up year after year to describe a countryside 'reeling under', 'in the grip of' or 'afflicted by' drought. The suffering, real and intense, comes through in a few revealing images —people elbowing each other out of the way in the frenzied race towards the water tanker; the worn and dehydrated faces of labourers toiling mechanically at 'drought relief works' while their babies crawl around in the heat and the dust, sad-eyed, fodder-starved cattle lined up for the short journey to the slaughterhouse . . .

The people of Rajkot and Jamnagar are facing the worst drinking water scarcity in living memory. Broken pipelines and ditches in the middle of the road are a common sight in Rajkot. People run after water tankers, like crazy animals, while some racketeers mint money by selling water pilfered from the pipeline right under the nose of the government. Private operators provide as much as two lakh gallons of water to the needy in Rajkot at about Rs. 150 per 10,000 gallons . . .

[In Karnataka] on account of both the kharif and rabi crops failing this year, about 30 per cent of the targeted food production has been lost and most farm labourers, along with a large number of small and marginal farmers, have lost their means of livelihood. In over 12,000 villages in 110 talukas spread over 17 districts, the average crop yield per acre has been less than 25 per cent. The State has witnessed the distress sale of tens of thousands of cattle last winter . . . the State's economy is in a shambles and resource mobilisation has been severely hit . . . One area in which the government has scored heavily is the provision of drinking water, as a result of a massive operation, which included sinking borewells, implementing mini-water supply and piped water supply schemes . . . [But] it appears that the government has not been able to go beyond the conventional concept that relief works mean mainly the building and repair of roads . . . One consolation is that as many as 32,213 hectares have been covered under afforestation schemes. But this is too small an area compared to the vast 'treeless' areas of the northern districts. (*Indian Express*, Sunday magazine section, 1 June 1986)

A 1600 km drive through some of the badly hit districts brought this reporter face to face with that agonising reality. Of the State's 175 taluks, 154 are reeling under the drought. Nearly 1.59 crore [15.9 million] people and 90 lakh [9 million] head of cattle are affected. Both kharif and rabi output has been hit and the shortfall in the targeted production of 85 lakh tonnes is expected to be a staggering 45 lakh tonnes. An estimated 15 lakh people need to be sustained daily on relief employment until the South-West monsoon in June. As much as Rs. 160 crores has already been funnelled from Government coffers into relief measures.

All one hears from the demoralised peasants is an endless narration of misery . . . It is being described as the worst drought of the century, though few have called it a 'famine' mainly because people, though not cattle, have so far escaped starvation . . .

Gaollara Kyathanna of Dodderi village in the almost barren Chellekere taluk of Chitradurga district is an illiterate marginal farmer who does not even know his age. He looks past 70. The three bagas of sajje, a coarse grain his sons had grown last year on their dry land, were not sufficient to feed the family of six. Now the family lives on the Rs. 7.80 a day one of the sons and his wife each earns on a Government relief work. Village-level officials have not issued the family the most sought-after 'green card' which ensures a ration of about 10 kg of grain a month besides clothes . . . The distress, coupled with the abolition of the . . . mid-day meal schemes, has affected school attendance. When those who have studied up to the SSLC are jobless and are tending goats, why should we send our children to school, ask the Harijans of Purlihalli in Chellakere taluk. Inducements like free education, text-books and uniforms work only during 'fair weather'.

All over northern Karnataka people complained of a sharp spurt in the prices of foodgrains. The revenue authorities maintain that the situation is not so grave as to warrant the opening of gruel centres . . . Some women scratching the scorched land were seen near Madhugiri town in Tumkur district. They were looking for groundnuts in the roots of plants harvested last season. One of them, Gowramma, had got four nuts after the morning-to-noon drudgery. Peanuts? But that is how the poor literally eke out a living. . . .

Karnataka, which has received migrants from the dry tracts of tamil Nadu and Andhra Pradesh for ages, is sending out its people this year to other States . . . Aggravating the problem in Kolar and Tumkur districts is the inflow of people from the Rayalaseema region of Andhra Pradesh which is also facing drought . . . Karnataka has wet patches and dry expanses . . . The crucial period is March to June. For the present, the rural and urban folk scan the spotless blue skies for that speck of cloud that might bring some succour. (A. Jayaram, 'On a Tour of Drought-Hit Areas', in *Frontline*, 22 February–17 March 1986)

In the state of Andhra Pradesh the 1985–6 drought was very widespread, with 250 taluks out of 330 declared drought affected. Telugu newspapers such as *Andhra Bhoomi*, *Andhra Prabha*, and *Eenadu* provided detailed and lively coverage of the impact on crops, cattle, and the conditions of the most vulnerable sections of the rural poor. So did the English language newspapers.

Detailed and sensitive coverage of a drought, its early signals, its effects in terms of the conditions of life and work of the people affected, and governmental performance in this crisis has for long been a strength of the independent Indian press, its local as well as national, its small as well as medium-sized and big components.

In his study of the political responses to the Bihar 'famine' of 1966–7, the political scientist Brass (1986) found that both 'the press reports about the developing crisis situation and the responses of the politicians and authorities to the situation turned the Bihar Famine of 1966–67 into a political drama in which many of the principals self-consciously played their roles on the public stage'. And more specifically:

framing the whole drama—commenting on it, in fact, virtually creating it—were the local and national press. The Bihar press, particularly two Patna English-language dailies, *Searchlight* and the *Indian Nation*, adopted vigorously critical positions towards the Congress Government and the administration of the State. Their correspondents toured the countryside during the drought and wrote numerous reports of famine conditions and starvation deaths that contradicted the statements of the Government and the administration, which said that the situation was under control.

Brass discovered that the reporters who accompanied Ministers and political bigwigs on their tour of the crisis-affected areas set the tone for the strong descriptions and characterizations of the overall situation and, in fact, created or evoked the language of 'unprecedented' crisis. For example, in one sample scrutinized by Brass, the reporter was moved to describe 'the rice-belt of Bihar' near Patna as looking 'like the desolate wastes of the Rann of Kutch in mid-summer'.

In this particular case, there were several weaknesses in the press coverage of the 'famine': Brass's study showed 'no systematic reports . . . at this time [October 1966] of various other signs and symptoms of famine, such as wandering, migration, increases in criminal activity, and the like. At this stage, much of the expressed concern was premonitory rather than immediate.'

More serious was the fact that the Bihar newspapers did not or could not see through official attempts to explain the major crisis in terms of 'drought-induced crop failure that led to a further food availability decline [FAD] in an already food-deficit State' whereas the evidence, including official statistics, clearly argued otherwise. Brass's analysis suggests that in such cases, the retention of the FAD theory as an explanation of 'famine' and scarcity

serves three important functions for the authorities . . . first, it equalises need within the area defined as famine-stricken or suffering from scarcity. All regions and all classes are said to suffer equally, if in different ways. . . . Second, the theory serves to minimise the ability of the authorities and people to help themselves, thereby justifying external assistance. Third, the theory diverts attention from inequalities and suffering that exist in normal times in particular regions and among disadvantaged social groups.

Nevertheless, for all the weaknesses and distortions in the response to the crisis that it allowed itself to reflect, the Bihar press in 1966–7 played a significant democratic role. Brass's study poses for us sharply the issue of the relationship between the severity of the 'famine'/drought/scarcity situation and its 'informatization' (a clumsy, but unavoidable, word in this context) and politicization; it highlights the world of difference which relatively independent information and news media can make to the consequences and impact of a crisis. One of Brass's conclusions relates to the 'high degree of politicisation' of the Bihar crisis of 1966–7. This point is vital to our analysis: 'Famine and scarcity have occurred before and since the Bihar Famine, and both have occurred with a lesser degree of politicisation or have been ignored by politicians and the press . . . In a democratised crisis, the crisis for the people becomes a crisis for the politicians as well.'

Several local and national newspapers covered actively, and generally with a greater sense of sophistication and nuance than in the Bihar case, the Maharashtra droughts of 1970–3. In particular, the *Times of India* distinguished itself in this coverage. There were numerous reports, editorial page assessments, and leaders over this period. In the 1980s, food crises which have developed or threatened to develop elsewhere, in other states and localities, have tended to get covered in increasing detail by various sections of the press which have provided growing evidence of being aware or conscious, in a professional or institutional sense, of the adversarial role performed. The contemporary coverage of the extensive situation of drought (in the summer of 1987) by various newspapers round the country appears to be a data-rich field that can be examined systematically by scholars interested in this role.

Tendencies of overstatement and sensationalism

There is increasingly, in sections of the Indian press, a tendency to dramatize and sensationalize the coverage of poverty and hunger on a mass scale, usually when a crisis threatens, but also in the 'regular', persistent form. While the approach might seem to serve a positive function in that it highlights the problem and brings it to the fore, the quality of the treatment, the obscuring of contours and certainly nuances, the blurring of definitions and specifics, and the dramatizing of poverty and hunger lowers credibility among serious readers and, from the standpoint of serious analysis, proves counter-productive. Unfortunately, international experience demonstrates that tendentious or 'populist' journalism and also propaganda tones can make a mark and set the pace and some of the trends in a quite competitive field.[28]

A widely read example in mainstream Indian journalism of sensationalizing a crisis and, in fact, transforming through journalistic overstatement (with propaganda tones) a widespread drought into an unprecedented 'famine' is the cover story in the *Illustrated Weekly* of 16 January–1 February 1986 by Nikhil Lakshman. The feature titled 'Hunger' carries the cover page announcement: 'As the Republic Celebrates Its 36th Anniversary, 100 Million Indians are Threatened by Famine.' The ten-page article treats as quite 'academic' any boundary line between *drought* and *famine*, predicts the direst consequences for India—including 'ecological disaster'—and indicts the government for remaining 'cool to the famine' (up to the time of writing of the article) and for playing 'semantic games'.

[28] The most detailed and trenchant criticism of the interrelationship between the structure, content, and tendencies of the American media come from an insider, Bagdikian (1983), who argues that the monopoly structure and control of the media have produced 'social and political sterility' in the reporting of events and 'silence on fundamental forces behind major news events'. Unfortunately, the media monopoly fosters viability and great commercial success in the market. Bagdikian (1983) concludes that 'the news media—diluted of real meaning by apolitical and sterile context, homogenised with the growth of monopoly, overwhelmingly more of service to merchants than to the audience, and filled with frivolous material—are a threat to their own future but also to the body politic . . . When the news is designed to exclude a third or a half of the population, it has sacrificed much of its standing as a democratic mechanism' (pp. 206–9). Again, Bagdikian (1985) observes, 'Gross propagandising, it is true, can reduce profits. But where monopoly reigns, as in 98 per cent of the cities with local papers, consumers have no alternative and owners have great latitude . . . The major media have enormous political and social influence. Those who control the media can make the most empty-headed political hack sound like a Founding Father and the most self-serving piece of legislation resemble the Golden Rule' (pp. 16–17). And so on. Some of these assessments might sound like overstatements, but there is little question among the serious Western media critics that bad journalism sells and, under certain circumstances, is quite capable of edging the better product out of the market. In India itself the *Hindustan Times*, which is generally recognized by professionals as having the weakest content among the major English language national dailies, is an established commercial success, especially in the national capital where it reigns as the top-circulated newspaper.

The feature claims to be based on an 'investigation' by one journalist into the phenomenon of unprecedented mass hunger in 1985–6—'now it's famine. Spreading its tentacles across nine States; affecting the lives of millions of men, women and children.' The article is right through a mixture of some well-observed verities and obvious exaggeration, with a turn of phrase, a quote, a verbal sweep, a stroke of journalistic breathlessness heightening the effect. The contrast between 'a nation which is held up as an example of agricultural glory in the Third World', a nation of 'foodgrain surpluses' on the one hand and a nation in which mass hunger is 'an unpleasant but integral part of our lives', is drawn legitimately enough. But the assertion that famine threatens 100 million people in nine states goes along with the rather tame statement that 'accurate information is unavailable' on starvation deaths—which are guessed to be over 500 in Orissa, 'victims of the epidemics that inevitably accompany the pestilence'.

The cover feature in the *Illustrated Weekly* charges that 'so far, the [Rajiv] Gandhi Government has remained cool to the famine and not taken any steps to channelise some of the excess stock toward scarcity-hit areas. It has been hostile to the States' urgent appeals for aid as well . . . three years into a crisis on a war footing, the government has chosen to play semantic games. This is a dangerous trend.' Aside from the centre, state government after state government is indicted for doing too little, too late. And such breathless assertions back up the argument:

Rajasthan, according to Chief Minister Harideo Joshi, is in the vice-grip of the worst famine in living memory . . . the overall situation in Maharashtra continues to be grim . . . In Orissa . . . large areas continue to be battered by famine with the result that cultivators have lost their zest for agriculture . . . For Karnataka, it is the worse famine this century . . . 27 out of the 45 districts in Madhra Pradesh are presently victims of famine . . . Gujarat was in trouble . . . [with] famine conditions existing in . . . 17 districts.

Only in the case of Andhra Pradesh does the writer settle for the lesser term, *drought*, and there too it is asserted for Rayalaseema that 'the current famine is the 20th in the last 28 years'.

There is in the article no careful examination of the specifics of mass hunger and distress, no attempt to identify possible factors that might have brought about the collapse of employment, purchasing power, and the economy of these people. The criticism of the central and state governments fails to be specific and becomes a stance of alleging that they were slow to recognize the symptoms of the phenomenon of 'famine' or tried to cover them up, moved far too slowly into miserably inadequate action, did not take efficient measures (in most cases) to implement the relief schemes, and did not, at any rate, have any worthwhile long-term or 'permanent' policy to combat the phenomenon.

Has not more land been brought under the plough and under irrigation over the past three decades? Have not cropping patterns diversified and foodgrain production *in toto* been raised rather impressively? Has not agricultural technology been transformed in important parts of India, making self-sufficiency in food a going proposition? And is there not evidence of some kind of impact of all this on rural poverty and hunger? Does not this objective side of the picture have to be taken into account while evaluating the poor record of the government in relation to the challenge of doing away with crisis hunger 'permanently'? Our journalist will have none of this. Nor does he look seriously at the other side of the picture and raise questions and issues that Indian economists have been discussing for long relating to a bleak development record in combating endemic 'regular' hunger.

The *Illustrated Weekly* article on the Great Indian 'Famine' of 1985–6 highlights another tendency in current Indian journalism: the meshing of *instant economics*[29] with *instant ecology*,[30] with the latter increasingly emphasized. The basic explanation advanced for the crisis, aside from government inaction and stupidity, is *ecological*. The 'ecological crisis', it is asserted, will intensify with man-induced 'gradual desertification of the terrain' which is generally regarded as the function of the current agricultural strategy. 'Authorities' and 'experts' are selectively cited to allege 'destruction of water resources' (by 'land mismanagement' and various other blunders), a wholesale neglect of the vital importance of afforestation, dangerously ill-conceived irrigation schemes, totally misplanned cropping patterns, and 'a steady erosion in our national resources'. Anil Agarwal, a writer who has made some sort of input into ecological journalism in India and is treated as a kind of cult figure by

---

[29] For an excellent discussion of what *instant economics* could mean to public policy in the field of food economics and hunger, see Sen (1985b): '"Practical" people are easily convinced that they know precisely what the problem is, and even though what they "know" with such certainty varies from person to person, they are impatient with the economists' tendency to use complicated ideas to tackle apparently simple problems. What may be called "instant economics" has always appealed to the quick-witted layman impatient with the slow-moving economist. In the field of hunger and food policy, the need for speed is of course genuinely important, and this impatience does have considerable sense. But instant economics is also dangerously deceptive, particularly in this field. Millions of lives depend on the adequacy of the policy response . . . Past mistakes of policy have been responsible for the death of many millions of people and the suffering of hundreds of millions, and this is not a subject in which short-cuts in economic reasoning can be taken to be fairly costless.'

[30] *Instant ecology* is a tendency that has surfaced in the Indian press over the past decade, although there is little doubt that there are parallel developments in other parts of the world. Some of the concerns might be progressive or legitimate, and in this sense some of the press coverage, particularly on ecological and political controversies such as the *Silent Valley* episode, has performed a worthwhile public service. Typically, however, the ecologically orientated journalist in India, recognizing a 'soft' and permissive field (in contrast to development economics), makes the most sweeping and extravagant claims about what he or she knows will be the ecological impact of, say, the new technology in agriculture, the effects and linkages with other problems, and plays the role of a pundit. Ecological overstatements, and assertions about desertification, the impact on rainfall trends, and so on that the journalist need not even bother to attempt to substantiate (beyond quoting some 'specialist' in a field where specialists might differ considerably), abound in certain sections of the Indian press. Such trends have obviously been influenced by international currents of instant ecology which Indian journalists and intellectuals are exposed to.

several of his followers, is quoted as saying: 'India is on the road to ecological, economic and social disaster.'

Articles of this kind, and the sensational manner of featuring them, lower the credibility of Indian magazine journalism with respect to socio-economic problems and issues and appear to be misconceived and misdirected responses to the need to provide support to anti-hunger strategies.

Coverage of endemic, 'regular' hunger

We shall begin this section by citing the opinions of some professionals on the role the Indian press plays in highlighting (or not highlighting) the problem of persistent 'regular' hunger and in motivating (or not motivating) public opinion to push for sustained and intelligently targeted anti-hunger policies.

[On] the point whether newspapers are sensitive to the problems connected with poverty or . . . other problems facing the majority of the people in this country . . . my own impression is that the English language newspapers do more in this respect than the regional language newspapers . . . the distance from the area of conflict or the type of readership which a particular paper might be catering for plays a part. (Nikhil Chakravartty, editor, *Mainstream*, and Chairman of the first NAMEDIA conference, 1983, in an interview 'Is the Indian Press Free and Fair' published in *Communicator*, 15/2, April 1980)

In an article titled 'News Coverage and Values in Official Media' published in *Mainstream*, 24/29, 22 March 1986, M. V. Desai, a veteran in the media field, noted that Indian newspapers reported much 'official' news, even if they were often critical of government action. They provided little news from mofussil towns and villages. As for news about hunger as in the recently high-lighted case of the people of Kalahandi in Orissa, it was not broken until after the visit of a VIP (Prime Minister Rajiv Gandhi who visited the area in July 1985).

Drought, food, sales and starvation deaths in Kalahandi did seem to scandalise mediamen throughout the country. Almost every national English daily wrote editorials condemning the situation—State government officials, local politicians and journalists however are not surprised at the situation and ask why the nation's press has suddenly taken up cudgels on behalf of the starving people of Kalahandi who have been suffering from two decades of chronic drought. (Saibal Dasgupta, 'Orissa: In the Shadow of Neglect', *Indian Express* magazine, 25 August 1985)

We shall take up the sòmewhat rhetorical question posed at the end of this last evaluation by the journalist. In the main, Indian newspapers probably take a less 'low-key' approach to persistent hunger—and to the 'deadly conflicts' over capturing enough food to eat and survive—than they did a decade ago. However, the problem of persistent hunger and conflicts over access to food remaining, in effect, a 'tame issue' to Indian newspapers continues. The journalistic rationalization of this might run as follows. Since poverty and hunger have been around for a long time and since they exist on a forbiddingly vast scale in this society, newspaper coverage of them has to carry some element of novelty, some unusual facet, some waking-up quality in order to qualify as more than a 'tame' or 'soft' item. In newspaper parlance, you need some kind of news or topical peg to hang your hunger and poverty story on—if you are to convince your news editor or editor. Slowly and sporadically, this conception of journalism has begun to change, but the old approach is bolstered by news/editorial values and the impression that the space constraint and presumed reader interest do not make anything other than the present approach realistic.

Another occupational problem which is widely recognized by the critics is the 'essential dilettantism' of journalism. Now it is true that changes in the nature and scope of news coverage, the emphasized interest in science and technology, the importance of finance, economic journalism, and so on have pushed reporters into more specialization as *journalists* than used to be the case. At least in the more serious news organizations in India, the search is on for increasingly sophisticated science reporters, economic reporters, legal and industrial relations correspondents, energy, defence, and national security affairs writers, and so on. Even so, some familiarity with the content of the economic/financial/business newspapers in India suggests that there is no persuasive evidence that this supposedly specialized branch of Indian journalism does any deep-going, sustained investigation into the situation of persistent hunger and extreme deprivation in the land.

There is another basic problem inherent in the practice of journalism whether it is in a developing society such as India or a highly developed society such as the United States. For all its advantages and clout, journalism as a profession deservedly carries a reputation for *superficiality*, so much so that in English language usage, to be 'journalistic' is to merit a certain kind of condescending or otherwise unflattering response from serious intellectuals, scholars, and so forth. The insider critics point to the press's preoccupation with action, sensation, measurable developments, organized movements, personalities, surprises, and novelties as limiting its quality, role, and impact. Journalists might, to themselves and to superficial external observers of the profession, seem constantly to be participating in the making of history, but they clearly lack—as a professional group—the sensitivities, the nuances, and the rooted opportunities of the participant observers. The caricature of the successful journalist would be that of a fleet-footed participant observer who comes, sees, scribbles notes, conquers news space—and then moves on to something else.

This general observation can be related to an interesting small-scale phenomenon that has surfaced in Indian journalism during the last decade and a half: the journalist who turns researcher and undertakes to offer deeper insight, a better class of analysis, and more meaningful prescriptions on socio-economic subjects than garden variety colleagues. To the extent that this move by a small section of journalists who have made some kind of mark in their professional field is triggered by a restlessness with the superficialities and staleness of routine journalism it would seem to hold some promise. But the specific results of this move 'beyond journalism', to the extent they can be sampled in the columns of readily available publications, are not inspiring thus far.

Finally, we shall cite this influential example of socially sensitive journalism making a difference.

The *Indian Express* has, on several occasions, brought to the fore cases of bonded labour, the cruelty and indignity imposed on indigent women in specific rural contexts, starvation deaths in parts of the country, and so on. In 1985 it took the lead among national newspapers in covering starvation deaths amidst appalling socio-economic circumstances in Kalahandi district in Orissa. Kalahandi is one of the seventy-four vulnerable areas identified and covered by the Drought Prone Areas Programme. The first revelation of the long persistent hunger and of starvation deaths here appeared in the national media around the time of Prime Minister Rajiv Gandhi's visit to the area in July 1985. On 26 July 1985, the *Indian Express* (Madras edition) brought out a front page news item titled 'Starvation Deaths in Kalahandi District' with a Komna (Orissa) dateline. It reported the death on account of starvation of at least six persons in the preceding fortnight and the struggle for life of many more in the Komna block of Kalahandi district. Details of the dead were provided. It was noted that hungry people in Komna and surrounding villages had been eating leaves and roots for want of foodgrains after the crops failed three months earlier in the locality.

The failure of government to bring such a grave situation to light was noted. The Chief Minister of Orissa, it was reported, got first-hand knowledge of four deaths on 20 July 1985 but kept it to himself. The tribal people complained to the newspaper's correspondent that they were not provided with work or relief despite the Chief Minister's visit. All they got was a little foodstuff for babies under the drought feeding programme, but 'that is inadequate', they pleaded. On 28 July 1985, reports appeared in various newspapers round the country on the Prime Minister's visit to Phulbani district, and his fifteen-minute conversation with Parasi Punji, the woman who had sold her sister-in-law on account of an inability to support her, made the national media headlines. The tribal people were also reported to have told Rajiv Gandhi about the roots and wild leaves they were eating and to have complained that no official had ever visited their villages. 'Emaciated' Adivasi men and women were quoted as pleading with the Prime Minister's wife: 'Ma, give us food and work.'

The *Indian Express* continued its survey work in the area. In its issue of 7 August 1985 appeared a story by Saibal Dasgupta headlined 'Orissa Tribes live on Seeds and Leaves'. It described the 'traditional famine food' of tribal people in Koraput and Kalahandi districts—cakes made of powdered tamarind seeds, dried kernel or mango, mushrooms, wild leaves, mahua flowers, bamboo shoots, and tuberous roots—but noted that even when there was no drought, large sections of the people sustained themselves on a miserable diet. Once again, criticism was recorded of the official attitude and performance. There was an independent follow-up by the newspaper, and on 23 August 1985 fourteen more starvation deaths in just one Kalahandi village were reported. Feature articles in the newspaper's magazine section, other reports, and responses from readers demonstrated that a serious, independent, and sustained journalistic effort in such matters did make a difference to public opinion and did put pressure on impervious official hides.[31]

The fairly detailed coverage in the press of the issues concerning the midday meal (free school lunch) scheme which was introduced in 1982 in the southern state of Tamil Nadu and expanded to cover some nine million preschool and school children between the ages of 2 to 15 and which cost the state exchequer approximately Rs. 2,000 million annually represents another example of relevant journalism focusing on nutrition and hunger, even if the evaluations are somewhat divided. The motivations, implementation, financing, and impact have made it a target for political and media controversy, but there is a clear and persistent strand of support within an influential section of the press for such policy interventions in the vast arena of malnutrition and hunger.

Another example is the active interest taken by various newspapers and magazines in 1986 in exposing the story of injustice meted out to hundreds of bonded labourers, living under conditions of semi-starvation and social isolation, in the Kodaikanal area in Tamil Nadu. In this case, the press acted in association with official and unofficial allies in the democratic system to make a difference to a specific case of gross inequity and hunger. The Supreme Court's intervention in favour of the bonded labourers—clearly recognizing their entitlements, interpreted in a minimum sense, as justiciable rights—is likely to encourage the practice of such socially sensitive journalism.

In the most recent period, there has been a new interest shown by national newspapers in the content and methodology of the Left Front government's land reform and rural relief programme in West Bengal. With the interest heightened in the wake of the Left Front's decisive electoral victory in the state in March 1987 (for the third successive time) the experiment is widely recognized as a more imaginative and serious response to the challenge of chronic hunger and inequity in the countryside than the responses seen in other states. Studying the results of such broad-based socio-economic and political experiments in a relatively objective way, without ideological obfuscation or the mediation of crude prejudices, will undoubtedly represent an advance for Indian journalism.

Such cases provide insights into the strengths, but also the inadequacies, of Indian journalism in relation to endemic, regular hunger. Press coverage

---

[31] The situation in Kalahandi continued to figure on magazine covers a couple of years after the problem was highlighted by a daily newspaper. See for example, 'The Sorrow of Kalahandi' by S. N. M. Abdi in the *Illustrated Weekly* of 26 April–2 May 1987.

makes an observable difference, but almost invariably the press comes in only after another source of investigation has set in motion the events or triggered the controversy. A perceptive essay on the Indian judicial system by an American scholar, Galanter (1986), makes the point that the practice of law in India, for all the courtroom skills and sophistication it exhibits, suffers from serious inadequacies: for example, there is no tradition of independent investigation developed for situations outside the courtroom, technical specialization, and so on.[32] Such a criticism would apply even more to Indian journalism in relation to socio-economic fields where its independent or internal resources are clearly inadequate. With respect to exploring hunger and poverty across the land and yielding popular support to anti-hunger strategies, a major line of advance for the independent press would be directed towards bringing about a purposeful, critical, precisely targeted interaction between intelligent journalism and the relevant specialized disciplines in the social sciences or in other fields. This could help provide some focus, nuance, and sophistication in description, analysis, and prescription to journalistic coverage of complex socio-economic realities. Journalists must, making a decisive break with the tendencies we have remarked on in this paper, demonstrate a willingness to seek the aid of specialists in a much bigger way in the knowledge that *self-reliance* in this profession is guaranteed to push journalism further in the direction of superficiality, misleading analysis, and habitually missing the mark. On the other side, economists, historians, sociologists, anthropologists, political scientists, those involved in the study of science and technology and various other disciplines relevant to the concerns of wide-ranging journalism must show a willingness to utilize and develop the channels available in the relatively independent press (and perhaps even in the non-independent electronic media) to popularize the knowledge and insights they have gained from serious research. This they must do especially if they are concerned with influencing public policy in directions they deem desirable.

To an extent, the *Economic and Political Weekly* (*EPW*), a unique publication in the developing world, has promoted such an interaction over the years. Taking some kind of vantage position between journalism and the scholarly world, it has drawn from both and, perhaps, to that extent influenced sections

---

[32] Galanter (1986) offers an excellent review of the strengths and weaknesses of the Indian judicial system. He observes: 'The Indian lawyer is primarily a courtroom advocate, rather than advisor, negotiator, planner, or investigator . . . Lawyering revolves around courtroom manœuvre and argument with hardly a trace of the investigative, fact-development side of law practice. Lawyers do not employ specialist investigators or para-legals trained to conduct factual inquiries. Experts in scientific and technical fields with the exception of medicine are seldom utilised. Factual investigation is generally considered the responsibility of clients rather than of their lawyers. The low priority to fact-gathering and research is reflected in lawyers' fee arrangements: Lawyers typically charge their clients by the court "appearance" . . . India's lawyers are far from unenterprising. But it is an inventiveness within the severe limits imposed by the present format of law practice.' This criticism is of obvious relevance to the 'fact-development' side of journalistic practice in India.

of Indian journalism and also introduced the academic researcher to some of the requirements and strengths of serious journalism. Especially in the field of hunger, food economics, and poverty, the *EPW*—which, one must assume, has an influence beyond its limited circulation and is taken seriously by policy makers—has distinguished itself over the years in both its academic and journalistic sections. If there has been one major theme running through its issues it is the structural inadequacy of anti-hunger strategies pursued in India; its criticism of official policies has been detailed, sensitive, and credible. (However, in the recent period, the *EPW* has also tended to reflect trends in *instant economics* and *instant ecology*.) Provided the standards are not consciously lowered in an attempt to gain circulation and provided the temptation to compete with non-comparable publications on purely journalistic terms is resisted, there is clearly a future for this type of informed, research-orientated journalism. *South* magazine is another example of this intellectually serious approach to journalism, with some differences from the *EPW* in terms of focus, length of articles, and presentation and also international reach. (A deficiency in comparison with the *EPW* seems to be a less clearly focused critical editorial standpoint.)

If the capabilities and role of the independent press *vis-à-vis* hunger and poverty are to be strengthened, practical attention must be bestowed on the task of systematic interaction between journalism and specialized disciplines. If scholars who want to go public, or reach a wider audience, have something to learn from journalism, the press has a great deal to learn from academic disciplines on questions of sources, substantiation, precision, making a distinction between narration, description, descriptive richness, and analysis, and focusing on issues.

For too long has India's independent press got by on the strength of empiricism (if so eclectic an activity can be given that description), an inchoate realization of its own history, accumulated strengths, and unrealized potential, and a methodology that is *ad hoc* and, on most issues, hit-or-miss. What it needs to acquire in order to develop further is an active consciousness, a coherent theory of its own role in relation to society, a better informed socio-political and ethical[33] side to its practice, a break with the illusion of professional self-sufficiency, a systematic critical monitoring of its own performance, an internal accountability to higher intellectual standards, a more precise and less breathless style, and an active public advocacy of its own role as an indispensable part of the striving for a democratic, just system. Our study of the role of India's independent press in relation to hunger and poverty and the direction of public policy points strongly to these conclusions.

---

[33] Two recent studies of the ethical side of journalism, as it is practised in America, are Goldstein (1985) and Lambeth (1986); the findings would be, in some cases, of recognizable relevance to the practice of the Indian press. The first is a revealing critique and exposé of 'how journalists compromise their ethics to shape the news', and the second is a more formal academic treatment on 'enduring principles' and 'an ethic for the profession'.

6.3. Conclusions

1. It is an attractive intellectual proposition that information, and especially the news media, can play a substantive and progressive role in shaping public policy combating hunger. Our study, which is confined to the role of an independent press in relation to two kinds of hunger—a 'crisis' such as drought or famine on the one hand, and 'regular', endemic hunger and subhuman poverty on the other—substantiates this impression. It demonstrates that where the political system and practice allow it, timely and relevant journalism does make a real difference. Further research is required to explore why this role is so unevenly developed in the Third World. This case-study of the Indian experience yields a highly positive conclusion on the role of an independent press, but cautions against overestimating this role, especially as measurement of influence is virtually impossible. The contrast with the contemporary experience of much of Africa suggests a framework in which the 'power' of a relatively independent press—with a long-established tradition of playing a credible-informational and also a critical-adversarial role in relation to official authority—can be contrasted usefully with the absence of any such tradition and current role.

2. The role of an independent press such as India's must be viewed and analysed as part of a wider institutional value and ideological-political context. Alert, informative media coverage, if it is to be effective, must form part of an ideological and political context of attitude, feeling, and critical democratic values and practice; but merely to emphasize this would appear to undervalue the initiative or trigger that media coverage can provide to influencing the public mood or public opinion in a particular direction. Where the system allows no role for an independent press, policies could take a damaging course—at least in part on account of this absence.

3. The Indian press experience set in a broader framework suggests an analytical distinction between the 'credible-informational' and 'adversarial' or 'destabilizing' roles of an independent press in a developing country context. The first function has usually to do with a rule of law tradition, but it must be assumed that it can also be 'learned'; the more progressive 'adversarial' role that a press may be able to play with respect to public policy and in defence of mass entitlements and their expansion needs much stronger ideological and political nourishment. The first role appears to be a prerequisite for the second; but without the latter, which might imply some kind of 'adversarial' function in relation to government under typical circumstances, the former role might fade away through sheer disuse. Discussion of the independent strengths of a press in terms of these two roles does not imply ruling out a certain autonomy for the development of professional journalism. At its best, an independent press combines the two roles with professional competence and sophistication and works in favour of the stabilization of crisis-averting policies. But even under the best conditions, performance of the roles with professional serious-

ness might involve tensions and strains in the relationship with the government and in the arena of public policy making. Possibly the most important application of our positive finding is in the field of anti-hunger strategies.

4. A study of the historical and current performance of the independent Indian press in relation to hunger and poverty does seem to validate the 'dichotomy' suggested by Amartya Sen in his analysis of the essential experiences of India and China. The analysis suggests that while India's record in eliminating endemic, non-acute hunger contrasts unfavourably with the record of some other countries, such as China and Sri Lanka, independent newspapers along with opposition parties play a valuable role in making governments in India face realities and take steps in time to prevent famine. On the other hand, the disastrous Chinese experience of 1959–62 suggests that the absence of effective opposition parties and independent newspapers could, under certain circumstances, leave a government free to pursue disastrous policies even if they cause, or are unable to avert, a famine. The historical record of the Indian press with respect to a sudden outbreak of hunger on a mass scale—with famine as the worst case possibility—is a solid and valuable one. Recent and current coverage of crises such as droughts has been a strong point in the performance. On the other hand, the criticism that 'regular', chronic hunger and subhuman poverty are 'tame' issues to the Indian press is legitimate, even if recent coverage does suggest some improvement. The reasons for the 'low-key' treatment of endemic hunger and poverty must be explored in terms of policy orientation and bias, professional routine, the ideological and political predilections of journalists, influential or trendy currents in the literature journalists are exposed to, and a variety of practical constraints. But the basic problem seems related to inadequate intellectual and methodological resources and competence to investigate complex, mixed-up socio-economic realities in a non-superficial way. If this problem is addressed, the qualitative performance and impact could be improved significantly even within the context of the other limitations and constraints.

5. The Indian experience suggests that while the overall role and concerns are valuable, habits of imprecision, exaggeration, and oversimplification might detract from this role. There is a tendency to dramatize and sensationalize the coverage of poverty and hunger on a mass scale while missing out deeper structural features and processes. This tends to lower credibility among serious readers and, from the standpoint of serious analysis, proves counterproductive. The inherent problems of journalism—the constant search for a 'wake-up' quality for the less serious reader, dilettantism, and built-in tendencies of superficiality—make sensitive and sustained coverage of complex socio-economic realities difficult.

6. Aside from working towards a better material basis on which to develop, the independent press in India needs to go beyond the informational and methodological capabilities it has acquired professionally. A major line of advance would be stronger and more systematic interaction between serious

journalism and specialized disciplines, especially the social sciences; the pursuit of self-reliance in journalism would clearly be retrograde. The press also needs an internal accountability to higher intellectual standards, a more precise and less breathless style of work, and public advocacy of its role as a vital part of the striving for a democratic, just society. Provided these tasks can be undertaken seriously, it has a real future—even if majority practice in the Third World suggests that the Indian experience will be very hard to extend or replicate.

References

ARNOLD, D. (1979), 'Looting, Grain Riots and Government Policy in South India 1918', *Past and Present*, 84.

BAGDIKIAN, B. H. (1983), *The Media Monopoly* (Boston: Beacon Press).

——(1985), 'The Media Grab', *Channels*.

BRASS, P. R. (1986), 'The Political Uses of Crisis: The Bihar Famine of 1966–1967', *Journal of Asian Studies*, 45.

GALANTER, M. S. (1986), 'Affidavit in the United States District Court, Southern District of New York in Union Carbide Corporation Gas Leak Disaster at Bhopal, India', in *Mass Disasters and Multinational Liability: The Bhopal Case* (Bombay: Indian Law Institute).

GILL, P. (1986), *A Year in the Death of Africa: Politics, Bureaucracy and the Famine* (London: Paladin Grafton Books).

GOLDSTEIN, T. (1985), *The News at Any Cost: How Journalists Compromise Their Ethics to Shape the News* (New York: Simon & Schuster).

HAMELINK, C. J. (1983), *Cultural Autonomy in Global Communications* (London: Gollancz).

HANCOCK, G. (1985), *Ethiopia: The Challenge of Hunger* (London: Gollancz).

Independent Commission on International Humanitarian Issues (1985), *Famine: A Man-Made Disaster?* (London: Pan Books).

LAMBETH, E. B. (1986), *Committed Journalism: An Ethic for the Profession* (Blooming-ton, Ind.: Indiana University Press).

SANTHANAM, K. (1943), *The Cry of Distress: A First-Hand Description and an Objective Study of the Indian Famine of 1943* (New Delhi: The Hindustan Times).

SEN, A. K. (1981), *Poverty and Famines: An Essay on Entitlement and Deprivation* (Oxford: Oxford University Press).

——(1982), 'Coromandel Lecture' (New Delhi: as published in the *Hindu*).

——(1985a), 'Some International Comparisons', in *Commodities and Capabilities* (Amsterdam: North-Holland).

——(1985b), 'Food, Economics and Entitlements', mimeo (WIDER); reproduced as ch. 2 above.

SONTAG, S. (1978), *On Photography* (Harmondsworth: Penguin).

7

Adapting to Undernourishment: The Biological Evidence and its Implications

Partha Dasgupta and Debraj Ray

7.1. *Introduction*

In estimating the prevalence of undernourishment in a region or country it has been common practice to choose a benchmark—or, as some would say, a critical limit—which reflects nutrition requirements and then to calculate the percentage of the population falling below the benchmark. (See e.g. Dandekar and Rath 1971; Reutlinger and Selowsky 1976; and FAO 1978.) The logic underlying the choice of the benchmark has varied across studies. But a common driving hypothesis has been that a person's long-run nutrition requirements are more or less fixed and that the variation in requirements often observed across otherwise similar people is to be explained largely by differences in their innate physiological characteristics. In other words, it has been assumed that the magnitude of *inter*personal variations in nutrition requirements dwarf adaptive variations within the individual, or what has been called *intra*personal variations. This common hypothesis has been given its sharpest articulation in a study by Reutlinger and Alderman (1980) who, in estimating the extent of world-wide undernourishment, have dispensed with the exclusive use of overall regional benchmarks and have worked directly with a statistical distribution of individual intakes and requirements.

This common underlying hypothesis has recently come under sharp attack (Sukhatme and Margen 1978, 1982; Sukhatme 1981). The attack is easy to describe, but its validity is far from simple to assess. It consists of the claim that the nutrition *requirement* of any given individual varies in the long run over a wide range, and that this variation is achieved through an autoregulatory process of adjustment of body metabolism. In other words, variations in nutrition *intake* within this range do not involve any significant alteration in the person's weight, or in his body composition, or indeed in his physical and mental capabilities. Or, to put it in yet another way, the claim is that within a wide range a reduced nutrient intake triggers an autoregulatory mechanism which permits the individual to adapt to the reduction in a costless manner. The claim is, then, that observed variations in nutrition intakes among otherwise similar persons, engaged in similar activities, are not to be explained

We have benefited greatly from discussions with Devaki Bhaya, Avindam Das Gupta, Jean Drèze, Barbara Harriss, Michael Lipton, Siddiq Osmani, Manoj Panda, Philip Payne, A. Vaidyanathan, and John Waterlow.

by interpersonal differences in requirements, but rather by intrapersonal variations occasioned by the autoregulatory mechanism. It follows from this that existing nutrient benchmarks, or norms, such as population average requirements, as used for example by Dandekar and Rath (1971) and Reutlinger and Selowsky (1976), and person-specific requirements, as in Reutlinger and Alderman (1980), overstate greatly the extent of undernourishment and must therefore be reduced so as to encompass the fact of autoregulation.[1] This claim, and the question of its incorporation in the measurement of the extent of undernourishment, has caused such a furious debate in the development literature that the disentangling of rational arguments from polemics and submerged value judgements is a difficult task. Nevertheless, our concern in this article is to try and assess the claim.

The measurement of poverty and undernourishment is not the only issue at stake. If a regulatory mechanism exists, it has important implications for the positive economic theory of labour markets and involuntary unemployment in resource-poor economies. They have to date been largely unexplored. (For a preliminary analysis of these issues see Dasgupta and Ray 1986, 1987.) A second task of this article is to study some of these implications.

One might well ask, given that there has been so much debate over these matters, what all the fuss is about. We all know that quantitative estimates are fuzzy, if for no other reason than the serious limitations imposed by the raw data. Why bother with an exact choice of minimum nutrition requirements? Precise quantitative estimates are unnecessary: what matters is qualitative changes, such as those occurring over time.

There are several reasons why quantitative estimates matter. First, one must note that a limited data set is no excuse for failing to construct a comprehensive system of measurement. Second, the choice of nutrition requirements (or, more generally, a poverty line) is not only theoretically capable of altering dynamic trends, it has done so in practice. Finally—and this is a most serious consideration—even if different nutrition requirements, or poverty lines, agree over time, the question of *which* line to use is of crucial importance. Government planners, policy makers, business groups, social activists, and the person in the street use these figures to discuss the economy, to press their own cases, and to allocate funds. To argue, therefore, that quantitative estimates do not matter is to misrepresent reality at a most basic level. The controversy that we shall assess has had a tremendous impact on individuals and institutions. It is no mere academic debate.

---

[1] Reutlinger and Alderman (1980), using the 1978 FAO estimates of average energy requirements in various regions and assuming a normal distribution of requirements with a coefficient of variation of 15%, calculated that in the mid-1970s the total number of undernourished people in the world was about 800 million. For a comparison of the methods used by FAO (1977), Reutlinger and Selowsky (1976), and Reutlinger and Alderman (1980) in estimating the extent of global undernourishment see Beaton (1981). See also Beaton (1983).

The paper is organized as follows. In section 7.2 we will discuss the statistical and measurement issues associated with autoregulation. Our central concern will be with the arguments advanced by Dr P. V. Sukhatme, a major proponent of the autoregulation hypothesis. Our conclusion will be that, unless an extremely strong notion of autoregulation is employed, the methodology espoused by Sukhatme is not correct. And even if this strong notion (see below) is invoked, there is a clear confusion of statistical thresholds with physiological thresholds that invalidates the main argument. However, the presence of autoregulation might influence measurement, and we indicate how this may be incorporated. Accordingly in section 7.3 we will turn to an examination of the biological evidence concerning autoregulation. Both adjustment and adaptation mechanisms will be discussed there. We will show that the evidence does point to certain areas of the human system where adjustment and adaptation are distinct possibilities. It also points to other areas where the system may move in the opposite direction. *Furthermore, there is also evidence that if adaptation exists, it is purchased at a cost.* The cost involves, among other things, a reduction in the capacity for sustained physical and mental activities, and a greater susceptibility to infection and disease.

These conclusions imply that if one wishes to adopt the approach of using a cut-off line (followed by a headcount) to measure undernourishment, then there is little merit in the suggestion that the nutrition norm be reduced substantially from population-average requirements. For the suggestion either involves a refusal to call an individual undernourished unless the evidence for doing so is overwhelmingly strong in a probabilistic sense, or exhibits a high tolerance for the risks and dangers of adaptation.

Of course, substantial *interpersonal* variations in requirements and some knowledge of the joint distribution of intake and requirement may require the use of modified headcount measures that are different from those implied by population-average cut-offs (see section 7.2(a), equation (2)). And as mentioned above, there are ways of incorporating (potentially costly) auto-regulatory behaviour into measures of undernourishment. We will discuss these matters in section 7.2(e).

Section 7.3 also raises the issue of short-term adjustment. The tentative conclusion we will reach is that most adjustment takes place through the action of the storage mechanism, depositing or running down energy in bodystores in the form of fat or protein. In particular, short-term changes in the efficiency of energy metabolism do not appear to be significant (see also WHO 1985: 13, 50). The implications of this finding are discussed, most especially in the context of its effect on long-term requirements.

In section 7.4 we will look at the implications of regulation for the positive economic theory of labour markets. We note that while the existence of regulation does not compel us to change our normative notions of poverty measurement, it can nevertheless have a significant impact on the way in which labour markets function in resource-poor economies. Both adjustment and adaptation are introduced into the existing nutrition-based theories of labour markets and involuntary unemployment in developing countries. These modifications appear to yield insights not obtainable from the current theory.

7.2. *Regulation: statistical and measurement issues*

(a)   *The background*

The measurement of undernourishment and poverty has recently been the subject of controversy.[2] Our objective in this section is to provide a survey of the statistical aspects of regulation, and to examine their implications for the measurement of undernourishment. To clear the route, we avoid one aspect of the debate, for the reason that it is irrelevant for our purposes: that concerning the distinction between undernourishment and poverty. Calorie-based poverty lines are common in India, as they are elsewhere. Whenever the actual energy intake of an individual unit (or group) is being compared to the calorie requirements of the poverty line, and headcounts below the line are being computed in this fashion, we shall say that we are dealing with the measurement of *undernourishment*. When the income (or expenditure) of the unit is being so compared, we shall call it the measurement of *poverty*.[3]

We will begin by covering well-known ground, with a brief discussion of the calorie-based methods that have been used for the construction of poverty lines. In the main we will restrict ourselves to the *headcount* measure, as the debate has largely centred on headcounts. There is, however, a link (which we will discuss briefly below) between our discussions and the considerations that have led to newer measures of poverty.[4]

The primitives for a nutrition-based poverty line must always be nutrients, though the requirements may occasionally be stated not in terms of calories, proteins, and so forth, but in terms of foods of various kinds.[5] We will restrict ourselves to nutrient specifications. In fact we simplify further and concentrate

---

[2] Much of this debate may be found in Sukhatme (1978, 1981a, 1981b, 1982a), Dandekar (1981, 1982), Dasgupta (1985), Zurbrigg (1983), Mehta (1982), Krishnaji (1981), Rao (1981a, 1981b), Gopalan (1983a), Chakravorti and Panda (1981), Paranjpe (1981), Seckler (1982), Payne and Cutler (1984), Chafkin (1985), and Vaidyanathan (1985). The *Bulletin of the Nutrition Foundation of India* has published articles relating to the controversy. Important examples are Gopalan (1982, 1983b) and Rand and Scrimshaw (1984). Other journals which have published much in this field are clinical journals such as the *American Journal of Clinical Nutrition*, and the *Ecology of Food and Nutrition*. Quite a few of our more important references are articles published in these journals.

[3] A failure to distinguish the two has led to added debate. See e.g. Rao (1977, 1981a, 1981b) and Dandekar (1981).

[4] See e.g. Watts (1968), Sen (1976), and Foster, Greer, and Thorbecke (1984). For a survey of these new measures and their axiomatic basis, see Foster (1984).

[5] In India (our main setting), the Indian Council for Medical Research (ICMR) provides one such example. They publish balanced-diet lists in addition to nutrient specifications.

on calorie requirements.[6] Now, the neglect of protein requirements is not a serious offence for the Indian case, or indeed for many developing countries.[7] More serious is the neglect of other nutrient requirements, in particular those of vitamin A, iron, and the B-group vitamins.[8] Their automatic supply is not ensured even if energy needs are met. Our only excuse for isolating calorie requirements and ignoring these other requirements is that the main debate on regulation and adaptation has focused on energy requirements.

The Food and Agricultural Organization (FAO), in a series of publications, has systematically revised calorie requirements downwards (see FAO 1957, 1963, 1973, 1977). Their 1973 estimate for the *reference man* stood at 2,600 Kcal for maintenance and 400 Kcal for 'moderate' activity, yielding a total of 3,000 Kcal per day. The FAO reference man was an adult male aged 20–39, weighing 65 kg, and living in a mean ambient temperature of 10°C. It is due largely to these specifications of the reference man that the FAO's more recent estimates of requirements in tropical regions have been much lower. (Their 1978 estimate for Asia was 2,210 Kcal per day. But see the joint report from WHO, FAO, and UNU,—WHO 1985—for the most recent set of estimates.)

The Indian estimates have varied considerably, but the more recent ones are not too different from the FAO figure. The Indian reference man (if one can at all point to one in a situation where nature and nurture intertwine closely to determine average weights and sizes[9]) weighs less than the FAO (1973) reference man and lives in an ambient climate with a mean temperature of around 25°C. Both these factors lower the energy requirement, the former by reducing energy needs to maintain body frame, and the latter by reducing the basal metabolic rate.[10] These observations should be qualified by the remark that unskilled labourers in India perform tasks that are at the very least on the hard side of 'moderate', indeed often those that are extremely strenuous.

These adjustments are the immediate ones that come to mind, and there are a great many more that are worth considering.[11] For this reason the variations

[6] Later, however, in our analysis of the clinical evidence, we shall consider protein requirements and the possibilities of regulation there.

[7] The writings of Sukhatme in this context have been justly influential. See Sukhatme (1970, 1972, 1974). For a more general discussion of the protein problem, see the references in Gopalan (1983*b*). The reason protein deficiencies can be overlooked for countries such as India is not because proteins are unimportant, but because the nature of the diets in these countries is such that protein requirements are almost always met when calorie needs are met. This statement needs to be qualified for diets which draw heavily on tubers, such as cassava and yam, where the fulfilment of calorie requirements says little about protein. This is why kwashiorkor is important in some African countries whereas the main manifestation of childhood undernourishment in India is marasmus.

[8] See Gopalan (1983*b*) for a useful discussion of these points.

[9] See e.g. Gopalan and Narasinga Rao (1974) and the discussion in Bliss and Stern (1978*b*).

[10] We define these terms and discuss the issues involved in more detail in s. 7.3.

[11] Bliss and Stern (1978*b*) provide an example of the possible margins of disagreement that might occur, by constructing suitable modifications of the early FAO figures.

in estimates of calorie requirement in India have been large. The Indian Council for Medical Research (ICMR), for example, recommends 2,800 Kcal per day (Gopalan and Narasinga Rao 1974), but even their recommendations have varied (see Rao 1981*a* for a description of how the ICMR criteria based on food baskets have themselves changed over a decade). Dandekar and Rath (1971) in their pioneering study on poverty used 2,250 Kcal per day as the per capita requirement for India, though this corresponds to a higher requirement when converted into a figure for the reference man (see below, section 7.2(*b*)). Bardhan's work on poverty in India (Bardhan 1973) described a food basket whose calorie value is estimated (in Bliss and Stern 1978*b*) to be 2,386 Kcal. The Planning Commission employs separate criteria for rural and urban sectors, placing these at 2,300 Kcal and 2,100 Kcal respectively. And there are many others,[12] but a complete enumeration of these figures is not central to our purpose here. What needs to be emphasized is that despite wide variations, these estimates share the common assumption that individuals have fixed requirements (barring interpersonal differences due to different genotypes). To understand the furore following Sukhatme's statement of his position, this point must be appreciated. It is not so much the lower requirements espoused by Sukhatme, rather, it is the idea of adaptation (to a history of low intakes) that goes with it, which has been the source of so much controversy.[13]

To establish Sukhatme's position clearly, we will quote extensively from his own writings. To many, he is the originator of the adaptation hypothesis, and certainly it is he who has been most active in expounding the implications of the hypothesis for the measurement of poverty. We will therefore study his argument in detail.[14] But in order to do that it is as well to introduce some notation and restate what we referred to as the 'common hypothesis' in the Introduction.

Let x denote a person's actual calorie intake and y his requirement. (We are assuming for the moment that people have fixed requirements.) Of course, requirement is not directly measurable, and so needs to be estimated from desirable energy expenditure. By the qualification 'desirable' we mean the energy expenditure of a person whose body weight and physical activity have been chosen at desirable levels and, in the case of a child, whose growth rate has been suitably targeted. For such a person, energy balance would imply an equality of intake with expenditure. Thus for such a person requirement, y, equals his desirable intake. And this can differ from his actual intake, x. Let $F(x,y)$ be the (probability) density of (x,y) pairs in the population under study. Now consider the level of calorie requirement of the 'reference man', as

---

[12] See e.g. Dasgupta (1985) and a survey of measures in Rao and Vivekanand (1982).

[13] As we have already observed, different estimates for requirements have coexisted relatively peacefully.

[14] Sukhatme's position is developed in a number of papers and lectures, especially in the course of the *Economic and Political Weekly* discussions referred to earlier (above, n. 1).

described in any one of the studies mentioned above. (Sukhatme focuses on Dandekar and Rath 1971). Call this β. This reference man is typically interpreted to be the *average* man. (See e.g. WHO 1985: 15.) Thus

$$\beta = \int_x \int_y y F(x,y)\, dx\, dy^{15}$$

As there must be genotypic variations within the population the standard deviation of y is positive. Let σ_m denote the standard deviation of requirements. Since individuals are assumed to have fixed requirements σ_m reflects interpersonal variations exclusively.

A crude index, I_1, of the headcount of the undernourished (see Dandekar and Rath 1971; Reutlinger and Selowsky 1976) is

$$I_1 \equiv \int_{x<\beta} \int_y F(x,y)\, dx\, dy. \tag{7.1}$$

This yields the percentage of the population with an intake less than β. The deficiencies of this index when requirements vary are fairly obvious.

For *this* model of nutrition the correct headcount index is I_2, where

$$I_2 \equiv \int_x \int_{y>x} F(x,y)\, dx\, dy \tag{7.2}$$

This yields the proportion of the population whose intakes are less than their requirements.[16] In practice, of course, we would have a *sample* of n observations on intakes, $x_1, \ldots x_n$. To apply a measure of the form (7.2), we would require some knowledge of the *conditional* distributions $F(y|x_i)$ for each i. The appropriate (sample) headcount index corresponding to (7.2) is then given by

$$\hat{I}_2 \equiv \sum_{i=1}^{n} \left[\int_{y>x_i} F(y|x_i)\, dy \right] \tag{7.2'}$$

See, for example, Reutlinger and Alderman (1980).

(b) Regulation and measurement: a challenge to the conventional wisdom

It is this formulation of the nutrition problem which has been challenged by Sukhatme. His analysis has its starting-point in the experimental observation (see Edholm *et al.* 1970; Sukhatme and Margen 1978; and the references in section 7.3 below) that 'Intake does not balance expenditure, even when

---

[15] By his reference to Arthur Bowley's work, where apparently half of England was dubbed undernourished because they were consuming below the average (see Sukhatme 1978), Sukhatme appears to imply that β is the average *intake* for the population. This implication is clearly unwarranted, as the calorie figures used by Dandekar–Rath and others are explicitly recognized to be (average) calorie *requirements*, not average calorie *consumption*.

[16] In equations (7.1) and (7.2), we are assuming a continuous probability density only for the purposes of exposition. Clearly more general distributions can be accommodated.

averaged over a week. This is tantamount to undermining the whole basis of investigating the energy balance by simultaneous measurement of energy intake and expenditure' (Sukhatme 1978). Sukhatme rejects the view that such large fluctuations can be the result of measurement error, and argues that this intertemporal 'intra-individual variance is the dominant part of the total variation', dwarfing interindividual variation of the kind that we have allowed for above. This leads to the second stage of Sukhatme's argument, which deals with the presence of substantial autocorrelation in individual energy balance data over time. This observation is first made for the Edholm et al. (1970) data set on energy balances, which, even though it is 'limited to three weeks with breaks after each week, [is] consistent with AR [autoregressive] series of order one with serial correlation of the first order' (Sukhatme 1978). The observation is then made for the nitrogen (N) balance study reported by Sukhatme and Margen (1978).[17] 'Statistical analysis of the series shows that N balance on successive days is correlated all along the series . . . In particular, the auto-correlation of the first order is found to have a fairly high value' (Sukhatme 1978).

Sukhatme then turns to the implications of autocorrelation. According to him, the major implication of serial correlation is the existence of a regulatory mechanism controlling the efficiency of energy use within the body. Rather than measurement error,

the more possible explanation in our view would appear to lie in the stochastic stationary nature of the physiological mechanism generating energy balance in a man maintaining body weight . . . the conclusion [from the experiments] is that a man is in balance in a probabilistic (homeostatic) sense in that his balance on any day is regulated by the balance on the preceding day and it varies between fixed limits independent of [the time period]. (Sukhatme 1978)

A similar implication is also drawn in Sukhatme and Margen (1978), where it is stated that serial correlation in the N balance *implies* that the daily N balance, *like energy balance*, is regulated' (emphasis ours).[18] Furthermore, Sukhatme (1982a) argues that

the only inference [he] can draw is that energy intake is used with variable efficiency by means of some homeostatic mechanism working for the good of the whole body and controlling body weight in the process . . . the body has reversible mechanisms to bring about for itself a change it needs over time for maintaining health and activity by slowing down or speeding up rates of metabolism to preserve homeostasis.

---

[17] One must be careful here, as we shall point out in s. 7.3. Nitrogen balance studies deal with protein intakes and expenditures. Extensions of the results obtained here to energy balance may simply not be valid.

[18] It is interesting that Sukhatme–Margen (1978) draws an analogy with the 'regulation' of energy balance, while the Sukhatme (1978) paper, postulating energy balance regulation, leans on the Sukhatme–Margen work for empirical support!

To sum up, autoregulation, in Sukhatme's view, appears to be the 'modification of requirements without detriment' (Rand and Scrimshaw 1984), and it is in his view a logical implication of serial correlation in energy balance.

The clinical basis for the existence of regulation will be examined a later section. Assuming for now that regulation of this sort is indeed implied, what are the implications for measurement? Again, it is as well to have Sukhatme's own words on the subject:

> When the observed intake for any day or period is therefore less than the average requirement, worked out from the FAO/WHO scale, it cannot be taken to imply that a man is undernourished, as Dandekar and Rath do, unless his intake is so low as to be below the lower limit of the confidence interval for the chosen level of significance . . . it follows that in any observed intake distribution on nutrition unit basis with a nutrition unit having the same daily requirement as the reference adult, namely β, the proportion of the population below $\beta - 2\sigma_w$ will determine the incidence of undernourishment and poverty. (Sukhatme 1978)

In the foregoing quotation, σ_w is the standard deviation of intrapersonal variation of intakes for the reference man. Sukhatme assumes a normal distribution of intakes and, as mentioned earlier, regards interpersonal variation (σ_m earlier) to be negligible. If it is in fact not negligible and if inter- and intrapersonal deviations are uncorrelated then the overall standard deviation, σ, would satisfy the relation,

$$\sigma^2 = \sigma_w^2 + \sigma_m^2. \qquad (7.3)$$

We have now at hand the key ingredients of the debate. The common hypothesis, mentioned in the Introduction, is that σ_m is far in excess of σ_w. The 'adaptationist' thesis is that σ_m is negligible when compared to σ_w. Thus, in choosing $\beta - 2\sigma_w$ as the benchmark—the cut-off level of intake in the measurement of undernourishment—Sukhatme is choosing, roughly speaking, the bottom of the range of intakes which in his view, any individual can safely adapt to.

Sukhatme's application of the undernourishment line so constructed leads to dramatic results.

First, he considers the requirement of 2,750 Kcal per consumer unit, which was adopted by the National Sample Survey (NSS) of the Government of India (NSS, 26th round) at the instance of FAO.[19] This estimate corresponds closely

[19] A consumer unit, which corresponds close to our notion of the reference man, is used to transform household data into 'adult equivalent' terms in the National Sample Survey. To illustrate, the National Sample Survey (NSS) (26th round, 1971–2) used the following equivalences between consumer units and persons in the households surveyed: 4.29 consumer units for 5.39 persons per rural household, 3.81 consumer units for 4.72 persons per urban household, which worked out to an all-India average of 4.19 consumer units for 5.26 persons per household. Therefore, if one wishes to translate a per capita requirement into a per-consumer-unit requirement, the former must be divided by the ratio 4.19/5.26, or approximately 0.8. In the text, we do precisely this for the Dandekar–Rath requirement of 2,250 Kcal per capita, to avoid confusion. It corresponds to a higher figure for the consumer unit.

to that of Dandekar and Rath (1971), whose figure of 2,250 Kcal is stated per capita, and not for the reference man or consumer unit (see e.g. Dandekar 1981). To transform this into a requirement per consumer unit (in the Indian case), we divide by 0.8 (see n. 19) to obtain approximately 2,800 Kcal per consumer unit.

Second, Sukhatme suggests a coefficient of variation of 15 per cent to capture the sum of intra- and interindividual variation in consumer units. That is, σ is 15 per cent of β, in our terminology. As the relevant data are given at the household level, and as there are about four consumer units to a household (n. 19), the 'mean minus two sigma' rule entails subtracting $2(\sigma/\sqrt{4})$ from β. Sukhatme does so, and arrives at his cut-off line of 2,300 Kcal per consumer unit.[20]

Applying this figure, urban Maharashtra's undernourishment headcount takes a plunge from 63 per cent to 33 per cent, Punjab's headcount 'falls' from 20 per cent to 10 per cent, and the all-India headcount now stands at the refreshingly 'low' figure of 25 per cent (urban) and 40 per cent (rural).

It is important to evaluate the argument. In the remainder of this section we will be concerned with the validity of Sukhatme's statistical reasoning. We will also discuss the implications that regulation has for the measurement of undernourishment. An examination of the biological basis for Sukhatme's argument is deferred to section 7.3.

(c) A simplified model of energy requirement

We begin by considering a simplified model of energy balance, in which we incorporate a variety of regulatory features, and which we will extend later (sections 7.3 and 7.4). Divide time into discrete periods $t = 0,1,2 \ldots$, and consider an individual with initial requirement β_0. This requirement is conditional on a prespecified level of activity.[21] Let us suppose that a constant amount q of energy is to be devoted to this activity, and that an amount r_t (at time t) is to be expended for basic metabolism and the maintenance of the frame of the body. We shall refer to r_t as the *resting metabolic rate* (RMR).[22] Let s_t be the energy released from (or stored in) the body, say, in the form of fat. Finally, let x_t denote the intake of the individual at time t. Ignoring waste for simplicity,

---

[20] Sukhatme's arithmetic is incorrect. The implied coefficient of variation needed to obtain 2,300 Kcal is 16.4%. We ignore this relatively minor slip, even though poverty calculations are known to be extremely sensitive to the line. Sukhatme's statement that the coefficient of variation is 15% is also open to a charge of inconsistency. Dandekar (1981) reports four different figures stated by Sukhatme in different papers, ranging from 300 to 400 Kcal (as estimates of intraindividual variation).

[21] We take it that this level of activity is determined by the demands of the individual's environment. After all, the question is one of living on lower intakes while '[engaging] in similar activity from day to day' (Sukhatme 1981a).

[22] In s. 7.3, we take up the concept of RMR in detail when discussing the clinical evidence concerning adaptation.

we have:

$$\delta_t x_t = r_t + q + s_t, \quad t \geqslant 0. \tag{7.4}$$

where δ_t is the efficiency of energy metabolism at time t. A lower value of δ signifies a lower efficiency of energy metabolism.

Let S be an exogenously given constant that stipulates the outer limit of 'borrowing' from the body; i.e. we postulate that *for continuing health of the individual*, it must be the case that

$$\sum_{t=0}^{T} s_t \geqslant -S, \qquad T \geqslant 0 \tag{7.5}$$

If this does not hold for some T, *we say that the individual is undernourished.*

We reiterate at this stage that the structure we are using is simplified for the purpose of exposition. The threshold S, for instance, has been chosen to be 'history-independent'. Moreover there is in reality no sharp threshold; what we have is a 'probability of breakdown' which is an increasing function of S, the extent of 'borrowing' from the body. However, these extensions, while complicating the analysis, add little to our understanding of the basic issues at this stage.[23] Furthermore, we have assumed that energy is stored as efficiently as it is run down (this assumption is implicitly embedded in the summation of s_t in (7.5)). In section 7.3 we shall consider the implications of relaxing this assumption.

The individual lives in an environment which gives (or denies) him access to food. The relevant scenario is that of an economic environment where the individual earns an income (perhaps in every period), which we suppose for simplicity to be all spent on food. We represent the income opportunities measured in 'energy units' as an exogenously given stochastic process $\langle z_t \rangle$. One could think of a number of examples in which the process $\langle z_t \rangle$ takes different forms. Under long-term employment, for instance, z_t is a fixed number (perhaps with a time trend). On the other hand, an individual who is a casual labourer might be unemployed each day (or week) with some probability. The corresponding random process of labour incomes is then represented by $\langle z_t \rangle$.

Given intakes and incomes, we define the sequence $\langle K_t \rangle$ by the condition

$$K_T = \sum_{t=0}^{T-1} (z_t - x_t) + K_0, \qquad T \geqslant 1 \tag{7.6}$$

where $K_0 \geqslant 0$ is exogenously given. We impose the feasibility condition that

$$K_T \geqslant 0, \qquad T \geqslant 0 \tag{7.7}$$

Equation (7.7) states that the current food budget plus past savings cannot be overstepped at any date. Finally, to close the system, we specify how r_t (the

---

[23] Sukhatme, too, makes a similar assumption as is evident from the excerpts above. Of course, he too is aware of the simplifications involved. He mentions that by his use of the term 'threshold, [he does] not imply that there is any sharp discontinuity in the distribution. All that is meant is that the risk of undernutrition remains about the same over a wide, though limited, range of intakes.'

RMR) and δ_t (the efficiency of metabolism) might vary over time. At the moment, we keep things general by noting that r_t and δ_t are functions (possibly degenerate) of the *history* of intakes (activity levels are constant). Writing $h_t = (x_0, \ldots, x_t)$, for $t > 0$ we have,

$$r_t = r_t(h_t), \qquad \delta_t = \delta_t(h_t)$$
$$r_0, \delta_0 \text{ given.}^{24} \tag{7.8}$$

Now, a few definitions within the context of this simple model. The body will be said to be *capable of adjustment* if $S > 0$. The body is *capable of adaptation* if $r_t(.)$ or $\delta_t(.)$ is a non-degenerate function. *Positive adaptation* will be said to exist if $r_t(h_t)$ is increasing in the components of h_t and δ_t is decreasing. And finally, we define *regulation* to be the entire complex of adjustment and positive adaptation.

Some comments on these definitions will be useful. Intuitively, it would seem reasonable to say that a body can *adjust* if it can vary its current intake around the 'going' requirement (for period 0 in this model it is $\beta_0 = q + r_0$), at least for a few periods. For the purpose of our analysis the downside variation is clearly important, and in our model this is possible if and only if $S > 0$.

Adaptation is a different matter altogether. This requires a change in the requirement itself or in metabolism efficiency as a function of past intakes. It is naturally captured in the non-degeneracy of the $r_t(.)$ and $\delta_t(.)$ functions.[25] Adaptation is then positive if a history of low intake is 'absorbed' by the body by a lowering of its requirements or by an increase in its metabolic efficiency. This is precisely how we have defined it above.

Nevertheless, we should reiterate that both adaptation and adjustment go deeper than is suggested by these definitions. In section 7.3 we will discuss possible sources of regulation in much greater detail. Speaking broadly, all regulatory features that permit the body to cushion itself against short-term fluctuations in intake will be labelled *adjustment*. Similarly, all regulatory features that allow the body to accommodate itself to a permanently lower intake will be termed *adaptation*.

It should be noted that adaptive mechanisms (such as changes in r_t or δ_t) may well have costs in other dimensions, such as effects on the probability of breakdown. The totality of these costs need to be considered in determining the level of 'acceptable adaptation'.

(d)   Regulation and measurement: a reconsideration

First, it should be pointed out that it is not clear from the totality of Sukhatme's writings exactly what he means by regulation. Of course, this is not all-

---

[24] The functions $\langle r_t(h_t)\rangle$ and $\langle \delta_t(h_t)\rangle$ can be taken to be random without adding anything to the analysis.

[25] This is not to suggest *unbounded* adaptation. None of the protagonists in the debate has suggested this and, needless to say, there is no evidence supporting it.

important; we are ultimately interested in the issues themselves. It is therefore our goal in this section to understand whether the various features of regulation can indeed be used in poverty measurement along lines similar to those of Sukhatme.

Nevertheless, it is important to settle (as far as this can be done) the matter of whether Sukhatme is addressing phenomena similar to those defined above. Some indicators (as well as a few ambiguities) may be obtained from the following excerpts; 'The test of health is regulation of energy balance and maintenance of body weight and level of desired activity and not the level of intake only, as long as the latter is above the threshold value' (Sukhatme 1981a). Here the concept of 'threshold value' is made operational by Sukhatme in the statistical manner that we have described above (that is, mean minus two standard derivation). Elsewhere, Sukhatme also notes that 'fortunately for most of us, unless the intake is too low, the basal metabolic rate is found to decrease as the intake decreases, and in consequence the efficiency of energy utilization is improved' (Sukhatme 1978).[26]

There are various interpretations of these (and other similar) statements, but it appears that they are all broadly consistent with the complex of regulatory phenomena that we have outlined above. Consider adaptation, as we have defined it. This notion is clearly present in the excerpts above and in Sukhatme's writings, in general, though there are minor points that are confusing.[27] Similarly, there is no way to rule out adjustment, even if body weight is to be 'maintained'. It all depends on what one means by 'maintaining body weight'. If the narrow view is taken that body weight is to remain constant at every instant of time, then adjustment is being ruled out as a possible source of regulation. If the broader view is taken that body weight must not have a declining trend, but that it can have some cyclical movements, then indeed adjustment can be accommodated under these statements.

We will comment on the implications of the entire complex of regulatory features for measurement of undernourishment. In the process, we shall also evaluate the method proposed by Sukhatme. Indeed, we retrace his argument, step by step.

1. *Intakes vary while expenditures are relatively stable.* While Sukhatme's use of the term 'expenditure' is unfortunate and has even lured some into thinking that he might be unaware of the First Law of Thermodynamics,[28] his intention is quite clear from the context. He is referring to expenditure on physical

[26] One should note, though, that there is a difference between basal and resting metabolism. See s. 7.3 for details.

[27] Consider e.g. the statement above that the 'basal metabolic rate is found to decrease . . . and *in consequence* the efficiency of energy utilization is improved' (Sukhatme 1987, emphasis ours). This latter is usually connected with factors other than a reduction of the *basal* metabolic rate. See our discussions below, s. 7.3, and indeed Sukhatme's own writings elsewhere (e.g. Sukhatme and Margen 1982).

[28] See e.g. Mehta (1982).

activity, and is suggesting that variations are absorbed by the regulatory process.[29] Equation (7.4) is being satisfied all along.

There can be no doubt, from the evidence to be discussed later, that Sukhatme's suggestion is valid so far as adjustment is concerned. And it appears that most of the protagonists in the debate accept this.[30] But adjustment to what extent? Sukhatme reports that this 'intraindividual variation' does not vanish when averaged over a week or two, a statement largely based on Edholm *et al.* (1970). But does this variation persist without substantial loss of body weight when intakes are averaged over a *month* or more? The reason this question would appear to be important is that the National Sample Survey data on expenditures and food consumption are monthly averages, and this is the database for the Dandekar–Rath study, and many other studies, including Sukhatme's own calculations. In terms of our model, this can be illustrated simply. Suppose that there is no adaptation, so that $r_t = r$ for all t, and define $\beta = q + r$. Then on using equations (7.4) and (7.5) a little algebra reveals that for all $T \geq 0$.

$$\left[\left(\sum_{t=0}^{T} x_t \right) / T \right] - \beta \geq -S/(T+1) \tag{7.9}$$

This places a bound on how far the time-averaged intake can fall *below* the requirement, as a function of the time period of averaging: the longer the period over which the averaging is done, the smaller is the permitted deviation between average intakes and requirements. Whether intraindividual variation persists for a month or more would therefore depend on the size of S. We will argue below (section 7.3) that there is little or no evidence that intraindividual variation of this order exists, and that where it does such variation does not involve substantial costs for the individual.

2. *Autocorrelation implies regulation.* As Scrimshaw and Young observe, 'Sukhatme never defines precisely what he means by regulation other than to state that it is a consequence of autocorrelation'. Nevertheless, as discussed above, there are enough indicators in Sukhatme's writings to incorporate both adjustment and adaptation. The presence of autocorrelation is, to him, a crucial indicator of regulation.[31]

The presence of autocorrelation is an important signal. It is important because it tells us that the (large) observed fluctuations in energy balance (intake minus dissipated output) are unlikely to be due to noise or measurement error. This must be qualified by the possibility that autocorrelation may simply be the result of long-term physiological trends within the body (see section 7.3). However, we find it difficult to understand how the presence of

---

[29] This includes both adjustment and adaptation, though some of the analytical issues are different. See below.

[30] For instance, Dandekar (1981) states that he has 'no difficulty admitting such variation'.

[31] See e.g. Sukhatme (1978, 1981a, 1982) and Sukhatme and Margen (1978, 1982).

serial correlation in intake (with relatively stable expenditure on physical activity) implies anything over and above the easily admitted phenomenon of (short-run) adjustment (see point (1) above). To see why autocorrelation implies nothing more, consider, for instance, the stylized example of a farmer. A farmer's physical activity is fairly stable through the year, certainly more so than his output of food, which is realized only at certain points in the year and that too with some randomness. If there are important limitations of the informal credit market and inadequate storage facilities, his 'income' at each date will be a stochastic process (our sequence $\langle z_t \rangle$) with cyclical properties. This process will also display substantial autocorrelation, for 'incomes' will be low for some periods before harvest, and high for some periods after harvest. Given the feasibility requirement (7.7) on intakes, the stochastic process $\langle x_t \rangle$ and the calorie balance process so generated will also have autocorrelation. But this is an autocorrelation imposed by the vagaries and inequities of the farmer's environment, providing him with an unstable income and demanding a steady expenditure of energy. Of course, the fluctuation in intakes implies some degree of forced physiological adjustment. But the autocorrelation? It implies nothing further about the biology of nutrition.

The example above is set in a somewhat extended time scale, and also places exogenous bounds on intakes. To argue the same point within a shorter time scale, consider the example where an individual receives a steady income. Suppose that he eats well, though with restraint, on weekdays, but indulges himself on weekends. Suppose, further, that he works at a steady pace through the week. The derived sequence of calorie balances will, no doubt, display excellent autocorrelation! But what does this tell us about adjustment (over and above the considerations discussed above) or about adaptation?

The use of the phenomenon of autocorrelation to suggest that regulation (especially in its costless adaptive form) exists has serious implications for the measurement of undernourishment that may well be wrong.

3. *The 'mean minus two standard deviations' rule for poverty measurement.* As we have already observed, Sukhatme proceeds to suggest that the FAO/WHO estimates should be reduced by two standard deviations (encompassing both intra- and interindividual variation) and that this should be used as the cut-off line. In fact, Sukhatme argues that one can place 'physiological meaning' on this new threshold, which has been established using the 'chosen level' of significance.

One can certainly extend or modify this straightforward rule in a number of ways,[32] but a crucial question needs to be faced. What is this 'chosen level' of

[32] Krishnaji (1981) for example modifies the Sukhatme rule by recognizing that different genotypes will have different intraindividual variations and so one cannot simply add the two variances to arrive at a measure of total variance. But there is an implicit acceptance of 'the chosen level of significance'. Chakravorti and Panda (1981) are well aware of the significance of the 'chosen level', but as part of their exercise they experiment with different intake-distributions, such as the beta.

significance and how is it established? The level $\beta - 2\sigma$ is a *statistical* cut-off. Sukhatme puts it forward as a *physiological* threshold. Now, a necessary condition for such a proposition to be valid is that costless regulation exists *and* intrapersonal variation (σ_w) is greatly in excess of interpersonal variation (σ_m). But no evidence is produced to show that σ_m is indeed negligible relative to σ_w (points (1) and (2) above). This necessary condition continues to remain a hypothesis, which we explore further in section 7.3.

In any event, the condition is *necessary* and by no means *sufficient*. For there is no explanation advanced as to why the extent of admissible regulation coincides so neatly with two standard deviations below the mean! Sukhatme is not only taking a qualitative position, he is also taking a quantitative one.

We first consider the social costs involved if the hypothesis happens to be wrong. Suppose, for example, that it is σ_w which is negligible as compared to σ_m. That is, *inter*personal variation is dominant. Then the 'mean minus two standard deviations' rule (over intakes) would carry with it the implicit null hypothesis that an individual is *not* undernourished. In this case the rule would demand Sukhatme's 'type one error'—classifying a person as undernourished when he is not—to be made with a probability of only 2.275 per cent. As Dandekar puts it,

It means that we will not accept the existence of undernourishment unless the evidence is overwhelming. If we meet a household whose energy intake is below the average requirement, we shall suppose that its particular requirement must also be below the average or in fact below its actual intake; it eats less because it needs less. We take cognisance of its low intake as possible evidence of undernourishment only if the intake is so low that the probability of the requirement being lower still is very low. (Dandekar 1981)

In response to Dandekar's comment, Sukhatme's answer 'is that the level of significance should indeed, be left to be chosen by "God" . . . So far as I am concerned, "God" resides in human values, not in the theory of statistical inference.' No comment is necessary.[33]

Next, consider regulation in the form of adjustment alone. Let us suppose that each observation is averaged over T periods (e.g. the NSS data on food consumption represent monthly averages). In that case, the appropriate cut-off level, if S is known, is given by

$$\beta - \frac{S}{T+1}$$

where S represents the outer limit on borrowing from the body (see (7.9)). Now S is presumably related to the body weight of the individual—for

---

[33] The ideological undercurrents in the debate have been much discussed. See e.g. Gopalan (1982), Dasgupta (1985), Payne and Cutler (1984), Banerji (1981), Chakravorti and Panda (1981), and Zurbrigg (1983).

simplicity, let us say that $S = \theta W$, where W is body weight and θ is a given fraction. In this case, to estimate the percentage of undernourished individuals, we must have some idea of the *distribution of body weights* in the sample being considered, as well as a physiological estimate of θ, and all this should be 'deflated' by the time period of averaging.

The resulting cut-off, in the absence of precise knowledge regarding body weights, is then again a statistical test, much like the one we have just described. Again, the choice of the cut-off is crucially dependent on the 'level of significance', and this in turn involves value judgements about the magnitude of type one errors the observer is willing to bear.

Finally, consider regulation in the form of adaptation alone. With no other sources of regulation, pure adaptation demands that the RMR and/or the efficiency of energy metabolism fully compensate for variations in energy intake, at least up to a lower limit of individual intake.

Two other conditions are relevant for what follows. First, the lower limit must be invariant with respect to the history of intakes. A fluctuating intake history may induce compensation for RMR/metabolic efficiency to a particular lower limit. If this intake history is replaced by a *steady intake at the lower limit*, there is no guarantee that the same adaptive mechanism will permit the system to compensate permanently for this low fixed intake (on this point, see Gopalan 1983*b*). The experimental studies cited by Sukhatme do not check for this feature.

Second, the compensating adaptive changes must not induce changes in other relevant dimensions, such as the incidence of morbidity, the general state of long-run health, and indeed the probability of survival. Again, Sukhatme does not cite experiments which correct for these possibilities. In section 7.3, we briefly discuss some of these issues.

If both these conditions are met, and adjustment is ruled out, then the lower limit of intakes may be used as a threshold for measurement of undernutrition. One must then estimate such a lower limit from careful physiological experimentation. Once the distribution of 'acceptable' intakes is known, then, in particular, a mean minus two sigma rule may be applied to *this* distribution.

Once the two conditions are not met, however, matters are somewhat more subtle. For illustration, let us continue to assume that compensating adaptive changes have no effect on relevant factors such as morbidity and mortality, but drop the first condition. In this case, the lower bound on requirements must be calculated by examining all stationary intake streams which the system can adapt to. In general, the minimum of such intakes will be higher than the minimum requirement generated by intake streams which occasionally or periodically offer higher intakes.

If, in addition, adaptive changes do have potentially adverse effects, such as an increased morbidity rate or lower probability of survival, then in no way does a rule such as Sukhatme's take these factors into account. Once again, by neglecting the possible attendant dangers of adaptation, such rules exhibit a high tolerance for the ill effects of a low nutritional intake.

To summarize:

1. Fluctuation in intakes with a relative stability in expenditure appears to be an experimentally verified occurrence. We have no difficulty in admitting that this implies adjustment but it still remains to be seen how persistent the feature of adjustment is. This is especially relevant when working with NSS household expenditure data which are effectively monthly averages.

2. Autocorrelation in intakes implies nothing over and above (1), barring the provision of evidence that the fluctuations described in (1) are not due to experimental error. And finally;

3. We discuss the implications for measurement. First, we note that adding the variances of inter- and intrapersonal variation to obtain the cut-off threshold is simply not permissible. For instance, when all variation is interpersonal, Sukhatme's measure reduces to a statistical test which allows 'type one error'—classifying a person as undernourished when he is not—to be made with extremely low probability. We argue that this implicitly involves value judgements that may be unacceptable to many. Second, even if all variation is intrapersonal, we need to distinguish between variation generated and 'buffered' by *adjustment*, and that compensated for by *adaptation*. In the case of the former, the measure is still basically statistical, though we argue that Sukhatme's specific rule is not applicable at all. In the case of the latter, a Sukhatme-type rule might apply if (*a*) full adaptation to fluctuating intakes can be 'mimicked' by full adaptation to the minimum of those intakes, and (*b*) adaptation has no adverse effects on related variables such as morbidity or mortality.[34]

We shall be discussing some of these issues further in section 7.3.

(e)   A new measure of undernourishment

We conclude this section with a brief discussion of the potential merits of Sukhatme's proposal. To do so, we ignore adaptation for the moment, and concentrate on the phenomenon of adjustment. Suppose, in fact, that adjustment is significant relative to the time period of measurement.[35] Simplify further and assume that individuals all have similar genotypes as regards nutrition: that is, everyone is the reference man. Finally, assume that we have an estimate (in the form of a distribution function) of the extent of intraindividual variation.

[34] Sukhatme (1982a) reports that 'already [their] work has aroused widespread interest among economists, statisticians, social scientists, biochemists, nutritionists and medical doctors. It has also aroused interest in the Planning Commission, the Indian Council for Medical Research and in the Department of Science and Technology.' Sukhatme's arguments also appear to have convinced such development economists as Srinivasan (Srinivasan 1981) and Lipton (Lipton 1983).

[35] In the context of NSS data, this would mean that adjustment is persistent on the time scale of a month or more.

Now consider a sample of individuals, and the corresponding sample of intakes for the time period under measurement. We specify—explicitly—the probability with which we are permitted to commit the error of classifying a person as well nourished when in fact he is not. (This probability will, of course, reflect our values concerning the importance that we attach to the problem of malnutrition and poverty.) A simple statistical calculation will then yield a level x^* below which we will call a person undernourished.

What we learn from Sukhatme's argument (although he does not explicitly say so) is that the level x^* *in no way reflects the calorie requirement estimated by nutritionists*. That line is given by β, the requirement of the reference man (see e.g. WHO 1985: ch. 2). It is important that the level x^*, which is a *statistical* threshold, be kept distinct from the *nutritional* norm given by β. Failure to do so has led to an unnecessary debate.[36] The level x^* not only reflects β, it attempts also to capture variations around that line and the value judgements of the social scientist that are embedded in the significance level of the hypothesis test. Its level can be higher or lower than that of β.[37]

These observations suggest a departure from the standard practice of headcount measurement. We motivate a new measure of undernourishment by noting first that in the foregoing discussion the observer has an implicit 'model' of undernourishment. What is this model? It is this. There are, first of all, two states: breakdown and good health. Given the observation (or a set of observations) on food intake, the observer assigns a value 1 (for breakdown) or 0 (for good health). It is the choice of the set of observations to which the observer should assign the value 1 that is at the heart of the debate. Given that this set has been chosen, the observer takes the average of all the ones and zeros in the population. This is the measure of undernourishment.

One can argue that it is precisely this insistence on assigning either a 'zero' or a 'one' which is responsible for a large chunk of the controversy. A more detailed statistical model, coupled with a better knowledge of, and appreciation for, the clinical literature would permit us to attach *probabilities* of breakdown to every observation. Some preliminary observations were made regarding this in section 7.2(*d*). Suppose that this is expressed as a function $p(x)$, where x is the observed intake. One possible measure of malnutrition is then

---

[36] A number of economists and nutritionists have accused Sukhatme of suggesting that a person living continually at the lower threshold can survive in a healthy way. And indeed his writings appear to imply such conclusions (see also Seckler 1982, 1984*b*). There is nothing in the statistical findings to support this form of adaptation. Moreover, we are arguing that it is unnecessary to invest what is a statistical threshold with a different meaning, namely, physiological requirement. One can call it a poverty line if one wishes, but it does not mean that the reference man living on a steady intake equal to this threshold can live a healthy life.

[37] Note e.g. the implicit value judgement in the statement of Rand and Scrimshaw (1984), 'If an individual's requirement varies over time, would he not need to be assured the highest level that he required rather than the lowest?' See also Chakravorti and Panda (1981).

$$M_1 = \left[\sum_{i=1}^{n} p(x_i) \right]/n, \qquad (7.10)$$

where x_i is the intake of person i in a sample population of size n.

Observe that this measure subsumes as a special case the one in which there are pure interpersonal variations. To see this simply interpret $p(x_i)$ as the probability that requirement exceeds the observed intake x_i, that is,

$$p(x_i) = \int_{y > x_i} F(y|x_i)dy$$

in the language of section 7.2(a), and now compare (7.10) with (7.2'). The simplest headcount measures using cut-offs, such as those used by Dandekar and Rath (1971) and Sukhatme (1978), are also special cases. (For any cut-off β, set $p(x) = 1$, for $x < \beta$ and $p(x) = 0$ for $x \geq \beta$.)

Our proposed measure also incorporates the possibility of (costly) autoregulation. To see this, assume for convenience that there are no interpersonal variations. Suppose, further, that the time period underlying the observation x_i is given. (For NSS, data x_i represents a monthly average.) Then $p(x_i)$ will stand for the probability that the body will break down (due to stress, infection, or disease), conditional on the observation that x_i has been the observed intake. A satisfactory quantification of $p(.)$ will require that available physiological data be put together in a consistent statistical way (see section 7.3). This measure can therefore be viewed from another angle, in that it is a way of seeing the basic disagreements which have fuelled the controversy.

Finally, one may be interested in a related measure. Suppose that there is some x such that $p(x) = 0$. Consider the minimum such x, call it x^*. A discriminating measure of undernourishment might be constructed to highlight further the risk $p(x_i)$ associated with some observation x_i. This is done by weighting the risk by the (proportionate) nutrition gap $(x^* - x_i)/x^*$. In doing so, we capture not only the extent of the risk faced by the individual but the difficulty of its alleviation. Our second measure is therefore

$$M_2 = \left[\sum_{i=1}^{n} p(x_i)(x_i - x^*) \right]/nx^*$$

There is a close formal similarity between M_2 and the new measures of poverty. If the observations are incomes and x^* is interpreted as a poverty income value, then $(x^* - x_i)/x^*$ is precisely the ith persons's proportionate income gap. The function $p(x)$ may be thought of as a weighting scheme, analogous to the way in which absolute deprivation would be captured in a poverty measurement.[38]

---

[38] In measures of relative deprivation one must use a set of weights where each weight is in some way sensitive to the positions of others. Sen (1976) uses the ranks of the poor as weight but this is only one possible weighting system, and there are other, equally persuasive, systems where the weights are dependent only on the absolute shortfall. See Kakwani (1980) or Foster (1984).

7.3 (a) Regulation: the biological evidence

The heated discussions in the pages of the *Economic and Political Weekly* (and elsewhere) might create the impression that Sukhatme (and Seckler) were the initiators of the regulation hypothesis.[39] This is not true. Adaptation to a reduced or infrequent supply of calorie has been the subject of study since the beginning of this century, dating back at least to the laboratory-controlled experiments of Benedict. One of the classic studies of the physiology of human adaptation to continuing calorie deficiency is that which was undertaken in 1950 by Keys and his colleagues (Keys *et al.* 1950). And there is a wealth of data on the effects of calorie deprivation in experimental animals (see Fabry 1969 for a detailed discussion). The survey by Grande (1964) summarizes some of this earlier literature. Other studies on calorie deprivation or on fluctuating calorie intake, such as Edmundson (1977, 1979) or Edholm *et al.* (1970), have received a more explicit treatment in the current debate. We will examine these presently.

Our discussion of the existing clinical literature is constrained in several respects. First, we are ourselves students in this area, and we cannot pretend that we understand, in detail, the many intricacies of the biological processes underlying regulation. Secondly, there is doubt that any satisfactory answer exists in the available literature. Not only does a great deal more empirical work need to be done to understand the implications of undernourishment for economic behaviour, there is much that is not understood at the more basic physiological level. Finally, there is an intriguing feature of the clinical studies that has crucial implications for the measurement of undernourishment, though not for the positive economic theory that one might construct from this.[40] This is the use of *adaptation* as a term to describe the change in the equilibrium of an organism (man, in our example) relative to the external environment (calorie intake history in the present context) as this environment is exogenously altered. This corresponds roughly to our usage so far. However, the use of the term permits a variety of 'adaptive' mechanisms to come under its rubric. This can cause a problem. For, when it is the undernourishment of man we wish to study and estimate, many of these mechanisms can legitimately be regarded as socially undesirable. For example, Fabry writes, referring to the Keys *et al.* (1950) study:

The final effect of adaptation [to low calorie intake] is a reduction of the total energy output . . . The greatest ratio of the 'actively' saved energy is accounted for by the reduced physical activity. Spontaneous reduction of movement, which in under-

[39] Sukhatme himself suggests that his work, along with that of Margen and Seckler, 'has caused an upheaval in the [current] philosophical and scientific concepts [that] will almost certainly imply a change in the nature and direction of future research' (Sukhatme 1981*a*).

[40] See s. 7.4 for a discussion of the implications of adaptation for the economic theory of labour markets and unemployment in resource-poor economies.

nourished subjects are part of the complex of marked behavioural differences . . . thus play a very substantial role in the adaptation to a reduced food intake. (Fabry 1969: 20–2)

'Adaptation' at the price of physical debilitation, manifested for instance in the 'spontaneous reduction of movements' carries very different ethical connotations from those the word normally suggests. This is certainly not to suggest that biologists are harsh, unfeeling creatures. But they have a well-defined clinical view of adaptation, which must not be taken out of context. This also makes our task more difficult. Which features of adaptation should be socially acceptable? Which features should be rejected? These are difficult matters, but they must not be evaded. In other words, we are arguing that there are types of adaptation which a defendable measurement theory should ignore. An act of measurement (of undernourishment) is thus a normative act.

Important, for instance, is the question: 'adapted' or not, does the person feel hungry? Does he experience suffering as a consequence of his low or fluctuating intake of food? However difficult these questions may be to translate into practice, they cannot be lost sight of. Of course, the 'adaptationists' in our debate recognize these points (not fully, though, as we shall argue). But even the concern with regulatory mechanisms which do not impair the ability of the individual to do productive work does not go far enough. For example, many Indian labourers perform back-breaking tasks in unhealthy, hostile environments.[41] There can be no question that they work hard relative to their low levels of energy intake. Even were they capable of adapting, could it be suggested that they do not go hungry? Banerji (1981) makes this point forcefully and clearly. His empirical work is perhaps the only real attempt there has been to quantify the extent of hunger in this basic sense. While registering our basic sympathy with this approach, we recognize that there are other dimensions to the problem, and it is to these we now turn.

We are interested in the existence of regulation and its positive and normative implications. To narrow down the vast area of coverage that is implied, we concentrate on the following specific issues:

1. What is the biological evidence for *adjustment* to a low or fluctuating intake of nutrients, especially of calories?
2. What is the biological evidence for *adaptation* to a low or fluctuating intake, in the sense that the ability to perform tasks remains unimpaired?
3. What implications do (1) and (2) have for the measurement of under-nourishment and poverty?
4. What implications do (1) and (2) have for economic behaviour, in particular, for theories of the labour market in resource-poor economies?

Issues (1), (2), and (3) will be the subject of study of this section. The study of (4) will be left to section 7.4.

[41] Durnin and Passmore (1967) note that rickshaw-pulling in Calcutta is among the most arduous tasks in the world in terms of energy requirement.

(b)   Components for the energy balance equation

We begin by extending the basic structure of section 7.2. Recall equation (7.4) (with time subscripts dropped):

$$x = r + q + s \qquad (7.11)$$

The components of this equation need to be studied in greater detail, and we proceed to do this.

1. *The Atwater factors and metabolizable energy.* Consider first the energy intake x, which represents the *metabolizable energy* available to the individual. Now, this does not equal the energy value of food ingested, v, say. From v, we must subtract losses of energy due to digestion (fecal losses). What is left may be called *digestible energy*. But this, too, contains further losses, due largely to incomplete oxidation of protein and other nitrogenous materials in the body. The resulting excretion of urea, creatinine, and uric acid contains energy. These urinary losses are deducted from digestible energy to yield x, the metabolizable energy.

It transpires that these losses, divided by the gross energy content of food intake, appear to be quite stable across individuals, though they depend, of course, on the type of food ingested. The percentage of retained energy varies between 90 and 95 per cent, and these (food-specific) coefficients are known as the *Atwater factors*.[42] The Atwater factors are used widely to provide information on the calorie value of various types of food.

2. *The resting metabolic rate and its components.* Consider, next, the term r in (7.11). We have defined this to be the *resting metabolic rate* (RMR). It has two significant components. The first is the *basal metabolic rate* (BMR). This is defined as the energy expenditure of an individual who is at rest in a thermoneutral environment and who has fasted for a period of fourteen hours.[43] It is the energy required to maintain body temperature, to sustain heart and respiratory action, to supply the minimum energy requirement of resting tissues, and to support ionic gradients across cell membranes. FAO (1973: 107) suggest a BMR of roughly 1,700 Kcal per day for its reference man. The BMR has certain broad properties (see Heim 1985). For instance, it is roughly a constant fraction of body surface area. Furthermore, expressed as a fraction of body area, it varies inversely with age and body weight. And finally, there are important links between BMR and undernourishment. We will explore this below.

---

[42] See e.g. Atwater and Benedict (1903). However, even in discussions on nutritionally healthy populations there are disagreements regarding the reliability of the Atwater factors, for example, when applied to foods containing large amounts of indigestible carbohydrates (dietary fibre). There are suggestions that the variability of retention may be higher, between 80 and 95% (see e.g. Heim 1985).

[43] See e.g. Heim (1985). By a thermoneutral environment we refer to the range of ambient temperatures within which the individual is in thermal balance, at a constant body temperature, with no net heat loss or production.

The second component of RMR is the increased metabolic rate resulting from the ingestion of food. Food ingestion causes a great deal of heat production and loss; this extra production will be called *diet-induced thermogenesis* (DIT).[44] The magnitude of DIT is certainly not negligible—probably around 600 Kcal per day.[45] It has been suggested that DIT mechanisms play an important role in regulation. These are controversial matters; we will nevertheless look into them briefly.

3. *Physical activity.* The term q in (7.11) represents energy requirements for physical activity. We now study this more closely. Let α denote a *type* of activity (carrying loads, harvesting, working on a conveyor belt, and so on) and λ its *level* (kilogram-miles per day, bushels per day, bolts tightened per hour, and so forth). The activity and its level will demand a certain amount of energy. In a given experimental situation, the energy cost of each activity may be directly measured[46] or obtained from published tables.[47] As a rough indicator, FAO (1973) suggested a requirement of 400 Kcal per day for moderate activity for their reference man, but activities requiring in excess of 1,000 Kcal per day would by no means be uncommon.

The energy requirements in physical activity depend on the genotype of the individual and his history. (An example of an important indicator is the body weight of the individual.) But the manner in which these requirements are affected is a complicated issue, and we will postpone its discussion for the moment. But we note that for a given activity α, its level λ and a given history h_t for the individual at time t, the energy requirement q_t is given by the function

$$q_t = e_t(\alpha, \lambda, h_t) \qquad t \geqslant 0 \tag{7.12}$$

4. *Storage.* The additions to (or running down of) body stores of energy are reflected in the final term of (7.11), which is s. At the risk of some simplification,[48] we postulate that given the weight w_t in period t and the magnitude of s_t (positive or negative), the weight in period $t + 1$ is determined by the relation

$$s_t = s(w_{t+1} w_t) \tag{7.13}$$

---

[44] The phenomenon is called by various names: specific dynamic action of food, thermic effect of food, post-prandial increase in heat production, and so on. See Heim (1985).

[45] FAO (1973) suggests 1.5 times the BMR as a reasonable approximation for energy required for pure maintenance. This being 2,600 Kcal for its reference man, one may infer that it regards the DIT of such a person to the be 866 Kcal per day.

[46] The measurement of oxygen consumed and carbon dioxide produced (and preferably also urinary nitrogen output) can provide a reliable indicator of energy expended on various activities. The Weir equation (Weir 1949) provides one link between these variables, and can be used for the estimation.

[47] See e.g. Durnin and Passmore (1967), Bannerjee and Saha (1970), and WHO (1985).

[48] The simplification essentially arises from the fact that we are ruling out feedback effects of history on the form of the function $s(.\ ,\ .)$. This does not appear to be important, as far as we can tell from the existing literature.

It should be noted that the function $s(.,.)$ (like our other functions) depends on the individual's genotype. In particular, the *form* in which energy is stored in the body may differ significantly among individuals. A large part of the storage is in the form of fat, but there are individuals who store significant amounts in the form of protein.[49] These factors will have a role to play in our later discussions.

We believe that if there are any mechanisms for adjustment or adaptation, their impact must be on one or more of the four categories described above. It may help the reader to know that most of the pleas for regulation come under items 2 and 4 (see, for example, our analysis above of the Sukhatme hypothesis). But we will consider each category in turn.

(c) *Metabolizable energy*

How reliable are the Atwater factors in giving us estimates of the metabolizable energy of various types of food? In undernourished populations, the answer appears to be: not very. In fact, the evidence is strong that undernourishment (especially coupled with episodes of acute diarrhoea[50]) leads to a significantly impaired ability to digest nutrients. The Atwater factors, which predict a nutrient digestibility of 95 per cent plus (barring protein), may be completely off the mark in these situations.

For the populations in less-developed countries, Atwater factors generally lead to overestimates of digestibility. Uauy (1985) observes that the mucosa of the small intestines of people living in these countries display changes that are characteristic of subclinical nutrient malabsorption, and that digestibility rarely exceeds 90 per cent as a result. In addition, undernourishment or recent episodes of acute diarrhoea can bring down nutrient absorption to below 80 per cent (Molla 1984).

But that is not all. Food intakes that have a high percentage of dietary fibre (crude fibre exceeding 10g per day) possess digestibility coefficients that are overestimated by the Atwater factors.[51] Fibre intakes exceeding 50g per day are not unusual in rural tropical populations or among vegetarians (Uauy 1975). This may decrease digestibility by a further 10 per cent, (Uauy 1985; Prynne and Southgate 1979).

All this is bad news for the 'adaptationists'. But the objection may be raised that this 'negative adaptation' is not significant quantitatively. So it is as well to

---

[49] Dugdale and Payne (1977) construct an interesting model where people are classified as metabolically fat or metabolically lean, depending on their genetic predisposition to store energy in the form of fat or protein respectively. This form of 'leanness' or 'fatness' has important implications for adjustment to fluctuating intake (see below).

[50] The connections between undernourishment and illnesses such as diarrhoea are discussed below.

[51] This is because foods containing large amounts of indigestible carbohydrates (dietary fibre) have detrimental effects on the digestibility of other nutrients, thereby reducing the metabolizable energy content of proteins and fats (Heim 1985).

see what order of magnitude is involved. Suppose an individual's daily requirement of metabolizable energy is 2,500 Kcal. Multiplication by an average Atwater factor of 95 per cent leads to a 'gross' requirement of approximately 2,600 Kcal per day. But now consider a rescaling of the digestibility coefficient along the lines suggested above. This would be anywhere between 70 per cent and 95 per cent, the lower figures being nearer the mark for undernourished people in tropical countries. Take a figure of 75 per cent and rescale the metabolizable energy requirement. The new gross requirement is approximately 3,300 Kcal per day, which is 700 Kcal per day higher.[52] It is clear then that the numbers involved are far from insignificant. (As a measure of relative magnitude, it might help to recall the FAO (1973) prescription of 400 Kcal per day needed solely for moderate activity of the reference man.)

(d) Resting metabolism

It is here the issue of regulation and its normative implications acquires its greatest complexity. One is concerned not only with the existence of adaptive mechanisms, one is concerned also with their normative interpretation. Rather than linger over these issues in the abstract, we go directly to the evidence.

Our starting-point is the classic Minnesota experiment of Keys and his colleagues on the biology of human starvation.[53] The analysis of Taylor and Keys (1950) with data drawn from the experiment is particularly instructive. Thirty-two subjects were investigated.[54] In the course of the control period they were in energy balance with an average daily intake of 3,492 Kcal. Over an experimental period of six-months, the food intake was lowered to 1,570 Kcal per day.[55] The effects were dramatic:

The subjects suffered a marked loss of strength and endurance as the starvation period progressed. The men commented that they felt as if they were rapidly growing old. They felt weak and they tired easily. They moved cautiously, climbing stairs one step at a time, and obviously reduced unnecessary movements to a minimum. (Taylor and Keys 1950)

---

[52] We are not suggesting that 75% is in fact the appropriate coefficient. Much work needs to be done on this problem before anything substantially precise can be said. Nevertheless, the orders of magnitude predicted by the preliminary evidence that we have quoted are striking, and deserve much more attention than they have received. The proponents of adaptation do not mention these issues, to the best of our knowledge.

[53] The basic reference is Keys et al. (1950). See also Taylor and Keys (1950), and the article by Young and Scrimshaw (1971) for an insightful account of the Minnesota experiment and related considerations.

[54] The subjects were resident in the Laboratory of Physical Hygiene for one year, where the experiments were carried out.

[55] This 'starvation diet' consisted of potatoes, cabbage, turnips, and cereals, with only a few grams of animal protein each week. The protein content of the diet was 54.5g per day, and adequate allowances of minerals and vitamins were provided (except for riboflavin and vitamin A).

Table 7.1 Energy saved by subjects after six months of calorie undernourishment

Source of saving	Energy saved (Kcal per day)	% of total calories saved
Basal metabolism	614	31.9[a]
DIT	192	10.0
Energy expected on physical activity	1,116	58.1[b]
Total saved	1,922	100.0

[a] 65% (i.e. 20.7% of total calories saved) for decrease of metabolizing tissue mass, and 35% (i.e. 11.2% of total calories saved) on account of lower tissue metabolism.
[b] 60% (i.e. 34.9% of total calories saved) on account of reduced physical activity, and 40% (i.e. 23.2% of total calories saved) on expenditure for work due to reduced body weight.
Source: Data from Taylor and Keys (1950), taken from Fabry (1969).

Body weight fell, but stabilized at the end of the six-month period, when a new energy balance had more or less been established. The average loss of body weight was 24 per cent. An average of 1,922 Kcal per day had therefore been 'saved' by the body. How was this saving accomplished? To see this, consider Table 7.1.

In comparison with the corresponding values in the control period, the basal metabolic rate (BMR) declined by 19 per cent, the energy expended on work fell by 71 per cent, and the specific dynamic effect of food (DIT) fell proportionately to the reduced intake, by about 50 per cent. In terms of calories saved, reduced physical activity was the largest contributor (58.1 per cent of total calories saved) with BMR a not-too-close second (31.9 per cent).

Now, the Minnesota experiment was not designed to answer the questions that we have been asking here, in particular, those concerning adaptation with *unchanging* physical activity levels. But it does raise the following question: what if the experiment were redone with the subjects being required to maintain a specified activity level? This experimental situation would mirror more closely the actual experience of low-intake labourers who are forced to work at specified levels in order to earn a living. After all, the reduced 'starvation' diet of 1,570 Kcal per day is close to the average energy intake of Kerala (approximately 1,600 Kcal per day), and is certainly as large as the nutrition intake of large sections of the Indian population.[56]

It may be argued that comparison with India is improper. Indians have been limited over generations to low intake and 'adaptations' have taken place on a corresponding time scale. The Minnesota experiment, using North Americans

[56] The Kerala figure is NSS data (see National Sample Survey, *Sarvekshana*, Jan. 1979), though it may be on the low side (see Kumar 1986). As for Indian nutrition-intake data, there is a good deal of information. See e.g. Rao (1977) and Dasgupta (1985).

with generations of comfortably high food intake, obviously does not mirror this situation. But one must be careful. A Lamarckian notion of intergenerational improvement, in the sense that the child acquires adaptation from the parent, is simply not tenable, though it may be granted that genotypes with lower needs have had advantages in the selection process. What is at issue in the present debate is the question of *phenotypic* adaptation. The underlying premiss is that the genotypes of people in less-developed countries (determining body size and weight) are not very different from their counterparts in developed economies.[57] The Minnesota experiment is, therefore, relevant to our enquiry, and the modified version, requiring unchanging activity, would have been especially so.

While it is difficult to speculate on the consequences of such a modification, it is worth noting that Taylor and Keys are themselves quite cautious in drawing implications from the experiment for 'positive' or 'beneficial' adaptation. They observe that much of the adaptation is obtained 'by the rather desperate expedient of reducing the mass activity of the organism. This mechanism . . . is entirely passive and produces major limitations and stresses of its own.'[58] Nevertheless, the experiment provides a key insight into one possible mechanism for positive adaptation: that occurring via a lowering of the basal metabolic rate. In the Minnesota experiment this fell by 19 per cent, and accounted for 31.9 per cent of the total calories saved.[59] A lower BMR has been observed in other experiments dealing with reduced calorie intake.[60] One influential study (Edmundson 1977, 1979)[61] identifies the basal metabolic rate as the fundamental adaptive mechanism under calorie deficiency. The study has received attention in the current debate[62] and merits discussion in some detail.

The subjects were 54 East Javanese farmers. Each subject was measured six times at two-month intervals (for one year) for a total of 324 man days of data.

---

[57] For example, Gopalan and Narasinga Rao (1974) write that 'it has been shown . . . that the growth potential of Indian children is not different from that of European or American children'. Then again, we have in WHO (1985: 36) that: 'A number of studies have attempted to assess the possibility of ethnic differences in BMR but these have failed to identify any differences that could not be related to the nutritional state or possibly to climatic conditions.' The increasing body sizes and weights of people in Japan and China also appear to support this assertion in a general way.

[58] Taylor and Keys (1950).

[59] This observation needs to be qualified, however, by the fact that the greater part of the reduction was accounted for by the reduced amount of metabolizing tissue (see n. *a* of Table 7.1). When calculated as a fraction of lean body mass, the BMR was only 15% lower (Taylor and Keys 1950).

[60] See e.g. Grande, Anderson, and Keys (1958) and the survey by Grande (1964). These experiments suggest that a lower BMR per unit of lean body mass participates in the improved energy balance, indicating a reduction of metabolic processes in tissues.

[61] A summary of these two papers may be found in Edmundson (1980).

[62] See e.g. Sukhatme (1982*a*).

Food intake was measured and its metabolizable energy content determined. Activities were recorded for each individual, and mean energy outputs were determined for ten basic activities. Work outputs for each individual were then calculated by multiplying the mean energy output per minute by the number of minutes each subject engaged in that activity.

The results were striking. While the mean energy intake (2,430 Kcal per day) corresponded closely to mean energy output (2,443 Kcal per day), there was no association between average intake and output for individuals. The ratio of energy intake to output (averaged over the six observations for each subject) ranged from a low of 0.59 to a high of 1.63. Edmundson concluded:

This implies that trained observers watched 54 villagers very closely for 324 days, with the specific purpose of carefully determining how hard these men were working, [and] could detect no discernible differences in the observed work output of men with high and low energy intakes. (Edmundson 1977)

Edmundson's second study (1979) is a continuation of the first. Eleven of the earlier 54 subjects were chosen for further testing. Most of them had exhibited unusually high or unusually low intakes in the earlier study, and the rest served as controls.[63] The subjects were so selected that average heights (and weights) in the high and low intake groups were similar. Basal metabolic rates of these subjects were measured, and a six-day average of energy intakes was constructed for each individual.

The BMR of the high-energy-intake group was found to be twice as high as that of the low-energy-intake group. Subjects enjoying high energy intake also expended greater energy in performing standard tasks, though the difference here was not as significant. Edmundson concluded that there is an adaptive increase in metabolic efficiency, in response to a prolonged period of low intake.

This study is certainly closer in spirit to the sort of issues we have in mind, and so it is worth discussion in a bit more detail. Consider the first experiment. While calorie intakes were measured individually, energy outputs were calculated for each subject by multiplying the number of minutes spent on a particular activity by the (group) *averaged* energy expenditure per minute on that activity. Now, this is a peculiar thing to do, for there is then no way to judge the work output of each individual per unit of time. Suppose you are ill-fed and hungry, and work at a lethargic pace for an hour. Your well-fed counterpart works for an hour, too, but gets a lot more done. Edmundson's technique of measuring energy outputs would give both of you the same

---

[63] Six of these had exhibited intakes below 2,000 Kcal per day in the early study, three had exhibited intakes greater than 3,000 Kcal per day, and two had intakes of about 2,500 Kcal per day.

number! It is no wonder, then, that the 'most efficient' low-intake subject in that experiment released 1.63 times the energy that he ingested.

In response to this one might invoke Edmundson's second experiment. Here, subjects with high energy intake expended more energy per minute for performing standard tasks. It might be argued, therefore, that this greater efficiency permitted low-intake subjects to work just as hard while using less energy. But this argument fails on two counts. First, of the two tasks, the lighter one did not exhibit differences in efficiency (between the two groups) that were significant at the 1 per cent level, though the heavier one did. In any case the differences are not high enough to allow one to argue that all subjects were working equally in the first experiment. Second, the tasks measure an efficiency *rate*. They do not measure the stamina, or the ability, to perform at a certain rate for prolonged periods of time.[64]

The Edmundson experiment therefore retreats into the same realm as the Minnesota experiment. While it is stated that there were 'no discernible differences' in physical activity, the measurement techniques used simply do not permit such an assertion to be made.

Now, one may ask: if our basic concern is with a possible adaptive mechanism in the BMR, why worry whether work output stays constant? After all, the BMR was undoubtedly lower in the low-intake subjects, and to the extent that this was due to a lower oxygen utilization of tissue,[65] it is indicative of some degree of adaptation, even though one needs to be careful in drawing any conclusions about the direction of causality involved.[66]

The answer is that we do not know whether a fall in the BMR as a response to undernourishment is at all separable from a decline in physical stamina and activity. Taylor and Keys (1950), for instance, warned that a great part of the decline in BMR may be due to the wastage of tissue. In particular, the heart may undergo considerable loss of muscle mass during periods of prolonged low intake. Young and Scrimshaw (1971) also observe that the heart size shrinks in these situations, and the effect of such a phenomenon on physical activity, especially on work that requires stamina, is not difficult to predict. And, at a more general level, Gopalan (1983) argues that for an adult, adaptation to a low

---

[64] It will help to disclose at this stage what these 'standard work tasks' were. The light task involved pedalling a bicycle ergometer at a rate of 50 watts per minute, while the heavy task involved pedalling to produce a work output of 100 watts per minute. Energy intakes in this process do give an index of efficiency, and with lower resting metabolism it is not surprising that low-intake subjects are more efficient. But this exercise reveals nothing about their capacity for doing sustained work.

[65] Recall that in the Minnesota experiment, a great deal of the fall in BMR was due to *wastage* of active tissue.

[66] Edmundson is careful. He recognizes that 'it is difficult to say whether the low-intake subjects eat less simply because their needs are less as a function of normal physiologic variability or whether their low BMR's represent a combination of short and long term adaptations to low energy intake' (Edmundson 1979: 193).

intake 'may not pose serious health hazards', but only if 'the inadequacy can be totally compensated by reduction in activity'.[67]

It is important to remember that an exhibition of a decline in the basal metabolic rate as a response to low intake is not an indicator of *acceptable* adaptation. For instance, children with marasmus or kwashiorkor are known to 'adapt' by lowering significantly their basal metabolic rates (Jaya Rao and Khan 1974).[68] This is not a normal state but a strategic response to a life-threatening environment.

How much of a change in the basal metabolic rate (following low calorie intake) can be treated as acceptable physiological adaptation, as opposed to a pathological response? This is a difficult question, and its satisfactory resolution requires careful study of a number of aspects. We have emphasized that the fall in BMR could be due to a wastage of tissue and not to a depressed oxygen utilization of active tissue.[69] The two situations are quite different. We can thus do no more than insist that there are basic uncertainties in interpretation which cannot be ignored. Whether the BMR adapts significantly to low intake in an acceptable way is still very much an open question. WHO (1985: 50) go further: 'The documented changes in metabolism when energy intake is altered suggest, therefore, that with the present state of knowledge the range of metabolic adaptation must be considered to be small.'

We conclude with diet-induced thermogenesis (DIT) as a possible adaptive mechanism.[70] The best-known experiments that have been conducted have addressed the effects of *overfeeding*, and thus inducing obesity. The aim here has been to study energy balance in subjects.[71] It has been conjectured that DIT mechanisms might play a part in energy balance regulation, and that obesity might be traced to a defect in these mechanisms (when DIT does not increase following high intake).[72] But all this is still controversial.

(e) Efficiency of energy metabolism

A related issue is the possibility of adaptation through changes in the efficiency of energy metabolism. Sukhatme and Margen (1982) advance this as a

---

[67] Gopalan goes on to state that in the case of a child, not surprisingly, a total reduction of activity in fact hampers its physical and intellectual growth and development. See the references in Gopalan (1983). See also WHO (1985).

[68] One can argue, in fact, that the marasmic infant adapts better. For in the case of marasmus, the child discards its muscles in order to protect the more important organs (liver, pancreas, and intestines), while these organs are damaged in the child with kwashiorkor (see Gopalan 1983).

[69] As Jaya Rao and Khan (1974) observe (but do not carry out), expressing BMR as a fraction of lean body mass may help to isolate a little better the degree of adaptation involved.

[70] These observations are largely taken from Rand, Scrimshaw, and Young (1985).

[71] See e.g. Sims (1976), Jung *et al.* (1979), and Schutz *et al.* (1984).

[72] See Jung *et al.* (1979), Danforth (1981), Miller (1979), and Jequier (1983). It has been suggested that thermogenesis in brown adipose tissue might be the principal energy buffer (Himms-Hagen 1984), but this area is controversial, as the high metabolic rate of this tissue may not be significant for the organism as a whole (Uauy 1985).

hypothesis. But the assertion is based on little or no cited evidence (the details we relegate to a footnote[73]). Rand, Scrimshaw, and Young (1985) test the Sukhatme–Margen hypothesis with the original data from five sets of long-term metabolic studies. There were 42 subjects in all, who were examined for periods of 63–90 days.[74] In each study, crude estimates of energy intake required to maintain body weight for each subject were arrived at. During the study, the amounts of energy estimated were supplied at an unchanged level. The subjects were asked to maintain their usual level of physical activity in order to achieve a relatively constant energy expenditure in this sphere.

These studies attempt to minimize daily variations in energy intake and physical activity. Therefore, if there is a regulatory aspect to energy metabolism which adjusts to short-term fluctuations in body needs (or intakes) while maintaining body weight, this would presumably manifest itself in the observation that most subjects quickly settle down to a constant body weight.

This did not happen. In 19 out of 42 subjects there were significant increases in body weight, and another 14 displayed significant declines in weight. (Sixteen of these 33 individuals had body weight increasing or decreasing throughout the length of the study.) Of the remainder, 8 subjects showed fluctuating body weight with no apparent trend, and only 2 maintained a stable body weight. It was therefore clear that for the great majority of the subjects, 'the apparently modest imbalance between energy intake and expenditure was not effectively buffered by adaptive thermogenesis',[75] or by changes in the efficiency of energy metabolism.

(f) Physical activity

We now turn to our third category of energy use: physical activity. Recall that one of the requirements of 'acceptable' adaptation in the studies we have been commenting upon is that physical activity at the ongoing level should not be lowered. To capture this, fix the activity (α) and its level (λ). The question of

---

[73] The body does not take energy directly from food. For example, glucose is converted into ATP, which is then broken down to supply the body's energy needs. In the process of ATP formation, a large fraction of energy is dissipated as heat. This fraction is at least as large as 45–50%, but in many individuals it is higher. Sukhatme and Margen (1982) argue that high-intake individuals are relatively inefficient in this conversion. For example, they state that an individual with an intake of 1,900 Kcal per day will have an efficiency of 50%, whereas in an individual consuming 3,200 Kcal per day the efficiency is 30%. For an intermediate intake of 2,550 Kcal per day the efficiency factor is 37%. These numbers are plucked from the air and do not seem to have any experimental basis. It is worth noting, too, that when these intakes are multiplied by the respective conversion factors, they all give the same figure—about 950 Kcal! This 'backcalculation' also appears to suggest (unintentionally, perhaps) a belief that all adaptive changes are due to changes in energy metabolism.

[74] The five studies dealt with dietary nitrogen and energy intake for 16, 8, 6, 6, and 6 subjects for 63, 84, 82, 90, and 82 days respectively. See the references in Rand, Scrimshaw, and Young (1985).

[75] Rand, Scrimshaw, and Young (1985).

adaptation in this sphere may now be rephrased thus: do low-intake subjects require less energy to perform the given activity at the given level, relative to their high-intake counterparts?

Now, there are a number of ways in which an individual's nutrition history might affect current work-efficiencies, but we will simplify and focus on two particular aspects of a low-intake history: small body size and low body weight. There is much evidence that both these factors are consequences of a history of low intake, the former more so in the case of childhood undernourishment.[76] Our question then simplifies to whether people of small stature and weight are more sparing in their energy use, when asked to perform the task (α, λ). This is also connected to the debate on the 'small but healthy' hypothesis, a revealing title fashioned by Seckler.[77]

The evidence on this issue is limited. We have observed that Edmundson's (1979) study yielded a better efficiency rate (measured as the ratio of work output to energy consumption) for people with low intake. But there are studies that indicate no such efficiency difference. For instance, Spurr et al. (1984) studied the effect of malnourishment on treadmill walking, using a sample of school-aged Colombian boys. They concluded that there was no evidence to indicate that shorter, lighter people are mechanically more efficient than their larger counterparts. This is not surprising. There is no doubt that, ceteris paribus, a heavier or bigger person uses more energy simply to 'carry' his larger dimensions along. This would tend to raise work efficiency of smaller people. On the other hand, there are many tasks where physical strength is an asset. Activities such as stone-cutting, sugarcane harvesting, and carrying loads come easily to mind. There are many others. A heavier person may well get more work accomplished on the treadmill, though he may also use more energy per unit of time. But there is no reason to expect a significant difference in the ratio of work to energy, though Seckler (1984), contrary to Spurr and his · colleagues, feels 'the limited evidence indicates that, down to a low limit of size, small people are more efficient workers'.

In any event, one may ask: why should work efficiency be the sole criterion? Comparisons of efficiency do not answer our basic question, which is couched in terms of a fixed activity and a given level of that activity. Work capacity is equally relevant. We therefore turn to a brief discussion of studies dealing with this issue.

Areskog et al. (1969) used as their subjects six groups of Ethiopian males of varying ages. Anthropometric and other laboratory data were taken. The

---

[76] Familiar scales for grading protein-calorie malnutrition (PCM) are based on these observations. The well-known Gomez scale (Gomez et al. 1956) uses weight for age as a percentage of the Harvard standard (for normal, healthy individuals). The Waterlow scale (Waterlow 1976) uses height-for-age (as a percentage of the Harvard standard) for grading chronic PCM. See also Downs (1964) and Vaidyanathan (1985).

[77] See e.g. Seckler (1980, 1982, 1984), Payne and Cutler (1984), and Chafkin (1985).

capacity to do work was then measured on a bicycle ergometer, with the work load being increased stepwise at six-minute intervals. The physical work performed at a heart rate of 170 per minute was taken as an index of work capacity.[78] A high positive correlation between body weight and work capacity was obtained.[79]

Other studies on malnutrition and reduced work capacity agree with this finding. Noteworthy is a study undertaken by Desai et al. (1984) on marginal malnutrition, body size, and work capacity.[80] The subjects were migrant adolescent males in Southern Brazil. A local group of well-to-do adolescent boys of the same age served as controls. Dietary data revealed that energy and nutrient intakes were marginally lower in the migrants, and that they had lower reserves of fat and muscle mass relative to the controls. Work-load experiments were undertaken in a manner similar to that in Areskog et al. (1969). The results were that, at submaximal work loads, the migrants exhibited oxygen consumption and work efficiency similar to that of the controls but achieved this at a higher fraction of their work capacity. This manifested itself in heart rates that were significantly higher. Physical work capacity (measured at work at a heart rate of 170/min.) was one-third lower in the migrants.[81]

Dutra de Oliveira et al. (1985) summarize some of this literature. They conclude by observing that

The implications of the association between small body size and impaired productivity are now becoming evident. Our studies in Brazil, and those of others in India, Colombia and Guatemala clearly suggest that small body size due to inadequate dietary intake and the resulting decreased productivity in the lower socioeconomic classes could perpetuate their poverty through a vicious cycle . . .[82]

Again, while nothing definite can be said, the trust of these studies is all too clear. A history of low intake that manifests itself in small body size and/or low weight is unlikely to create adaptive advantages for the individual in the sphere of physical activity. While the results on work efficiency are somewhat ambiguous, those on work capacity are quite sharp, suggesting that there is a reduction of work capacity in conditions of undernourishment.

These issues concerning physical activity can be depicted in a simple manner

---

[78] An ECG was done at regular intervals and the respiration rate and blood pressure were also measured. The work done at a heart rate of 170/min. was obtained by linear interpolation from the data. Wahlund (1948) discusses principles for the measurement of work capacity.

[79] Similar results were obtained by Satyanarayana et al. (1977), who found that work capacity was correlated with weight, height, and habitual physical activity. Weight accounted for 64% of the variation in work capacity.

[80] Dutra de Oliveira et al. (1985) provide a concise summary of this and related literature on body size and work capacity.

[81] Satyanarayana et al. (1979) found a similar reduction in the work capacity of Indian boys with a history of undernourishment during childhood.

[82] References to these studies may be found in Dutra de Oliveira et al. (1985).

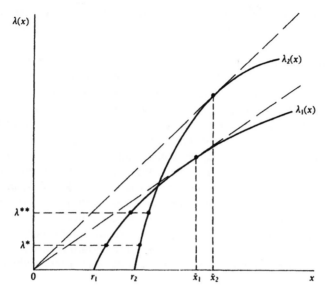

Fig. 7.1.

(see Fig. 7.1). We consider two individuals, one with a history of low intake, the other, high. We hold the weight of each individual as a constant, and so, for each individual, equation (7.4) reduces to

$$x_i = r_i + q_i, \qquad (i = 1, 2), \qquad (7.14)$$

where i is the label of the person. Now, the level of activity, λ_i, depends upon q_i, and it is an increasing function of q_i *for a given person.* Write this as $\lambda_i(q_i)$. It is, by definition, zero when q_i is nil, and remains zero if x_i falls short of r_i. Using (7.14) then we may construct the function $\lambda_i(x_i)$ and in Fig. 7.1 we present two such functions, one for each of the persons under review. In Fig. 7.1 we have assumed that the RMR (r_i) of person 1—the one with a history of lower intakes—is lower than the RMR (r_2) of person 2. λ^* and λ^{**} are two levels of physical activity. As drawn in Fig. 7.1 the two functions relating work output to calorie intake, $\lambda_1(x)$ and $\lambda_2(x)$, are consistent with what is often inferred from Edmundson's experiments: the ratio of work output to energy consumption is higher for the person with the lower intake at each of the two levels of work output, λ^* and λ^{**}. But it is not at all clear why we should jubilate over this. For note that person 2 has a greater *capacity* to work. At high enough intakes he can do more work per unit of time than his rival. Of greater significance, person 2 is intrinsically more efficient; in that the maximum ratio of work output to energy consumption that 2 can offer (at intake level $\bar{x}_2$) exceeds the *maximum* ratio that 1 can offer (at intake level $\bar{x}_1$). The implications of this for the operations of the labour market, and thus of employment opportunities, are explored in a preliminary way in section 7.4. (See also Dasgupta and Ray 1986.)

To be sure, there are other possible configurations of such curves. It depends on the activity in question. But before we think of other configurations we should remind ourselves that the poor in less-developed countries are often engaged in strenuous activities, not sedentary. It is a cruel play upon words which labels them the 'weaker' members of society, when what they are forced to do in order to earn a livelihood is often back-breaking work.

Over and above this is a more general observation that needs to be made. The issues that are raised by Fig. 7.1 are very much the ones that need to be raised when debating economic policy. We need to have some idea of the shape of the curves in Fig. 7.1 over a wide range of energy consumption. Even if it were true that the person with a history of low intakes is more efficient *at certain specified activity levels*, it would not, on its own, be a matter of significance. As we noted earlier, biologists use the term 'adaptation' in a certain manner. This usage does not carry with it the connotation that adaptation is necessarily 'costless'.

(g) Storage

This brings us to our last source of regulation: that occurring through *adjustment*. In a sense we have come full circle, for in section 7.2 it was the issue of adjustment and its implications for measurement that was our principal concern. Here, we will limit ourselves to some observations on adjustment through storage, and to some remarks on the possible effects of fluctuating intake on long-term requirements.

We begin with a discussion of the experiment performed by Edholm and his colleagues (Edholm et al. 1970). This study has received much attention in the debate on regulation.[83] The subjects were 64 British infantry recruits observed at 6 centres for 3 weeks. Energy intake was measured every day for each recruit, and daily energy expenditure was recorded for 35 of these men. The mean daily intake was 3,850 Kcal and the mean daily expenditure was 3,750 Kcal.

While there was a significant relationship between (time) average intake and expenditure for individual subjects, there was no relationship between food intake and energy expenditure on the same day (nor with one-day lags).[84] Moreover, the variability of daily expenditures was considerably smaller than that of intake in all the six centres. Daily weight and daily calorie balance were positively and significantly related, and the correlation was enhanced when these variables were averaged over five to seven days.

These observations suggest some degree of adjustment on a day-to-day

---

[83] See above, s. 7.2.

[84] However, Edholm et al. report a 'slight tendency' for a day of high intake to be followed by a day or two of low intake, and the same was true of expenditure, though to a lesser extent.

basis, with a significant part of the adjustment being effected by body weight changes. Sukhatme's assertion (see Sukhatme 1978) that there exists a physiological regulatory mechanism 'maintaining body weight' is therefore not unambiguously borne out by the Edholm *et al.* (1970) data, even though Sukhatme leans heavily on this data for his arguments. Moreover, we have earlier discussed the study of Rand, Scrimshaw, and Young (1985) which suggests strongly that there is no adjustment mechanism over and above the storage mechanism, and this necessitates changes in body weight.

A related experiment by Sukhatme and Margen (1978) deals with protein intakes and outputs. This may appear anomalous at first blush; for there is no apparent connection between energy regulation and 'regulation' in the case of protein use. Nevertheless, this study has been used as a basis by Sukhatme for his postulate of energy regulation, and so merits attention.

Nitrogen inputs and outputs are a proxy for protein use, and the term *nitrogen balance* is employed to describe the underlying 'protein balance'.[85] Sukhatme and Margen report nitrogen-balance time-series for six subjects.[86] Nitrogen intake was controlled by the experimenters, and was held fixed for various periods. It was observed that nitrogen output fluctuated from day to day, with no apparent trend. The authors argue against the possibility that these fluctuations are simply the result of measurement error, or represent uncorrelated noise. In particular, nitrogen balances on adjacent days were found to be correlated, with the extent of serial correlation diminishing as pairs of values further separated in time were examined. This intraindividual variation persisted even when output was averaged over two weeks. The authors concluded that the protein requirements of an individual maintaining his body weight[87] will vary 'from week to week' with 'stationary variance'. The resulting chain of statistical implications that is drawn from this and the Edholm *et al.* experiment has already been examined in section 7.2.

Let us suppose, for the sake of argument, that experiments dealing with protein use can be extrapolated to energy balances, although there are problems with such a drastic supposition.[88] Here, then, is indirect evidence

---

[85] See e.g. Sukhatme and Margen (1978), Rand, Scrimshaw, and Young (1979, 1985), and many other protein-use experiments. Protein use in the body is signalled by nitrogen excretion in the urine and faeces; the former is quantitatively dominant and it is this that is usually employed as a measure of total nitrogen output. See Torun (1985) for an illuminating introduction to the chemistry and metabolism of proteins. See also WHO (1985).

[86] For subjects 1 and 2, the series was 84 days long, and for the remainder they were between 30 and 40 days.

[87] The subjects were given a calorie diet that was chosen to maintain body weight.

[88] Rand and Scrimshaw (1984), among others, express strong reservations about such an analogy. One reason for its inappropriateness is the fact that there is a tremendous recycling of old proteins occurring continuously in the body. The fresh dietary intake accounts for only a small fraction of the aminoacids that are being synthesized at any one point of time. There is therefore more scope here for variation in the balance, a scope not shared by energy balances (see e.g. Torun 1985).

supporting short-term adjustments without the need for body weight changes. It is necessary, though, to look at the phenomenon of autocorrelation once again. Recall from section 7.2 the use of autocorrelation as an identifying device for regulation, and our criticism of it in the context of the Edholm *et al.* (1970) experiment. That criticism no longer applies here, for intakes in the Sukhatme–Margen experiment were controlled by the experimenters.

· However, suppose that there are long-term trends in body requirements of energy and protein that are not being corrected for. These trends may arise, for instance, from a change in body composition over time (Rand, Scrimshaw, and Young 1979). Energy or nitrogen outputs would then mirror this trend and induce autocorrelation in the balance. But such serial correlation is clearly not symptomatic of any form of regulation.

Rand, Scrimshaw, and Young (1979, 1985) examine this line of reasoning. Their (1979) experiment used 21 subjects, who were given controlled diet with fixed nitrogen intake.[89] The daily urinary nitrogen excretion was measured and corrected for a linear trend, to minimize possible effects of alteration in body composition. After this was done, only two out of 21 subjects showed significant serial correlation in daily nitrogen balance. Therefore the residual variation (after the trend is removed) has no direct implications.

Rand, Scrimshaw, and Young (1985) redo these calculations for five sets of long-term metabolic studies (see details above) with 42 subjects in all. The subjects were supplied with unchanged amounts of protein in each study, and their daily (urinary) nitrogen excretion was measured. Uncorrected nitrogen excretion data exhibited autocorrelation in 19 out of 42 individuals. The data was then 'corrected'. The major correction was for trend, which was done by fitting various polynomials to the data. The resulting data displayed daily variation, but no autocorrelation except in only four subjects. The authors concluded that for most individuals daily variations in nitrogen excretion are random and not indicative of any form of adjustment.

While no definite conclusions are possible, the available evidence appears to indicate that Rand, Scrimshaw, and Young are correct. That adjustment possibilities exist cannot be doubted; the human body can smooth out short-term fluctuations. But it can do so largely through changes in body weight, that is, by using up stores of fat or other sources of energy. And it is plain that an adjustment mechanism cannot go on working permanently 'on the down side'. For that, one has to invoke adaptation.

(h) The energy costs of fluctuating intakes

We conclude with some remarks on the possible impact of a fluctuating calorie intake on long-term average requirements. We will assume here that fluctu-

---

[89] The subjects were divided into two groups. Group 1 (resp. 2) consisted of 16 (resp. 5) subjects and was examined for 8 (resp. 11) weeks. See Rand, Scrimshaw, and Young (1979) for more details.

ations are mediated by changes in the body stores of energy (since this is the tentative conclusion from the available data).

Storage mechanisms add to the energy content of the body when there is surplus intake, and draw on the body stores when there is a deficit. The major energy store is in the form of fat, followed by energy stored in the form of protein.[90] The proportion stored in each form appears to be a genotypic characteristic of the individual, with the fat stores accounting for perhaps 85 per cent of the total, on average.[91]

Now, storage is not free, though the cost of running the stores down is low. Data on the cost of building up stores is hard to come by; nevertheless one can get some information from studies of children and adolescents recovering from malnutrition.[92] Heim (1985) states that to deposit a gram of protein requires 8.7 Kcal of energy, while a gram of fat costs 12 Kcal. Drawing down a gram of protein releases 4 Kcal, while a gram of fat releases 9 Kcal. These differences have an obvious implication: a person with a fluctuating energy intake will need, on average, more than a person with a fixed intake. But this qualitative statement needs to be buttressed by some notion of its quantitative significance. To provide some idea of the magnitudes involved, we use our algebraic framework, together with the knowledge gleaned from the available evidence. Assume, for simplicity, that the resting metabolic rate is a fixed number (r) and that the energy required for physical activity is fixed at q. We may then write the following special case of equations (7.4) and (7.13):

$$x_t = r + q + A(w_{t+1} - w_t), \qquad \text{if } w_{t+1} < w_t \qquad (7.15)$$
$$= r + q + B(w_{t+1} - w_t), \qquad \text{if } w_{t+1} \geq w_t$$

with $B > A > 0$. These inequalities reflect the storage cost.

If intakes are fixed for all time, requirement is simply $r + q$. Now consider a fluctuating intake; specifically, one that fluctuates between a low value (x^1) and a high value (x^2), with $x^1 < r + q < x^2$. The long-term average intake is $x^* = (x^1 + x^2)/2$. A little algebra shows that for body weight on average to remain constant

$$x^* = (r + q) + [(B - A)(x^2 - x^1)]/2(A + B) \qquad (7.16)$$

so that x^* is clearly greater than $r + q$. Now we take an example from Sukhatme and Margen (1982). Using an average requirement of 2,550 Kcal—$(r + q)$

---

[90] See e.g. Young and Scrimshaw (1971). There is also a very small supply of energy (a few hundred calories) in the form of glycogen in the liver and muscle. The store of glycogen in the liver is in fact the first source of energy release when there is a drop in food intake, or a large gap between meals.

[91] See e.g. Dugdale and Payne (1977), who place the modal value of the protein store (as a fraction of the total) at 0.05–0.10, but admit that the distribution has a 'long tail'. Their definitions of metabolically fat and lean people are based on this ratio. Young and Scrimshaw's data puts the average at 0.15.

[92] See the references in Heim (1985).

—for the reference Indian male, Sukhatme and Margen calculate the lower 'threshold' to be 1,900 Kcal per day (x^1). What does this imply for the value of the larger intake and for the average? The numbers above for storage yield values of 8.25 for A and 11.5 for B.[93] Using these values in (7.16), x^2 and x^* turn out to be 3,456 Kcal and 2,678 Kcal respectively, implying an average intake 130 Kcal per day higher than that resulting from a fixed intake. This is no small number. It is about a third of the amount that the FAO (1973) prescribed for moderate activity (see section 7.2(a)).[94]

(i) Summary of the clinical evidence

We summarize these findings in the context of our original question: what are the implications for the measurement of undernourishment and poverty?

Take the phenomenon of adjustment first. We have argued in section 7.2 that even if adjustment is shown to exist, its impact on the statistical cut-off line for determining poverty is ambiguous. But does adjustment which can proceed by 'maintaining body weight' exist at all? It appears that the answer is 'no'. Granted, there is a mechanism which is capable of adjustment by regulating the energy stores of the body. But such a mechanism cannot justify a downward revision of human requirements. In fact, it can quite conclusively be established that long-term requirements will *increase* as a result of fluctuating intake (section 7.3(h)).

We are then left with adaptation. In summary, the clinical literature indicates the following observations. First, undernourishment, especially among rural populations in tropical countries, is likely to lower the digestibility of food. Conversion coefficients such as the Atwater factors are not terribly relevant in these contexts. The effect of lowered digestibility is an increase in the energy needs of individuals, as measured by the energy content of food that they consume. The quantitative magnitude of the revision may be quite large (section 7.3(c)).

Second, there is almost certainly a reduction in the basal metabolic rate under conditions of sustained low intake. The magnitude of this reduction is uncertain, and so is the extent to which the reduction is achieved by better oxygen utilization of tissue (rather than loss of tissue). It is also unclear whether and to what extent this reduction interferes with physical activity. It may be tentatively concluded that while there is some adaptation here, it is achieved at the cost of some compromise, involving a greater stress on the body. Other related forms of adaptation include diet-induced thermogenesis and changes in the efficiency of energy metabolism. The former is not too well-understood,

---

[93] These numbers are Kcal per gram. We have assumed that energy is released from protein and fat in the same ratio as it is deposited.

[94] There is another possible effect of fluctuating intake on long-term requirements. Fabry (1969) argues that intermittent feeding has very different effects from those of a sustained low intake. His experiments with rats suggest that the basal metabolic rate increases in situations of fluctuating intake (see esp. pp. 84–9).

while the latter does not appear to be particularly significant (sections 7.3(*d*) and (*e*)).

Finally, low intakes may lead to reduced body weight and body size. The impact of this on work *efficiency* is ambiguous, with the results appearing to depend on the type of activity. However, the impact on work *capacity* is fairly unambiguous. This is lowered in situations of undernutrition (section 7.3(*g*)).

What implications do these findings have for the measurement of poverty? The existence of adaptation is far from clear. Indeed, where some form of adaptation can be shown to be present (such as in the BMR), it finds a countervailing form of 'negative' adaptation, such as reduced work capacity. But the point we wish to make here is different. Let us grant that the foregoing evidence can be construed to weigh in favour of adaptation. Does this imply that we should reduce the figures for nutritional requirements?

This problem brings us back to the centrepiece of section 7.2, the logic of statistical inference. It is necessary to describe explicitly the risks that we are willing to turn a blind eye to when measuring undernourishment. It is evident even from our cursory examination of the evidence that adaptation is not purchased free of charge. Besides, we have not even considered the vast literature on the well-established links between low intake and illness. There is not only no question that the 'malnutrition–infection complex' exists (Keusch 1980), but every indication points to the fact that the relationship is a synergistic one.[95] Undernourishment increases susceptibility to infection, just as surely as a history of illness aggravates the symptoms of undernourishment.

Undernourishment precipitates infection. The most common mechanism is the impairing of defence systems. Such impairment may well be a price that has to be paid for adaptation to a reduced intake. The body is weakened in its capacity to form antibodies against an infection. The result is a fatality rate for common diseases and respiratory infections that is unbelievably high.[96] The incidence and severity of illnesses such as diarrhoea also increase with malnutrition.

These connections are reinforced by observed statistical correlations between morbidity and calorie intake. For the case of India, Kumar's careful study of the village of Vembayan in the Trivandrum District of Kerala reveals 'that the frequency of illness lessens as incomes pick up' (Kumar 1986). Noting, too, the predominance of respiratory and gastric ailments, he concludes that there is 'evidence of stress on the system—and amongst those engaged in heavy manual work—an indication that a combination of physical exertion and inadequate nutrition are taking their toll'. The pattern is similar

[95] See Latham (1975) for an introduction to the issues involved. There is also the important connection between malnutrition (especially in children) and subsequent risk of mortality. See e.g. Chen *et al.* (1980).

[96] Latham (1975) reports that the fatality rate from measles in many poor countries is over 15%. In Mexico, the fatality rate is 180 times the US rate. The corresponding ratios for Guatemala and Ecuador are even higher—268 and 480 respectively.

even if one considers very general interstate figures on per capita intake and morbidity in India. Vaidyanathan (1985) does precisely this and obtains an inverse relationship between the two variables.

Illness aggravates undernourishment. Apart from the obvious costs in terms of inability to work during periods of illness, there are serious metabolic costs associated with fever that do not disappear overnight.[97] Bacterial infections are known to lead to an increased loss of nitrogen from the body, and there is a general depletion of body protein, especially from muscles. This leads to a marked reduction in the ability to work. Infections with fever are known to lead to anorexia, characterized by a loss in appetite which leads to a reduced food intake. Intestinal parasites play a central role in the feedback from infection to malnourishment. For example, hookworms cause intestinal blood loss, leading to a considerable loss of iron and thus to iron-deficiency anaemia. And that most common of all parasites, the roundworm, has huge metabolic needs of its own and takes them from the host. Gastrointestinal diseases, especially diarrhoea, are important in precipitating both kwashiorkor and marasmus in children.

The evidence that we have taken some pains to describe is there for all to see. The issue is this: is it justifiable to undertake a reduction in the calorie-based poverty line, Sukhatme-style, on the basis of the available literature? For us, the answer is 'no'. Nevertheless, one might decide that Sukhatme was 'correct', after all, and might thus proceed to revise requirements downwards. In doing so, he must not run away from the implicit value judgements that are involved, in the manner described in this and the preceding section. These judgements are bound up in turn with the risks that the observer deems tolerable for millions of people living and working from day to day on a low intake of food. In particular, the larger the downward revision, the greater is the implied tolerance for these risks.

In terms of the value judgements that we are making, we find these risks unacceptable. The statistical logic that is involved in Sukhatme's measurement rule is now clear and certainly lowers the line for measuring undernourishment. But, in the words of Gopalan (1983b), 'Those interested in building a strong vigorous nation, of healthy productive adults, and of active children who can run, play and bounce about, grow and develop into healthy adults, may however *not* be prepared to buy such a prescription.'

7.4. *Implications for the theory of labour markets*

(a) *Malnutrition, unemployment, and the distribution of assets*

The connection between nutrition and work productivity (as in Fig. 7.1 above)

---

[97] Each degree centigrade rise in temperature is associated with a 13% increase in BMR, and the figure is probably higher for children (Heim 1985).

leads to a very different economic theory of labour markets.[98] Leibenstein (1957) was probably the first economist to explore this connection in a formal way, and subsequent contributions were made, largely in a partial equilibrium setting, by Mirrlees (1976), Stiglitz (1976), Bliss and Stern (1978a), and others. The studies here have mainly been of two types. There is the question of allocation of food among members of a poor utilitarian family farm when nutrition affects productivity (Mirrlees 1976; Stiglitz 1976), and the problem of labour employment by a monopsonistic firm (Leibenstein 1957; Stiglitz 1976; Bliss and Stern 1978a). In both these problems the nutrition–productivity relation has a fundamental effect. In the former, the allocation problem under the utilitarian criterion necessitates unequal division amongst *ex ante* identical people. In the latter situation, the result is involuntary unemployment, with employed workers receiving a higher wage than their reservation wage.

In our earlier work (Dasgupta and Ray 1986, 1987), we developed the implications of the nutrition–productivity relation in a competitive general equilibrium setting. Involuntary unemployment was shown to be linked to the incidence of malnutrition, and these to be related in turn to the production and distribution of income and thus ultimately to the distribution of assets.[99] It was established there that despite the presence of involuntary unemployment, market equilibrium in the theoretical economy is Pareto efficient. It follows that short-run programmes of employment generation must necessarily involve the redistribution of assets, or food transfers.

These are strong results. But they are based on the assumption that there is a link between current nutrition and current productivity. As we have seen from our survey, this assumption is not correct, unless a person is already weakened from inadequate intakes in the past. Adjustment and adaptation may act to mediate a fluctuating or low intake. It is therefore important to examine how these results are affected when the nutrition–productivity relationship is modified to incorporate regulation.

This is not the place to rework the general equilibrium theory that we have described above, although this can be done. We will instead concentrate on the central feature that is common to all these models—the labour market and involuntary unemployment. Readers familiar with the literature mentioned here will be able to extend the modifications implied for labour market models to the more general theories.

Notice first that our attitude is seemingly contradictory. In sections 7.2 and 7.3 we have been wary of drawing the conclusion that *acceptable* adjustment or adaptation exists. And now we are proposing to conduct an exercise on the

---

[98] It is not our purpose to survey the literature here, so we shall only indicate the main references.

[99] It may be worth noting that there is a strong empirical relationship between the extent of malnutrition and the ownership of land assets. See e.g. Valverde *et al.* (1977), or Bairagi (1983).

modifications necessary for an understanding of decentralized resource allocation mechanisms occasioned by the phenomenon of regulation. In fact there is
no contradiction. In a market with profit-maximizing firms, an employer could
not care less whether the adjustment or adaptation that he is exploiting is
socially acceptable. Consequently, while regulation of the sort examined here
might not affect our theory of poverty measurement, it may well cause us to
rethink the positive economic theory of labour markets.

Note next that many of the models mentioned above employ two sets of
assumptions to put the theory to work. The first, as we have already observed,
postulates a relationship between current intake and productivity. The second
postulates that employers are actually aware of and exploit this relationship.
There is an empirical literature exploring the validity of the second assumption, but the evidence is mixed.[100] However, in a competitive environment this
second assumption is unnecessary as long as piece-rates are paid for tasks and
as long as the employer can observe, or monitor, the number of tasks
performed. Our work uses this alternative construction. (See Dasgupta and
Ray 1986 for a more detailed discussion.) To simplify our analysis, we will
consider separately the phenomena of adjustment and adaptation. Our arguments will be expository and heuristic in parts; a formal model can easily be
constructed along the lines that we suggest.

(b) Adjustment and the labour market

First consider adjustment. We restrict ourselves to short-term labour contracts
here. It is clear that in the case of long-term contracts (say those lasting for a
period of months), adjustment makes little or no difference to the theory
developed in Dasgupta and Ray (1986).

We suppose that the resting metabolic rate of the individual is fixed at the
level r, and the energy required for a given activity level is history-independent
(no adaptation). Assuming a single activity and combining equations (7.4),
(7.11), and (7.13) we have:

$$x = r + e(\lambda) + s(w', w), \qquad (7.17)$$

where w is the initial weight of the individual, w' the weight at the end of the
period, and $e(\lambda)$ the energy expenditure associated with the activity level λ.
Here, weight is to be viewed as a store of energy for the individual, and as an
index of general well-being. Remember that we are concerned with situations
where obesity is not at all relevant.[101]

---

[100] See e.g. Rodgers (1975), Bliss and Stern (1978b), and Bliss and Stern (1982). For short-term
contracts, the situation is unclear, though the predominance of partial payments in terms of meals
at work may be taken as indirect evidence that the employer attempts to shift the intrafamily
distribution of food in favour of the worker. For long-term contracts (slavery being the best
example) the evidence is stronger and favours the postulate.

[101] It is, of course, not being suggested that a small body weight is an unambiguous sign of ill
health. People may be genetically small and healthy. We are saying that, given the genotype of the
individual, a smaller weight is indicative of greater debility. It goes without saying that these
remarks are not valid in the range of obesity.

Consider first the situation where there is no work requirement and no food intake for the entire period under consideration. In this case, next period's weight w' is given as a function of initial weight w—call this $f(w)$—where $f(w)$ solves[102]

$$s(f(w), w) + r = 0 \tag{7.18}$$

Presumably, if the individual fails to find a job that earns him income and demands physical activity from him, he will have some source of energy intake (denoted by x^0) to fall back upon. We assume that to obtain this intake, the individual does not require to supply any significant amount of physical work.[103] If unemployed his end-of-period weight is given by a function $k(w)$ which is the solution to

$$x^0 - s(k(w), w) = r \tag{7.19}$$

Clearly, as long as $x^0 > 0$, $k(w) > f(w)$.

Given the ranges of weight, the activity, and the economic group we are studying, the continued well-being of the individual (at whatever level) is of primary importance to him.[104] So it is reasonable to postulate that the individual will not accept a job which drags his end-of-period weight w' *below* the level $k(w)$, which is what he can guarantee himself. Once that is guaranteed, he prefers a larger income to a smaller one. So our postulate is that the individual's 'preferences' are lexicographic. He first attempts to guarantee a certain level of well-being ($k(w)$). Once that is done, he tries to maximize income.[105]

The level of activity λ in employment determines the total income of the individual (which is assumed to be equal to his food intake).[106] In other words, we are supposing that there is a *piece wage rate* μ which is paid for each unit of the activity (often called an efficiency unit) that is supplied. Assume that firms (or employers) are perfectly competitive. Then standard methods yield the existence of a downward sloping derived demand curve for 'efficiency units of labour', E, as a function of the piece-rate. Call this $D(\mu)$.

Return to the individual labourer. We impose some structure on the energy function for physical activity in equation (7.17) by describing its inverse

---

[102] We are assuming for simplicity that such a weight can be defined; i.e. that the worker is not already on the borderline of starvation.

[103] Strictly speaking, this assumption is unnecessary. All that is required is that the individual earns this 'reservation intake' from an activity which has relatively low energy demands (begging, odd jobs, living off friends and relatives).

[104] We are abstracting here from questions of family size and food distribution within the family. These add very little to the analysis (see Dasgupta and Ray 1986).

[105] Given our definition of well-being (not to be confused with the individual's 'utility'), increasing well-being and increasing income are not the same thing.

[106] These assumptions can be relaxed with no difficulty (see Dasgupta and Ray, 1986).

function (call it $\lambda(e)$).[107] Specifically, we assume that $\lambda(e) = 0$ for $0 \leqslant e \leqslant e^0$,[108] and it is increasing, continuous, and bounded for $e > e^0$.[109]

Now suppose that the individual faces a piece rate of μ. He checks first whether he is able to supply a positive amount of work λ *and* attain an end-of-period weight of at least $k(w)$. This is equivalent to checking that the equation

$$\mu\lambda = r + e(\lambda) + s(k(w), w) \qquad (7.20)$$

has a solution with $\lambda > 0$. If it does not, then his labour supply at that wage rate is zero. If it does, then the individual chooses the maximum λ consistent with the satisfaction of (7.20). This yields the 'supply curve' of efficiency units at the individual level. Call it $S(\mu)$.

For simplicity, consider a continuum of identical individuals, each indexed by a point on the interval $[0, m]$. The aggregate supply curve is then given by $mS(\mu)$. We will now establish the following result:

If m is large enough, there will be a subset of individuals denied access to the labour market, though they are able and willing to work at the going piece-rate. There is involuntary unemployment in the sense that those who find jobs are better off than those who do not. Despite this, the piece-rate does not fall.

The argument that drives this result is easy to describe verbally. Consider the individual's decision at each piece-rate μ. Suppose that (7.20) has a solution with positive λ. Then $S(\mu)$ is positive. Now lower μ. There will come a point—call it μ^*—when $S(\mu^*)$ is positive, but for any μ less than μ^* (7.20) does not have a solution with positive λ; and so $S(\mu) = 0$ (see Fig. 7.2). *At this threshold $S(\mu^*)$ is positive.* This follows from the postulate that either $k(w) > f(w)$ or $e^0 > 0$ (any one of these conditions will do). Denote $S(\mu^*)$ by S^* (Fig. 7.2). We may conclude that the aggregate supply curve has the property that $mS(\mu) \geqslant mS^*$ if $\mu \geqslant \mu^*$, and $mS(\mu) = 0$ if $\mu < \mu^*$. Thus the aggregate supply curve of 'efficiency units'—that is, the supply of aggregate activity level—is discontinuous at μ^* (see Fig. 7.3).

It is now easy to see that if m is large enough—so that mS^* is large enough—the equilibrium piece rate will be μ^*, since the market demand curve, $D(\mu)$, for labour activity will pass through the gap in the supply function at μ^*. At this piece-rate everyone is capable of working, but not everyone will get a job. The fraction of employed people will be $D(\mu^*)/mS^*$.[110] The

---

[107] This (together with a translation to include r) is precisely the function used in the models we have described, and in Fig. 7.1.

[108] The number e^0 may be equal to zero. All we require for our analysis is *either* $k(w) > f(w)$ or $e^0 > 0$. (See Fig. 7.1 above.)

[109] These correspond to the assumptions made in Bliss and Stern (1978a) and Dasgupta and Ray (1986, 1987).

[110] The critical size of the labour force is $D(\mu^*)/S^*$. If m exceeds this there is involuntary unemployment.

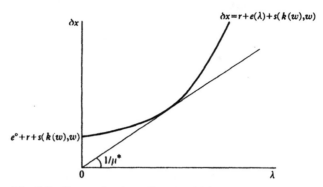

Fig. 7.2. Determination of lowest viable piece-rate, μ^*

piece-rate cannot fall because at a rate lower than μ^* workers cannot supply any effort. The unemployment is involuntary. People who find employment consume more than people who are unemployed and are therefore distinctly better off.

The reader can easily extend this analysis to the case where there is a heterogeneous labour group, or to the case of a monopsonistic employer. But what is clear from all this is that the standard analysis (as in Dasgupta and Ray 1986) is robust against the phenomenon of adjustment. There are, of course, new issues arising from the explicit inclusion of adjustment. For instance, the lower is the 'reservation weight', $k(w)$, the quicker will be the deterioration of people who are subject to the whims of a casual labour market. Adjustment is a curse in disguise if the labour market is short term and its workings are influenced by adjustment in the way we have just described. To the extent that people are driven to lower and lower values of $k(w)$ by the lack of alternative opportunities, their ability to adjust in the short term drives them to work for a reduced piece-rate. The combination of adjustment, high labour supply, and a casual labour market can be disastrous in the long run.

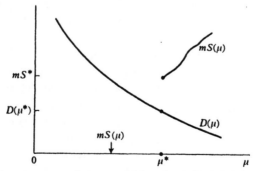

Fig. 7.3. Involuntary unemployment arising from food–productivity link: $[mS^* - D(\mu^*)]/mS'$ is % of workforce unemployed

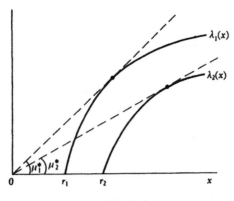

Fig. 7.4.

(c)   Adaptation and the labour market

We turn to the implications of adaptation. We analyse this by neglecting adjustment. However, r will now be explicitly a function of history.

Consider an individual at period t. Let $A_t = (x_0 + x_1 + \ldots + x_{t-1})/t$ denote the average intake of the individual. We will write r as an increasing function $r_t(A_t)$ of the history of intakes. This corresponds to positive adaptation. Moreover, we allow for the possibility that the current energy-requirement function for physical activity also depends on average intake, though we do not specify its direction yet. For an individual at time t, we write

$$x_t = r_t(A_t) + e(\lambda, A_t) \tag{7.21}$$

Now consider two types of individuals, 1 and 2, with 1 having a *history* of lower intakes than 2. Suppose that there is a large number in each group. At time t, suppose that both these groups are trying to sell their services on the *casual* labour market, where a going piece-rate has been announced. What will be the nature of the market equilibrium?

First suppose that history does not affect the energy requirements for physical activity: i.e., that A_t does not affect $e(.\,,\,.)$.[111] Then it is easy to establish the following result:

If the number of people in each group is large, equilibrium in the casual labour market involves the complete absence of group 2 workers. A fraction of group 1 finds employment and the remaining fraction is involuntarily unemployed.

The reasoning behind this claim is simple. Persons in group 1—those with a history of low intakes—have a lower resting metabolic rate. But we have assumed that a person's nutrition history does not affect the energy expended at any given level of activity; that is, e_t is independent of A_t. Fig. 7.4 presents

---

[111] Recall that in Fig. 7.1 we assumed that A_t *does* affect $e(.\,,\,.)$.

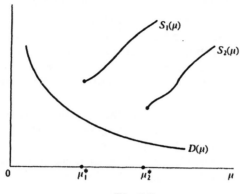

Fig. 7.5.

for a person in each of the two groups the maximum level of activity he is capable of achieving as a function of his calorie intake. It is immediate from the figure that every piece-rate which permits a person in group 2 to provide a positive level of activity is also a viable piece-rate for a person in group 1. It is also immediate that there exist viable piece-rates for persons in group 1 that are not viable for the others. These features are translated to Fig. 7.5, which presents the supply functions of the two groups. As in Fig. 7.3, each supply function has a discontinuity, at μ_1^* and μ_2^* respectively, but the discontinuity for group 2 occurs at the larger piece rate, μ_2^*. If the number of persons in each group is large the market demand curve for labour activity will pass through both the discontinuities, and no group 2 person will find employment in this labour market. A fraction of group 1 will.

Now this is seemingly paradoxical, the conclusion being that it is those with a better nutrition history who are entirely excluded from the labour market in question, while those who have the worse history have at least some chance of being employed.[112] It suggests that there are future advantages to being ill-fed now!

In fact there is no paradox here. What the result indicates is that if there is significant adaptation (never mind its 'social acceptability'), and if there are no changes in the energy function for physical activity, then low-intake people may well find a temporary buffer in the short-term, casual labour market.

Moreover, we cannot conclude from this that the casual labour wage rate will settle at a level that permits continued well-being. At the lowered rate of metabolism these labourers may have drastically increased susceptibility to infection and disease. But the casual labour market is insensitive to all this. By its very nature, it is a myopic market.

These statements must be qualified by the possibility that the energy

[112] For vividness one might imagine that a lottery is used to determine which people in group 1 are employed.

requirements for physical activity may be affected by history (as in Fig. 7.1). If the activity is such that a history of low intakes reduces efficiency, then there is a trade-off involved and the end result is ambiguous. In addition, if work capacity is considered, the results described here might be reversed as would be the case if the curves are as in Fig. 7.1. One might tentatively conclude that the results of our example here will apply to activities where a reduced weight is not a huge disadvantage.

What of longer-term contracts? Here, the considerations are very different and are similar to the ones offered in Dasgupta and Ray (1986). Any such model must include the possibility that a person with a history of low intakes is more easily prey to illness. One such bout of illness imposes a cost on the long-term employer, which he cannot afford to ignore. It seems very likely such considerations will dominate. We conjecture that the relative desirability of the two groups from the point of view of employers is likely to be the complete reverse when we consider long-term contracts. Here, the well-nourished person is at a premium. Moreover, the wage rates in the two markets will reflect this premium. Casual labour wage rates will be lower on two counts. First, due to the adaptation that results in a lowering of the piece-rate, and second, due to the intrinsic myopia of short-term contracts, created by the fact that an illness of the worker imposes no cost on the employer. (See the remarks in Dasgupta and Ray (1986: section V).)

The theory modified to include adaptation is richer, although more complicated. A full account of this theory is not available. But the considerations that we have mentioned permit us to draw a few broad conclusions, with which we end.

People with a history of low intake are progressively excluded from the more lucrative long-term labour contracts in the economy. The exclusion is progressive because of the wage gap that is likely to persist between casual and long-term markets, resulting in greater disparities over time. However, these excluded people will not lower the poverty rates in the economy by simply dying off. There are markets to absorb such people. These are the casual labour markets, offering a precarious source of living, where underfed, undernourished people by virtue of their 'adaptation' actually find a place. But there are no inbuilt mechanisms in these markets that will reduce their undernourishment. Short-term contracts simply do not look ahead.

References

ARESKOG, N., *et al.* (1969), 'Physical Work Capacity and Nutritional Status in Ethiopian Male Children and Young Adults', *American Journal of Clinical Nutrition*, 22.

ATWATER, W., and BENEDICT, F. (1903), 'Experiments on the Metabolism of Energy and Matter in the Human Body', *Bulletin of the Office of Experimental Stations*, 136 (Washington, DC).

BAIRAGI, R. (1983), 'Dynamics of Child Nutrition in Rural Bangladesh', *Ecology of Food and Nutrition*, 13.

BANERJEE, B., and SAHA, N. (1970), 'Energy Cost of Some Common Daily Activities of Active Tropical Male and Female Subjects', *Journal of Applied Physiology*, 29.

BANERJI, D. (1981), 'Measurement of Poverty and Undernourishment', *Economic and Political Weekly*, 16, 26 Sept.

BARDHAN, P. (1973), 'On the Incidence of Poverty in Rural India of the Sixties', *Economic and Political Weekly*, 8, Feb.

BEATON, G. H. (1981), 'Numerical Descriptors of the Nutrition Problem: An Analytical Comparison of FAO and World Bank Approaches', mimeo (Faculty of Medicine, University of Toronto).

——(1983), 'Energy in Human Nutrition: Perspectives and Problems' (W. O. Atwater Memorial Lecture), mimeo (Faculty of Medicine, University of Toronto).

BENEDICT, F., MILES, W., ROTH, P., and SMITH, H. (1919), 'Human Vitality and Efficiency under Prolonged Restricted Diet', Carnegie Institute Publication No. 280 (Washington, DC).

BLISS, C., and STERN, N. (1978a), 'Productivity, Wages and Nutrition, Part I: The Theory', *Journal of Development Economics*, 5.

————(1978b), 'Productivity, Wages and Nutrition, Part II: Some Observations', *Journal of Development Economics*, 5.

————(1978c), *Palanpur: Studies in the Economy of a North Indian Village* (Oxford: Oxford University Press).

CHAFKIN, B. (1985), 'Bashing Nutritionists: The "Small but Healthy?" Hypothesis', *Economic and Political Weekly*, 20, 18 May.

CHAKRAVORTI, S., and PANDA, M. (1981), 'Measurement of Incidence of Undernourishment', *Economic and Political Weekly*, 16, 1 Aug.

CHEN, L., CHOWDHURY, A., and HUFFMAN, S. (1980), 'Anthropometric Assessment of Energy-Protein Malnutrition and Subsequent Risk of Mortality among Preschool Aged Children', *American Journal of Clinical Nutrition*, 33.

DANDEKAR, V. (1981), 'On Measurement of Poverty', *Economic and Political Weekly*, 16, 25 July.

——(1982), 'On Measurement of Undernourishment', *Economic and Political Weekly*, 17, 6 Feb.

——and RATH, N. (1971), 'Poverty in India', *Economic and Political Weekly*, 15.

DANFORTH, E. (1981), 'Diet-Induced Thermogenesis: Control of Energy Expenditure', *Life Science*, 28.

DASGUPTA, P., and RAY, D. (1986), 'Inequality as a Determinant of Malnutrition and Unemployment: Theory', *Economic Journal*, 96.

———— (1987), 'Inequality as a Determinant of Malnutrition and Unemployment: Policy', *Economic Journal*, 97.

DASGUPTA, R. (1985), 'Nutrition Situation in India: A Statistical Analysis', *Economic and Political Weekly*, 19, 7 Sept.

DESAI, I. D., WADDELL, C., DUTRA, S., DUTRA DE OLIVEIRA, S., DUARTE, E., ROBAZZI, M. L., CEVALLOS ROMERO, L. S., DESAI, M. J., VICHI, F. L., BRADFIELD, R. S., and DUTRA DE OLIVEIRA, J. E. (1984), 'Marginal Malnutrition and Reduced Physical Work Capacity of Migrant Adolescent Boys in Southern Brazil', *American Journal of Clinical Nutrition*, 40.

DOWNS, J. (1964), 'A Study in Nutritional Dwarfing', *American Journal of Clinical Nutrition*, 15.

DUGDALE, A., and PAYNE, P. (1977), 'Patterns of Lean and Fat Deposition in Adults', *Nature*, 266, Mar.

DURNIN, J., and PASSMORE, R. (1967), *Energy, Work and Leisure* (London: Heinemann).

DUTRA DE OLIVEIRA, J., DOS SANTOS, J., and DESAI, I. (Commentary) (1985), in O. Brunser *et al.* (eds.), *Clinical Nutrition of the Young Child* (New York: Raven Press).

EDHOLM, O. G., ADAM, J. M., HEALY, M. J. R., WOLFF, H. S., GOLDSMITH, R., and BEST, T. W. (1970), 'Food Intake and Energy Expenditure of Army Recruits', *British Journal of Nutrition*, 24.

EDMUNDSON, W. (1977), 'Individual Variations in Work Output per Unit Energy Intake in East Java', *Ecology of Food and Nutrition*, 6.

———— (1979), 'Individual Variations in Basal Metabolic Rate and Mechanical Work Efficiency in East Java', *Ecology of Food and Nutrition*, 8.

———— (1980), 'Adaptation to Undernutrition: How Much Food does Man Need?', *Social Science and Medicine*, 14D.

FABRY, P. (1969), *Feeding Pattern and Nutritional Adaptations* (Butterworths Academia).

FAO (1957), *Calorie Requirements*, Nutritional Studies 15 (Rome: FAO).

———— (1962), *Nutrition and Working Efficiency*, Freedom from Hunger Campaign Basic Study 5 (Rome: FAO).

———— (1963), *Third World Food Survey*, Freedom from Hunger Campaign Basic Study 11 (Rome: FAO).

———— (1973), *Energy and Protein Requirements*, Report of a Joint FAO/WHO *ad hoc* Expert Committee (Rome: FAO).

———— (1977), *Fourth World Food Survey* (Rome: FAO).

FOSTER, J. (1984), 'On Economic Poverty: A Survey of Aggregate Measures', in R. L. Basmann and G. F. Rhodes (eds.), *Advances in Econometrics* (Greenwich: JAI Press).

————GREER, J., and THORBECKE, E. (1984), 'A Class of Decomposable Poverty Measures', *Econometrica*.

GOMEZ, F., GALVAN, R., FRENK, S., CRAVIOTO, J., CHAVEZ, R., and VASQUEZ, J. (1956), 'Mortality in Second and Third Degree Malnutrition', *Journal of Tropical Pediatrics*, 2/77.

GOPALAN, C., (1982). 'The Nutrition Policy of Brinkmanship', *Bulletin of the Nutrition Foundation of India*, Oct.

———— (1983a), 'Small is Healthy: For the Poor not the Rich', *Economic and Political Weekly*, 18/15.

——(1983b), 'Measurement of Undernourishment: Biological Considerations', *Bulletin of the Nutrition Foundation of India*, July.

——(1985), 'The Mother and Child in India', *Economic and Political Weekly*, 20, 26 Jan.

——and NARASINGA RAO, B. (1974), 'Dietary Allowances for Indians', Special Report Series No. 60 (National Institute of Nutrition, ICMR).

GRANDE, F. (1964), 'Man under Caloric Deficiency', in D. Dill *et al.* (eds.), *Handbook of Physiology, Section 4: Adaptation to the Environment* (Washington, DC: American Physiological Society).

——ANDERSON, J., and KEYS, A. (1958), 'Changes in Basal Metabolic Rate in Man in Semi-starvation and Feeding', *Journal of Applied Physiology*, 12.

HEIM, T. (1985), 'Energy Metabolism: Theoretical and Practical Aspects', in O. Brunser *et al.* (eds.), *Clinical Nutrition of the Young Child* (New York: Raven Press).

HIMMS-HAGEN, J. (1984), 'Thermogenesis in Brown Adipose Tissue as an Energy Buffer: Implications for Obesity', *New England Journal of Medicine*, 311.

JEQUIER, E. (1983), 'Does a Thermogenic Defect Play a Role in the Pathogenesis of Human Obesity?', *Clinical Physiology*, 3.

JUNG, R., SHETTY, P., JAMES, W., BARRAND, M., and CALLINGHAM, B. (1979), 'Reduced Thermogenesis in Obesity', *Nature*, 279, May.

KAKWANI, N. (1980), *Income Inequality and Poverty: Methods of Estimation and Policy Applications* (New York: Oxford University Press).

KEUSCH, G. (1980), 'Homing in on Interventions in the Malnutrition–Infection Complex', *American Journal of Clinical Nutrition*, 33.

KEYS, A., BROZEK, J., HENSCHEL, A., MICKELSON, O., TAYLOR, H., *et al.* (1950), *The Biology of Human Starvation*, vols. i and ii (Minneapolis: University of Minnesota Press).

KRISHNAJI, N. (1981), 'On Measuring the Extent of Undernourishment: A Note on Sukhatme's Procedure', *Economic and Political Weekly*, 16, 30 May.

KUMAR, G. (1986), 'Malnutrition and Infection in Economic Development', in P. India', mimeo (University of Oxford).

LATHAM, M. (1975), 'Nutrition and Infection in Economic Development', in P. Abelson (ed.), *Food: Politics, Economics, Nutrition and Research* (Washington, DC: American Association for the Advancement of Science).

LEIBENSTEIN, H. (1957), *Economic Backwardness and Economic Growth* (New York: John Wiley).

LIPTON, M. (1983), 'Poverty, Undernutrition and Hunger', World Bank Staff Working Paper No. 597 (Washington, DC: World Bank).

MEHTA, J. (1982), 'Nutritional Norms and Measurement of Malnourishment and Poverty', *Economic and Political Weekly*, 17, 14 Aug.

MILLER, D. (1979), 'Prevalence of Nutritional Problems in the World', *Proceedings of the Nutrition Society*, 38.

MIRRLEES, J. (1976), 'A Pure Theory of Underdeveloped Economies', in L. Reynolds (ed.), *Agriculture in Development Theory* (New Haven: Yale University Press).

MOLLA, A. (1984), 'Absorption of Macronutrients during the Cause Stage and after Recovery from Diarrhoea of Different Aetiologies', *Food and Nutrition Bulletin*, 10 (Suppl.).

PARANJPE, H. (1981), 'How Poor are we?', *Economic and Political Weekly*, 16.

PAYNE, P., and CUTLER, P. (1984), 'Measuring Malnutrition: Technical Problems and Ideological Perspectives', *Economic and Political Weekly*, 19, 25 Aug.

PRYNNE, C., and SOUTHGATE, D. (1979), 'The Effects of a Supplement of Dietary Fibre on Faecal Excretion by Human Subjects', *British Journal of Nutrition*, 41.

RAND, W. and SCRIMSHAW, N. (1984), 'Protein and Energy Requirements: Insights from Long-Term Studies', *Bulletin of the Nutrition Foundation of India*, Oct.

——and YOUNG, V. (1979), 'An Analysis of Temporal Patterns in Urinary Nitrogen Excretion of Young Adults Receiving Constant Diets at Two Nitrogen Intakes for 8 to 11 Weeks', *American Journal of Clinical Nutrition*, 32.

——(1985), 'Retrospective Analysis of Data from Five Long-Term Metabolic Balance Studies: Implications for Understanding Dietary Nitrogen and Energy Utilization', *American Journal of Clinical Nutrition*, 42.

RAO, V. K. R. V. (1977), 'Nutritional Norms by Calorie Intake and Measurement of Poverty', *Bulletin of the International Statistical Institute*, 47/1, Proceedings of the 41st session invited papers.

——(1981a), 'Some Nutritional Puzzles: A Note', *Economic and Political Weekly*, 16.

——(1981b), 'Reply to Dandekar', *Economic and Political Weekly*, 16.

——and VIVEKANAND, M. (1982), 'Calorie Norm Controversy', *Economic and Political Weekly*, 17.

REUTLINGER, S., and ALDERMAN, H. (1980), 'The Prevalence of Calorie-Deficient Diets in the Developing Countries', *World Development*, 8.

——and SELOWSKY, M. (1976), *Malnutrition and Poverty: Magnitude and Policy Options*, World Bank Staff Occasional Papers, No. 23.

RODGERS, G. (1975), 'Nutritionally Based Wage Determination in the Low-Income Labour Market', *Oxford Economic Papers*, Mar.

ROTHWELL, M., and STOCK, M. (1981), 'Regulation of Energy Balance', *Annual Review of Nutrition*, 1.

SATYANARAYANA, K., NAIDU, A., CHATTERJEE, B., and NARASINGA RAO, B. (1977), 'Body Size and Work Output', *American Journal of Clinical Nutrition*, 30.

——————and NARASINGA RAO, B. (1979), 'Nutritional Deprivation in Childhood and the Body Size, Activity and Physical Capacity of Young Boys', *American Journal of Clinical Nutrition*, 32.

SCHUTZ, Y., BESSARD, J., and JEQUIER, E. (1984), 'Diet-Induced Thermogenesis Measured over a Whole Day in Obese and Non-obese Women', *American Journal of Clinical Nutrition*, 40.

SECKLER, D. (1980), 'Malnutrition: An Intellectual Odyssey', *Western Journal of Agricultural Economics*, 5, Dec.

——(1982), 'Small but Healthy: A Basic Hypothesis in the Theory, Measurement and Policy of Malnutrition', in P. Sukhatme (ed.), *Newer concepts in Nutrition and Their Implications for Policy* (Pune: Maharashtra Association for the Cultivation of Science).

——(1984a), 'The "Small but Healthy?" Hypothesis: A Reply to Critics', *Economic and Political Weekly*, 19, 3 Nov.

——(1984b), 'The "Small but Healthy" Hypothesis: An Invitation to a Refutation', in P. Narain (ed.), *Impact of P. V. Sukhatme on Agricultural Statistics and Nutrition* (New Delhi: Indian Society of Agricultural Statistics).

SEN, A. (1976), 'Poverty: An Ordinal Approach to Measurement', *Econometrica*, 44.

SIMS, E. (1976), 'Experimental Obesity, Dietary-Induced Thermogenesis, and Their Clinical Implications', *Clinics in Endocrinology and Metabolism*, 5/2.

SPURR, G., BARAC-NIETO, M., REINA, J., and RAMIREZ, R. (1984), 'Marginal Malnutrition in School-Aged Colombian Boys: Efficiency of Treadmill Walking in Submaximal Exercise', *American Journal of Clinical Nutrition*, 39.

SRINIVASAN, T. (1981), 'Malnutrition: Some Measurement and Policy Issues', *Journal of Development Economics*, 8.

STIGLITZ, J. (1976), 'The Efficiency Wage Hypothesis, Surplus Labour and the Distribution of Income in L.D.C.'s', *Oxford Economic Papers*, 28.

SUKHATME, P. (1961), 'The World's Hunger and Future Needs in Food Supplies', *Journal of the Royal Statistical Society*, 124.

——(1970), 'Incidence of Protein Deficiency in Relation to Different Diets in India', *British Journal of Nutrition*, 24.

——(1972), 'Protein Strategy and Agricultural Development', presidential address, *Indian Journal of Agricultural Economics*, Jan.–Mar.

——(1974), 'The Protein Problem, its Size and Nature', *Journal of the Royal Statistical Society*, Ser. A (general), 137.

——(1978), 'Assessment of Adequacy of Diets at Different Income Levels', *Economic and Political Weekly*, 13 (Special No.).

——(1981a), 'On Measurement of Poverty', *Economic and Political Weekly*, 16, 8 Aug.

——(1981b), 'On the Measurement of Undernutrition: A Comment', *Economic and Political Weekly*, 16, 6 June.

——(1982a), 'Measurement of Undernutrition', *Economic and Political Weekly*, 17, 11 Dec.

——(1982b), *Newer Concepts in Nutrition and Their Implications for Policy* (Pune: Maharashtra Association for the Cultivation of Science).

——and MARGEN, S. (1978), 'Models of Protein Deficiency', *American Journal of Clinical Nutrition*, 31.

————(1982), 'Autoregulatory Homeostatic Nature of Energy Balance', *American Journal of Clinical Nutrition*, 35.

TAYLOR, H., and KEYS, A. (1950), 'Adaptation to Caloric Restriction', *Science*, 112.

TORUN, B. (1985), 'Proteins: Chemistry, Metabolism and Nutritional Requirements', in O. Brunser *et al.* (eds.), *Clinical Nutrition of the Young Child* (New York: Raven Press).

UAUY, R. (1985), 'Commentary', in O. Brunser *et al.* (eds.), *Clinical Nutrition of the Young Child* (New York: Raven Press).

VAIDYANATHAN, A. (1985), 'Food Consumption and Size of People: Some Indian Evidence', *Economic and Political Weekly*, 20, Review of Political Economy, 27 July.

VALVERDE, V., MARTOREL, R., MEJIA-PIVARAL, V., DELGADO, H., LECHTIG, A., TELLER, C., and KLEIN, R. (1977), 'Relationship between Family Land Availability and Nutritional Status', *Ecology of Food and Nutrition*, 6.

WAHLUND, H. (1948), 'Determination of the Physical Working Capacity', *Acta. Med. Scand.* 215 (Suppl.).

WATERLOW, J. (1976), 'Classification and Definition of Protein-Energy Malnutrition', in G. Beaton and J. Bengoa (eds.), *Nutrition in Preventive Medicine: The Major Deficiency Syndromes* (Geneva: WHO).

WATTS, H. (1968), 'An Economic Definition of Poverty', in D. P. Moynihan (ed.), *On Understanding Poverty* (New York: Basic Books).

WEIR, J. (1949), 'New Methods for Calculating Metabolic Rate with Special Reference to Protein Metabolism', *Journal of Physiology*, 109.

WIDDOWSON, E. (1947), 'A Study of Individual Children's Diet', Special Report Series No. 257 (London: Medical Research Council).

WHO (1985), *Energy and Protein Requirements*: Report of a joint FAO/WHO/UNU Expert Consultation, Technical Report No. 724 (Geneva).

YOUNG, V., and SCRIMSHAW, N. (1971), 'The Physiology of Starvation', *Scientific American*, 225.

ZURBRIGG, S. (1983), 'Ideology and the Poverty Line Debate', *Economic and Political Weekly*, 18.

8

Nutrition and the Economics of Food: Implications of Some Recent Controversies

S. R. Osmani

8.1. Introduction

Economists have had a long-standing interest in matters of nutrition. Many of their concepts and policy deliberations are based on ideas borrowed from nutrition science. For example, the concept of absolute poverty has, at least since the turn of this century, been explicitly defined as the failure to satisfy a minimum standard of nutritional requirement (Rowntree 1901). To the extent that such failure constrains the physiological and behavioural performance of human beings, it also has a bearing on the welfare-theoretic notions of 'functioning', 'capabilities', and 'quality of life' (Sen 1985). Moreover, practical application of these concepts often requires the use of anthropometric indicators of nutritional status and the comparison of observed status with some desirable 'standard'. Finally, both 'requirement standards' and 'nutritional status indicators' are also of relevance in formulating food and nutrition policies in so far as they provide a tool for assessing the incidence of food deficits and nutritional deprivation among population groups (FAO 1985; World Bank 1986).[1]

In all these matters the economists of course rely on what they perceive to be the nutrition profession's best judgement on how to set up 'requirement norms' and 'status indicators'. In recent years, however, it has become increasingly apparent that the 'best judgement' depends very much on which authority an economist happens to turn to. The differences do not merely consist in the magnitude of this or that 'requirement' or 'standard'. More basic disagreements on the very foundations of concepts and theories are also involved. Naturally, economists cannot help looking ruefully across the border as they feel the loss of bearing for some of their own concepts and theories. This paper is an attempt by a concerned economist to regain his own bearings in an alien territory which is apparently in a state of flux.

Our main objective however is not to resolve the basic disagreements; even to attempt such a task would be impertinent for an outsider. Our interest really is a rather parochial one: we wish to assess whether the current controversies in

The author is grateful to Peter Svedberg and especially to Jean Drèze for extremely helpful comments on an earlier version of the paper.

[1] Some formulations of the positive theory of labour market also have nutritional foundations. Dasgupta and Ray (1987) have recently taken a fresh look at this issue.

nutrition literature warrant any serious rethinking in two specific areas of
interest to the economists, namely (1) the methodology for assessing poverty
and capability and (2) the orientation of food policy in the developing world. It
has been claimed by most protagonists in the 'Great Nutrition Debate' that
much is at stake in both these areas depending on how one perceives the
concepts of requirements and standards. This is then where our enquiry will
begin: differing perceptions of these basic nutritional concepts and the
presumed scientific basis of these perceptions.

In section 8.2, we take up the concept of 'energy requirement' and the
controversies surrounding its definition and measurement.[2] The conceptual
and scientific issues raised in this debate bear on the practical question of how
to set up appropriate nutritional standards which could be used as a yardstick
for the measurement of undernutrition. A furious debate has been raging over
the last decade on the issue of whether or not the traditional concept of
'requirement' leads to a gross overestimation of actual undernutrition. This
debate is reviewed in this section. Next, in section 8.3, we look at the
relationship between food intake, non-food environment, and physical activity, and their implications for assessing nutritional status. In particular, it is
noted that these relationships make for a multi-faceted nature of both the
origin and the outcome of nutritional deprivation. This is seen to have some
rather important implications for deciding exactly what is to count as a state of
undernutrition. The insights developed from these sections are then brought
together in section 8.4 to shed light on the question of our primary interest,
namely what changes, if any, are warranted in our approaches to poverty,
capability, and food policy? Finally, section 8.5 offers a brief summary and a
few concluding remarks.

8.2. In search of a nutritional standard

The concept of a 'standard'

The human body requires energy for performing both internal functions
(chemical as well as mechanical works within the body) and external work on
the environment. The required energy is supplied mostly by the food consumed; but, if necessary, additional supplies can also be obtained by burning
up reserve stores of energy inside the body. Conversely when the ingested food
yields more energy than is expended by the body, the excess energy is stored
inside. Any imbalance between intake and expenditure thus causes an equivalent variation in energy stores. This is reflected mainly in a corresponding
change of body weight, but partly also in the composition of the body, i.e. in

---

[2] The focus on energy, to the exclusion of all other nutrients, is consistent with the prevailing
view that energy deficiency is the most pervasive form of nutritional deficiency in the developing
world. It is also appropriate in a discussion from the perspective of poverty because it is arguable
that poverty has a more direct impact on the intake of energy than of any other nutrient (Osmani
1982: 112).

the proportion of different forms of energy-stores such as fat (adipose tissue) and lean body mass.

When a person is in a state of 'energy balance', i.e. intake equals expenditure at a given level of physical activity, his body weight and composition remain unchanged; as such he can be said to be in a state of equilibrium. However, to be in equilibrium is not the same thing as being blessed with adequate nutrition. Different levels of equilibrium may imply different levels of achievement of various functional capabilities (e.g. the ability to avoid disease or to perform physical activities). Only when these capabilities are deemed to be adequate by some criteria can a person be said to be in a state of adequate nutrition. Accordingly, the standard of 'minimum requirement' can be defined as the level of intake that is associated with the minimum level of equilibrium at which all the functional capabilities can be maintained at desirable levels.

Since equilibrium is defined as a state where the body weight remains unchanged at a given level of activity, the 'requirement standard' can also be conceived as the level of intake that is necessary to maintain a body weight and a level of activity which are consistent with full functional capabilities.

Accordingly, the latest expert committee on nutritional standards offers the following definition. 'The energy requirement of an individual is that level of energy intake from food which will balance energy expenditure when the individual has a body size and composition and level of physical activity, consistent with long-term good health and which will allow for the maintenance of economically necessary and socially desirable physical activity' (FAO/ WHO/UNU 1985: 12). Several comments on this definition are in order.

First, it espouses what may be called the *functional* view of requirement: the 'standard' is supposed to indicate the level of intake at which the set of nutrition-dependent functions achieves a satisfactory level. The contrast is with what may be called the *normative* view of requirement. For example, a society may decide, in view of alternative claims on scarce resources and its value judgement about the worth of alternative claims, that no more than a certain amount of resources can be devoted to improving the level of nutrition within the plan period. This will lead to a target level of intake, which may justifiably be viewed as a requirement norm in the planning context. Alternatively, a society may wish to achieve, perhaps in the long run, a certain level of intake that other societies have already been able to achieve. That target may again be taken as the requirement norm. As opposed to these normative views, it is the functionalist view that the nutritionists generally subscribe to.[3] It is not

---

[3] The matter is actually a little more complicated than that. A group of nutritionists allege that the traditional establishment view takes a normative approach by basing requirement norms on Western standards. On the other hand, the traditionalists argue that theirs is a truly functionalist view, and accuse the heretics of aiming for an unacceptably low level of functional achievement. We shall come back to this debate (the so-called adaptationist debate) time and again. But suffice it to note at this stage that each camp, in its own judgement, is adhering to the functionalist view.

suggested that the other concepts are altogether inappropriate, but merely that the search for a 'functional' standard is very much a legitimate scientific concern for the nutritionists. Accordingly, undernutrition, which is defined as the failure to meet the standard, is also viewed as a functional concept. A person is said to be undernourished if and only if he fails to achieve a satisfactory level of all the nutrition-related functions. Those who fail to achieve 'normative' targets not explicitly based on functional achievements may be underfulfilled in some sense but not necessarily 'undernourished' in the sense of nutrition science. By the same token, those who fulfil a normative target are not necessarily well nourished.

Secondly, while we have drawn a contrast between the 'functional' and 'normative' concepts of requirement, it should be pointed out that the 'functional' standard is not necessarily independent of normative judgements. There are various routes through which such judgements may enter. One such route is particularly emphasized by a group of nutritionists who believe that it is futile to look for a level of intake at which all the functions will simultaneously reach a satisfactory level in some absolute sense. According to them, there is always a trade-off whereby some functions are enhanced at the expense of others.[4] Consequently, the specification of a standard is perforce said to require a normative judgement about the acceptable trade-offs (Pacey and Payne 1984). In contrast, the establishment view by and large takes the position that it is possible to identify a standard at which all functions are expected to be simultaneously satisfactory in an absolute sense. However, they too recognize the role of normative judgements, especially with regard to the specification of a 'socially desirable' level of activity.[5] This is particularly true in respect of 'discretionary' or non-economic activities on which different societies may have different norms and values as to what is a desirable minimum.[6] Thus, one way or the other, normative judgements inevitably appear in the specification of a 'functional' standard. However, what still distinguishes it from the 'normative' standards, as defined earlier, is the fact that it is explicitly linked to the achievement of optimum levels of functions, whereas the latter may have some other goals in mind ('catching up with the West', for instance).

The contrast between functional and normative standard does however tend to get blurred when one takes the 'planning goal' view of a requirement norm.

[4] For instance, it is argued that with high levels of intake, children may achieve a higher level of functions that accrue from a larger physical stature, but only at the risk of greater obesity which may have fatal consequences. There is thus supposed to exist a trade-off between physical stature and longevity.

[5] This recognition has led the FAO/WHO/UNU (1985) expert committee to conclude their report with the advice that before setting up a requirement norm one should first seek an answer to the question of 'requirement for what?'.

[6] There is also a related issue of whether it is at all sensible (or possible) to allow for any positive level of activity in defining the requirement standard. This issue is discussed in s. 8.3.

We have described it as normative; but it may also have a functionalist property if it is based on an 'optimal' level of functions given the resource constraint as well as society's value judgements on the trade-offs between alternative claims on resources. Is it then justified to distinguish between normative and functionalist approaches? Some nutritionists (notably Philip Payne and his colleagues) argue that it is not. While being avowedly functionalist, they also insist that a nutritional standard cannot but be normative in the planning sense. They link it up with their view that a trade-off between functions is unavoidable, and argue that the optimal trade-off, and hence the optimal level of functions, can only be determined in the light of resource constraints and value judgements.

According to this view, therefore, there can be no unique functional standard even for a given society with unchanged value judgements—it will depend on the level of resources. As more resources become available, the standard will be raised. Thus the whole notion of undernutrition becomes resource-dependent (in addition to being dependent on value judgements, which, as we have seen, it must be).

We shall argue however that a functional standard does not have to be normative in the planning sense. More precisely, while value judgements are indeed unavoidable, one does not have to make the standard contingent on resources as well, even if one believes à la Payne that trade-off between functions is inevitable. Given the nature of trade-offs and society's value judgements about them, one can define an unconstrained optimum at which the functions would achieve the most satisfactory level from a particular society's point of view. This is the level of nutrition the society would aim for, if its objective was to maximize the level of functions. It is this unconstrained optimum that in an obvious sense qualifies to be the truly functional standard.

Of course, if the resources are too meagre to achieve the unconstrained optimum, it will certainly be legitimate to aim for a constrained optimum (one that is contingent on both resources and value judgements) as a target for the planning horizon. But it does not seem sensible to use the latter as the defining criterion of undernutrition. The use of such a resource-dependent criterion will lead to the perverse result that more undernutrition may be observed at higher levels of resources, even if the functions of every individual happen to improve. Conversely, the simplest way to eliminate undernutrition will be to declare that no resources were available to improve the level of nutrition![7]

The particular feature of a resource-dependent criterion that seems to appeal to its proponents is the fact that it helps to isolate the most deserving cases (Pacey and Payne 1984; Dowler et al. 1982). To elaborate, if $\hat{l}$ stands for the constrained optimum given by an egalitarian social welfare function, then it follows from definition that the scarce resources can be best utilized by

---

[7] Sen (1983) used the same argument to dispose of similar attempts to define poverty in relation to a resource-dependent concept of the poverty line.

bringing those below $\hat{I}$ up to the level of $\hat{I}$, leaving aside for the moment all those whose functional levels lie above $\hat{I}$ but below the unconstrained optimum, I^*. The latter group, which is relatively better off, can be dealt with later, when the resource position improves. This is of course a perfectly sensible policy. But for this policy to operate, it is not necessary to call the latter group well nourished and recognize only the former as undernourished. We can call all of them undernourished, grade them according to their degree of undernutrition (as measured by the distance from I^*), and pick up only the severest cases (those below $\hat{I}$) for remedial action during the plan period. In other words, while $\hat{I}$ is a perfectly legitimate selection criterion for immediate action, it need not at the same time be a defining criterion of undernutrition.

In sum, while a functional standard is not independent of normative judgement, it should not, like a 'planning goal', be made contingent on resources as well. In the jargon of economics, the functional standard represents an unconstrained optimum, while the planning goal is a constrained optimum. The latter is a valid target for the plan period as well as an attractive selection criterion for immediate remedial action; but only the former is a sensible criterion of undernutrition.

The final comment regarding the definition relates to its domain of application—in particular, whether it is applicable to individuals or population groups. In principle, it should be applicable to every single individual, provided one can stipulate an appropriate body weight and activity level for the person and also find the minimum level of intake that could sustain the stipulated levels of weight and activity. In practice, however, it is extremely difficult to achieve this objective, for a number of reasons.

First, even if all the relevant characteristics (age, sex, etc.) of a person are fully specified, one cannot pin down a single body weight which is ideal for him. The nutritionists can only tell that the healthy individuals of a given type usually maintain body weight within a certain range. The average of this (fairly narrow) range is a useful basis for computing the average requirement of a group of individuals of a given type, but there is no basis for computing the specific requirement of a single individual. Secondly, there is a similar problem with the level of activity. In principle, it should be possible to specify the desirable level of activity for any single individual. But when one is dealing with a large population, it may be practically unfeasible to elicit the required information for every single person. The best one can do is to classify the population into certain major groups (in terms of age, sex, and occupation) and specify an average level of activity for each group. Once again, one can only compute the average requirement of individuals of a given type. Thirdly, even when a particular body weight and level of activity are specified, one is not able to find a particular level of intake that is most appropriate. The nutritionists only know that a sample of healthy individuals of a given body weight and activity will be found to have intakes within a certain range, but no single level of intake can be declared as ideal. Once again, one can only say, provided the range is fairly narrow, that the average intake of the sample is a useful measure of the average requirement of the group.

Therefore, in practice, the standard is applicable only as an average requirement of groups of individuals of particular types. By considering as detailed a typology as possible one can reduce the error of approximation that is inevitably entailed by the use of an average. But one cannot pronounce (except in probabilistic terms) on the specific requirement and thus the nutritional status of a particular individual picked up at random.

The schism: intraindividual variation in requirement

Some fundamental problems with the concept of requirement still remain even if it is agreed that the norm should be defined with respect to an optimum level of functions and that it should refer to the unconstrained optimum rather than a constrained optimum determined by resources. One set of problems relates to the issue of whether a unique level of intake can be associated with the given optimum of functional achievements. If not, then one will have to accept that there is no fixed requirement for any given individual. Whether this is in fact the case or not has been a matter of intense controversy over the last decade or so.

By and large, the mainstream view in nutrition science takes the position that the level of intake required for optimum functions (or ideal health, to put it differently) can be assumed for all practical purposes to be unique for any given individual. This obviously leads to the notion of a fixed requirement. It is of course granted that two apparently identical individuals (of the same age, sex, body weight, and composition, performing the same level of activity, and living in the same environment) can have different requirements. This is attributed to inherent genetic differences in the efficiency of energy utilization. It is a well-known fact that the human body cannot fully utilize the energy content of food intake—a large part of it (nearly 60 per cent) is dissipated as heat. How much is actually utilized (i.e. the efficiency of utilization) depends on genetic composition. Therefore, apparently identical individuals with different genetic compositions may be endowed with different metabolic efficiencies and hence may require different levels of intake to maintain the same level of health. Consequently, there arises the possibility of *inter*individual variation in requirement. However, there is believed to be no scope for *intra*individual variation in requirement once such parameters as age, sex, activity, and environment are specified.

This well-known model of fixed requirement has recently been challenged by what may be called the homeostatic theory of nutrition. According to this theory, a person may be able to maintain the same state of health ('homeostasis') at different levels of intake. This theory thus emphasizes the possibility of intraindividual variation in requirement. Two different mechanisms have been postulated which can presumably allow for such variation. One such mechanism is principally associated with the names of P. V. Sukhatme and his colleagues.[8] They invoke the concept of efficiency of energy utilization and argue that this efficiency can vary intraindividually even if none of the defining characteristics of a person (namely age, activity, body weight, etc.) undergoes any change. Variable efficiency in turn implies that different levels of intake can yield the same amount of 'utilized' energy and hence the same level of functional achievement. Therefore, according to this view, no unique level of intake can be associated with the given optimum of functions, and consequently requirement must be recognized to be variable intraindividually.

The other mechanism relates to the energy requirement for children. The issue at stake is how much energy is needed for satisfactory growth at different stages of childhood. Once again the mainstream view postulates a fixed requirement model, on the ground that there is a unique rate of growth that is ideal for a given child (although different children may have different ideal rates of growth determined by genetic characteristics). In contrast, the homeostatic theory suggests that within a certain range different rates of growth can sustain the same state of health for any given child. Accordingly, the energy requirement of a child is believed to be variable intraindividually. This hypothesis has been advanced most forcefully by David Seckler and has come to be known as the 'small but healthy' hypothesis.[9]

The possibility of intraindividual variation in requirement is not a mere scientific curiosity. It has rather remarkable implications for the empirical assessment of undernutrition in the real world. There are basically two major approaches towards the measurement of undernutrition, namely the dietary approach and the anthropometric approach. In the dietary approach, the energy intakes of individuals or households are compared with the requirement norm and those having intake below the norm are identified as undernourished. In the anthropometric approach, which is applied mostly to the case of children, certain indicators of physical growth are compared against some norms of desirable standards and if those indicators fall short of the standards then undernutrition is said to have occurred. The assessment of undernutrition through either of these approaches can be extremely sensitive to the decision as to whether the possibility of intraindividual variation in requirement is to be allowed or not.

Take the case of the dietary approach first. Those who believe in the fixed requirement model usually compare energy intake with some norm of average requirement. Various international organizations (e.g. FAO and WHO) periodically provide revised estimates of average requirements for different types of people (a type being defined by age, sex, and activity level). The idea behind taking the average is to allow for the possibility of interindividual variation in requirement among people of the same type. There is however no

---

[8] See Sukhatme (1977, 1978, 1981a, 1982a, 1982b), Sukhatme and Margen (1982), and Sukhatme and Narain (1982), among others.

[9] See Seckler (1980, 1982, 1984a, 1984b).

room for intraindividual variation here, each person being assumed to have a fixed requirement. Arguing from the perspective of the homeostatic theory, Sukhatme has launched a crusade against this practice of using the average requirement as the cut-off point for identifying the undernourished. He has suggested that if one is interested in setting a cut-off point, then one should set it, not at the average value, but at the lower end of what he calls the range of homeostasis (i.e. the range of intraindividual variation in requirement). He denotes this lower cut-off point as $\mu - 2\sigma$ where μ stands for average requirement and σ stands for the standard deviation of intraindividual variation. Using this cut-off point he was able to show that the incidence of nutritional poverty in India was less than half of what Dandekar and Rath (1971) had estimated earlier by using the average norm. By sheer reconceptualization of energy requirement, the magnitude of poverty was cut down at a stroke from an enormous 46 per cent to a more innocuous-looking 15–20 per cent. Hence the furore over the theory and measurement of requirement.

The dietary approach is also affected by the decision as to whether or not to accept Seckler's variant of the homeostatic theory. If, as Seckler suggests, there is a range of growth rates, rather than a unique ideal rate, which are equally compatible with optimum nutritional functioning, then the minimum energy requirement for the children should be such as to allow for the minimum growth rate within the homeostatic range.[10] This implication of homeostatic theory is in sharp contrast with the traditional approach where the requirement norm for the children is set on the principle of allowing for the maximum possible growth rate permitted by the genetic potential.

Seckler's hypothesis has similar implications for the traditional anthropometric approach to the measurement of undernutrition, and it is in this context that this hypothesis has been mostly debated. The norms against which actual anthropometric measurements (e.g. weight, height, arm circumference, etc.) are compared are usually derived from actual measurements on children who are presumed to have achieved their full genetic potential. The obvious implication of using such norms is that anyone whose physical growth falls short of genetic potential must be deemed to be undernourished. In contrast, the homeostatic theory would suggest that retardation of growth can be indicative of undernutrition only when it is severe enough to fall below the range of homeostasis. The practical implication of these differences in terms of measurement of undernutrition can be quite staggering. For example, from the perspective of genetic potential theory, Gopalan (1983b) finds that the majority of children in India are undernourished, whereas Seckler contends on

---

[10] It is however not suggested that the minimum growth rate is what society should aim to achieve, but merely that undernutrition would occur only when the diet is incapable of meeting the requirement even for this minimal growth rate. The concept of requirement here is a diagnostic rather than a prescriptive one. This distinction is further discussed in s. 8.4.

the basis of his homeostatic theory that only 15–20 per cent of Indian children can be called undernourished in the functional sense.

It is thus clear that the theory of homeostasis—both Sukhatme's and Seckler's—conflicts with the traditional approach by suggesting a significantly lower cut-off point for the assessment of undernutrition. Not surprisingly, it has generated an exceedingly heated controversy—the proponents of the theory blaming the mainstream tradition for grossly overstating the magnitude of undernutrition and being blamed in turn for dangerously underplaying the extent of human misery.

In the rest of this section we shall briefly evaluate the two variants of the homeostatic theory, and try to arrive at a judgement on whether the lower cut-off points suggested by this theory should be accepted or not.[11]

The rationale of $\mu - 2\sigma$

There has been a lot of confusion over how precisely to interpret Sukhatme's arguments. It appears to us that there are actually two different ways in which he has tried to justify the use of $\mu - 2\sigma$. We shall refer to them as Mark I and Mark II versions respectively. The Mark I version follows from the theory of autoregulatory homeostasis proposed by Sukhatme and Margen (1982). This theory suggests that the efficiency of energy utilization varies over time in an autocorrelated manner; and if a healthy person is economically or otherwise unconstrained in his intake of calories and if he remains engaged at a fixed level of activity while maintaining his body weight, then his intake will also be seen to vary over time in an autocorrelated manner. The Mark II version also relies on the idea of variation in the efficiency of energy utilization, but in a manner that seems to abandon the *autoregulatory* model altogether. It seems more accurate to describe it as the *adaptive* model. Sukhatme of course tries to justify this mutation on the ground that the latter model follows logically from the former, but we shall argue that this is not really so.[12]

In order to see how the logic of $\mu - 2\sigma$ was derived from the autoregulatory model, it will be useful to begin by noting three important implications of autocorrelated intakes that this model predicts an unconstrained healthy person to have:

1. An autocorrelated variable is generated by a stochastic stationary distribution, i.e. a distribution with constant mean and variance. Because of the constancy of the mean, it can be expected that if a large number of observations are taken over time, the observed average of intakes will approach the theoretical mean of the distribution. This theoretical mean can be shown to be nothing other than a person's long-term average requirement. It follows

---

[11] For a considerably more detailed evaluation, see Osmani (1987) where the arguments are more fully developed as well as supported by necessary documentation.

[12] Mark I is of an earlier vintage, being most visible in the writings of 1977 and 1978. Mark II is more of a product of the 1980s, developed largely in response to the criticisms of Mark I.

therefore that although an unconstrained person's intakes will vary from day to day, in the long run his average intake will equal his average requirement (unless some extraneous factor intervenes).

2. Autocorrelation also implies that the variance of the mean of intakes does not decline rapidly to zero as the period over which the mean is taken is increased. Therefore, if the mean is taken over a relatively short period, say a week, then the mean intake will have a significantly non-zero variance. In other words, the weekly mean intake will not as a rule be equal to the 'true' mean. From Edholm et al.'s (1970) data Sukhatme has estimated that the coefficient of variation of weekly mean is in the order of 12–15 per cent. Recalling that intake equals requirement for healthy people, one could therefore say that requirement varies intraindividually with a coefficient of variation of 12–15 per cent (when the reference period is a short span of time, such as a week).

3. When autocorrelation is allowed for in the daily intakes (or, requirements) of the healthy subjects in Edholm's experiments, most of the variation seems to originate from intraindividual rather than interindividual variation. From this Sukhatme concludes that intraindividual variation in requirement is a far more important phenomenon than interindividual variation which the traditional view tends to emphasize.

Armed with these implications of the autoregulatory model, Sukhatme then proceeds to confront the conventional approach to the measurement of undernutrition. As mentioned before, a person is conventionally identified as undernourished if his mean intake (m) over a sample period falls short of some norm of average requirement (μ), i.e. if $m < \mu$. Also recall that μ is obtained in practice from interindividual average of requirements over a sample period. But according to the third implication of autocorrelation mentioned above, these interindividual differences are really the reflection of underlying intraindividual variation. Therefore μ can be taken to be an estimate of intraindividual average requirement over the long term.[13] Accordingly, the inequality $m < \mu$ can be interpreted as an instance of a person's weekly intake falling below his long-term requirement. Now we know from the second implication of autocorrelation that the weekly intake of a healthy unconstrained person may easily deviate from his long-term requirement. Therefore it will be wrong to treat everyone with m less than μ as undernourished.

One really has to distinguish between two separate cases that may generate the inequality $m < \mu$: (1) the case of unconstrained healthy people eating less in the sample period simply because their requirement has fallen below μ in the normal course of intraindividual variation, and (2) the less fortunate case where the inequality reflects some constraint on intake. The first case is evidently not one of undernutrition, for although the observed intake is less than μ, the 'expected' intake over the long term will be equal to μ (by the first implication of autocorrelation); in the words of Sukhatme, the variation in intake is in

[13] Assuming of course that the intradistribution of requirements is the same for everyone.

'statistical control'. However, in the second case, where the intake is constrained, there is a possibility of failure in 'statistical control', i.e. the 'expected' intake may in fact turn out to be less than μ. Only such cases should be treated as undernutrition.[14] We therefore need a criterion for determining who are and who are not in 'statistical control' of intake variation over time. But how do we find such a criterion?

Sukhatme's strategy was to look for a characteristic feature of the intakes of healthy unconstrained people. This feature was then to be used as the criterion for distinguishing the well-nourished people from the undernourished ones. The particular feature that he used for this purpose was the 'range of homeostasis', i.e. the range of variation within which the intake of a healthy person can be expected to lie. As it happens, 95 per cent of healthy people can be expected to have intake within the range μ ± 2σ, assuming that efficiency varies in a normal distribution. If an intake falls outside this range, one can be reasonably confident that it is not the intake of a healthy person. Thus argues Sukhatme (1978: 1383), 'Clearly, most individuals in health in the framework of this model will have an intake between μ ± 2σ. It follows that the proportion of individuals below the lower critical limit may be taken to represent the estimate of the incidence of undernutrition'. This is the Mark I rationale for using μ − 2σ as the criterion of undernutrition.

There is however a serious flaw in this logic. In order to claim that undernutrition occurs only when intake falls short of μ− 2σ, it must be established that everyone with intake in the range of homeostasis is well-nourished. But Sukhatme's premiss (the first proposition in the quotation above) does not ensure this. It only ensures that if a person is healthy his intake will lie between μ ± 2σ. From this it does not follow that anyone who has intake within this range is necessarily healthy. For example, if some extraneous constraint on intake rather than variable efficiency brings down someone's intake in the sample period below μ (albeit above μ − 2σ), and if the nature of the constraint is such that it is going to persist over time, then clearly average intake will not equal μ even in the long run. Such people must be considered undernourished by Sukhatme's own criterion, namely the failure of 'statistical control'. Consequently, the cut-off point of μ − 2σ will in general lead to an underestimate of total undernutrition.

The mistake basically lies in the failure to see that to have one's intake within the range of homeostasis is only a *necessary* condition for being well nourished. It is by no means *sufficient*. Yet it is sufficiency that is needed to justify the claim that everyone with intake above μ − 2σ should be considered well nourished. The failure of 'Mark I justification' is thus seen to lie in an elementary confusion between 'necessity' and 'sufficiency'.

This particular logical problem seems to be taken care of, however, in the

[14] 'Clearly, undernutrition must be defined as the failure of the process to be in statistical control' (Sukhatme 1978: 1383).

subsequent Mark II version. Here Sukhatme brings in the notion of adaptation in order to justify the claim that everyone with intake above $\mu - 2\sigma$ must indeed be considered well nourished. Drawing on the concept of 'dietary-induced thermogenesis' proposed by Miller (1975), Sims (1976), and others, he argues that the efficiency of energy utilization can adapt to the variation of intake. In particular, it is suggested that as intake falls from the level of average requirement, the body responds by reducing wasteful dissipation of heat and thereby increasing the efficiency of energy utilization. Since such adaptation simply takes the form of reducing wastage, there is no apparent cost involved in the process; in particular although the intake is reduced, the body continues to utilize the same amount of energy as before. As a result, on the one hand body weight remains intact and on the other the level of activity can be sustained at the old level. Since neither body weight nor activity is affected, an erstwhile healthy person must be considered to remain healthy as long as the decline in intake can induce a fully compensating increase in efficiency. The range of intakes within which such fully compensating variation is actually possible is called the range of costless adaptation. Obviously, any intake within this range is consistent with good health and therefore one cannot stipulate any fixed requirement for any given individual. The range of costless adaptation is thus conterminous with the range of intraindividual variation in requirement. Only when intake falls below this range can it be said that requirement is not being met and thus a person is undernourished.

Sukhatme then goes on to suggest that the range of costless adaptation is given by $\mu \pm 2\sigma$ which he had earlier described as the range of autoregulation. Hence he argues that $\mu - 2\sigma$ is the appropriate cut-off point for measuring undernutrition.

Now the description of $\mu \pm 2\sigma$ as the range of adaptation, and not merely as the range of autoregulation, is a particularly significant departure. We have seen that in the autoregulation framework one could only say that the intakes of healthy people will mostly fall within the range of $\mu \pm 2\sigma$. One could not assert the reverse, and that created a logical problem in accepting $\mu - 2\sigma$ as the cut-off point. But it is different if $\mu \pm 2\sigma$ is viewed as the range of costless adaptation. Give a man any intake within this range; his efficiency will adapt accordingly to bring expenditure into equality with his intake, without any effect on body weight or activity. If that is so, then everyone with intake (m) above $\mu - 2\sigma$ must be considered adequately nourished.[15] In other words, the inequality $m > \mu - 2\sigma$ is now both necessary and sufficient for a person to be well nourished. The logical flaw in the Mark I rationale thus seems to be neatly avoided in the Mark II version.

But this achievement is more apparent than real. It is true of course that if $\mu - 2\sigma$ could be established as the limit of costless adaptation, it would indeed

---

[15] 'It follows that a person *must* be considered in energy balance *whenever* his intake falls within homeostatic limits of balance' (Sukhatme 1982b: 39; emphasis added).

be the correct cut-off point. But as we have noted, $\mu \pm 2\sigma$ was originally described as the 'range of autoregulation' i.e. the range within which the intake of a healthy *unconstrained* person can be expected to lie. In contrast, the 'range of adaptation' refers to a range within which a person can costlessly adapt even if his intake is *constrained* to deviate from the average. They are apparently not the same thing. Yet Sukhatme assumes that the two 'ranges' are exactly the same; and in doing so, he takes recourse to the argument that autoregulation implies adaptation.[16] But we shall argue that autoregulation does not imply adaptation and that *a fortiori* the range of autoregulation cannot be identified with the range of adaptation.

Sukhatme makes the transition from autoregulation to adaptation by hinging on the fact that both phenomena are characterized by a common mechanism, namely, variation in the efficiency of energy utilization. But this transition is not logically valid because the qualitative nature of 'efficiency variation' is not the same in the two cases. In particular, the causal relationship between intake and efficiency is exactly the opposite.

In the autoregulation model efficiency is supposed to vary 'as a matter of course' within a stochastic stationary distribution. This leads to corresponding variation in requirement, so that in the case of an unconstrained person '. . . *intake is regulated* in autoregressive manner to meet his needs' (Sukhatme 1981a: 1318; emphasis added). The causation thus runs from variation of efficiency to change of requirement and then finally to intake ('to meet his needs'). It all starts with prior spontaneous variation in efficiency as a stochastic process.[17] In 'adaptation' however the line of causation is completely reversed: 'When total energy is less, the body wastes less, thus using the intake with greater efficiency. As intake increases, wastage also increases and the energy is used with decreased efficiency' (Sukhatme 1982b: 38).[18] Indeed, adaptation is by definition a phenomenon where variation in efficiency is induced by prior variation in intake, whereas in autoregulation efficiency varies in a *spontaneous* manner, and intake merely follows suit.

Since spontaneous and induced variation in efficiency cannot be the same

---

[16] 'It is apparently the autoregressive mechanism in daily expenditure in maintaining body-weight which enables a man to adapt his requirement to intakes without affecting the net energy needed for maintenance and physical activity' (Sukhatme 1982b: 39).

[17] The idea of spontaneous variation comes out most clearly when one considers the analogy drawn by Sukhatme and Margen (1978, 1982) between their models for energy and protein. They found autocorrelation in both models and claimed that these are similar biological phenomena. It is however significant that intake was kept fixed in the protein model, and yet expenditure varied in an autocorrelated manner due presumably to similar variation in the efficiency of protein absorption. There was thus no scope for efficiency to vary in response to intake. If the analogy is to be retained, one must then admit that efficiency of energy utilization varies in a spontaneous manner; intake merely follows suit when it is free to vary. See Mehta (1982) on this point, p. 1335.

[18] Note the contrast in the causation in autoregulation, '. . . a healthy person varies his or her intake, increasing it when wastage is larger, and decreasing it when it is lower' (Sukhatme and Margen 1982: 109).

biological phenomenon, it is clear that autoregulation cannot imply adaptation. It is nevertheless possible that adaptation may exist regardless of autoregulation. If it does, then of course it is the lower end of the range of costless adaptation rather than the average value that can claim to be the correct cut-off point for identifying the undernourished. However, it will no longer be legitimate to deduce the limit of adaptation from the value of Sukhatme's $\mu - 2\sigma$, derived as it was from the autoregulatory model inferred from Edholm's data. It must be based on an independent assessment of the biological evidence on adaptation. But is there any such evidence?

There is of course no disputing the fact that all living organisms, including human beings, adapt in various ways in the face of adversity, such as a shortfall in food intake. They may for instance reduce their level of activity or settle down to a lower body size so as to bring down their energy expenditure and achieve a new equilibrium at the lower level of food availability. That is however not the kind of adaptation that is relevant to the issue at stake. Since we are interested here in the possibility of adaptation that would enable a person to meet his requirement equally within a range of intakes, the adaptive mechanism must not affect either body weight or activity, because if either of them changes from the stipulated desirable levels then a person can no longer be said to be meeting his requirement. The truly relevant type of adaptation can only occur through variation in the efficiency of energy utilization, unaccompanied by any change in either body weight or activity. This is what we call the case of costless adaptation in the present context. The relevant question therefore is: what is the evidence for such costless adaptation?

The adaptationists often refer to a considerable body of cross-sectional evidence which shows that people at different levels of habitual intakes can maintain similar body weight while remaining engaged in apparently similar activities. In fact, as high as twofold range in the variation of energy intake is not at all uncommon (Rose and Williams 1961; Widdowson 1962; Edmundson 1977, 1979). This has sometimes been interpreted as a priori evidence that people can adapt costlessly to low food intakes by using energy more efficiently. There is however a serious problem with this interpretation. As Edmundson (1980) rightly notes, one can never be sure from cross-sectional data whether the observed variation in intake is indicative of adaptive behaviour or merely a reflection of genetic differences in the efficiency of energy utilization.[19]

In order to circumvent this problem, what one really needs is longitudinal

[19] The genetic differences may of course be the outcome of evolutionary adaptation over a long period, in which only the more efficient genes come to survive in an environment of nutritional stress through the process of Darwinian selection, while the less efficient genes continue to survive in a more bountiful condition. As distinct from such genetic adaption, however, what is relevant for the present context is the notion of phenotypic adaptation, i.e. the ability of the same person to adapt in his own lifetime. The point here is that cross-sectional evidence is inherently incapable of distinguishing between genotypic and phenotypic adaptation.

evidence on the condition of the same person experiencing deviation from habitual intakes. Some insight can be gained in this respect from the experimental evidence on the effects of overfeeding and underfeeding. There appears to exist enough evidence to show that the efficiency of energy utilization does respond adaptively to alterations in food intake; but it is almost invariably accompanied by alterations in body weight as well.[20] The case for costless adaptation is therefore not yet established.

It should however be borne in mind that in all these experiments, calorie intake was either severely reduced or grossly blown up. They do not therefore rule out the possibility that at moderate levels of deviation, costless adaptation in efficiency may still occur.[21] Future experiments may throw light on this possibility. But at the present moment there is no scientific basis for arguing that a significant scope for costless adaptation exists, far less for making a quantitative assessment of the limits of adaptation.

We are thus left with the judgement that the hypothesis of intraindividual adaptation in requirement à la Sukhatme is not yet substantiated by scientific evidence, although the possibility cannot be ruled out altogether. On the other hand, there is ample evidence of interindividual variation in requirement. What all this implies for some of the concerns in economics is discussed in section 8.4.

The homeostatic theory of growth and the measurement of undernutrition

Let us now turn our attention to the second mechanism of homeostasis which, according to Seckler, invalidates the traditional approach of measuring undernutrition among children. Recall that the homeostatic theory of growth challenges the orthodox view that a child must be considered undernourished if it fails to achieve the maximal possible growth permitted by genetic potential. Instead, it posits the hypothesis that, within a range of shortfall from the genetic potential, a child is 'small but healthy'.[22]

Before assessing the merit of this hypothesis, it is necessary to note a couple of confusions that have bedevilled the controversies surrounding it.

First, the precise content of Seckler's hypothesis has not always been

---

[20] See the reviews in Apfelbaum (1978), James and Shetty (1982), Norgan (1983), and Dasgupta and Ray (1987). See also a number of related papers in Blaxter and Waterlow (1985).

[21] Rand et al. (1985) have produced evidence which shows that even at moderate levels of deviation, adaptive variation in efficiency does not seem to operate without accompanying change in body weight. But as the authors point out, there are problems of interpretation. One difficulty is that the levels of physical activity were not monitored, which makes it difficult to ascertain if the failure to maintain weight was due to failure of adaptation or to alteration in activity.

[22] More precisely, the hypothesis can be stated as follows: if two persons of different body sizes (one having achieved his genetic potential and the other falling short by a margin to be specified below) are living in the same environment and receiving an intake that is commensurate with their respective body size and (desirable) activity, then the smaller person will enjoy the same level of functional capability as the bigger person, despite having failed to achieve his genetic potential; smallness per se (within a range) does not matter.

correctly appreciated. He does not propose that good health consists in being small (as opposed to being big), but that being small (up to a point) may be just as healthy as being big. The operative phrase is therefore 'small *but* healthy' and not 'small *is* healthy' as has sometimes been misconstrued.[23]

Secondly, Seckler's initial formulation suffered from a lack of rigour which has caused much confusion regarding the domain of his hypothesis. He defined as 'small but healthy' (SBH, for short) all those who are suffering from mild to moderate malnutrition (MMM) according to conventional standards (Seckler 1980, 1982). But this is imprecise, because the set of MMM may be different for different types of anthropometric measurements, of which there are quite a few. The most widely used measures are weight for age (Gomez classification), height for age, and weight for height (Waterlow classification).[24] Weight for height is a measure of 'wasting' and height for age is a measure of 'stunting' whereas weight for age may reflect both wasting and stunting. It is clear from Seckler's writings that the domain of SBH was meant to be confined to the case of pure 'stunting' unaccompanied by 'wasting'. Thus, for instance, he claimed that '. . . about 90% of all the malnutrition found in these countries involved people with low height for age *but with the proper weight for height ratio*' (Seckler 1980: 223, emphasis original), and wondered '. . . if there is anything wrong with these small people other than their smallness' (p. 223). Yet he often talked of mild to moderate malnutrition as if it were an undifferentiated category. The imprecision has since been rectified, and Seckler (1984*b*) has recently defined SBH explicitly as referring to the mild to moderate degrees of pure stunting (i.e. between 80 and 100 per cent of the 'Harvard median standard' for height for age with normal weight for height ratio). However, the confusion in the mean time has taken its toll, and much of the critique of SBH has simply gone astray by bringing in evidence that was not quite relevant.

The distinction between 'wasting' and 'stunting' is in fact quite a crucial one. Both are indicative of retarded growth in a general sense, but of two quite different kinds. 'Wasting' represents depletion of body tissue, whereas 'stunting' indicates slower rate of new tissue deposition. They thus represent two distinct biochemical processes whose functional consequences need not be the same. It is generally recognized that 'wasting' is much more harmful than 'stunting'. But Seckler goes a step further and suggests that *moderate* stunting is not harmful at all.

This proposition is based on the following kind of reasoning. If the level of nutrition is not consistent with normal body weight at the genetically permissible maximal height and if yet such height is to be attained, then equilibrium will have to be achieved by depleting body tissue (i.e. by 'wasting') in order to

---

[23] This confusion seems to permeate much of the critique by Gopalan (1983*a*, 1983*b*), who even goes as far as using evocative phrases like 'small is beautiful' in presenting a caricature of Seckler's views, and takes him to task for 'pleading the virtues of smallness'.

[24] An excellent account of alternative measures and their relative usefulness can be found in Waterlow (1972).

supply additional energy. This will admittedly have adverse functional consequences. But 'stunting' offers an adaptive mechanism to avoid these consequences by reducing height and thereby reducing nutrient demand in keeping with supply. At this low-level equilibrium, existing tissues need not be depleted to supply additional energy, and normal body weight for height can be maintained. Therefore, it is argued, if stunting is within a moderate range, 'There are no impairments because this range represents an adaptive response of bodysize to adverse conditions *in order to avoid these impairments*' (Seckler 1980: 224; emphasis original).

But this argument is not entirely convincing. Just because adaptation is designed to avoid some adverse consequences, it does not follow that it has no adverse effects of its own. It is at least conceivable that more severe consequences are averted at the cost of less severe ones. There is thus no a priori reason to believe that an adapted state, such as 'stunting', is necessarily costless.

Thus on the purely conceptual ground, the plausibility of homeostatic theory remains wide open. It is, in the final analysis, by the empirical evidence on the relationship between stunting and functional impairment that the issue must be judged.

Several kinds of nutritional functionings are relevant in this respect. Two of them, namely immunocompetence and cognitive development, relate directly to the stunted children. However, looking at the children alone is not enough. Since a stunted child is very likely to grow into a small adult, it is necessary to investigate what adverse effects the small adult size might have in later life. In this context two specific functions are often singled out for detailed scrutiny, namely physical productivity of men and the reproductive efficiency of women.

Is any of these functions adversely affected by small physical stature? Generally speaking the answer is: yes, all of them are. However, one has to be extremely careful in using the empirical evidence for passing judgement on the homeostatic theory of growth, for this theory does not postulate a general invariance relationship between physical stature and nutritional functions; it only predicts the specific relationship that pure stunting of a moderate degree does not impair nutritional capability. It means that not all kinds of evidence on the relationship between physical stature and functions are relevant for testing this theory. For instance, if small stature is due to wasting rather than stunting alone, or even in the case of pure stunting if the degree of retardation happens to be severe, then the evidence is not relevant for our present purpose. As it happens, most of the evidence is actually of this kind, which gives rise to the general notion that small physical stature adversely affects nutritional functions. In contrast, the genuinely relevant type of evidence, involving pure moderate stunting, is in fact quite scanty. We have looked into the available studies in some detail elsewhere (Osmani 1987), and the findings are described in a nutshell below.

In respect of three of the four functions mentioned above, namely immuno-competence (i.e. susceptibility to morbidity and mortality), reproductive efficiency of women, and physical productivity of men, there is no reason to believe that pure moderate stunting has any discernible adverse effect. There is however some ambiguity regarding the fourth function, namely cognitive development of children. On the one hand, there is no direct clinical study to show that the neurological system has actually been impaired in some instance of pure moderate stunting. On the other hand, a large number of empirical studies reveal a positive relationship between height and mental functions, a relationship that exists even in the case of moderate height retardation. It is the interpretation of this correlation that is subject to ambiguity. The retardation in height is certainly due to nutritional deprivation, but the associated mental retardation may not be so. It may arise from a different source, namely the lack of stimulus. It is generally recognized that cognitive development is a function of both nutrition from within and stimulus from outside. Furthermore, in the actual socio-economic conditions in which impoverished children live, both nutrition and stimulus are often simultaneously deficient. It is therefore difficult and often impossible to determine to what extent, if at all, nutrition *per se* is responsible for slow mental development.

If stimulus is really the culprit, i.e. if the biochemical processes involved in physical stunting have nothing to do with cognitive retardation, then one will have to conclude in line with the other three functions mentioned above that moderate stunting does not impair cognitive function either. Will it then lead to the judgement that a moderately stunted child is nutritionally healthy? Not necessarily. Consider the case of cognitive function again. Even if one accepts that stimulus rather than height is the causal factor behind cognitive retarda-tion, it does not follow that a stunted child is nutritionally healthy, because the lack of stimulus may itself be a result of inadequate nutrition. The relationship between stimulus and nutrition arises from the fact that the former depends a great deal on a child's exploratory activities, of which play is a very important medium; and activity is very much a function of nutrition. Therefore, the very same phenomenon of nutritional constraint that leads to stunting through the pathway of biochemical processes may also retard mental development through the pathway of activity. It means that even if it is right to say that moderate stunting does not cause any functional impairment, it will not be right to say that a moderately stunted child is necessarily healthy from a nutritional point of view.

Accordingly, we find it necessary to make a distinction between two possible interpretations of the 'small but healthy' hypothesis, namely that (1) moderate stunting does not impair any nutritional capability, and (2) a moderately stunted child does not suffer from any impairment of nutritional capabilities.

The first is a causative statement; and we feel inclined to treat it sympatheti-cally in view of our findings on all the functions mentioned above. The second is an associative statement; and here our discussion on cognition points to the need for caution. We should not simply assume that a moderately stunted child is nutritionally sound, even if we accept the statement (1).

The causative statement is relevant for the dietary approach to the assessment of nutritional status, while the associative statement is relevant for the anthropometric approach. The validity of the causative statement would imply that there is room for intraindividual variation in requirement through costless adaptation in the rate of physical growth. Accordingly, the minimum dietary needs of children ought to be based on a growth rate which lies at the lower end of the homeostatic range rather than at the top of genetic potential, provided the diet allows for an adequate level of activity commensurate with proper cognitive development.

On the other hand, the doubt over the associative statement leaves one in quite a quandary. While one cannot accept that a stunted child is necessarily healthy, neither can one go back to embrace the genetic potential theory because the falsity of the associative statement does not imply the truth of the converse. In other words, one cannot assume that a stunted child has necessarily suffered from nutrition-constrained cognitive retardation. That would depend on whether the child had actually reduced his activity at the same time that it became stunted. For all we know, it may not have done so and may have actually absorbed the entire nutritional constraint through adaptive stunting. By looking at anthropometry alone, one cannot be sure.

In fact the relationship between nutrition and activity creates quite a general problem for anthropometry, not just in the context of the homeostatic theory of growth. We pursue this general problem further in section 8.3 and discuss some of its implications in section 8.4.

8.3. Food, environmental hygiene, and physical activity[25]

The problem of incomplete measurement

Assume for the moment that all the debates on adaptation in both efficiency and physical growth have been satisfactorily resolved. So we know how to set up minimum dietary standards and how to define anthropometric norms below which function of some kind is expected to be impaired. We may simplify further and assume away any genotypic variation in the energy requirement among individuals of the same age, sex, and physical parameters. Can we now measure the extent of undernutrition by using either dietary standards or anthropometric norms?

The answer unfortunately is still 'no'. In fact, we shall presently demonstrate that the following three propositions are generally true:

1. Neither the dietary approach nor the anthropometric approach fully captures the set of undernourished population.

---

[25] Parts of this section and the next draw heavily from the author's previous unpublished work which was used as background material for preparing the Technical Appendix in FAO (1985).

2. Each approach captures a different subset of undernourished people, although there may be a partial overlap between the two.
3. Even a combination of the two approaches cannot capture the complete set of undernourished people.

Let us take up the anthropometric approach first. Once the appropriate anthropometric standards have been identified, any observed deficiency relative to those standards would certainly be an indication of undernutrition. But the problem consists in the fact that the converse is not necessarily true, i.e. adequate anthropometric status does not ensure that a person is well nourished. Recall that the body needs energy both for maintaining its internal functions and to undertake physical activity in the external environment. If the available energy is less than minimum requirement, then the body has two options: either to reduce body size below the minimum desirable level or to reduce physical activity. (Of course, some combination of the two is also possible.) If the first option is chosen, we shall observe the outcome as an anthropometric shortfall. But if only the second option is chosen, anthropometric status will be maintained at a satisfactory level. Yet we must say that the person is undernourished for the simple reason that the energy available to his body was not enough to meet the minimum requirements for maintaining both his body and his physical activity at the stipulated levels.

The anthropometric approach is thus intrinsically incapable of measuring the complete set of undernourished people.[26] What it ideally measures can be called *physiological dysfunction*.

The dietary approach too yields an incomplete measurement, but in a different sort of way. Recall that dietary standards are usually set up with reference to either Western populations or laboratory subjects who happen to live in a near-ideal condition of environmental hygiene. Most people in the developing world however live in poor hygienic conditions and are much more susceptible to infections and disease, which is now being recognized to have a most profound effect on nutritional status.[27] Some researchers even tend to accord a greater role to environmental hygiene compared to access to food in explaining the present state of undernutrition in the developing world (Mata 1978).

In general, infection may precipitate undernutrition by affecting both intake and requirement of food. Anorexia (loss of appetite) is the principal mechanism through which infections and disease reduce the intake of food; some cultural practices also play a contributory part in reducing the food allocation for a child when it is taken ill. Mata (1978) has shown in a celebrated study of

<hr>

[26] This has been one of the recurring themes of Beaton's recent writings on nutritional measurement. See Beaton (1983, 1985).

[27] For a description of the mechanisms through which infection may affect nutrition, see Beisel *et al.* (1967), Scrimshaw *et al.* (1968), Mata (1975), Beisel (1977), Scrimshaw (1977), and Chen and Scrimshaw (1983), among others.

the children of Santa Maria Cauqué (in Guatemala) that it is the reduced food intake due to illness that explains most of the nutritional deficiency.

Requirement on the other hand is affected in a number of ways. Firstly, malabsorption of food, especially in diarrhoeal diseases, through either vomiting or increased fecal and urinary losses, reduces the effective utilization of food. Secondly, parasitic elements thriving in the gastro-intestinal tract claim a share of the food and reduce the amount available to the body.[28] Thirdly, requirement is increased directly because of increased tissue catabolism and diversion of energy for the production of various host-protective factors.

Now in so far as infection affects actual food intake, the dietary approach can in principle take note of it, and the assumption of ideal environment does not make any difference. But not so in the case of requirement; here it does make a difference. The worse the environment (i.e. the greater the frequency and severity of infection), the greater is the need for energy.[29] Consequently, the usual dietary standards necessarily underestimate the energy requirement appropriate for the prevailing conditions in the developing world. People who are consuming adequate food according to these standards may still be undernourished, because their actual requirement may be higher due to poor environmental hygiene. The dietary approach is thus incapable of capturing the full set of undernourished people.

If should be noted, however, that unlike the limitation of the anthropometric approach this limitation is not intrinsic to dietary measurement. For after all what stops us from devising requirement standards appropriate to the environmental condition of each region or country in the world? In principle of course this can be done, but there are very serious practical problems. The difficulty consists in the fact that people do not live in a similar environment even in a small locality, not to speak of country or region. This diversity cannot be glossed over, because even the interhousehold differences in microenvironment can make enormous differences in susceptibility to infection. The need to take note of this diversity creates two kinds of informational problem.

First, we shall have to know a great deal about each household's or person's microenvironment. This is no simple task, especially because the relevant environment is not defined by a single factor but by a multitude of factors (such as water supply, housing, sanitation, etc.) many of which are not even easily quantifiable.

Secondly, we shall be required to quantify on the one hand the relationship between environmental quality and the risk of infection, and on the other the

---

[28] In a sense, the effect of the first two factors can be seen either as reduced effective intake or as increased requirement. But since dietary intake is recorded at the level of ingestion rather than absorption, it is proper to view it as increased requirement specially in the context of dietary measurement of undernutrition.

[29] This does not however mean that supplying additional energy is necessarily the best strategy for dealing with poor environmental hygiene. The question of *strategy* will be discussed in the next section. Here we are concerned with the *assessment* of deficiency in a given environment.

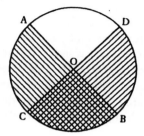

Fig. 8.1. Relationship between dietary and anthropometric measurements

relationship between degrees of infection and nutritional requirement. The present state of knowledge is woefully inadequate to permit any of these quantifications with any reasonable degree of confidence.

Therefore for all practical purposes the dietary standards must assume, for at least some time to come, an ideal level of environmental quality, and hence must fail to measure undernutrition in its entirety.[30]

It is thus clear that both anthropometric and dietary approaches would fail to measure undernutrition completely even if all the adaptationist arguments were resolved. But it is important to note that each fails in a rather different way. In fact, the failure of one happens to be the strong point of the other. Thus, while anthropometry fails to capture undernutrition when it is manifested in reduced activity, dietary approach can capture it quite successfully. For the latter is concerned only with the imbalance between need and intake; and how the imbalance is manifested does not make any difference to it. On the other hand, the failure of dietary approach to deal with a variety of microenvironments is no problem for anthropometry at all. Whatever the environment in which a person lives, if the food intake in the given environment leads to physical undernutrition, anthropometry can (ideally) capture it.

In a sense, therefore, the dietary and anthropometric approaches are complementary to each other. But unfortunately it does not follow that, when used in tandem, they will together provide the correct picture. For, firstly there is likely to be a partial overlap of unknown magnitude, and secondly there is one part of the undernutrition set which is out of reach for both approaches. These relationships can be shown schematically by Fig. 8.1.

The full set of undernutrition is shown by the area within the circle ACBD. Whatever the microenvironment of a person, if his intake is less than the requirement for that environment, he belongs to this set, regardless of whether the actual outcome is suboptimal body weight or suboptimal activity. The dietary approach misses out those whose intake is enough for the chosen level

---

[30] Some pioneering attempts are being made under the auspices of the United Nations University to develop dietary standards appropriate to the actual conditions of developing countries, but there is still a long way to go. See Turun *et al.* (1981) and Rand *et al.* (1984).

of environmental quality, but not enough for their particular environments. Let such people belong to the subset ADB, so that the subset actually captured by dietary approach can be represented by the area ACB. On the other hand, the subset captured by anthropometry is shown by the area DBC. These are the people whose energy deficiency relative to their respective environments has led to physical undernutrition, with or without accompanying reduction in activity. The overlapping area COB represents those whose intake is not enough even for the ideal environment and the resulting deficiency is manifest in physical undernutrition.

The out-of-reach area is shown by AOD. The situation here is the exact reverse of the overlapping area COB. Here the people have enough intake for an ideal environment, but not enough for their actual environment (hence out of reach of the dietary approach), and the resulting imbalance has been manifested entirely in reduced activity (hence out of reach of the anthropometric approach).

A matter of definition?

When we claim that neither the dietary nor the anthropometric approach can measure undernutrition fully, we are taking what we believe to be a widely accepted notion of undernutrition. This notion is characterized by its exclusive focus on the quantitative relationship between needs and intake. Neither the genesis nor the particular outcome of this relationship matters in defining a person as undernourished.[31] That is why we call a person undernourished when infection creates deficiency by raising his requirement, even though he may be apparently eating well. Similarly, if the outcome of deficiency turns out to be reduced activity rather than reduced body size, we still call him undernourished.

In contrast to this all-embracing notion of undernutrition, Payne and his colleagues have recently been arguing for a more restrictive concept. Although they present it as a matter of definition, we wish to get the matter straight, firstly because the subject-matter is already confusing enough without the help of different meanings being attached to the same name, but especially because the proponents seem often to mix up definitional issues with matters of substance.

One of the recurring themes in Pacey and Payne (1984) is the advocacy of the idea that undernutrition occurs only when the outcome of deficiency is manifest in some physiological dysfunction; the level of activity has nothing to do with it. Thus they quote approvingly from Jelliffe (1966: 8) who defined malnutrition as a state of nutritional imbalance that is '. . . clinically manifested, and detected *only* by biochemical, anthropometric or physiological tests' (emphasis added).

---

[31] But of course it is extremely important to know about both genesis and outcome, if only because they do matter in policy formulation. More on this in s. 8.4.

It should be noted however that Jelliffe was giving a general definition of malnutrition arising from deficiency of any of the essential nutrients, not just of energy. Moreover he was writing in an era when nutrients other than energy were of primary concern.[32] In that context, his definition had some obvious merit. All the nutrients, other than energy, are needed by the body for functions *within* the body. Naturally, deficiency in these nutrients will be necessarily manifested in some internal disorder. But not so in the case of energy. As Beaton (1985) pointedly reminds us, energy has the unique feature that, unlike other nutrients, it supports both internal and external work. Deficient energy can therefore cause either internal or external dysfunction. Accordingly, the same functional concept of undernutrition that focuses exclusively on physiological dysfunction in the context of other nutrients should take into account both internal and external function in the case of energy. It is interesting to note that Pacey and Payne fully condone the functional concept of undernutrition. Yet when they talk of function they only mean internal function. This is patently inconsistent with a truly functional concept of undernutrition.

Pacey and Payne seem to claim that their restricted definition follows from the adaptationist view of nutrition. This is where definition gets mixed up with matters of substance. Note first of all that they take a much broader view of adaptation than most other people who bring the idea of adaptation to bear upon the criterion of undernutrition. Sukhatme, for instance, is interested primarily in adaptation in energy efficiency, and Seckler in physical growth. But Pacey and Payne talk about a 'total strategy of adaptive responses' which 'comprises individual and social changes in behaviour as well as changes in bodyweight, body composition and metabolic regulation' (p. 63). A person is said to become undernourished only when all these adaptive mechanisms get exhausted.

Of particular interest here is the idea of adaptation through 'individual and social changes in behaviour' which essentially means reducing the level of physical activity. Now if this particular adaptive mechanism gets exhausted (i.e. comes down to zero) and energy deficiency still persists, then obviously there is no option but to suffer from physiological dysfunction. In this sense the choice of physiological dysfunction as the exclusive criterion of undernutrition would seem to follow from the notion of 'total adaptation'. In fact, Pacey and Payne make this logic quite explicit while explaining their choice of a dietary criterion of undernutrition. In general, they do not have much faith in the dietary criteria at all, but if a choice has to be made they would prefer the cut-off point of 1.2 BMR used by FAO (1977).[33] Now the interesting point

---

[32] The realization that energy deficiency is the most serious aspect of the nutritional problem in the developing world is a relatively recent phenomenon. See e.g. McLaren (1974).

[33] Actually, Payne's advice was influential in persuading FAO to use this criterion in the first place.

about this cut-off point is that it does not allow for any physical activity. It is based on the notion of 'maintenance requirement' which is placed at 1.5 BMR and is deemed to be just adequate to maintain body weight when a person is doing nothing more than eating and sleeping. After allowing for adaptation in metabolic efficiency, the critical limit is then set at 1.2 BMR (i.e. two standard deviations below 1.5 BMR). Pacey and Payne call it the 'absolute limit of adaptation' and count as undernourished only those whose intake falls below this limit. Obviously, all such people would suffer from physiological dysfunction even after they have 'adapted' their activity down to zero.

But is it right that the 'adaptationist' view should lead to a definition of requirement which assumes a zero level of activity? Recall that what is relevant for defining a requirement standard is not just any form of adaptation but only those which do not entail any functional cost. Thus Sukhatme proposed to bring down requirement because adaptation of efficiency, in his view, allowed a person to reduce his intake without incurring any functional cost. One can similarly argue that activity can be adapted down to a certain extent without any cost. But unless one makes the absurd suggestion that it can be driven down to zero without any cost, one must define requirement with reference to some positive level of activity. One will then have to recognize that deficient energy can lead to either internal disorder or reduced activity. Naturally, it will then be quite wrong to define undernutrition exclusively in terms of physiological dysfunction.

Elsewhere, Payne and Cutler (1984) seem to concede this point by using the term 'social cost malnutrition' to describe the situation where deficient energy leads to unacceptable reduction in activity. But they are still opposed to the use of a dietary criterion incorporating a positive level of activity. Their argument is that such a criterion will fail to distinguish those whose low activity is due to energy constraint from those whose activity as well as intake are constrained by external factors such as employment opportunity; and in their view it is only the former category that deserves to be called (social cost) malnourished.

There is indeed a problem here. But it has nothing to do with the principle of whether or not some positive level of activity ought to be chosen. It is rather a problem of how to choose an activity norm in a world of less than full employment. There are actually two possible options to choose from: either (1) to choose an activity level that is commensurate with the employment opportunity that is actually open to a person given the constraints on demand for labour, or (2) to choose a socially desirable level of activity commensurate with the kind of gainful employment that we would ideally like him to have. There are those, such as Beaton (1985), who would prefer the second option. In doing so, they of course recognize that low energy is not necessarily the limiting constraint on activity for all those who are found to have both low intake and low activity. But they still consider such people to be inadequately nourished, while Payne and Cutler refuse to do so. We believe that there is room for genuine disagreement here. But this is not germane to the issue at hand. If

Payne and Cutler insist on their particular notion of 'social cost malnutrition', all they have to do is to choose the first option of defining an activity norm. In no way does this justify the position that the criterion of undernutrition should altogether disregard the level of activity.

It is thus clear that undernutrition cannot be equated with physiological dysfunction either by invoking the adaptationist view of nutrition or by pointing to the difficulty of choosing an activity norm. The two can be equated only by definition. However, as we have argued, such a definition will not be fully consistent with the functional view of nutrition which Payne and his colleagues happen to expound.

Of course, the concept of physiological dysfunction is an important one in its own right, and it is certainly worthwhile to try and identify the set of people who are afflicted with this syndrome. What we object to is the attempt to reduce the concept of undernutrition to the narrower concept of physiological dysfunction.

8.4. Implications for economics: concepts and policies

In this section, we propose to piece together the preceding discussions on nutritional controversies and explore some of their implications for economics. Specifically, we shall try to assess the implications for the concept of poverty line (and the measurement of poverty), the assessment of capabilities, and the formulation of food and nutrition policies.[34]

Poverty line and the measurement of poverty

As is well known, the absolute poverty line is usually defined in relation to a norm of nutritional requirement, frequently of calories alone. Accordingly, a person is said to be absolutely poor if his income or diet is inadequate to achieve the desired norm of calorie requirement. The measurement of poverty is thus closely linked to the dietary measurement of undernutrition. We shall presently, see that they are not necessarily the same thing, but the linkage is obvious enough. We shall therefore proceed by first noting the problems in the measurement of undernutrition as such, and then explore the implications for the measurement of poverty.

Our discussion in the preceding sections suggests that the use of an 'average' calorie norm for the dietary measurement of undernutrition has to contend with three major difficulties:

1. The use of an average norm is unjustified if one allows for adaptive intraindividual variation in requirement. We have seen in section 8.2 that the particular adaptive mechanism of variable metabolic efficiency (à la Sukhatme

---

[34] The implications for yet another aspect of economics, namely the positive theory of labour market, have recently been explored by Dasgupta and Ray (1987).

Mark II) is not borne out by scientific evidence. But it is not quite so easy to dismiss the possibility of intraindividual variation in requirement arising from adaptation in the rate of physical growth (à la Seckler).[35]

2. The use of 'average' cannot allow for interindividual variation in requirement arising from genetic differences. Note that such variation will continue to exist even if we allow for intraindividual adaptation in defining the requirement norm. The allowance for adaptation simply means that the requirement norm is to be set at the lower end of the range of adaptation. But the range of adaptation can vary interpersonally due to genetic differences, thus leading to interindividual variation in requirement.

3. The existing requirement standards are based on ideal environmental conditions, and are hence inappropriate for those whose requirement is increased by poor environmental hygiene (see section 8.3).

All three problems lead to a common consequence, namely the misclassification of the undernourished. The first problem leads to the error of overestimation because if requirement adapts intraindividually, then the appropriate criterion of undernutrition is the minimum and not the average of the range of adaptation. The third problem on the other hand creates the opposite error of underestimation; many undernourished people living in a poor environment will not be classified as such because their intake, while being inadequate for their own environment, may be high enough in relation to an ideal environment. The second problem also creates a problem of misclassification, but the direction of bias is indeterminate in this case. If different people have different requirements, then some of those classified as undernourished by the criterion of average requirement will not actually be so, while some of the truly undernourished will not be classified as such.[36] Whether the net effect will be overestimation or underestimation, or whether the biases will cancel each other out, cannot be predicted a priori.[37]

What does this problem of misclassification imply for the measurement of poverty when the same 'average norm' is used to determine the poverty line? Clearly it implies that the set of the poor, defined with reference to such a

---

[35] This follows from the observation that the *causal* interpretation of the 'small but healthy' hypothesis cannot be refuted in the light of existing evidence (s. 8.2).

[36] The various expert committees which calculated the recommended dietary allowances were always aware of these possible errors and explicitly warned against using the average norm as the criterion for assessing undernutrition. The use of an average, in their view, lay in the assessment of aggregate food deficiency and in planning overall food supply. See Hegsted (1972).

[37] While using the average norm, Reutlinger and Selowsky (1976) had expressed the hope that the biases would offset each other. But Srinivasan (1981: 10) and Lipton (1983: 27) later conjectured that overestimation is the more likely outcome. Kakwani (1986: 10) has recently provided a formal proof of this conjecture for the typical case where average requirement is higher than the mode of intake distribution. But the result is valid only for the special case of zero correlation between intake and requirement. Once the existence of correlation is acknowledged, the direction of bias can be shown to be indeterminate. See the results of simulation in Kakwani (1986: 57).

poverty line, will not in general be identical to the set of the undernourished.

Note that in the actual estimation of poverty, the divergence between the poor and the undernourished can arise from yet another source. It has to do with the usual practice that the poverty line is defined, not as the calorie norm itself, but as an income (or expenditure) level that would satisfy this norm. Now the problem arises from the fact that income and calorie intake are not monotonically related across individuals; what one actually uses in practice is an average relationship between income and intake. But the lack of monotonicity implies that having an income above the poverty line is no guarantee that calorie intake too will be above the required level. Similarly, having an income below the poverty line does not indicate that calorie intake is actually deficient. Thus, once again, there arises a divergence between the poor and the undernourished. This was in fact one of Rao's (1977, 1981) criticisms of Dandekar and Rath's (1971) estimation of poverty in India.[38]

But how damaging is this problem of divergence, from whichever source it may arise? Does this invalidate the traditional way of measuring poverty? We shall argue that the answer depends, not surprisingly, on how one perceives the conceptual foundations of poverty.

Consider the general concept of living standard, of which poverty is merely one end of the spectrum. As Sen (1984a) has recently argued, the concept of living standard can be interpreted in at least three different ways: in terms of either utility, opulence, or capability. Of the three, the last two interpretations are particularly relevant in the present context. In the opulence approach, the focus is on the commodity bundle a person happens to enjoy; he is said to be more opulent with a bundle x than with y if he prefers x to y.[39] In the capability approach on the other hand, the focus goes beyond the commodity bundle and looks at the way the possession of commodities enables a person to carry out various functions; if the bundle x gives him a greater capability to function than does y, his living standard is said to be higher with x than with y.

Poverty then can be interpreted as either the lack of opulence or the lack of capability, 'lack' being defined in either case as shortfall from a chosen standard. Also, in both cases, the chosen standard may be linked to a norm of nutritional requirement. However, the appropriate norm may not be the same in both cases. This is a consequence of the fact that a shortfall from the norm (i.e. poverty) would have different connotations in the two cases (functional impairment in one case and undesirable commodity status in the other), and

---

[38] Sukhatme (1978: 1383) also notes this problem, but he attributes it wrongly to the neglect of intraindividual variation in requirement. Actually, variation in requirement has nothing to do with this particular problem. Even if there were no inter- or intravariation in requirement, misclassification would still arise from the use of an income standard simply because of the lack of monotonicity between income and calorie.

[39] Despite an apparent similarity, this is not the same thing as evaluation of utility; at best it can be thought of as evaluation of *the commodity basis* of utility. For a lucid exposition of the subtle but fundamental difference between the two, see Sen (1984).

the norms should be such as to permit the respective connotations. This observation has crucial implications for the relevance of nutritional problems in the measurement of poverty.

In particular, it implies that 'average' requirement need not be an inappropriate norm for the measurement of poverty from the opulence perspective, even though it may create serious problems in the measurement of undernutrition. This is so for the simple reason that poverty in the opulence perspective need not entail any functional impairment, only a 'less preferred commodity bundle' compared to the one associated with the chosen nutritional standard. Consequently, while one may accept that the 'average norm' approach to the measurement of poverty will fail to capture the truly undernourished people, that in itself will not constitute a case for rejecting this approach. As a matter of fact, arguments based implicitly on the opulence view have frequently been put forward to defend the traditional way of measuring poverty against criticisms arising out of the recent nutrition debate.

Consider for instance the problem created by the lack of monotonicity between income and calorie. Dandekar (1981) is aware that in assuming away this problem through the use of an average relationship between income and calorie, his poverty line income implicitly assumes an average standard of household management. Accordingly, he recognizes that some of the poor may be able to satisfy their calorie needs by a better than average standard of household management, while some of the non-poor may fail to do so through poor management. But that does not worry him, because poverty for him is not the phenomenon of a household actually failing to meet calorie needs, but of living '. . . on *such levels of consumer expenditure* that *judged by average standards of household management*, it could not provide for itself diet adequate even in terms of calories' (p. 1243; emphasis added). Here the concern is clearly with opulence or the lack of it, not with nutrition as such.

A similar argument has been made by Sen (1980) in response to the problem created by interindividual variation in requirement. He argues that 'Malnutrition can provide *basis* for a standard of poverty without poverty being identified as the extent of malnutrition. The level of income at which an average person will be able to meet his nutritional requirements has a claim to being considered as an appropriate poverty line even when it is explicitly recognised that nutritional requirements vary interpersonally around the mean.' Clearly, poverty defined in this way will not reflect the extent of undernutrition, but it will enlighten us 'on an income deprivation related to some average standard'. Like Dandekar, Sen is taking here the opulence view of poverty.

The remaining two problems, i.e. those due to intraindividual adaptation in requirement and to variation in environmental hygiene, can also be dealt with in a similar manner. One only has to define the poverty line as a point in the scale of opulence which in an ideal condition of environmental hygiene will just satisfy average calorie requirement under average household management and without obliging a person to take recourse to his adaptive capacity. There is then in principle nothing wrong in accepting the usual figures of calorie requirement as the basis of a reference standard. Poverty is now simply defined as *income deprivation* in relation to this standard. Obviously, income deprivation in this sense may or may not reflect nutritional deprivation, and conversely nutritional deprivation may occur even when income deprivation does not. But that need not worry us when we take the opulence view of poverty.

One may however ask: is opulence or the lack of it the most appealing interpretation of poverty? Sen (1983) has in fact argued convincingly that capability rather than opulence can claim to be a more natural interpretation of poverty. It is after all the notion that poverty consists in the lack of some basic capabilities that gives it an absolutist core and makes it different from relative inequality. Therefore, if we are interested in measuring absolute poverty, it would seem natural to measure it on the scale of capabilities. From this perspective, we can no longer view the divergence between poverty and undernutrition with the same equanimity which we could afford in the opulence perspective. For, when one uses the yardstick of nutritional capability, the content of poverty is nothing other than undernutrition. Of course, one could wish to take a much broader view of poverty, covering more than nutritional capability. In that case, a person could be poor without being undernourished. But an undernourished person must be considered poor, as long as the lack of nutritional capability remains one of the defining criteria of poverty.[40] The problem of misclassifying the undernourished then becomes a matter of concern.

Naturally, the traditional way of measuring poverty on the basis of 'average norm' will no longer do. We shall have to face all the problems of measuring undernutrition that we mentioned earlier. Serious problems of empirical estimation will arise in the process. But, the principles of an appropriate methodology can be easily described.

Firstly, the problem of lack of monotonicity between income and calorie may be tackled by abandoning the intermediation of an income standard and comparing actual calorie intakes directly with the required level.

Secondly, intraindividual adaptation in requirement can be taken care of by setting the requirement norm at the lower end of the range of adaptation. The practical problem, however, is that the range of adaptation is not yet known with any reasonable degree of confidence.

The remaining problems of interpersonal variation in requirement due to

---

[40] Strictly speaking, one can still draw a distinction between poverty and undernutrition in so far as there is a distinction between the *capability to be nourished* and being *actually nourished*. Sen (1984a) makes the point starkly by giving the example of an ascetic who might choose to fast and become undernourished despite his being rich and having the means of being excellently nourished. In most cases, however, people will be undernourished not because they choose to be so, but because they are constrained to be so. For all practical purposes, therefore, the capability view of poverty (in the nutritional dimension) can be identified with the concept of undernutrition.

genetic differences as well as different environmental conditions are much more difficult to handle. As we have noted earlier the use of an average, or any other single, figure of requirement will fail to identify correctly those who are actually unable to meet their respective requirements. Technically, the solution lies in evaluating a joint probability distribution of intake and requirement, which in simple terms means counting how many people have intakes below their respective requirements. This approach has sometimes been used for measuring the extent of nutritional deficiency (e.g. Reutlinger and Alderman 1980). But is suffers from serious informational constraints. Basically, four types of information are needed for its application: the parameters of the intake distribution function, the parameters of the requirement distribution function, the correlation between intake and requirement, and finally the functional forms of intake and requirement distributions. Among these, information on intake distribution is perhaps the easiest to obtain, although that too can pose serious problems when it comes to individual as distinct from household distribution. Something is also known about the mean and variance of requirement distribution arising from genetic differences; but these relate primarily to ideal environmental conditions. The nature and extent of variation due to different environmental hygiene are as yet in the realm of unknown. So too are the parameters of correlation between intake and requirement, and the functional form of requirement distribution. Useful insights can be gained by simulating with different values of parameters and different functional forms, as Kakwani (1986) has done with Indian data. But the main stumbling block remains the almost complete lack of knowledge about the differences in environmental hygiene which people actually experience and the variation in requirement arising from that.

On the whole then, one may conclude that the measurement of poverty in the sense of capability is faced not so much with conceptual problems as with informational constraints, but with constraints that would appear to be well-nigh impossible to overcome in our existing state of knowledge. This is however an argument not for abandoning the capability concept of poverty, but for strengthening our efforts to elicit the required information.

Assessment of capability

The concept of capability is of course of interest in itself, not merely as a basis of poverty. In comparison of welfare between population groups, capability has a claim to be the essence and the measure of welfare.[41] From this perspective, the issues relating to the assessment of nutritional capability are of direct concern to the welfare economist.

We have already noted some of the problems of assessment in the context of measuring poverty from the capability perspective. Many of the problems in

---

[41] Sen (1985) has argued forcefully for accepting capability as the conceptual basis of social welfare in preference to alternative bases such as utility or opulence.

fact arose from the fact that the assessment was being done indirectly through a comparison between intake and requirement, and this was rendered difficult by the variation of requirement across individuals. But this particular problem does not arise when capability is assessed directly. Whatever the nutrient requirements may be, and however they may vary, the relationship between intake and requirement will be revealed in capabilities. If we can measure capabilities, we need not worry about requirements, nor for that matter about intakes.

However, the measurement of capability is not all that simple. As we have seen, nutritional capabilities can span several dimensions, e.g. immunocompetence, physical work capacity, cognitive skill, etc. Assessment of these functions demands a great deal of time, expertise, and resources. When large population groups are involved, the exercise may become practically infeasible. But we have also seen that anthropometry is often used as a convenient short-cut, especially in the case of children, on the assumption that the achievement of physical growth is a reliable indicator of functional achievement. In his pioneering attempts to apply the concept of capability in actual comparisons of welfare, Sen too has sometimes used anthropometry as an indicator of nutritional capability, and has actually expressed a preference for anthropometry over the intake-requirement approach.[42] This preference is of course understandable in view of the problems with the latter approach discussed earlier. But our discussion in sections 8.2 and 8.3 suggests that there are good reasons to be wary about the anthropometric approach too.

In the first place, any attempt to use anthropometry as an indicator of welfare will have to contend with the homeostatic theory of growth, the so-called 'small but healthy' hypothesis. What this theory does is to challenge the assumption of a monotonically increasing relationship between anthropometry and nutritional capabilities and to suggest instead that capabilities remain invariant within a range of anthropometry. We have seen (in section 8.2) that there is a lot of force in this proposition when interpreted in a causal sense, i.e. it seems quite plausible that moderate stunting within a certain range may not *cause* any impairment of functional capabilities. However, we have also seen that within this range, lower anthropometry may well be *associated* with a lower level of one particular type of nutritional capability, namely cognitive skill. Consequently, while one cannot assume a monotonically increasing relationship, neither can one be sure that all capabilities will actually remain invariant within the specified range. One would not therefore be able to ascertain what really is the status of nutritional capabilities within the range of causal invariance. This does obviously create a problem in using anthropometry for the assessment of nutritional capability.

One way of getting around this problem would appear to lie in using

[42] As, for instance, in exploring the issue of sex bias in the allocation of household resources. See Sen (1988) and Sen and Sengupta (1983).

anthropometry as an index of general capabilities, incorporating nutritional capability but going beyond it. It is generally agreed that whether or not a stunted child lacks any nutritional capability, he is certainly more deprived in a general sense compared to a normal child. If he were not in fact more deprived in terms of food and environmental status he would not have been stunted in the first place. That is why even those who question the use of traditional anthropometric standards for the assessment of nutritional status do not hesitate to add that anthropometry is nevertheless one of the most reliable indicators of general social deprivation (Goldstein and Tanner 1980; Dowler et al. 1982). In terms of capabilities it means that whatever the status of nutritional capability, a stunted child is most likely to lack other capabilities associated with food and environmental quality.[43] Therefore, regardless of whether the 'small but healthy' hypothesis is valid or not (either in the causative or the associative sense), an economist would appear to be right in using anthropometry as long as he is aware that he is assessing a much broader range of capabilities than those associated with nutrition alone.[44] Except, that is, for one problem.

The idea of taking the route of general capabilities was to ensure that an overall monotonic relationship could be postulated between anthropometry and capability even though the same could not be done for the nutritional capabilities as such. This strategy will work as long as each type of capability is either monotonically increasing or invariant with anthropometry, and at least some capabilities are strictly monotonically increasing (as the non-nutritional capabilities are expected to be). But a problem will arise if some of the capabilities turn out to be inversely associated with anthropometric achievement. Paradoxical as it may seem, this is indeed possible in respect of some nutritional capabilities. This becomes clear as soon as one recognizes the possibility of a trade-off between physical growth and physical activity (section 8.3).

Consider two children of the same genotype living in the same condition of adverse 'food and environmental status'. They are obviously facing the same nutritional stress, but each may respond differently by choosing a different combination of physical retardation and activity reduction. Assume that one of them has become physically retarded by maintaining a high level of activity, while the other has avoided physical retardation by reducing activity. A

[43] Food, for instance, can be used, in addition to yielding nutrition, 'to give eating pleasure and to provide support for social meetings' (Sen 1985: 9).

[44] The implication of this distinction between nutritional and general capabilities has not always been correctly understood. Thus, for example, Gopalan (1983a), Beaton (1985), Martorell (1985), and several others have used the argument of general deprivation to dispose of the 'small but healthy' hypothesis. As Beaton explains his position: 'not because small is bad in itself, it is deprivation that is harmful' (p. 230). But surely being deprived in terms of general capabilities is not the same thing as being 'unhealthy'. The argument of general deprivation could be brought against a hypothesis like 'small but well-off' which no one proposes; but in order to question the 'small but healthy' hypothesis the battle must be fought on the plane of nutritional capabilities alone.

striking example of the latter possibility was provided by Rutishauser and Whitehead (1972) who described a Ugandan child population in which physical growth was maintained at reasonable levels in the face of an apparent low intake; and 'further examination of the community suggested that one way in which this was achieved was by a very low level of activity, play' (Beaton 1983: 11).

Clearly, anthropometry would be a misleading indicator of capability in this case. Considering nutritional capability first, the child with 'high anthropometry, low activity' is more likely to suffer from cognitive retardation. Moreover, quite apart from its effect on cognition, the 'capability to play' may be valued in itself; and in that regard too he would be suffering a greater loss of nutritional capability. Thus even though his physiological functions may happen to be superior by virtue of a better physical stature, nothing can be said about his overall nutritional capability without introducing relative value weightings for different functions. As for non-nutritional capabilities, there is no reason for the two children to fare differently since by assumption they belong to the same 'food and environmental status'.

It is thus clear that anthropometry by itself would be a poor indicator of capabilities. It will generally be necessary to obtain additional information on the activity patterns of the populations concerned.

Food and nutrition policy

Arguments over the presumed policy implications of differing views on nutrition have aroused a great deal of passion in recent years. Much of it however has been sadly misplaced and many false battles have been fought, although, as we shall see, there are also some useful lessons to be learnt from all this.

Most of the controversies have centred around the implications of 'adaptationist' views, with both sides of the camp often hitting out against the wrong target. A more substantive debate has sprung from the realization that the genesis of undernutrition is a much more complex phenomenon than was traditionally thought; but this too has got mixed up with the adaptationist debate. The issues covered in the process can be divided up into two broad categories, namely (1) whether the adaptationist view warrants any diminution in the policy concern with poverty and (2) what should be the content of policy for different groups of population. The first issue has generated an entirely false debate, while the second contains elements of both false and genuine claims.

One of the reasons why the debate over adaptation has generated so much heat is the fear that by showing the magnitude of malnutrition and poverty to be much less than what it is believed to be, the adaptationists might encourage a potentially dangerous complacence on the policy front. A typical expression of this fear can be found in Zurbrigg's (1983) statement that 'Sukhatme's argument can lead to politically expedient redefinition of poverty' (p. 2083). Now, politicians do of course manipulate academic ideas if they find it expedient to do so. But ideas must be judged on their own merit; and in this particular case they do not logically warrant the kind of fears expressed.

The adaptationists have generally been careful in drawing a distinction between nutritional poverty (i.e. undernutrition caused by poverty) and general socio-economic poverty. A person who has adapted to a low level of intake may have avoided nutritional poverty; but in doing so he does not become non-poor in a general sense, for it is his general poverty that has forced him to adapt in the first place.[45] In other words, the necessity of adapting is itself an indication of poverty. By this criterion, Sukhatme reckons that most of the people in rural India could be counted as poor, although undernutrition due to poverty may be no more than 15–20 per cent (Sukhatme 1982c: 248).[46] One may disagree with the second part of the statement (in view of our discussion in section 8.2), but there is certainly nothing in it to encourage a complacent view of poverty.

Similar confusion has surrounded the views of Seckler. Because he considers the stunted children to be 'healthy', he has often been interpreted to imply that stunting is not a matter of policy concern. Thus Martorell (1985: 25) interprets him as arguing that 'planners should concern themselves with wasting and not with stunting'; and Gopalan (1983b: 34) raises the alarm that to accept Seckler's views 'is to acquiesce (however unwittingly) in the preservation of the status quo of poverty, ill-health, undernutrition and socio-economic deprivation'. Once again, what the critics fail to notice is the distinction between undernutrition and general deprivation that the adaptationists are trying to highlight. Seckler (1984a) in fact states quite categorically that whether or not we call the stunted children undernourished, the fact that they have been forced to become small indicates that they are generally deprived; and as such they are certainly a cause for policy concern.

Encouraging complacence on the policy front would therefore hardly seem to be a necessary consequence of the views espoused by the adaptationists. However, they do claim that the adaptationist perspective calls for certain reorientations in the content of policy. We shall argue that some of the suggested reorientations are indeed deserving of serious consideration, but their merit in no way depends on the scientific validity of the adaptationist perspective.

Three specific issues have figured prominently in this context: (1) prioritization, (2) identifying a target group for feeding programmes, and (3) relative emphasis on food versus non-food policies.

[45] In view of our discussion earlier in this section, this position would imply either the acceptance of the opulence view of poverty, or the adoption of a broad-based capability view incorporating a wider range of capabilities than those associated with nutrition alone.

[46] By the same token, Sukhatme (1982c) also questions the usefulness of the traditional dietary approach for the measurement of poverty (quite apart from questioning its usefulness for the measurement of undernutrition). In doing so, he is implicitly adopting the 'broad-based' capability view of poverty.

1. *Prioritization*. One of the recurring themes running through the writings of all the leading adaptationists, such as Sukhatme, Seckler, and Payne, is the claim that the acceptance of their view will lead to a more equitable allocation of resources. The argument runs briefly as follows: those who have successfully adapted are indeed deprived, but those who have failed to adapt and become undernourished are even more so. Thus the people identified as 'truly under-nourished' by their criterion would usually belong to the neediest section of the population; by identifying them, one is helping to channel scarce food and other resources to those who need them most. By implication, it is suggested that the non-adaptationist view does not make any distinction between degrees of need and is not concerned with priorities. This point is in fact made most explicitly by Payne and Cutler (1984) who claim that in the genetic potential theory, as in Paretian neo-classical economics, one is not concerned with whether the benefit goes to the severest or the least severe cases of deprivation as long as somebody benefits without worsening anyone else's condition.[47]

This is clearly a rather curious argument. The desire to concentrate on the most deprived cases has nothing to do with the nutritional phenomenon of adaptation. It arises simply from the value judgement that the gain of the neediest should be valued most. A devout non-adaptationist can equally hold this value judgement and may decide to give top priority to those farthest from the genetical potential even though he may believe that anyone below the potential is undernourished to some extent. Obviously, the difference in nutritional perspective need not entail any difference in policy as far as ranking of priorities is concerned.

2. Identifying a *target group for feeding programmes*. It has also been suggested that 'adaptation' makes certain types of policies unsuitable for certain categories of people. The criticism has mainly centred on the nutrition intervention policies such as supplementary feeding programmes which have traditionally enjoyed a great deal of support from the nutritionists. It has been argued from the perspective of the 'small but healthy' hypothesis that such feeding programmes are inappropriate for the purely stunted children. The argument can be summed up as follows. Since the moderately stunted children do not have any obvious nutritional disability, additional food will do them no good. In fact, if one catches them late in their childhood when the scope for catch-up growth is practically nil, supplementary feeding will only serve to make them obese.[48] If caught early, they may of course get out of the stunted growth path and get back to normal growth; but in order to keep them there,

---

[47] Elsewhere, Pacey and Payne (1984) take the precaution of pointing out that this is not a necessary implication of the genetic potential model, but that it could be interpreted in this way by unscrupulous policy makers. This is of course sheer polemics. But if one wants to play the game, one should also face the retort that the unscrupulous policy makers can misinterpret the adaptationist model too to feel complacent about the 'adapted'.

[48] A recent review by Beaton and Ghassemi (1982) shows that supplementary feeding of school-age children has seldom resulted in any objective signs of nutritional improvement.

either the feeding programmes will have to continue until adulthood which they seldom do, or one will have to do something about the basic socio-economic deprivation which produced stunting in the first place. It is therefore suggested that feeding programmes should be targeted primarily towards the 'wasted' children (or the severely stunted ones showing clinical lesions), and the problem of moderate stunting should be tackled through broader socio-economic policies which can strike at the root of poverty.

We believe there is a great deal of sense in this proposition. But one does not have to believe in the 'small but healthy' hypothesis in order to appreciate it. As we have noted earlier (section 8.2), a child which has achieved equilibrium with his environment through stunting can be said to have successfully avoided the evils of wasting. If he is now 'unstunted' by temporary feeding and then thrown back to the original environment, he will achieve new equilibrium with his higher height only with a lower weight for height ratio, i.e. through wasting. Such acts of temporary feeding will be considered inappropriate if the original equilibrium is preferred to the new. But in order to have this preference it is not necessary to believe that only wasting is bad and stunting carries no evil; all that is needed is the undisputed proposition that wasting is a greater evil than stunting. Therefore, the wisdom of targeting feeding programmes primarily towards the wasted children should be equally visible from all perspectives.[49] It is however true that the inappropriateness of bringing stunted children into the network of feeding programmes has seldom been appreciated in designing actual programmes. This is reflected in the widespread use of the Gomez classification by weight for age, which as a selection criterion fails singularly to distinguish between wasting and stunting. Much more discerning criteria ought to be used if the feeding programmes are to reach the genuine target group.

3. *Food versus non-food policies.* Recent discussions on nutrition policy have frequently challenged the conventional wisdom that nutrition policy is basically about increasing access to food. In the emerging new perspective, non-food factors such as occupational pattern, environmental hygiene, etc. may be of equal if not greater importance than access to food.

As Pacey and Payne (1984) rightly point out, the constraint imposed on a mother's time by occupational patterns may be an important cause of child malnutrition in many poor societies. The nature of diet in poor societies is often such that the calorie content is very low in proportion to the bulk, so that a child has to be fed several times a day in order to ensure adequate calorie intake. A mother may not be able to maintain the required frequency, if occupational demand keeps her away from home for long periods of time. In that case, the child will either go unfed or will have to make do with food prepared in bulk early in the day. In the latter case, the food is likely to become infested with germs given the poor condition of environmental hygiene; and

---

[49] See e.g. the judgement of a leading non-adaptationist, Scrimshaw (1982: 103).

given the fact that a child is most vulnerable to infection during the weaning stage, he is very likely to fall victim to infection-induced undernutrition. Giving the household more food in this condition will not help much to save the child. More fundamental measures are needed that will remove the occupational constraint on the mother's time.

Similarly, emphasis has tended to shift away from access to food to access to better environmental quality (i.e. freedom from infection). We have seen in section 8.3 that infection can widen the divergence between intake and requirement by both restricting intake and increasing requirement. The traditional emphasis on access to food seeks to bridge the gap by acting on the intake side of the inequality. In contrast, the new perspective emphasizes the importance of tackling the problem from the requirement side (and also of relaxing the infection-constraint on food intake) through policies aimed at improving environmental hygiene. Clearly, the fight against infection is no less a nutrition policy than the struggle to ensure access to food. However, the relative importance of the two approaches has not always been judged on the basis of sound analysis. The adaptationists, for example, have been particularly forceful in advocating the case that nutrition policy should focus primarily on the environmental front, especially in countries like India where infection rather than food is in their view more of a limiting constraint. But it has not been appreciated that the choice of strategy does not simply follow from the nature of the limiting constraint. The general nature of the problem can be illustrated with the help of Fig. 8.2.

The combination of a person's food intake and the environment in which he lives is represented by a point in this diagram. Food intake is measured along the horizontal axis and the factors denoting environmental hygiene (and

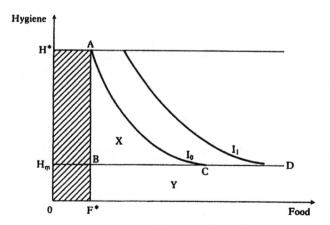

Fig. 8.2. Interaction between food and hygiene

somehow expressed as a composite index) are measured along the vertical axis. The curves I_0, I_1 etc. belong to a family of what may be called isonutrition contours. All points on a curve denote the same level of energy available to the body for its normal maintenance and external work, and hence the same nutritional status. The downward sloping segment of the curve signifies that as the non-food environment worsens more intake is required for providing the body with enough energy for normal maintenance and external work, after meeting the additional needs due to infections and disease. This captures the idea that energy requirement is increased when non-food environment worsens.

There are two critical points, H^* and H_m, on the vertical axis. H^* represents an ideal condition of environmental hygiene, so that the isonutrition contours are shown truncated from above at this point. The other point H_m represents such a poor state of hygiene that additional food intake beyond a certain level gets wasted and therefore cannot contribute to the improvement of nutritional status.[50] In other words, when an isonutrition contour gets below the point H_m it becomes horizontal at some stage.[51] It also means that if I_0 happens to be the highest contour to become horizontal, all the contours above it will approach $H_m D$ asymptotically.

Let I_0 also be the contour on which just enough energy is available to the body for maintaining body size and activity at the minimum desirable level. It can be described as the minimal desirable isonutrition contour which provides the basis for estimating food requirements at different levels of environmental hygiene.[52] Recall that the usual requirement standards refer to ideal hygiene, i.e. to a point like H^*. The corresponding food requirement is given by F^*, and the population identified as undernourished by this criterion will belong to the area $H^* O F^* A$. Obviously, actual undernutrition will be much more than this because, by definition of the minimal desirable isonutrition contour, any point to the left of or below I_0 indicates undernutrition. The special characteristic of the subset $H^* O F^* A$ is that, unlike the rest of the undernourished, these people face a limiting food constraint because their food intake is not enough even for an ideal environment. In fact, depending on the nature of the limiting constraint, the whole set of undernourished people can be split up into four subsets: (1) $H^* H_m BA$, (2) $H_m O F^* B$, (3) the area X which is below AC and bounded from below by the lines AB and BC, and (4) the area Y which is below BD and bounded from the left by the line BF_m.

---

[50] This may happen for instance in the case of acute diarrhoea when extra food will literally go down the drain, or in the presence of parasites which eat up a large share of the food.

[51] Presumably, the lower the contour, the lower will be the level of food intake at which it becomes horizontal.

[52] The particular curve I_0 is chosen for this purpose purely for the sake of diagrammatic simplicity. It can be easily checked that none of the arguments below will be altered in essence if any other curve either above or below I_0 were chosen.

As we have just noted, for the people belonging to H^*H_mBA, more food is a binding necessity; their undernutrition cannot be removed by exclusive reliance on environmental measures. Those belonging to the area Y on the other hand have such a wretched environment that no amount of extra food will help on its own; for them, improvement of health environment is an absolute necessity. For those belonging to H_mOF^*B, more food and better environment are both binding necessities, neither will suffice by itself. Finally, for those in the area X, there is no binding constraint; their problem can be solved either by acting on food or environment alone or through a combination of the two.

Now if one accepts that only a small proportion of the undernourished face a limiting food constraint, it would mean that those belonging to the subsets H^*H_mBA and H_mOF^*B (i.e. those identified as undernourished by the dietary criterion) are much fewer in number than those belonging to the other two subsets. But would that by itself indicate what strategy is optimal for the majority of the undernourished? Obviously not. Consider first the area X where there is clearly a trade-off between provision of food and improvement of hygiene. The economically optimal way of bringing a person on to the I_0 curve can only be determined by an analysis of the relative cost-effectiveness of alternative policies. For this one will have to know the exact location of the undernourished in relation to the I_0 curve, the cost of food *vis-à-vis* environmental provision, and the total amount of resources available for the purpose. In fact, a similar economic analysis will be needed for each of the other three categories as well. Although one or the other (or both) of food and non-food factors can be viewed as limiting constraint in these cases, there is almost always a choice between alternative combinations of food and non-food endowments. Thus even when environmental improvement is an absolute necessity (as in area Y), one cannot maintain a priori that the choice of environmental measures alone is the optimal strategy; nor can one make even the milder statement that most of the resources should be devoted to environmental improvement. By the same token, neither can one claim that more resources should be necessarily committed on the food front even for the food-constrained population. Allocation of resources between alternative strategies is a distinct exercise from identification of the limiting constraint.

In any case, the relative emphasis to be placed on alternative strategies is quite independent of the notion of adaptation. If adaptation provides a buffer against nutritional stress, it does so irrespective of whether the stress arises from food constraint operating on the intake side or from the non-food factors operating on the requirement side. In terms of Fig. 8.2, it merely has the effect of uniformly lowering the minimal desirable isonutrition contour. That by itself does not alter the relative importance of food and non-food factors. Conversely, there is nothing in the conceptual framework of the non-adaptationists that should prevent them from according a greater role to environmental policies. For example, Mitra (1978) clearly recognized the primacy of environmental policies from a non-adaptationist perspective. Gopalan (1983a) has also noted how wrongly the adaptationists have been trying to usurp the case for environmental improvement as if its importance can only be perceived from their own perspective.

However, the fact remains that when it came to actual formulation of policy, the traditional nutritionists seemed almost always to accord the pride of place to the provision of food. Two of the most celebrated intervention programmes, namely the INCAP project in Guatemala (Scrimshaw et al. 1969) and the Narangwal experiment in India (Kielmann et al. 1978), added personal health care to the provision of food, but environmental hygiene was left out in both. The successes achieved in these projects are now recognized to have been much too meagre compared to the resources deployed.[53] It is also recognized that the relative failure of these programmes is probably explained by the failure to address the limiting constraint of poor sanitation and water supply. It is thus clear that policies aimed at the improvement of environmental hygiene will have to be accorded a much greater role than has been done in the past. However, as Scrimshaw (1983: 222) rightly observes, environmental hygiene will be of little help if personal hygiene does not improve at the same time. Perhaps education can play a role here in promoting cleanliness (which will help both environmental and personal hygiene) as well as generally raising the nutritional consciousness of the people.

A broader view of the food problem

Finally, we would like to draw attention to an issue which in a sense is a matter of semantics, but can have an important impact on one's perception of the problem. The recognition that nutritional stress can arise as much from poor hygiene as from inadequate access to food often leads to a propensity to distinguish between a food problem and a hygienic problem as two distinct aspects of the general problem of nutrition. As a consequence of making this distinction, the emerging emphasis on hygiene is sometimes accompanied by a corresponding de-emphasis on the food problem in the context of malnutrition in the developing world. We find it a somewhat misleading way of looking at the problem. There is, we believe, a strong case for looking at the whole of the nutrition problem (especially that of protein-calorie malnutrition) as a problem of inadequate food. After all, the very notion of a food *problem* can only be conceived as the inequality between intake and requirement of food. Anything that contributes to this inequality can be said to constitute a food problem. Poor hygiene aggravates the inequality by raising requirement (or by restricting intake), thus making the food intake inadequate and hence causing a food problem. Therefore, instead of distinguishing between *food problem* and *hygienic problem* as two separate factors impinging on the problem of nutrition, it would seem more logical to distinguish between *access to food* and *access to*

---

[53] See the reflections of a leading architect of the INCAP project, Scrimshaw (1983).

hygiene as two entitlements both of which have a bearing on the common problem of food and nutrition. Accordingly, even when we recognize that poor hygiene is the more important limiting factor or that more resources should be committed to environmental policies than to the provision of food, that by itself should not lead us to take a diminished view of the magnitude of food problem.

However, it does require us to take a much broader view of the concept of the food problem than we have done in the past. It forces us to recognize that the food problem is not a problem merely of low intake, but also of high requirement due to poor environmental quality. Even when the focus is on intake, we should no longer perceive it to be solely a matter of economic access to food; for, as we have seen, intake may be constrained by other factors such as anorexia as in the case of the children of Santa Maria Cauqué (Mata 1978) or the constraint on the mother's time as in the example of Pacey and Payne (1984). Accordingly, the solution of the food problem should be seen to lie not solely in enhancing the absolute entitlement to food, but in a much broader spectrum of policies including health and environmental measures as well as educational measures which may be necessary to enhance the effectiveness of other measures. Pointing to this need for broadening the concept of the food problem (and its solution) is perhaps the single most important contribution in the field of policy made by recent advances in our understanding of human nutrition.

8.5. *Summary and conclusions*

We set out to understand the logical and scientific basis of some current controversies in the assessment of nutritional status. The objective was to explore in what way, if at all, these controversies affect some of the concerns of economics, specifically in the assessment of poverty and capability and in the formulation of food and nutrition policy.

Three specific nutritional issues were covered in the process, namely (1) whether the phenomenon of variable efficiency of energy utilization warrants a downward revision of the requirement norm from its customary 'average' value (a great deal of current controversy over the assessment of poverty springs from this issue); (2) whether the functional capabilities of a person remain invariant within a range of physical growth achieved in childhood (this issue has relevance for both dietary assessment of poverty and anthropometric assessment of capability); (3) the complications arising from the fact that undernutrition has both a non-unique origin and a non-unique outcome (both assessment of poverty and capability as well as formulation of policy ought to take note of these complications).

The principal conclusions emerging from our analysis can be summarized as follows: .

1. The claim that the norm for energy requirement should be set two standard

deviations below the average cannot be sustained. Sukhatme tried to justify this claim by using two quite different models of variable efficiency—one stochastic and the other adaptive. In the stochastic model, efficiency of energy utilization varies in a *spontaneous* manner and intake varies *pari passu*, whereas in the adaptive model variation of efficiency is *induced* by prior variation in intake. The justification of the lower cut-off point in terms of the stochastic model is logically wrong because this model only ensures that to have one's intake above the point is a necessary condition for being well nourished, but it does not ensure sufficiency. If on the other hand the adaptive model is accepted, then it would be logically correct to set the norm at the lower limit of adaptation rather than at the average value. But the limit of adaptation cannot be identified with Sukhatme's cut-off point which was derived from the stochastic model. This is a consequence of the fact that stochastic variation is not the same thing as adaptation, for the simple reason that spontaneous and induced variation in efficiency cannot be the same biological phenomenon. The limit of adaptation must be found from independent scientific evidence on 'pure' adaptation in efficiency. However, the existing scientific knowledge does not provide any evidence in support of pure adaptation of this kind.

2. On the controversy over the possibility of costless adaptation in physical growth, we found it useful to distinguish between two interpretations of the 'small but healthy' hypothesis—one causative and the other associative. The causative interpretation was found difficult to refute in the light of existing evidence, which implies that the dietary assessment of nutritional status ought to recognize the possibility of intraindividual variation in requirement arising from physical adaptation among children. However, one cannot be equally sanguine about the associative interpretation because physical retardation may be *associated* with the loss of one kind of nutritional function (namely cognitive skill) even within the range of causal invariance. This doubt raises serious problems for the anthropometric measurement of nutritional status.

3. Even if all the debates on adaptation in energy efficiency and physical growth were to be satisfactorily resolved, both dietary and anthropometric approaches will fail to capture the set of undernourished people fully. The dietary approach will fail to capture those who have an intake that is high enough for an ideal environment, but not high enough to meet the higher requirement associated with the poor environment in which they live. The problem essentially is that undernutrition has multiple origins, in which both food and hygiene have a role to play, but the dietary approach focuses on food alone by assuming ideal hygiene. On the other hand, the trouble with the anthropometric approach is that undernutrition has also multiple outcomes, and anthropometry picks up only one of them. Faced with a nutritional stress, a person may reduce either his body size or his level of activity. Concerned as it is with body size alone, anthropometry will fail to identify those who have responded to the stress by reducing activity.

4. The review of nutritional issues (as summarized in the preceding three

points) indicates that the traditional dietary approach to the measurement of undernutrition using average requirement as the cut-off norm has to contend with at least three difficulties: intraindividual variation in requirement arising from adaptation in physical growth, interindividual variation in requirement due to genetic differences, and variation in requirement due to differing conditions of environmental hygiene. The common consequence of all three problems is a very likely misclassification of the undernourished. Its implication for the measurement of poverty is that the set of poor will not in general be identical to the set of the undernourished. The question then arises: does the divergence between the poor and the undernourished render the use of an 'average' norm an inappropriate method of measuring poverty? We have argued that the answer depends on how one perceives the conceptual foundations of poverty. If one takes the opulence view of poverty, then there is in principle nothing wrong in persisting with the traditional approach. However, if the capability view is accepted, the methodology will have to be revised quite radically.

5. In the recent development of the capability approach to welfare, anthropometry has come to play an important role. It is used as an indicator of capability on the assumption that there exists a monotonically increasing relationship between physical growth and nutritional capabilities. However, the possibility of trade-off between physical growth and physical activity invalidates this assumption. As a consequence, anthropometry by itself turns out to be an uncertain indicator of capability. Proper assessment of capability requires information on both anthropometry and activity of the populations concerned.

6. Much of the policy debates arising from the recent nutrition controversy appears to be a classic case of much ado about nothing. Examples are the claim that the adaptationist view will encourage complacence on the policy front and the counter-claim that only the adaptationist perspective can ensure the most rational as well as equitable use of scarce resources. However, a couple of useful lessons come out quite clearly. First, supplementary feeding programmes should be targeted more specifically to the wasted children (and the severely stunted ones), leaving the problem of moderate stunting to be taken care of by broader socio-economic policies. Secondly, policies aimed at the improvement of environmental and personal hygiene should be accorded a much greater role than has been done in the past.

7. The stress on hygiene points to the need for taking a much broader view of the food problem (and its solution) than has been done in the past. There was a time when the solution of the food problem was seen to lie in higher rates of aggregate production of food. Recently, the focus has rightly shifted from aggregate availability to individual entitlement to food. It would now appear that one ought to go one step further and recognize that entitlement to food is not all that there is to the problem of food and nutrition. Entitlement to hygiene is an equally important dimension of the food problem confronting the

developing world. Both of these entitlements need to be addressed simultaneously, although the appropriate balance between the two will depend on the relative cost-effectiveness of alternative policy mixes. However, there is also a significant political economy dimension in the choice of strategy. In many societies, entitlement to food can be radically improved only by a drastic redistribution of productive assets which is bound to come up against resistance from powers-that-be. On the other hand, entitlement to hygiene can often be improved at least up to a point even within a given structure of ownership of assets and the balance of power that goes with it (*vide* the case of Sri Lanka). Thus the emphasis on hygiene is not only justified in its own right, it also makes a lot of tactical sense in the face of the socio-political constraints which are holding down the quality of life in much of the Third World.

References

APPELBAUM, M. (1978), 'Adaptation to Changes in Calorie Intake', *Progress in Food and Nutrition Science*, 2.

BEATON, G. H. (1983), 'Energy in Human Nutrition', *Nutrition Today*, Sept.–Oct.

——(1984), 'Adaptation to and Accommodation of Long Term Low Energy Intake: A Commentary on the Conference on Energy Intake and Activity', in E. Pollitt and P. Amante (eds.), *Energy Intake and Activity* (New York: Alan R. Riss).

——(1985), 'The Significance of Adaptation in the Definition of Nutrient Requirements and for Nutrition Policy', in Blaxter and Waterlow (1985).

——and GHASSEMI, H. (1982), 'Supplementary Feeding Programs for Young Children', *American Journal of Clinical Nutrition* (Suppl.), 35.

BEISEL, W. R. (1977), 'Magnitude of the Host Nutritional Responses to Infection', *American Journal of Clinical Nutrition*, 30.

——SAWYER, W. D., RYLL, E. D., and CROZIER, D. (1967), 'Metabolic Effects of Intracellular Infections in Man', *Annals of Internal Medicine*, 67.

BLAXTER, K., and WATERLOW, J. C. (eds.) (1985), *Nutritional Adaptation in Man* (London: John Libbey).

CHEN, L. C., and SCRIMSHAW, N. S. (eds.) (1983), *Diarrhoea and Malnutrition* (New York and London: Plenum Press).

DANDEKAR, V. (1981), 'On Measurement of Poverty', *Economic and Political Weekly*, 16.

——and RATH, N. (1971), 'Poverty in India', *Economic and Political Weekly*, 6.

DASGUPTA, P., and RAY, D. (1987), 'Adapting to Undernutrition: The Clinical Evidence and Its Implications', Working Paper No. 10 (Helsinki: WIDER).

DOWLER, E. A., PAYNE, P. R., SEO, Y. O., THOMSON, A. M., and WHEELER, E. F. (1982), 'Nutritional Status Indicators: Interpretation and Policy Making Role', *Food Policy*, 10.

EDHOLM, O. G., ADAM, J. M., HEALY, M. J. R., WOLFF, H. S., GOLDSMITH, R., and BEST, T. W. (1970), 'Food Intake and Energy Expenditure of Army Recruits', *British Journal of Nutrition*, 24.

EDMUNDSON, W. (1977), 'Individual Variations in Work Output per Unit Energy Intake in East Java', *Ecology of Food and Nutrition*, 6.

——(1979), 'Individual Variations in Basal Metabolic Rate and Mechanical Work Efficiency in East Java', *Ecology of Food and Nutrition*, 8.

——(1980), 'Adaptation to Undernutrition: How Much Food Does Man Need?', *Social Science and Medicine*, 14D.

FAO (1977), *Fourth World Food Survey* (Rome: FAO).

——(1985), *Fifth World Food Survey* (Rome: FAO).

——/WHO/UNU (1985), *Energy and Protein Requirements*, WHO Technical Report Series 724 (Geneva: WHO).

GOLDSTEIN, H., and TANNER, J. M. (1980), 'Ecological Considerations in the Creation and the Use of Child Growth Standards', *Lancet*, 15 Mar.

GOPALAN, C. (1983a), 'Measurement of Undernutrition: Biological Considerations', *Economic and Political Weekly*, 18, 9 Apr.

——(1983b), 'Small is Healthy: For the Poor not for the Rich', *Bulletin of the Nutrition*

Foundation of India, Oct.; also repr. in *Future* (autumn 1983) (page references relate to the reprint).

HEGSTED, D. M. (1972), 'Problems in the Use and Interpretation of the Recommended Dietary Allowances', *Ecology of Food and Nutrition*, 1.

JAMES, W. P. T., and SHETTY, P. S. (1982), 'Metabolic Adaptation and Energy Requirements in Developing Countries', *Human Nutrition: Clinical Nutrition*, 36C.

JELLIFFE, D. B. (1966), *The Assessment of the Nutritional Status of the Community* (Geneva: WHO).

KAKWANI, N. (1986), 'On Measuring Undernutrition', Working Paper No. 8 (Helsinki: WIDER).

KIELMANN, A. A., TAYLOR, C. E., and PARKER, R. L. (1978), 'The Narangwal Nutrition Study: A Summary Review', *American Journal of Clinical Nutrition*, 31.

LIPTON, M. (1983), 'Poverty, Undernutrition and Hunger', World Bank Staff Working Paper No. 597 (Washington, DC: World Bank).

MCLAREN, D. (1974), 'The Great Protein Fiasco', *Lancet*.

MARGEN, S., and OGAR, R. A. (eds.) (1978), *Progress in Human Nutrition*, vol. ii (Westport: AVI Publishing).

MARTORELL, R. (1985), 'Child Growth Retardation: A Discussion of Its Causes and Its Relationship to Health', in Blaxter and Waterlow (1985).

MATA, L. J. (1975), 'Malnutrition–Infection Interactions in the Tropics', *American Journal of Tropical Medicine and Hygiene*, 24.

—— (1978), *The Children of Santa Maria Cauqué: A Prospective Field Study of Health and Growth* (Cambridge, Mass.: MIT Press).

MEHTA, J. (1982), 'Nutritional Norms and Measurement of Malnourishment and Poverty', *Economic and Political Weekly*, 17.

MILLER, D. S. (1975), 'Thermogenesis in Everyday Life', in E. Jequier (ed.), *Regulation of Energy Balance in Man* (Geneva: Medicine & Hygiene).

MITRA, A. (1978), 'Revolution by Redefinition of Parameters', in Margen and Ogar (1978).

NORGAN, N. G. (1983), 'Adaptation of Energy Metabolism to Level of Energy Intake', in J. Parizkova (ed.), *Energy Expenditure under Field Conditions* (Prague: Charles University).

OSMANI, S. R. (1982), *Economic Inequality and Group Welfare: A Theory of Comparison with Application to Bangladesh* (Oxford: Oxford University Press).

—— (1987), 'Controversies in Nutrition and Their Implications for the Economics of Food', Working Paper No. 16 (Helsinki: WIDER).

PACEY, A., and PAYNE, P. (eds.) (1985), *Agricultural Development and Nutrition* (London: Hutchinson).

PAYNE, P. R., and CUTLER, P. (1984), 'Measuring Malnutrition: Technical Problems and Ideological Perspectives', *Economic and Political Weekly*, 19.

RAND, W. M., SCRIMSHAW, N. S., and YOUNG, V. R. (1985), 'Retrospective Analysis of Data from Five Long-Term Metabolic Balance Studies: Implications for Understanding Dietary Nitrogen and Energy Utilization', *American Journal of Clinical Nutrition*, 42.

—— UAUY, R., and SCRIMSHAW, N. S. (eds.) (1984), *Protein-Energy-Requirement Studies in Developing Countries: Results of International Research* (Tokyo: UNU).

RAO, V. K. R. V. (1977), 'Nutritional Norms by Calorie Intake and Measurement of Poverty', *Bulletin of the International Statistical Institute*, 47.

—— (1981), 'Some Nutritional Puzzles: A Note', *Economic and Political Weekly*, 16.

REUTLINGER, S., and ALDERMAN, H. (1980), 'The Prevalence of Calorie-Deficient Diets in the Developing Countries', *World Development*, 8.

—— and SELOWSKY, M. (1976), 'Malnutrition and Poverty: Magnitude and Policy Options', World Bank Occasional Paper No. 23 (Washington, DC: World Bank).

ROSE, G. A., and WILLIAMS, R. T. (1961), 'Metabolic Studies on Large and Small Eaters', *British Journal of Nutrition*, 15.

ROWNTREE, B. S. (1901), *Poverty: A Study of Town Life* (London: Macmillan).

RUTISHAUSER, I. H. E., and WHITEHEAD, R. G. (1972), 'Energy Intakes and Expenditure in 1–3 Year Old Ugandan Children Living in a Rural Environment', *British Journal of Nutrition*, 28.

SCRIMSHAW, N. S. (1977), 'Effect of Infection on Nutritional Requirements', *American Journal of Clinical Nutrition*, 30.

—— (1982), 'Programs of Supplemental Feeding and Weaning Food Development', in Scrimshaw and Wallerstein (1982).

—— (1983), 'Importance of Infection and Immunity in Nutrition Intervention Programs and Priorities for Intervention', in B. A. Underwood (ed.), *Nutrition Intervention Strategies in National Development* (New York: Academic Press).

—— BEHAR, M., GUZMAN, M. A., and GORDON, J. E. (1969), 'Nutrition and Infection Field Study in Guatemalan Villages, 1959–1964, IX: An Evaluation of Medical, Social and Public Health Benefits, with Suggestions for Future Field Study', *Archives of Environmental Health*, 18.

—— TAYLOR, C. E., and GORDON, J. E. (1968), *Interactions of Nutrition and Infections*, WHO Monograph Series 57 (Geneva: WHO).

—— and WALLERSTEIN, M. B. (eds.) (1982), *Nutrition Policy Implementation: Issues and Experience* (New York and London: Plenum Press).

SECKLER, D. (1980), 'Malnutrition: An Intellectual Odyssey', *Western Journal of Agricultural Economics*, 5; also repr. in Sukhatme (1982*d*).

—— (1982), 'Small but Healthy: A Basic Hypothesis in the Theory, Measurement and Policy of Malnutrition', in Sukhatme (1982*d*).

—— (1984*a*), 'The "Small But Healthy?" Hypothesis: A Reply to Critics', *Economic and Political Weekly*, 19.

—— (1984*b*), 'The "Small But Healthy" Hypothesis: An Invitation to a Refutation', in P. Narain (ed.), *Impact of P. V. Sukhatme on Agricultural Statistics and Nutrition* (New Delhi: Indian Society of Agricultural Statistics).

SEN, A. K. (1980), 'Levels of Poverty: Policy and Change', World Bank Staff Working Paper No. 401 (Washington, DC: World Bank).

—— (1983), 'Poor, Relatively Speaking', *Oxford Economic Papers*, 35.

—— (1984*a*), 'The Living Standard', in D. A. Collard, D. R. Helm, M. F. G. Scott, and A. K. Sen (eds.), *Economic Theory and Hicksian Themes* (Oxford: Oxford University Press).

—— (1984*b*), 'Family and Food: Sex Bias in Poverty', in A. K. Sen, *Resources, Values and Development* (Oxford: Basil Blackwell); P. Bardhan and T. N. Srinivasan (eds.) (1988), *Rural Poverty in South Asia* (New York: Columbia University Press).

—— (1985), *Commodities and Capabilities* (Amsterdam: North-Holland).

—— and SENGUPTA, S. (1983), 'Malnutrition of Rural Indian Children and the Sex Bias', *Economic and Political Weekly*, 18.

SIMS, E. A. H. (1976), 'Experimental Obesity, Dietary-Induced Thermogenesis, and Their Clinical Implications', *Clinics in Endocrinology and Metabolism*, 5/2.

SRINIVASAN, T. N. (1981), 'Malnutrition: Some Measurement and Policy Issues', *Journal of Development Economics*, 8.

SUKHATME, P. V. (1977), *Malnutrition and Poverty*, Ninth Lal Bahadur Shastri Memorial Lecture (New Delhi: Indian Agricultural Research Institute).

——(1978), 'Assessment of Adequacy of Diets at Different Income Levels', *Economic and Political Weekly*, 13.

——(1981a), 'On Measurement of Poverty', *Economic and Political Weekly*, 16.

——(1981b), 'On the Measurement of Undernutrition: A Comment', *Economic and Political Weekly*, 16.

——(1982a), 'Measurement of Undernutrition', *Economic and Political Weekly*, 17.

——(1982b), 'Poverty and Malnutrition', in Sukhatme (1982d).

——(1982c), 'Improving Living Conditions in Villages: Interview with the Press', in Sukhatme (1982d).

——(ed.) (1982d), *Newer Concepts in Nutrition and Their Implications for Policy* (Pune: Maharashtra Association for the Cultivation of Science).

——and MARGEN, S. (1978), 'Models of Protein Deficiency', *American Journal of Clinical Nutrition*, 31: 1237–56; also repr. in Sukhatme (1982d).

—— ——(1982), 'Autoregulatory Homeostatic Nature of Energy Balance', *American Journal of Clinical Nutrition*, 35: 355–65; also repr. in Sukhatme (1982d) (page references are from the reprint).

——and NARAIN, P. (1982), 'The Genetic Significance of Intra-individual Variation in Requirement', in P. S. R. S. Rao and J. Sedransk (eds.), *Research Work of William J. Cochrane Memorial Volume* (New York: John Wiley).

TURUN, B., YOUNG, V. R., and RAND, W. M. (eds.) (1981), *Protein-Energy Requirements of Developing Countries: Evaluation of New Data* (Tokyo: UNU).

WATERLOW, J. C. (1972), 'Classification and Definition of Protein-Calorie Malnutrition', *British Medical Journal*, 3.

WIDDOWSON, E. M. (1962), 'Nutritional Individuality', *Proceedings of Nutrition Society*, 21 (London).

World Bank (1986), *Poverty and Hunger* (Washington, DC: World Bank).

ZURBRIGG, S. (1983), 'Ideology and the Poverty Line Debate', *Economic and Political Weekly*, 18.

9

Food and Standard of Living: An Analysis Based on Sri Lankan Data*

Sudhir Anand and Christopher Harris

9.1. *Introduction*

Many questions in public economics require comparisons to be made between the living standards of people. For example, if one is interested in measuring poverty, or in tracking its evolution over time, or in devising policies to reduce it, a criterion will be needed to distinguish the poor from the non-poor. Governments frequently resort to redistributional policies of various types —e.g. direct income transfers in some developing countries, the Food Stamp Scheme in Sri Lanka, and so on. Who should be eligible for such transfers or how should the target population be defined? (A family income and size criterion was applied to determine the beneficiaries of food stamps in Sri Lanka.) These questions necessitate the search for a welfare indicator, at least one which enables us to decide whether one household is better off than another; in other words, we seek an ordinal level-comparable indicator.

If such an indicator can be found one can then go on to explore the characteristics of households ranked from the poorest to the richest, say according to decile. Such characteristics can include food and non-food expenditure patterns, non-monetary variables such as the physical quantities of food necessities consumed, quality of housing, and possession of basic clothing and other durable goods. (It can also include socio-economic and demographic variables such as occupation, employment status, educational attainment, age, race, and so on.) This profile can be examined to determine whether the poorest households have the lowest satisfaction of basic needs in each dimension. Is it the case, for instance, that the poorest households have the lowest food consumption?

* The arguments in this paper were first presented in January 1985 at a workshop in Colombo under the research project 'Evolution of Living Standards in Sri Lanka', funded by the Swedish International Development Agency and other Nordic countries. Our report for that project (Anand and Harris 1985) outlines our approach to ranking individuals according to per capita food expenditure. This ranking method has since been used without acknowledgement by a parallel research team on that project (Bhalla and Glewwe 1986: 57 and n. to Table 9)—despite the fact that one of them (Bhalla) was both a participant at the Colombo workshop and the project manager to whom our April 1985 report was submitted!

Apart from the Food Strategies Conference at WIDER in July 1986, this paper has been presented at seminars at the London School of Economics and Oxford University (Nuffield and All Souls Colleges). For valuable discussions or comments, we are grateful to Jean Drèze, Jack Duloy, Terence Gorman, Siddiq Osmani, Maurice Scott, Paul Seabright, and Nick Stern. We owe a special debt of gratitude to Amartya Sen, whose very perceptive and detailed comments at every stage have helped us to sharpen as well as extend the analysis.

The urgency of finding the right welfare indicator can be illustrated by considering four different ranking variables of households—per capita income, per capita total expenditure, per capita food expenditure, and food share in total expenditure (an inverse welfare indicator)—and comparing the estimates they yield of the food expenditure of the lowest decile of individuals. For the Sri Lankan household budget survey data on which this chapter is based, we find that the bottom 10 per cent of individuals in the urban sector have a monthly per capita food expenditure of Rs. 116.45 when individuals are ranked by per capita income; Rs. 95.48 when per capita total expenditure is used as the ranking variable; Rs. 88.39 when per capita food expenditure is used; and Rs. 171.27 when food share in total expenditure is used. These widely differing predictions of the food consumption of the lowest 10 per cent (assuming them to be the target group for food strategies) will clearly affect our assessment of the magnitude of the problem of hunger. The reasons for such divergences in estimates are to be found in the relative variability of the different indicators, an issue which is of central concern in this chapter.

So far we have posed the problem of finding a welfare indicator in general terms. The precise nature of the solution is likely to be dependent on the particular country and the particular data set. As mentioned above, this chapter investigates the problem with reference to Sri Lanka—using the Consumer Finance Survey (CFS) 1981/82 conducted by the Central Bank of Ceylon. Naturally, some of the considerations we employ here will be specific to the data set and the country. However, in most cases analogous considerations are likely to arise with other data sets and other countries.

The CFS 1981/82 is a sample survey which was carried out in four rounds during October 1981 to September 1982 using a stratified two-stage sample design.[1] A total of 8,000 households was sampled, of which 7,927 responded fully—i.e. for whom all sections of the survey questionnaire could be 'completed satisfactorily'. For the purposes of the present chapter we have dropped a further 348 households, those with multiple 'spending units'. This reduces our effective sample size here to 7,579 households (38,883 individuals), but does not bias the comparison of alternative ranking variables in any way (see section 9.2(f) and Appendix 9.1(f)).

The plan of the chapter is as follows. Section 9.2(a) explains the concept of welfare we have in mind when we speak of a welfare indicator. Sections 9.2(b) and (c) introduce and discuss in general terms the four indicators with which we shall principally be concerned in this chapter—namely, income per capita, total expenditure per capita, food expenditure per capita, and foodshare. Section 9.2(d) outlines the criteria for choosing between them. Sections 9.2(e) and 9.2(f) describe the CFS data categories and the CFS subsample used in the empirical analysis. Section 9.3 treats the four indicators in turn, one subsection being devoted to each indicator. It presents the calculations we have carried out

---

[1] For a detailed evaluation of the survey—including its sample design, concepts, definitions, field enumeration, and quality of data—see Anand and Harris (1989).

using the CFS data, and expands on the themes introduced in sections 9.2(*b*)–(*d*). Section 9.4 is in conclusion.

9.2. *Methodology*

In this chapter we investigate the problem of finding a suitable proxy for the utility, or welfare, of individuals. We shall refer to such a proxy as a welfare indicator. In the present section, we: (*a*) indicate how we understand the term utility or welfare; (*b*) consider four proxies for it that can be estimated from typical household survey data; (*c*) discuss the problems in their empirical use; (*d*) explain the methodology we use in comparing alternative welfare indicators; (*e*) outline the CFS data categories that correspond to these indicators; and (*f*) briefly discuss the CFS subsample on which our investigation is based.

(*a*)   *Utility: scope and timespan*

Our concept of utility is restricted in scope to the physical well-being of an individual, and in timespan to the long run. We expand below on the nature of these restrictions, and the reasoning behind them.

We shall take it that the utility of an individual is determined by what he or she consumes. Furthermore, we shall define consumption as consisting of (1) food, (2) non-food non-durable goods and services, and (3) the flow of services obtained from durables. Thus we take no account of externalities in consumption—the possibility that an individual may derive pleasure or displeasure from the consumption of others. In particular, we would not regard a voluntary gift (monetary or in kind) from one individual to another as contributing to the donor's utility; for while he or she may derive altruistic pleasure from the gift, it is not directly productive of physical well-being.

We would justify this narrow definition of utility by the observation that poverty and deprivation should be seen in terms of the fulfilment or non-fulfilment of very basic physical requirements. But we would also qualify this defence by noting that the definition does not really make an adequate allowance for illness—which does affect an individual's well-being.

Certainly it can be argued that underconsumption causes illness. For example, illness could arise as the direct consequence of inadequate consumption of food (undernourishment), inadequate consumption of preventive drugs (or inoculation), and inadequate consumption of fuel (to boil water). The truth of the matter, however, would seem to be that inadequate consumption merely results in a higher risk of illness. The actual occurrence of illness is inherently random. Hence, of a group of individuals with the same consumption, some will suffer from illness while others will not. The former are clearly worse off.

It can also be argued that illness is taken into account in another way. An individual who is ill has a reduced earning capacity, and hence a reduced command over resources. His or her illness will therefore be reflected in lower consumption. (On this argument, our accounting captures illness through its *effect* on consumption, rather than having low consumption as its *cause* as in the previous paragraph.) But once again it would seem that the utility reduction associated with the illness will be greater than the utility reduction due merely to the lower consumption.

Turning to the timespan of utility, we focus on long-run (average) utility rather than short-run (instantaneous) utility;[2] our concern is to identify people who face *chronic* poverty. We do not want to identify those who happen just to be temporarily badly off.[3] To see why not, consider an imaginary economy in which there are two groups (e.g. occupations). Those in the first group have a constant but low short-run utility. Those in the second group experience large (e.g. seasonal) fluctuations in utility. At the low point, the utility of the latter is even lower than that of the former, but on average it is higher. If we were to focus on short-run utility we could single out the second group as the target for poverty relief. The result would be to raise the standard of living of the better-off even further.

(b) Proxies for utility

Of course, an individual is likely to attempt to smooth the flow of short-run utility by ironing out consumption over time (see the simple model in Appendix 9.1(*a*)). If he or she succeeds in doing so perfectly, then short-run utility will be equal to long-run average utility, and both will be equal to the utility corresponding to the individual's long-run average income (assuming no saving for the next generation).[4] In this case the distinction between short-run and long-run average utility will not be important.

While capital markets in Sri Lanka are far from perfect, there is at the same time considerable evidence of extensive borrowing and repayment, and saving and dissaving (see section 9.3(*a*)). The most serious fluctuations in short-run utility are thus likely to be smoothed. This, together with the fact that we are only seeking an *ordinal* welfare indicator, motivates us to identify long-run average utility with long-run average income. We recognize that individuals may be unable to smooth their consumption streams completely, and that they may even be unable to smooth out some relevant fluctuations. But here we assume that they can, in order to avoid making what is already a long and involved chapter yet longer and more complicated.

Even in the absence of any utility connotations, long-run average income may be regarded as a reasonable indicator of 'standard of living'; it determines an individual's long-run command over resources, and the consumption level that can be

---

[2] Short-run or instantaneous utility may not even be a well-defined concept if utility over the lifetime is not separable period by period.

[3] Included in the latter category may be people caught by the survey at an unusually bad time of year for them.

[4] In Friedman's (1957) terminology, this is the utility corresponding to the individual's 'permanent income'.

sustained.[5] Unfortunately, whether it is identified with utility, or simply treated as being of interest in its own right, it suffers from the problem that it is unobservable. For any empirical exercise, therefore, we shall need to find a proxy. One obvious proxy is *short-run income*. Although observable—and observed in many household surveys—it is, unfortunately, likely to be variable relative to long-run average income.[6] This variability results from several causes, among which are the absence of regular employment for many people, the seasonality of employment generally (especially in agriculture), and life-cycle effects.

Another approach to seeking a proxy for long-run average utility is to focus on short-run utility. The latter will approximate the former if there is smoothing of the flow of short-run utility over time. Thus short-run utility can be considered a proxy for long-run average utility, just as short-run income is a proxy—albeit noisy—for long-run average income. Indeed, total consumption, which is closely related to short-run physical utility,[7] will be a better proxy for long-run average income than is short-run income if consumption is dampened relative to short-run income.

The problem with total consumption is that while it is in principle observable, in practice it is not directly observed. For example, the typical household budget survey does not canvass comprehensive information on stocks of durable items, and hence the flow of services from them cannot be estimated.[8] In particular, using the CFS 1981/82 data it is impossible to estimate total consumption; apart from the stocks of a few major consumer durables (see Schedule I, Part 2, of the CFS 1981/82 questionnaire), the only data relate to changes in the value of durables.

What we can estimate, however, is *total expenditure*. (For this to approximate total consumption, durable expenditure must be defined as purchases plus maintenance less sales of durable items.) But durable expenditure is lumpy, due to the indivisibilities inherent in most durable goods; hence total expenditure will be a noisy indicator of long-run average income. Another problem with total expenditure (and to some extent, total consumption) is that it is likely to track short-run income. Expenditures on durables, and on some non-essential consumables (such as entertainment), will tend to be made at times when income is high.

[5] Indeed, if the reader is unhappy with our identification of long-run average utility and long-run average income, he or she should treat this chapter as an investigation of long-run average income.

[6] A formal definition of one indicator being variable relative to another indicator is provided in section 9.2(*d*). The consequences of such variability are also discussed there, and a formal treatment is given in Appendix 9.1.

[7] By total consumption is meant the monetary value of the following three categories: (1) food; (2) non-food non-durable goods and services; and (3) flow of services from durable goods. Physical utility differs from total consumption in that it is determined (non-linearly) by quantities consumed, while total consumption values these quantities at prices.

[8] Nor is the typical survey likely to collect price and quality information on durable goods.

This suggests that we should try to eliminate the problem categories. These comprise all durable items, including those that should properly be regarded as durable (e.g. clothing and other apparel which in CFS are classified as non-durable), and those non-durables which are liable to vary systematically with income (e.g. communication, recreation and entertainment, holidays, and possibly pilgrimages and ceremonial expenditure). After such elimination, the single largest category of expenditure remaining is food expenditure; in the CFS 1981/82 it accounts for 72 per cent of the remainder.

The use of *food expenditure* as an ordinal proxy for long-run utility can make a good deal of intuitive sense. As an item of consumption, food is likely to be adjusted last—and least—of all in face of short-run fluctuations in income. In terms of a hierarchy of needs, food almost certainly comes at the top; thus people will marshal their food expenditure with tenacity.[9]

In the language of neo-classical consumer theory, the case for food expenditure may be stated in the following terms. Food expenditure is suggested as being monotonically related to utility, in turn determined by long-run average income. Holding relative prices constant, this is equivalent to assuming that food is a normal good, where food is treated as a single or Hicksian composite commodity. Even if relative prices can vary within certain limits, there still exist utility functions whose Hicksian demands generate a food expenditure function monotonic in utility.[10] In terms of elasticities of demand, food has a positive elasticity of demand with respect to long-run average income; but, for a given level of long-run average income, food has a zero elasticity of demand with respect to short-run income.[11] Again, holding long-run average income constant, and in the range of price variation permitted if a utility function with the required property is to exist, food has a Marshallian price elasticity of demand less than minus one (and a Hicksian price elasticity of demand equal to minus one). In principle, these are testable implications; however, in practice, they pose considerable difficulties because long-run average income is unobservable.

[9] We can interpret this in terms of neo-classical consumer theory as follows. Suppose that the (short-run) utility function is additively separable into utilities from individual goods (or groups of goods). Then the income elasticity of demand for any good (or group of goods) will be inversely related to the curvature of its subutility function, i.e. to the elasticity of its marginal subutility function. Goods with a more concave subutility function will have a lower income elasticity of demand, and will therefore be adjusted (proportionately) less to fluctuations in income. A hierarchy of needs can thus be specified in terms of an ordering of goods by the degree of concavity of their subutility function. We are saying that in comparison to other goods food probably has the most concave subutility function.

[10] It is easy to show that if relative prices were allowed to vary *without* limit, no utility function would exist with the above property. For if such a function existed, the Hicksian demand for food, say $h_1(p, u)$, where food is commodity 1 and p is the vector of commodity prices, would satisfy $p_1 h_1(p, u) = f(u)$ independent of prices $p >> 0$ with $f(.)$ monotonic increasing in utility u. But then $h_1(p, u) = f(u)/p_1$, which is homogeneous of degree (-1) in p, not homogeneous of degree 0 in p as a Hicksian demand function must be.

[11] According to this view, ordinary least squares estimates from cross-section budget data of the elasticity of demand for food with respect to short-run income will tend to be underestimates of the true elasticity with respect to long-run income (by the usual errors-in-variables argument).

We shall also consider an (inverse) indicator of welfare that has been very popular in the literature—the share of food expenditure in total expenditure, or *foodshare*. This is suggested by Engel's (1895) Law (a frequently verified empirical relationship), according to which the foodshare typically decreases with income or total expenditure. From this observation, one is led to ask whether the foodshare might be inversely correlated with welfare too.[12] According to Deaton (1980: 59):

Thus arose the idea of using the food share to indicate welfare, and it is still a widely-used concept, e.g. the food share is widely used as a dimensionless indicator of welfare in international comparisons, while the U.S. government implicitly defines its official poverty level by the expenditure corresponding to a food share of 1/3.

(c) Problems in empirical use of the indicators

Our object in searching for an empirical welfare indicator is to compare the standard of living of different individuals, so as to determine which individuals are better off and which worse off. But to use any of the above four indicators in practice requires us to assume that people (1) have identical physical preferences, and (2) face identical prices. A third problem is that the data for estimating these indicators of an individual's welfare will be available only at the household level. We comment on each of these three problems in turn.

First, individuals cannot be taken to have the same preferences. Indeed, the physical needs of individuals might be expected to vary with age and sex. They will also vary with occupation. For example, a high level of food consumption by a male manual labourer should be discounted to some extent since the extra calories provide the energy for him to undertake his work—they are not directly productive of utility. Secondly, the prices faced by individuals may vary from location to location, and from season to season. Worse still, we do not have complete information on all the prices that they face, e.g. the prices of non-food goods and services. Thirdly, the household budget survey data do not contain information on how the total expenditure and income of a household are actually distributed among its members. In particular, we do not know whether they are distributed in proportion to the members' needs.

Our response to these problems will be rather crude in this chapter.[13] As far as the first and third problems are concerned, we shall assume that an adequate estimate of each monetary indicator (income, total expenditure, and food expenditure) for an individual within a sector is obtained by dividing the household total of the indicator by the size of the household to which the individual belongs. (Engel's foodshare is in any case calculated at the level of the household; we assume that each individual in a household enjoys the welfare level corresponding to the household's foodshare.) The per capita

[12] Note how the use of foodshare is suggested more by an association of ideas rather than by a theoretical argument. In theory, there may be no convincing reason why foodshare should correctly indicate welfare; the hypothesis may not be rooted in any plausible model of behaviour.

[13] Various refinements are considered in our book (Anand and Harris 1989).

adjustment effectively ignores both problems. Regarding the second problem of price variation, we make a partial response by disaggregating our calculations to the level of sector.

Disaggregation by sector also helps address the most serious distortion created by the first problem—that of physical needs varying with occupation, level of physical activity, climate, and health status. The estate sector, which is relatively homogeneous and consists predominantly of households in the tea estates in the hill country, is very different from the other two sectors. The main differences lie in the nature and intensity of work undertaken, participation rates (especially among women), ambient temperature, and incidence of (especially bowel) infections. All these factors cause the energy requirements for people in the estate sector to be considerably higher than for the other sectors.[14] Treating each sector separately therefore avoids the need to compare the monetary indicators of people with systematically different requirements. A crucial caveat follows: the tables in section 9.3 of this chapter relating to various per capita monetary indicators must not be used for intersectoral welfare comparisons.

One can think of more sophisticated responses to some of the problems. For example, even within sectors, one could try to estimate a measure of the different needs of individuals of different ages, sexes, and occupations on the basis of 'scientific' data. For instance, detailed calculations of the nutritional requirements of individuals by age, sex, and activity level are available for Sri Lanka (see Anand and Harris 1987). These estimates could be made the basis for the construction of equivalence scales. The welfare of a household could then be taken to be the monetary indicator for the household per equivalent adult. (Note that this approach continues to ignore the third problem of distribution within the household.) A more sophisticated response to the second problem of price variation, for example, would be to correct the monetary indicator according to some regional and seasonal price index. Alternatively, one could disaggregate one's calculations still further than the level of sector.

Before undertaking such additional corrections, however, we feel that it is important to address a methodological point. Without correction, the indicator will be at best a noisy measure of welfare. Next, the correction is made using data that are themselves noisy. Hence, if the effect for which the correction is being made is small relative to the errors in the data used for correction, the corrected version of the indicator will actually be a worse measure of welfare than the uncorrected version. We therefore feel that, before undertaking any corrections, three conditions should ideally be satisfied. First, there should be evidence to show that the effect for which the correction is to be made is significant. Secondly, it should be known that the data used for the correction are reliable. Thirdly, there should be evidence to show that making the correction actually results in an improvement.

[14] We have elsewhere estimated the average energy requirements in the estate sector to be several hundred calories higher than in the other two sectors (Anand and Harris 1988).

We mention finally that we have made a preliminary examination of the more sophisticated responses to the first and second problems. The examination suggests that the use of equivalence scales may lead to the kind of deterioration envisaged in the preceding paragraph. This is entirely consistent with the uncertainties known to be associated with calculations of nutritional requirements. As for the use of price indices, there is some evidence that the use of sectoral price indices leads to a slight improvement in intersectoral comparisons. The improvement is, however, small.[15]

(d) Criteria for choice of indicator

We are searching for an ordinal indicator, a monotonic transform of which is as close as possible to long-run average income.[16] In other words, the monotonic transform of the indicator should vary as little as possible around long-run average income. Since the latter is unobservable, we cannot directly measure variability around it. Hence, in choosing such an indicator, we are forced to rely mainly on a priori and pragmatic considerations. However, in the case of some indicators, these considerations can be supplemented using a simple statistical model which predicts certain consequences of variability that *are* observable. These can be tested by calculations on our data set.

Before stating the consequences of variability, we must define the concept precisely. Variability is a relative concept; one indicator is only variable *relative to* another. We use the Rothschild–Stiglitz (1970) definition of one indicator being variable relative to another. Thus, by definition, Y is said to be *variable relative to* η if Y is equal to η plus noise; formally,

$$Y = \eta + \varepsilon$$

where ε is a random variable with the property that

$$E(\varepsilon|\eta) = 0$$

for all η.[17] In other words, Y is equal to η plus a disturbance term (uncorrelated noise). Here Y could be given the interpretation of short-run income, and η long-run average income.[18]

[15] It is of the same order of magnitude as the improvement obtained by replacing total expenditure with 'smoothed' total expenditure—see section 9.3(b).

[16] In the case of the indicators *income* and *total expenditure*, the monotonic transform is simply the identity mapping.

[17] Rothschild and Stiglitz (1970) say that Y is riskier than η if Y is equal *in distribution* to $\eta + \varepsilon$, where ε satisfies $E(\varepsilon|\eta) = 0$. For us, equality in distribution is not enough. For example, if Y were equal in distribution to $\eta + \varepsilon$, but independent of η, then it would contain no information about η whatever! Hence we require actual equality. Suppose, however, that we are given two indicators Y_1 and Y_2, both of which are variable relative to η (i.e. for each i, $Y_i = \eta + \varepsilon_i$ where $E(\varepsilon_i|\eta) = 0$). Then we can say that Y_2 is more variable than Y_1 (relative to η) if Y_2 is equal in distribution to $Y_1 + \varsigma$, where $E(\varsigma|Y_1) = 0$. For now both Y_1 and Y_2 contain information about η, and the only question is whether Y_1 contains more. The reader will find more on this in Appendix 9.1(d).

[18] More generally, an indicator ϕ is variable relative to η if there is a strict monotonic transform $m(.)$ such that $m(\phi) = \eta + \varepsilon$, where $E(\varepsilon|\eta) = 0$ for all η.

Any proxy for long-run average income will at best be a noisy indicator for two reasons. First, there will be the usual measurement error in estimating the indicator. Secondly, the indicator itself (or monotonic transform of the indicator) will be an imperfect proxy for, and thus variable relative to, long-run average income. What are the effects of such noise?

To fix ideas, we examine the predictions obtained from our simple statistical model (Appendix 9.1(b)) when short-run income Y is used as the welfare indicator. (Similar considerations will apply for the other indicators.) In this model an individual faces an income Y that fluctuates around its long-run average η. Individuals are not homogeneous—η varies from person to person. However, by virtue of the definition of long-run average, if we know η for a given individual then the expectation (over time) of $\varepsilon = Y - \eta$ conditional on this information is zero. Finally, a person must divide Y between consumption C and savings S. He or she does so in such a way as to maintain C at the maximum sustainable level. Thus $C = \eta$ and $S = \varepsilon$.

We expand briefly on the interpretation of the model. We have already mentioned that individuals are heterogeneous in that η varies from person to person. However, the model can be interpreted to include further heterogeneity. Individuals with the same η may face different patterns of short-run income—perhaps because they have different occupations. Overall, the model incorporates at least three kinds of heterogeneity: different long-run average incomes; different types of individual with the same long-run average income; otherwise identical individuals sampled at different points in the year or in their life cycle.[19]

The prediction made by the model is as follows. Suppose that a large number of individuals is selected at random, that they are ranked according to their income Y, and that for some p between 0 and 1 the bottom ($100p$) per cent of individuals so ranked is chosen. Then if $S = Y - C$ is averaged over the chosen individuals, the result will be negative.

The intuition behind the prediction is straightforward. Define group 1 to consist of the bottom ($100p$) per cent of individuals ranked by Y. Let the highest value of Y for this group be y; in other words, group 1 consists of those individuals for whom $Y \leqq y$. Next, define group 2 to consist of those individuals for whom $\eta \leqq y$. In moving from group 1 to group 2, two kinds of changes can occur. First, an individual in group 1 may fail to be in group 2. For such an individual, $Y \leqq y$ and $\eta > y$. It follows that for him or her, $S < 0$. Secondly, an individual who is not in group 1 may be in group 2. For such an individual, $Y > y$ and $\eta \leqq y$, i.e. $S > 0$. Thus in moving from group 1 to group 2 some individuals with $S < 0$ leave group 1, while others with $S > 0$ join it.

---

[19] Consider the following concrete example of three people with the same η: a government clerk in regular employment, who probably has an ε close to zero; a farm-machinery operator sampled just before harvest-time, who probably has a negative ε; and a construction worker sampled at the peak of his or her working life, who probably has a positive ε.

These two effects are mutually reinforcing, and ensure that the average of S over group 2 exceeds the average of S over group 1. But the average of S over group 2 is zero. Hence the average of S over group 1 is negative.

Further implications of our statistical model are explored in Appendix 9.1. Three types of proposition are demonstrated there. First, as the variability of an indicator relative to long-run income tends to zero, the predicted deficit (negative savings) of the bottom ranges will tend to zero (Proposition A.9). Secondly, a positive (instead of zero) propensity to save out of long-run income makes deficits in the bottom ranges less likely (Appendix 9.1(c)); the occurrence of deficits in the sample will thus be all the more significant. Finally, some kinds of increase in variability lead to an increase in deficits.[20] It is not true in general, however, that an increase in variability always leads to an increase in the deficit (see Fig. 9.1 in Appendix 9.1(d)). Hence, in the absence of more detailed information on the nature of the variability of different indicators, the fact that one indicator yields a higher deficit than another cannot be treated as conclusive evidence that it is more variable.

(e) CFS data categories

In this subsection we summarize the composition of the relevant CFS data categories, and consider how well they lend themselves to estimating the proxies for utility discussed in section 9.2(b). The CFS monetary aggregates are used largely unadjusted here; this approach allows comparison with other studies (in Sri Lanka and elsewhere) which have used existing survey categories. The CFS categories are described more fully in the survey *Report* (Statistics Department, Central Bank of Ceylon 1984).[21]

The first aggregate is *income* (Schedule VI of the CFS questionnaire). Income data were collected for two reference periods—the last one month and the last six months immediately preceding the interview. A comprehensive definition of income was used, including income received in cash and in kind from seventeen different income sources. The latter covered, *inter alia*: income from employment; income from property (including imputed rent if living in own house); interest, dividends, and pensions; transfers from government, from abroad, and from local friends or relatives; and the imputed value of own produce consumed.

The second aggregate is *food expenditure* (Schedule IV). This category recorded the value of food actually consumed by each household during a seven-day reference period. (In particular, the use of the term 'food expenditure' rather than 'food consumption' is something of a misnomer.) Value and

---

[20] Most notably, deficits increase with a uniform increase in variability—see Proposition A.8 in Appendix 9.1(d).

[21] Some details of the procedures adopted during field enumeration are given in the CFS 1981/82 *Instructions to Investigators* (Statistics Department, Central Bank of Ceylon 1981?). An exhaustive discussion and evaluation of the CFS categories is contained in Anand and Harris (1989).

(where possible) quantity data were obtained on a total of 200 separate food items, including drink, tobacco, and meals bought outside. Where a visitor was present for some meals, food expenditure of the household was reduced by the amount consumed by the visitor.

The third aggregate is *non-food non-durable expenditure* (Schedule V, sections 1 to 14). This category recorded the actual expenditure by the household during the last one month preceding the interview. Additionally, for many items of expenditure, a longer reference period of either the last six months or the last one year was also used. The items covered in this category were, *inter alia*: housing (including imputed rent); clothing, footwear, and other apparel; fuel and light; transport and communication; education; recreation and entertainment; ceremonial expenditure; laundry and cleaning; gifts and donations; personal expenditure; payments to servants in cash and kind; litigation; medical expenses; and infants' requirements.

The fourth and final aggregate is *durable expenditure* (Schedule V, section 15). This category recorded the purchases and sales of, and maintenance expenditure on, durable goods during the last one month as well as the last six months preceding the interview. The durable goods included a total of 41 items such as radios, bicycles, fans, sewing machines, kitchen equipment, and furniture.

The definition of durable expenditure that we use in this chapter is purchases plus maintenance minus sales. This definition is intended to avoid the kind of double counting that would otherwise be associated with a sale of durables the proceeds of which went towards further purchases of durables. (The effects of such double counting are particularly clear at the aggregate level where, if no allowance were made for sales, durable expenditure would increase in proportion to the number of times durable goods changed hands!)

The distinction between non-durable and durable expenditure within the overall category of non-food expenditure is slightly blurred. Certainly the economic life of all the items treated as durables is much longer than any of the reference periods used in the survey, and they should indeed be regarded as durable. Similarly, the non-durable items include many goods that were undoubtedly consumed within the reference period: firewood, kerosene, gas, train fares, postage, daily expenses associated with schooling, visits to the cinema, newspapers, and soap. But the non-food non-durable category also includes goods whose lifetime is greater than the longest reference period used for such items (six months)—e.g. clothing, footwear, mattresses, rugs, sports goods, and umbrellas. Finally, it includes housing.

The actual distinction being drawn in the CFS between durable and non-durable goods appears to be as follows. Those items classified as durables seem to be so classified because their purchase is mainly an investment which will result in a flow of services for a long time into the future (several years). There is no sense in which the expenditure on them in the reference period (last one month or last six months) provides a meaningful estimate of the value of the services derived from them during this period. But housing is classified as a non-durable because it is possible to value the flow of services derived from it. The awkward intermediate group of items that are somewhat but not very durable (clothing, footwear, etc.) have been classified as non-durable because a significant fraction of the total services to be derived from them could be expected to be obtained during the intermediate reference period of six months.

It can also be seen that the three major categories of expenditure in the CFS do not correspond exactly to the three categories of consumption that we have taken as the determinants of short-run physical utility. First, non-food non-durable items such as mattresses or umbrellas, which actually have a significant durable element, should be put in the durables category. Secondly, gifts to other households are included in non-food expenditure. Such gifts should be excluded from the non-food expenditure of individuals if one is interested, as we are, in measuring their physical well-being. Thirdly, it is debatable whether items such as litigation and medical expenses should be included in non-food expenditure. (We would be inclined to include the latter but exclude the former.)

We shall not, however, make any adjustments to these expenditure categories for two reasons. First, these are the categories that have been used by other researchers (in Sri Lanka and elsewhere) without adjustment. We wish to explore the strengths and weaknesses of these categories as a check on earlier work. Secondly, although it is possible to envisage all sorts of fine tuning,[22] the effects of such adjustment need to be compared with a reference case. Fine tuning is not worth undertaking for its own sake; we must show that it results in an improvement relative to the reference case. The natural reference case to choose consists of the existing categories.

(f) The CFS subsample

The subsample of households from CFS 1981/82 on which the calculations in this chapter are based is fractionally smaller than the full sample available. This subsection briefly explains our decision to drop certain households and why this makes no difference to the comparison of alternative welfare indicators. The households excluded from our subsample are those with multiple spending units.

As for budget surveys in other developing countries, a *household* in the CFS was defined as a group of persons living together and sharing common cooking arrangements. The concept of a spending unit, however, is peculiar to the CFS. A *spending unit* was defined to consist of one or more persons who are members of the same household and share a major part of their income and expenditure (not just food). They act as a unit in making the principal spending

---

[22] Of course, for some items—especially durable goods—the information required for fine tuning is simply absent from the CFS.

decisions, and can include either the whole household or a part of it. For instance, the families of two brothers may form a household, but if one brother's spending is independent of the other's they will form separate spending units. All domestic servants, boarders, etc. within a household form separate spending units.

There are both conceptual and practical difficulties in estimating the consumption and income of spending units in households with more than one spending unit. These difficulties stem from the existence of transfers between the spending units, implicit or explicit. At the conceptual level, for example, we must determine how to attribute the flow of services from a durable such as a radio or TV purchased by one spending unit and enjoyed also by other spending units in the household. Even with housing (which is less of a public good), the correct method of imputation of housing services by subsidiary spending units needs to be properly established. At the practical level, there are problems of discovering the actual transfers that have been made between spending units of a household, and of matching transfers to the specific purposes for which they have taken place.[23] For example, all expenditure relating to the rent or upkeep of the house is presently recorded under the primary spending unit, with any contribution by the subsidiary spending unit(s) entered elsewhere.[24] Unfortunately, transfers of the latter type cannot be distinguished from transfers to, and receipts from, spending units outside the household: the CFS questionnaire does not provide separate headings dedicated to the recording of intrahousehold transfers.

In contrast, great care was taken to ensure that food consumption was correctly attributed to the various spending units of a household.[25] The actual expenditure incurred by each spending unit on non-food items was also correctly recorded. But because intrahousehold transfers are difficult to isolate on a consistent basis, the true consumption and income of spending units cannot be established accurately. For the same reason, the total consumption and income of the households containing these spending units will be

[23] Detailed evidence on these problems is contained in an appendix of Anand and Harris (1989), which scrutinizes the characteristics (including transfers) of multiple-spending-unit households. In the CFS 1981/82 data there are 348 multiple-spending-unit households which contain among them 809 spending units (2,568 individuals). There are 263 households with 2 spending units; 62 households with 3 spending units; 19 households with 4 spending units; 3 households with 5 spending units; and 1 household with 6 spending units.

[24] Such lodging costs for the subsidiary spending unit(s) could have been recorded under the expenditure heading of 'Boarding Fees' or 'Gifts and Donations to Other Spending Units', and would have been received as income by the primary spending unit under the heading of 'Transfer Income from Local Friends/Relatives' or 'Other Transfer Income'. As the data presently stand, therefore, both the income and consumption of the primary spending unit will be overestimated.

[25] An elaborate system of 'food points' was used with each meal assigned a different weight. The CFS investigator recorded the number of persons present from each spending unit and from outside the household for meals each day. Food consumption was then allocated according to the number of food points for each spending unit after netting out visitors' food points.

inconsistently estimated if we aggregate up the spending units into household, and choose thereby to ignore intrahousehold inequality.[26]

In view of these difficulties we have decided, for the purposes of the present chapter, to drop the 348 multiple-spending-unit households from the full CFS sample of 7,927 households.[27] This exclusion will not bias the comparison of alternative welfare indicators undertaken in section 9.3 provided that households do not adjust their composition in response to short-run fluctuations in income. We take this to be an uncontroversial assumption. (A precise formulation of the conditions under which our analysis will be unaffected is given in Appendix 9.1 (f).)

9.3. *Empirical estimation*

In this section we investigate the properties of four potential welfare indicators. These indicators are based directly on major categories of the CFS 1981/82 data. They are: income per capita; total expenditure per capita; food expenditure per capita; and foodshare.

(a) *Income per capita*

As mentioned in section 9.2(*b*), (short-run) income per capita is likely to be variable relative to long-run average income. Although short-run income may approximate long-run average income for those in regular employment, and with no independent and unpredictable source of income such as home produce, this will be the case for only a minority of households in Sri Lanka. For others such as those in a rural household, much of whose income derives from agricultural employment or is in the form of agricultural produce, variability of short-run income will be particularly marked. (We emphasize that the CFS was conducted during the course of a year; hence different households were sampled during different seasons.)

There may be a second kind of variability associated with short-run income. An individual in middle age is likely to earn more than his or her lifetime average income. Similarly, an older individual is likely to earn somewhat less than his or her lifetime average income. If the middle-aged individual saves against retirement then income for him or her will overstate total consumption.

---

[26] Such inequality is likely to be particularly serious in a household some of whose spending units are servants.

[27] If our search for a welfare indicator results in a measure (per capita income, for instance) that cannot be calculated consistently for multiple-spending-unit households, then it will not be possible to draw representative conclusions about living standards in Sri Lanka from the CFS 1981/82 data. Such a result would nevertheless suggest that certain changes to the questionnaire design of future surveys are desirable. If, however, our search results in an indicator that can be calculated for multiple-spending-unit households (per capita food expenditure, for instance), then it will be possible to return to the full CFS sample, and compute representative estimates of living standards in Sri Lanka for 1981/82.

An elderly individual, on the other hand, may consume out of savings. Income for such an individual will therefore understate consumption. These are the kinds of effects emphasized by the life-cycle hypothesis of saving (Ando and Modigliani 1963). The seriousness of these effects in the CFS data may be mitigated by the tendency in Sri Lanka of different generations of the same family to live in a single household, but it is unlikely that they will be wholly absent.

It is possible to test for the variability of short-run income relative to long-run average income by comparing CFS estimates with the prediction of negative savings in bottom ranges obtained from the simple statistical model (section 9.2(d) and Appendix 9.1(b)). Thus we rank the individuals in our CFS subsample by their per capita household income, divide them into ten deciles, and compare the per capita income of the resulting bottom ranges with their per capita non-durable expenditure (rather than with total consumption, which is not observed). The results of such a calculation are given in Table 9.1. The table shows the actual values of non-durable expenditure and income in order to provide an adequate perspective on the magnitude of the difference between them.

Naturally we cannot expect the prediction to be verified perfectly—for two reasons. First, non-durable expenditure is, if anything, an underestimate of total consumption since it makes no allowance for the flow of services derived from durables. Indeed, the average of net durable expenditure over a sector probably gives some indication of the value of the flow of services derived there from durables. This average is positive in all three sectors and in the island as a whole (see Table 9.2). Secondly, there is net saving in the urban and rural sectors, and in the economy as a whole (see Tables 9.1 and 9.2), whereas the model leading to deficit ranges is predicated on zero net saving in the relevant population.[28] Both of these facts operate in the same direction. They make it less likely that a bottom range will exhibit a deficit in its income relative to its non-durable expenditure (Appendix 9.1(c)).

Table 9.1 shows that in the urban and rural sectors, and in the island as a whole, all bottom ranges up to and including the bottom 90 per cent show a deficit. Thus the number of surplus ranges is the minimum consistent with the qualifications of the preceding paragraph. In the estate sector all bottom ranges are in deficit. This is not necessarily significant since the sector as a whole is in deficit.

Table 9.1 also shows in parentheses the per capita income and non-durable expenditure of each decile separately. In the urban sector seven deciles are in deficit, while in the rural sector the number is eight. Since the surplus of

---

[28] Positive net saving would be predicted on the basis of the life-cycle savings hypothesis in a country whose population is growing—as is that of Sri Lanka. In this case the number of middle-aged individuals saving for their retirement exceeds the number of elderly individuals running down their savings.

Table 9.1 Per capita non-durable expenditure and per capita income of the lowest (100p) per cent of individuals in each sector ranked by per capita household income (Rs. per month)

Lowest (100p) per cent, $p =$	Urban sector		Rural sector		Estate sector		All island	
	Per capita non-durable expenditure	Per capita income	Per capita non-durable expenditure	Per capita income	Per capita non-durable expenditure	Per capita income	Per capita non-durable expenditure	Per capita income
0.1	**155.74**	**97.09**	**144.41**	**74.97**	**183.00**	**100.72**	**146.04**	**79.21**
	(155.74)	(97.09)	(144.41)	(74.97)	(183.00)	(100.72)	(146.04)	(79.21)
0.2	162.20	117.97	146.33	94.44	189.67	119.09	152.63	99.16
	(168.61)	(138.70)	(148.24)	(113.91)	(196.34)	(137.45)	(159.21)	(119.11)
0.3	176.50	136.47	154.95	109.33	201.55	131.53	160.31	114.48
	(204.83)	(173.13)	(172.17)	(139.07)	(225.66)	(156.79)	(175.68)	(145.12)
0.4	191.88	154.53	163.87	122.91	208.32	142.82	170.33	128.49
	(238.25)	(209.00)	(190.62)	(163.64)	(228.12)	(175.78)	(200.33)	(170.47)
0.5	206.93	172.32	173.48	136.04	217.95	152.45	180.87	142.02
	(266.78)	(243.03)	(211.93)	(188.57)	(256.53)	(191.05)	(223.08)	(196.19)
0.6	224.22	192.01	183.89	149.32	226.84	162.27	192.88	155.97
	(310.76)	(290.53)	(235.99)	(215.79)	(271.50)	(211.62)	(252.86)	(225.65)
0.7	243.21	214.75	195.58	164.24	237.44	173.18	205.11	171.69
	(357.19)	(351.33)	(265.82)	(253.85)	(300.40)	(237.99)	(278.50)	(265.98)
0.8	266.16	242.51	210.39	182.28	246.70	185.04	220.75	190.85
	(427.37)	(437.49)	(313.76)	(308.23)	(312.89)	(269.77)	(330.27)	(325.11)
0.9	294.49	281.75	229.48	208.07	258.27	199.67	241.04	218.25
	(520.54)	(594.80)	(382.25)	(414.42)	(349.44)	(314.97)	(403.23)	(437.24)
1.0	352.77	389.33	256.47	288.03	277.50	227.52	274.87	301.61
	(874.48)	(1,352.45)	(499.27)	(1,007.35)	(448.88)	(475.75)	(579.33)	(1,051.75)
TOTAL	352.77	389.33	256.47	288.03	277.50	227.52	274.87	301.61

Notes: The figures for non-durable expenditure and income are based directly on the CFS definitions. Thus non-durable expenditure is the total of the entries in Schedule IV and in sections 1–14 of Schedule V of the CFS 1981/82 questionnaire, and income is the total of the entries in Schedule VI.

The figures in parentheses are averages for the corresponding decile. For example, Rs. 238.25 is non-durable expenditure per capita of individuals in the fourth decile of the urban sector.

Bold-face entries denote deficit situations where non-durable expenditure exceeds income (for the bottom range or the decile).

The sample size on which this table is based is: urban sector—6,837 individuals; rural sector—29,330 individuals; estate sector—2,716 individuals; and all

Table 9.2 Net durable expenditure, net disinvestment, and net loans taken per capita for deciles of individuals in each sector ranked by per capita household income (Rs. per month)

Per capita income decile	Urban sector					Rural sector				
	Net durable expenditure (1)	Net financial and physical disinvestment (2)	Net loans taken (3)	Resources generated (3) + (2) − (1)	Deficit from Table 9.1	Net durable expenditure (1)	Net financial and physical disinvestment (2)	Net loans taken (3)	Resources generated (3) + (2) − (1)	Deficit from Table 9.1
1	−7.58	36.33	44.55	88.46	58.66	0.62	26.34	32.53	58.25	69.45
2	−0.90	4.76	26.50	32.16	29.91	0.44	14.00	20.15	33.71	34.33
3	−2.35	4.36	27.29	34.00	31.70	−0.97	17.84	16.71	35.52	33.10
4	1.22	−1.03	39.96	37.71	29.25	1.55	8.65	23.15	30.25	26.98
5	12.50	11.38	66.63	65.51	23.75	1.06	6.95	20.49	26.38	23.36
6	12.83	16.52	80.39	84.08	20.23	4.61	−14.06	26.02	7.35	20.20
7	44.97	38.17	34.60	27.80	5.86	5.44	3.96	27.84	26.36	11.97
8	11.20	−57.09	47.42	−20.87	−10.12	15.13	−2.30	40.67	23.24	5.53
9	54.33	39.07	37.28	22.02	−74.25	13.58	−18.23	29.84	−1.97	−32.16
10	151.66	−233.81	98.23	−287.24	−477.97	69.85	−372.71	25.56	−417.00	−508.07
TOTAL	27.87	−14.24	50.31	8.20	−36.57	11.14	−32.97	26.30	−17.81	−31.56

Table 9.2 (continued)

Per capita income decile	Estate sector					All island				
	Net durable expenditure (1)	Net financial and physical disinvestment (2)	Net loans taken (3)	Resources generated (3) + (2) − (1)	Deficit from Table 9.1	Net durable expenditure (1)	Net financial and physical disinvestment (2)	Net loans taken (3)	Resources generated (3) + (2) − (1)	Deficit from Table 9.1
1	−7.06	15.35	56.15	78.56	82.28	−0.92	27.09	33.18	61.19	66.83
2	0.83	−5.29	59.02	52.90	58.90	0.09	17.70	25.43	43.04	40.10
3	2.03	−1.49	60.76	57.24	68.86	−0.80	11.33	22.34	34.47	30.56
4	1.20	−3.99	47.64	42.45	52.34	1.07	5.71	24.86	29.50	29.87
5	1.52	1.45	67.23	67.16	65.48	1.27	0.23	26.71	25.67	26.89
6	2.31	2.61	51.23	51.53	59.89	4.18	−7.70	33.45	21.57	27.22
7	4.57	3.65	71.67	70.75	62.42	8.05	4.51	46.09	42.55	12.53
8	7.49	−2.02	58.19	48.68	43.12	20.71	6.85	41.18	27.32	5.17
9	9.31	35.99	49.12	75.80	34.47	16.05	−28.71	33.66	−11.10	−34.01
10	37.23	−7.87	40.77	−4.33	−26.86	87.48	−307.93	39.13	−356.28	−472.42
TOTAL	5.97	3.88	56.14	54.05	49.98	13.72	−27.10	32.60	−8.22	−26.74

Notes: All figures presented in the table relate to a reference period of one month.

Net durable expenditure is defined as durable purchases plus durable maintenance minus durable sales.

Net loans taken is defined as loans taken less loans repaid less interest paid on loans (section 10 of Schedule VII). This category is intended to capture the net resources made available via loans.

Net financial and physical disinvestment is a catch-all category. It includes an estimate of the resources made available to the household from the disposal of assets (sections 1–8 of Schedule VII), but it excludes tax payments (section 9 of Schedule VII).

The sample size on which this table is based is: urban sector—6,837 individuals; rural sector—29,330 individuals; estate sector—2,716 individuals; and all island—38,883 individuals.

income over non-durable expenditure expressed as a ratio of non-durable expenditure is 10 per cent in the urban sector and 12 per cent in the rural sector, the larger number of deficit deciles in the rural sector may be due to greater variability there of short-run relative to long-run income. The relative size of the deficit of corresponding deciles in the rural and urban sectors may also be due to the same reason.[29] For example, in the rural sector the deficit of the first decile as a fraction of its non-durable expenditure is 48 per cent, while the corresponding figure in the urban sector is 38 per cent. Finally, once account is taken of the overall deficit in the estate sector, the figures suggest that variability there may be rather lower.

The magnitude of the deficits of the lower deciles is startling. One is therefore led to consider how the households that make up these deciles have generated the resources needed to finance the deficits. Three principal mechanisms suggest themselves: the sale of consumer durables, financial and physical disinvestment (other than consumer durables), and the taking of loans.[30] Table 9.2 presents figures on these three mechanisms. It will be seen that they do generate the required resources. For example, the third decile of the urban sector has a deficit of Rs. 31.70 per capita. This deficit is covered by Rs. 27.29 of loans, Rs. 4.36 of disinvestment, and Rs. 2.35 worth of durable sales. In the seventh decile of the same sector, the resources available from loans, disinvestment, and the substantial net expenditure on durables are more than sufficient to cover the small deficit of Rs. 5.86.[31]

The balance in Table 9.2 is generally not exact. In the examples of the previous paragraph, resources generated actually exceeded recorded expenditure. The opposite imbalance also occurs. For example, in the eighth decile of the urban sector, income exceeds non-durable expenditure by Rs. 10.12. Yet payments for the acquisition of durables and financial and physical assets, net of loans taken, amount to Rs. 20.87. A full explanation of these discrepancies

[29] This is only an informal statement because the 'variability' being compared relates to the distribution of long-run average incomes in different sectors. Even for the same population, a larger deficit need not necessarily imply greater variability—see Appendix 9.1(d).

[30] Schedule VII of the CFS 1981/82 questionnaire on 'Savings, Investments, Loans and Taxes' records data on changes in assets (for the last one month and the last six months preceding the interview) under 10 major sections: (1) Financial Assets (e.g. savings accounts and certificates, fixed deposits, bonds, securities, and shares); (2) Physical Assets (e.g. buildings, machinery, and equipment); (3) Contributions (e.g. life insurance premiums, Employees Provident Fund, Cheettu); (4) Loans Given; (5) Assets and Liabilities representing Advances and Arrears; (6) Cash Assets and Stocks (including cash in hand, and stocks of agricultural and industrial products); (7) Capital Transfers (including gifts of a capital nature such as dowry, stocks and shares, land and buildings, etc.); (8) Capital Losses (of physical and business assets due to natural causes including destruction and theft); (9) Income Tax (including licensing fees, death duties, and other taxes); (10) Loans Taken (e.g. from boutiques, including amounts borrowed, repayments, and interest payments).

[31] Note that income tax payments (section (9) of Schedule VII) were not subtracted in calculating available resources. A more accurate estimate of the resources available to finance deficits will be found in Anand and Harris (1989).

would require a detailed discussion of the survey concepts and methodology (relating to Schedule VII of the CFS questionnaire) that is not germane to the main purpose of the present chapter.

Table 9.2 does seem to show, however, that the deficits are not caused by underdeclaration of income. Indeed, the table suggests a more general conclusion. To the extent that calculations such as those of Table 9.1 have formed the evidence for the belief that income is underdeclared, that view is weakened. For such calculations are more plausibly explained as the consequence of a rather less contentious factor—the variability of short-run relative to long-run income.[32]

It is worth pursuing the question of under- or overdeclaration of income a little further. It is conceivable that a high-income household, mistrusting the motives of a survey, might underdeclare its income. It is, however, unlikely that such a household would be so naïve as to declare its expenditure truthfully, thereby creating an obvious discrepancy. Hence underdeclaration of income by high-income households cannot be used to account for a deficit. Furthermore, there is a limit to the extent to which such a household can plausibly underdeclare its income.[33] This extent would not be sufficient to place it in the lowest deciles, where the deficits are greatest.

The case of low-income households is only marginally more problematic. Such a household might exaggerate its consumption out of pride. But once again it seems likely that it would do the same for its income. Another factor reducing the size of any deficit arising from exaggeration of consumption is the fact that a significant proportion of a poor household's total expenditure will be consumption in kind (e.g. home produce). Any such consumption is automatically entered by CFS investigators as income in kind too.[34]

Thus, while over- or underdeclaration may be present, it is unlikely to be relevant to explaining the discrepancies between income and expenditure. Although it would certainly be interesting to try to detect such misdeclaration, we are uncertain as to how this might be done. In particular, our investigations of the data so far have not uncovered any evidence of it. Ultimately we must rely on the training and motivation of the investigators. Such reliance would appear to be well placed (see Anand and Harris 1985: Appendices 1.A, 1.D, and 1.E).

[32] The conclusion that it is variability that is at fault will be reinforced in the following subsections where we examine ranking variables which are less variable than income.

[33] A household making obviously implausible responses to the questionnaire would be deemed by the survey team not to have 'responded satisfactorily', and would have been excluded from the final sample.

[34] A low-income household might, however, try to underdeclare its income—and expenditure—for fear of losing its entitlement to government subsidies, i.e. food stamps, even though such entitlements were established and eligibility was finalized well before the CFS 1981/82 was carried out.

(b) Total expenditure per capita

In the previous subsection we examined the usefulness of per capita income as a welfare indicator, and concluded that it was undesirably variable relative to long-run average income. In this subsection we investigate the performance of total expenditure per capita as a welfare indicator. Our definition of total expenditure is food expenditure plus non-food non-durable expenditure plus durable expenditure (where durable expenditure is defined as purchases plus maintenance minus sales).

As in the permanent income hypothesis, we would argue that a household's consumption is likely to relate more closely to its long-run average income than to its short-run income. At the very least, the household will attempt to iron out some of the fluctuations in its income. Even if it does not succeed in holding consumption constant, it is likely to dampen the variability of consumption relative to short-run income. In months when it receives a low income, it will dissave, take loans (often from the local boutique[35]), and sell jewellery or some other durable item.[36] In this way it will maintain its consumption.[37] On the other hand, in months when it receives a high income, it will save, repay loans, and redeem or repurchase durable items. But it will not necessarily increase its consumption. This suggests the use of total consumption as a welfare indicator.

Total expenditure, unfortunately, differs from total consumption in two important respects. These relate principally to the treatment of durables. First, total expenditure incorporates information on *changes* in the stocks of durables, whereas total consumption requires information on the stocks themselves (e.g. their level and economic life). Secondly, the expenditure on a durable does not provide a direct estimate of the value of the flow of services from it. To obtain such an estimate a knowledge of the expected economic life of the durable is needed. To take a hypothetical example, suppose that two durables cost Rs. 1,200 each but one lasts ten years and the other five. Then, to a first approximation, the flow of services from the first is Rs. 10 per month and the flow from the second is Rs. 20. Despite these problems, total expenditure does nevertheless seem close enough to total consumption to be worthy of consideration.

The crucial question from our point of view, of course, is how variable total expenditure is relative to long-run average income. It is convenient to divide

[35] 'Boutique' is the common word in Sri Lanka for a small local shop or booth selling selected food and other items of everyday use.

[36] The acquisition and disposal of jewellery is a common form of saving and dissaving among poor households in Sri Lanka.

[37] Notice that if a household sells a durable item then there will be a reduction in its consumption of durable services. But the resources generated will exceed the value of the reduction. Hence the household can actually increase its total consumption if it wishes.

this variability into two components: the variability of total expenditure relative to total consumption, and the variability of total consumption relative to long-run average income.[38] The nature of the first component is seen most clearly when we emphasize the aspect of a durable good as an investment in a flow of services. Indeed, consider the following hypothetical example. Suppose that there exists a durable that provides precisely the level (and mix) of flow of durable services that a household requires, that the lifetime of this durable is one year, and that there are perfect capital markets. Then once a year the household will make a large expenditure to purchase a replacement, and the rest of the time it will have no durable expenditure. That is, its total expenditure will vary about its total consumption.

The nature of the second component is seen most clearly when we emphasize the aspect of a durable as a form of saving. If a household relies principally on durable purchases and sales as a means of saving and dissaving, then its stock of durables—and the associated flow of services—will adjust passively in response to fluctuations in short-run income. As a result its total consumption will track short-run income and vary relative to long-run average income. An extreme example of this use of durables is furnished by poor households, who deliberately use the purchase and sale of jewellery as a means of saving and dissaving. The second component can, however, arise in other ways. For example, the use of certain durables (e.g. clothing) can be prolonged until income is sufficiently favourable to replace them. Or again, expenditures on non-essential consumables (e.g. entertainment) will tend to be made at times when income is high. Finally, if—contrary to the hypothetical illustration of the previous paragraph—individuals cannot adjust their durable stocks to precisely the level (and mix) they require because of indivisibilities, then they will sometimes consume too many, and sometimes too few, durable services.

Overall, total expenditure should lie somewhere between long-run average income and the undesirably variable indicator, short-run income. We can express this somewhat more formally by augmenting the simple statistical model of section 9.2(d)—which underlies section 9.3(a)—where $Y = \eta + \varepsilon$ with $E(\varepsilon|\eta) = 0$. In addition to this, we now conclude that $Y = T + \zeta$ and $T = \eta + \theta$, where T represents total expenditure, and $E(\zeta|T) = E(\theta|\eta) = 0$.

---

[38] In talking of the variability of total consumption relative to long-run average income we are implicitly allowing for the breakdown of the permanent income hypothesis. It is, however, possible to reconcile some variability in total consumption with our identification of long-run average utility and long-run average income. To see this, consider an individual whose utility function takes the form $\Sigma_{t=1}^{T} u(\phi_t) + v(\Sigma_{t=1}^{T} \omega_t)$, where T is the lifetime, ϕ_t is food consumption in period t, and ω_t is consumption of non-food goods and services in period t. If the individual's income stream is not too uncertain compared with the opportunities to borrow and save, but is sufficiently uncertain to prevent ω_t being kept constant over time, then the required situation arises. (Note that, for the terminology long-run *average* utility to make sense here, $v(.)$ would have to be a linear function. Long-run, or lifetime, utility might be a better terminology.)

Table 9.3 Per capita non-durable expenditure and per capita income of the lowest (100p) per cent of individuals in each sector ranked by per capita total household expenditure (Rs. per month)

Lowest (100p) per cent, p =	Urban sector		Rural sector		Estate sector		All island	
	Per capita non-durable expenditure	Per capita income	Per capita non-durable expenditure	Per capita income	Per capita non-durable expenditure	Per capita income	Per capita non-durable expenditure	Per capita income
0.1	123.34	117.71	101.92	99.22	134.41	119.78	106.25	103.59
	(123.34)	(117.71)	(101.92)	(99.22)	(134.41)	(119.78)	(106.25)	(103.59)
0.2	141.06	137.45	118.93	118.47	157.86	139.06	123.77	121.83
	(158.78)	(157.18)	(135.88)	(137.65)	(179.88)	(157.16)	(141.30)	(140.08)
0.3	159.28	153.33	133.35	132.28	170.95	148.71	139.03	136.72
	(195.17)	(184.64)	(162.20)	(159.91)	(197.38)	(168.19)	(169.49)	(166.42)
0.4	177.14	176.07	146.41	145.02	183.88	157.77	152.71	150.88
	(230.60)	(244.13)	(185.63)	(183.26)	(222.05)	(184.52)	(193.78)	(193.38)
0.5	194.32	194.13	158.72	160.02	195.88	170.99	165.80	168.20
	(262.83)	(266.14)	(207.96)	(220.02)	(243.69)	(223.62)	(218.13)	(237.50)
0.6	211.97	214.71	171.27	175.19	207.94	181.31	179.20	181.87
	(299.88)	(317.18)	(233.93)	(250.91)	(267.76)	(232.53)	(246.18)	(250.18)
0.7	231.83	241.16	184.66	192.60	220.47	189.98	193.87	199.04
	(351.23)	(400.28)	(265.10)	(297.21)	(295.23)	(241.73)	(281.93)	(302.11)
0.8	255.56	266.14	200.18	209.54	233.71	198.56	210.39	216.85
	(422.31)	(441.57)	(308.79)	(328.08)	(327.27)	(259.15)	(326.13)	(341.61)
0.9	287.74	305.93	219.50	235.79	250.07	207.46	231.76	242.73
	(544.44)	(623.43)	(373.77)	(445.39)	(382.02)	(279.31)	(402.39)	(449.37)
1.0	352.77	389.33	256.47	288.03	277.50	227.52	274.87	301.61
	(924.92)	(1,135.94)	(589.08)	(757.96)	(519.06)	(404.13)	(662.59)	(831.15)
TOTAL	352.77	389.33	256.47	288.03	277.50	227.52	274.87	301.61

Notes: The total expenditure of a household is defined as food expenditure plus non-food non-durable expenditure plus durable expenditure, where durable expenditure is defined as purchases plus maintenance minus sales.

The reference period for durable expenditure is one month.

Figures in parentheses are averages for the corresponding decile.

Bold-face entries denote deficit situations.

The sample size on which this table is based is: urban sector—6,837 individuals; rural sector—29,330 individuals; estate sector—2,716 individuals; and all

In other words, in addition to Y being variable relative to η, we are requiring that Y be variable relative to T and that T be variable relative to η.[39]

As in the case of income, we can test for variability in total expenditure by ranking individuals by per capita total household expenditure, dividing them into deciles, and comparing the income with the non-durable expenditure of the bottom ranges obtained. Table 9.3 presents the results of such a calculation. (The validity of this test, where the definition of deficit is still the difference between non-durable expenditure and income, depends in part on the assumption that $E(\zeta|T) = 0$ and is discussed in n. 39). There is still evidence of variability, with the bottom 50 per cent of the urban sector—and the bottom 40 per cent of the rural sector and of the island as a whole—being in deficit. But the improvement relative to income (Table 9.1) is striking. For example, in the rural sector only the bottom 40 per cent exhibits a cumulative deficit compared with the bottom 90 per cent previously, and the deficit of the first decile has fallen from Rs. 69.44 per capita to just Rs. 2.70.

It is also interesting to examine the effects of an adjustment that is frequently made to durable expenditure. Durable expenditure was recorded for two reference periods, the last one month and the last six months. In view of the lumpiness of durable expenditure, it is argued that the durable expenditure component of total expenditure should be calculated as an average over six months.[40] Such 'smoothing' should have the effect of reducing that part of the variability of total expenditure that arises from durable expenditure. Thus we might expect a reduction in the deficits of bottom ranges in terms of our model.

There is a second, incidental effect on variability associated with this adjustment to total expenditure. It arises in our data set from the apparent memory lapse in recalling durable expenditure over six months compared with one month. Some idea of the extent of memory lapse resulting from the longer reference period can be obtained by comparing net durable expenditure over the last month with one-sixth of net durable expenditure over the last six months. Figures on this are given in Table 9.4. The figures suggest that the extent of the lapse may exceed 30 per cent.

The effect of such memory lapse can be interpreted as equivalent to a

---

[39] This has the following consequence. The deficits calculated in Table 9.1 are (slight) overestimates of expectations of the form $E(Y - \eta|Y \le y)$, because non-durable expenditure is (slightly) less than η. Proposition A.2 in Appendix 9.1 shows that such an expectation is negative. The deficits in Table 9.3, however, correspond to expectations of the form $E(Y - \eta|T \le t)$. Proposition A.2 does not in general apply to such an expectation. But if Y is variable relative to T, then $E(Y - \eta|T \le t) = E(T + \zeta - \eta|T \le t) = E(T - \eta|T \le t)$ because $E(\zeta|T) = 0$. Since, moreover, T is variable relative to η, Proposition A.2 allows one to conclude that $E(T - \eta|T \le t) \le 0$. Hence $E(Y - \eta|T \le t) \le 0$.

[40] In the CFS data, purchases of some non-durable items were also recorded for a reference period longer than one month. The main such category was clothing, purchases of which were recorded for a six-month reference period. One could consider 'smoothing' clothing expenditure too, but we have not done so here. In this way we retain comparability with earlier work such as that of Deaton (1981).

Table 9.4 Net durable expenditure per month for one- and six-month reference periods (Rs. per month)

	Urban sector	Rural sector	Estate sector	All island
One month	27.87	11.14	5.97	13.72
Six months	16.81	7.68	3.73	9.01
Lapse in six-month figure as a percentage of one-month figure	40%	31%	38%	34%

reduction in the variability of one component of total expenditure, i.e. durable expenditure. Indeed, the component is just a scaled-down version of its former self. This type of reduction in variability always leads to a reduction in the deficits of bottom ranges (Proposition A.8 in Appendix 9.1(d)).[41]

Table 9.5 ranks individuals according to their smoothed per capita total household expenditure, and shows the per capita non-durable expenditure and income of bottom ranges thus determined.[42] Given the two effects described above which operate to reduce variability, it is surprising to observe how little change there is between Table 9.5 and Table 9.3. With the exception of non-durable expenditure of the bottom 20 per cent in the estate sector, no figure for the lowest three deciles changes by more than two rupees. Nevertheless, the general drift is towards marginally lower deficits in the bottom ranges (and a reduction in size of the largest bottom range in deficit in the urban sector—from 50 per cent to 30 per cent).

(c) Food expenditure per capita

It was argued in the previous subsection that total expenditure is an imperfect indicator of total consumption because durable expenditure does not provide a direct measure of the value of the flow of services from durables. This lack of correspondence seemed likely to manifest itself in a degree of variability. Moreover, evidence of variability was provided by the continued existence of deficit bottom ranges. One is led, therefore, to explore other indicators that are free of the undesirable features associated with durable expenditure.

The most natural approach is to continue with the general idea of an expenditure-based indicator, but to exclude durable expenditure from it. This could be justified on the grounds that the investment aspect of durable

[41] If the 'smoothed' (average over six months) durable expenditure ε_1 is 30 per cent less than the unsmoothed (one month) durable expenditure ε_2 for everyone, then in terms of the statement of Proposition A.8 $\varepsilon_2 = \lambda\varepsilon_1$ with $\lambda = (1/0.7) > 1$.

[42] Note that the analogue of Table 9.5 for spending units (including those in multiple-spending-unit households), which appears as Table 2.2 in Anand and Harris (1985), exhibits various anomalies. These anomalies result from the difficulties associated with multiple-spending-unit households mentioned in section 9.2(f) of the present chapter.

Table 9.5 Per capita non-durable expenditure and per capita income of the lowest (100p) per cent of individuals in each sector ranked by 'smoothed' per capita total household expenditure (Rs. per month)

Lowest (100p) per cent, p =	Urban sector		Rural sector		Estate sector		All island	
	Per capita non-durable expenditure	Per capita income	Per capita non-durable expenditure	Per capita income	Per capita non-durable expenditure	Per capita income	Per capita non-durable expenditure	Per capita income
0.1	**121.16**	**117.32**	**102.31**	**99.56**	**132.24**	**121.53**	**106.12**	**103.09**
	(121.26)	(117.32)	(102.31)	(99.56)	(132.24)	(121.53)	(106.12)	(103.09)
0.2	**140.91**	**137.96**	**118.98**	**118.05**	**154.56**	**140.17**	**123.78**	**122.55**
	(160.30)	(158.33)	(135.66)	(136.54)	(176.64)	(158.60)	(141.40)	(141.97)
0.3	**158.56**	**154.09**	**133.47**	**132.41**	**169.28**	**149.77**	**138.81**	**136.95**
	(193.83)	(186.32)	(162.41)	(161.11)	(198.66)	(168.93)	(168.86)	(165.74)
0.4	176.10	177.09	146.45	144.42	182.76	159.40	152.55	149.86
	(228.99)	(246.46)	(185.41)	(180.48)	(223.15)	(188.25)	(193.76)	(188.55)
0.5	193.58	195.54	158.84	159.86	195.70	173.49	165.74	168.20
	(263.37)	(269.19)	(208.34)	(221.53)	(246.66)	(228.99)	(218.45)	(241.53)
0.6	211.57	216.12	171.41	175.42	207.56	182.66	179.16	181.75
	(300.99)	(318.42)	(234.21)	(253.12)	(267.02)	(228.61)	(246.25)	(249.50)
0.7	230.76	238.69	184.73	192.38	219.77	194.01	193.67	198.35
	(346.90)	(375.29)	(264.68)	(294.13)	(293.70)	(262.76)	(280.67)	(297.91)
0.8	255.16	265.18	200.10	208.67	233.47	200.05	210.16	216.70
	(424.65)	(449.19)	(307.65)	(322.66)	(328.76)	(241.99)	(325.62)	(345.18)
0.9	286.90	304.88	219.56	234.42	249.78	208.13	231.52	242.20
	(541.43)	(623.18)	(375.25)	(440.52)	(379.93)	(272.62)	(402.42)	(446.19)
1.0	352.77	389.33	256.47	288.03	277.50	227.52	274.87	301.61
	(942.40)	(1,145.38)	(588.56)	(770.30)	(525.58)	(401.09)	(664.85)	(836.07)
TOTAL	352.77	389.33	256.47	288.03	277.50	227.52	274.87	301.61

Notes: The definition of 'smoothed' total household expenditure is non-durable expenditure plus durable purchases plus durable maintenance minus durable sales for the reference period of the *last six months*.

Figures in parentheses are averages for the corresponding decile.

Bold-face entries denote deficit situations.

The sample size on which this table is based is: urban sector—6,837 individuals; rural sector—29,330 individuals; estate sector—2,716 individuals; and all island—38,883 individuals.

Table 9.6 Per capita non-durable expenditure and per capita income of the lowest (100p) per cent of individuals in each sector ranked by per capita household food expenditure (Rs. per month)

Lowest (100p) per cent, p =	Urban sector		Rural sector		Estate sector		All island	
	Per capita non-durable expenditure	Per capita income	Per capita non-durable expenditure	Per capita income	Per capita non-durable expenditure	Per capita income	Per capita non-durable expenditure	Per capita income
0.1	**127.80**	**130.94**	**103.64**	**101.61**	**144.69**	**134.82**	**109.00**	**108.18**
	(127.80)	(130.94)	(103.64)	(101.61)	(144.69)	(134.82)	(109.00)	(108.18)
0.2	145.68	148.18	122.59	122.72	169.41	143.62	128.44	128.41
	(163.44)	(165.28)	(141.55)	(143.86)	(193.68)	(152.26)	(147.88)	(148.65)
0.3	167.52	178.16	138.20	140.33	183.68	153.78	144.22	145.50
	(210.92)	(237.74)	(169.34)	(175.44)	(212.79)	(174.53)	(175.74)	(179.64)
0.4	186.53	193.34	152.03	153.70	196.59	167.96	159.53	160.79
	(243.38)	(238.75)	(193.54)	(193.85)	(234.31)	(209.37)	(205.45)	(206.68)
0.5	210.38	220.69	165.68	169.16	206.34	176.07	173.65	176.79
	(305.72)	(329.99)	(220.31)	(230.99)	(245.84)	(208.95)	(230.12)	(240.76)
0.6	228.98	237.93	178.55	184.26	218.80	184.84	187.32	193.25
	(321.95)	(324.10)	(242.92)	(259.83)	(280.36)	(228.16)	(255.63)	(275.47)
0.7	246.86	259.59	191.90	201.04	228.92	194.66	202.45	210.44
	(354.67)	(390.22)	(271.93)	(301.64)	(289.25)	(253.19)	(293.19)	(313.59)
0.8	272.86	292.39	206.60	220.96	241.42	201.29	218.57	230.67
	(454.94)	(522.09)	(309.32)	(360.14)	(330.45)	(248.49)	(331.41)	(372.27)
0.9	303.54	330.02	225.94	250.89	255.26	212.49	239.83	260.78
	(549.00)	(631.09)	(380.60)	(490.26)	(364.01)	(300.53)	(409.94)	(501.67)
1.0	352.77	389.33	256.47	288.03	277.50	227.52	274.87	301.61
	(792.05)	(918.60)	(531.29)	(622.26)	(477.32)	(362.56)	(590.11)	(668.94)
TOTAL	352.77	389.33	256.47	288.03	277.50	227.52	274.87	301.61

Notes: The figures in parentheses are averages for the corresponding decile.
Bold-face entries denote deficit situations.
The sample size on which this table is based is: urban sector—6,837 individuals; rural sector—29,330 individuals; estate sector—2,716 individuals; and all island—38,883 individuals.

expenditure greatly outweighs all other aspects. Furthermore, it is conceivable that a suitably chosen subset of total expenditure might prove to be monotonically related to total consumption. In this subsection we investigate a particular subset of total expenditure—namely, food expenditure.

We begin with a brief return to the statistical model of section 9.2(d). Suppose that total consumption is an exact monotonic increasing transform $m(.)$ of food expenditure ϕ, and suppose that total consumption is maintained constant at the level of long-run average income η, so that $m(\phi) = \eta$. Then the bottom decile of individuals ranked by ϕ will be the same as the bottom decile ranked by η, which is by definition the poorest decile. As before, we expect the non-durable expenditure per capita of this decile to yield an accurate estimate of the corresponding categories of consumption. Similarly, we expect net durable expenditure per capita of this decile to provide an accurate estimate of the flow of services derived from durables. This flow may be small, but it cannot be negative. If, on the other hand, there is noise in the relationship between ϕ and η we may observe deficit deciles, much as we did in section 9.3(b). (More precisely, this will be the case if $m(\phi) = \eta + \theta$ and $Y = m(\phi) + \zeta$, with $E(\theta|\eta) = E(\zeta|\phi) = 0$.)

Table 9.6 presents calculations for individuals ranked by food expenditure analogous to those for income and total expenditure given in Tables 9.1 and 9.3, respectively. Even compared with Table 9.5 for smoothed total expenditure, there is a marked improvement. In the urban sector no bottom range is in deficit, compared with a deficit among the bottom 30 per cent in Table 9.5. Indeed, the bottom decile has a Rs. 3.14 surplus compared with a Rs. 3.94 deficit in Table 9.5. In the rural sector only the bottom 10 per cent is in deficit, compared with the bottom 40 per cent before. Finally, corresponding figures for the island as a whole are 20 per cent and 40 per cent.

The discussion of the previous paragraph shows that food expenditure performs better than income or total expenditure on the criterion of minimizing the size of bottom range in deficit. We should like to emphasize, however, that we do not believe that this is the only relevant criterion for the selection of a welfare indicator. In particular, it would be a mistake simply to select the indicator which performed best on this criterion, no matter how obscure that indicator might be. This can be seen most clearly in terms of a hypothetical example. Suppose that we created an artificial indicator by assigning a random number to each individual, and then ranked all individuals by this indicator. Because of the size of the sample, the deficit of each decile would approximate the overall average deficit, which is actually a surplus of Rs. 26.74 per capita. That is, no decile would be in deficit.

Let us therefore consider another criterion. Let us examine the estimates obtained for consumption of durable services by deciles determined in turn by the three principal indicators used so far—income per capita, total expenditure per capita, and food expenditure per capita. These estimates are presented in Table 9.7. Since we know a priori that consumption of durable

Table 9.7 Net durable expenditure per capita for deciles of individuals in each sector ranked by household per capita income, per capita total expenditure, and per capita food expenditure (Rs. per month)

	Ranking variable											
	Per capita income				Per capita total expenditure				Per capita food expenditure			
Decile	Urban sector	Rural sector	Estate sector	All island	Urban sector	Rural sector	Estate sector	All island	Urban sector	Rural sector	Estate sector	All island
1	-7.58	0.62	-7.06	-0.92	-16.42	-8.26	-3.21	-9.08	1.18	0.35	0.67	0.39
2	-0.90	0.44	0.83	0.09	-0.49	0.28	-4.94	0.14	4.72	0.47	2.16	1.50
3	-2.35	-0.97	2.03	-0.80	-0.37	0.27	1.02	-0.31	2.88	3.45	3.36	4.37
4	1.22	1.55	1.20	1.07	-0.02	0.35	-1.11	0.38	2.26	4.16	5.49	3.11
5	12.50	1.06	1.52	1.27	1.75	1.30	0.25	1.24	24.85	4.03	1.00	3.93
6	12.83	4.61	2.31	4.18	4.26	1.38	1.23	1.53	13.15	5.31	-2.47	4.39
7	44.97	5.44	4.57	8.05	2.42	2.48	1.18	1.92	11.07	5.56	17.23	11.04
8	11.20	15.13	7.49	20.71	9.33	3.69	5.57	4.76	78.71	4.85	3.45	11.58
9	54.33	13.58	9.31	16.05	15.25	8.11	7.80	9.02	71.92	25.72	9.83	35.53
10	151.66	69.85	37.23	87.48	261.63	101.70	51.09	127.49	67.64	57.44	18.78	61.32
TOTAL	27.87	11.14	5.97	13.72	27.87	11.14	5.97	13.72	27.87	11.14	5.97	13.72

Notes: Net durable expenditure is defined as durable purchases plus durable maintenance minus durable sales.

The reference period for purchases, maintenance, and sales of durables is one month.

The sample size on which this table is based is: urban sector—6,837 individuals; rural sector—29,330 individuals; estate sector—2,716, individuals; and all island—38,883 individuals.

services cannot be negative, the performance of per capita income is disappointing. Negative estimates are obtained for three deciles in the urban sector and for one decile in each of the rural and estate sectors.

The performance of per capita total expenditure is worse, with four negative estimates in the urban sector, three in the estate sector, and one in the rural sector. Furthermore, the general pattern of the estimates suggests that net durable expenditure has played a significant role in determining the decile into which a household ultimately falls. If it happens to have made a large durable sale, it moves a long way down in the ranking. If it has made a large durable purchase, it moves a long way up. Finally, the performance of per capita food expenditure is much the best. There is only one negative estimate, in the estate sector. The table as a whole does, however, give the impression that durable expenditure is lumpy relative even to the enormous samples used to construct the estimates (see the sectoral sample sizes in the Notes to Table 9.7).

Once again we must bear in mind that random ranking of individuals would probably result in a positive estimate for consumption of durable services in almost all deciles. What is significant in the findings of Table 9.7 is that an indicator that was obtained via a coherent chain of economic reasoning should have this desirable property when other indicators reached by other coherent chains of reasoning do not.

In conclusion, if one is examining a group of individuals who face fairly homogeneous prices, then the claim that food expenditure will bear a monotonic relationship to total consumption or long-run average income is highly plausible, and food expenditure will be a good welfare indicator for that group. An example of such a group would be a group of households from the same sector which were visited at approximately the same time. Any given sector of our sample, however, contains households visited at different points during the survey year. It is possible that the price of food items varied relative to that of non-food items during the course of the year. If it did, then substitution effects might conceivably have upset the monotonic relationship between food expenditure and long-run average income.[43]

Unfortunately we cannot check for variations in the relative price of food and non-food items, since we do not have adequate non-food price data. What we can say is that if variations in the relative price of food did occur, and if they did affect the relationship between food expenditure and long-run average income, then the resulting problem for food expenditure is less serious than the problem for total expenditure caused by the lumpiness of durable expenditure —less, that is, on the criteria we have been using. Furthermore, this conclusion appears to be robust against the inclusion of another potential source of variation in relative prices—that between sectors.

---

[43] See the elasticity conditions discussed in section 9.2(b).

(d) Foodshare

In sections 9.3(*a*) to (*c*) we investigated various welfare indicators, all of which
were monetary. This feature caused no immediate problems since households
sampled from the same sector in the same year could be regarded as facing the
same prices, at least to a first approximation. If, however, one wished to
compare welfare levels over time, account would have to be taken of changes in
the general price level in each sector. This causes problems for income and total
expenditure. First, there are the well-known general problems of both a
conceptual and a practical nature associated with the calculation of non-food
price indices (e.g. quality variation and appropriate quantity units). Secondly,
there is a problem specific to Sri Lanka—the only non-food price index relates
exclusively to Colombo.

In the case of food expenditure there is certainly no problem in calculating
appropriate price indices. Detailed price data exist, and adequate quantity data
can be obtained from the Consumer Finance Surveys conducted over time by
the Central Bank.[44] Their intertemporal use must, however, rely on an implicit
premiss. One such premiss would be that the price of food items does not vary
too much relative to that of non-food items. Unfortunately, to test this premiss
requires information on changes in non-food prices. Furthermore, if it were
true, one might as well apply the food price index to income and total
expenditure too. An alternative premiss would recognize that the quantity of
food consumed indeed varied with changes in the relative price of food, but
that income and substitution effects were such as to keep food expenditure in a
monotonic relationship with the value of total consumption (at least over the
relevant range of variation in the relative price of food—see section 9.2(*b*)).

Considerations similar to those applying to food expenditure apply to
another variable—foodshare. This was suggested as a possible welfare indicator by Engel (1895). To quote Deaton (1981: 1):

. . . the share of food in total expenditure can be regarded as an (inverse) indicator of
welfare. It is . . . a very convenient indicator, since its definition as a dimensionless
ratio renders it comparable over time periods and between geographical locations, at
least if the relative price of food does not vary too much. However, the real interest in
the food share is that it may be capable of acting as a *better* indicator of welfare than
measures based on income or expenditure alone.

It should be emphasized that Deaton is not necessarily advocating the use of
foodshare. The tenor of his remarks is that it is worth exploring it as a welfare
indicator. The present subsection is devoted to a discussion of the performance
of foodshare as a welfare indicator.

Foodshare, or rather inverse foodshare σ, is easily introduced into our

[44] See Anand and Harris (1985: Tables 3.1, 3.2, 3.3) for examples of intersectoral and
intertemporal food price indices we have constructed from the Consumer Finance Surveys of
1973, 1978/79, and 1981/82.

statistical model. We simply set $\sigma = T/\phi$ where, as above, $m(\phi) = \eta$ for some strictly monotonic function $m(.)$. It turns out to have two interesting properties. First, the bottom $(100p)$ per cent of the population ranked by σ can be expected to show a deficit. This is an immediate consequence of the variability of total expenditure T (see Corollary A.11 in Appendix 9.1(e)). Secondly, the average food expenditure of the bottom $(100p)$ per cent of the population ranked by σ exceeds the corresponding average obtained when ranking by T, which in turn exceeds the true average.[45]

The intuition behind the first observation is very similar to that behind the deficits observed when ranking by income. The intuition behind the conclusion that the average food expenditure obtained when ranking by T exceeds the true average is simple too: the assumption that η is a monotonic function of ϕ means that the true average is also that obtained for the ranking by food expenditure, which of course gives the lowest conceivable average for any population subgroup of size $(100p)$ per cent. The intuition behind the conclusion that the average obtained when ranking by σ exceeds that obtained when ranking by T is slightly more subtle. Imagine dividing the population initially into two groups: the bottom $(100p)$ per cent ranked by T, and the top $100(1 - p)$ per cent. Now re-rank them by σ. The place of any individual who is initially a member of the bottom group, but moves to the top group on re-ranking, must be taken by an individual who is initially a member of the top group—and vice versa. Let the total expenditure and food expenditure of the first individual be T_1 and ϕ_1, respectively, and let the corresponding values for the second individual be T_2 and ϕ_2. By choice of the bottom group, $T_2 > T_1$. Hence, if $\sigma_2 = T_2/\phi_2 < \sigma_1 = T_1/\phi_1$, this must be because $\phi_2 > \phi_1$. But then the average food expenditure of the bottom group has increased.[46]

We begin by investigating the prediction that bottom ranges will be in deficit. Table 9.8 presents calculations of the non-durable expenditure and income per capita of bottom ranges of individuals ranked (in decreasing order) by the food share of the household to which they belong. We compare Table 9.8 with Table 9.3, the corresponding table for per capita total expenditure. The size of the largest bottom range exhibiting a deficit remains the same as in that table in the urban and rural sectors, at 50 per cent and 40 per cent, respectively. The only change occurs in the 'all island' figures, where the size increases from 40 per cent to 50 per cent. What is suspicious, however, is the steep increase in the magnitude of the deficit of the deficit deciles. For example, the bottom deciles of the urban and rural sectors, and the bottom decile of the island as a whole, exhibit deficits of Rs. 23.57, Rs. 12.82, and Rs. 17.92 per capita, respectively. These compare with deficits of Rs. 5.63, Rs. 2.70, and Rs. 2.66 per capita for the corresponding deciles of Table 9.3. Overall, the prediction seems to be well borne out.

[45] See Proposition A.12 in Appendix 9.1(e). The true average is by definition the average obtained when ranking by η.

[46] A more careful discussion will be found in Appendix 9.1(e).

Table 9.8 Per capita non-durable expenditure and per capita income of the lowest (100p) per cent of individuals in each sector ranked by inverse household foodshare (Rs. per month)

Lowest (100p) per cent, p =	Urban sector		Rural sector		Estate sector		All island	
	Per capita non-durable expenditure	Per capita income	Per capita non-durable expenditure	Per capita income	Per capita non-durable expenditure	Per capita income	Per capita non-durable expenditure	Per capita income
0.1	**201.49** (201.49)	**177.92** (177.92)	**181.47** (181.47)	**168.65** (168.65)	**221.48** (221.48)	**185.44** (185.44)	**190.41** (190.41)	**172.49** (172.49)
0.2	**200.01** (198.72)	**187.54** (197.10)	**178.82** (176.16)	**169.32** (169.98)	**228.96** (236.40)	**194.46** (203.45)	**186.63** (182.86)	**173.45** (174.41)
0.3	**205.87** (217.34)	**192.37** (201.98)	**183.28** (192.19)	**176.76** (191.61)	**230.81** (234.54)	**195.33** (197.07)	**190.67** (198.74)	**180.16** (193.55)
0.4	**214.36** (239.82)	**204.77** (241.94)	**185.86** (193.59)	**185.10** (210.10)	**228.20** (220.43)	**193.64** (188.63)	**193.67** (202.68)	**188.25** (212.61)
0.5	**226.49** (275.05)	**222.88** (295.35)	**192.31** (218.11)	**194.51** (232.13)	**234.16** (258.01)	**197.60** (213.41)	**199.95** (224.99)	**197.45** (234.09)
0.6	**242.39**	**244.46**	**199.39**	**203.93**	**237.57**	**203.29**	**207.19**	**207.61**
,	(321.68)	(352.09)	(234.78)	(251.00)	(254.47)	(231.52)	(243.41)	(258.50)
0.7	**257.57** (348.88)	**267.85** (408.57)	**207.32** (254.92)	**215.63** (285.92)	**246.56** (300.14)	**210.18** (251.23)	**216.99** (275.86)	**221.72** (306.44)
0.8	**275.12** (398.04)	**289.46** (440.81)	**216.64** (281.82)	**228.40** (317.74)	**251.98** (289.81)	**213.09** (233.39)	**227.48** (300.75)	**235.35** (330.59)
0.9	**301.57** (512.39)	**318.16** (546.85)	**229.52** (332.58)	**247.15** (397.09)	**262.91** (352.20)	**218.42** (262.01)	**242.55** (363.11)	**255.65** (418.00)
1.0	**352.77** (813.31)	**389.33** (1,029.62)	**256.47** (498.91)	**288.03** (655.78)	**277.50** (405.47)	**227.52** (307.31)	**274.87** (565.57)	**301.61** (715.00)
TOTAL	**352.77**	**389.33**	**256.47**	**288.03**	**277.50**	**227.52**	**274.87**	**301.61**

Notes: Foodshare is defined as food expenditure divided by total expenditure, where total expenditure is defined as in Table 9.3.

Individuals are ranked in order of increasing inverse household foodshare (or decreasing household foodshare).

Figures in parentheses are averages for the corresponding decile.

Bold-face entries denote deficit situations.

The sample size on which this table is based is: urban sector—6,837 individuals; rural sector—29,330 individuals; estate sector—2,716 individuals; and all island—38,883 individuals.

Turning to estimates of the average food expenditure of bottom ranges, we must raise an obvious caveat. The predictions that the average food expenditure of the bottom ($100p$) per cent of individuals ranked by per capita food expenditure will be lower than the corresponding average when individuals are ranked by per capita total expenditure, and that this average will in turn be lower than that obtained using inverse foodshare, are vacuous. They will be true for any distribution, because our arguments apply just as well to the CFS data as they do to a population distribution. The interest of Table 9.9, which presents these averages disaggregated by sector, thus lies in the magnitude of the changes that occur when re-ranking takes place. For example, the food expenditure per capita of the bottom decile in the island as a whole changes from Rs. 78.80 to Rs. 83.01 to Rs. 164.37 as re-ranking occurs. The first change is of the order of 5 per cent, while the second represents a near doubling. This example is representative of the rest of the table, and shows that ranking by inverse foodshare is a totally inappropriate way of arriving at an estimate of the food expenditure of the poor. More broadly, it suggests that foodshare should be used as a welfare indicator only with caution.

It is natural to ask to what extent the effects we have just described are sensitive to the precise definition used of foodshare. For example, in his own work Deaton (1981) defined foodshare as the ratio of food expenditure to 'smoothed' total expenditure. We have investigated this second definition also. It gives results very similar to those of Table 9.8. Deaton (1981: 41) further suggested that in some cases it may be better to exclude lumpy purchases altogether. We have made calculations analogous to Table 9.8 for the ratio of food to non-durable expenditure (not shown as a table in this chapter). The resulting changes can be summarized as follows. The size of the largest bottom range in deficit in the urban sector falls from 50 per cent to 40 per cent, while the corresponding figures for the rural sector and the island as a whole remain the same. Next, the new deficits of the bottom deciles of the urban and rural sectors, and of the island as a whole, are Rs. 14.17, Rs. 11.49, and Rs. 14.08, respectively. This is a small improvement on the corresponding figures from Table 9.8. However, the new estimates of food expenditure per capita for the same deciles are Rs. 169.29, Rs. 158.29, and Rs. 165.12, respectively. They are not an improvement on the figures obtained using the original definition of foodshare.

We conclude the present subsection with some observations for which we have not yet been able to find a complete explanation. First, from Table 9.9 we see that in the urban and rural sectors, and in the island as a whole, food expenditure first decreases and then increases with inverse foodshare. (The picture for the estate sector is somewhat untidy, and it is difficult to point to a definitive pattern without using more elaborate econometric techniques.) This suggests that the underlying relationship between food expenditure and foodshare may not be monotonic. (By the underlying relationship we mean the theoretical regression $E(\phi \mid \sigma)$. It must be borne in mind that $E(\phi \mid \sigma)$, regarded

Table 9.9 Per capita food expenditure of the lowest (100p) per cent of individuals in each sector ranked alternately by per capita food expenditure, per capita total expenditure, and inverse foodshare (Rs. per month)

Lowest (100p) per cent, $p =$	Urban sector Per capita food expenditure	Per capita total expenditure	Inverse foodshare	Rural sector Per capita food expenditure	Per capita total expenditure	Inverse foodshare	Estate sector Per capita food expenditure	Per capita total expenditure	Inverse foodshare	All island Per capita food expenditure	Per capita total expenditure	Inverse foodshare
0.1	88.39	95.48	171.27	76.02	79.89	157.10	101.02	105.92	191.42	78.80	83.01	164.37
	(88.39)	(95.48)	(171.27)	(76.02)	(79.89)	(157.10)	(101.02)	(105.92)	(191.42)	(78.80)	(83.01)	(164.37)
0.2	103.04	107.78	166.38	90.03	92.93	151.55	117.29	124.63	195.52	93.21	96.47	157.86
	(117.60)	(120.09)	(161.53)	(104.05)	(105.91)	(145.99)	(133.26)	(142.19)	(199.59)	(107.61)	(109.95)	(151.36)
0.3	116.13	122.11	167.16	100.47	103.49	152.31	128.09	134.54	194.64	104.07	107.58	158.17
	(142.13)	(150.35)	(168.69)	(121.29)	(124.63)	(153.82)	(150.14)	(154.54)	(192.88)	(125.77)	(129.73)	(158.79)
0.4	127.61	134.13	169.87	109.61	112.84	151.73	137.51	143.78	190.03	113.65	117.59	157.78
	(161.94)	(170.09)	(178.00)	(137.03)	(140.91)	(150.01)	(165.03)	(171.08)	(176.34)	(142.42)	(147.65)	(156.61)
0.5	138.07	144.37	174.82	117.97	121.27	154.03	146.25	152.94	192.35	122.43	126.16	159.71
	(179.90)	(185.20)	(194.65)	(151.43)	(155.00)	(163.21)	(181.69)	(189.40)	(201.62)	(157.53)	(160.45)	(167.41)
0.6	148.30	154.03	181.83	125.90	129.26	156.46	154.59	160.67	192.23	130.84	134.70	162.06
	(199.44)	(202.14)	(216.78)	(165.58)	(169.11)	(168.62)	(195.76)	(199.05)	(191.64)	(172.86)	(177.38)	(173.79)
0.7	158.32	164.25	187.00	133.96	137.32	158.98	162.52	168.57	195.45	139.49	143.51	165.53
	(218.75)	(225.69)	(218.09)	(182.29)	(185.77)	(174.11)	(209.83)	(215.64)	(214.65)	(191.38)	(196.36)	(186.41)
0.8	169.41	175.52	191.60	142.75	146.14	161.57	170.85	175.52	195.01	148.82	152.73	168.44
	(247.06)	(254.69)	(223.82)	(204.16)	(207.88)	(179.68)	(230.18)	(224.69)	(191.95)	(214.12)	(217.35)	(188.71)
0.9	182.59	188.24	197.53	153.24	156.52	164.87	180.95	184.56	197.19	159.90	163.61	172.32
	(288.04)	(289.72)	(244.82)	(237.11)	(239.37)	(191.27)	(260.26)	(257.47)	(215.01)	(248.58)	(250.48)	(203.39)
1.0	204.02	204.02	204.02	169.81	169.81	169.81	195.98	195.98	195.98	177.65	177.65	177.65
	(395.27)	(345.35)	(262.43)	(318.93)	(289.33)	(214.20)	(331.00)	(296.50)	(185.32)	(337.29)	(303.91)	(225.59)
TOTAL	204.02	204.02	204.02	169.81	169.81	169.81	195.98	195.98	195.98	177.65	177.65	177.65

Notes: Figures in parentheses are averages for the corresponding decile.

The sample size on which this table is based is: urban sector—6,837 individuals; rural sector—29,330 individuals; estate sector—2,716 individuals; and all island—38,883 individuals.

as a function, will in general not be the inverse of $E(\sigma|\phi)$ similarly regarded. Hence this concept of underlying relationship must be used with care.)

Secondly, we have calculated Spearman rank correlation coefficients among six of the indicators that have been considered in this paper. These are presented in Table 9.10. An obvious feature of the table is the way in which the correlation between income per capita and the other monetary indicators falls as the transient components of the budget are progressively removed. A more interesting feature can be read from the table provided one is prepared to accept for the sake of discussion that food expenditure per capita is monotonic in long-run average income, i.e. $\phi = m^{-1}(\eta)$ in terms of the statistical model. For then, on dividing total expenditure $T = \eta + \theta$ by ϕ to obtain inverse foodshare σ, one observes a dramatic drop in the Spearman rank correlation coefficient with η (i.e. ϕ) from 0.907 to 0.280.

We do not as yet have a rigorous explanation for this phenomenon, but can offer the following heuristic argument. For the purposes of this argument it is convenient to introduce a new function $r(\eta) = m^{-1}(\eta) = \phi$. Our idea is that the tendency for changes in relative position to occur at any given level of η when the population is ranked by T rather than η can be measured by the ratio of the noise θ to the intensity of the underlying relationship $E(T|\eta)$, as measured by its slope. Similar remarks apply to σ. Carrying out these calculations we obtain θ in the case of T (because $E(T|\eta) = \eta$ with noise θ), and $\theta/(1 - \eta r'/r)$ in the case of σ (because $E(\sigma|\eta) = \eta/r(\eta)$ with noise $\theta/r(\eta)$). If the elasticity of food expenditure with respect to long-run average income $\eta r'/r$ is positive, as we believe to be the case, and less than unity, then the second tendency is greater. In this case, inverse foodshare will be a more variable indicator than total expenditure per capita.

The assumption that the elasticity of food expenditure with respect to long-run income is less than unity is equivalent to requiring that Engel's Law hold for the share of food in long-run average income. If, however, Engel's Law does not hold, i.e. $\eta/r(\eta)$ is not monotonic in η, then this constitutes a direct reason to expect a low Spearman correlation coefficient between η and σ.[47] It may be that a direct reason of this kind is required in order to explain the scale of the effect.

Next, the magnitude of the Spearman correlation coefficient between inverse foodshare and either of the standard welfare indicators, per capita income and per capita total expenditure, is low—of the order of 0.5. It may therefore be unreasonable to espouse, say, both per capita total expenditure *and* inverse foodshare as good welfare indicators.

Finally, lest the difficulties with foodshare that we have enumerated be regarded as casting doubt on the suitability of food expenditure itself as a

[47] Table 9.9 suggests that the underlying relationship $E(\phi|\sigma)$ was not monotonic. We emphasize again that this does not tell us anything directly about $E(\sigma|\phi)$, which is the relevant underlying relationship here. We are currently investigating this second relationship by non-parametric regression techniques (see Anand and Harris 1989).

Table 9.10 Spearman rank correlation coefficients between pairs of indicators: all island

Indicator	Per capita income	Per capita total expenditure	Per capita 'smoothed' total expenditure	Per capita food expenditure	Inverse foodshare	Inverse share of food in 'smoothed' total expenditure
Per capita income	1.000	0.808	0.806	0.741	0.513	0.516
Per capita total expenditure	0.808	1.000	0.986	0.907	0.601	0.598
Per capita 'smoothed' total expenditure	0.806	0.986	1.000	0.910	0.584	0.609
Per capita food expenditure	0.741	0.907	0.910	1.000	0.280	0.289
Inverse foodshare	0.513	0.601	0.584	0.280	1.000	0.957
Inverse share of food in 'smoothed' total expenditure	0.516	0.598	0.609	0.289	0.957	1.000

Note: The sample size on which this table is based is 38,883 individuals.

welfare indicator, we conclude by pointing out that there is no necessary relationship between the two indicators.[48]

9.4. Conclusion

The purpose of this chapter has been to investigate the problem of finding an empirical welfare indicator. We have done this in the context of a particular data set, the Consumer Finance Survey (CFS) 1981/82 conducted by the Central Bank of Ceylon. Because of a minor difficulty specific to the CFS, we had to discard a small subset of the households surveyed—the multiple-spending-unit households.

Our first potential welfare indicator was per capita income. It is widely believed that income varies about its long-run average. We argued that if such variability is present, then, when individuals are ranked by their per capita household income, there will be bottom ranges for which average consumption exceeds average income. Our calculations on the CFS data revealed that the bottom 90 per cent in each of the urban and rural sectors, and in the island as a whole, exhibited this phenomenon (despite substantial saving in the aggregate). This was striking confirmation of the view that income is very variable.

One undesirable consequence of using such a variable indicator is likely to be an overstatement of the food consumption (and other measures correlated with long-run average income such as housing and educational attainment) of the poor,[49] an understatement of the food consumption of the rich, and an understatement of the disparity in food consumption between the rich and the poor. A second consequence of using a variable welfare indicator will be an overstatement of inequality.[50,51]

Turning to a more promising indicator, per capita total expenditure, we argued that it has certain defects resulting from its inclusion of durable

[48] For food expenditure to be monotonic (increasing) in welfare requires the elasticity of food with respect to long-run average income to be positive. For foodshare to be monotonic (decreasing) in welfare requires the elasticity of food with respect to long-run average income to be less than unity.

[49] By the poor we mean those individuals having the lowest welfare, i.e. long-run average income. By, say, the housing conditions of the poorest decile we mean the average housing conditions of the bottom decile of the population ranked by welfare. This magnitude will in general be greater than the average housing conditions of the bottom decile of the population ranked by housing conditions itself: different individuals with the same welfare will have different consumption patterns, including housing.

[50] By inequality is meant the inequality of welfare, i.e. of long-run average income. This should be estimated by applying an inequality measure directly to welfare space. If it is calculated instead by applying such a measure to short-run income, then the result will be an overestimate: the distribution of long-run average income Lorenz-dominates that of short-run income because the latter can be obtained from the former by a series of mean-preserving spreads.

[51] Superficially there appears to be a contradiction in saying that the use of short-run income as a welfare indicator can lead to both an understatement of the disparity of living standards between the rich and the poor, and an overstatement of inequality. The apparent contradiction should,

expenditure. First, durable expenditure arises from adjustments in the stock of durables; it does not relate directly to the stock itself. Secondly, durable expenditure is more an investment than an expenditure on current services; as such it is likely to track income. Thirdly, durable expenditure is lumpy. These features of durable expenditure seemed likely to result in some variability in total expenditure itself. Once again we found evidence of such variability.

The difficulties associated with durable expenditure led us to try a third possibility—per capita food expenditure. Our choice of food expenditure was motivated by the feeling that it is likely to be a very stable element in a household's consumption. That is, it seems likely that food expenditure will bear a monotonic relationship to long-run average income, and thus provide the basis for a good ordinal welfare indicator. This view was confirmed by the fact that in the case of per capita food expenditure there was hardly any evidence of variability. In particular, when individuals were ranked by per capita food expenditure, no bottom range was in deficit in the urban sector, only one in the rural sector, and two in the island as a whole including the estate sector.

The claim that per capita food expenditure should provide a stable welfare indicator is very plausible in the context of a group of households facing homogeneous prices. However, the CFS was conducted over the course of a year. It seems possible that there are seasonal variations in the relative price of food to non-food items. We cannot test for such variations since we do not have, and cannot construct, adequate non-food price indices. But if variations are present, and if they do upset the hypothesized monotonic relationship between food expenditure and long-run income, then the resulting problems for per capita food expenditure appear to be less severe than those caused for per capita total expenditure by its inclusion of durable expenditure.

Overall, then, per capita food expenditure is likely to be a good ordinal welfare indicator. This conclusion is encouraging in at least two respects. First, it happens to be free of the difficulties to do with the income and total expenditure of multiple-spending-unit households; hence it can be used for the entire CFS sample. Secondly, it allows an estimate of the range within which the true food consumption of the poorest decile must lie. The ranking by per capita food expenditure must of course yield the lowest conceivable estimate of

---

however, disappear once the meaning of the terms 'living standards of the poor' and 'inequality' as set out in nn. 49, 50 is considered. For example, suppose that the underlying relationship between housing conditions and long-run average income is monotonic increasing. Divide the population into the bottom ($100p$) per cent, say the 'poor', and the top $100(1 - p)$ per cent, say the 'rich', according to long-run average income. Then reclassify the population according to short-run income. On average, those who are now misclassified as poor (by short-run income) will have better housing conditions than those who are misclassified as rich. Hence the disparity in housing conditions will be underestimated. (This example assumes implicitly that the deviation of housing conditions from the underlying monotonic relationship with long-run average income is uncorrelated with the fluctuations in short-run income about long-run income. This assumption seems reasonable in the case of housing conditions.)

the food expenditure per capita of the poorest decile of individuals, simply by virtue of its definition.[52] The estimate obtained using per capita total expenditure, on the other hand, is likely to be too high because of the variability of that indicator.[53] The ranges obtained in this way for the three sectors and the island as a whole are, respectively, Rs. 88.39 to 95.48, Rs. 76.02 to 79.89, Rs. 101.02 to 105.92, and Rs. 78.80 to 83.01.

There are also practical advantages to using per capita food expenditure as the welfare indicator. First, its informational requirements are more limited than those of total expenditure, since food expenditure is a strict subset of total expenditure. Secondly, food expenditure data are more accurate (certainly in the CFS) than non-food data. Thirdly, food price indices are more reliable than non-food price indices, allowing the possibility of intertemporal and intersectoral food consumption comparisons.[54]

Finally, there is a more general implication of our finding for Sri Lanka that re-ranking individuals by per capita food expenditure leads to a drastic reduction in the phenomenon of dissaving among the bottom ranges (and a complete disappearance in the urban sector). Numerous studies of household survey data for other developing countries have reported the finding that expenditures tend to exceed income for typically the bottom 80 to 90 per cent of the population ranked by (per capita) income. Explanations for this observed behaviour—by now a stylized fact—range from calling into question the quality of the underlying data to invoking or constructing models of indebtedness among the poor. But we regard *chronic dissaving by large groups* as intrinsically implausible, and believe that the widespread phenomenon of dissaving reported for the bottom ranges in developing countries arises from the use of an incorrect welfare indicator. Ranking individuals by an indicator more closely related to long-run average income should lead to a sharp reduction, if not disappearance, of the phenomenon. We conclude that re-ranking similar to this chapter's by per capita food expenditure is clearly warranted on other countries' data sets.

[52] By appealing to the analytic result that ranking by food expenditure yields the lowest conceivable estimate, we are implicitly acknowledging that food expenditure may not be in a monotonic and deterministic relationship with welfare. Such a relationship might break down because of measurement errors, or because of variations in taste. However, we believe that any such errors will be small, and that the estimate obtained in this way is consequently close to the true estimate (cf. Proposition A.12).

[53] This argument must be treated with care. In n. 51 we argued that the estimate of housing conditions obtained by ranking by a variable indicator would be an overestimate. The argument depended on the assumption that any fluctuations in housing conditions were uncorrelated with fluctuations in the indicator. In the case of food expenditure and total expenditure, however, the fluctuations are likely to be positively correlated. Such correlation between fluctuations will tend to offset the overestimation that results from the misclassification of households when they are ranked by total expenditure per capita. But as long as the fluctuations in food expenditure are small compared with those in total expenditure then, even if the fluctuations are perfectly correlated, the result will be an overestimate of the food expenditure of the poor.

[54] Notwithstanding these advantages, we are obviously not recommending that future household surveys in Sri Lanka and elsewhere should cease to collect non-food data!

Appendix 9.1

In this Appendix we set out the simple optimizing model that underlies our arguments concerning deficit deciles. This model is almost trivial. We state it only in order to emphasize the simplicity of the point that we are making. We also present a simple statistical model suggested by the optimizing model. In terms of this second model we show that:

(1) the calculations presented in the text are strongly consistent estimators of certain parameters of the underlying population distribution;
(2) deficit bottom ranges arise when short-run income is used as a ranking variable;
(3) the existence of a positive propensity to save out of long-run income makes deficit deciles less likely, and therefore all the more striking when they do occur.

Next, we discuss the proposition that greater variability in short-run income leads to larger deficits. We show that:

(4) for some kinds of increase in variability, deficits do increase;
(5) deficits do not in general increase with increasing variability;
(6) deficits tend to zero when variability tends to zero.

Thirdly, we discuss the implications of using foodshare as a welfare indicator for deficits and for estimates of the food expenditure of the poor. We show that:

(7) using foodshare as a welfare indicator will lead to deficit bottom ranges;
(8) estimates of the food expenditure of the poor obtained by using food-share as a welfare indicator will be even higher than those obtained by using total expenditure, which itself gives rise to overestimates.

Finally, we make precise the statistical relationship that must hold between the number of spending units in a household and other characteristics of the household if our model is to be unaffected by the decision to drop multiple-spending-unit households from the CFS sample.

(a)   The optimizing model

We begin with the optimizing model. In this model a household lives for T periods. In each period t, $1 \leqq t \leqq T$, it receives an income $y_t \geqq 0$. This income is divided between consumption c_t and savings s_t. If y_t is not sufficient to cover desired consumption then the household can borrow against future earnings. In such a case s_t is negative. Overall, the household

$$\text{maximizes} \sum_{t=1}^{T} u(c_t)$$

$$\text{subject to} \sum_{t=1}^{T} c_t \leqq \sum_{t=1}^{T} y_t.$$

In this problem, u, the household's utility of consumption in a given period, is strictly concave and independent of t. The solution obviously involves setting $c_t = \eta$ in every period, where $\eta = (1/T)\Sigma_{t=1}^{T}y_t$ is long-run average income.

(b) The statistical model

We turn now to the statistical model. We imagine drawing a household from the population. The crucial determinant of the household's welfare is its long-run average income η. If we could observe η we would know that the expectation of its income Y given η was just η. Unfortunately, we observe only Y, which is η plus an error ε. Thus our model is a model with errors-in-variables.

More formally, consider a sample of H households drawn independently from the same population. Household h is characterized by the triple $(Y_h, \eta_h, \varepsilon_h)$, where $\varepsilon_h = Y_h - \eta_h$. We take it that in the underlying population:

(P1) $E(\varepsilon)$ exists;
(P2) $E(\varepsilon|\eta) = 0$ a.s. (almost surely);
(P3) the distribution of Y is diffuse.

Assumption (P1) is needed to ensure that the conditional expectation $E(\varepsilon|\eta)$ is well defined. To require that $E(\varepsilon|\eta) = 0$ a.s. in (P2) is equivalent to requiring that $E(Y|\eta) = \eta$, and merely states that η is the long-run average of Y. Assumption (P3) means that the distribution function F of Y is continuous. It can be dispensed with, but if this is done then the statements and proofs of our results become more complicated.

Motivated by Table 9.1, we pick $0 < p < 1$ and find C_H such that $|p - C_H/H| < 1/H$. Next, let Z_H be the C_H^{th} order statistic of the sample $\{Y_1, \ldots, Y_H\}$. That is, let Z_H be the C_H^{th} lowest observation. Then define

$$X_H = \frac{1}{D_H} \sum_{Y_h \leq Z_H} \varepsilon_h,$$

where $D_H = \#\{h|Y_h \leq Z_H\}$. (Note that $D_H = C_H$ a.s. when (P3) holds.) If $p = 0.1$ then X_H is the average savings (negative deficit) of the bottom decile.

Proposition A.1: *Suppose that (P1) and (P3) hold. Then*

$$X_H \overset{a.s.}{\to} E[\varepsilon|F(Y) \leq p].$$

That is, X_H is a strongly consistent estimator of $E[\varepsilon|F(Y) \leq p]$.

The interest of Proposition A.1 derives from the fact that we can say something about $E[\varepsilon|F(Y) \leq p]$ using (P2), namely that $E[\varepsilon|F(Y) \leq p] \leq 0$. This is a special case of the following proposition.

Proposition A.2: *Suppose that (P1) and (P2) hold, and let y be such that $p = prob\{Y \leq y\} > 0$. Then $E(\varepsilon|Y \leq y) \leq 0$. (In the case where (P3) holds, we can take y to be any number such that $F(y) = p$.)*

Proof: We have by definition that

$$E(\varepsilon|Y \leqq y) = E[\varepsilon I_y(Y)]/prob\{Y \leqq y\},$$

where I_y is the indicator function of the set $\{x|x \leqq y\}$. But

$$\begin{aligned}
E[\varepsilon I_y(Y)] &= E[\varepsilon I_y(\eta + \varepsilon)] \\
&= E[\varepsilon I_y(\eta + \varepsilon)I_y(\eta) + \varepsilon I_y(\eta + \varepsilon)(1 - I_y(\eta))] \\
&\leqq E[\varepsilon I_y(\eta)]
\end{aligned}$$

(since $\eta \leqq y$ implies $\varepsilon I_y(\eta + \varepsilon) \leqq \varepsilon$ and $\eta > y$ implies $\varepsilon I_y(\eta + \varepsilon) \leqq 0$)

$$\begin{aligned}
&= E[E[\varepsilon I_y(\eta)|\eta]] \\
&= E[I_y(\eta)E(\varepsilon|\eta)] \\
&= 0
\end{aligned}$$

since $E(\varepsilon|\eta) = 0$ a.s. $\square$

Notice how the proof mimics the intuitive argument of section 9.2(*d*).

It is also interesting to know when the inequality of Proposition A.2 will be strict.

Proposition A.3: *Suppose that (P1) and (P2) hold, and let y be such that* $0 < p = prob\{Y \leqq y\} < 1$. *Suppose in addition that:*

(1) the support of η *is connected;*

(2) there exists a scalar $\sigma^2 > 0$ *such that var* $(\varepsilon|\eta) \geqq \sigma^2$ *a.s.;*

(3) $Y \geqq 0$ *a.s.*

Then $E(\varepsilon|Y \leqq y) < 0$.

Note that we do not need to assume that $var(\varepsilon|\eta)$ is everywhere finite.

Proof: Certainly $E(\varepsilon|Y \leqq y) \leqq 0$, so assume for a contradiction that $E(\varepsilon|Y \leqq y) = 0$. Let $[\underline{\eta}, \bar{\eta}]$ be the support of η, and suppose first that $y > \bar{\eta}$. Because $p < 1$ we have $prob\{Y > y\} > 0$, and the expectation $E(\varepsilon|Y > y)$ is well defined. Since $Y > y$ implies $\varepsilon > 0$, $E(\varepsilon|Y > y) > 0$. Finally,

$$\begin{aligned}
0 &= E(\varepsilon) \\
&= prob\{Y \leqq y\}E(\varepsilon|Y \leqq y) + prob\{Y > y\}E(\varepsilon|Y > y) \\
&= prob\{Y > y\}E(\varepsilon|Y > y)
\end{aligned}$$

(by the hypothesis $E(\varepsilon|Y \leqq y) = 0$)

$$> 0.$$

This is a contradiction.

Suppose therefore that $y \leqq \bar{\eta}$. Examining the inequality in the proof of Proposition A.2 we see that $\varepsilon \leqq y - \eta$ for almost all $\eta < y$. Next, picking $\delta > 0$, $prob\{y - \delta^2 < \eta < y\} > 0$. Hence we may condition on the event $y - \delta^2 < \eta < y$. Combining these two observations we have

$$E(\varepsilon^+|y - \delta^2 < \eta < y) \leqq \delta^2$$

and

$$E(\varepsilon^- | y - \delta^2 < \eta < y) \geqq \delta prob\{\varepsilon < -\delta | y - \delta^2 < \eta < y\},$$

where ε^+ is the positive part of ε and ε^- is its negative part. Also, (P2) implies that

$$E(\varepsilon^+ | y - \delta^2 < \eta < y) = E(\varepsilon^- | y - \delta^2 < \eta < y).$$

Hence

$$prob\{\varepsilon < -\delta | y - \delta^2 < \eta < y\} \leqq \delta.$$

Finally,

$$\begin{aligned}
0 < \sigma^2 &\leqq E[var(\varepsilon|\eta) | y - \delta^2 < \eta < y] \\
&= E[(\varepsilon^+)^2 + (\varepsilon^-)^2 | y - \delta^2 < \eta < y] \\
&\leqq \delta^4 prob\{\varepsilon > 0 | y - \delta^2 < \eta < y\} \\
&\quad + \delta^2 prob\{-\delta \leqq \varepsilon \leqq 0 | y - \delta^2 < \eta < y\} \\
&\quad + y^2 prob\{\varepsilon < -\delta | y - \delta^2 < \eta < y\} \\
&\leqq \delta^4 + \delta^2 + y^2\delta.
\end{aligned}$$

Letting $\delta \to 0$ we obtain the required contradiction. $\square$

Before turning to the proof of Proposition A.1, we note that an analogue of Proposition A.1 holds for intervals other than simply the bottom $(100p)$ per cent of the population for $0 < p < 1$. For example, the average deficit of households in the third decile converges to $E(\varepsilon | \underline{z} \leqq Y \leqq \bar{z})$, where $F(\underline{z}) = 0.2$ and $F(\bar{z}) = 0.3$. The distributional assumptions required in order to sign such expectations are naturally rather stronger than those of Proposition A.2. We do not pursue this question.

The reader who is not interested in the proof of Proposition A.1 is advised to skip to Appendix 9.1(c) at this point.

We need some notation. Let F_H be the empirical distribution function of the sample $\{Y_1, \ldots, Y_H\}$. Let $\bar{y} = max\{y | F(y) = p\}$ and $\underline{y} = min\{y | F(y) = p\}$. Let ε_h^+ (ε_h^-) denote the positive (negative) part $max\{0, \varepsilon_h\}$ ($max\{0, -\varepsilon_h\}$) of ε_h.

Lemma A.4: *Suppose that (P3) holds. Then $F_H(Z_H) \to p$ a.s.*

Proof: By construction of C_H, $C_H/H \to p$. On the other hand, because the distribution of Y is diffuse, the occurrence of ties in the sample $\{Y_1, \ldots, Y_H\}$ is a zero probability event. Hence $D_H = C_H$ a.s. But $F_H(Z_H) = D_H/H$. $\square$

Lemma A.5: *We have a.s. that $F_H \to F$ uniformly as $H \to \infty$.* $\square$

Lemma A.5 is simply the Glivenko–Cantelli lemma on the convergence of empirical, or sample, distributions to the population distribution.

Lemma A.6: *Suppose that (P3) holds. Then we have a.s. that*

$$\underline{y} \leqq \liminf_{H \to \infty} Z_H \leqq \limsup_{H \to \infty} Z_H \leqq \bar{y}.$$

Proof: It obviously suffices to prove that $F(Z_H) \to p$. To this end, we restrict attention to the event on which $F_H(Z_H) \to p$ and $F_H \to F$ uniformly. (By Lemmas A.4 and A.5, this event has probability one.) Then, for any $\varepsilon > 0$, there exists H such that

$$p - \varepsilon < F_H(Z_H) < p + \varepsilon$$

and

$$F_H(y) - \varepsilon < F(y) < F_H(y) + \varepsilon \quad \text{for all } y.$$

Substituting $y = Z_H$ in the latter inequalities, and combining them with the former, we have

$$p - 2\varepsilon < F(Z_H) < p + 2\varepsilon$$

as required. $\square$

Proof of Proposition A.1: We have: (1) $D_H/H \to p$ a.s.; (2) $E[\varepsilon | F(Y) \leq p] = E(\varepsilon | Y \leq y)$ by (P3); (3) $E(\varepsilon | Y \leq y) = E[\varepsilon I_y(Y)]/p$ by definition. Hence it will be sufficient to show that

$$\frac{1}{H} \sum_{Y_h \leq Z_H} \varepsilon_h \overset{\text{a.s.}}{\to} E[\varepsilon I_y(Y)].$$

(For the remainder of the proof we drop the qualification 'a.s.' whenever it relates to the sample distribution, but not when it relates to the population distribution.)

Consider the sum

$$\frac{1}{H} \sum_{Y_h \leq Z_H} \varepsilon_h^+.$$

Since $\liminf Z_H \geq \underline{y}$ we have, for any $\delta > 0$ and for H sufficiently large,

$$\frac{1}{H} \sum_{Y_h \leq Z_H} \varepsilon_h^+ = \frac{1}{H} \sum_h I_{Z_H}(Y_h) \varepsilon_h^+$$

$$\geq \frac{1}{H} \sum_h I_{\underline{y}-\delta}(Y_h) \varepsilon_h^+.$$

But the latter quantity converges to $E[\varepsilon^+ I_{\underline{y}-\delta}(Y)]$ by the strong law of large numbers. Hence

$$\liminf_{H \to \infty} \frac{1}{H} \sum_{Y_h \leq Z_H} \varepsilon_h^+ \geq E[\varepsilon^+ I_{\underline{y}-\delta}(Y)].$$

Finally, since $prob\{Y = \underline{y}\} = 0$ by (P3), $\varepsilon^+ I_{\underline{y}-\delta}(Y) \to \varepsilon^+ I_{\underline{y}}(Y)$ a.s. as $\delta \to 0$. Hence

$$\liminf_{H \to \infty} \frac{1}{H} \sum_{Y_h \leq Z_H} \varepsilon_h^+ \geq E[\varepsilon^+ I_{\underline{y}}(Y)],$$

by Lebesgue's dominated convergence theorem.

An argument analogous to that of the previous paragraph shows that

$$\limsup_{H \to \infty} \frac{1}{H} \sum_{Y_h \leq Z_H} \varepsilon_h^+ \leq E[\varepsilon^+ I_{\mathcal{Y}}(Y)].$$

But $I_{\underline{y}}(Y) = I_y(Y) = I_{\mathcal{Y}}(Y)$ a.s. We have therefore shown that

$$\frac{1}{H} \sum_{Y_h \leq Z_H} \varepsilon_h^+ \to E[\varepsilon^+ I_y(Y)].$$

Combining this with the analogous conclusion for ε^- gives the result. $\square$

(c) Positive savings

In this Appendix we show that when households have a positive propensity to save out of long-run income, deficits become less likely. More precisely, we introduce consumption C and savings S into the model, with $C + S = Y$. We assume that C is a deterministic function of $\eta : C = c(\eta)$. Since consumption above η is not sustainable, $c(\eta) \leq \eta$. The change in the deficit resulting from this behaviour on the part of households is

$$E(Y - C | Y \leq y) - E(Y - \eta | Y \leq y)$$
$$= E(\eta - C | Y \leq y)$$
$$= E[(\eta - C)I_y(Y)]/prob\{Y \leq y\}.$$

But

$$E[(\eta - C)I_y(Y)]$$
$$= E[E[(\eta - C)I_y(Y) | \eta]]$$
$$= E[(\eta - c(\eta))E[I_y(Y) | \eta]]$$
$$\geq 0,$$

since $\eta - c(\eta) \geq 0$ and $I_y \geq 0$. That is, a deficit is less likely in the presence of a positive propensity to save.

It is straightforward to generalize the derivation above to the case in which C is no longer a deterministic function of η, but rather $E(C|\eta) \leq \eta$ and C is conditionally independent of Y given η. (For a discussion of conditional independence see Appendix 9.1(f).)

(d) The influence of increases in variability on deficits

In section 9.3(b) we argued informally that total expenditure is variable relative to long-run average income, but less so than (short-run) income. This could be summarized by saying that total expenditure $T = \eta + \theta$ and income $Y = T + \zeta$, where $E(\zeta|T) = E(\theta|\eta) = 0$ a.s. The purpose of Appendix 9.1(d) is to investigate this statistical model.[55]

The main question we wish to tackle is that of whether we can say anything about the savings (negative deficit) $E[Y - \eta|F(Y) \leqq p] = E[\theta + \zeta|F(Y) \leqq p]$ obtained when individuals are ranked by income as compared with the savings (negative deficit) $E[Y - \eta|G(T) \leqq p] = E[\theta + \zeta|G(T) \leqq p]$ obtained when individuals are ranked by total expenditure. (Here G is the distribution function of T.) In approaching this question, the first point to note is that, because $E(\zeta|T) = 0$ a.s., $E[\theta + \zeta|G(T) \leqq p] = E[\theta|G(T) \leqq p]$. Hence the problem reduces to determining the dependence of $E[\varepsilon|F(Y) \leqq p]$ on Y and ε, where Y and ε vary over all random variables such that $Y = \eta + \varepsilon$ and $E(\varepsilon|\eta) = 0$ a.s. Concerning this dependence we give two special cases in which an increase in the variability of Y leads to a decrease in $E[\varepsilon|F(Y) \leqq p]$, i.e. to an increase in the deficit. Next, we give a counterexample to show that increases in variability do not in general lead to a decrease in $E[\varepsilon|F(Y) \leqq p]$, i.e. an increase in the deficit. Finally, we show that $E[\varepsilon|F(Y) \leqq p]$ tends to zero when variability tends to zero.

We depart from the notation of Appendix 9.1(b), according to which random variables Y_i and Y_j with $i \neq j$ represented independent drawings from an identical underlying population distribution. These random variables should now be thought of as representing different population distributions. Thus, for each i, $Y_i = \eta + \varepsilon_i$, where the expectation of ε_i exists and $E(\varepsilon_i|\eta) = 0$ a.s., but the distribution of ε_i may vary with i. Let F_i be the distribution function of Y_i.

Suppose first of all that we are given two indicators ϕ_1 and ϕ_2, with $m_i(\phi_i) = Y_i$ for a suitable strictly monotonic function $m_i(.)$ for each $i = 1,2$. Then ϕ_2 will be said to be *more variable than* ϕ_1 if there exists ζ such that Y_2 is equal in distribution to $Y_1 + \zeta$ and $E(\zeta|Y_1) = 0$ a.s. (cf. Rothschild and Stiglitz 1970).[56] (Note that since we are using our indicators only to obtain *ordinal* rankings, two indicators that are related by a monotonic transform are equivalent.)

Proposition A.7: *Suppose that Y_1 and Y_2 are both diffuse, that ϕ_2 is more variable than ϕ_1, and that η is a.s. constant. Then*

$$E[\varepsilon_2|F_2(Y_2) \leqq p] \leqq E[\varepsilon_1|F_1(Y_1) \leqq p].$$

---

[55] In Appendix 9.1(a) we had a simple optimizing model corresponding to the statistical model of Appendix 9.1(b). In the same way, it is possible to design optimizing models corresponding to the present statistical model. However, the issues arising in the design of such a model are more complex, and their proper discussion would take us too far afield. We do not, therefore, present such a model here.

[56] The underlying idea here is that an indicator ϕ is an imperfect indicator of η if a monotonic transform of it, $m(\phi)$, is equal to η plus noise. Mathematically, it would be more natural to write $\phi = q(\eta) + \psi$, where $q(\eta) = E(\phi|\eta)$, and to require that $q(.)$ be strictly monotonic. The problem with such an approach is that, unlike ε, ψ does not correspond to anything observable.

That is, if all individuals have the same long-run average income then deficits increase with variability.

Proof: We may assume without loss of generality that $Y_1 = \varepsilon_1$ and $Y_2 = Y_1 + \zeta$ a.s. Let A_2 be the set of (ε_1, ζ) such that $F_2(\varepsilon_1 + \zeta) \leqq p$. Then $prob\{A_2\} = p$ by the diffuseness of ε_2, and there exists y such that $\varepsilon_1 + \zeta \leqq y$ for all $(\varepsilon_1, \zeta) \in A_2$ and $\varepsilon_1 + \zeta > y$ for all $(\varepsilon_1, \zeta) \notin A_2$. (Take y to be any scalar satisfying $F_2(y) = p$.) Next, let A_1 be the set of (ε_1, ζ) such that $F_1(\varepsilon_1) \leqq p$. Then, $prob\{A_1\} = p$ too. Furthermore,

$$pE[\varepsilon_2 | F_2(\varepsilon_2) \leqq p]$$
$$= pE[\varepsilon_1 + \zeta | F_2(\varepsilon_1 + \zeta) \leqq p]$$
$$= E[(\varepsilon_1 + \zeta)\chi_{A_2}]$$
$$= E[(\varepsilon_1 + \zeta)(\chi_{A_2 \setminus A_1} + \chi_{A_1 \cap A_2})]$$

(where χ_A denotes the indicator function of A)

$$\leqq y \, prob\{A_2 \setminus A_1\} + E[(\varepsilon_1 + \zeta)\chi_{A_1 \cap A_2}]$$
$$= y \, prob\{A_1 \setminus A_2\} + E[(\varepsilon_1 + \zeta)\chi_{A_1 \cap A_2}]$$

(since $prob\{A_1 \setminus A_2\} = prob\{A_2 \setminus A_1\}$)

$$\leqq E[(\varepsilon_1 + \zeta)(\chi_{A_1 \setminus A_2} + \chi_{A_1 \cap A_2})]$$
$$= E[(\varepsilon_1 + \zeta)\chi_{A_1}]$$
$$= E(\varepsilon_1 \chi_{A_1})$$

(since A_1 is ε_1-measurable and $E(\zeta | \varepsilon_1) = 0$ a.s.)

$$= pE[\varepsilon_1 | F_1(\varepsilon_1) \leqq p].$$

This is the required result. $\square$

Proposition A.8: *Suppose that Y_1 and Y_2 are both diffuse, with Y_1 equal in distribution to $\eta + \varepsilon_1$; and suppose that there exists a scalar $\lambda > 1$ such that Y_2 is equal in distribution to $\eta + \lambda\varepsilon_1$. Then*

$$E[\varepsilon_2 | F_2(Y_2) \leqq p] \leqq E[\varepsilon_1 | F_1(Y_1) \leqq p].$$

That is, uniform increases in variability lead to increases in the deficit. (Actually it will be clear from the proof that the increase in the deficit is more than proportional to the increase in variability.) Note that if the relationship between Y_1 and Y_2 is as described in Proposition A.8, then Y_2 is in particular more variable than Y_1. (We do not prove this here.)

Proof: We may take it that $\varepsilon_2 = \lambda\varepsilon_1$ a.s. As before, let A_i be the set of Y_i such that $F_i(Y_i) \leqq p$. Once again there exists y such that $Y_2 \in A_2$ if and only if $Y_2 \leqq y$. Hence we have on $A_2 \setminus A_1$ that $\eta + \lambda\varepsilon_1 \leqq y$ and $\eta + \varepsilon_1 > y$, and so that $\varepsilon_1 < 0$. Similarly, $\varepsilon_1 > 0$ on $A_1 \setminus A_2$. It follows that

$$pE[\varepsilon_2|\,F_2(Y_2) \lessgtr p]$$
$$= E[\lambda\varepsilon_1(\chi_{A_2\setminus A_1} + \chi_{A_2\cap A_1})]$$
$$\lessgtr E(\lambda\varepsilon_1\,\chi_{A_2\cap A_1})$$
$$\lessgtr E[\lambda\varepsilon_1\,(\chi_{A_2\cap A_1} + \chi_{A_1\setminus A_2})]$$
$$= \lambda pE[\varepsilon_1|F_1\,(Y_1) \lessgtr p].$$

But we know from Proposition A.2 that $E[\varepsilon_1|F_1\,(Y_1) \lessgtr p] \lessgtr 0$. The proposition follows. $\square$

Propositions A.7 and A.8 show that in certain cases an increase in variability will lead to an increase in the deficit. That this is not a general result follows from the counterexample shown in Fig. 9.1. It is easily checked that with $p = 0.75$, $E[\varepsilon_2|F_2(Y_2) \lessgtr p] = -d/3$ while $E[\varepsilon_1|F_1(Y_1) \lessgtr p] = -c/3$. Hence the required inequality is reversed when $c > d$. (The constraints $c > 2b$ and $2b + d > c$, which are implicit in Fig. 9.1, must also be satisfied.)

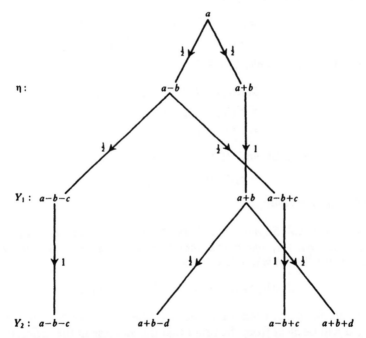

Fig. 9.1. Example in which increasing variability decreases the deficit

We conclude this section by showing that if income is always positive then deficits tend to zero when variability tends to zero. To this end, suppose that we are given a sequence of random variables $\{Y_n\}$, with Y_n equal in distribution to $\eta + \varepsilon_n$, where $E(\varepsilon_n|\eta) = 0$ a.s. Let F_n be the distribution function of Y_n, and let F be the distribution function of η.

Proposition A.9: *Suppose that: (1) $Y_n \geqq 0$ a.s.; (2) $\varepsilon_n \to 0$ in distribution; (3) η is integrable; (4) $prob\{F(\eta) \leqq p\} > 0$. Then*

$$E[\varepsilon_n | F_n(Y_n) \leqq p] \to 0.$$

Note that we do not assume that the Y_n are diffuse. Note too that the proposition could be stated in other forms. For example, (1) and (3) could be replaced by an assumption that the ε_n are uniformly integrable, while (4) could be replaced by an assumption that η is diffuse.

Proof: We may assume as usual that $Y_n = \eta + \varepsilon_n$. Passing to a Skorohod representation (see Grimmett and Stirzaker 1982) if necessary, we may also assume that $\varepsilon_n \to 0$ a.s.

Since $Y_n \to \eta$ in distribution, $F_n \to F$ at points of continuity of F. Hence, using (4), *liminf prob$\{F_n(Y_n) \leqq p\} > 0$*. We need therefore only show that $E[\varepsilon_n I_p[F_n(Y_n)]] \to 0$. This we do by an application of Lebesgue's dominated convergence theorem.

Let $y \geqq 0$ be a point of continuity of F such that $1 \geqq F(y) > p$. Let $\varepsilon = (F(y) - p)/2$. Because $F_n \to F$ at points of continuity of F, we have for all n sufficiently large that $|F_n(y) - F(y)| < \varepsilon$. For such n, $F_n(Y_n) \leqq p$ implies that $Y_n \leqq y$, and also that $|\varepsilon_n| = |Y_n - \eta| \leqq |Y_n| + |\eta| \leqq y + |\eta|$. On the other hand, $F_n(Y_n) > p$ implies that $I_p[F_n(Y_n)] = 0$. Overall then, $\varepsilon_n I_p[F_n(Y_n)]$ is dominated by the random variable $y + |\eta|$ for all n sufficiently large. The proposition therefore follows from the almost sure convergence of ε_n to zero. □

(e)   Foodshare and variability

Appendix 9.1 (*e*) explores two predictions that the model of this chapter makes concerning statistics based on foodshare, and is a supplement to section 9.3(*d*). The first prediction is that variability in total expenditure will result in deficits for bottom ranges of individuals ranked by inverse foodshare. The second is that estimates of the food expenditure of bottom ranges of individuals obtained by ranking by inverse foodshare will be higher than estimates obtained by ranking by total expenditure.

To avoid ambiguity, we begin with a description of the model. An individual has total expenditure T, long-run average income η, and food expenditure ϕ. We assume that $T = \eta + \theta$ where the expectation of θ exists and $E(\theta|\eta) = 0$ a.s.; that $\phi = m^{-1}(\eta)$, with $m(.)$ a strictly monotonic function; and that the expectation of ϕ exists. Furthermore, we assume that $\phi > 0$ a.s. This enables us to define inverse foodshare σ as T/ϕ, which definition reflects the idea that foodshare is an *inverse* welfare indicator.

We state our first proposition in a somewhat general form.

Proposition A.10: *Suppose that a function $f = f(\eta, T)$ and a scalar s are given. Suppose that f is non-decreasing in its second argument, and that $prob\{f(\eta, T) \leqq s\} > 0$. Then*

$$E[\theta | f(\eta, T) \leqq s] \leqq 0. \quad \square$$

The formal proof of this result closely follows that of Proposition A.2, and is therefore omitted. The intuition behind the result is a generalization of that behind Proposition A.2. Indeed, suppose that the population is initially divided into those for whom $f(\eta, \eta) \leqq s$ and those for whom $f(\eta, \eta) > s$. Then the deficit $E[\theta|f(\eta, \eta) \leqq s]$ of the bottom group must be zero because $E(\theta|\eta) = 0$ a.s. Suppose now that the population is reclassified according to $f(\eta, T)$. Two types of misclassification can arise. First, individuals with $f(\eta, \eta) > s$ may have $f(\eta, T) \leqq s$. Because f is non-decreasing in its second argument, such individuals must have $\theta < 0$. Secondly, other individuals with $f(\eta, \eta) \leqq s$ may have $f(\eta, T) > s$. For them, $\theta > 0$. These two effects are mutually reinforcing, and generate the required result.

Corollary A.11: *Suppose that* $prob\{\sigma \leqq s\} > 0$. *Then*

$$E(\theta|\sigma \leqq s) \leqq 0.$$

That is, variability in total expenditure will lead to deficits when individuals are ranked by foodshare.

Proof: Set $f(\eta, T) = T/m^{-1}(\eta)$. $\square$

Our second proposition relates to estimates of food expenditure. Before stating it we need some notation. We denote the distribution functions of η, T, σ, and ϕ by $F_\eta, F_T, F_\sigma,$ and F_ϕ, respectively.

Proposition A.12: *Suppose that the distributions of* η, T, *and* σ *are diffuse, and that* $T = \eta + \theta \geqq 0$ *a.s. Let* $1 > p > 0$. *Then*

$$E[\phi|F_\eta(\eta) \leqq p] \leqq E[\phi|F_T(T) \leqq p] \leqq E[\phi|F_\sigma(\sigma) \leqq p].$$

Two observations are made in order. First, the ($100p$) per cent of the population who have the lowest welfare are precisely those for whom $F_\eta(\eta) \leqq p$. Hence $E[\phi|F_\eta(\eta) \leqq p]$ is the true estimate of their average food expenditure. The proposition then states that the estimate obtained by ranking by T is an overestimate, and that that obtained by ranking by σ is higher still. Secondly, a version of the proposition is still true when ϕ is no longer a strictly monotonic function of η, namely $E[\phi|F_\phi(\phi) \leqq p] \leqq E[\phi|F_T(T) \leqq p] \leqq E[\phi|F_\sigma(\sigma) \leqq p]$.[57] This case is of rather less interest. For while $E[\phi|F_\phi(\phi) \leqq p]$ provides a lower bound for the true value $E[\phi|F_\eta(\eta) \leqq p]$, it does not appear to be possible to obtain an upper bound.

Proof: Because the distributions of η, T, and σ are diffuse, we can find y, t, and s such that $prob\{\eta \leqq y\} = prob\{T \leqq t\} = prob\{\sigma \leqq s\} = p$. Let A_η be the event $\{\eta \leqq y\}$, $A_T = \{T \leqq t\}$, and $A_\sigma = \{\sigma \leqq s\}$. Then

$$pE[\phi|F_\eta(\eta) \leqq p] = E(I_{A_\eta}\phi)$$
$$= E(I_{A_\eta \cap A_T}\phi + I_{A_\eta \setminus A_T}\phi)$$
$$\leqq E(I_{A_\eta \cap A_T}\phi) + prob\{A_\eta \setminus A_T\}m^{-1}(y)$$

---

[57] We must also assume that the distribution of ϕ is diffuse.

$$= E(I_{A_\eta \cap A_T}\phi) + prob\{A_T \setminus A_\eta\}m^{-1}(y)$$
$$\leqq E(I_{A_\eta \cap A_T}\phi) + E(I_{A_T \setminus A_\eta}\phi)$$
$$= E(I_{A_T}\phi)$$
$$= pE[\phi|F_T(T) \leqq p].$$

This establishes the first inequality. (Note that the assumption that $m^{-1}(.)$ is a monotonic function of η was used.)

Next, because $T \geqq 0$ a.s. and $\phi > 0$ a.s., we must have $t, s > 0$. Also, on the event $A_T \setminus A_\sigma$ we have $\eta + \theta \leqq t$ and $\eta + \theta > s\phi$, whence $\phi < t/s$. Similarly, on the event $A_\sigma \setminus A_T$ we have $\phi > t/s$. This gives the second inequality. (Note that this time the assumption that $m(.)$ is monotonic was not used.) $\square$

(f) Omission of multiple-spending-unit households

In this Appendix, we add a fourth random variable N to the statistical model of Appendix 9.1(b). N is the number of spending units in the household. (N would be expected to be discrete!) In terms of this model, a sufficient condition for our model to be unaffected by the selection of any subsample based exclusively on the value of N is that $E(\varepsilon|\eta, N) = 0$ a.s. A sufficient condition for $E(\varepsilon|\eta, N) = 0$ in turn is that ε and N be conditionally independent given η.

The reader will recall that two random variables A and B are independent if and only if

$$E[f(A).g(B)] = E[f(A)].E[g(B)]$$

for all bounded measurable functions f and g. By analogy with this definition, A and B are said to be conditionally independent given a third random variable C if and only if

$$E[f(A).g(B)|C] = E[f(A)|C].E[g(B)|C] \quad \text{a.s.}$$

for all such f and g. (Compare Dellacherie and Meyer 1978: II.3, pp. 30–7.) The latter condition is known to be equivalent to requiring that

$$E[f(A)|B,C] = E[f(A)|C] \quad \text{a.s.}$$

for all f such that $f(A)$ is integrable. Our sufficient condition, namely that $E(\varepsilon|\eta, N) = 0$ a.s., follows at once by setting $f = $ the identity mapping, $A = \varepsilon$, $B = N$, and $C = \eta$.

Requiring that ε and N be conditionally independent given η has the following informal interpretation. Let us pick out all households with a given value of long-run average income η, and compare the excess in their short-run incomes Y over η with the number of their spending units N. Then there should be no systematic relationship between $(Y - \eta)$ and N. Alternatively, if we pick a particular household then we should not observe any systematic relationship between ε and N over time. A special case of this would be that in which a household does not adjust its composition at all in response to short-run fluctuations in its income.

References

ANAND, S., and HARRIS, C. J. (1985), 'Living Standards in Sri Lanka, 1973–1981/82: An Analysis of Consumer Finance Survey Data', mimeo (Oxford), April.

————(1987), 'Changes in Nutrition in Sri Lanka, 1978/79–1981/82', mimeo (Helsinki: WIDER).

————(1988), 'Issues in the Measurement of Undernutrition', mimeo (Helsinki: WIDER); forthcoming in (ed.) S. R. Osmani, *Nutrition and Poverty*, to be published by Oxford University Press, Oxford.

————(1989), 'Food, Nutrition and Standard of Living: Methodology and Applications to Sri Lanka', MS under preparation for WIDER, Helsinki; forthcoming book to be published by Oxford University Press, Oxford.

ANDO, A., and MODIGLIANI, F. (1963), 'The "Life Cycle" Hypothesis of Saving: Aggregate Implications and Tests', *American Economic Review*, 53.

BHALLA, S. S., and GLEWWE, P. (1986), 'Growth and Equity in Developing Countries: A Reinterpretation of the Sri Lankan Experience', *World Bank Economic Review*, 1.

DEATON, A. S. (1980), 'Measurement of Welfare: Theory and Practical Guidelines', LSMS Working Paper No. 7 (Washington, DC: World Bank).

—— (1981), 'Three Essays on a Sri Lanka Household Survey', LSMS Working Paper No. 11 (Washington, DC: World Bank).

DELLACHERIE, C., and MEYER, P.-A. (1978), *Probabilities and Potential* (Amsterdam: North-Holland).

ENGEL, E. (1895), 'Die Lebenskosten belgischer Arbeiter-Familien früher und jetzt', *International Statistical Institute Bulletin*, 9.

FRIEDMAN, M. (1957), *A Theory of the Consumption Function* (Princeton, NJ: Princeton University Press).

GRIMMETT, G., and STIRZAKER, D. (1982), *Probability and Random Processes* (Oxford: Oxford University Press).

ROTHSCHILD, M., and STIGLITZ, J. E. (1970), 'Increasing Risk I: A Definition', *Journal of Economic Theory*, 2.

STATISTICS DEPARTMENT, CENTRAL BANK OF CEYLON (1981?), 'Instructions to Investigators—Consumer Finance and Socio-Economic Survey 1981/82', mimeo (Colombo) (referred to as CFS 1981/82, *Instructions to Investigators*, in the text).

——(1984), *Report on Consumer Finances and Socio-Economic Survey 1981/82, Sri Lanka*, Parts I and II (Colombo) (referred to as CFS 1981/82, *Report*, in the text).

10

The Intrafamily Distribution of Hunger in South Asia

Barbara Harriss

10.1. *A narrative string of quotations*

All actions stem from food . . . Food depends on food. (Rig-Veda; Taittiriya Upanishad, III.ix.1)

Food is a language of power. (Macdonald 1955)

The logic of the hearth is the logic of the Hindu cosmos in miniature. (Appadurai 1985)

The concept of 'the Indian family' has no analytical value. (Mies 1980: 73)

The son is oneself, the wife is one's friend but the daughter is indeed a humiliation. (Mahabharata Adi, 159.11)

Men owe their birth to women; O ungrateful wretches! How can happiness be your lot when you condemn them? (Bratsamhita (74) of Varahamira)

In India and Bangladesh . . . a pattern of sex bias—against women—in the distribution of food . . . has come through strikingly. (Sen 1985a: 15)

The data clearly demonstrate the non existence of sex discrimination in the intrahousehold allocation of food to women beyond what can be accounted for by body size, activity and physiological differentials. (Abdullah 1983: 143)

The primary target group . . . of relatively deprived individuals . . . has been identified beyond doubt as the child of either sex in the age group from 7 to 18 months. (Cantor *et al.* 1973: i.92)

Food is an emotional and moral meta-language . . . To miss the abstract notion of food is to see the place of practice very differently. (Khare 1976a: 5, 267)

These quotations commend themselves because they show the extent to which this essay will thread its way through a maze of both subtle ambivalences and gross contradictions with respect to a number of social issues which bear upon any discussion of food distribution within the South Asian household. These are the *modus operandi* of patriarchy, the measurement and interpretation of hunger, the cultural meanings of material phenomena, and the conception of the policy process. We shall consider these issues, in the course of this essay.

I am very grateful to Erica Wheeler, Simon Strickland, Philip Payne, and Mary Griffiths of the Department of Human Nutrition, London School of Hygiene and Tropical Medicine, for their helpful responses to earlier versions; to Amartya Sen, Qaiser Khan, Judith Heyer, and especially Jean Drèze for comments at and after the WIDER Conference in Helsinki (1986); to Terry Byres, Chris Langford, and Maureen Mackintosh who reacted to it elsewhere; to ICRISAT, especially Tom Walker, for permitting access to their food intake data; and to Nicola Dunn of the London School of Hygiene and Tropical Medicine who reworked some of the ICRISAT data for WIDER, though I alone am responsible for this revision.

10.2. The context

Malnutrition has been related to low household income and to inadequate entitlement to food at the level of the household.[1] But some members of households with inadequate aggregate food intake may not be malnourished,[2] and not all malnourished individuals come from households with inadequate aggregate food intake.[3] Shares within the household are unequal throughout the entire world including Western referents. Although it is necessary to explain the aetiology of malnutrition in terms of factors operating on the household, malnutrition does not often affect every household member equally at any given time.[4]

If malnutrition is difficult to define (a social construct as much as a biological state or process, an economic input as well as an outcome), it is even more the case with the idea of hunger. As Payne has observed, 'hunger is a euphemism for want and deprivation, an expression of appetite, a manifestation of the biological regulation of energy balance'.[5] Lipton has identified hunger as a probabilistic state of energy deprivation not intense enough to cause physiological damage through severe undernutrition, which is a state he associates with ultrapoverty.[6] We shall define 'hunger' carefully, restrictively (and with reference to its opposite), when we come to its measurement (section 10.3).

There is a widely held set of views about the allocation of food and nutrients within the South Asian household, summarized recently by Wheeler.[7] This is:

- that men take a disproportionate share of household food resources at the expense of other members and that women and children get less both than adult men and than what they need physiologically;
- that the consequences of getting less are more serious in households with insufficient food entitlements;
- that women permit this distribution and therefore acquiesce to the reproduction of malnutrition.

The reasons for this are thought to be not only material but also related to Hindu cultural principles.[8] So we begin by examining the culture of food in South Asia, after which we turn to the material relations of provisioning. Great interpretative caution is needed. While fine ethnographic accounts have been

[1] Respectively Lipton (1983); Sen (1981); Khan (1984).

[2] Mathews (1979: 100–3).

[3] Munoz de Chavez et al. (1974); Ryan et al. (1984: 30, 39).   [4] Sen (1985a, 1985b).

[5] Payne (1985a).   [6] Lipton (1983: 23).   [7] Wheeler (1984).

[8] 'Hindu' refers here to what Khare has called 'para-ideology': although Hindu does not mean Indian 'it is wrong to assume that there are as many types of cultural genesis of food problems as regional, religious or cultural communities'. For long, there has been exchange of information and technique such that people of all regions and religions are bound by interconnected effects with respect to the production and distribution of food (Khare 1976b: 173).

provided by Khare and by Appadurai,[9] it would seem that quantitative and gender aspects of allocation are so underresearched by anthropologists, and the small body of nutritional evidence is presented in such a timeless and classless way by nutritionists, that statements of general principle are made at one's peril. Caution is also needed over the discrepancies between what people say and believe, what they actually do, and what they think about these discrepancies.[10]

(a)   The control of food

It is often assumed that men make decisions about food production while women control household food budgets and food distribution.[11] Whitehead, however, has shown the household to be an arena of unequal material exchanges. These exchanges, and the control they involve, work to male advantage in both peasant society in Ghana and working-class households in the English Midlands.[12] That there are no equivalent studies in South Asia does not mean that her observation would not hold. Certainly both ancient customary law and modern practice show that the provision of a shared source of food appropriate to each member's needs is one of the obligations of the male householder. In practice, this distributive obligation involves the unequal work of almost all household members in rural society the needs of whom are culturally defined.[13] Control can be exercised over material stocks, over decisions about their use, and over their preparation within the household from the state of raw material to that of product, ready for consumption.

Attempts have been made recently to relate *female* control over food decisions to the class position of their households and their individual economic status as wage workers. Evidence exists from Maharashtra that the nutritional status of children is better if women rather than men directly control grain and/or cash with which to purchase grain.[14] The question at issue is whether cash or kind contributions by wage-working women to the household budget are translated into greater control over the use of that cash in subsistence decisions. Existing evidence suggests the answer is no. In three contrasted villages in North Arcot District of Tamil Nadu, although patterns of control were surprisingly diverse, the male household head enjoyed sole control of market decisions relating to domestic food in nearly 60 per cent of cases, and jointly with his wife in another 15 per cent. Women were responsible in a slight majority of households for the choice of ingredients, but with respect

[9] Khare (1976a, 1976b); Appadurai (1981, 1985).

[10] Khare (1976b); Dube (1983: 228).   [11] White (1984: 24).

[12] Whitehead (1981).   [13] Kane (1941: ch. 9, esp. p. 428); Greenough (1982: 215).

[14] ILO (1979). It is possible that factors other than female control (such as income) are involved in this relationship. There is evidence that nutritional status does not improve in female-headed households where female control is not a cultural artefact but a necessity in a slum in urban Bangladesh (Pryer 1987).

to quantities of food prepared there is no discernible pattern of control. Certainly women do not dominate quantitative decisions. There were no significant associations between female wage-work participation and their control over food expenditure and purchase decisions. Nor was there any consistent association between the gender of food controllers and their social class. In two villages women were more important controllers of food in the propertied classes while men dominated in assetless, labouring families.[15] This was not true for a third where male control was more frequent than joint or female control throughout the social spectrum.[16] This lends qualified support to a general conclusion made by Jain that 'income does not guarantee improved female status within household or society' if we understand 'status' to be defined at least in part by control over the most important expenditure head.[17]

(b)   The food cycle

The domestic preparation of food has developed elaborate structures based on principles of rank and hierarchy according to purity, social and ritual debt over the last two thousand years.[18] These structures testify to individual material rights and obligations which are not symmetrical, but which are not always easily reducible to female inferiority. Khare has described the preparation of a meal as a 'food cycle', and identified its elements and its social and cultural scope. Its rules, as derived from ethnographic material for Lucknow Brahmins, are recognized as 'remarkably similar' for Tamil Brahmins by Appadurai,[19] and so they may have wide geographical relevance. Khare's treatment of food cycles in poverty-stricken and/or low-caste households is to itemize and analyse the respects in which they deviate from Brahminical orthodoxy, an approach latent in Appadurai's most recent work on food cycles in poor agricultural households in Maharashtra.[20]

The elements of a food cycle consist of the food area, cook, utensils, technique, ingredients, feeding, and the reinstatement of purity by cleaning. To summarize: the cleaning of the food area is a female act; the food area may be subdivided into cooking, storing, and eating areas, the former generally female and the latter male. The cooking crews for the most exclusive food and in the most exclusive food area tend to be female.[21] Cooking utensils are

---

[15] Harriss (1986: 79–81).   [16] Gibbs (1986).   [17] Jain (1980: 4).

[18] On its history, see Chakravarty (1972: 33–7). Note that 'cooking' means an act of preparation not necessarily involving the application of heat, but almost invariably involving progressive social restrictions on consumption according to mode of preparation. Preparation without fire is more inclusive than with fire, and frying is more inclusive than boiling. Culinary expertise is derived from knowledge of the ritual rules of handling food rather than from any accomplishment in culinary aesthetics. Culinary orthodoxy rests with the individual not with the household (Khare 1976a, 1976b: 36; Appadurai 1985). The principles of orthodoxy, of purity, and of service are part and parcel of all other aspects of household behaviour (Dube 1983: 229–31).

[19] Appadurai (1981: 497).   [20] Appadurai (1985).

[21] Even in urban scavenging households it is women who 'cook' i.e. in this case who collect the food from their 'client' households (Trivedi 1976: 43).

classified in terms of material and context into a hierarchy of auspiciousness and gender. Cooking technique is not sophisticated, in contradistinction to its 'ontological mode' which is sophisticated and is not yielding to technological change.[22] 'To perfect the pampering of the body is to have labour lost for a decidedly trifling cause.'[23] Ingredients are subject to a large number of simultaneous and interacting classification systems, which we need to discuss later. But as Appadurai observes for the village of Vadi in Maharashtra, the provision of ingredients is not a task framed by rigid conceptions or measures of need or requirements but rather by seasonality of crops in relation to the cycle of village rituals and festivals, and to idiosyncratic household celebrations of the life-cycle rituals.[24]

'A meal' is consumed by different household members in different places at different times and with specific types of company. Eating is a ritually lowering act for the (male) eater and tends to be carried out after cleansing rather quickly and in silence.[25] For men to eat in the company of women has been considered improper since the first century AD.[26] In general, eating order obeys certain principles, with age and male sex taking precedence, and with husbands' relatives and patrikin taking precedence over wives' relatives and matrikin.[27] Women (not necessarily those who cook) serve using the right (male/pure) hand only, and they assign quantities despite male silence or refusal.[28] Whereas women eat last, the position of children is not so determined. They have been reported to eat in any order: before other household members (so that the wife serves her husband with undivided attention);[29] after men but before women (fed by other brothers and sisters; not subject to special favours from the server); and/or with the women.[30] In the latter circumstances, men

[22] Khare (1976a: 35–6, 70).

[23] Ibid. 63.

[24] Appadurai (1985). The classification of foods is often referred to derogatively by nutritoinists as 'food fads' or 'taboos'. Judgements of these systems as 'pernicious', 'detrimental to good nutrition', 'deplorable' (e.g. Cantor et al. 1973: i. 116, 120) may have been informed by the concept of the balanced diet which has come under criticism for its tendency to equate food types with types of nutrient.

[25] Khare (1976a: 8).

[26] Chakravarty (1972: 37).

[27] Khare (1976a: 76). Ambiguities of rank in large joint families with systems of cross-cousin marriage, resolved by statements with portions and ingredients, are the subject of Appadurai's 'Gastropolitics' (1981). See also Sharma (1983) for Rajasthan; Abdullah (1983) for Bangladesh.

[28] The left hand is reserved for dealing with the impure opposite of food: faeces. Women are proscribed from either cooking or serving while menstruating (when the woman is most removed from the role of genetrix) at which point, in houses where there is no alternative, roles are reversed and the male cooks and serves. This reversal is observed by the cremator who is cook at death rituals (Khare 1976a, 1976b).

[29] A case-study for Bengal is by Chakravarty (1972: 100–2).

[30] Khare (1976a) for north India, Appadurai (1981: 498); McNeill (1986: ch. 3.1); Thiagarajan (1973: 80) for south India.

will not know the quantities of food consumed by their women and children. Age and sex play a role in the degree of indulgence displayed over infantile transgressions of food rules. Women may in turn themselves obey an eating (and serving) order based on age and husband's rank within the household, or may eat communally at their convenience with 'prolonged gossiping'.[31]

Special food for women is often called 'leftovers'. Husband's leftovers are appropriate for the wife alone, otherwise polluted. But it is worth understanding that there are at least three types of leftover, only one of which has the wife eating the scraps on her husband's leaf or plate. The others are unserved residues: uneaten food in the serving pots and unserved reserves in the kitchen.[32]

There is a category of food recognized throughout South Asia as signifying status or prestige. Although the precise items vary, we tend to be referring with this concept to meat, fish, and sometimes milk products, fruit, and 'English' (temperate) vegetables. North Indian evidence suggests that this food is either never eaten by women, or reserved for men if supplies of it are scarce.[33] In Sharma's poor households in Rajasthan even vegetables were eaten mainly by men, and pulses were not given to young children.[34] However Khare cautions that meat, milk, and status vegetables are 'seldom encountered delicacies', not of great quantitative importance in the daily diet. Moreover, dietary variety does not by itself indicate variety or appropriateness of nutrients. A further caution comes from evidence from the south of an absence of gender difference in food variety in agricultural castes in Tamil Nadu, among scheduled castes in Kerala, and tribals in Andhra Pradesh. Finally, items taboo to women may also include narcotics and other appetite suppressants.[35] Given such variations and given trade-offs and substitutions between quantities and prices of food items in male and female diets it is not possible to make assumptions or generalizations about gender differences in the costs of nutrients in South Asia.

Three major sources of change in this model of daily food behaviour have been noted by ethnographers. One, poverty, appears to lead to a relaxation of rules with respect to every element. However, the orthodox rules are observed in ceremonial feasting by the poor, which is taken to signify their importance as reference points.[36] The second source of change is commensal derestriction. This has been described as practised by men, opposed by women, and understood not as a change in the rules but as a flouting of them.[37] The third is the education of women which may lead to a change in the rules surrounding

---

[31] Chakravarty (1972: 100–1); Khare (1976a: 76); Caldwell et al. (1983).

[32] Chakravarty (1972: 33); Khare (1976a: 76); Appadurai (1981: 498).

[33] Thiagarajan (1973); Abdullah (1983); Gulati (1978); Appadurai (1985).

[34] Sharma (1983).

[35] Khare (1986: 95); McNeill (1986: ch. 3); Trivedi (1976: 41); Gillespie (1986; personal communication).

[36] Khare (1976a: 65–99).   [37] Ibid. 245–54.

food as in those surrounding other aspects of domestic life.[38] We shall return to discuss certain policy implications of these changes later.

(c) Gender, food cycles, and life cycles

The food cycle is further shaped by culturally defined needs associated with equally culturally defined stages of life.[39] From birth, the gender of an infant testifies to its cultural needs. While a child is breast-fed he or she gets a nutritionally balanced diet with anti-infective properties. No evidence yet exists that gender affects the number or duration of feeds while a suckling is breast-fed. But evidence from villages as dispersed as Morinda in Punjab, Matlab thana in Bangladesh, Karnataka and DR Kuppam in Tamil Nadu suggests that male babies are breast-fed for longer than females. In the southern case the difference was five months. The difference between the most propertied and the assetless classes was a further five months so that a male child in a landed household would be likely to be breast-fed for ten months longer than a female child in an agricultural labouring household.[40] The decisions to wean and to cease breast-feeding, as Caldwell et al. also report with respect to the decision to end post-natal sexual abstinence, have until recently been a matter for female elders rather than for the mother herself and may be being taken over in some areas by husband or by husband and wife together.[41] Despite the listing of special diets for weaning in ancient texts, it is rare to find their use now and it is apparently usual to find children weaned on to a bland version of 'household food' (if this term can now be used). The relatively low energy density of such food is thought to result in frequent, time-consuming feeding of the weanling. Das Gupta, in her surveys of Ludhiana villages in Punjab, notes a tendency towards daughters being weaned on to a vegetarian diet and sons on to a non-vegetarian one.[42] Levinson, however, reminds us that gender differences in weaning do not necessarily signify nutritional differences. In the richer Jat households in Morinda the weaned girl was on a par with the semi-weaned boy in terms of total nutrients. This was not true of the poorer Ramdasia caste, where girls were at a disadvantage from an early age.[43]

[38] Dube (1983: 230–6) attributes this to the anomic nature of institutions of education and to the dissolving effect on domestic life of the intrusion of various forms of secular state institutions into it.

[39] Greenough (1982). Even at birth a distinction is made. The *dhai* in Kodiur village in Tamil Nadu is paid twice as much for a boy as for a girl (Mathews 1979: 150). Useful accounts of food and the life cycle are given for two villages in Tamil Nadu by Krishnamurthy (1973) and Thiagarajan (1973). Comparisons of different regions are made by Apte (1973).

[40] Levinson (1972); McNeill (1984); Caldwell et al. (1983); Koenig and d'Souza (1986); Visaria (1987).   [41] Caldwell et al. (1982).

[42] Das Gupta (1987).

[43] Levinson (1972). See also Chakravarty (1972) and Mathews (1979: 103–7). The Tamil Nadu Nutrition Study reports no gender discrimination in food behaviour, notes a large number of foods as being recognized as good for the weanling and concludes that cultural practices limit quantity rather than variety (Cantor et al. 1973: i. 123).

Appadurai reports that the gastropolitical socialization of children into roles of demand, aggression, and authority (boys) and deference, meekness, stoicism, and self-preservation (girls) proceeds from the age of about 5.[44] The Caldwells additionally observe gender differences in foraging for food and in snacking (both done more by boys). Children in their Karnataka studies were reported to eat together (in such a way as to make gender differences in the socialization of eating difficult to administer) until the age of 6 among the rich but until adolescence among the poor.[45]

Unless unusually poor nutritional status throughout childhood delays menarche, the girl reaches the stage of adulthood at puberty and several years before the boy.[46] If married prior to puberty she now migrates (if not, she is married) and starts to climb from the bottom the rungs of rank in her husband's household. This climb depends on the outcomes of her pregnancies. Food restrictions, commonly imposed in pregnancy and lactation,[47] actually leave a wide range of food available for women made to observe these rules. Evidence from a North Arcot village shows increases in food variety for pregnant and lactating women, together with slight increases in energy intake and marked compensating reductions in activities involving high energy expenditure in the third trimester.[48] According to Khare, the mother of a girl is freed from post-natal dietary restrictions earlier than is that of a boy because at birth the girl is less polluting. During lactation however the mother of a boy is allowed greater dietary variety than that of a girl[49] (though recall that dietary variety *per se* indicates nothing necessarily about nutrition). Other aspects of food behaviour for adults in the sexually active, working, householder stage of life have been described earlier.

The elderly are defined demographically as over 44 and supposedly postmenopause ('dried-out' is a common description in Indian languages). Calorie needs are thought to begin declining after the age of 55. About the diet of the elderly (who have been found recently to have major and time-consuming roles. in child care[50]) little is known. In Kodiur, a village also in North Arcot, an orthodox widow in an agricultural caste would eat but one meal a day composed of a highly restricted range of foods.[51]

[44] Appadurai (1981: 498).

[45] Caldwell and Caldwell (1987).

[46] Evelath (1985); Greenough (1982: 247).

[47] Mathews (1979); Krishnamurthy (1973); Thiagarajan (1973).

[48] Sundaraj and Pereira (1973, 1975); McNeill (1986); see also Roberts *et al.* (1982) for activity reductions during pregnancy in Gambia.

[49] Khare (1976a: 162).

[50] McNeill (1984). In India as a whole, however, 65% of male children are cared for by their mothers in contrast to 55% of female children (Nagaraj 1986: 65–6).

[51] Mathews (1979: 226–31); see also proscriptions on meat, fish, and alcohol in old age, in Chakravarty (1972: 36).

The food cycle is embellished not simply by life cycles but also by responses to illness. Errors in the food cycle *inter alia* are also widely understood to cause illness. 'The local medical system' (though there are at least three non-allopathic systems) 'encourages a view of a good diet which centres on food type rather than food quantity.'[52] This is because health is understood as a balance between three elements composing the material and spiritual body and corresponding broadly with three types of food.[53] Most major diseases recognized by allopathic medicine including those of malnutrition therefore have a dietary explanation vested in type of food rather than quantity.[54] Treatment accordingly is not conceived in terms of quantity but instead in terms of food items with qualities opposite to those manifested by the illness. For instance, the practice in DR Kuppam village of feeding millet rather than rice to workers engaged in heavy agricultural labour and vulnerable to malnutrition is understood in terms of millet's quality of 'coolness' which makes it appropriate for work in hot weather.[55]

While nutritionists have strained to study the quotidian food cycle, anthropologists have devoted attention to ceremonies. For our purposes a few points suffice. Firstly festivals, whether to do with the calendar, or with national, village level, or household religious occasions, or with life-cycle rituals, are numerous and involve increased consumption of food, 'perpetuating the myth of abundance and dissipating collective scarcity', as Khare puts it. Secondly they involve a social expansion of every aspect of the food cycle extending in the case of marriages to public meals. And they are not captured, indeed they are studiously avoided, in dietary surveys by nutritionists, so their positive quantitative effects are unknown.[56]

The converse is also true. Nutritionists have also avoided fasting subjects when studying the diets of so called 'free living' people. A fast, like a leftover, needs defining. Fasting means the abstinence from 'exciting' food (spices, fried and/or salty food) or from food raised through ploughing for half or a whole day. Boiled potatoes, tapioca, milk and its products, including sweets and fruit, are all fasting foods. So fasting involves changing the source of energy intake but not always reducing it. There are strong gender differences in fasting, male fasts being for individual spiritual purpose and female fasts being for the auspiciousness of the household collective (i.e. for husband, son,

[52] McNeill (1986: ch. 3.2); Mathews (1979: 96–141) according to whom other causes of illness are supernatural; injury, accident, and stress; dirt and pollution; and cultural errors in the practice of sexual intercourse.

[53] Marriott (1978); Kakar (1982: 219–51); Caldwell *et al.* (1982); Thiagarajan (1973: 84–6).

[54] Mathews (1979: 141); Krishnamurthy (1973: 60–4); see also Kynch and Maguire (1986) for evidence of reluctance to attribute disease to lack of food in Palanpur, UP.

[55] McNeill (1986: ch. 3.1); Krishnamurthy (1973).

[56] Excellent sources on food and feeding ritual in ceremonies can be found in Khare (1976a: 162–228); Appadurai (1981: 502–5; 1985); and Mathews (1979: 211–63).

brother).[57] In Vadi in Maharashtra 'most households have at least one member who fasts on at least one day a week and if it is just one person who fasts it is likely to be the senior female'.[58] Female fasts according to Khare are more varied, numerous, and austere than those of men. In Lucknow in the north, out of a total of 105 possible fasting days in the year, orthodox Brahmin women observed fasts on average on 55 days, while poor urban women observed from 5 to 15. Yet in DR Kuppam in the south, McNeill found no gender difference in those having fewer than three meals a day (whether voluntary on involuntary).[59] Both Khare and Appadurai remark that fasting among the poor may be an occasion for sociability and supportive exchange by the women of the immediate neighbourhood.[60] Again the quantitative negative effects of fasting on adult men and women are unknown.

This review of Hindu food behaviour lends very qualified support to the generalizations marshalled by Wheeler to the effect that women are residual claimants and that their lack of eligibility to certain types of food leads to malnutrition. Women and girls tend to act domestically according to a paradigm of service (both sexual and culinary). But just as there is great variety in types of household and types of food cycle so there is great variety in structural types of woman. Our model of subordination in food allocation is the bride. The new bride and apprentice cook in an orthodox house may well eat last and alone (less likely in tribal and/or Dravidian society and among the very poor). As the mother of a son she may eat well and in the company of her mother-in-law.[61] As a widow she may eat, taking precedence but separately, close to the biological minimum for survival. The separate interactional worlds of women both dictate gender differences in eating patterns and permit nutritional subterfuge. Small children appear to be a collective responsibility in a joint family, with elderly male and female relatives and/or older children, aunts, and servants figuring as importantly in their general care and their feeding as the mother, so often assumed to be the sole feeder. Notions of female rank and deconstructions of female gender have not by and large informed nutritionists' classifications of adult women and seem to be outside the range of their policy prescriptions.[62] Perhaps this is because rank and gender are modified by region, poverty, and caste or tribal group, in complex ways not easily accommodated by the policy process.

(d) Material aspects of patriarchy

Food behaviour and culture have been interpreted as manifestations of patriarchy[63] and, consistent with other indicators, as manifestations of rela-

---

[57] Macdonald (1955); Khare (1976a: 130–3); Dube (1983: 229).

[58] Appadurai (1985).   [59] McNeill (1986: ch. 3).

[60] Khare (1976a: 144–9); Appadurai (1985).   [61] Appadurai (1981: 500).   [62]ICSSR (1977).

[63] For example Mies (1980); Bardhan (1985). On the general phenomenon of patriarchy, see Mackintosh (1981).

tions and states of 'discrimination' and female subordination.[64] Pursuit of evidence of these states and indicators contextualizes food behaviour with other aspects of life inside and outside the household. With apologies to authors and readers of a large literature, we have to be brief. The oft-quoted law of Manu belies a profound ambivalence towards women in the minds of the male makers of and commentators on customary law, an ambivalence also attested by contemporary psychologists.[65] (The customary rights of the male householder over children of either sex, we also ought to note, are said to have been as absolute as those over women until earlier this century.[66]) The material subordination of women and children has operated through male control over land, property, labour and the expression of sexuality. It has had historically specific outcomes in welfare as measured by health and nutritional status, by mortality, in particular by the age distribution of excess female or male mortality rates.

Despite the enactment of legislation after Independence in India and Bangladesh to guarantee equal inheritance rights to men and women, the control of women over property is thought to have diminished throughout the subcontinent over the past fifty years, although there remain notable differences between 'the south' and 'the north', with southern (and possibly tribal) women having greater access to property than northern women.[67] Similarly despite the Dowry Prohibition Act of 1961, the practice of transferring resources on marriage as dowry is said to be increasing in both prevalence and size and colonizing the south of the subcontinent, where previously bride price was more common.[68] Controversial issues include the economic significance of the dowry,[69] the nature of the north–south difference in marriage transfers, whether or not dowry is diffusing south,[70] and whether its diffusion is related to a decline in female participation in the wage labour force.[71] But there is

[64] The dictionary definition of discrimination is the 'observation of distinct differences'. Sen does not distinguish between states and indicators of discrimination in his concept of (measurable) 'functionings' (Sen 1985b).

[65] Manu (v. 146–8): 'In childhood a female must be subject to her father, in youth to her husband, when her lord is dead to her sons. A woman must never be independent.' The ambivalence between scorn (of her pettiness) fear (of her sexuality), and veneration (of her as a mother of sons) is magnificently discussed in relation to customary law in Kane (1941: vol. ii, part 2, chs. 9–11) and see also Sharma (1980) for contemporary evidence for northern India. (Male) ambivalence towards the nurturing, protective, and destructive role of the mother is equally well described in Kakar (1981: 53–112).

[66] Kane (1941: 507).   [67] Omvedt (1978); Cain (1977); Miller (1981).

[68] Rajaraman (1983).

[69] Dowry can be interpreted economically as a rotating capital fund; as a compensation for an economically unproductive member; as a symbolic selling; as a response to a shortage of marriageable men; and as a premortum inheritance for the bride (Woodley 1986).

[70] Dyson and Moore (1983); compare Sharma (1980) for the north with Gough (1981) for the south.

[71] Compare Rajaraman (1983) with Randeria and Visaria (1984).

agreement that the commercialization of females via resource transfers at marriage is punitive for households with a preponderance of daughters.

Also material and real for those women to whom it pertains is the practice of seclusion. This may restrict the secluded woman to the interior of the home. It may prohibit interaction of any sort between a young woman and senior men. It may restrict public movement, participation in the labour force, and the making of cash transactions.[72] A sociological verdict on its operation in a Hindu village in central India is that it creates a smaller yet much more intricate interactional world than that of men.[73] Other ways by which female behaviour may be controlled in exogamous patrilineages include age differences between spouses, distance from the natal home, and frequency of natal visits (the latter regarded by demographic anthropologists of South Asia as having crucial bearing upon female welfare).[74]

Female disadvantage is expressed in wage work. In many parts of central and south India, for instance, men and women play a roughly equal role in the labour inputs to agricultural production, yet women are remunerated less for it both because more of their productive agricultural work is unwaged, and because daily wage rates are lower, in the region of 50–70 per cent of those of men.[75] Male control over the labour process is argued to render acceptable both the exclusion of women from secure work and a greater probability of involuntary unemployment. Other restricted sectors of female activity such as petty production and trade are dependent on male sanction for physical premises, credit, and prices.[76] This male control has implications for female welfare.

Girls' survival chances have been related to their anticipated earnings as adults and to the size of the gender gap in daily earnings.[77] Yet legislation in certain states expresses acceptance of this gender difference.[78] These differences cannot be explained by productivity. For a start, it is impossible to

---

[72] Respectively Sharma (1978, 1980) for north India; Gough (1981: 383–5) for the south; Cain *et al.* (1979) for Bangladesh.

[73] Appadurai (1985).

[74] Das Gupta (1987); Jeffery *et al.* (1987); and Visaria (1987) who records that in Kachch District of Gujarat a shroud is commonly given with a dowry, symbolic of the complete lack of future contact on the part of the bride with her natal home.

[75] See Parthasarathy and Rama Rao (1973); Ryan and Ghodake (1984), Behrman and Deolalikar (1986a) for evidence in agriculture, and Harriss (1981) for evidence in trade and agroprocessing.

[76] Harriss (1976a).

[77] Rosenzweig and Schultz (1980). See also Bardhan (1987) and Bardhan (1985). On gender differences adverse to women in rural trade see Harriss (1976a); on greater insecurity and on the lack of relation between participation rates and the probability of employment for women in contradistinction to men, see Ryan and Ghodake (1980); on a general statement about women's subsidy to capitalist exploitation, see Deere (1979).

[78] Bardhan (1982).

measure gender productivity when, as in agricultural production, the gender division of labour requires men and women to perform non-comparable tasks; and where jobs are comparable, productivity differences have been found not to determine wage rate differentials.[79] Whether wage rates are determined by supply and demand is still unresolved despite a substantial econometric input,[80] and the gender division of labour, within which supply and demand operates, is taken as given in this work.

Striking regional variations in the extent, forms, and conditions of female participation have been mapped, and attempts have been made to explain them materially. Although higher rates of female participation in wage work are observed in the south and east than in the north and north-west, explanations based on regional variations in agricultural ecology and on the labour needs of agriculture have not stood the test of empirical scrutiny.[81] This failure has strengthened the hand of those invoking the power of the varied manifestations of patriarchy.

Trends toward declining female participation have been observed from as far back as the 1911 census. This trend has been carefully reinterpreted as not being an artefact of the several census redefinitions of work.[82] Attempts have been made to relate the male control of new production technology in agriculture to the recent displacement of female labour and the intensification of capitalist production relations.[83] It is likely, however, that several contradictory processes are involved: changes in the gender division of labour; changes in the crop composition of certain farming systems with implications for the gender division of labour; 'voluntary withdrawal' of upper-class rural women; and forced displacement of women from assetless households.[84] There is incontrovertible evidence of massive masculinization and net labour displacement due to technological change in post-harvest processing.[85]

Women combine waged and unwaged productive work with unwaged reproductive work for much of their lives. While biological production and field work may be the preserve of adult women, social reproduction and household production is carried out by girls, adult women, and the elderly.

[79] Rosenzweig (1984).

[80] Ibid.; Binswanger and Rosenzweig (1984).

[81] Miller (1981); and see literature which qualifies her 'agrarian determinist' explanation of female participation: Mencher and Saradamoni (1982); Gulati (1975a, 1975b) in Kerala; Harriss et al. (1984); Ryan and Ghodake (1980) for central and southern dryland agricultural villages. For complicating and contradictory effects of poverty see Sen (1982); of caste see Gulati (1978); of dependency see Cain et al. (1979); of urban and rural location see Kynch and Sen (1983).

[82] ICSSR (1977: 5–6); Omvedt (1978).

[83] Mies (1980); Mencher (1980); Agarwal (1984).

[84] Agarwal (1984); Sharma (1980); Maclachlan (1983).

[85] See Sharma (1980) for Punjab and Himachal Pradesh; Harriss (1976b) for Tamil Nadu; Harriss (1982) and Mukherjee (1983) for West Bengal; Harriss (1979) and Greeley (1986) for Bangladesh.

This unremunerated work has been argued to subsidize wages paid to both male and female labour. Recent trends towards the nuclearization of the household in rural north India have been shown to have contradictory effects upon female autonomy. While on the one hand the relative power of the adult woman *vis à vis* the adult relatives in her household over decisions pertaining to provisioning, birth spacing, and child care may be increased, on the other hand so also are her burden of work and her energy needs, particularly about the time of childbirth. It is possible to generalize neither about trends in household composition and type nor about their implications for female autonomy.[86]

Given that female education may be a major source of change in domestic productive and reproductive behaviour (especially fertility decisions) advantageous to the welfare of women, the rise in their literacy rates and the increasing confinement of illiteracy to those over the age of 25 indicates the possibility of a rise in female status over the next two decades. Yet female literacy lags behind that of males, especially in the north and centre of India in areas with a high concentration of scheduled castes and tribes. In the latter case, there are high adult female participation rates in wage work to which low education may be expected to act as a countervailing force.[87] The relationship between education and demographic indicators of welfare is not clear cut. The Caldwells show for Karnataka that rising female educational status is associated with a reduction in child mortality rates but with no reduction in male–female differentials. Das Gupta presents evidence from Ludhiana region where there is a relatively high rate of female literacy that education has no impact upon either child mortality rates or gender differentials. Behrman finds that the ICRISAT data for villages in central and southern India reveals the educational status of the male household head as being positively associated with pro-male bias in the food allocation and intake of children under 13, an activity actually undertaken by women.[88]

Well-being, measured most directly by mortality, is the outcome not only of work burdens and status, and of education, but also crucially of the interaction between nutrition, physiological state, and disease. While female mortality rates in excess of male rates in the reproductive years are likely to reflect the hazards of childbirth,[89] and while high levels of parity and reproductive wastage are well-acknowledged health risks, the evidence for differential morbidity which is not directly or indirectly related to reproduction is not clear. On the one hand there is historical data to show greater female mortality

---

[86] Jeffery *et al.* (1987); Wadley and Derr (1987).

[87] Dube (1983); Caldwell *et al.* (1982); ICSSR (1977); Khan (1985); Jain and Nag (1986).

[88] Caldwell *et al.* (1983); Das Gupta (1987); Behrman (1986). An indication of the importance of countervailing factors to that of education is found in Sri Lanka where the far less well-educated Tamil women have lower fertility than more highly educated Sinhalese women (Langford 1982).

[89] ICSSR (1977: 4–7); Karkal (1987).

from epidemics of plague and influenza.[90] Closer to the present time, evidence on morbidity from the Calcutta Metropolitan Development Area shows that while 1.9 per cent of men were 'clinically ill', 2.2 per cent of women were 'clinically ill'.[91] On the other hand, Chen et al. and Koenig and d'Souza in Bangladesh, and McNeill in Tamil Nadu, all conclude that while there is no gender difference in the incidence of disease, there may be gender differences in the duration and intensity of illness.[92] Gender differences in sanitation have also been hypothesized as having an impact on morbidity in rural (north) India where the quantity, source, and degree of (faecal) contamination of bathing and clothes-washing water may be gender specific. Gender differences in quality of and expenditure upon clothing may also influence health status.[93]

Perceptions of health are another matter. Sen reports Bengali women as much more unwilling to declare indifferent or ill health than men. Gillespie shows that health is perceived by men of the Koya and Lambardi tribes in Andhra Pradesh as an individual state related to occupation and task. By contrast, tribal women see health as a collective household state related to household environment.[94]

Less ambiguity surrounds female disadvantage in the treatment of disease. We want to emphasize six aspects of this type of female disadvantage because of their implications for nutrition. First, lack of establishment of and/or access to maternity facilities represents a significant female disadvantage.[95] Second, if gynaecological and obstetric disorders are removed from data sets, it would seem that, while the gap between female and male treatment per death is narrowing, the gender gap in treatment of disease remains. But the evidence is not all one-way. In cases from north India and Bangladesh, a marked gender imbalance in health expenditure on children has been recorded (Das Gupta noting a factor of two for infants under 12 months). Females also appear to be less often referred for allopathic treatment than are males. Females are more often treated using the three other indigenous health systems (though we have to note criticisms about the iatrogenic character of rural primary health care interventions of whatever system of medicine). By contrast, in Karnatakan

[90] Kynch (1985a). These excess deaths may have been modified by relative lack of treatment, while the reasons for excessive female mortality from plague were ascribed by the British authorities not to poorer nutrition but to female service roles which brought them into contact with soiled clothes, infested grain, and which had them living in poorly ventilated rooms (ibid. 25).

[91] See Sen (1985b: 101–4). Here the relative excess of women suffering a combination of indifferent and ill health was only very slightly greater than the gender ratio for ill health by itself. Interestingly, the gender ratio for ill health was more adverse to women in improved slums than it was in unimproved slums and it was adverse to men in the town and villages surrounding Calcutta.

[92] Chen et al. (1981); McNeill (1986); Koenig and d'Souza (1986).

[93] Das Gupta (1987); Pettigrew (1987).

[94] Gillespie (1986).

[95] ICSSR (1977).

villages the Caldwells note no gender differences in treatment; and much more controversially neither does Visaria for infants and children in Gujarat.[96] Third, the (northern) gender gap seems to be greater for children than for adults.[97] Fourth, Mitra found that gender differences in child mortality rates from respiratory, gastrointestinal, and vitamin deficiency diseases arise not from gender differences in morbidity or differences in treatment but from the relatively later stage in illness at which girls were brought for treatment.[98] Fifth, mortality rates are highest in regions where the provision of health facilities and public expenditure on health per capita are lowest.[99] Gender differences in mortality rates have been shown to vary positively with distance of home from centre of treatment.[100] Lastly, it has been found in Bangladesh (and remains a hypothesis for testing elsewhere) that mothers of sons are less morbid than mothers of only daughters.[101]

Disadvantage in female access to treatment, especially at a young age, may be the most important influence on female health, a matter to which we need to return later. But as a corollary here we should note that these gender differentials in access to state medical facilities may be extended into other types of access to the state and into political life at village level and beyond.[102]

It comes as no surprise then that there is gender bias in basic demographic indicators (such as life expectancy, mortality, and the sex ratio) in South Asia. Although life expectancy has increased from the 1930s, when it was very low (mid-twenties) and had no marked gender bias, up to the present (when it is in the early fifties), improvement for women historically has lagged behind that for men. Aggregate female life expectancy, however, has been on a convergence course with that of men since the 1970s and is estimated actually to have converged in 1987.[103] Regional and social differences in this trend require research.

Similar general trends and relations are observed in mortality rates. The sex ratio is unusually masculine in South Asia and has become more masculine during this century.[104] Dyson concludes from a careful scrutiny of the Indian

---

[96] Singh et al. (1962); ICSSR (1977: 29); Aziz (1977); Aziz and Rassaque (1987); Caldwell et al. (1983); Kynch and Sen (1983); Kynch (1985a); Das Gupta (1987); Visaria (1987).

[97] Wyon and Gordon (1971); Chen et al. (1981); Chen (1982); Kielmann et al. (1983); Das Gupta (1987).

[98] Mitra (1978).

[99] Bardhan (1974).

[100] Rahaman (1982).

[101] Koenig and Wojtnyiak (1987). Whether this relation stems from the intrinsically more auspicious state of the mother of sons, or whether it is her sons who pay for her treatment, is a matter of conjecture.

[102] ICSSR (1977); Sharma (1978, 1980); Gough (1981).

[103] ICSSR (1977: 3, 19). Women's survival may have been affected by the gender of their children. The sex ratio is more masculine the greater the age of the respondent (Dyson 1987).

[104] Bardhan (1974); Padmanabha (1982); Sen (1985b: 85–6); Sen (1986); Nagaraj (1986).

data that the increasing masculinization of the sex ratio in successive censuses since 1921 is associated with the trend of decline in the general mortality rate *per se* 'independent of any change in the relative life chances between the sexes'.[105] Mortality is related to fertility and this too is declining. As a rule of thumb for South Asia, male neonatal mortality rates exceed those of females but are about-turned at one month of age. Excess female mortality persists through most of childhood and throughout the reproductive, householder stage of life. Roughly one-third of excess female mortality occurs during the first twelve months of life, another third occurs in the years 1–4, and the remaining third is spread throughout reproductive adulthood.[106] Recently, the life chances of females above the age of 5 have increased as have those of women at ages beyond the prime reproductive years. By contrast, excess male mortality in the age group above 35 has been rising rapidly, reasons for which are underresearched.[107] The sex differential, however, is never the most important component of mortality. Regional location is.

States with highest general mortality rates have the highest excess female mortality rates: Punjab, Haryana, and Uttar Pradesh. But, as Dyson and Das Gupta have each concluded, despite these very important redoubts, excess female mortality is declining and being gradually reduced to certain age groups, certain regions, and within them certain types of vulnerable female, notably the second and third daughters.[108] Historical case-studies in north-western India emphasize the role of female infanticide in the acquisition and retention of social and economic power and hint that despite legislation prohibiting this practice, it may still occur occasionally.[109] In the south, by contrast, gender differences in aggregate and infant mortality approach parity and even favour females in a number of districts in Tamil Nadu and in Kerala.[110] A spatial trend from parity in the sex ratio in the south-western extremity towards high masculinity in the north has been well described.[111] But the trend is less visible when data are disaggregated by caste or income

[105] *Pace* ICSSR (1977: 21). In Utopian agricultural conditions, if all mortality were slowly banished, a population sex ratio would increase to approach that at birth (approximately 105) (Dyson 1987).

[106] See Sathar (1985) for Pakistan; Koenig and d'Souza (1986) and Koenig and Wojtyniak (1987) for Bangladesh; Dyson (1987) for India; and Langford (1984) for Sri Lanka. Even in Sri Lanka, where the male mortality rate has exceeded that of the female since 1971, there is still excess female mortality among the under-5s (Langford 1984).

[107] Sen (1985*b*: 94–5); Padmanabha (1981, 1982); Chen *et al.* (1981); Dyson (1987).

[108] Bardhan (1974, 1987); Visaria and Visaria (1973) show that complications to this surface trend arise if the data are disaggregated according to social class.

[109] Clark (1983); Parry (1979): 'Mians do not feel it necessary to repudiate their past conduct and even view the allegation that the practice is not altogether extinct with a certain amount of complacency' (ibid. 215).

[110] Caldwell and Caldwell (1987); Das Gupta (1987).

[111] Miller (1981); Sopher (1980).

group. Regional variations in factors such as the age of marriage, the under-enumeration of women in censuses, the distance and frequency of visits to natal home, patterns of fertility and morbidity, gender and social differentials in the extent of assetlessness and poverty, property rights, the age and gender division of work and work burdens, have been invoked to explain regional variations in the sex ratio, and muddy the simple picture.[112]

So what? Far from being a digression, this summary of the *modus operandi* of patriarchy in South Asia shows that there is a material base to religiously justified son preference. Food behaviour cannot usefully be abstracted (either for analytical or for 'policy' purposes) from the social relations of patriarchy. The discriminatory practices of patriarchy may be unrelated to the wealth and economic status of households.

Female disadvantage which was most strikingly manifested in the sex ratio is not the necessary and inevitable result of underfeeding alone. A bundle of reciprocally causing variables, in particular reproductive burdens, work burdens, sanitation, and the treatment of disease, interact with the need for food to affect mortality. Lastly gender-based categories cannot be universalized even under the South Asian brands of patriarchy. There would appear to be sufficient contrariness in the relationships between the culture of food and the material subordination of women to justify a re-examination of nutritional evidence of intrahousehold food allocation. This forms the burden of the next section.

10.3.   The measurement of hunger within the household

'Hunger' or food-related deprivation in populations is measured by nutrient intakes, heights, weights, and ages, interpreted against yardsticks representing norms or averages.[113] Although we shall examine the intake of micronutrients, we focus on energy. The reasons for this are (1) that almost all components of the diet (including protein) are broken down to energy in the normal course of events, (2) that there are few deficiency diseases of which low energy intake is not a correlate, and (3) that appetite is probably most closely related to energy sufficiency.[114]

Hunger within the family is exceptionally difficult to research. Much

[112] ICSSR (1977: 4–5); Dyson and Moore (1983); Harriss and Watson (1987). It has been recently suggested by the Caldwells that 'north' and 'south' are misleading regionalizations, and that the more influential contrasts are between, on the one hand, regions of long-settled peasant agriculture with strongly differentiated age and sex roles, high fertility, and lower rates of fertility decline and, on the other, southern frontier agriculture with less-differentiated sex roles and lower fertility Caldwell and Caldwell 1987).

[113] Clinical signs and symptoms conventionally indicate micronutrient deficiency rather than hunger.

[114] Payne (1985a); LSHTM (1985: 7, 24). This also means that most nutrient deficiencies can be rectified straightforwardly with an increase in the usual diet.

research (and also much policy advocacy) assumes the identity of the mal-nourished and sets out to verify the prevalence and intensity of malnutrition.[115] Hence there is a disproportionate number of studies on samples of pregnant and lactating women and on infants and preschool children (the latter often undifferentiated by sex)[116] and correspondingly a dearth of measurements on adult men, older children and adolescents, and the elderly, let alone whole households.[117] This situation limits the inferences that can be made about gender differences for they cannot be sustained by evidence from children alone.[118] It also qualifies inferences about gender differences according to stages of life, whether physiologically or culturally defined.

That said, two types of measurements may be made on individuals within a household: (1) their food intake, subsequently converted to nutrients, and (2) their heights and weights (and ages), subsequently converted into anthro-pometric indices. Sen, concerned to evaluate ways of measuring function and capability, has put the case against food intake and for anthropometry for the measurement of well-being. In essence this case rests on measurement preci-sion, the intervention of other, possibly confounding (physiological), factors preventing a direct stimulus–response relationship between food intake and well-being, and the interpretation of measurements given the ragged state of standards for evaluation.[119]

Yet exactly the same comments may be levelled at anthropometry.[120] First, measurements of heights, weights, and especially ages in children are as practically difficult and subject to as many sources of error as are those of food intake.[121]

Second, diagnosis based on anthropometric status does not reflect aetiology. Malnutrition is a combination of inadequate food intake and infections.[122] Feedback relations operate through increased needs for energy in fever and

---

[115] Gopalan (1985).

[116] Waterlow (1972, 1973). Two recent examples from north-east India where disaggregation by gender would have been very helpful are Khan (1980) and Chattopadhyay (1985).

[117] See Satyanarayana *et al.* (1979, 1980) for adolescents; McNeill (1986) and references therein for adults and the elderly; and Dugdale (1985) for household measurements.

[118] Birth weight is influenced by maternal nutritional status (Prema 1978; Sibert *et al.* 1978). Interestingly, Tanner *et al.* (1970) show that there are even different degrees of gender difference in birth weight according to maternal body weight. The influence of the environment comes into play from early in infancy.

[119] Sen (1985b: 83). Sen also discusses other welfare indicators including mortality, morbidity, and clinical signs and symptoms.

[120] To call the result of anthropometry 'nutritional status' is as misleading as to call it 'health status' (Deolalikar 1984), and to use the anthropometric status of children as the basis of inferences about the 'nutritional status' of whole populations is an act of perhaps misleading heroism because of health events specific to childhood (Payne 1985a).

[121] Abdullah (1983) and McNeill (1986) have carried out both methods of assessment and discussed them critically.

[122] Pacey and Payne (1985: ch. 5).

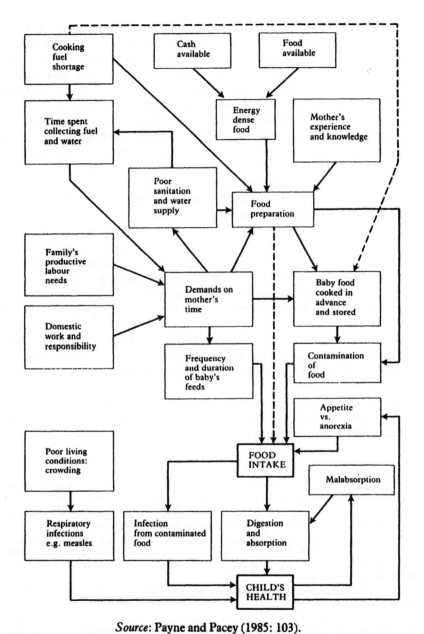

Source: Payne and Pacey (1985: 103).

Fig 10.1. Factors operating at the household level which affect the state of nutrition of children

tissue repair, reduced absorption of (up to 9 per cent of) nutrients because of intestinal dysfunctions, and reduced food intake because of mouth lesions, anorexia, and the withholding of food from the sick. All these mechanisms may serve to reduce the capacity to cope with infection.[123] The nutritional outcome of these feedback relations upon need and upon appetite for food cannot be generalized. Feedback relations are of course the basis of non-allopathic theories of illness. The complexity of environmental influences on both food supply and infection is traced in Fig. 10.1. Apropos of which, we have already seen how morbidity may be modified by gender differences in health care. It may be affected further by the quality of childcare.[124]

Third, the interpretation of anthropometric indices is problematic. Conventional arbitrary cut-offs for different grades of malnutrition (other than severe) are not helpful for assessing individuals because of interindividual variation in genetic potential. Local standards derived from populations affected by sex bias would lead to evaluations which are underestimates of discrimination. The meaning of mild to moderate malnutrition both for risk of current clinical conditions and for the probability of adverse current, seasonal, or long-term future effects on earnings, physical productivity, physiological and mental function is not clear.[125] Nor is the significance for adult functioning of the duration and incidence of the severe category of malnutrition during the period of growth.

Anthropometry cannot tell us whether there is 'failure in the equity of intrahousehold food distribution' but it can tell us about growth differences in children. We will not throw this particular baby out with the methodological bath water, so let us turn to what the South Asian data show (Map 10.1).

(a) The anthropometric evidence

Some of this evidence is not socio-economically disaggregated but indicates gross regional variations. At the extremities of the subcontinent, in the Nepalese Terai and in Sri Lanka, there are no gender differences in the growth

[123] LSHTM (1985: 63). According to Sukhatme, in a given population, barely half the variance in anthropometric status is linked to nutritional history, the rest is because of illness or it is genetic (1981: 6). Martorell, reviewing the literature on anthropometric status and risk of infection, also finds that anthropometric status affects the intensity of illness but not the risk (1985: 22).

[124] Nagaraj (1986); Visaria (1987).

[125] For the interpretation of grades see Gworinath Sastri and Vijayaraghavanlk (1973). For difficulties in matching anthropometric grades with clinical signs and symptoms, see Pacey and Payne (1985: 84–94) and Montgomery (1977). For problems with the concept of genetic potential see Payne and Cutler (1984). For controversy over the possible relationships between childhood malnutrition and adult productivity see Immink *et al.* (1984); Gwatkin (1983); Viteri (1971); Satyanarayana *et al.* (1979, 1980); Lipton (1983). On controversies over the relationships between childhood anthropometric status and physiological function see Pereira *et al.* (1979); Madhavan (1965); Rajalakshmi (1981); Klein (1981); Freeman *et al.* (1980); Evelath (1985); McNeill (1986). On anthropometric status and mental performance see Madhavan (1965); Rajalakshmi (1981). On seasonal changes in anthropometric status being socio-biological adaptation to the duration and periodicity of physical work, see Dugdale and Payne (1986).

retardation of children.[126] There is a conflict in the results from Bangladesh. On the one hand Chen et al. find that whereas 14.4 per cent of girls under 5 years old were 'severely malnourished' in terms of weight for age, only 5.1 per cent of boys were.[127] Abdullah, however, found no gender distinctions in anthropometric status for children of any age. Male children under 5 (and male adults) in labouring households were more likely than their female counter-parts to lose weight in the scarce seasons.[128] Sen, discussing the impact of the 1978 floods in West Bengal, shows that girls bore the brunt of the growth retardation in children under 6 years.[129] Kynch and Maguire in Palanpur village of Uttar Pradesh also found that young girls had a lower frequency distribution of anthropometric status than young boys and more frequent seasonal weight losses for girls against boys; but they noted a progressive decline in the status of boys with increasing age such that adult men were of as much concern as young girls.[130] In the north-west, in Kuchch District of Gujarat, no significant gender differences in anthropometric status have been found among preschool children.[131] Pushpamma and colleagues, investigating differences among adolescents in the three cultural and ecological regions of Andhra Pradesh, also found no gender differences.[132] In Tamil Nadu Pereira noted that girls' weights were closer to standards than boys',[133] and McNeill found the same relationships with respect to adult body mass indices, and found insignificant seasonal changes and no seasonal differences between the sexes.[134]

These findings are commonly presented in a historically decontextualized manner. They show regional variations but they are curiously classless. Gender differentiation in growth retardation among children appears to be a phenomenon confined to the north of the subcontinent and not always evident there.

Less field work is concerned with the social profile of anthropometric status. A general hypothesis about female economic status has been borrowed for testing from the mortality literature: excess female mortality (and hence anthropometrically measured female neglect) is greatest not among the poor but among the asseted where women are banned from participation in productive agricultural work.[135] This tends to be refuted in the 'north'.

---

[126] Martorell et al. (1984) for Nepal; Perera (1983) for Sri Lanka.

[127] Chen et al. (1981).   [128] Abdullah (1983).   [129] Sen (1981).

[130] Kynch and Maguire (1986).   [131] Visaria (1987).

[132] Pushpamma, Geervani, and Lakshmi Devi (1982).   [133] Pereira et al. (1979).

[134] McNeill (1986), thereby casting doubt on Chambers et al.'s model of the effects of seasonality of energy expenditure, input food stocks, and disease on nutritional status (Chambers et al. 1981). See also Behrman and Deolalikar (1986b) for similar results using the ICRISAT data for rural households in central and south India.

[135] Miller (1981). Bardhan (1987) finds a correlation coefficient of -0.82 between Bhatia's index of son preference and the statewise proportion of households possessing assets of less than Rs 1,000.

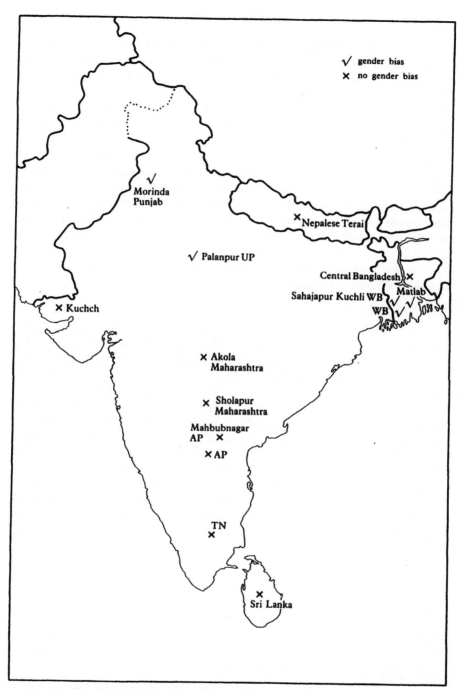

√ gender bias

✕ no gender bias

√ Morinda
Punjab

✕ Nepalese Terai

√ Palanpur UP

Central Bangladesh ✕

Sahajapur Kuchli WB   Matlab

WB   √

✕ Kuchch

✕ Akola
Maharashtra

✕ Sholapur
Maharashtra

Mahbubnagar
AP   ✕

✕ AP

TN
✕

✕
Sri Lanka

Sources: Abdullah (1983); Chen *et al.* (1981); Kynch and MaGuire (1986); Levinson (1972); Martorell *et al.* (1984); Perera (1983); Pushpamma *et al.* (1982); Ryan *et al.* (1984); Sen (1981); Sen and Sengupta (1983).

Map 10.1 Gender bias in anthropometric status in S. Asia

Sen and Sengupta's study in two contrasting villages of West Bengal reveals
gender differences in growth status which were greatest in landless labouring
households.[136] Khan shows that whereas the heights and health status of
Bangladeshi males aged 5 to 19 were not affected by household energy
supplies, those of females were.[137] In Punjab, Levinson found anthropometric
gender differences to be pronounced only among the poor Ramdasia
caste.[138]

In central and southern India there is evidence of gender bias, but not in the
expected direction. Ryan et al.'s anthropometric research in six villages
selected as representative of agrarian conditions in the semi-arid tropics shows
gender differences confined to the children of landless and small farmer
households where it was boys who were at a disadvantage.[139] Such results
reinforce the view of some demographic anthropologists that it is not economic
hardship or aggregate energy availability per se which cause discrimination
against the female sex. Rather, where it happens, it is to be considered the
outcome of kinship and culture.[140]

(b) Indicators of intake

But our subject is hunger. Hunger is a direct appetite for an input, hence
the appropriate measure is nutrient intake. As is the case with basic micro-
economic data (income, employment, time allocation, costs of production,
etc.), this is easier said than done. Data for individuals comprising households
sampled throughout a local society are needed because it cannot be assumed
that hunger is not felt within families identified in terms of their aggregate
energy supply as being adequately supplied with food. Seasonal data are
needed because intake, work loads and activity levels, and maintenance
requirements are known to vary seasonally. It is not to be supposed that food
allocations will be constant over the labouring year. Female interviewers are
appropriate for female respondents and are more likely to gain access to the
individual portions, necessary for weighing and for subsequent biochemical
analysis. Continuous on-site observation captures subsidiary feeding and
gender specific supplements to main meals. Exceptional events bias 24-hour

---

[136] Sen and Sengupta (1983).

[137] Khan (1984).

[138] Levinson (1972). Village-level data on excess female mortality are consistent with the north
Indian anthropometric results for cases in UP (Jeffery et al. 1987; Wadley and Derr 1987); and
Pakistan (Sathar 1985). But in Punjab, Das Gupta (1987) finds that although the landless are not
distinguished by greatest total excess female mortality, the mortality rates for the second daughter
are highest in this group. By contrast Houska finds no gender bias in mortality among sweepers in
Allahabad (1981).

[139] Ryan et al. (1984); confirmed by Behrman (1986). With respect to mortality, the Caldwells
found less gender bias among the landless in Karnatakan cases than among the landed (1987).

[140] Das Gupta (1987).

observations unless supplemented with food frequency information based on recall. Periods of measurement of between three and seven days are therefore necessary. The subject cannot be investigated, as nutritionists are wont to do, by taking random samples of men, women, and children, measuring their portions separately in different households, aggregating and contrasting the results, and leaving the readers free to recreate model households under their own assumptions about composition. Ideally each household member's food must be compared with others in the same household. This is rarely done.

As with anthropometry, there are many ways in which measurement errors may creep in. The methods by which intake is measured are said to suffer from trade-offs between precision and cost and invasiveness.[141] Errors of omission include 'snacking' (which may be the normal way of feeding little children), the measurement of consumption of breast milk, condiments, and spices, eating outside the household, and the exclusion of extraordinary food cycles.[142] Errors of commission may arise from the standardization of volumetric measurements, and from variations in the nutrient content of foods (especially consequent to cooking with heat), in its digestibility, in the accuracy of food composition tables, in dietary duplication for chemical analysis, and in behavioural modifications in 'subjects' due to their being observed.[143] Comparisons of recall with weighing have produced estimates of error of 10 to 40 per cent, though recent comparative studies tell of low levels of error.[144] To acknowledge the possibility of errors does not mean however that we can wish away the results of careful research.

A fair distribution of food among members of a household is not an equal one. Intakes attain significance (and 'nutritional justice' is achieved) in relation to need. Analysis of interindividual adequacy requires information about individual need. Need is arguably the most controversial concept in human nutrition. Need is thought to consist of three components: growth, activity, and maintenance. Body maintenance is by far the largest and most constant

---

[141] The methods are recall over 24 hours, record keeping, food frequency listing, with or without the testing of local household volumetric measures, the weighing of stated inventories for individuals, the weighing of cooked portions, and chemical analysis. Combinations of these methods are frequently used (Ferro-Luzzi 1982). 'There is no perfect method' (Pekkarinen 1970).

[142] Khare (1976a) describes the more or less numerous and casual meals fed to under-4s in his Lucknow households. See also Sundaraj and Pereira (1973, 1975). In studies on the allocation of food, breast milk is not conventionally measured and sometimes children under 2 are omitted from the analysis. However, for children above the age of 2, the energy from breast milk is not thought to introduce 'normally' a major error. (But for evidence to the contrary, see Ryan et al. 1984.)

[143] Ferro-Luzzi (1982); Pushpamma, Geervani, and Usha Rani (1982); Chacko et al. (1984). Note that in economic research the conversion of expenditure data into quantities introduces errors due to assumptions made about prices.

[144] See McNeill (1986) for a review of research. Her own work suggested that weighing methods lead to the omission (if at all) of drinks, pickles and chutneys, and (fried) snacks which are of significant importance to energy intake. Recall leads to the omission (if at all) of meal accompaniments (rasam and side dishes) which are not of importance to energy estimates.

component of need.[145] Women are known to be physiologically more efficient than men (even girls under 5 seem to be more efficient than boys under 5) and therefore to need less, and an 'average' Western man expends and needs to eat about 36 per cent more energy each day than his female counterpart.[146] Growth is a very small component of need even in children.[147] Evidence of the energy costs of pregnancy shows considerable variation.[148] It is the energy cost of activity which displays greatest interindividual variation.[149] Here there are many traps for unwary makers of assumptions. Time allocation studies may show that adult women have both much longer working days and less seasonal variation than can be accounted for by either wage work or farm work because of their widespread responsibility for the reproduction of the household.[150] But this may be set against physiological evidence that the energy costs of women's common daily activities (which subjectively seem quite demanding) are low.[151]

In the orthodox model of human nutrition, needs are converted into requirements[152] as a yardstick by means of which the adequacy of intakes may be evaluated. Requirements are defined as an estimated average value of a given nutrient intake and refined, according to further estimates, in relation to body weight, sex, activity, growth, and physiological state. From this account it will be evident that these estimates are subject to different margins of

[145] These are at present assumed not to interact or to vary with the composition of the diet (Rivers and Payne 1982). Activity accounts for only about 13% of energy need in a moderately active adult; growth accounts for only 4% of the intake of an average 1-year-old, only 2% after infancy. Growth accounts for only 18% during recovery from severe malnutrition in infancy (LSHTM 1985: 15).

[146] The female is physiologically more efficient because she is genetically smaller, has a lower proportion of metabolically active lean tissue and therefore, cet. par., lower protein and energy requirements. For reasons as yet unknown, her energy costs for activity are also lower, even per unit of lean body mass (Rivers 1982; LSHTM 1985: 18; Nelson 1986).

[147] On growth, see the Gambian studies of Flores et al. (1984); Gorsky and Calloway (1983). Ferro-Luzzi (1982) queries conventional deductions in energy requirements for ageing. Empirical evidence shows no reduction in energy intakes and wide variation in intakes with increasing age.

[148] Estimates of the energy needs of pregnancy vary from 27,550 calories (Ebrahim 1979) through the official 61,600 calories (UK, Colombia, and Guatemala) to 141,120 (Canada); see Lipton (1983). Both Lipton and McNeill conclude that there is no need for a special energy allowance for pregnancy, the calorie needs of the third trimester being straightforwardly compensated for by reductions in activity.

[149] Ferro-Luzzi (1982); Lawrence et al. (1985).

[150] McGuire (1979); Immink et al. (1984); Batliwala (1982, 1985); Ryan et al. (1984); McNeill (1986: ch. 4).

[151] Lawrence et al. (1985).

[152] Requirement (estimated average) must be distinguished from recommendation (set at above average to cater for people whose requirement is greater than average). Intake (what is eaten) must also be distinguished from allowance (what should be provided) (Waterlow 1979). In practice there is much confusion over the use and meaning of these terms.

error[153] not to mention variability,[154] sheer ignorance,[155] and political manipulation.[156] Furthermore, individual need (supposing it is normally distributed) will be below estimated requirements quite legitimately in half the cases. So requirements are abused if applied to individuals.

The revolutionary concept of adaptation has set the cat among these pigeons. 'Adaptation' arose from attempts to explain observations of habitual low and variable energy intake, capacity to adjust to which has been thought to be 'a form of fitness'.[157] Adaptation means many things. It can be behavioural, as when intake does not change during the third trimester of pregnancy but activity is much reduced.[158] It may be physiological: changes in body composition accompanying changes in intake.[159] But it may also involve the human body's adjusting the efficiency with which it metabolizes energy in a benign autoregulatory manner over a range of levels of supply, which puts paid to the concept of a fixed efficiency machine, a fixed requirement, and a determinate entitlement.[160] Adaptation could involve a combination of these factors. Beaton[161] notes a 'general failure to demonstrate metabolic adaptation' and Lipton, while acknowledging its conceptual importance, reckons that its quantitative impact may be small.[162]

In relation to intrahousehold food allocation, an adaptationist interpretation of low individual shares would be a counsel of caution against concluding that they are the result of 'discrimination'. In this study, since the range of intakes comprising thresholds for adaptation has not been specified, we do not have any option but to proceed to evaluate the sharing of food against requirements.

[153] Requirements of vitamins and minerals are set by evidence on intakes and deficiency diseases; the minima associated with disappearance of deficiency diseases (Anon. 1976).

[154] Recommended daily allowances for 41 countries show massive variations (as much as the variations in RDAs in the 19th century (Rivers and Payne 1982; Anon. 1976)) because of different assessments of the needs of age, sex, physiological status, different concepts of RDA, different criteria of adequacy, and different foods.

[155] Ignorance is deepest for aminoacids, trace elements, and minor vitamins; and for nutrients for the child from 6 months to 5 years, for adolescents, and for adults. Knowledge is most advanced with respect to energy, protein, calcium, iron, and vitamins A, B, and D and for young adults and the infant from birth to 6 months (Anon. 1976). See Lipton (1983) for a convincing argument that Western requirements are set too high and that modifications for body weight, activity, pregnancy, and climate are also exaggerations (pp. 13–29).

[156] Rivers and Payne (1982).   [157] Payne (1985a); Payne and Cutler (1984).

[158] Gorsky and Calloway (1983); Waterlow (1985).   [159] McNeill (1986).

[160] Sukhatme (1981, 1982); Seckler (1982); Payne (1985a, 1985b).

[161] Beaton (1985: 225); see also McNeill (1986).

[162] The idea has also been criticized as a tautology ('So long as you are not dead you are adapted' (Waterlow 1985)), and for its policy implications ('adaptation generates the impression among policy makers that undernutrition is not a serious problem in the country any more' (Gopalan 1983)). But the counter-arguments to these are that it is serious undernutrition that is 'the problem' and that it is neither accurate nor responsible to describe what is actually a process, as being a pathological state, by implication amenable to rectification (Rivers and Payne 1982; Payne 1985a, 1985b).

We derive a certain consolation from the fact that the Indian requirements estimates are among the most carefully determined and most regularly revised. They indicate that the female adult needs 85 per cent of the male's energy intake. Comparison with Western norms and recent empirical research (which suggest, respectively, that adult females need 27 and 32 per cent less than men[163]) open up the possibility that the Indian norms err on the side of generosity to women. In which case using them as a standard will tend to lead to overestimation of anti-female discrimination.

10.4. *Results*

Our search, which does not pretend to be exhaustive and extends to 1986, unearthed 24 cases of household surveys in India and Bangladesh relevant to the subject of food allocation (Table 10.1). They may be considered representative in regional terms, but they proved impossible to standardize. Sample sizes vary from 50 to 2,800 households. Sample selection varies from taking a population (Abdullah in Bangladesh), through random sampling of a preidentified stratum of the poor (Sharma in Rajasthan; Gopaldas in Gujarat; Pushpamma in Andhra Pradesh); spatially stratified random sampling (Tamil Nadu Nutrition Study); a combination of representative, purposive sampling for the landed and random sampling for the landless (ICRISAT in Madhya Pradesh, Maharashtra, and Andhra Pradesh) to purposive selection for accessibility (Chen in Bangladesh). With the exception of the Tamil Nadu study (estimated to be carried out in 1971–2) they date from the late 1970s and early 1980s. Only in Abdullah's and ICRISAT's 6 village cases is there any socio-economic disaggregation.[164] The length of observation varies; 3 sets (done by nutritionists Abdullah in Bangladesh, Pushpamma in AP, and Sharma in Rajasthan) consist of 72-hour continuous observation, the rest of 24 hours. Only 3 cases (the two Bangladesh studies and ICRISAT's 6-village one) comprise seasonally repeated observations. All aim for precision by weighing and/or volumetric estimation supplemented by recall, except for the Tamil Nadu Nutrition Study which relies only upon recall.[165] Coverage of micronutrients, classification by age, and disaggregation by sex are all unstandardized. Frustratingly few studies present disaggregates by sex for children under 13 and even fewer give data separately for the elderly. The routine inclusion of elderly men who

---

[163] LSHTM (1985); Nelson (1986).

[164] It should be pointed out that the Rajasthan, Gujarat, and AP case-studies are confined to the poor and permit little further disaggregation.

[165] The Tamil Nadu Nutrition Survey (Cantor *et al.* 1973, while being a model for detailed presentation, is the result of the least accurate method of measurement and contains what one suspects are at least a few spuriously precise and arbitrary results. Note an idiosyncrasy characteristic of the entire data set: that the results which deviate most from expectations (especially in relation to micronutrients) are for the smallest cell sizes in their samples.

Table 10.1 Household surveys on food allocation in India and Bangladesh

Source	Location	Sample	Method	Problems
Abdullah (1983); Abdullah and Wheeler (1985)	Bangladesh: an unnamed village 85 kms from Dhaka selected for isolation and unmodernized agriculture	53 households, being the population of households with one or more children under 5, surveyed four times (seasonally) in 1983	3 consecutive days of 24-hour weighing of total raw and cooked food and of individual portions of cooked food plus recall of snacks	Micronutrients omitted except retinol/carotene
Chen *et al.* (1981)	Bangladesh: 4 villages of Matlab thana	130 households purposively selected to be accessible and with one or more children under age 5, surveyed 1978–9	Bimonthly 24-hour measurement of household food supplies prior to intake and individual food intake via volumes of cooked food in vessels before and after each serving	No measurement for calcium, iron carotene, thiamine, riboflavin, and ascorbic acid
Sharma (1983)	Rajasthan: a drought-affected village in Jodhpur	100 households randomly selected from among small and marginal farmers, share-croppers, and landless agricultural labour households	66% of households subject to weighment of raw and cooked portions over 3 days. 33% of households subject to 24-hour recall (no significant difference between the 2 methods)	

Table 10.1 *cont.*

Source	Location	Sample	Method	Problems
Gopaldas *et al.* (1983)	Gujarat: 5 hamlets purposively selected for socio-economic representativity among Rathwakoli tribals	78 households, means of sampling not stated, surveyed in October 1980	25-hour recall plus one day's weighment of raw food	No gender difference in data presentation prior to adulthood, no adult non-pregnant non-lactating women. Vitamin A presented as retinol equivalents and not as carotene
Sadasivam *et al.* (1980)	Tamil Nadu: village 20 kms from Coimbatore	50 households randomly sampled (36% of which were agricultural labour, 38% industrial labour)	3-day measurement of cooked individual portions, subjected to biochemical analyses	Gender not distinguished prior to age 13
Pushpamma, Geervani, and Lakshmi Devi (1982); Pushpamma, Geervani, and Usha Rani (1982)	Andhra Pradesh: 18 semi-arid villages	280 households: 3% of small and marginal farms	3-day consecutive weighings of individual portions	
Cantor *et al.* (1973)	360 villages and 240 urban blocks selected randomly subject to a minimum of 16 villages per district in rural cases	12,953 individuals from 2,800 households with pregnant and/or lactating women and/or with children under 13, surveyed in 1971–2	One 24-hour recall of individual quantities of ingredients	Least accurate method together with a certain arbitrariness in the numbers

| Ryan et al. (1984) | Madhya Pradesh, Maharashtra, Andhra Pradesh: 6 villages purposively selected so as to represent typical conditions of 3 agro-ecological zones of the semi-arid tropics | 240 households selected as follows: in each village 30 cultivator households representative of all size categories of farm plus 10 randomly selected landless households, surveyed from Sept. 1976 to Jan. 1978 | 24-hour recall at 3–4-month intervals supplemented by volumetric estimations by respondents using 13 local size/volumetric vessels | Aggregation of different, village-specific size categories for types of cultivator; aggregation of random and representative samples with different sampling fractions; no gender classification prior to age 13; inclusion of breast-fed children but not of nutritional composition of breast-milk intakes in group 1–3; results are of 4 × 1 day's recall rather than of measurement or recall over longer periods though fasting and feasting were ignored in the surveys; no data for iron or calcium |

may both need and eat less energy than younger adults leads to underestima-
tions of the shares of male household heads in their reproductive years. A
lamentable state of methodological disarray, but no worse than that of most
areas of microeconomic rural research in South Asia and elsewhere.

All analysis of such data suffers bias. We have adopted the following method
to pick our way through this minefield and construct an index of the intrafamily distribution of hunger.

Average (actual) nutrient intakes for individuals in specific age and sex
groups have been expressed as a proportion of the average (actual) nutrient
intake of the adult male group, yielding ratios of *relative intake* (RI). Sources of
bias here are, first, the mean and extent of variation of the adult male intake
unstandardized for occupation, income, age, and activity, and second, as we
have observed, the accuracy of measurement. To facilitate a comparative
evaluation, each RI is then expressed as a proportion of the corresponding
recommended relative intake (RRI), where the latter is defined as the proportion
of the recommended intake for the group under consideration to the recommended intake for adult males. Recommended relative intakes are derived
from the latest (1981) recommendations for moderate activity levels of the
Indian Council of Medical Research. The *index of relative intake* (IRI) is the
ratio of actual relative intake (RI) to recommended relative intake (RRI).

The index of relative intake so constructed indicates the relative deprivation
of specific groups compared to adult males, where deprivation is seen in terms
of the deficit of intake in relation to need. Thus, an IRI of 1.0 indicates that the
relevant group has the same share as that recommended by the ICMR. An IRI
greater than unity indicates a favourable share of food, and conversely for an
IRI lower than unity.

Extreme deviations of IRI from unity, ranging from 0.1 to 2.44, are
observed for carotene (Map 10.7) and are characteristic of vitamin consumption. The ICMR index of RRI must be acknowledged as merely a probabilistic
criterion of evaluation, and is biased by the degree of accuracy of
recommendations.[166] Cells with the largest number of observations have been
mapped (Maps 10.2 to 10.7). We shall compare our interpretation with those of
the authors concerned. We then proceed to a reworking at the household level
of some of ICRISAT's data. This exposes further methodological problems,
and untoward results.

(*a*) *The regional geography of intrafamily energy and protein allocation*

No group of adult women consumed absolutely more energy or protein than
adult men, but our concern is with distribution rather than with absolute
intake. Two pieces of research from Bangladesh provide the strongest evidence
of low IRIs for young children (especially for girls under 4 years who are

---

[166] Nelson (1986) gives a full treatment of such analytical problems in relation to a UK
case-study.

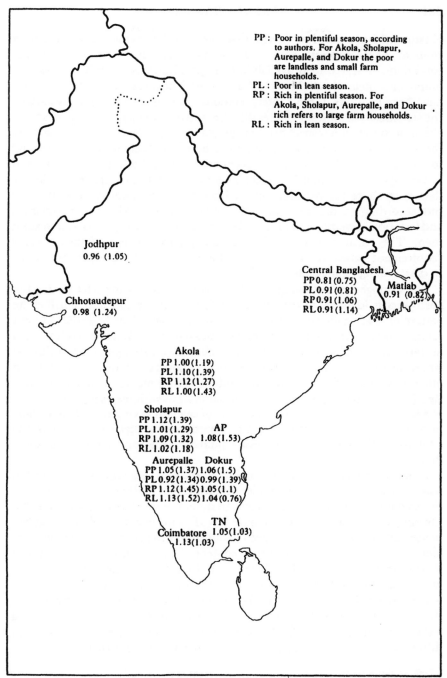

PP : Poor in plentiful season, according
to authors. For Akola, Sholapur,
Aurepalle, and Dokur the poor
are landless and small farm
households.
PL : Poor in lean season.
RP : Rich in plentiful season. For
Akola, Sholapur, Aurepalle, and Dokur
rich refers to large farm households.
RL : Rich in lean season.

Jodhpur
0.96 (1.05)

Central Bangladesh
PP 0.81 (0.75)
PL 0.91 (0.81)   Matlab
RP 0.91 (1.06)   0.91 (0.82)
RL 0.91 (1.14)

Chhotaudepur
0.98 (1.24)

Akola
PP 1.00 (1.19)
PL 1.10 (1.39)
RP 1.12 (1.27)
RL 1.00 (1.43)

Sholapur
PP 1.12 (1.39)
PL 1.01 (1.29)   AP
RP 1.09 (1.32)   1.08 (1.53)
RL 1.02 (1.18)
Aurepalle   Dokur
PP 1.05 (1.37) 1.06 (1.5)
PL 0.92 (1.34) 0.99 (1.39)
RP 1.12 (1.45) 1.05 (1.1)
RL 1.13 (1.52) 1.04 (0.76)

TN
Coimbatore   1.05 (1.03)
1.13 (1.03)

Sources: Central Bangladesh: Abdullah (1983); Matlab: Chen *et al*. (1981); Jodhpur:
Sharma (1983); Chhotaudepur: Gopaldas *et al*. (1983); Akola, Sholapur, Aurepalle, and
Dokur: Ryan *et al*. (1984); AP: Pushpamma, Geervani, and Usha Rani (1982);
Pushpamma, Geervani, and Lakshmi Devi (1982); Coimbatore: Sadasivan (1980); TN:
Cantor *et al*. (1973). On the construction of the indices, see text.
Map 10.2 Indices of relative intake of calories: adult women and (in brackets)
adolescent girls (aged 13–18)

obtaining 16 per cent less energy than boys on the average) and for elderly women. These relations seem most accentuated amongst the poor under conditions of scarce food availability (Maps 10.2–10.4). Similar trends are found for protein as well (Maps 10.5 and 10.6). Those responsible for this work have been cautious in their interpretations. Abdullah, while acknowledging the statistically significant gender difference in energy intake among preschool children, states with respect to other age groups: 'The data clearly demonstrate the non existence of sex discrimination in the intrahousehold allocation of food to women beyond what can be accounted for by body size, activity and physiological differentials'.[167] Chen and colleagues also compare their intake data with those for requirements, adjusted in a necessarily arbitrary way but according to the best state of knowledge, for body size, pregnancy, and lactation in women and for calorie increments necessary for labour in adult men. They also conclude: 'For all age groups male to female intake/ requirement ratios are near parity although marked male predomination persists among young children'.[168]

The average level of energy intake of adult males in the data set for the north-east is identical to that in the north-west of the subcontinent but the pattern of sharing differs (Maps 10.2–10.6). The data show high IRIs of both calories and protein for adolescent girls, rough parity of IRIs for adult women in Rajasthan, and low IRIs for elderly women in a tribal population in Gujarat where male and female children were already known to be treated, in food as in other aspects of life, with equality. Intakes of all measured nutrients were significantly different from those of the adult head with the exception of those of adolescent males in Rajasthan and that of calcium in Gujarat. Their authors have concluded respectively: 'The major portion of the diet was received by the adult male';[169] 'The head of the family did receive the lion's share of the family diet'.[170]

Adult male energy intakes average about the same amount in central India, where the research carried out under the auspices of ICRISAT's village studies programme reveal a different pattern. In the entire set of cases from ICRISAT the age group under 5 appear to have low IRIs for energy. Children who are being partially breast-fed have been included in this group but when notional allowances are made for the energy content of breast milk, their nutritional deficits are said to be greatly reduced.[171] In these four villages it is adult males who appear to have low IRIs compared with adult women and adolescent girls, while protein RIs are close to RRIs throughout the age and sex distribution. Regression analysis and t-testing for 10 nutrients for 938 children has provided a statistical basis for ICRISAT's own conclusion that 'There is no significant difference between boys and girls in the intake of the 10 nutrients'.[172]

---

[167] Abdullah (1983: 134).   [168] Chen et al. (1981: 63).

[169] Sharma (1983: 5).   [170] Gopaldas et al. (1983: 73).   [171] Ryan et al. (1984: 25).

[172] Ibid. 38.

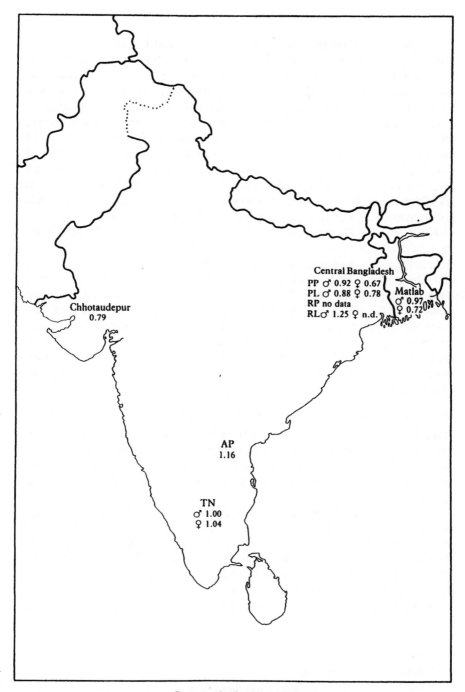

Central Bangladesh
PP ♂ 0.92 ♀ 0.67
PL ♂ 0.88 ♀ 0.78
RP no data
RL♂ 1.25 ♀ n.d.

Matlab
♂ 0.97
♀ 0.72

Chhotaudepur
0.79

AP
1.16

TN
♂ 1.00
♀ 1.04

Sources: As for Map 10.2

Map 10.3 Indices of relative intake of calories: the elderly

Somewhat the same pattern is revealed from two of ICRISAT's villages in south India together with two other studies. Here, the average energy consumption of the adult male is at least 300 calories less per day than elsewhere in the subcontinent. A given RI thus refers to absolutely less. Adult men seem to have relatively low intakes judged by the IRIs of all other age–sex groups. In Pushpamma et al.'s survey of 18 villages in Andhra Pradesh adult men receive 40 calories per kg of body weight contrasted with adult women who eat 44 calories per kg.[173] Exceptions to this trend occur among the poorest of ICRISAT's sample in the lean season where adult women (though not adolescent girls) are slightly disfavoured. In the southernmost villages again it is children of both sexes under 13 who have low IRIs. By contrast protein RIs are close to RRIs, except for poor preschool children in Aurepalle village.

While ICRISAT's conclusions have already been set out, and while Pushpamma et al. find adolescents of both sexes to be consuming absolutely more than male adults, Sadasivam and colleagues note the reverse. Adolescent girls and adult women are found to consume lower absolute levels than adolescent boys and adult men. They do not pursue this aspect of their interpretation further.[174] The authors of the Tamil Nadu Nutrition Study evaluated consumption by comparing absolute intakes with FAO references and concluded that weanlings of both sexes were subject to greatest deprivation while children under 4, adolescents, and young adults of both sexes but especially pregnant women were disadvantaged. Intake–requirement ratios rose with age: a system of gerontocratic favouring.[175]

(b) *Seasonal and social aspects of energy and protein allocation*

It is difficult to disentangle seasonal effects from those of socio-economic status because most of the data sets which disaggregate for the one disaggregate for the other. Hence both will be considered here, greatly facilitated by evidence that income or seasonal trends in shares are usually consistent throughout the age ranges.

Testing the hypothesis that if food is given preferentially to active participants in the wage labour market, then unproductive people (women and children in Bangladesh) will receive lower shares when overall food supply to the household is scarce than they do at times of plenty, Abdullah and Wheeler found cause to reject it.[176] A seasonal analysis of RIs of household energy in a village in central Bangladesh showed that the intake of women varied as a constant percentage of that of men at all seasons. Furthermore whereas the

[173] Pushpamma, Geervani, and Usha Rani (1982).

[174] Sadasivam et al. (1980: 250).

[175] Cantor et al. (1973: i. 79–86); also Pushpamma et al. (1981). But note that McNeill, studying adults but not children, found the reverse (1986: ch. 7).

[176] Abdullah and Wheeler (1985).

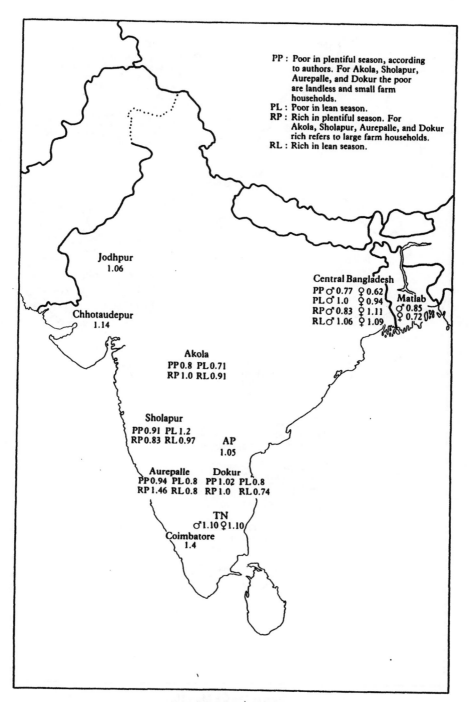

Sources: As for Map 10.2

Map 10.4 Indices of relative intake of calories: children under 5

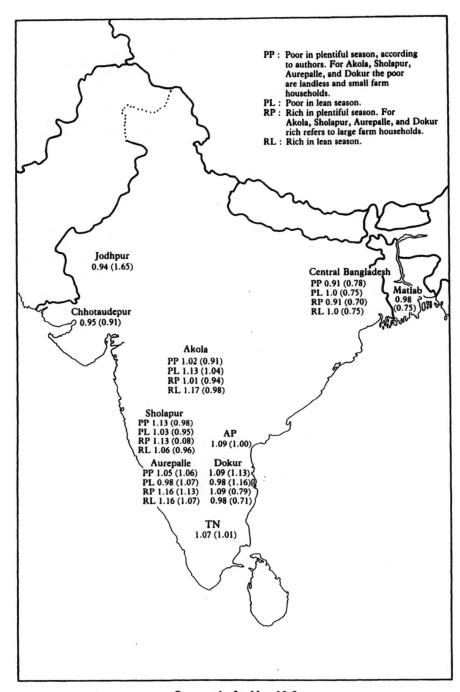

Map data labels:

Jodhpur
0.94 (1.65)

Central Bangladesh
PP 0.91 (0.78)
PL 1.0 (0.75)
RP 0.91 (0.70)
RL 1.0 (0.75)

Matlab
0.98
(0.75)

Chhotaudepur
0.95 (0.91)

Akola
PP 1.02 (0.91)
PL 1.13 (1.04)
RP 1.01 (0.94)
RL 1.17 (0.98)

Sholapur
PP 1.13 (0.98)
PL 1.03 (0.95)
RP 1.13 (0.08)
RL 1.06 (0.96)

AP
1.09 (1.00)

Aurepalle   Dokur
PP 1.05 (1.06)   1.09 (1.13)
PL 0.98 (1.07)   0.98 (1.16)
RP 1.16 (1.13)   1.09 (0.79)
RL 1.16 (1.07)   0.98 (0.71)

TN
1.07 (1.01)

PP : Poor in plentiful season, according to authors. For Akola, Sholapur, Aurepalle, and Dokur the poor are landless and small farm households.
PL : Poor in lean season.
RP : Rich in plentiful season. For Akola, Sholapur, Aurepalle, and Dokur rich refers to large farm households.
RL : Rich in lean season.

Sources: As for Map 10.2

Map 10.5 Indices of relative intake of proteins: adult women and (in brackets) adolescent girls (aged 13–18)

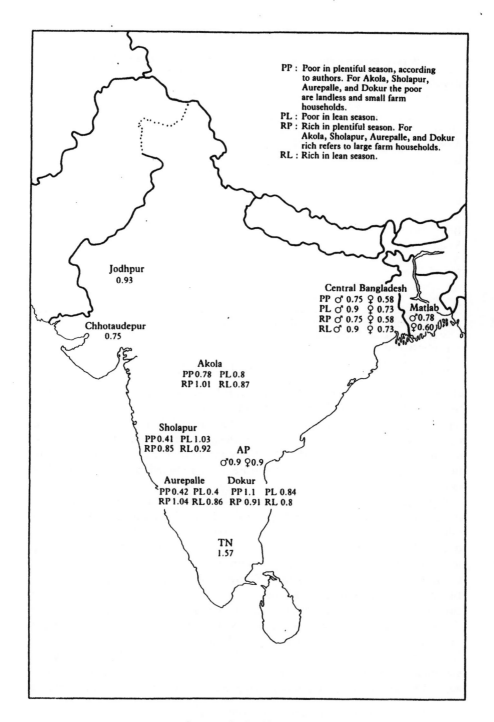

Within the map image:

PP : Poor in plentiful season, according to authors. For Akola, Sholapur, Aurepalle, and Dokur the poor are landless and small farm households.
PL : Poor in lean season.
RP : Rich in plentiful season. For Akola, Sholapur, Aurepalle, and Dokur rich refers to large farm households.
RL : Rich in lean season.

Jodhpur
0.93

Central Bangladesh
PP ♂ 0.75 ♀ 0.58
PL ♂ 0.9 ♀ 0.73
RP ♂ 0.75 ♀ 0.58
RL ♂ 0.9 ♀ 0.73

Matlab
♂0.78
♀0.60

Chhotaudepur
0.75

Akola
PP 0.78 PL 0.8
RP 1.01 RL 0.87

Sholapur
PP 0.41 PL 1.03
RP 0.85 RL 0.92

AP
♂0.9 ♀0.9

Aurepalle
PP 0.42 PL 0.4
RP 1.04 RL 0.86

Dokur
PP 1.1 PL 0.84
RP 0.91 RL 0.8

TN
1.57

Sources: As for Map 10.2

Map 10.6 Indices of relative intake of proteins: children under 5

Table 10.2 Seasonal and socio-economic relationships in energy intake, India

Region	Season	
	Lean	Plentiful
North		
A	$p < r$	$p \leq r$
B	$p \leq r$	$p < r$
Central		
A	$p = r$	$p \geq r$
B	$p > r$	$p > r$
A	$p < r$	$p = r$
B	$p = r$	$p = r$
South		
A	$p > r$	$p < r$
B	$p < r$	$p < r$
A	$p = r$	$p < r$
B	$p = r$	$p > r$

Notes: A: absolute level of energy intake by male adult.
    B: relative intakes of other age/sex categories.
    p: poorest (landless).
    r: richest (landed).
    For 'Central' and 'South', data are given for two locations within the region.

absolute intakes of young children remained well below recommended levels, the RIs of the most disadvantaged (girls under 4 years) actually rose at times of scarcity in such a way as to suggest that the seasonal shortages were absorbed by men rather than by women. Whereas the poor increased their consumption in times of plenty, it seemed that the richer households reduced their consumption of energy, possibly commensurate with reduced activity levels after harvest.[177]

Aggregate data for six villages in central and southern India reveals no easily interpretable seasonal relationships (Table 10.2). In the four central Indian villages discrepancies in consumption between rich and poor individuals during the lean season are reduced during seasons of plenty, because of a drop in the consumption of the rich. By contrast, in the south the rich consume absolutely more in times of plenty. There is, however, no consistent trend in the RIs of other household members. Testing Chambers's hypothesis that there are marked seasonal variations in nutrient intake (calorie lows coinciding dysfunctionally with high work burdens, high levels of morbidity, and the peaking of energy costs of pregnancy and lactation), Ryan *et al.* partially reject it.[178] Their regression analysis, confined to the intakes of children, shows no significant seasonal effect on nutrient intake despite the highly seasonal agricultural ecology of the semi-arid tropics. Two comments are in order: first

[177] Abdullah (1983); Abdullah and Wheeler (1985: 1312).
[178] Ryan *et al.* (1984: 39).

their analysis excluded the intakes of adults.[179] Second, their aggregated regression analysis may mask (possibly contradictory) seasonal relationships specific to individual villages. With respect to income, their finding of an absence of any income effect on the consumption of energy or protein is hard to square with an absence of change in RIs attributable to increasing income.[180] Constant RIs should mean rising absolute consumption (if income relates positively to holding size) when holding size is positively associated with nutrient consumption, as is found. It is possible that the range of agricultural income is low in these villages. If so, this would indicate the important nutritional role of off-farm income. Behrman's reworking of ICRISAT's seasonal data on food intake, anthropometric status, and expenditure shows a 5 per cent pro-male bias in nutrient allocation in the lean season, a bias more marked in low-caste (low-income) groups. To put this in its context, it is a gender bias in allocation less than that found in the USA.[181] The Tamil Nadu Nutrition Study, which did not investigate seasonal effects, shows incontrovertibly that the pattern of RIs in this southern state does not vary with aggregate household intake or with differences in household income.[182]

An important socio-economic variable in the ICRISAT data set (with effects upon consumption that overrode those of other variables) is household size. As household size increases so the individual consumption of energy and protein (as well as certain micronutrients) decreases. This is a marked general effect while the specifics of birth order have no explanatory mileage for this set of 938 children.[183]

(c) Class and allocative behaviour in scarcity: a village-level case in central India

The issue of social differences in the intrafamily distribution of energy under seasonally varying conditions of household energy availability demands further attention. ICRISAT's data on energy intake can be reworked at the level of individual households to compute RIs and IRIs. These can be examined under extreme conditions of energy supply to households to investigate three aspects of this subject:

1. whether allocative practice changes in scarcity;
2. whether allocative reactions take different forms according to agrarian class position;

---

[179] Note that McNeill in her semi-arid village found no socio-economic difference in the share except for greater variability in the female share among the landless and marginal peasantry than in other classes (1986).

[180] Ryan et al. (1984: 35).

[181] Behrman (1986).

[182] Cantor et al. (1973: i. 100). But note that levels of intake were associated inversely with ritual status 'regardless of economic position' (ibid. 94).

[183] Ryan et al. (1984: 35).

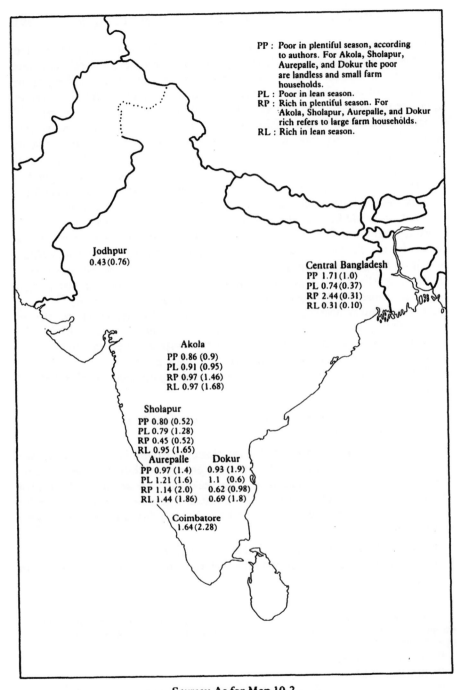

Map 10.7 Indices of relative intake of B carotene: adult women and (in brackets)
children under 5

3. whether such forms are generalized across different local agrarian ecologies.

The data set has already been introduced and discussed, both in the text and in Table 10.1, but further familiarity is advisable.

It has had to be assumed that ICRISAT's village-specific, different land-holding classes for categories of small, medium, and large farmers generate comparable economic groups and we worked with these categories (plus that of landless labour—four classes in all). It is also assumed that energy expenditure is more or less constant and moderate in all seasons. The type and size of samples make it clear that the possibility of non-trivial intervillage variation in nutrition was discounted when the field surveys began. This also has to be accepted. Disaggregated analysis by agrarian class in a given village shows that it is not possible to know whether some statistically insignificant results are 'real' or result from small cell sizes. This problem of cell size (along with a trial and error process of experimental aggregation) also informed our three age groupings (Table 10.3).

The first rock hit concerns the identity of the 'adult male' forming the referent for the construction of RIs and IRIs for all other household members. Social and economic power and decision-making responsibility do not require energy and may not be a characteristic of the male with the largest energy intake who is typically in his teens (as he is in the UK[184]). It is also possible for adolescent males to have an IRI exceeding 1.0.[185] In complex households, our household head is therefore the male between the age of 20 and 55 who consumes most energy. In the absence of such a male, it is a male over the age of 55. It is always possible that this nutritional household head is not the political head.

Another rock hit concerns seasons. ICRISAT classifies its four rounds of data as 'surplus' or 'lean' in season. T-tests, performed on the relative intakes for males and females under 3 and over 18, in order to examine whether interseasonal variation exceeded intraseasonal variation, demonstrated conclusively that ICRISAT's categories of 'surplus' and 'lean' are not meaningful indicators of household energy supplies in any social group. The variation in household energy supply between the two surplus seasons was more significant than any other seasonal difference. Thus it would seem that agricultural

---

[184] Nelson (1986).

[185] Seasonally female-headed households due to male migration are another problem, although in this case a quantitatively small one. In 2% of cases the RI ratio is constructed on the adult female. Another frustration, given our advocacy of the deconstruction of terms such as 'female', is our inability to do just that. We cannot distinguish between bride and daughter, between married elderly mother of sons and widow of daughters. Many big households in this data set include servants, kin, and guests. We have ignored their consumption in this exercise, though this is potentially researchable with ICRISAT's data set; as is the issue of deliberate discrimination against the second or third daughter (or son) in the subset of households simple enough to clarify this kinship relation.

Table 10.3 Statistically significant changes in indices of relative intake for calories in times of relative scarcity by agrarian class and sex, central Indian villages

| Landholding class | Females | | Males | | % mean deviation of RI from RRI in period of: | | | | | | Age–sex group compensating for change observed |
| | Age group | P value | Age group | P value | max. supply | | | min. supply | | | |
					%	SE	n	%	SE	n	
Aurepalle, Mahbubnagar Dt., AP											
III	≥20	0.008			+8	6.6	19	−18	5.3	18	M + F, 1–10; M ≥ 20
III + sf			1–10	0.03	−1	4.7	22	+19	8.0	16	F ≥ 20
mf			1–10	0.03	−2	3.1	8	+27	12.4	7	M HHH
lf	1–10	0.040			+2	4.8	5	+67	28.5	4	M HHH
lf	11–19	0.020			−9	2.4	8	+6	5.6	7	M HHH
mf + lf	11–19	0.050			−8	2.5	9	+34	1.8	10	M HHH
mf + lf			1–10	0.02	0	2.9	10	+25	8.8	11	M HHH
Dokur, Mahbubnagar Dt., AP											
III sf	11–19	0.030			−12	6.9	8	+10	16.0	18	F, 1–10
mf lf	1–19	0.060			−4	2.7	14	−17	23.6	13	M ≥ 20 + HHH
Kalman, Sholapur Dt., Maharashtra$_a$											

Kanzara, Akola Dt., Maharashtra

III	1–19	0.020			+2	2.6	11	–11	4.3	19	M HHH
sf					+8	8.8	9	–12	4.1	10	F, 11–19
III + sf	1–10	0.020	1–10	0.05	–1	2.7	11	–14	3.1	12	F, 11–19
III + sf	1–10	0.050	1–10	0.02	+5	7.5	11	–15	3.9	13	F, 11–19
mf	all				+5	3.4	22	–5	3.7	18	M HHH

Notes: III: landless

sf: small farm households (Aurepalle 0.21–2.5 ha; Dokur 0.21–1.0; Kalman 0.21–6.0; Kanzara 0.21–2.25).

mf: middle farm households (Aurepalle 2.51–5.25 ha; Dokur 1.01–3.0; Kalman 6.01–10.75; Kanzara 2.26–5.6).

lf: large farm households (Aurepalle >5.25 ha; Dokur ≥3.0; Kalman >10.75; Kanzara >5.6) (Jodha 1980).

HHH: household head.

M: male.

F: female.

SE: standard error.

n: cell size.

Age groups are as follows: 1–10; 11–19.

^{a} No significant changes.

Source: ICRISAT raw data.

production seasons cannot be assumed to be nutritional seasons in the diverse rural economy of the semi-arid tropics of South Asia. Nor will agricultural seasons in widely scattered villages be conterminous. Household energy entitlement will result from farm and non-farm assets, employment, other forms of exchange, and energy stocks stored. Disregarding ICRISAT's classification, the four sets of seasonal data for each household were therefore ranked according to aggregate household energy availability per consumption unit. Each household member's IRI in the period of maximum and minimum energy supply to the household was computed. Households were then grouped into agrarian classes, following ICRISAT's categories, and individuals within the households of given agrarian classes were grouped according to age and sex.

Four villages are studied separately here because of intervillage variation in their agricultural economies. Two, Aurepalle and Dokur, are on alfisols in a low rainfall region of Andhra Pradesh (Mahbubnagar District). Both have agricultural economies characterized by complexity and diversity in cropping patterns, which include monocropped paddy and monocropped and inter-cropped groundnut, sorghum, pearl millet, and pigeon pea.[186] Aurepalle has about a quarter of its cropped area irrigated by tank. By contrast Dokur has 60 per cent of its gross cultivated area irrigated by tank and well. Production resources tend to be concentrated upon irrigated land in Dokur where the specialized commercialization of monocropped agroindustrial crops such as sugarcane and cotton is on the increase. Large farms are those exceeding 5.25 ha in Aurepalle and 3 ha in Dokur (where average holding size is 2.6 ha). Both villages rely substantially upon female labour in production, Dokur, where labour inputs are twice as intense, more than Aurepalle. From 63 to 88 per cent of all hired labour is female and participation rates are (relative to other villages in the semi-arid tropics) high and stable. Female wages are, however, about 56 per cent of male wages.

Kalman village in Sholapur District of Maharashtra lies on deep vertisols, which, together with the bimodal pattern of the monsoons, means that land is fallowed during the rains. Only a tenth of the land is irrigated, upon which sugarcane, vegetables, and wheat are grown. The rest of the dryland is put to sorghum-led, complex intercropping. Large farms are those in excess of 10.75 ha. The intensity of labour use in Kalman is only one-fifth that of Dokur and a slight majority of the labour force is male. Female participation rates are lowest here, while the seasonal variability of both male and female employment is highest. Kanzara village in Akola District of Maharashtra has shallow soils and least irrigation (5 per cent of cropped land upon which cotton tends to be grown) but, like Dokur, it has a relatively assured moisture regime based in this case upon a dependable pattern of rainfall. The rainfed land, like that of

---

[186] Jodha (1980). Intercropping increases gross returns on rainfed land, evens out demand for labour, phases harvests with crops of different maturation (and thus phases actual or implicit income streams), and minimizes risk. It is particularly practised by small farmers.

Kalman, has sorghum- and chickpea-based intercropping. By contrast, the labour markets resemble those of the Mahbubnagar villages. The labour intensity, despite the domination of dry agriculture, resembles that of Aurepalle. Large farms exceed 5.6 ha.[187] Landless labourers account for 32 per cent of households.

We tested statistically the hypothesis that IRIs differ significantly in times of relative abundance and scarcity (as defined earlier). Separate tests were carried out for different cells disaggregated by sex, 3 age groups, 4 agrarian classes for each of four villages (96 tests), and also for experimental aggregations of classes and age groups to increase cell sizes. Of the 192 t-tests performed in all, only 14 were significant at the 5 per cent level and only 2 at 1 per cent. No significant changes in IRIs were recorded for Kalman village, one of the least irrigated and most uninnovative dryland villages, and that with the highest proportion of landless labour, the lowest female participation rate, and the greatest class variability in female employment. It was precisely in this type of village that we expected to find evidence of class-specific seasonal modifications to allocative practice. But such behaviour could not be detected. At the very least this calls

Table 10.4 Statistically significant changes in IRIs for calories by age group, central indian villages

Landholding class	Sex	Age group			
		1–10	11–19	1–19	≥20
Aurepalle					
III	F				D
III + sf	M	I			
mf	M	I			
lf	F	I	I		
mf + lf	F		I		
Dokur					
III + sf	F		I		
III + sf	F	D			
Kanzara					
III	F			D	
sf	F	D			
III + sf	F	D			
	M	D			

Notes: I: increase in RI.
 D: decrease in RI.
 RI: relative intake; for definition, see text.
 For other abbreviations see notes to Table 10.3.
Source: ICRISAT raw data.

[187] Jodha (1980); Ryan *et al.* (1980).

into question the value of female participation as a sensitive indicator of female advantage.

Age and gender groupings which showed statistically significant changes are recorded in Table 10.3 by sex and Table 10.4 by age. Table 10.3 also presents the deviation of RI from RRI for the class, both in times of abundance and in times of scarcity. On the right, the movements (rarely ones of statistical significance) in other gender and age groups' IRIs have been analysed to show the beneficiaries of, or the casualties from, the significant changes.

In the two Mahbubnagar villages significant changes in IRIs occurred among both sexes. In Aurepalle this change is complex. In the landless class, the RI of adult women was 8 per cent more than their RRI in the maximum time of plenty to each household, but dropped very significantly to 18 per cent less than RRI at the time of scarcity. Those to gain in times of scarcity were young children of both sexes (but especially boys) and adult men. In the asseted classes, the IRIs of young and adolescent girls increased in times of scarcity, as did those of young boys, at the expense of the male household head.

In Dokur, significant change was confined to girls and adolescent females and socially contradictory trends emerged. Among the labouring peasantry, adolescent girls increased their RIs from 12 per cent below the RRI in times of plenty to 10 per cent more than the RRI in times of scarcity. The casualties of this increase were girls under 10. Among the asseted, the share of young and adolescent girls decreased in scarcity. Adult men gained most from this.

In Kanzara, among labouring households young girls and boys under the age of 10 who had fair (girls) or 8 per cent more than fair (boys) shares in plenty saw their RIs reduced in scarcity by 13 per cent (girls) and 20 per cent (boys). The beneficiaries were girls aged 11 to 19. In the richer classes, there was a clear gender bias throughout all age groups. All female IRIs tended to fall in times of scarcity to the benefit of adult men, especially the male household head.

Analysis of variance tests (conducted on IRIs according to agrarian class, sex, and periods of maximum and minimum scarcity) showed that in the three latter villages agrarian class was the only significant variable affecting the IRIs. Gender and aggregate energy supplies to households (which must be affected by entitlements other than land) do not appear to be significant determinants of the pattern of intrahousehold shares.

It has been hypothesized from Bangladesh that, in times of scarcity, relative intakes will be chosen to relative needs, i.e. IRIs will be closer to unity (Abdullah 1983). The data examined here do not demonstrate any systematic relation of this sort, either according to age or gender, or between two villages in the same district, or within a social class. With the eye of faith we can discern two patterns. The changes in Dokur and Kanzara are somewhat similar. But Aurepalle is different. Separate trends are distinguishable for the asseted medium and large farm households on the one hand and the labouring peasantry (the small farm households and the landless labouring class) on the other. Among the labouring peasantry in Dokur and Kanzara, scarce food enables adolescent girls to increase their shares but young boys and girls to reduce theirs. Among the labouring people of Aurepalle, scarce food makes adult women reduce their share to the benefit of young children of both sexes and adult men. Among the richer households in Dokur, relative scarcity forces young and adolescent girls to reduce their shares in favour of the male household head. In Kanzara, it is all women who reduce their shares for the sake of the household head. By contrast in Aurepalle when food is relatively scarce, the male household head drops his share in favour of young children of both sexes.

It has also been hypothesized that unproductive people have lower relative intake in scarcity (Abdullah and Wheeler 1985). In the absence of information on economic participation, all we can report is that there is no social trend common to all four villages. While female children lose out in scarcity in all classes in Dokur and Kanzara, there is no change in Kalman. In Aurepalle, children of both sexes seem to be protected in scarcity (by mothers in poor families; and by fathers in those of the more propertied). Unfortunately there is no way of pursuing explanations for village- and class-specific behaviour, given the confines of the database.

We can now return to the three questions posed at the beginning of this section. With respect to the question whether allocative practice changes significantly with scarcity, we may conclude from the preponderance of insignificant results of t-tests that much allocative behaviour in these villages appears rather insensitive to conditions of aggregate household food availability. We are aware however that this conclusion, though based on a comparatively large sample, results from a disaggregation which has yielded many small cells. Yet by examining IRIs according to agrarian class and taking each village in turn, we do see certain significant changes in intrahousehold energy distribution. Certain classes in certain villages show age–sex responses in the allocation of energy which are most unlikely to be caused by chance. These allocative responses are to scarcity irrespective of the calendrical season of its occurrence. They are not responses to 'seasonality' *per se*.

So the answer to the second question (concerning the class specificity of allocative adjustments) is that some class-specific patterns have been distinguished in age–sex groups where allocative adjustments are significant. The answer to the third question (as to the similarity of class-specific behaviour across villages) is that this behaviour is so idiosyncratic as to defy generalization.

Such allocative patterns have not been revealed in previous analyses of the same data (Ryan *et al.* 1984; Behrman 1986). Other studies have focused upon absolute child intakes rather than the shares of each household member, and on the aggregate data set, which clearly masks varied and countervailing village- and class-specific trends. Other studies have assumed that agricultural seasons are congruent with nutritional seasons and that households do not have countervailing nutritional experiences during series of seasons defined as 'lean' and of 'plenty'. This case-study has exposed the limitations of such foci and assumptions. It has also exposed complex allocative behaviour explicable only by further field research. The specificities of the village economy, especially its class configurations, seem to be more powerful influences on changes in intrahousehold energy allocation than do levels of household energy intakes, agricultural seasons, or even gender *per se*. There is no quick fix for policy.

(d) The allocation of micronutrients

Imbalances in the shares of micronutrients in relation to estimates of need are far more marked and varied than those of energy and protein. They are also harder to interpret. The role of many vitamins is imperfectly understood. The absorption of certain minerals by the gut varies and is far from complete. It seems to depend as much on the presence or absence of other factors as on the mineral content of the diet. So the scientific basis for the RRIs is more uncertain than those for energy and protein. We present data for two minerals (iron and calcium (Table 10.5)) and for B carotene and vitamin A (Map 10.7).

Deficiencies in iron and in vitamin A are thought to be more significant for health than those of other vitamins and minerals.

Age/sex patterns in the allocation of iron and calcium are similar for the three cases for which we have evidence. Children under 5 have low IRIs (with relative intake about or under half the recommended norm). In disaggregated cases, girls and female adolescents get less than boys. Adult women have very low IRIs (with one exception for calcium).

Those familiar with policy-orientated debates over energy undernutrition may be interested in the conclusion of Ryan et al.:[188] 'The deficiency of vitamin A is probably the most serious nutrient deficiency in India.' Our data (22 cases, Map 10.7) show that, in the north, the aetiology of this deficiency is likely to be due to the way carotene is shared within the household, while in the south, it is likely to be due to very low absolute levels of household supply which are allocated relatively more equitably. Allocations lead to low IRIs for children of both sexes and for adult women in the north; and to low IRIs for adolescents and adult women in the central region. In 16 of the 22 cases, the IRI of adult women is more severely in deficit than that of children.

Data not presented here show that IRIs of thiamine (vitamin B1) follow a similar type of pattern with respect to age, gender, and the tendency for relative intakes to be more proportional to apparent need in the south, even though absolute levels may be low. The consumption of ascorbic acid (vitamin C) leads in the majority of cases to very low shares for children and to a lesser extent for adolescent and adult women. By contrast the sharing of riboflavin (vitamin B2) appears to discriminate in almost every case against adult men or is 'fair'.

An attempt to explain the absolute consumption levels of children (though not the intrahousehold shares) was made by Ryan et al.[189] It produced cases of

[188] Ryan et al. (1984).   [189] Ibid.

Table 10.5 Indices of relative intake for minerals

	Iron (µg)						Calcium (mg)					
	<5	10–12		13–18		≥18	<5	10–12		13–18		≥18
		m.	f.	m.	f.	(f.)		m.	f.	m.	f.	(f.)
Rajasthan	0.50	0.93	0.72	0.85	0.43	0.62	0.44	0.56	0.50	0.70	0.39	0.59
Gujarat	0.49	0.65		0.89		0.80	0.44	0.82		0.86		1.11
Tamil Nadu	0.56	0.91		0.98		0.54	0.36	0.64		0.62		0.80

Sources: Rajasthan: Sharma (1983); Gujarat: Gopaldas *et al.* (1983); Tamil Nadu: Sadasivam *et al.* (1980).

swings and roundabouts. On the one hand, it appears that the level of education of the mother accounts significantly and positively for the consumption of calcium and carotene by her children, by means, it is suggested, of her knowledge of the benefits to be gained from the consumption of milk (though there is an income as well as an education effect here). And the children of houses with larger agricultural holdings had larger absolute levels of consumption of calcium and all the measured vitamins; perhaps because land and labour could be spared for the vegetable garden. On the other hand, female participation in the agricultural wage labour force is associated positively with consumption of ascorbic acid. It is speculated that children who travel to the fields with their (uneducated and landless) mothers have ready access during the day to greens, chillies, tamarind, all rich in vitamin C. Furthermore, to the extent that they consume millet rather than milled rice their diets will probably be richer in iron and vitamin B1.

There are two further aspects to intrahousehold food distribution, for which we have to refer to information additional to that presented here. The first subject is alcohol. The second is food behaviour in times of crisis and famine.

(e)   Alcohol

The consumption of alcohol in non-tribal and, for different reasons, non-Muslim areas of South Asia is almost exclusively the preserve of males from their mid-teens to their late thirties.[190] It represents a private appropriation of costly calories (though it also dampens appetite and may lead to a reduction in food consumption).[191] About a third of male adults are estimated to drink.[192] The habit is not the preserve of harijans and is found throughout the social spectrum.[193] About half South Asia's drinkers drink heavily. Heavy or excessive drinkers tend to come from the social extremes in rural society.[194]

Drinking affects the household economy. Research from Punjab shows that the 'average' household with a heavy drinker spends 40 per cent less on food per capita than the average non-drinking household.[195] In two villages in

[190] Deb (1977: 1–9); Mohan *et al.* (1980); Mitchell (1984).

[191] Van Estenk and Greer (1985); Priyardarsiri and Hartjen (1982). Note that alcoholic drinks often contain sugar and small quantities of vitamins and minerals as well as alcohol (LSHTM 1985: 30).

[192] Thimmaiah (1979). Prevalence is higher in Sikh and Christian areas. Note that policy on alcohol consumption is a dilemma for the secular state, being a very important source of revenue (Mamoria 1980; Priyardarsiri and Hartjen 1982).

[193] Deb (1977); Harriss (1989). This is consistent with an account of a village in nearby Chinglepet (Djurfeldt and Lindberg 1975).   [194] Deb (1977); Harriss (1989).

[195] Deb (1977: 53). Deb also provides evidence that 'drinking households' spend less than non-drinking households on cash inputs to agricultural production, and on non-food consumption items (clothing, education, and medicine). Drinking is associated with lower gross income per acre from cultivation and with lower net income per capita. It is associated with higher expenditure on litigation (ibid. 41–53)!

North Arcot District, 10 per cent of households had both very low aggregate energy intakes and one or more drinkers. In these households there was a statistically significant negative relationship between expenditure on alcohol and expenditure per capita on food. A simulation of the diversion of alcohol expenditure to millet for the entire subsample of such households showed this would rectify household level energy deficits in every case.[196] Alcohol is usually excluded from dietary surveys, but it seems to lead to a reduction in food intakes for the household.

(f)   Famine

Extreme events have been interpreted by some as an accentuation of the 'normal order' and by others as a reversal of it.[197] By criteria of absolute mortality rates, the most vulnerable individuals during the 1878 famine in southern India were infants under 1, and people over 50. The least vulnerable were those aged between 12 and 50. In relief camps male mortality exceeded female mortality, and the population as a whole apparently became more feminine after the event. McAlpin has concluded from this that females have a survival capacity not affected by social factors.[198] The most vulnerable individuals during the 1943 Bengal famine appear to have been people over 50 and children aged 5 to 10. The least vulnerable were adults aged 20–40, men less than women.[199] Sen found greatest vulnerability among women of all age groups up to 61 in the wake of the West Bengal food emergency of 1978, and Bairagi found girls to be of lower nutritional status than boys after the food crisis in Bangladesh in the early 1980s.[200] Greenough explains that 'behind the cultural ideal of a co-resident sharing family' (an ideal which may not be practically manifest even in normal times) 'is a more powerful idea of family continuity held to depend on the adult male'.[201] Greenough argues that under conditions of acute scarcity the household is centralized into one agent, the householder, and other instruments are shed. Appadurai offers an alternative hypothesis that the destruction of the family during famine, including the abandonment of women and children by men, actually serves to maximize the life chances of individuals.[202] The evidence on the effects on food allocation

---

[196] Mitchell (1984: Appendices 12–15).

[197] Sen (1985a: 16–17 nn.); Appadurai (1985).

[198] McAlpin (1983: 56–63). See also Kynch (1985a) on the gender impact of colonial policy on famine relief which became more biased against women as time went on. And contrast with Caldwell et al. (1982) for contemporary Karnataka where the increasing cost of raising children is suggested as the reason for improved allocation to 'the weak' during crisis nowadays.

[199] Greenough (1982: 217–50).

[200] Sen (1984: 352–4); Bairagi (1986). Pryer (1987) also shows that even female-headed households in acute (personal) food crisis do not alter the bias in food allocation against girls in Khulna slums in Bangladesh.

[201] Greenough (1982: 224).   [202] Appadurai (1984: 484–5).

within the household of extreme food scarcity defies generalization about gender for South Asia. If one looks at absolute mortality rates by age and sex during famines, the very young and the elderly of both sexes seem most expendable. It is also possible to study age and sex patterns of increase in mortality during famines and to compare them with ordinary times. This approach can lead to quite different conclusions, in many cases children being protected. On this, see Drèze and Sen (1989).

(g) Conclusions

If the average actual relative intake ratios (RIs) of each of the 24 different sets of derived data on the allocation of calories according to age group and sex are plotted (Fig. 10.2), four tentative conclusions can be drawn which might best be regarded as hypotheses for further testing:

1. While the ratio of the adult woman's average energy intake to the adult male's is 0.85, the corresponding ratio for the '4 to 6 year old' (unfortunately the only non-adult category where the classification of age and sex groups gives us a useful number of variates (19)) is 0.47. These aggregate average ratios are commensurate with the RRI ratios obtained from ICMR recommendations.

2. However, whereas the variability of adult male and female absolute energy intake in these 22 regional cases appears similar (coefficient of variation: 15 per cent) that for 4- to 6-years-olds is over twice as great (37 per cent). This greater variability might be explained either by differences in the age distribution of children within this age group or by greater variability of energy

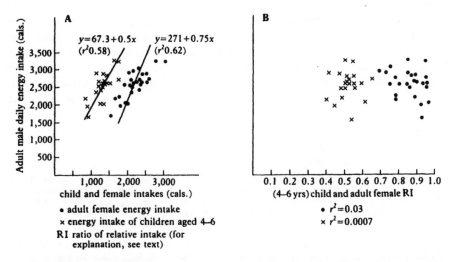

Fig. 10.2 Relationship between absolute adult male intakes of energy and absolute (A) and relative (B) intakes of adult females and children aged 4–6 years in South Asia

intakes, holding age constant (likely because of the feeding habits of this group), or by a combination of both.

3. About two-thirds of the absolute energy intakes of adult women and of children aged 4 to 6 appears to be explained statistically by the absolute level of intake of the adult male; so that one-third is to be explained by other factors, among which will feature intrahousehold allocation.

4. The absolute energy intake of adult men does not appear to explain the relative intake (the RI) of either adult women or children aged 4 to 6. Analysis of this data set (hedged crudely with *cet. par.* assumptions) does not support the hypothesis that in times of aggregate scarcity to a household there is a general trend towards intakes more proportional to need, despite the fact that individual cases such as Abdullah's (1983) show this behaviour pattern.

Other similarly tentative conclusions are:

5. Discrimination in energy and protein intakes through the allocation of food within the household seems to be greater in the north than in the south.

6. In the north it is least 'fair' for very young and very old females, and probably for adult women with special needs associated with pregnancy and lactation.

7. In the centre and south, where absolute intake is lower, shares are relatively low for weanlings, for young children of both sexes in the poorest households, and possibly, though controversially, for adult men.

8. Fifteen of the 31 observations of intakes of preschool children show relatively low shares, even among the comparatively rich and even among boys. This behaviour is concentrated in (though not exclusive to) the northeast and centre of the subcontinent. As with the mortality data, the greatest vulnerability is found in the 0–5 age group.

9. In the centre and south, socio-economic class rather than gender or aggregate household entitlement appears to be the most important influence upon distributional patterns within the family, though this does not necessarily mean that class position is the strongest influence upon anti-female discrimination.

10. Micronutrients are not distributed according to contemporary understanding of need. Children of both sexes and adolescent and adult (menstruating, pregnant, or lactating) women receive low shares, while adult men may be eating not only relatively large shares but also more than they are estimated to need, a factor especially important with respect to iron and vitamin A. There is more agreement about this aspect of food behaviour, although it is less strongly evident in central and southern India.

11. The consumption of alcohol, *ceteris paribus*, certainly reduces household food intake but its actual effects on the sharing of energy have not been measured.

10.5. The chronicle of explanations

In view of the contradictory nature of the evidence on intrafamily food allocation for South Asia as a whole, our approach here is to list the types of explanations (material then cultural) which have been put forward for low individual shares. Interestingly, little attention has been paid to the economics of the relative underfeeding of the elderly, who may perform important reproductive roles within the household, and may liberate adult women for wage work.

Earlier, in section 10.2(d) on patriarchy, we examined discrimination against the female sex as a whole, summarized by the sex ratio. Material explanations for its history and geography have involved notions of economic status and utility derived from female participation in wage work, or notions of autonomy derived from property rights and transfers. But existing ethnographic evidence shows the inadequacy of both types of explanation for regional variations in the masculinity of the sex ratio and tends to emphasize what the entire South Asian region has in common materially and culturally.

(a) Discrimination against women and children

Economic explanations turn around discrimination's being an efficient survival strategy (and presuppose scarcity of household food supplies, and a given gender division of labour). For south India, positive relationships between male anthropometric status and daily earnings from wage work, productivity on the household farm, or earnings from fish catches have been established.[203] The relative overfeeding of adult men has then been explained as necessary for the major income earner to secure work in uncertain and risky labour markets.[204] A disproportionate allocation to men is thus not a cause of (female) child undernutrition. Rather it is to be seen as a response to labour markets structured in favour of males and boys (and perhaps a means of contributing towards maintenance of women and children).

(b) Discrimination against the female child

Economic explanations focus on differentials in income or earnings and expenditure. State-level data show a significant relationship between low adult female earnings relative to those of adult men and the low survival chances of

---

[203] Ryan (1982); Deolalikar (1984); Abraham (n.d.); Ramprasad (1985).

[204] Lipton (1983: 54), though the introduction of uncertainty into the economic argument has to be squared with the facts—at least for the semi-arid tropics of India—that female hired labour is more important in production than is male hired labour, and that female labour markets are characterized by greater uncertainty than those for males (Ryan and Ghodake 1984; Harriss et al. 1984).

female children under 5.[205] Furthermore if the recurrent cost of raising boys is higher than that of girls, then girls, being cheaper to replace, may be more expendable.[206] The same may follow if boys have a greater earning power than girls prior to adulthood.[207] Calculations of future costs and returns may determine the reproductive strategy of a household. Girls may be disfavoured because their income earning capacity (in those regions where they participate in wage work) is removed from a household when they migrate at marriage. Conversely boys may be allocated preferential resources in order to attract brides.[208] The cultural corollary is that relative deprivation in food is part of the socialization of girls into the roles of deference and service that they will play as future daughters-in-law. In turn this involves authority and complicity on the part of the mother herself.[209] The religious role of the son upon the death of his parents is another crucially important cultural factor said to predispose households with children of both sexes to neglect the girl child in favour of the boy in times of scarcity.

(c) Discrimination against small children of both sexes

Discrimination against the male child when it occurs is the more extraordinary given the emotional and ritual centrality of the mother–son relationship in South Asia. A material explanation for discrimination against small children, whether male or female, is that feeding is part of a punitive conditioning appropriate to conditions of scarcity in adulthood.[210] There are also biological explanations, one termed the 'silhouette hypothesis': food is allocated according to the two-dimensional size of individuals, ignoring the higher rate of energy expenditure per unit of body weight in the young child, also ignoring

---

[205] Parthasarathy and Rama Rao (1973); Cain (1977); Miller (1981). It seems simplistic to confine measurements of costs and benefits to wage work. In rich households the male child may serve an unwaged apprenticeship in productive agriculture while female children in all conditions of household serve an unwaged apprenticeship which is both productive and reproductive. Caldwell et al. (1982) have used this type of reasoning to explain a relative shift in power and resources within households in Karnataka towards children and females. Children being more costly to raise (girls are increasingly being educated), they are not dispensed with as easily as before.

[206] Sen and Sengupta (1983).   [207] Kynch (1985b).

[208] Mies (1980: 93–100). Kane (1941: 510) quotes Bana the poet expressing parental caution over 'one whom one would never forsake, taken away all of a sudden by persons [husbands] who were till then quite unfamiliar'. But Abdullah uses this argument to explain the relative pampering of the prepubescent girl in Bangladesh (1983)!

[209] Lannoy (1971: 91–3). Feeding may be a similar sort of punitive experience as are bathing and disease, and, when combined with maternal indulgence, strengthens the child's ambivalence towards his/her mother.

[210] Cantor et al. (1973: i. 105–15). The silhouette hypothesis is used to explain their observation of the relative overfeeding of the ('inactive') elderly; though it must be said that their reference of need for the elderly may be underestimated; and that neither overfeeding nor the relative inactivity of the elderly has been confirmed more recently (McNeill 1986. See also LSHTM 1985: 18).

adult needs of activity, physiological state, etc.[211] A sociological explanation
for the underfeeding of small children, when it occurs in joint households, is
that it is not the mother but less well-motivated older siblings who help the
young child to eat.

This array of explanations suggests that they are best considered as specific
rather than as general, which is consistent with the variation found in our
evidence.

But, as Sen says, 'in dealing with within-family distribution, the perception
of reality—including illusions about it—must be seen to be an important part
of reality'.[212] Subjective and objective criteria of taste, sufficiency, satisfaction, and survival interact in nutrition. A meal can be nutritious but dissatisfying, satisfying but insufficient, or malnourishing as well as insufficient
and dissatisfying.[213] It is thus necessary to consider the cultural explanation of
scarcity, the meaning of deprivation to those who experience it.

(d) Cultural explanations of deprivation

'A cultural explanation, even if not yielding uniquely profound truth may
allow us to see how and why a culture may have failed in responding to forces of
reality.'[214] It is significant, then, that types of individual have not so far figured
in existing cultural explanations of deprivation and scarcity. The notion of
exclusion from items of food is a corollary of systems of classification of food
which simultaneously emphasize rank, periodicity, auspiciousness, and medicinal properties in an effort to achieve a state of satisfaction signifying personal
health.[215] As part of this effort, to have certain types of food forbidden
temporarily or permanently for purposeful, ritual reasons is the common
experience of life. Exclusion *per se* should not concern us so much as should the
deprivation associated with mass poverty. Khare, in seeking to explain why
chronic deprivation does not provoke a massive action for its removal in India,
has advanced the idea that it is because of the Hindu conception of food that
South Asian society tolerates extreme scarcity.

The first element in this cultural conception of food is that of the *jati* and
varna orders within which the food available to one depends on one's past
karma. These concepts offer stubborn resistance to forces of technological and
social change.[216] The second element is that of the Hindu myth of abundance.
'To eat and to feed are matters of inalienable moral responsibility.' Scarcity
therefore conveys a moral message. Even when food is scarce and nutritional

---

[211] Wheeler (1984).   [212] Sen (1985*b*: 83).   [213] Khare (1976*b*).

[214] Khare (1976*b*: 72).

[215] Ibid. 123. Food is 'an item of great semiotic virtuosity' (Appadurai 1981: 494). It may be
classified simultaneously in the following terms: purity and pollution; right- and left-handedness;
exclusiveness; organoleptic qualities; medicinal properties (heat, coolness, and windiness;
digestibility; weakness and strength); and auspiciousness over time (Kakar 1982: 219–68;
Chakravarty 1972: 41–53; Khare 1976*a*, 1976*b*).

[216] Khare (1976*b*: 168–70).

well-being is materialized only for few, abundance is thought by Khare to continue to be approximated both ceremonially and as an image of the future.[217] Hunger as a state of helpless deprivation does not receive any support in Indian cultural norms. The third element is the cultural 'taking for granted' of production. Cultural emphasis lies not in the material aspects of the production of food, but instead in invisible divine and moral aspects of the distribution of food within society to individuals whose nutritional needs are culturally prioritized according to the duties of the life stages.[218]

The nub of Khare's argument is this. Food produced by the farmer does not reach the eater without the observance of the moral order governing distribution. When this is weakened (as happens under conditions of material scarcity) there is no equally viable, universal, alternative regulation of distribution. 'Though we find profuse culturally backed incentives for distributing foods and feeding different types of members of society . . . we do not obtain any substantive or well focused idea that the cultural system had been geared to retaining sufficiency in foods.'[219] Moderation is thus simultaneously a value of luxury and a condition of necessity of the poor. Khare concludes that such cultural conceptions may reinforce the material neglect of production, may obscure the assessment of food shortage, and may contribute to apathy in the implementation of policy directed from the top down to remedying the problems of scarcity which appear.[220] Intrahousehold discrimination is thus culturally problematic only under deviant conditions of persistent scarcity when the provisioning responsibility of the male householder breaks down. Generalized subsistence for survival as substantiated for South Asia by food economists is for the cultural anthropologist an abnormality.

10.6. *Issues for policy*

Feeding is fundamental to biological, cultural, and political processes. Feeding is the expression of reproductive strategy. This can be expected to vary according not only to culture but also to class position. It is hardly surprising, therefore, that the literature cannot be construed as saying that there is a pan-Indian gender problem in the allocation of food. Evidence of discrimination in feeding practices and nutrient allocation within the family in South Asia certainly exists. It is rarely of a dramatic nature. Young children and the elderly are the groups most generally discriminated against. The absolute entitlement of the male household head, affected by the class position of the household, is probably the most important influence upon hunger within the family. Nutrient allocation is certainly problematic under conditions of

[217] Ibid. 169.

[218] Chapman (1983) provides a similar example of the interaction between different systems of knowledge about agricultural production in Bihar.

[219] Khare (1976*b*: 161–4).   [220] Ibid. 164–9.

scarcity, but no consistent allocative pattern emerges, even within the large class of the poor in times of scarcity. Instead, the age and gender impact of discrimination, its social and seasonal incidence and severity all vary regionally through the subcontinent. The scale of such geographical variation is below that at which the policy processes of agenda formation, authorization, and resource mobilization and allocation normally operate.[221] It is most unlikely that this conclusion would be changed by further research. As Gwatkin concluded after an exhaustive review of nutrition–productivity relations: 'The more thorough the study the lower the likelihood of an unambiguously positive result'.[222] What will be improved by future research on material strategies of reproduction is our understanding of the reasons for the apparent great diversity of allocative practice.

It can be objected that in the context of the reciprocally causing relations of patriarchy, it is counter-intuitive that there be no general sex bias in food intake. This chapter has shown, however, that discrimination in feeding does not automatically imply discrimination in nutrition, and that discrimination in nutrition does not automatically imply disadvantage in welfare. Females need absolutely less of most nutrients than do males. It is also clear that there are class, caste, and regional differences in the operation of patriarchy. Furthermore, discrimination may exist and yet not be picked up even in welfare indicators. That average life expectancy for example has probably reached gender parity in India says little about sex bias under patriarchy. Mortality and morbidity differentials can be explained by gender differences in access or entitlement to health care as well as by access or entitlement to nutrients. Then gender is not just a biological characteristic. It is also a social relationship affected by a material career, the content of both of which is undergoing change. Women are assumed to justify and condone 'inequitable distributions'. If, in a changing society, they actually do not condone allocative practice, they may be supposed to resist the system of ordering of power and subjugation at points where they may exercise certain control. Feeding is one such point.

We cannot assume therefore that the household is a castellated fortress defending patriarchy against the state. In fact, despite or because of the reciprocally causing relations of patriarchy, the household has long been sectoralized, split up, and relabelled for policy purposes, a process often undeterred by lack of information. In the case of intrafamily hunger: the nutritional vulnerability of children and the role of feeding practice in creating vulnerability were a basis for policy long before nutritional discoveries about vulnerability had been made. And, conversely, existing research is translated into clarion calls to planning in such a way as to make the policy analyst suspect that data often have a symbolic value rather than an informational role in the

---

[221] Schaffer (1984).   [222] Gwatkin (1983: 56).

process of policy. 'We need gender specific plans to improve the chances of survival of the girl child', concludes the *Indian Express*,[223] exemplifying the sort of faith in the ability of planning to deliver, in the ability of delivery systems to target, and in the ability of 'us' to benefit, that has been interpreted by Schaffer as institutional irresponsibility.[224] In fact there is no shortage of advocacy for more or less highly targeted therapeutic interventions to remedy nutritional discrimination. In this concluding section we shall describe the form it takes.

First, food behaviour is thought to be amenable to change by ideas and knowledge, hence nutrition education aimed at mothers is advocated. The paternalistic assumptions of maternal ignorance embodied in conventional nutrition education and the irrelevant and sometimes humiliating experience it can be for the target group have been exposed by Wheeler.[225] One could as well conclude from the evidence marshalled in this paper that men should be the target for education, especially about the allocation of micronutrients. More importantly there is no evidence that nutritional knowledge by itself can change the meaning of the food share, embedded in its culture. Others have argued further along these lines that women's education may change household culture. There is evidence that this is true among the rich but judgement must be reserved for the poor. 'The fact is clearer than the mechanics.' If women's education leads to an increase in their age at marriage and a reduction in the gap in age and experience between bride and groom, it may be more likely to change culture.[226]

A second strand of advocacy favours the extraction of the mother and child dyed or the child alone from the household for the administration of gender-neutral or positively discriminating nutritional therapy, as in on-site or take-home supplementary feeding schemes and mother and child health schemes. Free, decentralized, and locationally dispersed health care appears to reduce gender inequities in medical treatment. If nutritional therapy is successful, both absolute intake and relative shares within the household can be supplemented from outside. However, if the nutritional therapy is shared with untargeted household members or if it acts as a substitute rather than as a complement, changes in individual intakes and shares may not come about. Interestingly supplementary feeding has been most successful at reaching poor children, especially girls, in the south of the subcontinent where its need is arguably not the greatest, and amongst age groups which are not identified as most vulnerable, by schemes such as Tamil Nadu's Noon Meals Scheme which is minimally targeted, not beamed preferentially at girls, extremely costly, and which flouts many principles of good planning.[227] Alternatives to supplementary feeding have included feeding schemes for adult men, where the

---

[223] *Indian Express*, 17 Oct. 1985.   [224] Schaffer (1984).   [225] Wheeler (1985).
[226] Caldwell *et al.* (1982); Woodley (1986).   [227] Harriss (1986).

supplement is known to have 'leaked';[228] and schemes abstracting the child and offering an 'integrated' therapy not confined to food alone.

A third type of policy aims to increase the economic status of women via subsidized support: special credit, nurseries for working women, vocational training,[229] even reform of the gender division of labour and of gender differentials in wage rates[230] extending to the organization of women into trade unions and co-operatives[231] to claim *inter alia* land and property rights. But there is little evidence yet that improved economic status becomes translated into increased food shares, or that increased control by women over household resources changes their food behaviour. And with respect to the organization of women there is no evidence to date for this as a means of obtaining improved rights within the household.[232] As Sharma says: 'Women tend to see their position as problematic only when the machinery breaks down'. At this point they have little power and their customary forms of small-scale and individualized resistance are inadequate, against men within families and against the state in circumstances when it appears to be the castellated fortress defending patriarchy.[233]

A fourth tack is for the state to administer a general income supplement and an increase in aggregate household food supply through the public distribution system such that maldistributivist practices, if they exist, have less nefarious consequences. The public distribution system has no inevitable effect upon age or sex bias in food allocation. One example from Karnataka shows that a well-administered PDS may lead to a reorientation of the food-allocative priorities of households in time of scarcity.[234] But as PDS administered according to a perverse logic (supplies withdrawn in scarcity and increased at times of abundance, as has occurred elsewhere) could equally well have an opposite, retrenching effect.[235] Sex or age bias will not disappear with increases in income or household entitlement even if the visible, measurable welfare consequences of such biases do. An alternative but variable income supplement for about a third of rural households would be the prohibition of alcohol consumption.

Lastly, perusal of environmental linkages suggests a number of other policy options: measures to reduce female activity levels via a reduction in the energy costs of the acquisition of fuel and water, improving the efficiency of cooking stoves,[236] and reducing the 'secret sharers of food' by eliminating intestinal parasites.[237]

A few comments are in order. First, existing nutrition policy comprises interventions in the realms of incomes and prices (of changes to exchange

[228] Ryan (1982).   [229] ICSSR (1977); Nagaraj (1986).   [230] Lipton (1983: 54).

[231] Bardhan (1985).   [232] Ibid.   [233] Sharma (1980).

[234] Caldwell *et al.* (1982; 1987).   [235] Harriss (1985).   [236] Batliwala (1982).

[237] Lipton (1983).

entitlements) and not reforms of asset distributions (of changes to ownership entitlements). Second, it is still difficult to evaluate which options are available. There is no database for implemented policy such as to enable a technical choice between these options or permutations and combinations of them.

Third, the state has long addressed itself to the rectification of inequalities in rights, without demonstrating a corresponding capacity to discharge its legal obligations to other than a small proportion of the population.[238] All the states of South Asia are signatories of the Universal Declaration of Human Rights which includes a right to food, and to the International Covenant on Economic, Social and Cultural Rights guaranteeing the right to be free from hunger.[239] But the policy options which we have listed here have never been legal, mandatory obligations, and the international right appears tantamount to impossible to operationalize.[240] None the less, 'hunger within the family' can be reduced by supporting pressures on the state to make it more accountable to the organized claims of the hungry for those food-related resources that the state has professed itself obliged to provide. This requires an understanding of how state policy affects the organization and claims of different classes and types of women. It also entails understanding the interests of a given state in unequal allocations within different classes of households: a conceptual linking of reproductive strategy at the level of the family and at the level of the state.

---

[238] ICSSR (1977).
[239] Alston (1984).
[240] Zalaquette (1984).

References

ABDULLAH, M. (1983), 'Dimensions of Intra-household Food and Nutrient Allocation: A Study of a Bangladeshi Village' (Ph.D. thesis, Faculty of Medicine, London University).

——and WHEELER, E. F. (1985), 'Seasonal Variations and the Intra-household Distribution of Food in a Bangladeshi Village', *American Journal of Clinical Nutrition*, 41.

ABRAHAM, A. (n.d.), 'A Socio-economic Analysis of Food and Nutrition among Traditional Fishing Households (Kerala): Intra-family Food Allocation' (Brussels).

AGARWAL, B. (1984), 'Rural Women and High Yielding Variety Rice Technology', *Economic and Political Weekly*, Review of Agriculture, 19.

ALSTON, P. (1984), 'International Law and the Right to Food', in Eide *et al.* (1984).

Anon. (1976), 'Recommended Dietary Intakes and Allowances Around the World: An Introduction', *Food and Nutrition Bulletin*, 4.

APPADURAI, A. (1981), 'Gastropolitics in Hindu South Asia', *American Ethnologist*, 8.

——(1984), 'How Moral is South Asia's Economy? A Review Article', *Journal of Asian Studies*, 43.

——(1985), 'Dietary Improvisation in an Agricultural Economy' in Sharman *et al.* (1985).

APTE, J. (1973), 'Food Behaviour in Two Districts', in Cantor *et al.* (1973).

AZIZ, K. M. A. (1977), 'Present Trends in Medical Consultation Prior to Death in Rural Bangladesh', *Bangladesh Medical Journal*, 6.

——and RASSAQUE, A. (1987), 'Sex Differential in Mortality and Medical Consultation during 1975–1984: A Study in Matlab Upaz of Bangladesh', mimeo, paper presented at BAMANEH/American SSRC Workshop on Differential Female Mortality and Health Care in South Asia, Dhaka.

BAIRAGI, R. (1986), 'Food Crisis, Nutritional Status and Female Children in Bangladesh', *Population and Development Review*, 12.

BARDHAN, K. (1985), 'Women's Work, Welfare and Status', *Economic and Political Weekly*, 20.

BARDHAN, P. (1974), 'On Life and Death Questions', *Economic and Political Weekly*, 9.

——(1982), 'Little Girls and Death in India', *Economic and Political Weekly*, 17.

——(1984), *Land, Labor and Rural Poverty* (New Delhi: Oxford University Press).

——(1987), 'On the Economic Geography of Sex Disparity in Child Survival in India: A Note', mimeo, paper presented at BAMANEH/American SSRC Workshop on Differential Female Mortality and Health Care in South Asia, Dhaka.

BATLIWALA, S. (1982), 'Rural Energy Scarcity and Nutrition', *Economic and Political Weekly*, 17.

——(1985), 'The Energy, Health and Nutrition Syndrome', in Jain and Banerjee (1985).

BEATON, G. H. (1985), 'The Significance of Adaptation in the Definition of Nutrient Requirements and for Nutrition Policy', in Blaxter and Waterlow (1985).

BEHRMAN, J. R. (1986), 'Intra Household Allocation of Nutrients in Rural India: Are Boys Favoured? Do Parents Exhibit Inequality Aversion?', mimeo (Population Studies Center, University of Pennsylvania).

——and DEOLALIKAR, A. B. (1986a), 'Agricultural Wages in India: The Role of Health, Nutrition and Seasonality', mimeo, IFPRI/FAO/USAID Conference on Seasonal Causes of Household Food Insecurity, Annapolis, USA.

————(1986b), 'Seasonal Demands for Nutrient Intakes and Health Status in Rural South India', mimeo, IFPRI/FAO/USAID Conference on Seasonal Causes of Household Food Insecurity, Annapolis, USA.

BENERIA, L. (ed.) (1982), Women and Development: The Sexual Division of Labour in Rural Societies (Geneva: ILO).

BHATIA, J. C. (1978), 'Ideal Number and Sex Preference of Children in India', Journal of Family and Welfare, June.

BINSWANGER, H. P., and ROSENZWEIG, M. R. (eds.) (1984), Contractual Arrangements, Employment and Wages in Rural Labour Markets in Asia (New Haven, Conn.: Yale University Press).

BLAXTER, K., and WATERLOW, J. C. (eds.) (1985), Nutritional Adaptation in Man (London: John Libbey).

CAIN, M. T. (1977), 'The Activities of Children in a Village in Bangladesh', Population and Development Review, 3.

——SYED, S. K., and NAHAR, S. (1979), 'Class, Patriarchy and Women's Work in Bangladesh', Population and Development Review, 5.

CALDWELL, J. C., REDDY, P. H., and CALDWELL, P. (1982), 'The Determinants of Fertility Decline in India', Population and Development Review, 8.

—————— (1983), 'The Social Component of Mortality Decline', Population Studies, 37.

CALDWELL, P., and CALDWELL, J. (1987), 'Where There is a Narrower Gap between Female and Male Situations: Lessons from South India and Sri Lanka', mimeo, paper presented at BAMANEH/American SSRC Workshop on Differential Female Mortality and Health Care in South Asia, Dhaka.

CANTOR, S. M., et al. (1973), Tamil Nadu Nutrition Study (6 vols.) (Haverford, Penn.: Cantor Associates).

CHACKO, A., BEGUM, A., and MATHAN, V. I. (1984), 'Absorption of Nutrient Energy in Southern Indian Control Subjects and Patients with Tropical Sprue', American Journal of Clinical Nutrition, 40.

CHAKRAVARTY, I. (1972), Saga of Indian Food (New Delhi: Sterline).

CHAMBERS, R., LONGHURST, R., and PACEY, A. (eds.) (1981), Seasonal Dimensions of Rural Poverty (London: Frances Pinter).

CHAPMAN, G. P. (1983), 'The Folklore of Perceived Environment in Bihar', Environment and Planning A, 15.

CHATTOPADHYAY, B. (1985), 'Per Capita Per Diem Intake of Calorie Protein and Fat and Estimate of Clinical Undernutrition in Children for the Rural Paper in Selected Village Clusters of Districts in West Bengal', mimeo (Calcutta: Cressida).

CHEN, L. C. (1982), 'Where Have All the Women Gone?', Economic and Political Weekly, 17.

——HUQ, E., and D'SOUZA, S. (1981), 'Sex-Bias in the Family Allocation of Food and Health Care in Rural Bangladesh', Population and Development Review, 7.

CLARK, A. (1983), 'Limitations on Female Life Chances in Rural Central Gujarat', Indian Economic and Social History Review, 20.

CLAY, E. J., and SCHAFFER, B. B. (1984), Room for Manœuvre: An Exploration of Public Policy in Agriculture and Rural Development (London: Heinemann).

COHEN, R., GUTKIND, P. C. W., and BRAZIER, P. (eds.) (1979), *Peasants and Proletarians: The Struggle of Third World Workers* (London: Hutchinson).

COREA, G., *et al.* (eds.) (1985), *Man-Made Women* (London: Hutchinson).

DAS GUPTA, M. (1987), 'The Second Daughter: Sex Differentials in Child Mortality, Nutrition and Health Care in Punjab, India', mimeo, paper presented at BAMANEH/American SSRC Workshop on Differential Female Mortality and Health Care in South Asia, Dhaka.

DEB, P. C. (1977), *Liquor in a Green Revolution Setting* (Delhi: Research Company Publishers).

DEERE, C. D. (1979), 'Rural Women's Subsistence Production in the Capitalist Periphery', in Cohen *et al.* (1979).

DEOLALIKAR, A. B. (1984), 'Are There Pecuniary Returns to Health in Agricultural Work?', Progress Report No. 66, Economics Programme (Hyderabad: ICRISAT).

DJURFELDT, G., and LINDBERG, S. (1975), *Pills Against Poverty*, Scandinavian Institute of Asian Studies, Monograph Series No. 23 (London: Curzon Press).

DRÈZE, J., and SEN, A. K. (1989), *Hunger and Public Action* (Oxford: Oxford University Press).

DUBE, S. C. (1983), 'Changing Norms in the Hindu Joint Family', in O'Flaherty and Devett (1983).

DUGDALE, A. E. (1985), 'Family Anthropometry: A New Strategy for Determining Community Nutrition', *Lancet*, 21 Sept.

——and PAYNE, P. R. (1986), 'A Model of Seasonal Changes in Energy Balance', mimeo (London: London School of Hygiene and Tropical Medicine).

DYSON, T. (1987), 'Excess Female Mortality in India: Uncertain Evidence on a Narrowing Differential', mimeo, paper presented at BAMANEH/American SSRC Workshop on Differential Female Mortality and Health Care in South Asia, Dhaka.

——and MOORE, M. P. (1983), 'Kinship Structure, Female Autonomy and Demographic Behaviour: Regional Contrasts within India', *Population and Development Review*, 9.

EBRAHIM, G. (1979), 'The Problems of Undernutrition', in Jarrett (1979).

EIDE, A., EIDE, W. B., GOONATILEKE, S., GUSSOW, J., and OMAWALE (eds.) (1984), *Food as a Human Right* (Tokyo: UNU).

EVELATH, P. B. (1985), 'Nutritional Implications of Differences in Adolescent Growth and Maturation and in Adult Body Size', in Blaxter and Waterlow (1985).

FERRO-LUZZI, A. (1982), 'Meaning and Constraints of Energy Intake Studies in Free Living Populations', in Harrison (1982).

FLORES, R., *et al.* (1984), 'Functional Consequences of Marginal Malnutrition among Agricultural Workers in Guatemala 1984', *Food and Nutrition Bulletin*, 6.

FREEMAN, H., *et al.* (1980), 'Nutrition and Cognitive Development among Rural Guatemalan Children', *American Journal of Public Health*, 70.

GIBBS, C. (1986), 'Characteristics of Household Expenditure in a Tamil Village, South India' (BA dissertation, Newnham College, Cambridge).

GILLESPIE, S. (1986), 'Perceptions of Health and Seasonality in Two South Indian Tribal Groups', mimeo (London: London School of Hygiene and Tropical Medicine).

GOPALAN, C. (1983), 'Measurement of Undernutrition: Biological Considerations', *Economic and Political Weekly*, 18.

——(1985), 'The Mother and Child in India', *Economic and Political Weekly*, 20.

——and NADAMUNI, N. A. (1972), 'Nutrition and Fertility', *Lancet*, 18 Nov.

GOPALDAS, T., SAXENA, K., and GUPTA, A. (1983), 'Intrafamilial Distribution of Nutrients in a Deep Forest Dwelling Tribe of Gujarat, India', *Ecology of Food and Nutrition*, 13.

GORMSEN, E. (ed.) (1976), *Market Distribution Systems*, Mainzer Geografische Studien, No. 10.

GORSKY, R. D., and CALLOWAY, D. H. (1983), 'Activity Pattern Changes with Decreases in Food Energy Intake', *Human Biology*, 55.

GOUGH, K. (1981), *Rural Society in Southeast India* (London: Cambridge University Press).

Government of Sri Lanka (1983), *Nutritional Status: Its Determinants and Intervention Programmes* (Colombo: Colombo Food and Nutrition Policy and Planning Division, Ministry of Plan Implementation).

GOWRINATH SASTRY, J., and VIJAYARAGHAVANLK (1973), 'Use of Anthropometry in Grading Malnutrition in Children', *Indian Journal of Medical Research*, 61.

GREELEY, M. (1986), 'Rice in Bangladesh: Post Harvest Losses, Technology and Employment' (Ph.D. thesis, University of Sussex, Brighton).

GREENE, L. S. (ed.) (1977), *Malnutrition, Behaviour and Social Organization* (New York: Academic Press).

GREENOUGH, P. R. (1982), *Prosperity and Misery in Modern Bengal: The Famine of 1943–1944* (New York: Oxford University Press).

GULATI, L. (1975a), 'Female Work Participation: A Study of Interstate Differences', *Economic and Political Weekly*, 10.

——(1975b), 'Occupational Distribution of Working Women: An Interstate Comparison', *Economic and Political Weekly*, 10.

——(1978), 'Profile of a Female Agricultural Labourer', *Economic and Political Weekly*, 13.

GUPTA, S. C. (1986), 'Sex Preference and Protein Calorie Malnutrition', *Journal of Family Welfare*, 32.

GWATKIN, D. (1983), 'Does Better Health Produce Greater Wealth? A Review of the Available Evidence Concerning Health Nutrition and Output', mimeo, Report to USAID, Overseas Development Council (Washington, DC).

HARRISON, G. A. (ed.) (1982), *Energy and Effort*, Symposia of the Society for the Study of Human Biology (London: Taylor and Francis).

HARRISS, B. (1976a), 'Social Specificity in Rural Weekly Markets', in Gormsen (1976).

——(1976b), 'Paddy Processing in India and Sri Lanka: A Review of the Case for Technical Innovation', *Tropical Science*, 18.

——(1979), 'Post Harvest Rice Processing Systems in Rural Bangladesh: Technology, Economies and Employment', *Bangladesh Journal of Agricultural Economics*, 2.

——(1981), *Transitional Trade and Rural Development* (New Delhi: Vikas).

——(1982), *Transitional Trade and Rural Development* (New Delhi: Vikas).

——(1983), 'Food Systems and Society: The System of Circulation of Rice in West Bengal', *Cressida Transactions*, 2.

——(1986), 'Meals and Noon Meals in South India: Food and Nutrition Policy in the Rural Food Economy of Tamil Nadu State', Development Studies Occasional Paper No. 31 (Norwich: School of Development Studies, University of East Anglia); published as *Child Nutrition and Poverty in S. India* (New Delhi: Concept Pub. Co., 1990).

HARRISS, B. (1989), *Child Nutrition and Poverty in South India* (New Delhi: Concept).

——with CHAPMAN, G. P., McLEAN, W., SHEARS, E., and WATSON, E. (1984), *Exchange Relations and Poverty in Dryland Agriculture* (New Delhi: Concept).

——and WATSON, E. (1987), 'The Sex Ratio in South Asia', in Momsen and Townsend (1987).

HOUSKA, W. (1981), 'The Characteristics of Son Preference in an Urban Scheduled Caste Community', *Eastern Anthropologist*, 34.

Indian Council of Social Science Research (1977), *Critical Issues on the Status of Women* (New Delhi: ICSSR).

ILO (1979), *The Impact of Women Workers of the Maharashtra Employment Guarantee Scheme* (New Delhi: ILO).

IMMINK, M. D. C., VITERI, F. E., FLORES, R., and TORUN, B. (1984), 'Microeconomic Consequences of Energy Deficiency in Rural Populations in Developing Countries', in *Energy Intake and Activity* (New York: Alan Liss Inc.).

JAIN, A. K., and NAG, M. (1986), 'Importance of Female Primary Education for Fertility Reduction in India', *Economic and Political Weekly*, 21.

JAIN, D. (1980), *Women's Quest for Power* (New Delhi: Vikas).

——and BANERJEE, N. (eds.) (1985), *Tyranny of the Household: Investigative Essays on Women's Work* (New Delhi: Shakti).

JARRETT, R. J. (ed.) (1979), *Nutrition and Disease* (London: Croom Helm).

JEFFERY, P., JEFFERY, R., and LYON, A. (1987), 'Domestic Politics and Sex Differences in Mortality: A View from Rural Bijnor District, Uttar Pradesh', paper presented at BAMANEH/American SSRC Workshop on Differential Female Mortality and Health Care in South Asia, Dhaka.

JODHA, N. S. (1980), 'Some Dimensions of Traditional Farming Systems in Semi Arid Tropical India', in *Socio-economic Constraints to the Development of Semi Arid Tropical Agriculture* (Hyderabad: ICRISAT).

KAKAR, S. (1981), *The Inner World: A Psychoanalytic Study of Childhood and Society in India* (New Delhi: Oxford University Press).

——(1982), *Shamans, Mystics and Doctors: A Psychological Enquiry into India and Its Healing Traditions* (New Delhi: Oxford University Press).

KANE, P. V. (1941), *History of Dharmasastra*, vol. ii (Pune: Poona Bhandarkar Oriental Research Institute).

KARKAL, M. (1987), 'Differentials in Mortality by Sex', paper presented at the BAMANEH/American SSRC Workshop on Differential Female Mortality and Health Care in South Asia, Dhaka.

KHAN, M. (1980), 'Infant Feeding Practices in Rural Meheran, Comilla, Bangladesh', *American Journal of Clinical Nutrition*, 33.

KHAN, Q. (1984), 'Impact of Household Endowment Constraints on Nutrition and Health', *Journal of Development Economics*, 15.

——(1985), 'Household Wealth, Mother's Education and Female Child Mortality in South Asia: An Empirical Test of Intrahousehold Resource Allocation', Discussion Paper Centre for Analysis of Developing Economies, University of Pennsylvania).

KHARE, R. S. (1976a), *The Hindu Hearth and Home* (New Delhi: Vikas).

——(1976b), *Culture and Reality: Essays on the Hindu System of Managing Foods* (Simla: Indian Institute of Advanced Study).

——(1986), *The Indian Meal: Aspects of Cultural Economy and Food Use*, in Khare and Rao (1986).

——and RAO, M. S. A. (eds.) (1986), *Food, Society and Culture: Aspects of South Asian Food Systems* (Durham, NC: Academic Press).

KIELMANN, A. A., et al. (1983), *Child and Maternal Health Services in Rural India: The Naragwal Experiment*, vols. i and ii (Baltimore: Johns Hopkins).

KISHWAR, M. (1985), 'The Continuing Deficit of Women in India and the Impact of Amniocentesis', in Corea et al. (1985).

KLEIN, R. (1981), 'Relationship of Pre-school Nutritional Status, of Family Socio-economic Status and Preschool Ability to School Performance and School Age Intellectual Ability', mimeo (INCAP).

KOENIG, M. A., and D'SOUZA, S. (1986), 'Sex Differences in Childhood Mortality in Rural Bangladesh', *Social Science and Medicine*, 22.

——and WOJTYNIAK, B. (1987), 'Excess Female Mortality during infancy and Early Childhood: Evidence from Rural Bangladesh', mimeo, paper presented at BAMANEH/American SSRC Workshop on Differential Female Mortality and Health Care in South Asia, Dhaka.

KRISHNAMURTHY, L. (1973), 'A Life Cycle: Tiruvanmiyur Village, Chinglepet District', in Cantor et al. (1973).

KYNCH, J. (1985a), 'Some State Responses to Male and Female Need in British India', mimeo (Oxford: Institute of Economics and Statistics).

——(1985b), 'How Many Women are Enough? Sex Ratios and the Right to Life', *Third World Affairs*, 156–71.

——and MAGUIRE, M. (1986), 'Report on the Nutritional Status of Families in Palanpur, Uttar Pradesh, India', mimeo (Oxord: Institute of Economics and Statistics).

——and SEN, A. K. (1983), 'Indian Women: Well-Being and Survival', *Cambridge Journal of Economics*, 7.

LANGFORD, C. M. (1982), 'The Fertility of Tamil Estate Workers in Sri Lanka', International Statistical Institute, Scientific Report (Voorburg: World Fertility Survey).

——(1984), 'Sex Differentials in Mortality in Sri Lanka: Changes since the 1920s', *Journal of Biosocial Science*, 16.

LANNOY, R. (1971), *The Speaking Tree* (London: Oxford University Press).

LAWRENCE, M. L., SINGH, L., LAWRENCE, F., and WHITEHEAD, R. G. (1985), 'The Energy Cost of Common Daily Activities in African Women: Increased Expenditure in Pregnancy?', *American Journal of Clinical Nutrition*, 42.

LEVINSON, F. J. (1972), *Morinda: An Economic Analysis of Malnutrition among Young Children in Rural India* (Ithaca, NY: Cornell University Press and MIT).

LIPTON, M. (1983), 'Poverty, Undernutrition and Hunger', World Bank Staff Working Paper No. 597 (Washington, DC: World Bank).

London School of Hygiene and Tropical Medicine (1985), 'Basic Nutrition and Malnutrition', *Nutrition in Practice*, 1 (London: Department of Human Nutrition, London School of Hygiene and Tropical Medicine).

McALPIN, M. B. (1983), *Subject to Famine: Food Crises and Economic Change in West India, 1860–1920* (Princeton, NJ: Princeton University Press).

MACDONALD, A. W. (1955), 'Le Concept de Sambhogakaya', *Journal asiatique*.

McGUIRE, J. S. (1979), 'Seasonal Changes in Energy Expenditure and Work Patterns of Rural Guatemalan Women' (Ph.D. thesis, MIT, Cambridge, Mass.).

MACKINTOSH, M. (1981), 'Gender and Economics: The Sexual Division of Labour and the Subordination of Women', in Young *et al.* (1981).

MACLACHLAN, M. D. (1983), 'Why They Did Not Starve: Biocultural Adaptations in a South Indian Village' (Philadelphia: Institute for Study of Human Issues).

McNEILL, G. (1984), 'Energy Undernutrition in Adults in Rural South India', Progress Report, mimeo (London: London School of Hygiene and Tropical Medicine).

—— (1986), 'Energy Nutrition in Adults in Rural South India', Final Report to Ford Foundation, UNICEF, and ODA (London: London School of Hygiene and Tropical Medicine).

MADHAVAN, S. (1965), 'Age of Menarche of S. Indian Girls Belonging to the States of Madras and Kerala', *Indian Journal of Medical Research*, 53.

MAMORIA, C. B. (1980), *Social Problems and Social Disorganisation in India* (Allahabad: Kitabimahal).

MARRIOTT, M. (1978), 'Intimacy and Rank', mimeo, New Delhi Tenth Internal Conference of Anthropological and Ethnological Sciences.

MARTORELL, R. (1985), 'Child Growth Retardation: A Discussion of Its Causes and Its Relationship to Health', in Blaxter and Waterlow (1985).

—— LESLIE, J., and MOOCK, P. R. (1984), 'Characteristics and Determinants of Child Nutrition Status in Nepal', *American Journal of Clinical Nutrition*, 39.

MATHEWS, C. M. E. (1979), *Health and Culture in a South Indian Village* (New Delhi: Sterling Publications Pvt. Ltd.).

MENCHER, J. (1980), 'The Lessons and Non-lessons of Kerala; Agricultural Labour and Poverty', *Economic and Political Weekly*, 15.

—— and SARADAMONI, K. (1982), 'Muddy Feet, Dirty Hands: Rice Production and Female Agricultural Labour', *Economic and Political Weekly*, Review of Agriculture, 17.

MIES, M. (1980), *Indian Women and Patriarchy* (New Delhi: Concept).

MILLER, B. (1981), *The Endangered Sex: Neglect of Female Children in Rural North India* (Ithaca, NY: Cornell University Press).

MITCHELL, J. (1984), 'Patterns and Prevalence of Alcohol Consumption in Two Tamil Nadu Villages' (M.Sc. thesis, London School of Hygiene and Tropical Medicine).

MITRA, A. (1978), *India's Population: Aspects of Quality and control* (New Delhi: Abhinar Publications).

MOHAN, D., SHARMA, H. K., SUNDARAM, K. R., and NEKI, J. S. (1980), 'Patterns of Alcohol Consumption in Rural Punjab', *Indian Journal of Medical Research*, 72.

MOMSEN, J. and TOWNSEND, J., (eds.) (1987), *The Geography of Gender in the Third World* (London: Butler & Tanner).

MONTGOMERY, E. (1972), 'Stratification and Nutrition in a Population in Southern India' (Ph.D. thesis, Colombia University, Colombia).

—— (1977), 'Social Structuring of Nutrition in a South Indian Village', in Greene (1977).

MUKHERJEE, M. (1983), 'Impact of Modernisation on Women's Occupations: A Case Study of the Rice Husking Industry of Bengal', *Indian Economic and Social History Review*, 20.

MUNOZ DE CHAVEZ, M., *et al.* (1974), 'The Epidemiology of Good Nutrition in a Population with a High Prevalence of Malnutrition', *Ecology of Human Nutrition*, 3.

NAGARAJ, K. (1986), 'Infant Mortality in Nadu', *Bulletin, Madras Development Seminar Series*, 16.

NELSON, M. (1986), 'The Distribution of Nutrient Intake within Families', *British Journal of Nutrition*, 55.

O'FLAHERTY, W., and DEVETT, J. D. M. (eds.) (1983), *The Concept of Duty in Southern Asia* (New Delhi: Vikas).

OMVEDT, G. (1978), 'Women and Rural Revolution in India', *Journal of Peasant Studies*, 5.

PACEY, A., and PAYNE, P. R. (1985), *Agricultural Development and Nutrition* (London: Hutchinson).

PADMANABHA, P. (1981), 'Survey on Infant and Child Mortality (1979)', quoted in Kynch and Maguire (1986).

——(1982), 'Mortality in India: A Note on Trends and Implications', *Economic and Political Weekly*, 17.

PARRY, J. P. (1979), *Caste and Kinship in Kangra* (London: Routledge).

PARTHASARATHY, G., and RAMA RAO, G. D. (1973), 'Employment and Unemployment among Rural Labour Households: A Study of West Godavari', *Economic and Political Weekly*, 8.

PAYNE, P. R. (1985a), 'Public Health and Functional Consequences of Seasonal Hunger and Malnutrition', paper for Workshop on Seasonal Causes of Household Food Insecurity: Policy Implications and Research Needs, Washington, IFPRI.

——(1985b), 'Nutritional Adaptation in Man: Social Adjustments and Their Nutritional Implications', in Blaxter and Waterlow (1985).

——and CUTLER, P. C. (1984), 'Measuring Malnutrition: Technical Problems and Ideological Perspectives', *Economic and Political Weekly*, 19.

PEKKARINEN, M. (1970), 'Methodology in the Collection of Food Consumption Data', *World Reviews, Nutrition and Dietetics*, 12.

PEREIRA, S. M., SUNDARAJ, R., and BEGUM, A. (1979), 'Physical Growth and Neuro Integrative Performance of Survivors of Protein Energy Malnutrition', *British Journal of Nutrition*, 42.

PERERA, W. D. A. (1983), 'The Nutritional Status Surveys of Preschool Children in Sri Lanka', in Government of Sri Lanka (1983).

PETTIGREW, J. (1987), 'The Household and Community Context of Diarrhoeal Illness among the under Twos in the Rural Punjab', mimeo, paper presented at BAMANEH/American SSRC Workshop on Differential Female Mortality and Health Care in South Asia, Dhaka.

PREMA, K. (1978), 'Pregnancy and Lactation: Some Nutritional Aspects', *Indian Journal of Medical Research*, 68.

PRIYARDARSIRI, S., and HARTJEN, C. A. (1982), 'Legal Control and Alcohol in the United States and India', *International Journal of the Addictions*, 17.

PRYER, J. (1987), 'The Production and Reproduction of Malnutrition in a Bangladesh Slum', in Momsen and Townsend (1987).

PUSHPAMMA, P., GEERVANI, P., and KRISHNA KUMARI, K. (1981), 'Anthropometric and Dietary Pattern of Adults and Elderly Population of Andhra Pradesh', *Nutrition Reports International*, 23.

—— ——and LAKSHMI DEVI, N. (1982), 'Food Intake, Nutrient Adequacy and Anthropology of Adolescents in Andhra Pradesh', *Indian Journal of Medical Research*, 75.

—— ——and USHA RANI, M. (1982), 'Food Intake and Nutritional Adequacy of the

Rural Population of Andhra Pradesh, India', *Human Nutrition: Applied Nutrition*, 36A.

RAHAMAN, M. (1982), 'A Diarrhoea Clinic in Rural Bangladesh: Influence of Distance, Age and Sex on Attendance and Diarrhoeal Mortality', *American Journal of Public Health*, 72.

RAJALAKSHMI, R. (1981), 'Behavioural Development of Underprivileged and Malnourished Children', *Baroda Journal of Nutrition*, 8.

RAJARAMAN, I. (1983), 'Economics of Bride Price and Dowry', *Economic and Political Weekly*, 18.

RAMPRASAD, V. (1985), 'Food and Nutrition Assessment of Fishing Communities in Tamil Nadu', Bay of Bengal Fisheries Project Consultancy Report (Madras: FAO).

RANDERIA, S., and VISARIA, L. (1984), 'Sociology of Bride Price and Dowry', *Economic and Political Weekly*, 19.

RIVERS, J. P. W. (1982), 'Women and Children Last: An Essay on Sex Discrimination in Disasters', *Disasters*, 6.

—— and PAYNE, P. R. (1982), 'The Comparison of Energy Supply and Energy Need: A Critique of Energy Requirements', in Harrison (1982).

ROBERTS, S. B., PAUL, A. A., COLE, T. J., and WHITEHEAD, R. G. (1982), 'Seasonal Changes in Activity, Birth Weight and Lactational Performance in Rural Gambian Women', *Transactions of the Royal Society of Tropical Medicine and Hygiene*, 76.

ROSENZWEIG, M. R. (1984), 'Determinants of Wage Rates and Labour Supply Behaviour in the Rural Sector of a Developing Country', in Binswanger and Rosenzweig (1984).

—— and SCHULTZ, T. P. (1980), 'Market Opportunities, Genetic Endowments and the Infrafamily Distribution of Resources: Child Survival in Rural India', *American Economic Review*, 63.

RYAN, J. G. (1982), 'Wage Functions for Daily Labor Market Participants in Rural South India', Progress Report No. 38, Economics Programme (Hyderabad: ICRISAT).

—— BIDINGER, P. D., PRAHLAD RAO, N., and PUSHPAMMA, P. (1984), 'The Determinants of Individual Diets and Nutritional Status in Six Villages of Southern India', *Research Bulletin*, 7 (Hyderabad: ICRISAT).

—— and GHODAKE, R. D. (1980), 'Labor Market Behavior in Rural Villages of South India: Effects of Season, Sex and Socioeconomic Status', Progress Report No. 15, Economics Programme (Hyderabad: ICRISAT).

—— —— (1984), 'Labor Market Behavior in Rural Villages in South India: Effects of Season, Sex and Socioeconomic Status', in Binswanger and Rosenzweig (1984).

—— —— and SARIN, R. (1980), 'Labor Use and Labor Markets in Semi Arid Tropical Rural Villages of Peninsular India', in *Socio-economic Constraints to the Development of Semi Arid Tropical Agriculture* (Hyderabad: ICRISAT).

SADASIVAM, S., KASTHURI, R., and SUBRAMANIAM, S. (1980), 'Nutritional Survey in a Village of Tamil Nadu', *Industrial Journal of Nutrition Dietetics*, 17.

SATHAR, S. (1985), 'Infant and Child Mortality in Pakistan: Some Trends and Differentials', *Journal of Biosocial Sciences*, 17.

SATYANARAYANA, K., NADAMUNI NAIDU, A., and NARASINGA RAO, B. S. (1979), 'Effect of Early Childhood Undernutrition and Child Labour on Growth and Adult Nutritional Status of Rural Indian Boys around Hyderabad', *American Journal of Clinical Nutrition*, 32.

—— —— ——(1980), 'Agricultural Employment, Wage Earnings and the Nutritional Status of Teenage Rural Hyderabad Boys', *Industrial Journal of Nutrition and
Dietetics*, 17.

SCHAFFER, B. (1984), 'Towards Responsibility: Public Policy in Concept and Practice',
in Clay and Schaffer (1984).

SCRIMSHAW, N. S., and ALTSCHUL, A. M. (eds.) (1971), *Amino Acid Fortification of
Protein Foods* (Cambridge, Mass.: MIT Press).

SECKLER, D. (1982), 'Small but Healthy: A Basic Hypothesis in the Theory, Measurement and Policy of Malnutrition', in Sukhatme (1982).

SEN, A. K. (1981), *Poverty and Famines: An Essay on Entitlement and Deprivation*
(Oxford: Oxford University Press).

——(1984), 'Family and Food: Sex Bias in Poverty', in *Resources, Values and Development* (Oxford: Basil Blackwell).

——(1985a), 'Women, Technology and Sexual Divisions', *Trade and Development
(UNCTAD)*, 6.

——(1985b), *Commodities and Capabilities* (Amsterdam: North-Holland).

——and SENGUPTA, S. (1983), 'Malnutrition of Rural Indian Children and the Sex
Bias', *Economic and Political Weekly*, 18.

SEN, G. (1982), 'Women Workers and the Green Revolution', in Beneria (1982).

SEN, I. (1986), 'Geography of Secular Change in Sex Ratio in 1981', *Economic and
Political Weekly*, 21.

SHARMA, S. (1983), 'Food Distribution Pattern in Drought Affected Farm Families of
Rajasthan', M.Sc. thesis, University of Udaipur.

SHARMA, U. (1978), 'Women and Their Affines: The Veil as a Symbol of Separation',
Man, June.

——(1980), *Women, Work and Property in North-West India* (London: Tavistock
Publications).

SHARMAN, A., THEOPANO, J., CURTIS, K., and MERCER, E. (eds.) (1985), *Diet and
Domestic Life in Society*.

SIBERT, J. R., YADHAV, M., and INBARAJ, S. G. (1978), 'Maternal and Foetal Nutrition
in Southern India', *British Medical Journal*, 1.

SINGH, S., GORDON, J. E., and WYON, J. B. (1962), 'Medical Care in Fatal Illness of a
Rural Punjab Population: Some Social, Biological and Cultural Factors and Their
Ecological implications', *Indian Journal of Medical Research*, 50.

SOPHER, D. E. (ed.) (1980), *An Exploration of India* (London: Longman).

SUKHATME, P. V. (1981), 'Relationship between Malnutrition and Poverty' (New
Delhi: Indian Association of Social Science Institutions).

——(ed.) (1982), *Newer Concepts in Nutrition and Their Implications for Policy* (Pune:
Maharashtra Association for the Cultivation of Science).

SUNDARAJ, R., and PEREIRA, S. M. (1973), 'Diets of Pregnant Women in a South Indian
Community', *Tropical Medicine*, 25.

—— ——(1975), 'Dietary Intakes and Food Taboos of Lactating Women in a South
Indian Community', *Tropical Medicine*, 27.

TANNER, *et al.* (1970), 'Standards for Birth Weights at Gestational Periods from 32 to 42
weeks Allowing for Maternal Height and Weight', *Archives of Diseases of Children*,
45.

THIAGARAJAN, D. (1973), 'A Life Cycle: Olappalayam Village, Coimbatore Dt.', in
Cantor *et al.* (1973).

THIMMAIAH, V. (1979), *Socio Economic Impact of Drinking, State Lottery and Horse Racing in Karnataka* (New Delhi: Sterling Pub. Co.).

TRIVEDI, H. R. (1976), *The Scheduled Caste Woman: Studies in Exploitation* (New Delhi: Concept).

VAN ESTENK, P., and GREER, J. (1985), 'Beer Consumption and Third World Nutrition', *Food Policy*, 10.

VISARIA, L. (1987), 'Sex Differentials in Nutritional Status in a Rural Area of Gujarat States, India', mimeo, paper presented at BAMANEH/American SSRC Workshop on Differential Female Mortality and Health Case in South Asia, Dhaka.

VISARIA, P., and VISARIA, L. (1973), 'Employment Planning for the Weaker Sections in Rural India', *Economic and Political Weekly*, 8.

VITERI, F. E. (1971), 'Considerations on the Effect of Nutrition as the Body Composition and Physical Working Capacity of Young Guatemalan Adults', in Scrimshaw and Altschul (1971).

WADLEY, S., and DERR, B. (1987), 'Child Survival and Economic Status in a North Indian Village', mimeo, paper presented at BAMANEH/American SSRC Workshop on Differential Female Mortality and Health Care in South Asia, Dhaka.

WATERLOW, J. C. (1972), 'Classification and Definition of Protein-Calorie Malnutrition', *British Medical Journal*, 3.

——(1973), 'Note on the Assessment and Classification of Protein-Energy Malnutrition in Children', *Lancet*, 14 July.

—— (1979), 'Uses of Recommended Intakes: The Purpose of Dietary Recommendations', *Food Policy*, 4.

——(1985), 'What Do We Mean by Adaptation?' in Blaxter and Waterlow (1985).

WHEELER, E. F. (1984), 'Intra Household Food Allocation: A Review of Evidence', Bad Homborg, mimeo, paper presented at meeting on 'The Sharing of Food', London School of Hygiene and Tropical Medicine, London.

—— (1985), 'To Feed or to Educate: Labelling in Targeting Nutrition Interventions', in Wood (1985).

WHITE, B. (1984), 'Measuring Time-Allocation, Decision Making and Agrarian Changes Affecting Rural Women: Examples from Recent Resources in Indonesia', *IDS Bulletin*, 15.

WHITEHEAD, A. (1981), ' "I'm Hungry Mum": The Politics of Domestic Budgeting', in Young *et al.* (1981).

WOOD, G. (ed.) (1985), *Labelling in Development Policy* (London: Sage).

WOODLEY, R. (1986), 'Women's Marriage and Migration in Rural South India' (BA dissertation, Downing College, Cambridge).

WYON, J. B., and GORDON, J. E. (1971), *The Khanna Study: Population Problems in the Rural Punjab* (Cambridge, Mass.: Harvard University Press).

YOUNG, K., WOLKOWITZ, C., and McCULLOGH, R. (1981), *Of Marriage and the Market: Women's Subordination in International Perspective* (London: CSE Books).

ZALAQUETTE, J. (1984), 'The Relationship between Development and Human Rights', in Eide *et al.* (1984).

11

Rural Women and Food Production in Sub-Saharan Africa

Ann Whitehead

11.1. *Introduction*

The whole issue of the role of women in agricultural production in sub-Saharan Africa is currently a deeply politicized one.[1] From an obstinate silence about it, there has been an increasingly vociferous recognition in public development discourse of the work done by Africa's women farmers. In some quarters this is being described as an ever-increasing, and seemingly limitless, proportion of the total labour input to sub-Saharan African farming. The immediate source of this change lies of course in the severe crises in Africa's food supply brought about by the economic recession and highlighted by environmental disasters. Twenty years of recurring African famine have brought women's work to the fore of public debate. In responding to the continent-wide problems of intermittent famine and persistent hunger, there have been widespread speculations that the role of women in food production and the problems of agricultural output are in some way linked. In particular there is a widely held belief that food production has become 'feminized' in the twentieth century. This belief exists in two versions. There is firstly the view that socio-economic changes have progressively withdrawn men from food cultivation so that it is in the hands exclusively of women. A second view, more informed perhaps about the long-standing role of women in African agriculture, points to the predominantly male recruitment to commercial agriculture, and to much urban employment and entrepreneurship, to argue for the feminization, in a relative sense, of the food sector of modern agriculture. In whichever sense it is used, many commentators argue that feminization is contributing to the food problems of the subcontinent. Broadly this chapter seeks to address issues raised by this. I look at three main areas: (1) the contrast between some myths and counter-myths about the changing sexual division of labour in sub-Saharan Africa and the reality of the historical development of women's

I am grateful to Megan Vaughan for her helpful discussant's comments at the WIDER Conference and to Maureen MacIntosh and Gavin Williams for major comments on the initial text. I am also grateful to Alison Evans for several discussions of the themes of this paper, and to the comments of the audiences at seminars in Oxford, Sussex, and the Open University to whom versions of this paper were read during 1987.

[1] This paper will mainly exclude discussions of Southern Africa, where the political and economic effects of apartheid have created a specific regional form of some of the problems discussed here.

contemporary role in agriculture; (2) the effect of development projects on women, and some related problems in the economic modelling of peasant farming; and (3) what the economic structure of the African farm family implies for the constraints on and incentives to women increasing their agricultural output. The purpose is not to suggest that the sexual division of labour is the most important factor affecting the food crises in Africa. Many other factors play their part: among them national economies and political situations; environmental degradation; the level of productivity in agriculture; the form of agrarian stratification; and problems of the delivery of technological know-how and inputs. Nevertheless, as Berry (1984), Richards (1983a), and others have pointed out, the character of the social relations of the peasant sector has an important role in food production and food entitlement and these, in turn, may be critical elements in the agrarian crisis.

Food strategies, food production, and women: an orientation

The responses to the African food crises have included renewed international debate about the role of agriculture in national economic policies; a set of debates about what are currently the appropriate policies for African agriculture, as well as what were their past characters; and in some cases the development of coherent food strategies on a national basis. Some of these themes are apparent in other contributions to these volumes. Many of these debates are heated and unresolved for a number of reasons which include ideological and political differences underpinning some of the macropolicy approaches. These same differences underlie contestation about the extent of the agrarian crisis and its generality, a question which has been extensively explored by Berry (1984). In the midst of all this one reality is that in the last two decades far too great a proportion of the populations of a number of African countries have experienced persistent hunger and recurring famine. The decision to identify this situation as a 'real' crisis in food production rarely appears to have been a simple issue of how to interpret the inadequate statistics and database available to us. Nevertheless my starting-point is that urban and rural food security are central aspects of the debates about national food strategies because of the existence of this persistent hunger and intermittent famine.

That being said, women as a distinct set of social actors in the agrarian structure are irrelevant to many aspects of the debates about overall agricultural policy or about national food strategies. These must necessarily concern themselves with very broad-ranging economic and political issues. These include the debates about what is the most efficient way of increasing national income and purchasing power, as a prerequisite to solving issues of national food security, especially the relative roles of agriculture and industry; the place of agricultural pricing policy in raising output; the importance for food security of promoting non-food crops versus food crops; and the factors affecting the relation between national self-sufficiency and household self-sufficiency.

In most of these debates the character and social relations of the agrarian economy are of secondary importance. Where female (and male) farmers do become highly relevant is when we come to consider the role of food production itself within food strategies. Although the entitlement approach to food access, which focuses mainly on relations of distribution (Sen 1981), has been an important advance in elucidating the character of food deprivation, food production deficits may still be implicated in famine and hunger. The characteristics of the agrarian socio-economic systems and national economies of sub-Saharan Africa are critical in determining the comparative importance for the subcontinent of the contribution that food production makes to food availability. In sub-Saharan Africa agricultural policies and national food strategies must concern themselves directly with the character and conditions of food production for three main reasons.

Firstly, although this varies from country to country, domestic food production plays a central part in most of the national economies of sub-Saharan Africa. Because of the difficulty of raising foreign exchange earnings to the point where the purchase of cheaper imported food is possible on the scale required, domestic food production will continue to be important in economic planning.

Secondly, compared to other parts of the world, smallholder production by owner occupiers in sub-Saharan Africa makes up a much greater proportion of the forms of agrarian enterprises. This smallholder production is characterized by a variable degree of non-monetized self-provisioning, and is often set within a rural infrastructure which is markedly underdeveloped. The national food situation is determined both by the level of food production for self-provisioning and by factors influencing marketed food production in the smallholder sector. The incentives to market production are affected by the inadequacy of roads and transport, and also by the existence of market-places.

Thirdly, and finally, because of the history of agricultural investment and innovation, rural incomes will continue to depend on the production of food, until such time as agricultural investment produces a better profile of higher value crop mixes.

These characteristics which ensure that food production issues play a greater part in food security vary markedly between one African country and another. In each case the part that food production plays in increasing food security and food access is a matter for examination and never to be taken for granted. The way in which food production contributes to rural food security in Kenya may be very different from, say, Upper Volta. This examination needs to discriminate between the individual, household, and national levels, which then need to be integrated to produce a country perspective. That being said, there are few countries in the subcontinent where the conditions of smallholder production and the overall character of agrarian resource endowment are not significant aspects of food security problems.

In this chapter I wish to address these aspects of smallholder agricultural production from the particular perspective of the constraints and incentives to the women farmers of the subcontinent. It is not necessary to subscribe to the myth of feminization to recognize the importance of recent discussions which stress the significance for the productivity of African agriculture of the fact that production is undertaken by both women and men and that women's role within it is both little recognized and little understood (Lewis 1981; Dey 1984, 1985; Due and Mudenda 1984; Rogers 1980; Orstom 1985; Cloud 1986). Many recent studies of the peasant sector suggest that the conditions of the rural economy as they have developed in the last fifty years have placed on women a heavy burden of increasing work, often in deteriorating conditions (Kitching 1980; Henn 1984; Creevey 1986; Colson and Scudder 1988). Arguably, then, what I have termed the 'politicization of women's work' is directly related to changes in agricultural production and as well to increased comprehension of the problems that arise if women's work is ignored. These issues are addressed in this chapter in the following way.

In the first part I look at the character of contemporary rural women's work in sub-Saharan Africa, and its historical development. I show that there is considerable variation in women's role in agriculture and that descriptions of it in terms of dualistic models, especially those in which men are associated with the modern sector and women associated with, or, 'relegated to', an untransformed subsistence sector are misleading. I describe how the economic transformations characteristic of the twentieth century (mainly in the form of male migration, urban employment, and development of agrarian commodity production) have had a complex and varied effect on women's position in the farm household and on the sexual division of labour. I look closely at the way in which women's pre-colonial economic activities in the sexual division of labour took place within a structure of 'dual obligations' within the household. These were her obligations to work independently to produce an income or subsistence and at the same time to work for other members of the household in labour which was not directly remunerated (so-called family labour). I discuss how this dual responsibility has been affected by economic transformation, arguing that it has become increasingly difficult for women to undertake their independent farming, and that they have been progressively recruited into commodity production as family labour. This means that a woman has decreasing control over the proceeds of this production and in particular she is less able to protect the interests of her children.

I next turn to the part that development policies have played in these changes in rural women's work. One of the main themes here is how very often they appear to have worked to rural women's detriment. I argue that this is not only because of the 'invisibility' of women's work, which leads to a quite inadequate database from which to plan, but also because the economic modelling of most development planning seriously fails to capture the real conditions of women's farm work within the family. I point out that the farm household is often treated as a single economic unit and that women are incorporated into development projects as unpaid family labour. However the distributional patterns within the household are not changed in keeping with women's enhanced role as family labour. The evidence from evaluation studies of development projects tends to confirm the view that women farmers face resource problems for their independent farming, and incentive problems in their household farm work. I extend this argument by discussing in more detail the basis for women's economic decision making within the family, arguing that modelling based on purely economic considerations is inadequate. In the final section of the chapter I discuss various policy contradictions which arise out of a commitment to women's welfare in the context of the need to increase food production.

11.2 *Myths and counter-myths about the sexual division of labour*

'*Women grow all the food*': *what is female farming?*

Accounts of the role of women in agricultural production in sub-Saharan Africa have been marked by a tide of myth and counter-myth within which reality is difficult to discern. Until recently most agricultural planning and policy discussion has been dominated by only one of these myths. Although anthropological, historical, and microlevel case-studies have always testified to women's economic importance in the countryside, the planning discourse has treated women's work as wholly insignificant. Commonly the term 'farmer' was used to mean a man, and women's 'backyard farming' (or even subsistence production as a whole) was not the subject of agricultural policy. More recently we have seen the rise of a counter-myth—that of women's pre-eminence in sub-Saharan African food production—to the point that it is not uncommon to see it argued that women produce 60, 70, or even 80 per cent of sub-Saharan Africa's food (see, for example, FAO 1984). These claims have some polemical value. Nevertheless understanding African food production, and the role of women within it, is not advanced by generalized (and sometimes exaggerated) claims of this kind. There is an enormous variety in African women's role in food production and its relation to the rural household economy considered as a whole. This variety emerges not only out of the very different farming systems and patterns of agriculture which characterize sub-Saharan Africa, but also out of variation in the experience of the historical process of change, which has been so important in sub-Saharan Africa in the last century. Before I examine aspects of this historical record (in the next section), there are some important ideological and conceptual issues to be considered.

Emphasis on the female nature of sub-Saharan African food production has its modern genesis in the work of Esther Boserup (1970). Boserup character-ized sub-Saharan Africa as the great global area of female farming systems in which women, using 'traditional' (her term) hoe technology, have a substantial responsibility for the work of food production. She argued that the more productive 'traditional' farming technologies, and especially plough agri-culture, used mainly male labour. This association between gender and forms of 'traditional' technology took on new significance when, under the impact of state-directed innovation, the pace of technological change increased in the African countryside.

Subsequently there have been misgivings expressed about Boserup's ana-lysis. A number of recent discussions about African farming, notably those of Guyer (1983), Richards (1983b), and Wright (1983), have argued that it overstated the extent to which sub-Saharan African farming systems utilize female labour. Criticisms have also been made about the validity of the association she draws between which of the sexes does the work and whether hoes or ploughs are used 'traditionally' (Bryson 1981; Wright 1983; similar criticisms for South Asia in Agarwal 1985). Other writers have questioned her mode of explaining these gender associations within 'traditional' and 'modern' agricultural technologies (see Huntingdon 1975; Beneria and Sen 1981; Creevey 1986). Although Boserup's own writings are more subtle than stereo-typing sub-Saharan Africa as a single continuous female farming area, many popular and policy accounts now treat sub-Saharan African rural production as composed of 'female farming systems' in an exaggerated, stereotyped, and misleading way, citing her as their authority.

In some cases diagnosing sub-Saharan African farming systems as 'female' has served to invisibilize male labour input in farming. Indeed, Wright (1983) points out that when Boserup used the work of Baumann (1928) she played down his description of 'ancient patriarchal hoe cultures as a system in which male and female labour were mixed and balanced'. Although the most common male labour input in female hoe cultivation is for clearing the land, and there are many reports of the absence of this male labour making it difficult for women to farm, other apparently trivial inputs to the agricultural cycle (such as pest control) have been shown to be of considerable significance to agricultural yields in 'female farming areas'. 'Female' farming systems then, like their 'male' counterparts, are based on a complex interrelation of women's and men's work.

Notwithstanding this recognition that men also work in 'female' farming systems, not all sub-Saharan African farming can be characterized as even in this limited sense 'female'. Areas of traditional systems of grain production in which the dominant labour input to arable farming is from men are widespread and exist in environmentally and culturally significant areas. Similarly the association of women with hoes and men with ploughs in 'traditional' farming systems is overdrawn. For many hundreds of years a substantial amount of the labour time in farming has been performed by male farmers working with hoes. To a much lesser extent historical studies sometimes report women as using ploughs, while Wright's (1983) study of Southern Zambia and Venema's of Mali are examples in which women are found to use modern plough technology. Taking all these together, it may be concluded that, in relation to sub-Saharan Africa, the terms 'male' and 'female' farming systems on the whole conceal more than they reveal.

Nevertheless there have been major merits in the discussions generated by the idea of female farming. These have been firstly to emphasize the amount of productive work that women do; secondly rather crudely to draw attention to the variability of that role across the continent and within different farming systems; and thirdly to draw attention to the sexual division of labour as the basis of African agricultural organization. Some work on women's productive role goes beyond the simple assertion of its quantitative importance and explores its variability. Apart from the variability generated by differences in the experience of colonialism and commoditization (discussed below), ecological differences, slavery, and the development of trade all appear important. There do appear to be some broad associations between dominant crops, forms of social organization, and the sexual division of labour so that there are ecological or geographical areas in which specific crops seem to be associated with one sex or the other. However, these are area-specific patterns, and no one association is characteristic of the subcontinent as a whole. In examining these associations, Guyer (1983) has suggested that in some cases it is much less the technical and ecological aspects of the crops and farming systems than the historical development of cropping patterns, and the forms of labour organization that have been associated with these historical developments, which give rise to women's crops and men's crops. Work by Roberts (1985) covering francophone and anglophone West Africa shows that women's role in production in the pre-commodity economy varies according to the presence or absence of slave labour.

Another critical perspective which arises out of recent studies centring on women's work is the need to stress the importance of the total domestic economy as the context within which agricultural production is set. A good example of the significance of this more holistic approach to the domestic economy is to be found in Guyer's demonstration that the effects of the introduction of cocoa as a cash crop to two different ethnic groups differed not because the work that men and women did in farming differed but because their other economic activities were markedly different (Guyer 1980*b*). Members of rural households may trade, produce other goods such as pots or baskets, and this other work affects the profile of farming activity.[2]

The implication of these findings is, however, only influential at the margins of development planning and policy. Despite studies showing the importance to the family's well-being and welfare of such a multifarious set of household

---

[2] Hill (1986) and Kitching (1980) both stress the importance of this point in a wider context.

activities each of which consumes the labour time of household members, case-studies of the effect of development intervention still often exhibit a myopic concentration on agricultural production *per se* and much rural development planning is severely affected by failing to take the whole domestic economy into account. In this context farming systems research, in which some aspects of the household economy were seen to be linked in a systematic way, constituted an important conceptual advance, but recent discussions suggest that it remains an inadequate perspective from which to examine rural women's work (Richards 1986; University of Florida 1986; University of Wageningen 1988). It should also be noted here that despite the promise of new household economics which adopts a holistic approach to the domestic economy, it also contains significant limitations as an approach to the sub-Saharan farm household. (See especially discussion in Folbre 1986; Evans 1987). None of these approaches has assimilated the idea of the sexual division of labour as a conceptual tool.

The sexual division of labour

It is apparent from the earlier description of the relationship between female labour input and male labour input in farming systems that the sexual division of labour can operate not as a simple descriptive term, but as a core concept for the analysis of women's work (see Edholm, Harris, and Young 1977; Whitehead forthcoming *a*). As well as foregrounding detailed empirical enquiry into how the work between men and women is divided in all facets of the domestic economy, the concept of the sexual division of labour raises several analytical points about the interdependence and interrelation between men and women's work. It suggests that even in farming systems where women's work plays a large part, women's role in food production cannot be examined in isolation from the other work that men are engaged in. Where men and women are jointly engaged in farming, different crops and cropping patterns may exhibit quite different technical forms of the interrelation between men's tasks and women's tasks. The distinction I have made elsewhere (Whitehead 1981*b*, 1985) between sex sequential (i.e. crops produced by men and women working in sequence) and sex segregated (separate crops for each gender) patterns of relation between men's and women's tasks is very important in affecting the outcome of changes in agricultural practices. The concept of the sexual division of labour also draws attention to the issue of the social forms within which men and women are linked in such sexually ascribed tasks. There is an implicit assumption in much of the literature that the site of such divisions of labour is always the household or marriage (e.g. Sen 1985), but, of course, this need not be the case. Dey's study (further discussed in section 11.4) contains an example of women's work within the sexual division of labour being mainly for men in neighbouring households, and not part of the conjugal relationship (Dey 1981).

Understanding the sexual division of labour as a concept also assists in identifying its ideological character. Over and over again notions of sexual difference have been found to contain an important ideological component —that is to say that they may be more about what people believe than about what they do. This is especially the case when describing the past. But a sexual division of labour is rarely an unchanging prescription on human behaviour or, either contemporaneously or in the past, an immutable division of tasks between men and women. There are many examples of important historical shifts that have occurred in the balance and interlocking of men's and women's work, as well as numerous examples of more ephemeral departures from the conventions. The pattern of labour input into farming was almost certainly never as rigid as statements about who did what often imply, although there is some evidence that the sexual division of labour has rigidified. Wright (1983) argues that Toga men and women of the Southern Zambia plateau certainly did not work in sexually exclusive ways at the turn of the century. The ideological character of the sexual division of labour suggests that careful interpretation of descriptions of changes in its form may be needed. These several theoretical points provide a helpful interpretative frame when we come to consider another widespread myth about Africa's women farmers.

'Relegation to the subsistence sector'

Boserup also contributed to another myth: one which recognizes the centrality of the sexual division of labour to the rural economy as a whole and that women's agricultural work is important, but which holds a highly stereotyped and mistaken view of the nature of contemporary African agriculture and of the positions of men and women within it. Boserup argued strongly that economic transformation has produced a dichotomy in African agriculture in which men are associated with a 'modern' sector while women are associated with an untransformed sector in which they use 'traditional' technology, to produce mainly for subsistence. This has produced the myth that 'modernization relegates women to the subsistence sector'. It is very common indeed to find twentieth-century economic changes being understood as having created a double dichotomy in the rural division of labour. The dichotomy is on the one hand between subsistence and cash cropping agriculture; and on the other hand between women and men who, respectively, work within these sectors.

This model embodies a dualistic view of African agriculture as divided into two self-contained, technically and economically different sectors, between which there is presumed to be a competitive relationship because agrarian resources have been, and are being, drained from food production into cash crop production. When women's work in the sexual division of labour is taken into account this model becomes overlain with a gender dimension. The archetypal female farmer scratches the impoverished earth around her homestead with a hoe to produce 'subsistence' crops. Her husband, meanwhile, manages the complex technology of hybrid seeds, small-scale irrigation schemes, tractors, etc. to produce export agricultural crops, and her son is a migrant labourer in the urban sector. So powerful is this image in contemporary thought that this structural economic dualism is often conceptualized as lying at the heart of the relations of men and women within the peasant household as well as at the heart of the link between the food crisis and the sexual division of labour.

The prevalent and mistaken dualism is made up of a number of interrelated sets of stereotypes, many of which separately employ dualism of one sort or another. It exaggerates, as already discussed, the extent of female farming, and suggests a greater segregation between the male and female labour forces than exists. It also exaggerates the division and competition between cash crop and subsistence crop sectors, and misunderstands the nature of cash crop production as well as of the so-called 'subsistence' sector in contemporary agriculture.

Food crops versus cash crops?

A recent review of various approaches to the food crisis in Africa points out that 'a strong current of thought in the literature holds that the inability of most sub-Saharan countries to produce sufficient food is primarily attributable to the dualistic structure of their agrarian economies' (Tabatabai 1986). In this view, an agriculture polarized in terms of its form of production and techniques is a consequence initially of the dependent development suffered by sub-Saharan Africa during its colonial history. Agricultural investment was biased towards agricultural export crops and food production was neglected. The economic imperatives faced by post-colonial governments have continued these overall policies and the dualistic theory holds that currently there exists 'a conspicuous division between large scale, relatively capital intensive production of a narrow range of export crops, and a labour intensive peasant sector which provides the bulk of the populations' food requirements' (Lochfie 1975).

In his examination of the plausibility of agrarian dualism in this sense being the source of the food crisis in sub-Saharan Africa, Tabatabai's review (1986) of agricultural production data suggests they do not show that during the last two decades (when the food crisis has deepened) the export sector has been thriving at the expense of the food sector. Tabatabi points out that although the generalization that the food sector was discriminated against in policies and practices 'captures the essence of colonial and post colonial government policies', the further implication of a sharp division between the way in which production is organized between food and export crops is not tenable. There are many countries and regions 'where the bulk of export crops are produced along with food crops by small holders using equally primitive technologies'. There are also a number of countries (e.g. Zambia, Zimbabwe, and Kenya) in which food production itself is not confined to 'backward' smallholder production, but is produced on large farms which employ wage labour and use modern technology. If the modern sector is not unambiguously about export crops and export crops are not unambiguously produced by large-scale farming, then ideas about the nature of the the smallholder food-producing sector need also to be re-examined.

There have been many repeated, and trenchant, criticisms of generalized notion of the peasantry, and of the ideological character of many accounts of peasant production. Hill (1986:9), for example, regards 'peasant in its contemporary usage [as] the semantic successor to native, incorporating all its condescending, derogatory and even racist overtones'. She points to the initial ambiguity in the notion of subsistence, and identifies critical misconceptions about the land and labour supply and economic imperatives of those African farmers who grow some of their own food for consumption. Ellis (1988), while wishing to retain a category of peasant untainted by these misconceptions and ideologies, looks at many of the same issues while Williams (1987) discusses the ideological dimensions to the identification of the character of African peasantries in Hyden's work. Despite these recent restatements, notions of subsistence and stereotypes of peasants are still widely used, especially in general discussions of the food crisis.

Presumptions about the character of 'subsistence' and/or 'peasant' production have one origin in the laudable aim of trying to specify ways in which decision making might be different for farmers who produce some of their consumption needs. However another source is the problematic nature of most economists' discussions of the relation between market and non-market activities despite the insights central to the idea of the new household economics. In looking at sub-Saharan African smallholders we need to retain the following ideas: that production for own consumption is an important, *but variable*, part of production objectives; that the labour supplied to the farm enterprise is largely (*though not entirely*) only indirectly remunerated; and that as well as producing raw products, self-provisioners are committed to undertaking the transformational processes which produce consumable food. One thing that must be abandoned is the idea that the subsistence sector is synonymous with a non-market sector. Although a high proportion of food consumed by self-provisioning farmers does not enter or derive from the market, markets are important in the self-provisioning sector. In the conditions of agricultural production in sub-Saharan Africa, self-provisioning has normally been met by consuming own grown product plus that obtained in local market exchanges. Perhaps more importantly, most self-provisioning farmers in the current agrarian structure of sub-Saharan Africa sell food. In fact there is considerable evidence that the poorer you are the more coercively you are engaged in selling food (Bernstein 1979; Williams 1980; Hill 1982; Whitehead 1984). This of course makes a complete nonsense of the apparently irradicable economist's habit of referring to that portion of the product which self-provisioners sell as 'surplus'. There should be no suggestion that subsistence needs are met before surplus is marketed, nor that the divide between market and non-market is the same as the divide between production for self-consumption and production for exchange.

Ideological 'feminization'

One of the problems with the use of the term 'subsistence production' to refer to the production of food for household consumption is the ideological character of the label. Ideological underpinnings are also apparent in the frequent use of the term 'domestic' to refer to these forms of partially self-provisioning household production. Labelling, as many commentators do, self-provisioning as non-market and domestic in character smuggles in a number of other meanings.[3] There is an assumption that self-provisioning does not need to be planned for—an instinct for survival and familial ideologies will ensure that output is maintained. But the term 'domestic' is also associated with women. The importance of women's role in sub-Saharan African farming is then incorporated into the dualisms by assuming that it is primarily the women in the household who engage in its non-monetized production. Any monetized production women engage in is thought to generate small cash returns used for daily family needs. But I would go further than this in attributing ideological force to the concept of the domestic. Use of the term 'domestic' often accentuates an idea not only that this production is done by women but also that women are bound into the family in certain ways—that domestic mores and values determine behaviour. It can for example imply that because within the domestic sphere women have a strong interest in their children's welfare they are less risk taking, less innovative, or less commercial in orientation. It is not a far step from thinking this way about women's domestic production to seeing 'subsistence' production as being bound up with femininity in a larger sense—that is as linked to the difficulty of understanding female rationality. I would argue that many contemporary discussions of the food crisis in sub-Saharan Africa manifest a powerful and insidious ideological feminization of food production for subsistence. The idea that the subsistence production is feminine serves to mystify the empirical and analytical accessibility of non-market or household-based production. This ideological 'feminization' enhances a view that it is difficult to understand the structure of constraints and incentives, or even the 'logic' itself of subsistence production.

Thus far I have argued that the idea of sub-Saharan African food production being overwhelmingly female in its labour input is a myth. I have instead emphasized the need to examine the interlinkage and interdependence between men's and women's work within the sexual division of labour, stressing its variability and the complexity of changes within it as the economic transformations of the twentieth century have progressed. It is these processes of historical change in the conditions of women's farm work which I wish to

[3] For an interesting more general discussion of this point see Harris (1981).

examine in the next section. The myth of rural women's relegation to the subsistence sector rests additionally on a set of heavily stereotyped views about the historical processes of incorporation into the world economy that sub-Saharan Africa has experienced.

11.3. The historical transformation of rural women's work in the twentieth century

The stereotype that sub-Saharan African women have been relegated to the subsistence part of a dualistic economy composed of separate, and to some extent competing, subsistence and market sectors rests on a combination of two main ideas about woman's position in the contemporary rural household: either that she is the 'left-behind wife' in a semi-proletarianized rural household from which the wage labourer husband is absent while she runs a subsistence farm in an uncommercialized rural economy; or that she is a wife in a peasant household which itself straddles the two sectors, so that she is responsible for self-provision, while her husband produces for the market. Criticizing the accuracy of these views requires explorations of both the form of women's economic roles in the farming household and the kind of economic transformation that Africa has witnessed.

Women's dual economic role in the farming household

One of the most important social facts about women's work which is hidden by the term 'female farming' relates to the question of within what social relations this work is done. The idea of a 'female' farming system is markedly ambiguous about how the sexual division of labour is linked to the organization of production. In particular it does not specify whether women work in agriculture as farmers in their own right, or on farms that belong to others, and notably, of course, on farms which belong to men.

Some of the implications of women farming independently are: that they have access to land and other means of production in their own right; that they can control their own pace and intensity of work; that they may have power over the disposal of the products and income from their farming. Conversely, working on the farms of others implies: an absence of independent access to the means of production; a pace and intensity of work which is determined at the very least by decisions which have been taken at much earlier points of the farming cycle or season, and possibly directly by the owner of the farm; probably no full rights to the farming product and income therefrom. How a woman is remunerated for this labour on the farms of others depends on the relationship which recruits her to that work (which could be wage labour relationship) as well as on the customary forms of reward within some of these relationships. Much work of this kind comes under the conventional economists' category of family labour, i.e. it is performed by women for members of their own household. As we shall see, the terms and conditions under which women do this work are very varied. Although it is generally not directly remunerated it occasionally may be.[4]

Across the variety of farming systems, ecological areas, and socio-cultural systems which make up sub-Saharan Africa, there is considerable variation in whether, within the sexual division of labour, women's farming work is undertaken independently or as household labour. Nevertheless it is fair to generalize that women's contemporary productive role in the smallholder family combines both kinds of work and that it is, in essence, a dual one. Most women work independently of other members of the household, having separate access to land and other resources for farming or other economic activities, at the same time as contributing to household production as unremunerated family labour.

The roots of this dual role lie in the form of obligations between married men and women in the economies and societies of the nineteenth century prior to modern transformation. At that time sub-Saharan African societies were very varied but lay on a continuum between closed economies, which were based on kinship collectivities producing entirely for self-provisioning and internal markets, and complex forms of pre-industrial state in which socio-economic differentiation, usually involving slavery and considerable production for exchange, had developed. Although, in societies with more complex social divisions of labour, slavery and forms of stratification played an important part in production, in all of them domestic and conjugal relations, plus kinship relations in the widest sense, were important economically.

Within these structures, four features of the sexes' position were important. Firstly men's and women's access to resources was symmetrical. A woman's resource rights in the pre-commodity economy were based on her position within the kinship structure and the household, and they were guaranteed by the forms of authority and power within these systems. However, although they were symmetrical in form, in terms of capacity to command and effective possession they were very different from and usually very much less extensive than were men's. This was most marked in societies where accumulation had occurred, as for example in bridewealth societies, where women never had the same rights to bridewealth livestock as did men.

A second important feature is that the resources of husband and wife were not merged. As Goody (1976) has examined in a detailed and illuminating way, no single conjugal fund or common conjugal property was established on marriage within most of the societies of the subcontinent, and this is in marked contrast to peasant practice in Europe and Asia. There is a lively and

---

[4] The microeconomics of resource holding within African rural households are complex and very varied. While the complete merging of the economic resources of husband and wife is uncommon, any implication in this description of its opposite—namely of complete economic separation—is to be strenuously avoided. For ethnographic descriptions see Poewe (1981), Longhurst (1982).

considerable literature discussing this characteristic economic separation in African rural households (see Guyer 1981 and Whitehead 1984). Its wider implications as an aspect of kinship structures are discussed at length in Goody (1976), while Dwyer (1983) looks at its implications for women's access to income and poverty.

Thirdly, the responsibilities for providing for children's well-being were divided up between husband and wife as father and mother. Societies differed in the extent to which the responsibility for feeding children was that of the mother, although in many cases it was hers solely. It was this responsibility for their children which required wives to be economically independent to some degree. It can be seen as structurally linked to polygyny.

Fourthly, marriage generally obliged women to work for households into which they had married, and often directly for their husbands. These rights over a wife's labour were more or less extensive, and while she usually worked in return for generalized rights to maintenance and sustenance they did sometimes entail her direct remuneration. A wife's rights to the use of the labour of male members of the household were generally less extensive, although a husband often had considerable labour obligations to his in-laws. These generalizations over labour use are particularly affected by socio-economic variability. High status, or wealthy, or slave-owning, women, or, in some cases, senior wives in polygamous households, could gain access to other labour in various ways, and used other labour to fulfil their obligations as wives (Creevey 1986; Roberts 1985).

In essence, then, contemporary rural women's dual economic role within the farm household derives from a pre-existing dual role within the pre-commodity economy. The analytical difference between these two economic roles is critical in understanding the factors affecting women's farming production. In so far as the social relations under which women work are not the same in the two cases, the factors affecting these two kinds of work may not be identical.[5] It is also critical that the economic transformation of the twentieth century has affected these two economic roles in different ways, and has had in many cases a marked effect on the balance between them.

The character of twentieth-century rural economic transformation

The stereotype that women have been relegated to a subsistence sector also rests on very over-general views about the impact of colonial policies on rural economies, especially in relation to the changes that were brought about in the use of male labour. Colonial policies are popularly thought to have mainly used rural areas as male labour reserves for urban migrant labour, or as the source of African labour for the expanding capitalist production on white settler farms and for the expansion of smallholder production of certain desired products (e.g. cocoa, palm oil). In this view the pre-colonial food economy remained

[5] This point has been discussed more fully in Whitehead (1981b and forthcoming a).

untouched. Recent studies in agrarian history have begun to uncover the extent to which all these changes had important effects on the food economy. The development of wage labour, and the growth of cash income for farm families, meant that the internal food market expanded markedly in many countries. Areas specializing in food production for the regional market, often in the hands of women, developed (Young 1977; Muntemba 1982; Vaughan 1986; Guyer 1987; Bryceson 1988). Kitching (1980), for example, shows women in Nyanza Province in Kenya producing maize for the market as early as 1918. There were thus very important changes in the sexual division of labour being brought about by a combination of all these changes, but these cannot adequately be described as women 'being relegated to the subsistence sector'.

One reason for the expansion of women's food farming was undoubtedly the absence of men working elsewhere. Male labour migration is found in many African rural communities today, and it builds on the previous construction of some rural areas as colonial labour reserves. Obviously this profoundly important characteristic affected the viability and development of sub-Saharan African agriculture. A number of anthropological studies of rural societies and economies during the colonial era examined their cultural and social organizational capacity to adapt to the absence of men. These early studies have recently been reassessed in Stichter (1985). She suggests that the major findings were that male migration had the effect of bringing women's hitherto 'under-utilized' labour into production, and that there were important changes in crops, techniques, and forms of labour organization as well as in marriage relations (Phillips 1953; Skinner 1965). In some cases the rural labour supply was found to be inadequate (Richards 1937). Recent work confirms many of these findings (Hay 1976; Bukh 1979; Pottier 1988).

However, as Stichter (1985) points out, the effects of rural male labour migration have been far from uniform. In particular, views that women's farming, or the feminization of farming as a result of the absence of men, goes hand in hand with agricultural stagnation have undergone something of a shift as a result of more recent scholarship. Stichter argues forcibly for the need, in interpreting the effects of rural labour migration, to take into account differences in the agrarian situations within which the loss of labour is/was occurring. In agreeing with her, I would wish to emphasize that the factors to be considered include not only the nature of the farming system; the degree of development of internal rural markets; cultural aspects of the sexual division of labour; the level, regularity, and length of time for which wages were earned; but above all the degree, kind, and pace of commoditization of the rural economy itself. One of the main problems with many earlier studies of labour migration was that they ignored the way in which commercial development in the agrarian economy itself, including but not confined to the production of food for sale mentioned above, was taking place side by side with feminization of food production and male labour migration.

Recent work in agrarian and agricultural history has also considerably enlarged our understanding of the complexity and variability of transformations taking place in the rural production systems of sub-Saharan Africa during this century.[6] While it is true that early colonial policies were essentially discriminatory, so that agricultural export crops were promoted (with investment, crop innovations, and improved agronomic techniques) at the expense of food production which was left unimproved, subsequent colonial and post-colonial policies, plus the investment strategies of indigenous farmers themselves, have resulted in a much more varied pattern of agricultural development. Commoditization of African production—i.e. the development of production for sale within agrarian households as farm enterprises—developed over different periods of time, proceeded slowly in some places, and fairly quickly in others, but mainly at an accelerating rate. It entailed many and different kinds of changes in agricultural practice and techniques, and in farm labour organization. In any given area the character of the transformation and its pace varied according to environmental and ecological factors and to the character of the colonial policies, but also according to the form of the pre-colonial economic system, including the prior degree of production for exchange within it and, associated with this, the form of the social divisions of labour, including those based on gender.

In sum, the character and degree of commercialization of farm enterprises in contemporary rural areas varies very markedly. It includes areas of fully commercial food production (e.g. parts of Zambia), although many African agricultural economies are still dominated by smallholder farming. These smallholders themselves differ markedly in the balance between crops grown for sale and self-provisioning; in the levels of productivity and techniques used; and in the sexual division of labour and reliance on female labour. Some smallholder farms employ wage labour as well as family labour, use highly productive techniques, and produce mainly cash crops. They border on the category of purely commercial farms. Yet others are primarily focused on production for own consumption and these tend to be operated at low levels of productivity and to use mainly unremunerated forms of labour. In almost all of these farms, off-farm incomes make an important contribution to household budgets and in some cases this is in the form of income from migrant labour. It is this smallholder sector and women's role in production within it that holds the key to African nations' food security.

The effects on rural women

The agricultural innovation and intensification experienced by the smallholder sector as a whole in the last fifty years has produced considerably increased incomes for some households. The combination of labour migration, investment in agriculture, and increased commodity production has been

[6] For a synthesis of these studies see Freund (1984).

accompanied by changes in the form of socio-economic inequality. The organization of rural production has been restructured around smallholder households and away from more wide-ranging social relationships. In some cases, e.g. where rural slavery has disappeared, this has entailed the levelling down of pre-colonial hierarchies. In many other cases it has produced economic inequality. The extent and character of this varies according to the nature of the crops produced, the terms on which access to resources is obtained, and access to off-farm incomes. The interrelation between these processes has been the subject of much academic research, although relatively little has examined the effects on women (Kitching 1980; Berger and Robertson 1986; Bujra 1986).

These socio-economic changes have produced considerable differences in the life trajectories of Africa's female farmers, as they have for men, and the forms in which women experience these processes of socio-economic differentiation are somewhat different. Policy and planning need to be sensitive to these emerging forms of female socio-economic differentiation. They mean, for example, that in those widespread areas of the subcontinent which in the nineteenth century lacked marked socio-economic differentiation, women can no longer be treated as a homogeneous category. Polarization is increasingly apparent, in many rural districts, between women who have benefited from increased rural incomes and those who have been marginalized as a consequence of the changed distribution of rural resources. Women have benefited as commercial farmers in their own right, or as wives of successful commercial farmers; and there have also been improved opportunities for trade and other forms of production, e.g. beer brewing. Although some accounts exist of women who manage large farms, or are commercial farmers (Hill 1963, Kitching 1980, Cheater 1981, Wright 1983), these are relatively few. They are not the focus of attention in this chapter which confines itself to women within the smallholder sector. However, much larger numbers of women belong to another developing stratum of rural households—namely that which absolutely lacks the resources to meet consumption needs. One of its main characteristics is that it contains a growing number of female-headed households. Recent work has emphasized how important these households are among the rural poor in sub-Saharan Africa (Yousseff and Hetler 1984; UNICEF poverty studies). Rural women are more vulnerable to resource depletion and resource loss than are rural men. There is now a large literature which stresses both male migrant labour and the effects of socio-economic differentiation in the countryside as a cause of this growth of poor female-headed households. (Safilios-Rothschild 1985; Kassoudji and Mueller 1983; Cliffee 1976; Jiggins 1980). The loss of the social security system provided by the more collective forms of responsibility in the pre-commodity kinship system (Guyer 1981) means that many women are increasingly to be found working for their neighbours in return for food (Pottier 1985a) and in other areas as wage labour.

Men's and women's experiences of the development of production for exchange were radically different. To a very large degree, and primarily as a result of their greater command over land, labour, and capital resources in the pre-colonial economy, many men were independent agents in this revolution. Conversely it became much more difficult for women to pursue their independent farming, at the same time as it became all the more important for them to do so as male labour seeped out of the self-provisioning sector to urban waged work and to commercial production. As more land was taken under cultivation and improved agronomic techniques were introduced, women's independent farming came under increasing pressure at the same time as there was an increasing demand for women to work on cash crops as unremunerated labour. The pressure on women's independent farming derives from a number of factors. Their initial comparative lack of overall resources has been critical in determining the ability of women to respond to new economic opportunities (see Pala 1980; Kitching 1980; Clark 1981; Whitehead 1984).

Contemporary studies find women complaining of lack of land and capital and document the disadvantaged position of women within the new market- and state-codified systems of land allocation (Pala 1979; Muntemba 1982; Caplan 1984; Women in Nigeria 1985). Resettlement or irrigation schemes entailing large changes in the land use seem most often adversely to affect women's land rights to a serious extent. They also have labour problems not only because men are away but also because they are less liable to mobilize wide-ranging social relations in the rural areas, including political links, for exchange work parties (Guyer 1983; Whitehead 1984; Pottier 1985b).

Simultaneously with these difficulties about women's independent farming, the increased cash production of male smallholders demands that their wives do more work as family labour. This is widely reported in microstudies (see Monsted 1976; Pala 1980; Muntemba 1982; Colson and Scudder 1988). These studies also report that in many cases the system of intrahousehold distribution has not changed to take account of the changed character of the labour that women perform. One effect of production for exchange is that what was once circulating within the family as goods now comes in as money to the husband. Norms about the sharing of money are rarely the same as norms about the sharing of, say, food. Distribution of income within the family becomes an intense field of dispute (e.g. Monsted 1976). At the same time the kinds of transactions that take place within many sub-Saharan African families are predicated on women continuing to fulfil their responsibilities especially for their children by independent work (McMillan 1986). This domestic resource separation, plus an obligation to do unremunerated labour, is a situation fraught with potential conflict between husbands and wives (Roberts 1979; Whitehead 1981a, 1981b, forthcoming b; Dwyer 1983; Jones 1986). This point will be returned to in the next section, but here it should be noted that the severity of this problem has become particularly clear in the last ten to fifteen years with the effect of the world recession on agrarian incomes. During this time, the economic pressures on the partially self-provisioning farmer have been felt more and more by women members of the household.

In this description I have tried to stress that the effects of economic transformation on rural women's farming work have been complex. Differences in the economic resources and power of men and women in the pre-commodity economy have been built on and magnified as the commoditization of rural labour time has been extended and deepened. At the same time important differences between women have emerged as rural differentiation has increased. Finally economic changes have acted differently upon the two kinds of work women do within the household which I have identified as constituting a dual economic role.

I have tried to depict this complexity in Table 11.1, where women's agricultural work is distinguished both according to whether it is family labour or independent farming and according to the type of household to which women belong in terms of position in the class structure as well as gender of the head. The table depicts women working in the commercial farm sector as wage workers, as independent commercial farmers, as farm managers for absentee husbands, and as unremunerated family labour. As wives, women do all four kinds of farming, but as female heads of household they are either working on their own account or wage employed. Most women are however in the smallholder sector, producing food crops and cash crops. Women are wholly responsible for family food production in some areas, but in others they share that responsibility with their husbands. They also provide a substantial proportion of the labour input into cash cropping (which may be of crops also used for food). This may be on their own fields or on those of others, notably of husbands. While they largely work with unimproved techniques and inputs on food crops for consumption, they may well be working with modernized inputs

Table 11.1 Types of rural women's agricultural work

	Independent farming	Labour for others
In smallholder production (producing for self-consumption and for sale.)	1. on own account as smallholders' wives 2. on own account as female heads of household	1. unremunerated 'family labour' 2. labour in kind or for cash for husbands, kin, and neighbours (esp. if female-headed households)
In commercial production (producing for sale)	1. own account farmers as wives 2. own account farmers as female heads of household	1. managers for absent husbands 2. casual or wage labour (wives or female heads of household) 3. unremunerated family labour

in the cash sector (Wright 1983). They also retain a very substantial responsibility for a wide variety of domestic tasks which entail essential transformations of raw commodities into food.

What this static account belies, however, is an important set of contradictory pressures on women's work which have been triggered by the historical process of the development of production for sale within farming households. Understanding the factors which today affect women's willingness and capacity to increase their work in farming depends critically on understanding the pushes and pulls of this set of contradictory processes. Because of the pressure on a woman's resource holding, and the demands on her labour time of production for exchange, which occur without commensurate changes in intrahousehold allocation and distribution, considerable strain has been introduced in the balance between each part of women's dual economic role within the family. This emphasizes how important it is to analyse not only emerging class relations, but also domestic and household relations, as the setting for rural women's work.

11.4. *Development policies and women's economic role*

The preceding discussion has given a broadly historical account of the effects of economic transformation on rural women in sub-Saharan Africa. In this section I wish to concentrate exclusively on planned economic change to examine situations in which direct political intervention in the rural economy has taken place. This discussion focuses on the role of administrative and political intervention in bringing about changes in the sexual division of labour, and on the practices of agricultural and development policy. I shall mainly examine the findings from a growing, and increasingly sophisticated, literature which evaluates the impact on African rural women of specific development projects.[7] But, since most development projects directly addressing themselves to women are concerned with welfare issues and not employment or income generation (see Feldman 1981; Dixon 1982; Buvinic 1984), the projects I am considering are not women's projects but largely the indirect effects on women of development projects which have been designed to increase rural productivity and/or rural incomes overall.

Sexual discrimination in agricultural services
At the most general level, examination of national and international development policy and planning practice suggests that men's attitudes, whether as

---

[7] This section is based on the following sources: Brain (1976); Bryson (1981); Burfisher and Horenstein (1985); Carney (1988); Conti (1979); Dey (1981); Dixon (1980); Jackson (1985); Johnson (1988); Jones (1986); Kandiyoti (1985); Lewis (1984); McMillan (1986, 1987); Palmer (1985a, 1985b); Spiro (1984, 1985); Vail and White (1977); von Bulow and Sorensen (1988).

planners, extension agents, or fellow farmers, are a very considerable stumbling block to women farmers' efforts to gain access to critical knowledge and inputs to improve their productivity. One significant finding in the literature is that of widespread straightforward discrimination against women. Within the extension services and agricultural innovation practices, for example, a large number of attitudes and practices coalesce to produce what amounts to a refusal to recognize women's role in agriculture as pertaining to the 'modern' sector. This is the counterpart of what I identified earlier as the myth that women's farming is in backward, low-productivity production of food for family consumption.

The most systematic study of discrimination is that carried out by Kathleen Staudt in Western Kenya (1975–6; 1978; 1979; 1985). She examined many facets of the services in relation to rural women, and in particular made careful study of the contact of extension workers with farmers and its effects on their farming. She noted, among other things, that in a district which had little contact with extension workers the productivity of men and women was about the same, whereas in a district with extension workers, the productivity of women had declined. She also examined samples of farms run by heads who were essentially the same in all respects, except their gender, and found that farms with male heads were four times more likely to have been visited by an extension worker than were female-headed ones. She also found that 'capable women were being ignored for non-innovative men'. She argued that greater resources in the agricultural delivery systems have a positive impact on innovation—but only for male farmers. Women farmers adopt hybrid maize *more* when there is *less* agricultural extension work, and rely on informal women's groups to learn the appropriate techniques. 'Once a farming population becomes more dependent on service, after a period of systematic neglect in support services or valuable aid such as loans, women's performance deteriorates.'

These findings amount to marked gender discrimination which is nevertheless of a fairly simple kind—the bias towards male farmers in agricultural extension services. More general studies suggest that there are few agricultural extension services directed at women, who are mainly the recipients of extension in the home economics field (Feldman 1981; Bryson 1980; Ashby 1981; Jackson 1985). Very few women farmers are contacted by agricultural extension workers (Fortmann 1981; Gaobepe and Mwenda 1980; Staudt 1974–5). The staff of agricultural extension services are overwhelmingly male (Safilios-Rothschild 1985; Fortmann 1981). This lack of attention directed to women is not because they are inferior farmers. Different studies show that they are neither less productive, less efficient, nor less modern than their male counterparts (Moock 1976; Fortmann 1981; Staudt 1979).

The sources of this systematic bias are many. Some seem to arise from ideas about men and women in the rural culture (Fortmann, discussing a situation in Tanzania, makes the illuminating comment, 'the conventional wisdom that women cannot reason as well as men reduces any incentive for working with women'), as well as from the strong bias towards men in state agricultural services. There is a very long history to the neglect by state planners and policy makers of women farmers. Colonial agricultural extension policies all concentrated exclusively on men and in many places this has continued in the post-colonial period (Muntemba 1982). It is of course part of a much wider and extremely sorry story in relation to state practices and women. This broader field includes the history of technological rural innovation, which until recently has been resolutely male orientated, and the wider content of educational provision for girls and women as a whole, as well as the central role of ideologies about femininity and sex roles within this. The sex bias of mission and colonial education is well researched but there are few studies of colonial and post-colonial ideologies and practices in relation to women's work.

Whatever the relative part played by pre-colonial and colonially inspired sex stereotypes, it is very important to recognize that contemporary international planning ideologies not only do very little to combat them, but are also themselves the site of highly stereotypical ideas about the roles of the sexes, as well as about femininity and masculinity. However, because of the often assumed natural quality of sex differences, and the assumption that conceptual and classificatory categories are sex blind (that is are suitable for examining both men's and women's behaviour), many of these values are hard to see. I have put this generalization in an assertive form because there is a strong take-for-granted quality in the stereotyping which underlies many conceptual problems apparent in both analytical and empirical investigations of gender differences. It seems to me that this is the inescapable conclusion to be drawn from the examples examined below.

The invisibility of rural women's work

One of the most significant examples of stereotyping about sex roles lies in the various treatments of rural women's work in international planning circles. At the project level this leads to the following findings in evaluation studies. In designing projects, planners by and large markedly fail to appreciate the extent of women's work in agricultural production in sub-Saharan Africa. In too many reported cases male farmers receive the inputs and extension advice for crops which only women grow and are responsible for. There is also a widespread failure to predict that innovations in one part of the farming system will have effects on the 'invisibilized' female labour that goes into other kinds of production. The way that new agricultural practices may make the subsistence or food crop production that women do very much more difficult or less rewarding is unexamined. However, in addition to the neglect of women's productive activities in agriculture there is also a wholesale neglect of the economic significance to household welfare of women's productivity and effectiveness in off-farm activities and also of course in the reproductive work of the farm household (for examples see n. 7). For example, Burfisher and

Horenstein (1985) predict the effect of some planned development on the Nigerian Tiv farm households. They point out that the criteria for project success were based on aggregate statistics for agricultural output, productivity, and economic return which were biased towards cash crops and household heads. They thus failed to take account of most of the work which Tiv women did.

The initial issue raised by this invisibilization is the relatively simple one of the difficulties in measuring rural women's work. The invisibilization of women's work in national statistics has been widely reported and discussed (Beneria 1981, 1982; Anker 1983; United Nations 1984; Instraw 1986; Dixon-Mueller and Anker 1988). A recent comprehensive study by Dixon-Mueller for the ILO has examined the reasons for the underreporting of women's work in agricultural statistics, especially those produced using ILO labour force participation conventions (Dixon-Mueller 1985). She argues firstly that international standards of what are work, employment, and production are biased towards urban and developed countries' notions of these activities. She points out that they are particularly not designed for enumerating self-employment, seasonal and casual work, or household production of non-market goods and services. In sub-Saharan Africa these biases are particularly significant and are relevant to the work of both men and women in the agricultural sector. They 'invisibilize' women's labour input more because women are more likely to be doing seasonal, casual, or non-market productive work. Measuring rural work depends then on measuring goods and services produced for self-consumption. Dixon-Mueller argues that farm censuses are not consistent in what they treat as self-consumption production and what not. This has important gender implications in sub-Saharan Africa in that women's economic activities are disproportionately found in the non-market sector, where they are more than likely to be underrecorded.

Dixon-Mueller also points out that few efforts are made to counter the potential bias against recording women's work entailed in the near universal practice of interviewing the head of the household for information about the work of all household members.[8] In male-headed households, the nature of women's work, especially where the sexual division of labour creates separate male and female economic spheres, may mean that men simply do not know about women's economic activities, and hence cannot report them.

Men may, however, have other reasons for underreporting than ignorance. The lack of significance attached to women's work in the culture at large may lead to it being ignored (see e.g. Pittin 1985). A good example of this is the use of the term 'garden' to describe women's farms. There are many widespread cultural evaluations that what women do is somehow not 'work' or not 'farming'. In particular the cultural evaluation of women's work as 'domestic work' or 'housework' is responsible for considerable underenumeration. As

---

[8] This is discussed more extensively in Hill (1986).

Dixon-Mueller says: 'because male interviewers and male and female respondents frequently consider many of the things that women do as "housework" regardless of their intrinsic nature, tasks that for men are labelled economic activity may not be so for women'.

I have argued earlier that one form of women's work which is particularly subject to forms of cultural evaluation is that which women do as 'family labour'. Dixon-Mueller finds not only that family labour is frequently culturally 'invisibilized' but also that statistical conventions are extremely variable in their treatment of it. Yet as we have seen earlier the obligation to do unremunerated household work is an important aspect of women's farming work in sub-Saharan Africa. One of the main issues behind women's under-enumeration as members of the agricultural workforce identified by Dixon-Mueller is classifying and enumerating this family labour. 'At the heart of the confusion [over how many women are in the agricultural work force] is the question of whether a woman who works unpaid on the family holding is counted as a member of the labour force or not.'

The main lesson to be drawn from Dixon-Mueller's study is that in order to capture statistically women's input to agriculture, it is necessary to revise our conceptualizations of what work is to take account of the particular character of Third World agriculture and to take account of the conditions of women's work. This revision must include the recognition of seasonal and casual work as having a central place in many farming systems; measuring the production of non-market goods and services; being careful to include all the productive activities in the measurement of farm work (for example care of animals); and devising ways of measuring family labour. Dixon-Mueller concludes that ways of collecting statistics which do try to take these features into account produce from two to ten times as many female agricultural workers as do censuses using more conventional criteria.

Economic modelling and women's work in partial self-provisioning

At the beginning of this section I described how evaluation studies had uncovered a set of linked problems in the failure of rural development projects to plan for women's work in the farm household. Perceptions of women's work are filtered through culturally specific rural ideologies of what work is, under what relations work is performed, and who 'works'. Within them, it seems that women's work as family labour is so often not seen as work because it is performed within a sexual division of labour based on household and family relationships. It is regarded as an essential part of a woman's obligations as wife, as mother, and as daughter—that is, it is not seen separately as 'work' but as a continuation of her primary social roles. In many cases what invisibilizes women's work as 'family labour' is its 'family' or 'domestic' character. Equally, however, this range of cultural evaluations within the rural community interacts with planning and policy discourses which themselves treat women's work as family labour not qualifying them to be recorded as members of the labour force. In other words planning and policy discourses contain their own ideologies about 'women', about 'work' and the 'domestic'. Considered in this wider sense, these values lead not only to inadequate measurement, but also to the forms of inadequate modelling which underlie the linked set of failures identified above. They lead, that is, to conceptualizations of women's work, especially in the context of partial self-provisioning, which, because they fail to capture its empirical reality, are poor predictive tools.

Since sub-Saharan African rural production is often smallholder production which combines production for sale with production for own consumption, peasants must necessarily be able to manipulate the interface between market and non-market economic forms and decisions. They make decisions in which both market and non-market modes of meeting consumption needs are intermeshed and they must choose an appropriate mix of market and non-market modes of organizing production. Much economics is poorly designed for modelling this state of affairs. Subsistence or non-market production is often described as taking place on the 'family farm', and within 'domestic' relations. Apart from the assumption that self-provisioning does not need to be planned for—that as part of domestic life it can be left to take care of itself, the idea of the domestic also implies a preponderance of female labour and accentuates the idea of family mores as the basis on which decisions about economic activity take place.

Yet it would not be an exaggeration to say that modelling situations of partial self-provisioning is the most important prerequisite for rural economic planning in sub-Saharan Africa. What projects require is that peasant farmers who are engaged in both market and non-market spheres change their patterns of economic activity. Planners must therefore make predictions which operate across the market–non-market interface, especially when they have to predict what labour could be available from the peasant household for these new patterns of time use and the necessary economic incentives for their adoption. Because of the important role of women's labour they must also pay particular attention to the basis on which women make their economic decisions within the farm household.

Many of the findings of the evaluation studies summarized above suggest that an important reason for the difficulties in modelling and conceptualizing women's work within the partially self-provisioning farm enterprise is that a main tool used is the notion of opportunity cost. I described earlier how the detrimental effects of innovation on women's economic activities were largely unpredicted in development projects. This is mainly because the planning assumption is that these activities have low opportunity costs. Because the concept of opportunity cost depends on price criteria it is rather difficult to assess the value of the forgone labour for non-market activities or to predict what the 'elasticity' of demand for them is. Since they do not enter the market most of these activities have no empirical prices attached to them. Although it is recognized that they cannot be entirely forgone, it is assumed that it is on the whole more sensible to choose income earning activities rather than not. But it is doubtful whether decisions about much domestic work and non-market production work in this way. Getting water and firewood and producing food often cannot be forgone, especially where these goods and services cannot be supplied to the household by purchase.[9] Except in the direst of circumstances they do represent an important constraint. The problem is to quantify this constraint. Project demands for women's labour time to be spent on marketed crops frequently underestimate the cost in terms of time (even though that cannot be priced) of the forgone household food production and processing and other domestic work. It is presumed that increased monetary income will enable these goods and services to be replaced, but in addition to the problem of whether a supply of them exists to be bought, there are considerable problems of who controls the disposal of the household monetary income (see in detail below).

It was, of course, precisely the problems associated with the market–non-market interface that the new household economics sought to account for in modelling consumer choice in Western societies. The essence of this approach is that the household not the individual is the basic analytical unit; time as well as money is a critical item in allocation decisions; the household is both a production and a consumption unit and within it in particular the non-market production of consumption goods goes on. Relatively little application of new household economics has been made to Africa with the exception of a recent analysis by Low (1986) in Swaziland where peasant farmers fail to use improved techniques and inputs to increase their income from marketed production. Low's study, which takes up many of the classic new household economics positions, reveals some of the latter's limitations for modelling most sub-Saharan African production situations. His analysis leans very heavily on arguments of comparative advantage in which he presumes that individual household members act out of self-interest to maximize their utilities. He also explicitly assumes that these individual interests, when bound together in a household form of collectivity, produce a common household interest with a common set of utilities. The major empirical findings of this paper undermine any notion of the corporateness of the African farm household, and any idea of an unproblematic unity of interests of household members.

This brings me to the final main problem diagnosed by studies of development projects—the lack of fit between the model of the social relations of the sub-Saharan family farm enterprise enshrined in development projects and the complex and particular forms that these social relations actually take. The planner's model centres heavily on conceptualizing the conjugally based household as an economic enterprise in which the members work together. The husband/father is regarded as managing the resources on behalf of other

[9] The points in this paragraph were made in Evans (1986).

members, and those others, conceptualized as his dependants, provide labour under his direction. But, as I discussed earlier, one of the most noteworthy characteristics of sub-Saharan African domestic organization is that conjugal and household relations are emphatically not of this kind. The African farm family was, and is, very far from being a simple joint resource holding unit in which responsibilities for production and reproduction and rights to consumption and maintenance were shared on some notionally equal basis. It is a major perversity of development projects that they persist in treating the farm household as a unit taking no account of these facts. This is shown, for example, in the manner in which they target inputs, in their assumptions about what happens to farm income, and especially through their requirements of family labour from household members (especially wives) other than the putative male head (Hanger and Moris 1973).

Some of the most important negative effects of development planning on women arise because most development projects are engaged in actively recruiting women's labour in the household as peasant wives' family labour. Despite the dual form of women's traditional domestic obligations, there are virtually no development projects which include the expansion of women's independent farming, although some resources may be provided for a presumed dwindling amount of production of food for direct consumption. Assumptions about wives' availability to work on husbands' crops are more or less universal.

These problems are illustrated in a largely unsuccessful attempt to introduce irrigated rice production in the Gambia (Dey 1981, 1982). The efforts to implement a large-scale rice development project were unsatisfactory for a large number of reasons external to the form of intervention in the household farming system. Dey argues, however, that they also stemmed from the model that was employed in which the husband was the farmer and his wife was 'family labour'. An initial assumption was made that the men were traditionally rice growers and that they had full control over the resources required to do so, but in reality women grew the rice for household consumption and exchange within a complex set of rights and obligations between husbands and wives. Backed by project officials, men established exclusive rights to the women's former rice lands, pushing the women rice farmers out to inferior scattered plots on which to continue cultivating traditional rice varieties. The levels of improved rice production were disappointingly low in part because women became reluctant to participate as family labour (their planned role) and husbands had to pay their wives to work on the irrigated rice fields.

More than one study has identified women's refusal to perform the family labour that the project has planned for or demanded of them as contributing to the failure of a development project (Brain 1976; Cloud 1986). This recruitment of women as family labour in smallholder production by development planners is a more consciously planned intervention than commoditization, which as we have seen sometimes had the same effects. It represents the construction of a considerably enhanced form of conjugal dependence for African women.[10] And again research finds that wide-ranging domestic conflicts are set off between men and women by these changes in contemporary rural women's conditions of work. These conflicts extend over a wide field but include struggles over the sexual designation of tasks; over the disposition of household labour, e.g. the labour input to cash cropping; over the distribution of household income; and more widely over the patterns of household spending and consumption (Henn 1986). Many of these conflicts are about the construction of the conjugal relation and sets of rights and obligations between household members in entirely new forms (Vail and White 1977). Their ubiquity confirms that what is being promoted by the form of development projects is an enormous upheaval in the domestic relations between men and women.[11] In planning discussion in the sub-Saharan African context the term 'family labour' should never be seen as unproblematic. Behind its bland and apparently inoffensive face lies all the seething and unpredictable discontent of changing domestic labour relations.

However, the changes are equally important because of their implications for rural welfare. Evaluation studies of development projects also widely report that husbands and wives are found to be competing for the changed and/or enhanced rewards that increased or changed labour allocation brings (Conti 1979; Carney 1988; von Bulow and Sorensen 1988). Increased time spent on husbands' farms is important because women, relative to their independent farming, lack control over the rewards for what they produce. It is rarely regarded that there should be a direct link between the amount of a wife's work and the proportion of the total household product or income of which she has access or control. The former set of conventions which governed the distribution of rewards in kind within the household (and which may not have been equitable in the first place) does not automatically lead to sharing when household product is in the form of money. A great many calls are made on this income, and it may be received by 'the household' in ways which give husbands considerable personal control over it. A very early study of a large irrigation and resettlement project in Kenya showed that women and children suffered because they could not control the money (Hanger and Moris 1973). The planners proposed in vain that some of the increased money income should be spent on food since much less was being produced as a result of the project making much less land and labour available for it. A very large number of studies imply that there may be differences of opinion between men and women as to how household income should be spent in the interests of household welfare. And a number of studies suggest that this is one significant

---

[10] It parallels, in form and historical significance, the construction of female dependence in industrial wage-working families in late 19th- and 20th-century Europe and America.

[11] Discussed further in Whitehead (forthcoming *b*).

source of rural malnutrition (Schofield 1979; Chambers and Singer 1980; Kumar 1984a; Longhurst 1984; Turshen 1984).

Equally frequently the reported studies find that because of the nature of the intrahousehold distributional mechanisms, and the developmentalists' construction of 'family labour', wives are having difficulty in getting access to income commensurate with their labour input. It is when this conjugal competition affects the success of the development project itself that the conflictual and difficult nature of the consequences for husbands and wives becomes apparent. This is shown for example in Tobisson's report from Tanzania. She describes how a programme to encourage the cultivation of hybrid maize through extension and the distribution of subsidized seed, fertilizers, and pesticides to men met with resistance from women farmers, who predominate in food crop production. The result was an increased workload for women without concurrent control over the income. There was also some resistance to the cultivation of pure stands (essential for hybrid maize) since maize is traditionally intercropped with beans or cassava (quoted in FAO 1984).

I have argued that some of the negative effects of development project planning on women arise from the inadequacy of the underlying modelling. This is a matter of considerable concern. Some indication that it is a correct assessment is to be found in the fact that resettlement schemes, or irrigation schemes entailing large changes in land use, seem to be the kind of project which most adversely affects women (Hanger and Moris 1973; Cloud 1986; Conti 1979; Jackson 1985; and see especially discussion in Palmer 1985b). These expensive projects must entail very comprehensive planning, in which every aspect of the domestic economy needs to be covered. They are, therefore, particularly dependent on accurate modelling of the economics of the partially self-provisioning farm household. This kind of large-scale project entailing comprehensive modelling of the production and consumption patterns of the farm household is repeatedly shown to have produced a poor response from rural women. They do not behave as predicted and often this itself undermines the viability of the project. The studies cited above show that there is usually not enough provision for women's independent farming, either in the form of too little land allocated to them, or the absence of marketing or other support for it. Neither is there proper planning for their other economic activities.

11.5. *The basis of women's economic decision making*

It has become clear in the course of my account that women's decisions about allocating their resources, including their labour time, depend on what I have identified as the dual nature of their economic roles in the family. The structure of constraints and incentives for women farmers varies according to whether we are considering their work as independent farmers or their work as unremunerated family labour. The form in which a woman's work is done affects the degree of autonomy over her economic decision making, the form in which she receives any benefits of increased output, and the amount of control she has over her own work.

A woman working her own farm has the major control of the use of its product and associated income, although she may be affected by all kinds of cultural values about how to spend her income which lead her to neglect her own self-interest. Probably the main constraints on her increased production are the absence of access to other resources (notably land and credit or capital) and the failure to improve the technology and agronomic practices she is working with. However, quite different factors come into play in relation to work undertaken as family labour. Attempts have been made to mobilize women as family labour in circumstances where the modes of sharing in the household do not assume a common economic enterprise between household members. Widespread conflict between husbands and wives is brought about by the changes in women's labour time use that are occurring either as a result of commoditization in general or of agricultural development planning in particular. In many cases women do not receive sufficient (let alone commensurate) reward for working harder. A woman may have to spend more income on consumption goods that she used to produce because of the failure to provide support for self-provisioning crops, or intrahousehold gender relations may be such as to alienate her from so-called 'household' income. Women's responses to the demand for their unremunerated labour may have a profound effect on the success of development projects.

Nevertheless, one feature of the evaluation studies summarized in the preceding section which was not brought out there is that women's refusal to work as family labour is not universal. In some cases they are found to increase their work on household cash crops as unremunerated labour. This is apparent from a study by Palmer (1985b), comparing three resettlement schemes in which important differences emerge between them. She looks at two schemes in Burkina Faso (when it was Upper Volta) (Cloud 1976 and Conti 1979) and one in Nigeria (Spiro 1984, 1985). In all three cases the projects paid insufficient attention to women's independent food production, to the role this played in the household budget, and to the importance of women's other sources of income. Their main input was envisaged as family labour. So the form of farming economy and resources to support it that was planned had disadvantages for the women farmers (conceptualized by the planners as 'farmer's wives'). However, there were critical differences in women's response in the two countries. In both Burkina Faso cases women's lack of co-operation was instrumental in making these schemes relatively unsuccessful. In the Nigerian case women were staying in the resettlement areas and co-operating to some extent with the project and their husbands.

In trying to examine the difference in these cases, we are hampered by the lack of reliable economic data. Data on returns to labour are either absent or not sufficiently comprehensive, and it is remarkable how little emphasis is placed on the level of intensification entailed in each particular package. However, we can discern important differences in these cases. In the Burkina Faso schemes, the male head of household was finding it difficult to make a success of farming under the conditions of the project and total income or food available to the household was very low. We can hypothesize that women in the Burkina Faso cases were leaving the scheme in order to safeguard their own and their children's welfare in the face of the schemes' failure to protect the family's subsistence and income.

In the Nigerian case the resettlement package was funded at a very high level, and the proposed income levels for the resettled households were very attractive by rural standards. Hence although women's capacity for independent income in some directions had been reduced they were better off overall. We can hypothesize that the disadvantage to women of the loss of autonomy entailed in the enhanced role as family labourers was offset by the enhanced welfare of the family as a whole. There are at least three possible ways in which women may benefit, or feel they benefit, so as to want to work harder in household labour. They may benefit directly, i.e. in their own right because they achieve a better standard of living as a consequence of the improved household income. It is also possible that they do not benefit directly, but that their children's welfare is improved, and they may regard this as an important gain. Or they may perceive long-term benefits to themselves, or their children, of working in a household that looks as if it has better overall economic prospects.

The dual structure of sub-Saharan African women's economic roles, plus their culturally derived responsibility for their children, mean that women have to balance between (1) allocating their resources to their independent earning capacity to provide for themselves and their children, and (2) allocating resources to their work as family labour, and providing for them more indirectly. How this trade-off is dealt with depends on a number of things. Straightforward economic considerations are, of course, important, especially the relative returns to labour in each choice, but in the case of family labour especially, getting access to the returns to labour has to be negotiated with other people—generally with husbands. Thus the considerations extend beyond the economic into the sphere of social relations. Put crudely, family labourers do not necessarily behave as wage labourers. Wives' labour is clearly subject to a different set of constraints and incentives from any other work relation. The control that is exercised is direct, and interpersonal, and may involve elements of male–female coercion.[12] Roberts (1983) has argued that wives' 'quality as unfree labour becomes increasingly important as commodity

[12] Whitehead (1981b) hypothesizes a large number of potential factors which might affect the capacity of male household heads to pass on the pressures associated with commodity production in peasant households to their wives, although few of these have been empirically examined.

relations destroy the bonds securing other non-free labour (e.g. of sons) to the peasant household'. Wives' labour is unfree in the sense that it is entered into as part of marriage; it is rarely directly remunerated; it can only be left by divorce. Roberts's work suggests that struggle between the sexes over women's labour has been very important in the historical development of market production in West Africa. Palmer's (1985b) suspicion is that the capacity of husbands to coerce their wives to produce more is often what is being deliberately harnessed in situations of economic change. Roberts (1983), however, implies that gender conflict in the household is not simply a struggle over the economic. What determines wives' work intensity is a complex of factors associated with other kinds of investment in the social relations under which the work is being performed: that is to say the social relations of the family, including the way in which women, and men, as part of a particular culture and society, interpret the responsibilities of motherhood.

Considering the basis for women's economic decision making, the central issue raised is what are women's 'interests' and how do they relate to a woman's position in the family and household? Models and theories which treat the household as a unit assume an identity of interests between its members and sometimes a single joint utility function. One assumed basis for these common interests is the interdependence, common goals, and a need for sharing that the roles of men and women as parents are thought to create. Some feminist writings on the household, on the other hand, imply total separation of interests of women and men, and presumably no agreed consumption goals. Common parenthood is not seen as creating common interests and if anything is seen as a source of separate interests between men and women. The implication of the Nigerian case is that neither approach is correct. Although it is unhelpful to treat a wife as wholly submerged in the household, the economic separation between husbands and wives must not be interpreted as total. Rural marriage is more than a means of making women work harder for men's benefit. A woman's own welfare may be sufficiently linked to the success of the market production part of the household farming enterprise that she may be prepared to intensify work effort on crops for which the returns for effort are not commensurate with the amount she puts in. Or she may have interests in the welfare of other household members which lead her to acquiesce in pressure to make her work harder. In either case it is not possible to separate her interests from those of other members of the household.

Predictive modelling and women's dual economic role

Modelling this complex state of affairs is very difficult for a number of reasons. In the first place, once we accept the interplay of social factors with economic factors as important goals in the decision making, these social factors are difficult to quantify. The model itself becomes indeterminate. But also since the number of relevant variables is very wide, there may be considerable variations between individual women who appear to occupy similar positions.

So that the way the trade-off works for one woman may be different from the way it works for another for all kinds of reasons. These include many factors outside the marriage and household—for example access to resources through other kin and friends; her own other skills and those of her children. It is thus very difficult to predict what the impact of particular policies will be as between one woman and the next. A final reason which makes modelling difficult is that responses at the margin may well be very different from the average. At the margin there may be little incentive for a woman to contribute to the collective endeavour.

The absence of predictability in relation to just how far women are willing to increase their work intensity as against the perceived benefits has been amply demonstrated above. One of the major points thrown up by considering the market–non-market interface as a problematic area for economic modelling is the extent to which, embedded as it is in the sexual division of labour, or in family relations, women's labour in the sub-Saharan African farm family requires a different theory of allocation. Many of the planning interventions analysed above which seek to change how peasant families allocate their labour essentially depend on the ability of the household head to persuade wives to work on their market crops. Thus, in strategies to raise smallholder marketed surplus understanding the factors which affect a husband's ability to do this may be critical for project success. The assumption that women will perform family labour is based not only on an assumption that market work, which produces an income, must be preferred to household work that does not, but also on the assumption that the sexual division of labour constitutes an unproblematic way of allocating the sexes to various tasks within the farm enterprise. Such an assumption can only be based upon models of the household and marriage which ignore the complex combination and separate and joint interests which we have identified as such an important feature of the African farm family.

11.6. Food strategies, food production, and women: discussion

At the beginning of this chapter I argued that food production strategies had an important part to play in some of the national food strategies of many sub-Saharan African states. I now wish to review what the findings of the previous sections imply for the role of African women farmers in meeting the goal of increased food production, especially of increased marketed food. This discussion focuses fairly narrowly on a set of issues which arise out of what I have described as the myth of feminization; namely what is it that prevents sub-Saharan African rural women producing more? Do women face particular problems which are different from those of male farmers? Is the structure of women's incentives different from that of men? If so, what is the implication for food strategy policies?

The crisis of relative underproduction of African food production is fortuitous for some of those scholars who, for nearly two decades, have been arguing that development has been having negative effects on women. There is a widely held belief that improvement in women's welfare and solving the deep-seated problems of rural or agricultural development neatly coincide. The nature of the food crisis tends to confirm the view that development is detrimental to the welfare of populations in the Third World. It particularly confirms a view that there is a link between the role that women play in food production in Africa and the evidence that rural women are a significant category of sufferers from rural development. The preceding analysis should, in fact, have made it clear that in its present form agricultural development policy aimed at increasing farm household production tends to be in contradiction to, rather than congruent with, a commitment to rural women's welfare.

One main reason for this is that the changes which have accompanied the development of marketed production in rural Africa have produced considerable socio-economic differentiation. Impoverishment is a significant restraint on agricultural production. Many of the poor female-headed households rapidly emerging in rural areas lack the resources to produce their own subsistence and there are few income earning possibilities. By and large policies which increase the amount of marketed food probably also increase rural differentiation. Food strategies which are centred on agricultural innovation and intensification and aim at greater food security need to take account of the likely enhancement of socio-economic differentiation. They do not create self-sufficiency, or the wherewithal to purchase food for all rural households. The gender dimension arises here because female-headed households are more often the food deficit households and women's earned incomes are very low.

How have women responded to planned and unplanned change?

This chapter has not followed the issues raised by female impoverishment and female-headed households very closely. The main body of the chapter has been a sustained examination of how married women have responded to planned and unplanned economic changes in the countryside. The historical record shows that rural wives have historically changed their labour time use quite considerably in response to the development of a market for rural products. They have taken up new positions in the sexual division of labour; they have adopted new crops, new crop mixes, and new techniques; and they have seized a large number of income earning opportunities. They have marketed crops and sold their labour power at the same time as seeking to maintain within their farming a viable food-producing element for self-consumption. This is very often associated with their role as the guardians of their childrens' welfare. These historical processes of innovation have been very varied and uneven, and they have entailed some contradictions. Women's intensified economic activity has occurred in their role as farmers in their own right, and in their role as family labourers. The increasing amount and proportion of women's labour time spent in production on their husbands' farms is one of the most common findings in studies of the effects of commercialization in African agriculture. Women members were able to make their contribution to the increased cash needs of rural households by increasing their work as family labourers, and to some extent as independent commodity producers and as traders.

Recent research has found that these changes have produced considerable gender conflict occurring mainly within the domestic and conjugal domain. This conflict between the sexes arises because in most forms of rural marriage the conventional patterns of resource sharing, and decision making about consumption and spending, are built upon there being separate spheres for wife and for husband. These separate spheres often coexist with a more joint household economic arena, but in this the husband (or household head if this is not the husband) generally has the greatest decision-making power. The result is that wives very often have to struggle quite hard to establish any control over the new income inputs that the changed profile of the domestic economy creates. This struggle is very important because, in many cases, women retain a primary responsibility for the welfare of the children of their marriages. So it would not be unreasonable to summarize the historical record as showing intensification of women's work producing not only benefits for some and disbenefits for others, but also a sharpening of gender conflict. The latter is about the disposition of women's labour, the distribution of the rewards from it, and the customary divisions of responsibility for spending. Underlying these struggles are the difficulties women have in changed economic circumstances of meeting the needs of family welfare. These conflicts have some bearing on the rate of creation of rural female-headed households and on rates of female labour migration.

However, if we turn to the conclusions to be drawn from the section of this chapter which looks at the evaluation studies of development projects, there is a somewhat different pattern of findings. Many development projects have a rather sorry record in relation to women. There are too many cases in which projects seem to have negative effects on women's and children's welfare. Most important for my argument, women who are caught up in development projects often fail to perform the economic role allotted to them, and, in contradiction to the historical record of innovation and intensification, appear to be unwilling to innovate or to increase their agricultural output. These problems arise because development planners, perhaps unwittingly, are making it very difficult for women farmers. On the one hand they undermine their independent farming which has provided income and food for self-consumption. On the other hand, they fail to ensure that women have adequate control over spending decisions where more domestic consumption must be purchased on the market. Indeed the institutional form of projects may considerably reduce the number of arenas of economic decision making that are in women's control. It is these changes which underlie women's resistance to the work project planners expect of them as family labourers. But not all projects have failed to mobilize women as family labour. Under some circumstances the structure of constraints and incentives can encourage women to increase their marketed output.

These findings thus confirm what has been shown in the historical studies, namely that there is nothing intrinsic to women which has created the sub-Saharan African food crisis. It is rather a failure of planning to understand and model how constraints and incentives operate for sub-Saharan African women farmers within the farm family.

Constraints on and incentives for female farmers

First of all let me dispose of two arguments which are commonly advanced as reasons which prevent sub-Saharan African women producing more, namely that cultural values bar women's entry to certain kinds of economic activity, and that there are severe constraints on women's time. Clearly cultural values about proper male and female behaviour may be important in determining activity within the sexual division of labour, particularly where they are associated with various kinds of religious beliefs. However, there are so many individual examples of cultural values of this kind changing under the impact of factors promoting change in the sexual division of labour that arguments that it is ideas about appropriate behaviour for women that alone prevent agricultural innovation (e.g. in relation to women using ploughs) cannot be sustained.

Somewhat more complex is the issue of whether the limits on increasing women's labour time input to agriculture have been reached. There are a number of discussions which imply, or say explicitly, that it is simply not possible to increase rural women's work burdens any further. It is true that an important proportion of the increased output from rural areas since the beginning of this century has derived from increases in women's work burdens. It is also true that the environmental conditions within which women are performing their domestic work relating to household maintenance have, in some cases (but not all), deteriorated. It is thus indisputable that many rural women are currently overworked and, as Henn points out (1984), we may genuinely be reaching the point at which the total number of hours women spend in economic activity cannot be increased. (And certainly not without adversely affecting nutritional standards—Longhurst 1984; Chambers and Singer 1981.) However, I would argue that there are rather few studies that have shown unambiguously, and distinct from other reasons, that women have failed to produce more because a limit to their labour time has been reached.

One study which set out explicitly to examine the hypothesis that women peasant farmers could not produce more for the market because of time constraints is that by Henn (1986). Her agroeconomic study compared two villages in the Southern Cameroon, which has a relatively strong traditional food sector, although with a recently falling output per person, and in which women are the main food producers. The main hypothesis investigated in the study was whether the falling output was related to the tight labour time constraints for women. Henn examined this by comparing the labour time input of men and women to their significant economic activities in two villages. Although the villages had essentially similar socio-economic and cultural configurations, they differed in their access to food markets; one having a new road providing quick and cheap access to an urban food market and the other being very remote and isolated. She found that, when they had access to a market, women increased the work they did in food crop production. This put up their total work hours to a very high number, although the productivity of the increased labour in food crop production was not very high.

Henn's study demonstrates that infrastructural provision is very important, but also that if they get income over which they have control, women will increase their already considerable hours of work.[13] The study also shows that the increased rewards for extra time spent on work do not have to be very great to act as an incentive. The effect here, as elsewhere, is to produce often very high work burdens which are 'intolerable' in the sense of being grossly to women's detriment. However the evidence that these work burdens are 'intolerable', in the sense that women's scarce labour time is then the major constraint on certain forms of increased output or agricultural innovation, is much less clear cut. A number of projects and studies show that women's high work burdens can be increased still further if they can be either directly or indirectly coerced, or if there are direct economic incentives. (This is the general point being made also by Henn 1984.)

What has become clear in the course of my account is that the structure of constraints and incentives for women farmers varies according to whether we are considering their work as independent farmers or their work as unremunerated family labour. A woman is much more likely to increase her work load if she is working her own farm and has some control of the use of its product and associated income. However, there are often major resource difficulties which act as a material constraint to her independent farming. In assessing this it is essential to disaggregate the household since women's access to resources cannot be read off from those of her husband or other household head. Although capital, land, labour, credit, and modern inputs are all in short supply for smallholders in general, this is particularly so for women as compared to men. In relation to work undertaken as family labour some women will produce more food, even where the rewards that they directly receive for the increased labour input are either not commensurate with what they put in, or are proportionally less than what the men receive. Nevertheless they often resist attempts by husbands to extract more labour from them. In development projects in particular, the form of the project may act as a distinct disincentive to women to increase their work as family labour. In order to

---

[13] Evans and Young (1988) argue that wives in N. Zambia engage in casual wage work for food and consumption goods which is of low status, because they control this income.

provide incentives in such projects, women's self-provisioning and their access to some extra income need to be protected. Attention should also be paid to the effects of the project design on female autonomy and the potentiality for conjugal coercion.

Policy contradictions

The analysis in this chapter suggests that there are at least two main ways in which women's agricultural production can be increased. Firstly by increasing their dependent role in the conjugally based household. This is in fact the most usual smallholder strategy for increasing production. There are, as we have seen, a number of problems with this trajectory. Policies which strengthen the capacity of the household head to improve the cash income of the household have been found to place demands on the labour of family members, many of whom are women. Empirically, this is found to create a struggle between men and women over whether women's labour should go into their independent farms or into these 'household' farms, and over the spending of the increased household income. Women's capacity to farm on their own account often loses out, thus increasing their dependency on their husbands.

So in some cases women exchange enhanced well-being for increased dependence, and the processes which have enhanced their relative disadvantage and loss of autonomy since the beginning of the century will be given a further boost. Very few studies give any sense of the struggle that is going on in the countryside over these issues (but see Roberts 1984; Vaughan 1984), partly because women's resistance has always been difficult to see. Do we know how much autonomy is valued? If we are not able to predict the basis on which women will decide between competing demands on their labour time, it may be because we are very far from being able to weigh up how far women experience as intolerable some of the forms of social relation which lie at the heart of the peasant (smallholder) household.

In yet other cases, there is no guarantee that this strategy will not produce a greater crisis of rural malnutrition. There are differential attachments to nutritional and welfare goals as between husband and wife, and women's leverage over consumption patterns when they have worked as family labour is not great. So women and children do not get enough of the extra resources and may get less than before. This may also happen because women do not have time to provision themselves and their families. However, to have policies which actively increase men's control over the disposal of household product and income might be in the interest of national food strategies.

The second strategy would be to increase a woman's capacity for food production in her own right. This would require directing efforts to improve radically the levels of productivity of her agronomic practices and ensuring that she has the resources to benefit from this. This can be done for women farming in women-only households and for women's own account farming as wives. But this also has clear difficulties attached to it. In the first place all the evidence suggests that shifting the balance of agricultural extension services and agronomic and technological research to provide improved inputs to women will be a very costly business. Not only are the current structures and budgets not set up to do this, it is also possible that it is intrinsically most costly to do this for women, given their 'inaccessibility'. A second major area of difficulty is of course the way in which this would conflict with male interests. Several authors have highlighted that even minimal efforts to direct agri-cultural projects and planning towards women either depend on men's co-operation, or can be sabotaged by men's diversion of the resources to themselves (Dixon 1980; Buvinic 1984; Roberts 1979). Uncomfortable though it may be, the requirement that Africa's food crisis be seriously addressed with a change in the pattern of resource allocation towards agriculture and towards smallholders necessarily raises these issues of discrimination and sexual politics.

References

AGARWAL, B. (1985), 'Work Participation of Rural Women in the Third World: Some Data and Conceptual Biases', in Young, K. (ed.), *Serving Two Masters* (London, New Delhi: Routledge & Kegan Paul, Macmillan).

ANKER, R. (1983), 'Female Labour Force Participation in Developing Countries: A Critique of Current Definitions and Data Collection Methods', *International Labour Review*.

ASHBY, J. A. (1981), 'New Models for Agricultural Research and Extension: The Need to Integrate Women', in Lewis (1981).

BAUMANN, H. (1928), 'The Division of Work According to Sex in African Hoe Culture', *Africa*, 1.

BENERIA, L. (1981), 'Conceptualising the Labour Force: The Under Estimation of Women's Economic Activities', *Journal of Development Studies*, 17/3.

——(1982), 'Accounting for Women's Work', in L. Beneria (ed.), *Women and Rural Development: The Sexual Division of Labour in Rural Soweto* (New York: Praeger).

——and SEN, G. (1981), 'Accumulation, Reproduction and Women's Role in Economic Development: Boserup Revisited', *Signs*, 7.

BERGER, I., and ROBERTSON, C. (eds.) (1986), *Women and Class in Africa* (New York: Africana Publishing Co.).

BERNSTEIN, H. (1979), 'Concepts for the Analysis of Contemporary Peasantries', *Journal of Peasant Studies*, 6.

BERRY, S. (1984), 'The Food Crisis and Agrarian Change in Africa: A Review Essay', *African Studies Review*, 27.

BOSERUP, E. (1970), *Women's Role in Economic Development* (London: Allen & Unwin).

BOULDING, E. (1983), 'Measures of Women's Work in the Third World: Problems and Suggestions', in M. Buvinic *et al.* (eds.), *Women and Poverty in the Third World* (Baltimore: Johns Hopkins).

BRAIN, J. (1976), 'Women in Resettlement Schemes in Tanzania', in Hafkin and Bay (1976).

BRYCESON, D. F. (1988), 'Food Insecurity and the Social Division of Labour in Tanzania, 1919–1985', D.Phil thesis, Oxford University.

BRYSON, J. C. (1980), 'The Development Implications of Female Involvement in Agriculture: The Case of Cameroon', MA dissertation, University of Manchester.

——(1981), 'Women and Agriculture in Sub-Saharan Africa: Implications for Development', *Journal of Development Studies*, 17/2.

BUJRA, J. (1986), 'Urging Women to Redouble their Efforts: Class, Gender and Capitalist Transformation in Africa', in Berger and Robertson (1986).

BUKH, Y. (1979), *The Village Women in Ghana* (Uppsala: Scandinavian Institute of African Studies).

BURFISHER, M., and HORENSTEIN, N. (1985), *Sex Roles in the Nigerian Tiv Farm Household* (West Hartford, Conn.: Kumarian Press).

BUVINIC, M. (1984), 'Projects for Women in the Third World: Explaining their Misbehaviour', mimeo (Office of Women in Development, USAID).

CAPLAN, A. P. (1984), 'Cognatic Descent, Islamic Law and Women's Property on the

East African Coast', in R. Hirschon (ed.), *Women and Property: Women as Property* (London: Croom Helm).

CARNEY, J. A. (1988), 'Struggles over Crop Rights and Labour within Contract Farming Households in a Gambian Irrigated Rice Project', *Journal of Peasant Studies*, 15.

CHAMBERS, R., and SINGER, H. (1981), 'Poverty, Malnutrition and Food in Zambia', Country Case Study for *World Development Report 1981*.

CHEATER, A. (1981), 'Women and their Participation in Commercial Agricultural Production: The Case of Medium Scale Freehold in Zimbabwe', *Development and Change*, 12.

CLARK, C. M. (1981), 'Land and Food, Women and Power in Nineteenth Century Kikuyu', *Africa*, 50.

CLIFFE, L. (1976), 'Rural Class Formation in East Africa', *Journal of Peasant Studies*, 4.

CLOUD, K. (1976), 'Report of Fact Finding Trip to Niger, Mali, Senegal and Upper Volta', mimeo (Washington DC Office of the Sahel Francophone West Africa Affairs, USAID).

——(1986), 'Sex Roles in Food Production and Distribution in the Sahel', in L. Creevey (ed.), *Women Farmers in Africa: Rural Development in Mali and the Sahel* (Syracuse, NY: Syracuse University Press).

COLSON, E., and SCUDDER, T. (1988), *From Prayer to Profit: The Ritual Economic and Social Importance of Beer in Gwembe District in Zambia 1950–1982* (Stanford, Calif.: Stanford University Press).

CONTI, A. (1979), 'Capitalist Organisation of Production through Non Capitalist Relations: Women's Role in a Pilot Settlement Scheme in Upper Volta', *Review of African Political Economy*, 15–16.

CREEVEY, L. (ed.) (1986), 'The Role of Women in Malian Agriculture', in *Women Farmers in Africa: Rural Development in Mali and the Sahel* (Syracuse, NY: Syracuse University Press).

CREHAN, K. (1983), 'North Western Zambia: From Producer to Housewife', *Review of African Political Economy*, 27–8.

DAUBER, R., and CAIN, M. L. (eds.) (1981), *Women and Technological Change in Developing Countries* (Boulder, Colo.: Westview).

DEY, J. (1981), 'Gambian Women: Unequal Partners in Rice Development Projects', in N. Nelson (ed.), *African Women in the Development Process* (London: Frank Cass).

——(1982), 'Development Planning in the Gambia: The Gap between Planners' and Farmers' Perceptions, Expectations and Objectives', *World Development*, 10.

——(1984), 'Women in Food Production and Food Security in Africa', *Women in Agriculture*, 3 (Rome: FAO).

——(1985), *Women in African Rice Farming Systems*, Proceedings of a Conference on Women in Rice Farming Systems, IRRO, Sept. 1983.

DIXON, R. B. (1980), 'Assessing the Impact of Development Projects on Women', AID Program Evaluation Discussion Paper No. 8 (Office of Women in Development).

——(1982), 'Women in Agriculture: Counting the Labour Force in Developing Countries', *Population and Development Review*, 8.

DIXON-MUELLER, R. B. (1985), 'Women's Work in Third World Agriculture: Concepts and Indicators', ILO Women, Work and Development Series No. 9.

—— and ANKER, R. (1988), 'Assessing Women's Economic Contributions to Development Training in Population', *Human Resources and Development Planning*, 6 (Geneva: ILO).

DUE, M. J., and MUDENDA, T. (1984), 'Women's Contribution Made Visible: Of Farm and Market Women to Farming Systems and Household Incomes in Zambia 1982', Illinois Agricultural Economic Staff Papers 84-E-285 (University of Illinois).

DWYER, D. (1983), 'Women and Income in the Third World: Implications for Policy', Working Paper No. 18 (New York: Population Council).

EDHOLM, F., HARRIS, O., and YOUNG, K. (1977), 'Conceptualising Women', *Critique of Anthropology*, 9–10.

ELLIS, F. (1988), *Peasant Economics: Farm Households and Agrarian Development* (Cambridge: Cambridge University Press).

EVANS, A. (1986), Briefing Paper on Women and Agricultural Development for Study Course 6, Women, Men and Development (Institute of Development Studies, Sussex).

——(1987), 'Household Economics in Agrarian Societies', paper for International Development Issues Seminar, Cambridge, Mar.

——and YOUNG, K. (1988), 'Gender Issues in Household Labour Allocation: The Transformation of a Farming System in Northern Province, Zambia', Report submitted to ODA.

FAO (1984), 'Women in Food Production and Food Security', paper for Government Consultation on Role of Women in Food Production and Food Security, Harare, Zimbabwe.

FELDMAN, R. (1981), 'Employment Problems of Rural Women in Kenya', unpublished paper prepared for ILO.

FOLBRE, N. (1986), 'Hearts and Spades: Paradigms of Household Economics', *World Development*, 14.

FORTMANN, L. (1981), 'The Plight of the Invisible Farmer: The Effect of National Agricultural Policy and Women in Africa', in Dauber and Cain (1981).

FREUND, B. (1984), *The Making of Contemporary Africa: The Development of African Society since 1800* (London: Macmillan).

GAOBEPE, M. G., and MWENDA, A. (1980), 'The Report on the Situation and Needs of Food Supplies, Woman in Zambia' (Lusaka: FAO).

GOODY, J. (1976), *Production and Reproduction: A Comparative Study of the Domestic Domain* (Cambridge: Cambridge University Press).

GUYER, J. (1980a), 'Household Budgets and Women's Incomes', Working Paper No. 28 (Boston: African Studies Centre).

——(1980b), 'Food, Cocoa and the Division of Labour by Sex in Two West African Societies', *Comparative Studies in Society and History*, 22.

——(1980c), 'Female Farming and the Evolution of Food Production Patterns amongst the Beti of Southern Central Cameroons', *Africa*, 50.

——(1981), 'Household and Community in Africa', *African Studies Review*, 24.

——(1983), 'Anthropological Models of African Production: The Naturalisation Problem', Working Paper No. 78 (Boston: African Studies Centre).

——(1984), 'Women in African Rural Economies: Contemporary Variations', in Hay and Stichter (1984).

——(1987), *Feeding African Cities: Studies in Regional Social History* (Manchester: Manchester University Press).

HAFKIN, N., and BAY, E. G. (eds.) (1976), *Women in Africa: Studies in Social and Economic Change* (Stanford, Calif.: Stanford University Press).

HANGER, J., and MORIS, J. (1973), 'Women and the Household Economy', in R. Chambers and J. Moris (eds.), *Mwea: An Irrigated Rice Settlement in Kenya* (Munich: Weltforum Verlag).

HARRIS, O. (1981), 'Households as Natural Units', in Young, K. (ed.), *Of Marriage and the Market* (London: CSE Books).

HAY, M. J. (1976), 'Luo Women and Economic Change during the Colonial Period', in Hafkin and Bay (1976).

——(1982), 'Women as Owners, Occupants and Managers of Property in Colonial Western Kenya', in Hay and Wright (1982).

——and STICHTER, S. (eds.) (1984), *African Women South of the Sahara* (London: Longman).

——and WRIGHT, M. (eds.) (1982), 'African Women and the Law: Historical Perspectives', Boston University Papers on Africa 7 (Boston, Mass.: Boston University).

HENN, J. K. (1984), 'Feeding the Cities: Women Farmers', *World Development*, 12.

——(1986), 'Intra-household Dynamics and State Policies as Constraints on Food Production; Results of a 1985 Agroeconomic Survey in Cameroon', paper presented at the Conference on Gender Issues in Farming Systems Research and Extension, University of Florida, Feb.

HILL, P. (1963), *The Migrant Cocoa Farmers of Southern Ghana* (Cambridge: Cambridge University Press).

——(1972): *Rural Hausa: A Village and a Setting* (Cambridge: Cambridge University Press).

——(1982), *Dry Grain Farming Families: Hausa (Nigeria) and Karnataka (India) Compared* (Cambridge: Cambridge University Press).

——(1986), *Development Economics on Trial: The Anthropological Case for a Prosecution* (Cambridge: Cambridge University Press).

HUNTINGDON, S. (1975), 'Issues in Women's Development: Critique and Alternatives', *Journal of Marriage and the Family*, 37.

IBRD (1979), *Recognising the Invisible in Development: The World Bank Experience* (Washington, DC: IBRD).

ICRW (1980), *The Productivity of Women in Development Countries: Measurement Issues and Recommendations* (Washington, DC: ICRW).

IDS Bulletin (1985), *Sub-Saharan Africa: Getting the Facts Straight*, 16/3.

INSTRAW (with United Nations Statistical Office) (1986), 'Improving Statistics and Indicators on Women Using Household Surveys', draft Working Paper (New York).

JACKSON, C. (1985), *The Kano River Irrigation Project* (West Hartford, Conn.: Kumarian Press).

JIGGINS, J. (1980), 'Female Headed Households among Subsistence Cultivators in the Central and Northern Provinces in Zambia', paper presented at the Ford Foundation Workshop on Women and Agricultural Production in Eastern and Southern Africa.

JOHNSON, S. (1988), 'Gender, Intrahousehold Relations and Agricultural Development in Sub Saharan Africa', unpublished manuscript submitted as part of M.Sc. for Department of Agricultural Economics, University of Reading.

JONES, C. W. (1986), 'Intra-household Bargaining in Response to the Introduction of New Crops: A Case Study from Northern Cameroons', in L. Moock (ed.), *Understanding Africa's Rural Households and Farming Systems* (Boulder, Colo.: Westview).

KANDIYOTI, D. (1985), 'Women in Rural Production Systems: Problems and Policies' (UNESCO).

KASSOUDJI, S., and MUELLER, E. (1983), 'The Economic and Demographic Status of Female Headed Households in Rural Botswana', *Economic Development and Cultural Change*, 31.

KITCHING, G. (1980), *Class and Economic Change in Kenya: The Making of an African Petite-Bourgeoisie* (New Haven, Conn.: Yale University Press).

KONGSTAD, P., and MONSTED, M. (1980), *Family Labour and Trade in Western Kenya* (Uppsala: Scandinavian Institute of African Studies).

KUMAR, S. (1984a), 'Household and Gender-Specific Preferences in Food Consumption and Child Nutrition', paper for Workshop on Conceptualising and Household in Africa, Harvard University, Nov.

——(1984b), 'Differential Control over Spending and Consumption as a Function of Productive Roles', paper given to a Workshop on Methods of Measuring Intrahousehold Resource Allocation at Tufts School of Nutrition, Oct.

LEWIS, B. (1981), *Invisible Farmers: Women and the Crisis in Agriculture* (Washington, DC: Office of Women in Development AID).

——(1984), 'The Impact of Development Policies on Women', in Hay and Stichter (1984).

LOCHFIE, M. F. (1975), 'Political and Economic Origins of African Hunger', *Journal of Modern African Studies*, 3.

LONGHURST, R. (1977), 'The Provision of Basic Needs for Women: A Case Study of a Hausa Village in Nigeria', Draft Report for ILO.

——(1982), 'Resource Allocation and the Sexual Division of Labour: A Case Study of a Moslem Hausa Village', in L. Beneria (ed.), *Women and Rural Development: The Sexual Division of Labour in Rural Soweto* (New York: Praeger).

——(1984), 'The Energy Trap: Work, Nutrition and Child Malnutrition in Northern Nigeria', Cornell International Monograph Series, No. 13 (Cornell University).

LOW, A. (1986), *Agricultural Development in Southern Africa: Farm Household-Economics and the Food Crisis* (London: Heinemann).

MCMILLAN, D. (1986), 'Distribution of Resources and Products in Mossi Households', in A. Hansen and D. E. McMillan (eds.), *Food in Sub-Saharan Africa* (Boulder, Colo.: Lynne Rienner).

——(1987), 'Monitoring the Evolution of Household Economic Systems over Time in Farming Systems Research', *Development and Change*, 18.

MAIR, L. (1969), *African Marriage and Social Change* (Frank Cass) (reprint of Part I of Phillips (1953)).

MONSTED, M. (1976), 'The Changing Division of Labour within Rural Families in Kenya', Project Paper 76.1 (Centre for Development Research).

MOOCK, P. (1976), 'The Efficiency of Women as Farm Managers: Kenya', *American Journal of Agricultural Economics*, 58.

MUNTEMBA, M. S. (1978), 'The Underdevelopment of Peasant Agriculture in Zambia: The Case of Kabwe Rural District, 1964–1970', *Journal of Southern African Studies*, 5.

——(1982), 'Women as Food Producers and Suppliers in the Twentieth Century: The Case of Zambia', *Development Dialogue*, 1–2.

Orstom-Cie (1985), *Femmes et politiques alimentaires*, Proceedings of an International Seminar held in Jan., Paris.

PALA, A. O. (1976), 'African Women in Rural Development: Research Trends and Priorities', Overseas Liaison Committee Paper No. 12 (Washington, DC).

——(1979), 'Women's Access to Land and Their Role in Agriculture and Decision Making on the Farm: Experience of the Jolo of Kenya', Discussion Paper No. 263 (Nairobi: IDS).

——(1980), 'Daughters of the Lakes and Rivers', in M. Etienne and E. Leacock (eds.), *Women and Colonisation: Anthropological Perspectives* (New York: Praeger).

PALMER, I. (1985a), 'The Impact of Male Outmigration on Women in Farming', in I. Palmer (ed.), *Women's Roles and Gender Differences in Development: Cases for Planners* (West Hartford, Conn.: Kumarian Press).

——(1985b), 'The Impact of Agrarian Reform on Women', in I. Palmer (ed.), *Women's Roles and Gender Differences in Development: Cases for Planners* (West Hartford, Conn.: Kumarian Press).

PHILLIPS, A. (1953), *Survey of African Marriage and Family Life* (Oxford: Oxford University Press).

PITTIN, R. (1985), 'Deconstructing the Household: Relations of Production and Reproduction in Rural Nigeria', paper presented to the WIN Annual Conference, Ilorin.

POEWE, K. O. (1981), *Matrilineal Idology: Male Female Dynamics in Luapula, Zambia* (London: Academic Press).

POTTIER, J. (1985a), 'Introduction', in J. Pottier (ed.), *Food Systems in Central and Southern Africa* (London: School of African and Oriental Studies).

——(1985b), 'Reciprocity and the Beer Pot: The Changing Pattern of Mambwe Food Production', in J. Pottier (ed.), *Food Systems in Central and Southern Africa* (London: School of African and Oriental Studies).

——(1988), *Migrants No More: Settlement and Survival in Mambwe Villages, Zambia* (Manchester: Manchester University Press).

RICHARDS, A. I. (1937), *Land, Labour and Diet in Northern Rhodesia: An Economic Study of the Bemba Tribe* (Oxford: Oxford University Press).

RICHARDS, P. (1983a), 'Farming Systems and Agrarian Change in West Africa', *Progress in Human Geography*, 7.

——(1983b), 'Ecological Change and the Politics of African Land Use', *African Studies Review*, 26.

——(1986), 'What's Wrong with Farming Systems Research?', paper given to Development Studies Annual Conference.

ROBERTS, P. (1979), 'The Integration of Women into the Development Process: Some Conceptual Problems', *IDS Bulletin*, 10.

——(1983), 'Feminism in Africa: Feminism and Africa', *Review of African Political Economy*, 27–8.

——(1984), 'The Sexual Politics of Labour and the Household in Africa', paper given at the Workshop on Conceptualising the Household in Africa, Harvard University, Nov.

——(1985), 'Rural Women's Access to Labour', paper given to BSA/DSA Study Group Workshop on Class and Gender in the Third World.

ROGERS, B. (1980), *The Domestication of Women: Discrimination in Developing Societies* (London: Tavistock Publications).

ROSE, T. (1985), *Crisis and Recovery in Sub Saharan Africa* (Paris: OECD).

SAFILIOS-ROTHSCHILD, C. (1985), 'The Implications of the Roles of Women in Agriculture in Zambia' (New York: Population Council).

SCHOFIELD, S. (1979), *Development and the Problem of Village Nutrition* (London: Croom Helm).

SEN, A. K. (1981), *Poverty and Famines: An Essay on Entitlement and Deprivation* (Oxford: Oxford University Press).

——(1985), 'Women, Technology and Sexual Divisions', *Trade and Development (UNCTAD)*, 6.

SENDER, J., and SMITH, S. (1987), 'A Report to ODA's Economic and Social Committee for Research on Smallholder Tea Production in the West Usambaras', now published as *Economic Development in Rural Tanzania: Class, Poverty and Gender in the Usambaras*, (Mbilinyi: Routledge, 1987).

SKINNER, E. P. (1965), 'Labour Migration among the Mossi of the Upper Volta', in H. Kuper (ed.), *Urbanization and Migration in West Africa* (Berkeley, Calif.: California University Press).

SPIRO, H. (1984), 'Agricultural Development Strategies: The Experience at Ilora', paper given at Workshop on Women in Agriculture, IITA Ibadan, Nigeria.

——(1985), *The Ilora Farm Settlement in Nigeria* (West Hartford, Conn.: Kumarian Press).

STAUDT, K. (1974–5), 'Women Farmers and Inequalities in Agricultural Services', *Rural Africana*, 29.

——(1978), 'Agricultural Productivity Gaps: A Case Study of Male Preference in Government Policy Implementations', *Development and Change*, 9.

——(1979), 'Women and Participation in Rural Development: Framework for Project Design and Policy Oriented Research', Occasional Paper No. 8 (Cornell University Rural Development Committee).

——(1985), *Agricultural Policy Implementation: A Case Study from Western Kenya* (West Hartford, Conn.: Kumarian Press).

STICHTER, S. (1985), *Migrant Laborers* (Cambridge: Cambridge University Press).

TABATABAI, H. (1986), 'Food Crisis and Development Policies in Sub-Saharan Africa', Rural Employment Policy Research Programme, WEP-10-6/WP72 (Geneva: ILO).

TOBISSON, E. (n.d.), 'Women, Work, Food and Nutrition in Nyamwigura Village, Mara Region, Tanzania', annotated in FAO (1984).

TRIPP, R. (1978), 'Economic Strategies and Nutritional Status in a Compound Farming Settlement in N. Ghana' (doctoral dissertation, Columbia University).

——(1981), 'Farmers and Traders: Some Economic Determinants of Nutritional Status in Northern Ghana', *Journal of Tropical Pediatrics*, 27.

TURSHEN, M. (1984), 'Food and Hunger in the Ciskei', paper to the 1984 *Review of African Political Economy* Conference on the Crisis in Africa.

UNICEF (1987), *The State of the World's Children* (New York: Oxford University Press for UNICEF).

United Nations (1984), 'Improving Concepts and Methods for Statistics and Indicators on the Situation of Women', Studies in Methods Ser. F, No. 33.

University of Florida (1986), Conference Papers on Gender Issues in Farming Systems Research and Extension.

University of Wageningen (1988), 'Is Farming Systems Research an Improvement?', Introduction to Lecture series (Brouwer and Jansen).

VAIL, L., and WHITE, L. (1977), '"Tawani Machembero": Forced Cotton and Rice Growing on the Zambezi', *Journal of Africa History*, 19.

VAUGHAN, M. (1984), 'Women, Men and Food Supply in the History of Southern Malawi', paper given to Workshop on Conceptualising the Household in Africa, Harvard University, Nov.

——(1986), *The Story of an African Famine* (Cambridge: Cambridge University Press).

VENEMA, B. (1986), 'The Changing Role of Women in Sahelian Agriculture', in L. Creevey (ed.), *Women Farmers in Africa: Rural Development in Mali and the Sahel* (Syracuse, NY: Syracuse University Press).

VON BULOW, D., and SORENSEN, A. (1988), 'Gender Dynamics in Contract Farming: Women's Role in Small Holder Tea Production in Kericho District Kenya', Project Paper 88.1 (Copenhagen: Centre for Development Research).

WHITE, L. (1984), 'Women in the Changing African Family' in Hay and Stichter (1984).

WHITEHEAD, A. (1981a), 'I'm Hungry Mum: The Politics of Domestic Budgeting', in K. Young *et al.* (ed.), *Of Marriage and the Market* (London: CSE Books).

——(1981b), 'A Conceptual Framework for the Analysis of the Effects of Technological Change on Rural Women', WEP Working Paper No. 79 (Geneva: ILO).

——(1984), 'Beyond the Household: Gender and Resource Allocation in a Ghanaian Domestic Economy', paper for Workshop on Conceptualising the Household in Africa, Harvard University, Nov.

——(1985), 'A Conceptual Framework for the Effects of Technological Change on Rural Women', in I. Ahmed (ed.), *Technology and Rural Women* (London: Allen & Unwin).

——(1986a), 'Women in Rural Food Production in Sub-Saharan Africa: Some Implications for Food Strategies', paper given at a Symposium on Food Strategies at WIDER, Helsinki.

——(1986b), 'Economic Transformation and the Sexual Division of Labour in Rural Production', paper to ESRC Conference on Economic Transformation in Tropical Africa, Centre for West African Studies, Birmingham.

——(forthcoming a), 'Women in Food Production in Sub-Saharan Africa', Training Module, EEC *Training for Trainers Project* (Sussex, IDS).

——(forthcoming b), 'Food Crisis and Gender Conflict in the African Countryside', in Bernstein, H., *et al.* (eds.), *The Food Question: Who gets What and Why* (London: Earthscan).

WILLIAMS, G. (1980), 'Inequalities in Rural Nigeria', Development Studies Paper 16 (University of East Anglia).

——(1987), 'Primitive Accumulation: The Way to Progress?', *Development and Change*, 18.

Women in Nigeria Editorial Committee (1985), *Women and the Family* (Zaria: Codesria Book Series).

World Bank (1981), *Accelerated Development in Sub-Saharan Africa* (Washington, DC: IBRD).

——(1983), *Sub Saharan Africa: Progress Report on Development Prospects and Program* (Washington, DC: IBRD).

WRIGHT, M. (1983), 'Technology, Marriage and Women's Work in the History of Maize Growers in Mazabuka, Zambia: A Reconnaissance', *Journal of South African Studies*, 10.

YOUNG, S. (1977), 'Fertility and Famine; Women's Agricultural History in S. Mozambique', in R. Palmer and N. Parsons (eds.), *The Roots of Rural Poverty in Central and Southern Africa* (London: Heinemann).

YOUSSEFF, N., and HETLER, C. (1984), 'Rural Households Headed by Women: A Priority Concern for Development', Women and Rural Development Paper No. 31 (Geneva: ILO).

NAME INDEX

SUBJECT INDEX